SCHOOL OF
ORIENTAL AND AFRICAN STUDIES
UNIVERSITY OF LONDON

Historical Writing on the Peoples of Asia

HISTORICAL WRITING ON THE PEOPLES OF ASIA

HISTORIANS OF THE MIDDLE EAST

Edited by

BERNARD LEWIS

Professor of the History of the Near and Middle East in the University of London

AND

P. M. HOLT

Reader in the History of the Near and Middle East in the University of London

LONDON

OXFORD UNIVERSITY PRESS

NEW YORK TORONTO

1962

Oxford University Press, Amen House, London, E.C.4

GLASGOW NEW YORK TORONTO MELBOURNE WELLINGTON
BOMBAY CALCUTTA MADRAS KARACHI LAHORE DACCA
CAPE TOWN SALISBURY NAIROBI IBADAN ACCRA
KUALA LUMPUR HONG KONG

PRINTED IN GREAT BRITAIN BY
WESTERN PRINTING SERVICES LTD., BRISTOL

PREFACE

Between the years 1956 and 1958 the School of Oriental and African Studies, University of London, held a series of study conferences to survey and evaluate the course and character of historical writing on the peoples of Asia. To bring this large subject down to manageable proportions the method of analysis by region was adopted, and South Asia, South East Asia, the Near, Middle and Far East were in turn examined. In historical depth the survey extended from the period of the early empires and literatures, through the age of Western dominance and the freedom movements down to the present day. Writings in both Western and Asian literatures were analysed.

The conferences brought together the leading authorities in these studies from Asia and the West and had the effect of making them more keenly aware not only of the underlying assumptions, predilections and prejudices of past writers but also of their own standpoints as historians. These investigations into the nature of historical objectivity are the more valuable and influential because they are taking place at a time when historians are seeking to rewrite Asian history and the peoples of Asia and the West are adjusting their relationships.

In preparing for each conference the same methods were used. Seminar groups, including a judicious balance of mature scholars and younger historians in training from Asian and Western countries, were established to analyse in detail the papers which had been prepared according to an agreed, comprehensive plan by the prospective members of the forthcoming conference. The business of the conferences therefore consisted not in reading papers but in attempting to solve the problems thrown up by the seminars.

Believing that these conferences have made a contribution to 'the well-being of mankind' I wish to affirm my deep appreciation of the Rockefeller Foundation, which provided the major part of the financial costs and also of the farsightedness and support of its officers, who contributed substantially to the effectiveness of the work done.

In the view that the papers which were submitted to the conferences possess an intrinsic and comparative value the School of Oriental and African Studies has generously provided funds for their publication and, suitably edited and introduced, they will appear under the following editors:

Professor W. G. Beasley and Professor E. G. Pulleyblank: China and Japan.

Professor D. G. E. Hall: South East Asia.

Professor B. Lewis and Dr. P. M. Holt: The Near and Middle East.

Professor C. H. Philips: India, Pakistan and Ceylon.

School of Oriental and African Studies

C. H. PHILIPS

CONTENTS

PART I

ARABIC, PERSIAN, AND TURKISH HISTORIOGRAPHY
TO THE 12TH/19TH CENTURY

PART II

EUROPEAN (INCLUDING RUSSIAN) HISTORICAL WRITING ON THE NEAR AND MIDDLE EAST FROM THE MIDDLE AGES TO THE PRESENT DAY

PART III

MODERN MIDDLE EASTERN HISTORICAL WRITING

PART IV

GENERAL THEMES

INTRODUCTION

The term Middle East was first used in 1902 by the American naval historian Alfred Thayer Mahan. In an article in the *National Review*, published in London, he suggested this new expression for the area between India and Arabia, with its centre in the Persian Gulf. The new term was taken up and employed, in *The Times* by its correspondent in Tehran, Valentine Chirol, and, later, in the House of Lords by Lord Curzon.[1] Its use abroad spread rapidly, and in British though not in American usage it almost entirely superseded the slightly older term Near East, with which, however, it sometimes remains in loosely defined association.

Both terms are of recent origin—the Near East is a product of nineteenth-century diplomacy, the Middle East of twentieth-century strategy. Both terms obviously derive from a world of which Western Europe was the centre and in which other regions had significance only as Western Europe saw them. Yet in spite of their recent origin, their rather parochial outlook, and their obsolete global projection, these terms, Middle East in particular, have won world-wide acceptance and are now used to designate these countries even in regions for which in fact they lie to the North, the West, or the South;[2] even, most remarkable of all, in the Middle East itself.

One may well wonder how it is that these upstart and rather colourless geographical expressions should have come to be applied to what is, after all, one of the most ancient regions of civilization in the world—a region with a long and famous history, with a distinctive and familiar personality.

Perhaps the reason may be sought precisely in the fact that this region was, for so very long a time, *the* East—the ancient, classical, and archetypal Orient which has been the neighbour and often the rival of Europe and the West from the days when the invading armies of the Persian Great

[1] Mahan, 'The Persian Gulf and International Relations', *National Review*, September 1902 (reprinted in idem, *Retrospect and Prospect*, London, 1903); V. Chirol, *The Middle Eastern Question* (London, 1903). For Curzon's reference in the House of Lords see *Hansard*, Lords, third series, vol. vii, col. 576. Our thanks are due to Professor J. C. Hurewitz for this information. The above was already written when R. H. Davison's 'Where is the Middle East?' discussing the same problem, appeared in *Foreign Affairs*, July 1960.

[2] In Russia, for example, the terms *Blizhnii Vostok* and *Srednii Vostok* (Near East and Middle East) are in current usage. In India the attempt has been made to replace these terms by the expression West Asia, which however has the disadvantage of excluding Egypt and other African territories in the Middle East. It is to be noted that in a recent book by an Indian author the Western term reappears (J. K. Banerji, *The Middle East in World Politics* (Calcutta, 1960)).

King first crossed to Greece until the last rearguard action of the Ottoman Empire. As late as the nineteenth century the countries of south-west Asia and north-east Africa were still simply the East, without need for further definition, and the problem of their disposal was the 'Eastern Question'.

It is only in comparatively recent times that, as Europe became involved in the affairs of a remoter orient, it became necessary to seek some closer definition of the ancient and familiar one. In antiquity the Greeks had first given the name Asia to the lands on the eastern shores of the Aegean, and then changed it to Asia Minor as a vaster Asia, in Persia and in the semi-mythical empires of India and China, loomed on their horizon. In the same way Europe, at the end of the nineteenth and the beginning of the twentieth century, began to qualify 'the East' as near and middle, in contrast to the further East that lay beyond it.

In spite of this recent and changing nomenclature, and of a continuing vagueness as to its precise geographical definition, the Near and Middle East is nevertheless an area with an unmistakable character and historic identity. It is a land of ancient civilizations—the river valley societies of Mesopotamia and Egypt, the plateau empires of Anatolia and Iran, that grew and commingled and were welded together in the empire of Alexander and the kingdoms of the Diadochi. It is the region which saw the birth of three of the great religions of humanity, Judaism and its two offspring, Christianity and Islam.

Since the seventh century it has been pre-eminently the land of Islam, in which the Muslim faith was born and the classical civilization of Islam was formed. It was here that the caliphs and sultans of the great universal Islamic empires lived, reigned and died, and that the three first peaks of Islamic civilization, those of the Arabs, the Persians, and the Turks, were attained; and, although these empires are all extinct, they still live in the common memory of Muslims as the classical and religious past of their own Muslim community. There have been other peoples, languages, and kingdoms in Islam since the classical Empires—in Asia, in Africa, even in Europe; but all of them are secondary, post-classical, in a sense colonial, related to the Middle Eastern heartlands of Islam as were the Americas to Europe. The classical civilization of Islam, in which the basic and characteristic common Islamic patterns and traditions were evolved, grew up in the Middle East, in the dominions of the caliphs and sultans, in lands that were predominantly of Arabic, Persian and Turkish speech.

This involves some change in the current political definition of the area. As used at the present time, the term Middle East includes Turkey, Persia, and perhaps Afghanistan, the Fertile Crescent, Arabia and north-east Africa, with a rather vague extension southwards and westwards from Egypt into Arabic-speaking Africa. In the larger historical sense it must be extended westwards to Morocco and, for a while, Spain, and northwards beyond the Turkish and Persian frontiers into those parts of Eastern Europe and Central Asia which, until the nineteenth century, were still part of the Middle East—countries inhabited by Turkish or Persian-speaking Muslims closely identified in their religious, cultural and political background with the lands of what we now call the Middle East; countries which once formed part of the great empires of Islam, in which such cities as Ganja, Samarqand and Bukhārā were as essential a part as Damascus, Baghdād or Cairo.

Islam is a religion with a strong sense of history. God himself, says the fifteenth-century Egyptian scholar, al-Sakhāwī, in his defence of history, told stories about the peoples of the past,[3] and indeed the Qur'ān is full of warnings from the lessons of history. 'We tell you stories of the Apostles, which will strengthen your heart, and thus bring you the Truth, an exhortation, and a memorial for the believers.'[4] Muḥammad was profoundly conscious of his place in the historic sequence of progressive revelations, and of the predicament of man in the vast design from Creation to Judgement. His mission was an event in history, and its purpose and meaning preserved and transmitted through memory and record. The later adoption of the doctrine of *Ijmā'*, according to which the divine guidance was transferred from the Prophet after his death to the Muslim community as a whole, gave a continuing significance to the acts and experiences of that community, in whose history could be discerned the unfolding of the divine purpose on earth. On a lower level, the immense authority and prestige attached to the Companions and Helpers of the Prophet provided a recurring incentive to the descendants of early heroes and the successors of early factions to ascertain, to adjust, and to rediscover the truth concerning the personalities and events of the beginning of Islam.

Islamic societies, since early times, have been conscious of their place in history and concerned about the record of it left for later times. Islamic rulers have been interested in the deeds of their predecessors, and anxious to record their own for their successors. Muslim historiography begins with the biographies of the Prophet and the sagas of the Arabian tribes. Thereafter almost every dynasty in Islam had annals or chronicles of some kind, and in many countries serious historiography begins with the advent of Islam.

The principal object of the Conference on Historical Writing on the Near and Middle East, held at the School of Oriental and African Studies, University of London, in 1958, was to investigate historiographical attitudes and preconceptions. The question of these arises whether one considers the original literary sources, the work of Western writers, or the more recent, Western-influenced historical writing in Arabic, Persian and

[3] F. Rosenthal, *A History of Muslim Historiography* (Leyden, 1952), p. 219.
[4] Qur'ān xi, 120.

Turkish. Some work has been done to reveal the outlook and preconceptions of the classical writers, and of those who followed their tradition down to the nineteenth century, although even here there is still room for a more subtle or a more sympathetic analysis. By contrast, the development of Western historiography on the Muslim peoples has received little attention. This deficiency does not affect academic circles alone. Fundamentally, ideas about the Islamic world held today by non-specialists in the West derive from obsolete European historical writing, and have been responsible for erroneous and imperfect judgements. The third subject of our enquiries, modern historiography in the Near and Middle East, has hardly been studied at all, although it has been profoundly affected by the impact of the West, and at the highest level has utilized the techniques of the Western historian. This is another deficiency in our knowledge which is of practical importance. The image of the past, both recent and remote, is a factor in the outlook of the Muslim peoples which the West tends to underestimate, and the image is both reflected in, and formed by, Muslim historical writing. In brief, to find a key to the outlook of modern Muslim peoples, we need to know far more about what they think of their history, its emotive power for them, and their attitude to it as mirroring their present group-consciousness. A further, if incidental, purpose of the Conference was to throw light upon the present situation in the discovery and use of historical materials, and to indicate lines for further research.

The papers that follow have as their common theme historical writing on the Middle East in the period since the rise of Islam.[5] There is of course no intention of attempting a full coverage of the subject. Our purpose has rather been to group together a number of studies of different topics and aspects, some of large general issues, some of particular problems of periods and places, genres and even individual authors. Within the field thus defined, the topics for study were classified in three main groups:

(1) Historical writing in the Muslim Middle East before the impact of Western influences—that is to say, in the indigenous Islamic tradition of historiography. This consists chiefly of various types of historical writing in Arabic, Persian and Turkish, with some attention to the historiography of religious and ethnic minorities.

(2) European, including Russian, historical writing on the Middle East, from the Middle Ages to the present day.

(3) Historical writing in the Middle East in the modern period, showing the impact of European ideas, and the reactions to them.

[5] The vast and variegated historical records of the pre-Islamic period would have involved an impossible extension of our subject. They have moreover been extensively treated elsewhere, notably in the recent symposium edited by R. C. Dentan, *The Idea of History in the Ancient Near East* (Yale, 1955).

The Conference began, appropriately, with a paper on the *Sīra*, the biography of the Prophet and the historical presentation, by Muslim writers, of the series of events with which Islamic history began. Ever since the *Sīra* was first made known to Western scholarship by Gustav Weil in 1843,[6] it has formed the subject of detailed investigations by a series of scholars. The first generation of Western orientalists who worked on the *Sīra* adopted, on the whole, a positive attitude. After discounting the obviously legendary passages, they were ready to accept most of the remainder as an accurate record of the life and work of Muḥammad. Since then, however, our knowledge of the Prophet's life has grown less and less as the progress of scholarly research has called one after another of the data of Muslim tradition into question. The positivist Leone Caetani and the Jesuit Henri Lammens, from their different points of vantage, subjected the tradition to a minute and sometimes captious historical and psychological analysis, while the meticulous scholarship of Tor Andrae was able to show the motives and influences which led the early Muslims to give a new shape and colour to the image they carried in their hearts of the last and greatest of the Prophets. Lammens went so far as to reject the entire biography as no more than a conjectural and tendentious exegesis of a few passages of biographical content in the Qur'ān, devised and elaborated by later generations of believers. Other scholars, while maintaining a critical attitude, reacted against this extreme formulation, and Becker in particular, rejecting many of Lammens's arguments, was prepared to accept elements of the tradition as long as they were not disproved and seemed historically reasonable. More recently, the studies of Professor Schacht on the legal traditions have thrown doubt on much of the biographical material. In his own words: 'A considerable part of the standard biography of the Prophet in Medina, as it appeared in the second half of the second century A.H., was of very recent origin and is therefore without independent historical value.'[7]

Professor Montgomery Watt in his paper re-examines this fundamental problem of Islamic historiography, and adopts a position rather closer to the Muslim tradition than that of recent, more radical criticism.

The question of Jewish and Christian elements in Islam has long occupied the attention of scholars. Professor Rosenthal in his paper considers the extent to which Biblical influences appear in Muslim historiography,

[6] In his *Mohammad der Prophet, sein Leben und seine Lehre*. The Arabic text was edited by Wüstenfeld in 1858–60, published in a German translation by Weil in 1864, and in English by A. Guillaume in 1955.

[7] J. Schacht, 'A Revaluation of Islamic Traditions', *JRAS* (1949), pp. 143–54. The point is developed in detail in the same author's 'On Mūsā b. 'Uqba's Kitāb al-Maghāzī', *A.O.* (1953), pp. 288–300. For general discussions of the literature on the *Sīra* see G. Levi Della Vida, 'Sīra', in *EI*[1]; idem, *Storia e Religione nell' Oriente Semitico* (Rome, 1924), pp. 111–37; R. Blachère, *Le Problème de Mahomet* (Paris, 1952), pp. 1 ff., and, from a Muslim point of view, M. Hamidullah, *Le Prophète de l'Islam* (Paris, 1959).

beginning with the impact of the Biblical idea of history on the Prophet himself, and examining both the role of Biblical conceptions and the place of Biblical themes in Muslim historical writings.

The accumulation of pious or legal tradition was not the only source of early Islamic historical writings. There was also the Arabian saga. The peninsular Arabs of pre-Islamic and early Islamic times lived and sang in the heroic style—tribal, nomadic, warlike, obsessed with battle and vengeance, honour and booty, death and destiny, personal, family and tribal pride. Their poetry and legends mirror the conceptions and pre-occupations of an heroic age. Muḥammad, the greatest of them all, was not only a Prophet; he was also an Arab hero, and before long writings appear celebrating the exploits and victories of the Prophet and his Companions in their wars against the unbelievers. These works, though perhaps nearer to history in character and purpose than the Traditions, are still far from being historiography in the true sense. They are subjective and episodic, presenting a series of heroic figures and incidents, without concern for chronology, sequence, or consistency—in a word, saga rather than history.

These elements of heroic saga made some contribution to the elaboration of the *Sīra*. Far more important, however, was their role in the development of another school of historiography, examined in Professor Duri's paper. Unlike the biographic tradition, which was primarily cultivated in Medina, the tribal historians flourished in Iraq, especially in the garrison cities of Kūfa and Baṣra, the main centres of the conquistador tribal aristocracy. In his paper Professor Duri shows how the conquerors' obsession with tribal honour, founded on the glorious deeds of their ancestors, led to a new interest in narratives of the past, and how these developed and evolved under the impact of the political, religious, social and regional rivalries of the early centuries of Islam, and of the new group alignments with which they were connected.[8]

The earliest Arabic chronicles are not continuous narratives of events but collections of separate narrations, each supported by a chain of authorities purporting to go back to an eyewitness or actor. To some extent these early narratives also relied on lists of events and of participants in them, related ultimately to the collective memory of the community, perhaps supported by some form of written record. From these early narrations other, more sophisticated forms of historiography in time developed—imperial and dynastic annals, universal histories, and a range of works with more restricted topics of various kinds.

The next paper, by Professor Sir Hamilton Gibb, deals with one of the most important and characteristic of these new genres. The biographical dictionary, as Professor Gibb points out, is 'a wholly indigenous creation of

[8] Professor Duri has developed these points further in his paper on al-Zuhrī in *BSOAS* (1957), xix, 1–12, and in his book *Baḥth fī nash'at 'ilm al-ta'rīkh 'ind al-'Arab* (Beirut, 1960).

the Islamic community', entirely different in both conception and execution from such earlier enterprises as the biographical sections of the Chinese dynastic histories or the Syriac Christian martyrologies. The Arabic biographical dictionaries developed as part of the main historiographic tradition, and in time reached an astonishing scale and diversity. Some are devoted to various classes of individuals, such as Companions of the Prophet, reciters of the Qur'ān, creators of Tradition, poets and men of letters, physicians, judges, mystics; others deal with persons connected with a city or region and merge with local history; others again, of a more annalistic type, are in effect collections of obituary notices, arranged in chronological sequence. In his paper Professor Gibb outlines the development, sources and value of these different categories, and makes some suggestions as to the attitudes and motives, in the Arab Islamic community, that led to their production.

The period between the tenth and thirteenth centuries was one of profound crisis and change, when Islam fought and won a mighty struggle against three successive enemies—against heresy, Christendom, and heathendom. The Shi'ites—Buyids and Fatimids, Twelvers and Ismā'īlīs—were overcome, and ceased to be a menace to either political legitimacy or religious orthodoxy; the Crusaders were held and thrown back, and, most important of all, the conquests and migrations of the heathen steppe peoples from the East were transformed, by religious conversion, into a new source of life and power.

In the course of these struggles, and the great Sunni revival that accompanied them, the Islamic state, society, and civilization were transformed, and life and culture in the Islamic lands began to flow in new channels. These changes were fully reflected in the historical literature of the time. Already under the caliphs the earlier type of history, presented in the form of religious traditions, had given place to a new and more sophisticated school of historiography, written by bureaucrats for bureaucrats, and based on official information rather than oral traditions. Under the Turkish dynasties a further change took place. History was no doubt still an essential part of the education of a civil servant, and was to some extent written with that in view—but the pious, *madrasa*-trained functionary of post-Seljuq times was a very different person from the elegant and worldly-wise *kātib* of 'Abbasid days of whom Professor Rosenthal remarks: 'He had to be acquainted with the eras of the three nations, the Persians, Byzantines and Muslims. He had to know the contents of the Persian *fürstenspiegel* such as *Kalîlah wa-Dimnah*, the 'Covenant' of Ardašîr, and the letters of Anûšarwân. He also had to be familiar with the biographies of the caliphs and their chronology, as well as the raids of the early years of Islam. All this made a perfect secretary of state. His letters and documents greatly gained from the insertion of examples drawn from a large collection of historical curiosities. For his own good, he should know the history of the wazîrs.'[9] It was in a very different spirit that Abū S̲h̲āma wrote history, as a reminder of mortality and a preparation for eternity.[10] It is no accident that so many of the great Arabic historians of the later middle ages—as Ibn al-Jawzī, Ibn al-At̲h̲īr, Abū S̲h̲āma, Sak̲h̲āwī, Ibn Ḥajar— were men whose main interest and reputation among their own contemporaries lay in fields other than history, and usually in the religious sciences. Though, as Professor Rosenthal points out, history did not actually become part of the syllabus of the *madrasa*, the historian had become a man of the *madrasa*. It was a change of no small significance.

The next three papers deal with closely related topics, and illustrate the development of historiography in the central lands during this period. Professor Cahen's paper, on the historiography of the Seljuq period, is mainly concerned with works written in Iraq and Iran; Professor M. Hilmy M. Ahmad deals with the historians of Syria and Egypt in roughly the same period; Professor Gabrieli deals with both, but in relation to their treatment of a single theme—that of the Crusades.

An important branch of Islamic historiography was local history, which began at quite an early date with the compilation of historical, biographical and topographical works relating to various cities and provinces of the Islamic Empire. This type of writing flourished especially in the East, where there were histories of K̲h̲urāsān and Transoxiana, as well as of Samarqand, Buk̲h̲ārā, Merv, Herāt, Balk̲h̲, Nīs̲h̲āpūr, Qumm, and other cities and regions in Iran. In the Arabic-speaking provinces, near to the imperial capitals and dominated by the centralized river-valley societies of Iraq and Egypt, local history developed rather later, and on somewhat different lines, but there too it produced important and sometimes immense works. Only two regions, Syria and Spain, are considered here, and form the subject of papers by Professor Sami Dahan and Professor Charles Pellat. Syria, so often disputed between the rulers of Iraq and of Egypt, enjoyed periods of relative independence from both; the fragmentation of her countryside by mountains, rivers and valleys led to the growth and persistence of strong local autonomies and loyalties. These are reflected in the local histories of Syria, where we may also at times detect some cherished recollection of her early and brief interlude of imperial greatness, under the Umayyad Caliphs. Spain, at the far Western extremity of the Islamic world, soon rejected even the nominal suzerainty of the eastern caliphs, and pursued her own independent political development. It is therefore all the more remarkable that, as Professor Pellat shows, her historiography should be so close to the oriental tradition, and so much dominated by oriental examples.

---

[9] Rosenthal, *History*, pp. 46–7.
[10] *Tarājim rijāl al-qarnayn al-sādis wa'l-sābi'* (Cairo, 1947), p. 5; cf. p. 93 below.

For the first few centuries of Islam historical works by Muslim authors were written exclusively in Arabic—even works by Persian authors on Persian subjects, such as the many city histories of Iran. From the eleventh century onwards, however, the use of Arabic for historical works was gradually restricted to the countries of Arabic speech, from Iraq to Spain, and a new historical literature began to develop in the Persian language, which became the dominant literary medium not only in Persia but also, for a time, in Turkey, central Asia, and Muslim India.

Four papers follow, on aspects of Persian historiography—or rather of historiography in the Persian language, since much of the earlier historiography in Arabic had been written by Persians, including historians of the calibre of Balādhurī, Yaʿqūbī, and Ṭabarī. It has been maintained by some scholars that Arabic historiography was deeply influenced by pre-Islamic Persian historical works which have been lost; some have gone so far as to attribute the very beginnings of Arabic historiography to the inspiration of Persian models. Professor Spuler, in a comprehensive paper on the evolution of Persian historiography, rejects this view; on the contrary, he maintains there is no evidence of the existence of any written historical works in Persia at the time of the Arab conquest, which could have influenced the historiography of Islam. When a Muslim Persian like Ṭabarī wrote history, he followed the methods of the Arabs because no others were known to him. In the same way when Persians began to write historical works in their own language they followed on the pattern of Arabic historiography. If a distinctively Persian historical view is sought, it must be found in the epics rather than in historical works which, whether written in Arabic or in Persian, continue to express the Arab-Islamic historiographic view. It was not until the Mongol period that a Persian historiographic pattern begins to emerge. By that time Persian history is written exclusively in Persian.

The next paper, by Dr. J. A. Boyle, deals with the two major Persian historians of the Mongol period, and discusses their work, examining in detail the sources on which they drew and their contrasting presentation of the same events. Another individual and rather exceptional historian was taken up by Professor Minovi who in his paper on Bayhaqī, presents a Persian writer of the pre-Mongol period with a style conspicuously different from that of historians writing in Arabic.

In the remaining paper in this section, Professor Lambton, taking up a theme clearly already considered for Arabic historiography by Professor Gibb, examines the Persian biographical literature and notes some of its characteristic features. On the whole, the Persian biographies confirm Professor Gibb's view that this literature expresses a conviction of the significance of the contribution of individuals to the building of Islam. In the Persian works, however, it is the *ʿulamā*ʾ who form the subjects of the overwhelming majority of biographies and very little attention is given to the ruling and official classes. This suggested, Professor Lambton remarked, that by the time this Persian material had been compiled, the community and the state had grown rather apart.

During the fourteenth and fifteenth centuries Turkish takes its place as the third major language, in order of emergence, of Middle Eastern Islam. In Turkey as in Persia, historiography began in an alien but classical language, and the first historical works of the Ottoman state were written in Persian. Soon works in Turkish, at first of a rather primitive character, began to appear, and in time developed into a rich Turkish historical literature.

Five papers were presented in this section. The first two, by Professor Inalcık and Mr. Ménage, both deal, in different ways, with the vexed and difficult problem of the origins of Ottoman historiography, and in so doing introduce a new type of historical composition not previously encountered —the historical calendar.

The remaining three papers deal with special topics—Professor B. Lewis with the use by Muslim, especially Ottoman, historians of non-Muslim sources, Dr. G. L. Lewis with the part played by the historian as propagandist and public relations officer, as exemplified in Ottoman victory-bulletins and similar writings, and Dr. Walsh with the presentation, in Ottoman and also Persian historical writings, of the great Ottoman-Safavid rivalry in the sixteenth and seventeenth centuries. This last paper also contains a number of broad comments and criticisms of Ottoman and indeed Islamic historiography in general.

The last theme considered in this first section was the historiography of minority communities living within the Islamic Empires. These writings, though in many ways poorer and thinner than the historical literature of the Muslims, could serve in several ways to supplement and even to control them. De Goeje and Wellhausen, in their studies on the Arab conquests of Syria, had shown how Christian writings could be used as a check on the chronology of the Arab sources, and sometimes could help in reaching a decision on the relative merits of conflicting versions. Cahen, in a different way, has shown how official accounts of taxation and administration could, with due caution, be amplified from the unofficial reactions of the taxed and administered.[11] Not all minority groups produced historical literature. A highly literate community like the Middle Eastern Jews, for example, though they left many historical documents, produced very little genuine historiography between the Roman and the Ottoman periods, when the influence of the European Renaissance is

[11] For example in his article 'Fiscalité, propriété, antagonismes sociaux en Haute Mesopotamie au temps des premiers 'Abbasides, d'après Denys de Tell-Mahré', *Arabica* (1954), i, 136–52.

discernible in their literature.[12] Some kind of focus seems to be required for the development of a historiographic tradition—a state or country, or a church, and a people like the Jews, who had lost the one without establishing the other, had no regional or institutional centre around which a historical literature, of the kind known in the medieval Middle East, could develop. The same factor may help to explain the relative poverty of the historical literature of Muslim minority groups like the Shīʿa and Kharijites.[13] The lack of interest in history among the Ismāʿīlīs goes even further, and even the literature of the Fatimid Caliphate, preserved among the Ismāʿīlīs of Arabia and India and recently rediscovered, contains remarkably little of straightforward historical content. Perhaps the reason for this must be sought in a different philosophical conception—that with the ending of the effective Imamate and the establishment of what was, for the Ismāʿīlīs, a usurping Caliphate, history had taken a wrong turning, and ceased to be of any value or significance.

Four papers were presented in this section. The first two deal with the Arab historiography of the Lebanon, seen from different viewpoints. Dr. Salibi's theme was the historiography of the Maronite Church, and the theological and communal preoccupations of its historians;[14] Mr. Hourani was concerned with the historiography of the Lebanon as such, which he traced through its successive phases—the Maronite church and nation, the feudal Lebanon, the Christian Lebanon of the nineteenth-century writers, and the multi-communal Lebanon of the present day. The two remaining papers deal with the two major historical literatures in non-Islamic languages—the Syriac chronicles, by Professor Segal, and the Armenian, by Dr. Dowsett. Both writers give a brief sketch of the general characteristics of these literatures, and of their value for the historian of Islam.

European historical writing on the Muslim Middle East arose from the challenge which Islam presented to Christendom. This was felt on two levels. There was, first, the challenge of Islam as a religion, subsequent to Christianity in its appearance, bearing certain resemblances to the older faith in its theological system, yet nevertheless claiming for itself a superior and final revelation. The common monotheism, and the Judaeo-Christian inheritance of Islam did not historically constitute a common ground of agreement between the two religions. The main body of Christian

[12] On Biblical historiography see Millar Burrows 'Ancient Israel', in R. C. Dentan, *The Idea of History*, pp. 99–132; on the post-Biblical literature, M. Steinschneider, *Die Geschichtsliteratur der Juden* (Frankfurt, 1905) (works in Hebrew only).

[13] Kharijite historiography has some importance for the history of the first great clashes out of which Kharijism occurred; for accounts of some of these sources see R. Rubinacci's articles in *AION*, 1949, pp. 431–8; 1952, pp. 95–110; Veccia-Vaglieri, ibid., 1952, pp. 1–94; and 1953, pp. 1–98; M. Kafāfī in *Bull. Fac. Arts. Cairo*, 1952, pp. 29–48. For other studies on sectarian literature see J. D. Pearson, *Index Islamicus* (Cambridge, 1958), pp. 86 ff.

[14] Since developed at greater length in his book *Maronite Historians of Medieval Lebanon* (Beirut, 1959).

orthodoxy saw in Islam at best an heretical aberration; the Christian image of Islam, largely derived from inadequate and distorted sources, has often ascribed to Muslim belief a malicious and even diabolical perversity.[15]

The challenge of Islam to Christianity on the theological level has been a constant factor in the relations between the Muslim and Christian communities for over thirteen centuries. It has in certain periods been reinforced by a challenge on the political level, at times of conflict between Muslim and Christian states. At such times, Islam became, not merely a rival system of theology but a topic of intense current political interest.

The most serious of these political challenges was that presented by the expansion of Ottoman power from a petty amirate in Anatolia to a great empire, ruling not only ancient Muslim territory but also lands which had long been Christian in south-eastern and central Europe. The impact of Ottoman expansion into Christendom was first felt by the Byzantines, who had already experienced the Arab and Seljuq conquests. The interest of Byzantine historians in the Ottomans, primarily as political opponents threatening the security of the Empire, is described in Sir Steven Runciman's paper, in which he stresses the importance of Byzantine writings of the fourteenth and fifteenth centuries as source-material for early Ottoman history.

With the continuing expansion of Ottoman power, after the absorption of the last Byzantine territories, the range of European historical writing on this topic increased. Mr. Parry's paper gives an account of the various types of material dealing with the Ottoman Empire, which have come down to us from the fifteenth and sixteenth centuries. He selects for detailed study Paolo Giovio (1483–1522), a Renaissance historiographer who was particularly well informed on contemporary Turkish affairs.

Meanwhile writing on Islam as a religion continued side by side with the discussion of the contemporary Ottoman problem. Two main approaches may be broadly distinguished. The first was that of the controversialists, who continued into the sixteenth and seventeenth centuries concepts of the Prophet and Islam still largely derived from the medieval Western corpus of beliefs. A subordinate use of Islam in controversy appears in the writings of such men as Prideaux, Voltaire and Gibbon, where the object of the writer is not to convert or confute the Muslims, but to discomfit other Christians, or to express in quasi-historical terms the anti-clericalism of the Enlightenment.

The second approach in this period is that of the scholars, concerned primarily to acquire and make known information about Islam and its

[15] The formation of the Christian view of Islam until the nineteenth century is described by Aldobrandino Malvezzi, *L'Islamismo e la cultura europea* (Florence, 1956). A more detailed study, relating particularly to the period 1100–1350, has recently appeared in Norman Daniel, *Islam and the West: the making of an image* (Edinburgh, 1960).

history. The collection and publication of texts by pioneer orientalists, such as Erpenius and Pococke in the seventeenth century, laid the foundations of an informed understanding of Muslim civilization. Although these early scholars showed a marked interest in Arabic historical writing, and historical texts were (with the Qur'ān) the first to be printed in Europe, they were for the most part not historians. Their influence is first to be seen in the gradual modification of the traditional Western image of Islam, as the polemicists began to take account of the more authentic information the Orientalists provided. As late as the eighteenth century, moreover, it was still impossible to draw a hard and fast line between the controversialist and the scholar. There was however a distinct shift in attitudes towards Islam in the seventeenth and eighteenth centuries. This is illustrated in Dr. Holt's paper on Prideaux, Ockley and Sale.[16]

Before the nineteenth century Muslim history did not emerge as an independent discipline. It was subordinated to linguistic and literary studies (themselves ancillary to Hebrew and Old Testament scholarship) or was regarded, for example by Gibbon, as an appendage to the history of the classical world. Two important pioneer works of historiography had appeared early in the eighteenth century, Ockley's *History of the Saracens* (1708–18) and Gagnier's *Vie de Mahomet* (1732). Not until a hundred years later do we reach the beginning of the modern flood of writing on the various periods and aspects of Muslim history.

A dominant influence upon European students of Islam in the nineteenth and early twentieth centuries was the concept of scientific historiography. Older attitudes however survived: the disparagement of the Prophet and of certain aspects of the religion, which goes back to medieval themes; the favourable contrast of Islam with Christianity, in the anti-clerical tradition of the Enlightenment. During the nineteenth century also Europe attained decisive military, political and material superiority over the Muslim East, but this precarious domination was soon undermined by the wars and revolutions of the twentieth century. The confidence of the earlier period, and the failure of nerve after the First World War, were reflected in the attitude of European writers towards Islam. These themes are treated by Professor Fück in his paper on Islam as an historical problem in European historiography since 1800.[17]

Professor Fück's delineation of the outlines of development is supplemented by four papers on more limited fields. Dr. Dunlop takes as his subject the first of the nineteenth-century scientific historiographers of

[16] Some aspects of the development of Islamic historical studies in the earlier part of the seventeenth century are discussed by P. M. Holt, 'The study of Arabic historians in seventeenth century England: the background and the work of Edward Pococke', *BSOAS* (1957), xix/3, 444–55.

[17] The general development of Arabic studies, including history, has been traced by Professor Fück in his work, *Die arabischen Studien in Europa bis in den Anfang des 20. Jahrhunderts* (Leipzig, 1955).

Islam, Gustav Weil, whose *Geschichte der Chalifen* was not only important in itself as a compendious history based on then largely unpublished material, but was a major source of Sir William Muir's history of the caliphate. Professor Salibi deals with a more controversial figure, Henri Lammens, who in his writings on the Prophet and early Islam combined the techniques of scientific historiography with an unsympathetic, and at times hostile, attitude to his subject matter: a combination of scholarship and prejudice which is reminiscent of Marracci in the late seventeenth century. The papers of Dr. Yapp and Mr. Hill are both concerned with non-academic historiographers. Dr. Yapp indicates how the pictures of Persian history drawn respectively by Malcolm and Sykes were influenced by their British background and the nature of their work in Persia. Mr. Hill's paper is largely a study in controversial historiography, the attitudes to modern Sudanese history adopted by writers who were strongly moved by opposition to slavery, or who either defended or opposed the Egyptian claim to rule in the Sudan.

Since the Communist Revolution of 1917, Russian historical writing has stood apart from the main body of European scholarship. The nature of Soviet historiography is examined in relation to two special fields by Professor Frye and Colonel Wheeler. Professor Frye is principally concerned with Soviet writing on Central Asia in the ninth and tenth centuries. He stresses the significance of detailed research into art, archaeology, numismatics and epigraphy, and the comparative freedom of such work from domination by Marxist ideology. A marked contrast appears, according to Colonel Wheeler's account, in the Soviet treatment of Persian history from 1906 to 1946. Here the presentation and interpretation of events is governed by ideological and political considerations.[18] While this period of Persian history is consistently seen as essentially a movement for national liberation, there have been considerable shifts of attitude in regard, for example, to Tsarist policy.

In the nineteenth and twentieth centuries a new epoch begins in Middle Eastern historiography, inaugurated by the impact, on Middle Eastern historians, of the historical literature of the West. The translation of Western works into Middle Eastern languages, and even more the growing familiarity of Middle Easterners with Western languages and literatures, profoundly affected the work of historians, who began to acquire new concepts, new methods, and new purposes in their work. Traditional historiography did not of course cease. On the contrary, it continued, often in a late and somewhat degenerate form, in all three languages of the area,

[18] An interesting study in the formation and revision of the official Soviet line on an historical problem is provided by Paul B. Henze, 'The Shamil problem', in Walter Z. Laqueur (ed.), *The Middle East in transition* (London, 1958), pp. 415–43. For Soviet historiography on Islam, see further, *A detailed analysis of An Outline of the history of Islamic studies in the U.S.S.R. by N. A. Smirnov*, Central Asian Research Centre (1956).

and at times even spilled over into Western languages, in works which, behind the outward forms of modern scholarship, revealed a concern with achievement rather than with development, a preference for compilation rather than analysis.

The most significant writings, however, are those which show some response to Western stimuli and some attempt to adopt and apply Western methods. As the new literature grows and expands, three major changes become apparent.

The first is the expansion of the field of interest, in time, in space, and in content alike. The historian becomes interested in times before the rise of Islam, and in lands beyond its borders; at the same time he seeks to penetrate below the surface movement of events to the deeper levels of institutional, social, and economic history. Thus in nineteenth-century Egypt we find Rifā'a Rāfi' al-Ṭahṭāwī writing the first serious Arabic account of the Pharaohs, while in Turkey Süleymān Pasha gives to Turkish readers the first Turkish account of their pre-Islamic past.[19] At the same time, interest was growing in the history of Europe. At first, this was concentrated on heroes—and heroines. Thus the first published translations were of works on Napoleon and the Russian Empress Catherine, produced in Egypt, but in the Turkish language, in 1829 and 1832.[20] Voltaire's *Peter the Great* appeared both in Persian (1846) and in Arabic (1849), while his *Charles XII* also awakened widespread interest.[21] This was followed by translations of more general works on European history, and then by original works on the same subject.

This new acquaintance with Western history and historiography eventually began to affect the writing of Middle Eastern history too. The first stages of change are well illustrated in two major historical works of the nineteenth century, the Ottoman histories of Aḥmed Jevdet Pasha (1822–95) and Muṣṭafā Nūrī Pasha (1824–89). Both are orthodox and traditional in appearance, but both show significant innovations. While Jevdet does not go very far from traditional historiography, he greatly widens the frame within which his history is presented. He deals at some length with European history—the French Revolution and Napoleon—and even with the American Revolution, thus showing a new kind of historical awareness and a realization that even the history of the Islamic Empire can only be made intelligible within the framework of a very much larger field of historical enquiry. In Nūrī Pasha's work, the extension of the frame of reference is of a different kind. Despite its traditional form and manner, his book reveals a clear awareness that great changes have taken place, and that the author is describing a world and a set of institutions which no

[19] Rifā'a Rāfi' al-Ṭahṭāwī, *Anwār tawfīq al-jalīl* (Būlāq, 1285/1868); Süleymān Pasha, *Tārīkh-i 'ālem* (Istanbul, 1293/1876). Both are based almost entirely on Western sources.

[20] See below, p. 190.

[21] See below, p. 191 and p. 424.

longer exist, and are therefore in need of explanation and interpretation. There is thus an enlargement of the time-dimension in Nūrī, as of the space-dimension in Jevdet. Both can be observed in the works of later historians, together with a further development of the scope and content of historical writing, as the precept and example of European scholarship became better known. Not least important was the influence of those Western scholars who had concerned themselves with Middle Eastern history—of the orientalists, whose works introduced to Middle Eastern readers and students a series of new ideas of how their own history should be studied and presented.

With these new themes came new methods and materials. The study of ancient history, in Egypt and elsewhere, rested largely on archaeology, and Middle Eastern scholars could not but be impressed and influenced by the immense work of discovery going on around them. Such men as Maḥmūd Pasha al-Falakī (1805–86) Aḥmad Pasha Kamāl (1851–1923), and ʻAlī Bahjat (1859–1924) did much to add to the new knowledge and, still more important, to bring it to their compatriots. Numismatics opened new paths even to historians of Islam, and the first pioneer work of the Turkish scholar ʻAbd al-Laṭīf Ṣubḥī, published in 1862, was followed by many others.[22] On the whole, however, these new historical auxiliary sciences made less impact than the textual and philological scholarship of the west, which, corresponding more closely to the indigenous scribal tradition, evoked a widespread response in the discovery and editing, with varying degrees of competence, of lost or forgotten texts and documents.

Closely associated with these changes in the scope and techniques of historical writing was a third, highly significant development, in the unit or entity of historical presentation. In nineteenth-century Egypt the term *waṭan*, hitherto home or domicile, for the first time acquires the political connotation of fatherland, and the attempt is made to write the history of Egypt—not of a dynasty, a religious community, a province, a city or the universal Islamic Empire, but of the land of Egypt, the *waṭan* of the Egyptians. This is a direct result of the importation of the West European idea of the secular and territorial fatherland, and of a profound and enduring relationship between the land and those who inhabit it. It led in turn to the assertion of identity with earlier, pre-existing local civilizations and for the first time Middle Eastern Muslims began to look back, for the roots of their historical and corporate identity, not only to the classical empires of Islam but also, beyond them, to the forgotten civilizations of pre-Islamic antiquity. In this movement, which would link Muslim Middle Easterners not only with their heathen ancestors but also with their

[22] On Ṣubḥī see F. Babinger, *Geschichtsschreiber der Osmanen* (Leipzig, 1927), pp. 368–70, and L. A. Mayer, *Bibliography of Moslem Numismatics*[2] (London, 1954), items 1734–6. Cf. below, p. 426.

Christian neighbours, members of the Christian minorities played an important part. Starting in Egypt, the movement spread to other countries, and produced a series of schools of national historiography, concerned with the history of Lebanon—and the Phoenicians; of Iraq—and the Assyrians; of Turkey—and the Hittites; of Iran—and the ancient empires of the Achaemenids and Sasanids. All these had of necessity to rely largely on Western research, and on the new methods and materials used by it.

The West European idea of the fatherland or *patrie* was not the only such innovation. From the polyglot empires of central and eastern Europe, where a more subjective and romantic loyalty—nationalism rather than patriotism—prevailed, came the idea of the nation as a folk or race, and with it a new historiography—not of Turkey, but of the Turks, not of Egypt or Syria or Iraq, but of the Arabs.

The first paper in this section, by Professor Ayalon, dealt with the Egyptian historian al-Jabartī, the last great historian of the traditional school and, in some ways, the first of the new. This paper, in an expanded form, has been published elsewhere and is therefore given here only in abridgement.[23]

Next come three papers, all dealing, in different ways, with the impact of the West in Middle Eastern historical writing. Professor Shayyal's theme is a broad one—Egyptian historiography in the nineteenth century.[24] Dr. Kuran's, roughly parallel, is concerned with Turkish historiography in the period 1839 to 1908; Dr. Kazemzadeh deals more specifically with Western influence, and with a somewhat later period—the late nineteenth and twentieth centuries. A comparison between these papers underlines the need for a closer correlation between studies of Arab, Turkish, and, to a lesser extent, Persian history in the nineteenth century, and in particular of the intellectual development of the three areas. Until very recently, a large proportion of the educated classes in the Arab countries of Asia knew Turkish, while those in Turkey read both Arabic and Persian. Many of the educated Arab élite, particularly in Syria and Iraq, received their education not so much from the French and American schools and colleges, the importance of which has perhaps been overstressed,[25] as from the educational institutions set up in the successive phases of the Ottoman reform. Consequently many developments can only be fully appreciated in this larger context. The translation movement, for example, shows such striking parallels and resemblances that they cannot possibly be dismissed

[23] David Ayalon, 'The Historian al-Jabartī and his Background', *BSOAS* (1960), XXIII, 217–49.

[24] Professor Shayyal has published his paper, together with much additional material, in Arabic: *al-Ta'rīkh wa'l-mu'arrikhuūn fī Miṣr fi'l-qarn al-tāsi' 'ashar* (Cairo, 1958).

[25] Notably in George Antonius's brilliant *Arab awakening*, first published in London in 1938, and in the whole school of historical advocacy that derives from it.

as wholly coincidental.[26] Professor Shayyal refers to the opening of the *Institut d'Egypte* in Alexandria in 1859, and the *Jam'iyyat al-Ma'ārif* in 1868. There must certainly be a connection between these and the Turkish *Enjümen-i Dānish*, established in Istanbul in 1851, and *Jem'iyyet-i 'Ilmiyye*, founded in 1860. *Jam'iyyat al-Ma'ārif* and *Enjümen-i Dānish* mean the same thing—Society of Knowledge—and the two did much the same work.[27]

The introduction of new methods and materials, and the response and reaction to the Western image of the past, helped in the emergence of a new, national historiography in the countries of the Middle East, with a new national self-image. Professor Faris's paper examines the treatment of one theme—the struggle between 'Alī and Mu'āwiya—in modern Arabic historiography, and shows how new problems and concepts have transformed the understanding and presentation even of the classical Islamic past.[28]

The Middle East is a land of myths, and even today the mythopoeic faculty is still working, among both those who dwell there and those who pass; new myths, in modern style, emerge and evolve to explain the inexplicable facts of nature and history. The contemporary image of the past in the Muslim world does not rest only on formal historical writings; it owes much also to popular works of various kinds, to novels, plays, the cinema, radio, and now television. Professor Rizzitano's paper deals with works of an Arab dramatist, and gives an interesting revelation of some of the political and emotional attitudes that affect the depicting of past events.

The problems of self-image and historical and corporate consciousness form the theme of the two final papers, by Professor von Grunebaum and Professor Cantwell Smith. While the first is concerned with the images of man and history in the minds of historians, the second attempts to elucidate the significance of the term Islam as used, in different periods, by Muslims. The discussion of the two was opened by Mr. Hourani, with an introductory statement that has been transcribed from the report of the debate, and is included in this volume.

The survey of historiography contained in these forty-odd papers is obviously far from complete. Several major topics are quite untouched—such as for example the classical Arabic historiography of the ninth and tenth centuries, the historians of Egypt under the independent dynasties

[26] Thus, for example, *Télémaque* appeared in Turkish in 1862 and in Arabic in 1867, *Paul et Virginie* in Arabic in 1872 and in Turkish in 1873, *Monte-Cristo* in Arabic in 1871 and in Turkish in 1871–3. The Turkish version of *Robinson Crusoe*, published in 1864, was translated from Arabic and not from English.

[27] See below, pp. 409 and 424. On the *Enjümen-i Dānish* see further B. Lewis, 'Andjuman' in *EI*².

[28] In 1959 a colloquium was held at the American University, Beirut, on Arab Historiography in the last hundred years, concerning medieval Arab History. The papers were published in the journal *al-Abḥāth* of June and September 1959.

from Tulunids to Mamluks, the historical literature of the Iranian cultural and political renaissance, the imperial Ottoman chronography of the great period, the historical literature in Hebrew from the sixteenth century to the present day, the local histories of North Africa, Arabia, Iraq, Anatolia, and many other places. The studies of European historical writing contain no account of the Muslim Near and Middle East in medieval Western Christian sources, nor any full treatment of the new specialist approaches of twentieth-century historians—the study of the region and its civilization from the sociological and anthropological angles. In a group-survey of this kind there is also inevitably some overlapping, notably in the papers of Professor Salibi and Mr. Hourani, those of Professors Cahen, Dahan and Hilmy Ahmed, and those of Professor Inalcık and Dr. Ménage. Here the difference in treatment and approach of the various writers made it desirable to retain their papers as they stood. All authors were given the opportunity to revise their contributions in the light of discussion in the Conference.

In the final session of the Conference, several proposals were made for further collaborative efforts, which, it was felt, would be of value for the advancement of our subject. These were:

(1) A revised and consolidated edition of the historical sections of Brockelmann's *Geschichte der arabischen Literatur*.

(2) A survey and bibliography of translations into Middle Eastern languages from Western languages in the nineteenth and early twentieth centuries.

(3) A calendar of archives and other documents of the minorities in the Middle East.

(4) A service for abstracting Russian publications on Islamic subjects.

(5) A dictionary of the use and development of political, social, and cultural terms in the Islamic World in modern times. This would include such words as 'nation', 'fatherland', and the like, the usage of which has changed very greatly since the beginnings of westernization, and still varies significantly from country to country, and from community to community. This, like the second proposal, would be of the greatest value for the understanding of the recent and contemporary Middle East.

The participants in the Conference felt, at the conclusion of their meetings, that it had contributed to clearing the way to more objective historical writing, both in the Near and Middle East, and in the West. By drawing the attention, both of scholars and of the wider public, to the problems involved, it had played a part in increased mutual understanding.[29]

[29] This is attested by several subsequent publications to which reference has already been made.

PART I

ARABIC, PERSIAN, AND TURKISH HISTORIOGRAPHY TO THE 12/19TH CENTURY

I. THE MATERIALS USED BY IBN ISḤĀQ

W. MONTGOMERY WATT

Reader in Arabic in the University of Edinburgh

1. *The State of the Problem*

Though a certain amount of work has been done on the life of Muḥammad during the last half century, there has been no comprehensive survey of the sources as such. Some continue to adopt what may be called the Lammens-Becker position, while others, like the present writer, have adopted a rather different position but without arguing for it extensively.[1] A study of the sources of the *Sīra* may therefore appropriately begin with C. H. Becker's account of the position of Henri Lammens:

> In its detailed accounts, which are often diffuse, the *Sīra* is not an independent historical source. It is merely *ḥadīth*-material arranged in biographical order. The individual *ḥadīths*, however, are either exegetical elaborations of Qur'anic allusions or later inventions of dogmatic-juristic tendency. The exegetical and dogmatic interest is older than the historical. The latter only arose when, in the face of the Christian historical sources which attest the miraculous figure and the divinity of Jesus, analogous historical sources seemed a desideratum for the founder of Islam likewise. The actual historical material is extremely scanty. So the allusions of the Qur'ān are taken and expanded; and, first and foremost, the already existing dogmatic and juristic *ḥadīth* are collected and chronologically arranged.[2]

Becker goes on to say that he agrees with Lammens on these general points (though differing from him considerably in their application in detail), and concludes with a diagram in which *tafsīr* and *ḥadīth* appear as the two types of material out of which the *Sīra* is formed.

When one looks at the pages of Ibn Isḥāq, it is easy to find sections and small passages which clearly belong to *tafsīr*. At the end of his account of the battle of Badr, for example, there is a section[3] about the *Sūrat al-anfāl*, giving the precise references of the various verses to incidents in the battle. But what is one to make nowadays of *ḥadīth*? Since Becker wrote, there has been the important work of Joseph Schacht on legal *ḥadīth*. In this special field, to which he is careful to limit himself (though his theory may have

[1] Cf. the working principle formulated in my *Muhammad at Mecca*, p. xiv.

[2] Becker, 'Grundsätzliches zur Leben-Muhammed-Forschung', *Islamstudien* (Leipzig, 1924), i, 520 f. (reprinted from *Der Islam* (1913), iv, 263 ff.).

[3] Wüstenfeld, pp. 476–85.

repercussions in other fields), Professor Schacht holds that it was not until the time of al-Shāfi'ī (d. 820) that it became the regular practice for legal rules to be justified by a *ḥadīth* reporting a saying or action of Muḥammad through a continuous line of transmitters. If this theory is correct or even roughly correct, then *ḥadīth* as they are found in the canonical collections were not in existence in the time of Ibn Isḥāq (d. 768). The Lammens-Becker position thus rests upon presuppositions which an important body of present-day opinion would dispute.

Whether one adopts the Lammens-Becker position or some other position, it would seem that the next step is to look again at the materials in the *Sīra*, especially those which are clearly not *tafsīr*, and to try to determine just what they are. At the same time attention must be paid to the motives of those who preserved, modified or fabricated them. Such a programme would require a book, and the present paper is therefore no more than a preliminary survey.

2. *The Expansion of the Qur'ān*

There is a certain conception of Muḥammad in the Qur'ān itself. He is there regarded as one of a long line of prophets, all sent by God to particular peoples with a message that in essentials was identical. Muḥammad's special task was at first thought of as the extension to the Arabs of the true religion of God. Latterly it was also the restoring of the true religion in its purity after it had been corrupted by Jews and Christians. This purified religion, as established by Muḥammad, is spoken of as continuing to the Last Day, though sometimes only as one of several religions. At other times Muḥammad is said to have been sent to all men,[4] and to be 'the seal of the prophets'[5] (though this phrase may not originally have had the connotation afterwards given to it). The claim is likewise made that Muḥammad's coming was foretold in the Jewish and Christian scriptures.

The conception in Ibn Isḥāq's *Sīra* of Muḥammad as prophet and messenger goes beyond that in the Qur'ān in various respects. While the Qur'ān had insisted that, though a warner and a bearer of light, he was only a mortal, in the *Sīra* various supernatural powers are attributed to him; he has knowledge of the future and is able to perform miracles. His coming is supposed not merely to be mentioned briefly in the Bible but to be widely known to religious scholars. And his religion is thought of as the final religion and one applicable to all men; this last point is witnessed to by the fact that important men, whose official positions prevented them from openly becoming Muslims, privately admitted that they believed in Muḥammad.

This theological development of the conception of Muḥammad may be attributed to general religious interests, and affects several types of

[4] 7. 158/157; 34. 28/27; cf. 21.107, 'a mercy to the worlds'. [5] 33.40.

material. In part this is doubtless due, as Becker argued,[6] to an attempt to meet the anti-Islamic polemic of Christians, and in particular to their arguments that Muḥammad could not be a prophet since his coming had not been foretold and his message was not attested by miracles. Without denying that the need to find some retort to the Christians was a strong motive, it should be noticed that a similar theological development might arise from a desire to assimilate Muḥammad to the conception of a religious leader current in the heartlands of the Islamic empire; men who held that any great religious leader must have had supernatural powers would look for these in Muḥammad and would tend unconsciously to see them where they were not really present.

Two types of material which might fall under the heading of *tafsīr* are relevant to the *sīra*. The first of these are expansions of Qur'anic references to earlier prophets. These are mainly based on the Bible and on extra-canonical works in the biblical tradition. For the prophets of 'Ād and Thamūd, however, it was necessary to go to Arab legend or to invent, while the stories connecting Abraham and Ishmael with Mecca could have had no other basis than the Qur'anic allusions. The second type of material is what is known as 'occasions of revelation', and this material, which must be derived from personal memories or invention, gives information not about pre-Islamic times but about the life of Muḥammad himself. The question of the truth or falsity of this material is thus quite different from that of the first type. There are contradictions in it, as when the same verse is said to have been revealed on two different occasions. On the other hand, there are many cases where there is no reason to doubt the traditional account of the circumstances in which a verse was revealed; this is usually so in passages concerned with the main events of the Medinan period. It is sometimes difficult to be certain how far a traditional account is genuine; e.g. the beginning of *Sūra* 80 is usually said to refer to Ibn Umm Maktūm, and this is probably true; but that the men to whom Muḥammad was talking were Abū Jahl and 'Utba b. Rabī'a is probably no more than the intelligent guess of some later transmitter.[7]

Both types of *tafsīr*-material were the product of a genuine religious interest. The Qur'anic allusions had to be elaborated into complete stories and the background filled in if the main ideas were to be impressed on the minds of simple men. The group of men who were primarily responsible for this were the *quṣṣāṣ* or 'story-tellers', who were really a kind of preacher and performed an important function in disseminating the ideas of the Qur'ān among the rank and file of the Muslims.[8] Their primary motive

[6] 'Christliche Polemik und islamische Dogmenbildung', *ZA* (1911), xxvi, 175–95 (=*Islamstudien*, i, 432–49).

[7] Ṭab., *Tafsīr*, ad loc.; Ibn Isḥāq says it was al-Walīd.

[8] Goldziher, *Muhammedanische Studien*, ii, 161–3; *Koranauslegung*, pp. 58 f.

must have been the spread of the Islamic religion, but in the course of their activity they were doubtless affected by the desire to assimilate the conception of Muḥammad to current conceptions of what a religious leader should be. The distorting effect of these secondary motives is to be seen not so much in the 'occasions of revelation' as in the 'theological' anecdotes to be considered under a later heading (7), for which the 'story-tellers' were in part responsible.

3. *Arab Genealogies and pre-Islamic Events*

The study of genealogy was a special branch of knowledge among the pre-Islamic Arabs (as indeed among later Arabs too), and along with poetry, with which it was connected, was one of their chief cultural achievements. The deepest feeling in their lives was tribal pride or zeal for the honour of the tribe, and this honour and nobility, was one of the chief topics of their poems. Honour and nobility, however, depended largely on descent; and therefore it was necessary to know who one's ancestors were and the noble deeds they had performed. Along with genealogy in the strict sense, therefore, went a knowledge of the 'days', that is, the battles, of the Arabs.

This knowledge was continued under Islam, and indeed in some respects developed. Abū Bakr was pre-eminent as a genealogist, and his knowledge doubtless contributed to Muḥammad's political successes. Several others are mentioned in early Umayyad times, notably 'Abīd b. Sharya who was at the court of Mu'āwiya.[9] The same motive of pride in one's tribe was still operative, especially when the conquests brought the tribes into much more frequent contact with one another. It seems to be a fact that under the Umayyads passions became attached to larger groupings that had seldom been spoken of previously, especially the 'northerners' ('Adnān or Ma'add) and the 'southerners' (Qaḥṭān or al-Yaman). Goldziher has argued that the interest in the rivalry between the north and the south arose from the rivalry between the *Anṣār* who were 'southerners' and Quraysh who were 'northerners'.[10] Even if other factors contributed to the interest in it, this rivalry of north and south certainly affected the study of genealogy and led to much 'tendential shaping' of the earlier legends and the earlier parts of genealogies. While the modern scholar must proceed with great care where such 'tendential shaping' is suspected, the wide-spread interest in genealogy is a guarantee of a high degree of accuracy in the genealogical details given about Muslims, and also in those for one or two generations before Muḥammad.

[9] *Fihrist*, ch. 3, ¶1 (Cairo, 1348, p. 132); cf. Goldziher, *Muh. Stud.*, index, s.v. 'Abīd.
[10] Op. cit., i, 89–98.

4. *The Main Events of the Maghāzī*

An important group of materials to which very little attention has been paid by Western scholars is what may be called for short 'the *maghāzī*-material'. This is to be taken to mean such information as the list of expeditions, the aim of each and the actual results, the leader, the number and, in so far as known, the names of the participants, the approximate date and relative chronological position. This information is usually given without any *isnād* both by Ibn Isḥāq and al-Wāqidī, and is generally distinct from the anecdotes connected with the various expeditions; the latter are part of the account of the expeditions as we have them, but deal with minor details and usually have some *isnād*, even if not a complete one. In the case of some of the major expeditions, such as the battles of Badr and Uḥud, the *maghāzī*-material includes an outline of the course of the battle.

Little of this material can be derived from the Qur'ān, where most of the expeditions are not mentioned. It must be the result of the work of the whole series of students of the *maghāzī*, questioning large numbers of persons and sifting and ordering the information thus obtained. This process, moreover, did not come to an end with Ibn Isḥāq. He knows of several expeditions[11] which he is apparently unable to date or place chronologically; but al-Wāqidī seems to have access to further information which enables him to do that. Ibn Hishām is often able to add to Ibn Isḥāq's account the name of the man left in charge of Medina when Muḥammad was absent. It is also to be noted that the writers named treat this type of information as ascertained fact, and that it was generally accepted as such by the Muslims as a whole. The authoritative position of Ibn Isḥāq is presumably due to the fact that there was practically nothing in his *Sīra* which the community could not accept (though modern scholars like Caetani think that al-Wāqidī has corrected him on some minor chronological details).

While the ordering of this material must have been the work of scholars, the preservation of it until the scholars collected it must have been the work of the Muslims in general or at least of some Muslims. What were their motives? First and foremost would be pride in the achievements of the Islamic community, and this feeling would be, as it were, a reincarnation of the pride of the pre-Islamic nomad in the achievements of his tribe. The early collectors of *maghāzī*-material were doubtless moved by such a pride, in combination with scholarly interests; since legal *ḥadīth* did not yet exist, their aim cannot have been to provide a framework for these. Some of the material may have been preserved not for its own sake but because it was implicit in some incident remembered by a particular

[11] W. 973–99.

family or clan because it redounded to their honour.[12] Some of the lists of men and similar matters, especially the lists of those at Badr, would be of importance for the administrators of the Islamic state, since priority in conversion affected the stipend due.

This consideration of motives shows little ground for doubting the truth of the main events of the *maghāzī*. The scholars and the administrators as a whole, whatever may have been the case with individuals, had no strong reason for distorting the facts. Family anecdotes would often exaggerate the importance of the member of the family featuring in them, but such exaggeration can be allowed for, and perhaps was often allowed for by men like Ibn Isḥāq; in any case the exaggerations in an anecdote would probably not affect the information implicit in it about the main events. Thus the *maghāzī*-material (in the special sense of the main outline of events, and omitting all anecdotes), though it has often been passed over in silence by Western scholars, is an essential foundation for the biography of Muḥammad and the history of his times. Without this material the Qur'ān is useless as a historical source. When this material is accepted as a basis, however, it is possible to give a coherent account of Muḥammad's achievements, and that is a further confirmation that it is in general true.

Analogous to the *maghāzī*-material, and best included under the same head, is a small amount of material about the chronological order of events before the Hijra.

5. *Poetry*

Not much requires to be said about the poetry, since, even if it is all authentic, it adds little to our historical knowledge. The information it gives us is mainly about the attitude of tribes and clans to one another. This is in the form of praise and blame, and only refers to events allusively. In many cases, though not in all, there would be little change in these attitudes in the first century or so of Islam; and in these cases the fact that a poem is not by the person to whom it is attributed but by some later member of the same clan does not affect the value of the information, since the actual writer has the same attitudes and has access to the traditional lore of the tribe. Where there has been a change of attitude, such as the increased animosity of the *Anṣār* against Quraysh, the value of falsely attributed poetry is different; but the question cannot profitably be discussed without more study of detail than is possible here. It has also to be kept in mind that false lines may have been interpolated into genuine poems.

[12] The view of Schacht that a family *isnād* for a legal *ḥadīth* is to be regarded as false presupposes that the handing down of anecdotes within a family had been a common practice.

6. *Documentary Material*

There is not much documentary material in Ibn Isḥāq. The most important document is the Constitution of Medina. It is possible, too, that his list of the Muslims at Badr may come from an official document, either directly or through previous scholars. For the purposes of the present study it is not necessary to do more than mention this type of material. (There are further documents, apparently authentic, in Ibn Sa'd, i/2.)

7. *Anecdotes*

All the remaining material in the *Sīra* of Ibn Isḥāq may be taken together under the heading of anecdotes, since it is in the form of stories about particular incidents. There are indeed some composite stories where Ibn Isḥāq conflates two or three accounts, and these stand halfway between anecdotes and *maghāzī*-material; it is easy, however, to apply to them what is relevant of the remarks under the two headings. In this discussion of the sources the title 'anecdotes' is to be preferred to 'Traditions' or *ḥadīth*, since there is not yet a coherent body of material studied and preserved by a particular group of people. Instead there is a very varied mass of material, preserved by different groups of people for different reasons.

The most important distinction to make is between anecdotes which have been modified or distorted by party-interests, political, theological or legal (including anecdotes which are sheer inventions) and anecdotes which have not been affected by interests of these kinds. Among the latter are anecdotes which have been preserved because of a general interest in the achievement of the Islamic community and those which have been preserved because of pride in the achievements of one's family or clan. As already noted, this last group of what may be called 'familial anecdotes' is liable to exaggerate the importance of the family or clan, but apart from that, unless some other motive is also present, it is not distorted.

Among the distorted or tendential anecdotes are some which appear to be sheer inventions. One such is the story derived by Ibn Isḥāq from his father about the brightness which was seen by a woman on 'Abdallāh's forehead just before he begat Muḥammad but which disappeared afterwards; this is clearly intended to contribute to the conception of Muḥammad as supernaturally endowed. Sheer inventions of this kind seem to be found chiefly where theological interests are involved, especially in developing the Qur'anic conception of Muḥammad (as described in 2). They take the form of stories about soothsayers, monks and wise men who knew about his coming beforehand and stories about his birth, childhood and early life. There are also stories about miracles performed by him during his maturity. The supernatural characteristics attributed to Muḥammad in these stories justify their complete rejection, since the Qur'ān insists that

Muḥammad is no more than a man. These stories are not without interest, however, in that they show the directions in which theological tendencies were developing the conception of Muḥammad.

The majority of the tendential anecdotes, however, are not sheer inventions, but are modifications to varying extents of true stories. The original incident is often something quite trivial. In many cases we have several different versions of a story, and are able, as it were, to see it growing. Thus, it appears to be the case that, when the wounded Sa'd b. Mu'ādh came to judge Banū Qurayẓa, Muḥammad said, 'Stand for your *sayyid*.' In itself this remark is trivial and of no historical significance, but one party said that it implied that the *Anṣār* were fit to rule over Quraysh, and the other party gave the story a little twist to rule out this implication, and so on.[13]

The story of Quzmān may be taken as another example of how a story is tendentially shaped. Ibn Isḥāq's version is ascribed to 'Āṣim b. 'Umar, a scholar from whom he obtained much information, and al-Wāqidī's is presumably from the same source, though he does not say so, since in it 'Āṣim's grandfather Qatāda is mentioned (but not mentioned here by Ibn Isḥāq). According to al-Wāqidī's version,[14] which is the most primitive, Quzmān arrived late at the battle of Uḥud, but fought bravely until he was mortally wounded; after a time, unable to bear the pain of his wounds any longer, he cut a vein with an arrow and died, whereupon Muḥammad remarked, 'He is one of the people of Hell, but God uses wicked men to further religion.' In this form the story may well be true, though it is also a warning against suicide; even if true it is historically unimportant. Ibn Isḥāq's version is similar except that before Uḥud, Muḥammad is said to have been in the habit of saying, 'He belongs to the people of Hell.'[15] The remark, then, instead of being a judgement on suicide, becomes an example of Muḥammad's foreknowledge—there is no suggestion that it is merely his reading of character—and this point is emphasized by the ending of the story in al-Ṭabarī's recension, though not in Ibn Hishām's. This is not the end of the matter, however. In the course of the theological discussions about predestination someone noticed that the version which exemplified Muḥammad's foreknowledge also implied that the man's fate was predetermined. The anecdote therefore appears in the canonical collections of Traditions among those concerned with predestination.[16] The theological version of the anecdote, however, differs from the others in that the historical details—the man's name and the 'expedition'—are omitted. While the opposite is conceivable, it is almost certain that the historical

[13] Cf. Montgomery Watt, 'The Condemnation of the Jews of Banū Qurayẓah', *Muslim World* (1952), xlii, 160–71; the conclusions of that article will have to be modified in the light of the distinction in this paper between *maghāzī*-material and anecdotes.

[14] Wellhausen, p. 109.

[15] Wüst., p. 578; cf. A. Guillaume, *Life of Muḥammad*, pp. 383 f.

[16] Al-Bukhārī, *Qadar* (82), p. 5.

versions are the original and that the theological version is derived from them. The theologians' lack of interest in historical details tends to confirm the view that the *Sīra* was not produced in order to provide a framework for theological, political and legal Traditions; Muslim scholars in the earlier period paid little attention to the kind of internal evidence this would have provided.

Among the criticisms made of Ibn Isḥāq in his own time and shortly after were the charges that he was a Shi'ite and a Qadarite. The chief evidence noticed for the latter is that he has two anecdotes given on the authority of the early Mu'tazilite, 'Amr b. 'Ubayd. Shi'ite sympathies may have led Ibn Isḥāq to include stories about Muḥammad's supernatural birth and to exclude anecdotes (found in al-Ṭabarī) making Abū Bakr or Zayd b. Ḥāritha the first male Muslim. On the other hand, in the recensions we have there is no trace of anecdotes supporting extreme Shi'ite views, such as the Khumm tradition.

This is a suitable point to refer to the quarrel between Mālik b. Anas and Ibn Isḥāq.[17] The latter claimed he was able to correct Mālik's Traditions, and this may well be so. The point is that Mālik was more interested in the juristic soundness of the Traditions (and of the inferences from them) than in their historical accuracy. Though the method of the *isnād* as later perfected by al-Shāfi'ī was not yet normal, Mālik must have preferred a doctrine based on the opinions of sound scholars to one arrived at by the methods of a historian who was ready to accept evidence from inadmissible people like Jews and Christians. The fact of this quarrel further confirms the independence of the historical interest from the theological and legal interests. The historian was not altogether free from political interests, however, since Ibn Isḥāq is said to have written his *Maghāzī* for the Caliph al-Manṣūr (754–75).[18]

The anecdotes, then, are a great mass of material, preserved by different groups of people, and of varying value. Some are inventions. Others are the tendential elaboration of a trivial remark or incident; whether the latter is genuine or not (e.g. Muḥammad's remark after Quzmān's death) is historically insignificant. Because there are many anecdotes of this sort, however, the scholar is not justified in rejecting all anecdotes found in the *Sīra*. On the contrary, there are many which are wholly or largely true; and these are usually also of greater historical significance than those which have been tendentially elaborated. This justifies the practical rule that anecdotes are to be accepted where they do not contradict other material and where there is no tendential elaboration. There will sometimes be difficulties in following out this rule, for example, in deciding to which category a piece of material belongs; but the general principle is clear.

[17] Cf. the biographies in Wüstenfeld, ii, ii–xxxiii; also Yāqūt, *Irshād*, vi, 400.
[18] Ibn Qutayba, *Ma'ārif*, p. 247; etc.

8. *The Structure of the* Sīra

The various types of material have now been enumerated. The material, however, has not merely to be collected; it must also be arranged. This matter too is worthy of consideration. While we can study the structure of Ibn Isḥāq's *Sīra* fairly adequately, it must be remembered that this structure cannot be attributed solely to him, since the scanty remains of his predecessors show that they had already arranged the material in much the same way as Ibn Isḥāq did.[19]

For the purposes of this study three parts may be distinguished in the *Sīra*, though these do not quite coincide with the subdivisions known to Arab scholars. These three parts are: (1) an account, based mainly on the Old Testament, of events from the creation of the world to the time of Ishmael; (2) events in Arabia from Ishmael to Muḥammad's call, based on Arabian genealogical and legendary material; (3) events from Muḥammad's call to his death. Each of these parts has a definite framework or principle of arrangement. For the first it is genealogies found in the book of Genesis; for the second it is mainly the genealogy of Muḥammad himself; for the third it is what has been called the *maghāzī*-material (including the slight amount of similar material dealing with the period from the call to the Hijra).

The framework having been thus provided, Ibn Isḥāq adds the other types of material at an appropriate place. After the account of the Hijra he places material concerning the conditions Muḥammad found in Medina on his arrival and his first dispositions, for example, the pairing of Emigrants and *Anṣār* as brothers, and the attitudes of various Jews. The presence of the Constitution of Medina here merely indicates that Ibn Isḥāq thought this an appropriate place, and therefore does not necessitate dating the document immediately after the Hijra.

To illustrate how the material is added to the framework Ibn Isḥāq's treatment of the battle of Badr may be analysed. It is subdivided as follows (Wüstenfeld's paging):

427	Introduction—*maghāzī*-material
428–75	Anecdotes interspersed with *maghāzī*-material[20]
476–85	Qur'ān and *tafsīr*
485–515	Lists (*maghāzī*-material)
516–39	Poetry
539	Concluding sentence (*maghāzī*-material)

Al-Wāqidī's arrangement is similar.

[19] Guillaume, *Life of Muḥammad*, xiv–xix.

[20] This concludes with a list of the Meccans who provided camels to feed the army (not, as Guillaume, the pilgrims—cf. Wāqidī-Wellhausen, p. 80).

As an example of a minor raid, the account of the expedition to Dhāt al-Riqā' may be examined in greater detail.[21] It consists of:

Summary of the events of the raid (*maghāzī*-material)

Anecdote about the 'prayer of fear' (partly *tafsīr*; this is found in al-Ṭabarī (i. 1454), but is omitted by Ibn Hishām, who instead has three other more legal anecdotes not from Ibn Isḥāq)

Anecdote about Muḥammad's trust in God in danger (there is an element of *tafsīr*, but it appears to be a later addition)

Anecdote about Muḥammad's kindness to Jābir (with one detail which could be regarded as miraculous)

Anecdote of man who finished reciting a *sūra* though wounded

Concluding sentence (*maghāzī*-material).

It is instructive to compare with this al-Wāqidī's account of the same expedition. This cannot be done here in detail, but the following points may be noted. Al-Wāqidī provides more of his material with an *isnād*, and the *isnāds* tend to be more complete; this makes it more difficult, however, to distinguish between *maghāzī*-material and anecdotes than in the work of Ibn Isḥāq. Al-Wāqidī has fuller details of names. While retaining most of Ibn Isḥāq's anecdotes (though often in different forms, which may indicate different sources), he adds a number of new anecdotes which illustrate Muḥammad's supernatural powers, or which have theological or legal implications.

The statement that the first part of Ibn Isḥāq's *Sīra* deals with stories from the book of Genesis requires some expansion. It involves regarding the book of *al-Mubtada'* or *al-Mabda'*, which is mentioned by Ibn al-Nadīm, Yāqūt and others, as part of the *Sīra*. Though neglected by Ibn Hishām, it is frequently quoted by al-Ṭabarī in his history.[22] It may be noted, too, that the *Sīra* of Ibn Sa'd begins with an account of the prophets from whom Muḥammad was descended, that is, from Adam to Abraham and Ishmael. Ibn Isḥāq follows Genesis more closely than al-Ṭabarī,[23] though even he has some additional material. The criticism of Ibn Isḥāq[24] that he took material from Jews and Christians reflects the later attitude of suspicion towards such sources and the tendency to avoid them (at least in theory).[25] Thus Ibn Sa'd prefaces his accounts of the Old Testament figures with remarks of Muḥammad about his ancestry, in which he speaks of God choosing the Arabs;[26] while al-Ṭabarī accepts the Tradition that the first thing God created was the Pen and rejects the account, based on Genesis, of Ibn Isḥāq on the grounds that it has no *isnād* and that a subject

[21] Wüstenfeld, pp. 661–5.

[22] Cf. *Indices*, s.v.

[23] E.g. the birth of Seth's son Enos (i, 164).

[24] Yāqūt, *Irshād*, vi, 401.

[25] Cf. Montgomery Watt, 'The Early Development of the Muslim Attitude to the Bible', *Transactions of the Glasgow University Oriental Society*, xvi, 50–62.

[26] i/1.2.

of this kind requires a *khabar* from God or the Messenger.[27] Similarly, Ibn Sa'd approves the opinion that it is wrong to pursue genealogies further back than Ma'add (though he himself quotes them right to Adam) and justifies this by saying that the earlier names are not remembered but are taken from *Ahl al-kitāb*.[28] It was doubtless the suspicion of Jewish and Christian information, coupled with reliance on the method of *isnād* to Muḥammad, which led to the disappearance of Biblical material from the *Sīra*, though it was retained by historians like al-Ṭabarī, al-Mas'ūdī, and Ibn al-Athīr.

The omission of the Biblical material, however, enhances the importance of the *maghāzī*-material, and suggests that the chief task immediately ahead for scholars in this field is to look more closely at this *maghāzī*-material and to study its relations to the various groups of anecdotes.

[27] 1.32.

[28] 1/1.29. The connexion of Arab genealogies with the Old Testament goes back at least to 'Abīd b. Sharya (al-Mas'ūdī, *Muruj*, iv, 89; cf. 112, not to go beyond Ma'add); the gap has to be filled either by identifying Arab names with Biblical (cf. al-Ṭabarī; i, 147 f., discussion whether the Persian Jayumart is Jāmir b. Yāfith b. Nūḥ), or by invention.

2. THE INFLUENCE OF THE BIBLICAL TRADITION ON MUSLIM HISTORIOGRAPHY

FRANZ ROSENTHAL

Professor of Semitic Languages, Yale University

'Biblical' is understood here to mean 'Judaeo-Christian', with the restriction of this term to its cultural-religious sense in which it is usually employed in historical contexts. This makes it possible for us to exclude from consideration such subjects as late Greek and Byzantine historiography and their possible influence upon Muslim historical writing.

The topics to be discussed in this paper are:

(1) The influence of the biblical *idea of history* on the Prophet.

(2) The use Muslim scholars made of the Prophet's idea of history in the *writing of history*. In this connection, it may not be entirely superfluous to state the obvious fact that possession of a historical view of the world and the production of historical works are two different things. The most profound historical view need not, and often does not, lead to the creation of a historical literature.

(3) The enrichment of the *contents* of Muslim histories through materials derived from the biblical tradition. It need hardly be said that this covers a very wide field and that for a detailed study of the subject a large number of Muslim historical works would have to be discussed. As this cannot be done here, a bare outline of some of the problems and materials involved must suffice.

(4) Similarities in the *form* of historical presentation that exist between biblical and Muslim historiography. Since common origin, or parallel development, is the most likely explanation here, to the exclusion of influence and dependence, we may restrict ourselves to merely touching upon this subject.

(1) *The Influence of the Biblical Idea of History on the Prophet*

The historical reflections expressed and implied in the Qur'ān are practically all connected with biblical figures and events. Moreover, they belong to the theological substance of Muḥammad's message, and, to all appearances, they also have no counterpart in pagan Arab thought. Thus, their ultimate Judaeo-Christian origin is assured.

However, when it comes to the discussion of particular points, we are up against the blank wall of our ignorance of details as far as Judaeo-Christian thinking in the central Arabian environment is concerned, an ignorance that is not compensated for by what we know from contemporary or near-contemporary Jewish and Christian literature in other parts of the world. Therefore, the extent of the Prophet's own contribution in responding to the stimulus he received from outside remains a matter of speculation. And when we try to become even more specific and attempt to dissect the biblical influence according to its Jewish and Christian components—with gnostic intermediaries remaining a possibility—our argumentation is apt to lose itself in a welter of preconceived ideas.

A somewhat simplified but on the whole, I believe, accurate description of Muḥammad's concept of the historical process, derived from the Qur'ān and largely disregarding developments in Muḥammad's thinking, runs as follows:

The world had its definite beginning and is moving towards its definite end. Everything in it, the stars, the earth, the oceans, the mountains, the plants, the animals, is there to fulfil a definite purpose in the unfolding of history in which they participate without themselves being exposed to any changes except during the final cataclysm. God has made and destined it this way, and everything, known to Him and observed by Him, is moving onward according to His plan. The framework of chronology, a year consisting of twelve months (9.36/36), has also existed since the beginning of creation and is to continue to the final end. Thus, the setting in which history unfolds is rigidly unchangeable.

Man is intended as the beneficiary of all these divine preparations. He becomes the sole agent of history in as much as in this world, he alone (together, to be sure, with such supernatural beings as the *jinn* and the devils) has a certain measure of freedom to act. How this freedom can be reconciled with divine omnipotence, foresight, and planning, is by no means clear; its existence is accepted as a fact proven by history. (There is an element of circular reasoning here: the freedom to act produces history, history proves the freedom to act. This is the inevitable consequence of the lack of clarity concerning the concept of freedom of action.)

The actions of man are stimulated and directed by his desires (*ahwā'*). Human desires have an inclination towards evil and that which is not acceptable to God. Whenever human actions are good and reflect true belief in God, prosperity will be the reward for them; if they are evil and actions of unbelief, punishment and destruction will follow. Reward and punishment may take place in this world or in life after death. The reality of mundane reward and punishment can be illustrated from history and is known from experience. There can be no doubt whatever as to the absolute certainty of an other-worldly retribution. Being operative among groups of people, and not merely among individuals, this causal nexus between goodness and reward on the one hand, and between evil and punishment on the other, constitutes history. Examples from the past abound, especially for the negative aspect. At various times in the past and in various localities (so as to show the universal validity of the historical experience), inspired men attempted to correct the sinful behaviour of their contemporaries and to guide them to the good life. They achieved no lasting success, or failed completely, with dire consequences, less for themselves than for the groups that sinned and suffered destruction.

Turning from the past to the present and future, Muḥammad's early preoccupation with the end of the world and his apparent belief in its imminent arrival—antedating in large part the historical views heretofore mentioned—soon gave way to an attitude more congenial to him. The Prophet's basic psychological outlook was one of supreme confidence and an indestructible optimism; we may recall, for instance, that he displayed no bitterness, such as comes from frustration, about his childhood experiences as an orphan, that the attacks of his enemies were met with aggressive defiance, that the joys of Paradise were given more prominence in the Qur'ān than the tortures of Hell. Now, Muḥammad saw himself as one of the periodical warners and prophets sent to mankind; undeterred by consistently inauspicious historical precedents, he considered himself as presenting his people with a unique opportunity for salvation and became more and more convinced that he would succeed where all the others had failed. He is the final prophet (if finality is the main idea implied by the disputed expression 'seal of the prophets' in 33.40/40). The path to a better future is prepared, though there still are, and always will be, many who do not see the light. The last days of the world will come in the wake of all the great happenings foreseen for the End, but when this will be has become less certain.

Taking the preceding brief outline as representative of Muḥammad's view of the world, we may ask ourselves how it compares with concepts of history prevalent in the Judaeo-Christian tradition. It has been said that in order to arrive at an adequate understanding of the Scriptures, it would be necessary to accomplish the impossible feat of forgetting the entire tradition of interpretation and exegesis. Here, the opposite applies. In order to have a suitable basis for comparison, it is necessary to forget all the critical efforts of modern scholars and attempt to see the biblical idea of history—the *one* biblical idea of history—with the eyes of the Jews and Christians of late antiquity.

The unchangeable physical setting of history and the coming of its final dissolution were accepted as true facts. The idea of the preponderance of man in creation had its firm biblical basis. History was God's plan for the salvation of humanity. Man's obstinacy and sinfulness led to the constant repetition of the same process: opportunities for salvation were offered by inspired men, but these opportunities were rejected and there was, as a result, renewed suffering. For Christians, the unique opportunity for ending this calamitous process had arrived in the coming of Christ; the opportunity continued to exist in the spiritual sense, but in this world, sin and concomitant suffering persisted. For Jews, the history of rejected opportunity, sin, and suffering had never been interrupted since man appeared in the world, but opportunity had ceased to be a reality in this world and become the hope, doomed from the outset, of occasional dreamers, while suffering was the almost constant fate of the Jews. The End was expected to come and follow its prescribed course; this was as certain as the interpretation of the biblical hints as to the exact time of its coming was uncertain.

The identity of this historical view with that of Muḥammad is obvious. Essentially, it also was the same among both Christians and Jews. The idea that the dismal spectacle of history was to be ended here and now by a saviour, points to a Christian inspiration for this important element of Muḥammad's thinking as long as there is no concrete evidence for Jewish Messianic beliefs in his environment.

The one meaningful difference between the biblical view and that of the Prophet lies in the fact that whatever its antecedents, the Judaeo-Christian attitude had come to be profoundly and lastingly pessimistic. It would seem that actual conditions were mainly responsible for this development. In the historical experience of the Jewish minority during the centuries preceding Islam, there assuredly was nothing that could have swayed the Jews from despair, and oriental Christianity, even in the rather short interval between pagan persecution and Muslim predominance, had little occasion to savour the exhilarating effect of worldly success and forget its contempt of this world. In contrast, the confidence Muḥammad had in himself and his cause proved justified by the tremendous political success of Islam. This made it possible for his buoyant optimism to triumph over the gloomy sin-and-retribution theory of history and to remain very much in evidence in later times when history was written. To be sure, the idea of reward and punishment finds expression in historical works, and even appears in prominent places. Near the beginning of his *History* al-Ṭabarī says:[1] 'Let us now discuss those who were the first to be given by God royal authority and to receive His bounty but who, then, were ungrateful, denied His Mastership, and behaved proudly and insolently towards their Master. As a consequence, God deprived them of His bounty and shamed and humbled them. Let us then continue with those who followed their example in this respect and imitated them, with the result that God wrought His vengeance upon them and, including them in the company of the former, made them share their shame and humiliation. We shall also mention those rulers, or messengers and prophets, who lived at the same time or after them, who obeyed their

[1] *Annales*, i, 78.

Master and led a praiseworthy life.' This biblical and Islamic view of life implied in al-Ṭabarī's statement was presumably shared by most Muslim historians but it had little influence upon their historical presentation. It certainly did not induce them to seek the motive of sin and retribution in every phase of Muslim history.

(2) *The Prophet's Idea of History and Muslim Historiography*

There can be no doubt that Muḥammad's interest in history, and the manner in which this interest found expression in his work, provided a powerful stimulus for the creation of an Islamic historiography. It may seem doubtful, though, whether his particular historical view had a decisive influence on the character of Muslim historiography and whether its influence upon Muslim historical thinking was an altogether beneficial and productive one. There is much evidence forcing us to answer both questions or, at any rate, the second one, in a negative sense.

As already mentioned, the Judaeo-Christian disappointment with history did not become an effective factor in Muslim historiography. Moreover, Muslim historians often followed their own short-range utilitarian ends which left little room for far-reaching speculations and belonged to a different level of historical activity. On the other side of the ledger there are clear indications of the influence exercised by Muḥammad's view of history. Most Muslim historians (with certain exceptions to be touched upon immediately on the following page) saw a definite break in history in the coming of Muḥammad and the events of his time; history could be divided into two great periods, the one before Muḥammad, and the one after his coming, and historical works were organized in accordance with this theory. A minor point is the inclusion of the history of the future (that is, of the end of the world) among historical subjects to be treated in detail; in this respect, Muslim historians drew their inspiration from the Prophet's theology of history and did so increasingly even at a rather late date. Above all, whenever they thought along world historical lines, the vast majority of Muslim historians closely adhered to the views that Muḥammad had derived from biblical tradition and made part and parcel of Muslim thinking.

It is hardly possible to weigh these factors and attribute greater importance to one side as against the other. However, the last of the points mentioned brings us to the aspect of Muḥammad's view of history that was decidedly harmful to historical thinking in Islam. His view of history was coherent and all-inclusive, and it became an integral part of most Muslim theologies. It could hardly be reconciled with other historical views, not even with such widespread, elementary theories as that of the cyclical character of history or the golden age theory of gradual deterioration. Consequently, it tended to discourage the formulation of different historical theories by Muslim historians. On the whole, it was tremendously successful in this respect. Occasionally, alternative historical theories were cautiously proposed, but whenever this was done, and no matter how guardedly, a slight tinge, at least, of the non-conforming, the unorthodox, was attached to these efforts. A good example is the historian Miskawayh and his *Tajārib al-umam*. Miskawayh completely eliminated God from history by the simple expedient of declaring the doings of the prophets—and Muḥammad's life work—something outside human experience, that is, history, and, therefore, not deserving the attention of the historian. While Miskawayh, it can be assumed, was motivated by a deep-seated dissatisfaction with the basic assumptions of Islam, the loyal devotion to traditional Islam of a later historian, Ibn Khaldūn, is beyond doubt. However, like Miskawayh, he had to divorce the traditional view from his own historical insights by assuming two different levels of existence, the supernatural or divine, and the human. Both levels, he contended, are normally separate. Human history moves in circles, determined by human material needs and psychological attitudes, and these circles are only very occasionally and irregularly disturbed by some arbitrary, if highly effective, supernatural interference. This theory, developed in the *Muqaddima*, was applied by Ibn Khaldūn, skilfully and, again, cautiously, to the historical presentation of the *'Ibar*. In an inconspicuous manner, he incorporated the biblical history into his world-wide scheme of racial groupings and societies and dismissed the period of Muḥammad as an intermission—a glorious and awe-inspiring one, to be sure—during which the *'aṣabiyya* was inoperative.

These two examples clearly show how dangerous the ground became for an author whose historical insight tempted him to abandon the biblical tradition. The temptations were many: Persian history, Greek philosophy, Shī'a theology. Slippery spots of potential danger to the traditional view often show up in Muslim histories and cause us to wonder what their authors might have thought. However, conscious, or unconscious but clean-cut, breaks with the biblical tradition as Muḥammad had interpreted it, are exceptional, and, as our hindsight enables us to see, their occurrence could hardly be expected.

(3) *The Biblical Material in Muslim Histories*

Historical, or pseudo-historical, material centring around biblical events and personalities gained the right of entry into Islam through the Qur'ān and its interpretation. This material is generally recognized to constitute the nucleus of the earliest Muslim historical writing. It quickly grew in size and had become very voluminous by the time the historical works with which we are familiar began to be written. Theological literature provided a home for a good deal of it. As far as historical writing is concerned, biblical stories entered world histories and certain types of local histories, such as those dealing with South Arabia and Egypt, and also appeared in the form of monographs.

We are fortunate in having a very recent discussion of the problems posed by the early stages of Muslim historiography in N. Abbott's magnificent publication, *Studies in Arabic Literary Papyri I: Historical Texts* (Chicago, 1957). The problems are many and difficult, and their solution is hardly yet in sight. The nine papyri published by Miss Abbott, in spite of their outstanding importance, do not by themselves contribute much substantial information concerning the history of the earliest historical efforts by Muslim scholars, coming as they do from a considerably later period. However, Miss Abbott used the papyri for a thorough re-examination of a large part of the material that is available for the study of the beginnings of Muslim historiography. Three of the nine papyri are ascribed to historical works dealing with biblical material. There may be some doubt as to the historical character, properly speaking, of the works to which the papyri in question originally belonged, but the rather large percentage of 'biblical' material seems significant. Miss Abbott's investigations also extend to discussing the period in which Arabic translations of works such as the Christian apocryphal stories of Adam and Eve and the Cave of Treasure, as well as Arabic translations of at least parts of the Bible, can be assumed to have been made. Early eighth-century dates are considered likely. An even more interesting feature of Miss Abbott's study is her skilful defence of the historical reality of early authorities, such as Kaʿb al-Aḥbār and Wahb b. Munabbih for the biblical, and ʿAbīd b. S̲h̲arya for the South Arabian material. The author also contends that historical material was transmitted in writing, and published commercially, at an early date, presumably, early Umayyad times. As far as the subject under discussion here is concerned, Miss Abbott's work is undoubtedly helpful in that it tends to confirm the early and important role that the biblical tradition played in the incipient Muslim historiography.

In addition to the chronological problem, the biblical material in Muslim histories raises other problems which can be formulated, briefly, as follows: where do the biblical stories come from, that is, are they stories derived from Jews and Christians, or stories of a different origin ascribed to biblical figures, or stories derived from Jews and Christians but greatly transformed? Secondly, what part does the original text of the Bible play in the historical presentation of Muslim historians? Finally, has the biblical material, either in its original form or transformed by means of more or less subtle changes, been used to defend and promote certain Muslim views of a historical or, more likely, theological character? Answers to these questions could probably be given with a great deal of assurance if we had a sufficient number of detailed studies dealing with individual biblical figures and elucidating the treatment they received in the available Muslim literature; since this is not the case, and we have to rely upon the comparatively few works published by modern scholars which are either too comprehensive or concerned with the one or other point of detail, much remains uncertain.

The original text of the Bible may have been a matter of little concern for the earliest historians, not so much because access to it may have been rather difficult, but because they were less interested in historical accuracy than in making a coherent whole of the fragmentary Qur'anic narrative by whatever means they could lay their hands on. Information derived from the Jewish and Christian Scriptures, nevertheless, entered Muslim historiography at an early date and stayed in it through the centuries. However, going back to the original sources required possession of a serious scientific spirit as well as a considerable amount of courage in view of the conflicts that might appear between the Bible and the text of the Qur'ān.

The scientific spirit was possessed, as a matter of course, by the great scholars who occupied themselves with chronology, such as, for instance, Ḥamza al-Iṣfahānī and al-Bīrūnī. They spent considerable effort to find and consult persons able to read the Bible or the relevant Jewish-Christian chronological works and explain their contents to them. Among the historians, there were, in the ninth century, men such as Ibn Qutayba. In his *Maʿārif* he contrasted the traditional information of Wahb b. Munabbih with the text of the Bible, which he quoted literally. Some accurate knowledge of the original is also evident in the History of al-Yaʿqūbī, although he admits much traditional material without questioning its genuineness. Unfortunately, the daring scientific spirit of these times had soon to contend not only with the natural sluggishness of the human mind but also, in the historical field, with the formidable authority of the great Ṭabarī. Al-Ṭabarī had a certain amount of accurate biblical information, but he ostensibly relied on the traditional Muslim material. His vast influence may be suspected to have tipped the scales in favour of that material, and against greater respect for the original sources, among most later historians. Occasional references to Torah and Gospel, spurious or genuine, were fashionable at all times. Even a late author, such as Ibn Kat͟hīr, who relied greatly upon tradition, may be found to quote 'what I have seen in the book that is in the possession of the People of the Book and which I think is the Torah'.[2] Ibn K͟haldūn, intellectually curious as he was, attempted to gain access to reliable sources, at least for certain phases of Judaeo-Christian history.[3] For a long time a strong feeling of

[2] *Bidāya*, i, 95.
[3] Cf. W. J. Fischel, in *I. Goldziher Memorial Volume* (Jerusalem, 1956), ii, 147–71.

aversion to the all too luxuriant growth of fabulous biblical legends, the 'Israelite stories', had also been spreading among scholars. But in spite of these sporadic critical efforts, the genuine desire to learn about the original sources, which in many cases could have been easily satisfied, is conspicuously absent from the vast majority of historical works that deal with the biblical material.

The provenience of much of this material from the *midrāsh* and the *haggādāh* of Jews and Christians is generally accepted by modern scholars. To be sure, the scholars who studied the question of origin were bent upon finding Judaeo-Christian parallels and sources and paid little attention, or none whatever, to the large mass of material that could not be identified in this manner. But there is a significant amount of proven relationship between the Muslim material and Judaeo-Christian literature; and, of course, the fact that no parallel text or source may be available cannot ever constitute a satisfactory argument against Judaeo-Christian provenience. Thus, unless it can be shown that a given story cannot have come to the Muslims from Jewish or Christian sources, the Judaeo-Christian tradition remains the most likely source of origin, in particular for all the older material.

A considerable amount of Muslim transformation and invention is clearly recognizable, as we would expect. Certain broad categories can be discerned. One of them includes stories that reveal too determined a desire to explain statements of the Qur'ān, especially in cases where several stories are offered in explanation, or where we are confronted with a conspicuous growth and accretion of details, as, for instance, in the enumeration of the names which God taught Adam; at least the details are obvious additions. Even more obvious are cases where the original tradition was replaced or transformed by references to Arabian conditions or Qur'anic data. For instance, when mankind's first language, spoken by Adam, is considered Arabic, instead of Hebrew or Aramaic, it seems likely that the transformation was due to Muslims; the assumption that it originated with Arabian Jews or Christians would require definite proof. Or there is the tradition that Adam took up residence in India or Ceylon when he was expelled from Paradise. This tradition, al-Ṭabarī tells us, 'is well established by the authority of Muslim scholars and the people of Torah and Gospel',[4] but he is suspicious of another tradition that places Eve in Jidda and Iblīs in Mesene. The location of the devil in southern Mesopotamia may not be an unfriendly allusion to the alleged devilishness of the people and the climate of that region but rather reflect Mesopotamian gnostic tradition.[5] However, the introduction of Jidda clearly had its

[4] i, 121.

[5] Cf. the Mandaean *Ginza*, trans. M. Lidzbarski, p. 281 (Gottingen-Leipzig, 1925), according to which 'the worlds of darkness are located in the lowlands of the south'.

origin in the desire to have a logical Arabic connection for the story of Adam; again, a Muslim origin seems more likely than the assumption that Arabic Jews and Christians were responsible for the creation of the legend, in particular, since the reference to Iblīs seems to indicate Mesopotamian connections. A more difficult problem is presented by such cases as the story that Yūsuf possessed nine-tenths of all the world's beauty. It is no doubt connected with the Talmudic statement that Jerusalem possessed nine-tenths of all existing beauty,[6] but how the transference of the motif from Jerusalem to Yūsuf took place is hard to explain. We may, however, recall that in another passage, Yūsuf's beauty is explained by the fact of his relationship to Sarah who possessed outstanding beauty.[7] Thus, given Yūsuf's beauty and the need of finding an explanation for it, the scholarly search for such an explanation apparently could take many directions.

Another category of stories for which Muslim origin seems indicated is constituted by practically all cases involving Arabic verses. Finally, we find that the monographs dealing with the *qiṣaṣ al-anbiyā'* succeed in presenting the history of the prophets in an almost coherent narrative; here, suspicion necessarily arises with regard to stories that serve to furnish the dramatic continuity. Thus, there existed a large number of biblical stories that owed their origin or form to Muslim inventiveness. Jews and Christians, from all intellectual levels, had long been occupied with elaborating on episodes of their holy history, and there certainly was nothing to prevent Muslims from following their example.

The use of the biblical tradition for purposes other than establishing true or alleged historical facts was almost inevitable. In this connection, we may refer to the transformation which, according to a widely-accepted scholarly theory, the picture of Ibrāhīm underwent at the hands of the Prophet himself. Another important development in this sense was the adaptation of the history of the prophets to the requirements of S͟hī'a theology. The tendency towards arabization has already been mentioned. Certain ideas also entered the presentation of biblical material by the historians via the interpretation of the Qur'ān and other branches of theology. On the basis of Qur'ān 7.172/171, for instance, the problem of predestination became part of the history of Adam.[8] In the earliest generations of historians, the intentional use of such material for definite purposes may have been rather common. In later times, it seems to have been obscured by the great mass of purely 'historical' information.

[6] Qidd. 49b, cf. M. Lidzbarski, *De propheticis, quae dicuntur, legendis Arabicis* (Leipzig, 1893), pp. 50 f.

[7] Al-Mas'ūdī (?), *Ak͟hbār al-zamān* (Cairo, 1357/1958), p. 200.

[8] Cf. al-Ṭabarī, i, 135 f., which may be contrasted with Ibn Kat͟hīr, *Bidāya*, i, 87 ff.

(4) *The Biblical Tradition and the Forms of Muslim Historical Writing*

Literary forms that occur in both the Old Testament and Arabic historical writing are a common inheritance from the second millennium B.C. when speakers of the languages known to us as Hebrew, Aramaic, and Arabic formed a closely related linguistic and social entity. The conservatism of the Arabic group in Arabia, particularly in the realm of language and literature (even if the idea scholars held in the past of the pervasiveness of that conservatism must be revised in details), suffices to account for the survival of forms which the other groups discarded for various reasons.

A distinctive form of historical writing is constituted by stories built around some verses of poetry which gave lustre to the events they celebrate and which the stories serve to explain. This literary form occurs sporadically in the Bible. In pre-Islamic Arabia, it was the main vehicle for the preservation of historical information. From the artistic point of view, it was highly effective and commended itself to Muslim historians who continued to use this form, with modifications, on a large scale. The episodic presentation of history thus came to dominate a large segment of Muslim historical writing.

A marked interest in genealogy is noticeable throughout the Old Testament and, in pre-Islamic Arabia, is the most eloquent testimony to the existence of a certain degree of historical consciousness there. This common trait proved to be of minor significance for the development of the forms of historical writing, for which genealogy as such can provide only the barest framework. When genealogical lore was adopted by Muslim historians for historical purposes, it chose forms of literary expression predetermined by the general development of Arabic historical literature.

The arrangement of historical information according to dynasties and the reigns of individual rulers is found in the Bible as well as in Islamic historiography. It is an obvious principle of organization, known practically all over the world. In Islam, it can be assumed to have been modelled after some precedent nearer to it in time than the remote period of the ancient Near East.

The preceding pages have shown, I believe, that the biblical tradition occupies a special place in the history of Muslim historiography. It provided Muslim historical writing with some of its most significant elements. It all but deprived it of the chance to experience great developments in historical thinking. The problems connected with the biblical tradition are often different from those which confront students of other aspects of Muslim historiography. Many of them spring from the darkness that surrounds the earliest period of Islam's intellectual and literary history. Others are obscured by the large mass of widely scattered and seemingly disparate materials. None seems incapable of an eventual solution.

3. THE IRAQ SCHOOL OF HISTORY TO THE NINTH CENTURY—A SKETCH

A. A. DURI

Professor of Islamic History in the University of Baghdad

Muslim historiography is a part of Muslim culture, and can only be understood when studied with reference to other cultural activities and developments. To study it alone leads only to a partial and vague idea of its origins and development.

Muslim historiography began after the rise of Islam. Pre-Islamic activities—the tales of the *Ayyām* and genealogy—indicate a line of interest and the beginnings of a technique of narration, but no idea of history.

The beginnings of historical studies followed broadly two lines which were distinct from each other—that of *ḥadīth*, and that of the tribes which is in a sense a continuation of pre-Islamic activities. These two lines reflect the two major currents in early Islamic society—the Islamic and the tribal, which influenced all aspects of life. Each line was followed widely in one centre—the *ḥadīth* primarily in Medina, the cradle of Islam; the tribal primarily in Kūfa and Baṣra, the two new garrison cities and centres of tribal traditions. Medina, Kūfa and Baṣra were the centres of scholarship in early Islam.

The Islamic line is not our concern here. It suffices to say that it began with Traditionists who paid special attention to the career of the Prophet (starting with ʿUrwa b. al-Zubayr), and who soon went on to a study of early Islamic history, and formed a school of *maghāzī* scholars. In addition, stories and anecdotes (*qaṣaṣ*) about the Prophet and the conquests were told and circulated. These did not, however, initiate any line of history; they supplied later, especially to Ibn Isḥāq, some data, and were looked upon with mistrust by serious scholars. The critical approach of this school is shown in their emphasis on authority and on the scrutiny of reporters. By the end of the first century A.H., the lines of the *Sīra* were laid and the bulk of the basic material collected. Many *qaṣaṣ* crept in after that and a tendency, from simple and factual data towards glorification, manifested itself. The writing down of notes began fairly early; by the end of the first century A.H. it was established by Zuhrī and henceforward sources were both oral and written.

The tribal type of history arose from an interest in tribal activities and affairs. In concept and style it was a direct continuation of the tales of the

Ayyām and genealogical accounts, directed mainly to the new *Ayyām* battles and conquests in Islam.

Arab culture was basically oral, and poetry was its documentary evidence and the best means of preserving traditions. References to records and archives of the kings of Ḥīra and Yaman (Himyarites) and to records and genealogies kept by some families in Yaman, utilized later, are exceptions.[1]

Anecdotes were related primarily in *majālis* (social gatherings) and were generally the common property of the family or the tribe. Some individuals, such as the *ruwāt* of poetry or the elders of tribes (*mashāyikh*), became the principal reporters. Initially, such anecdotes or reports (*riwāyāt*, *akhbār*) had no chain of authorities (*isnād*). They continued to be a part of general culture and a common concern. Such oral traditions, with much poetry, continued to circulate in early Islam as before.[2] Kūfa and Baṣra, being major tribal centres and in direct and continuous contact with the desert, played an important part in their circulation.

Islam, and the settlement of tribes in cities, gathered the tribes together in closer association, fostered new interests, and led to the spread of reading and writing. There is ample evidence to attest the resort to writing, to aid memory or to preserve traditions, before the end of the first century and during the first half of the second century.[3] The process of having written as well oral traditions had begun.

Early in the second century A.H. we hear of individuals (*ashyākh*, *ruwāt*) versed in the genealogies and deeds of their tribes, and of tribal monographs (*kutub*) which contain genealogies, poetry, and probably *akhbār* of some tribes. They were very likely collected by some *rāwī* and still considered the common property of that tribe. The poet Ṭirimmāḥ (d. 105/723) quotes the *kitāb* of Tamīm, while Ḥammād al-Rāwiya (*c.* 126 A.H.) has the *kutub* of Quraysh and Thaqīf.[4] These monographs and *ruwāt* provided data for later historians.

The interest of *ruwāt* grew broader in time. Local patriotism related to a *miṣr*, the living of many tribes in a city, and party politics, all had their impact. Besides, the creation of an empire and the feeling of a historical role fostered a new consciousness. All this helps to explain the process of transition from the simple tribal *ruwāt* to the early historians.

By the middle of the second century A.H. we meet with 'learned' *ruwāt*—*akhbārīs*, genealogists and philologists, who left historical works or a wealth of historical narratives. This was a period of pioneering scholars in different fields who started collecting poetry, *akhbār*, and *ḥadīth*. Abū 'Amr b.

[1] See Ṭabarī (Cairo), ii, 123; Ibn Hishām (Cairo), i, 381; Hamdānī, *Iklīl*, i, 5; x, 30–1, iii, 112.

[2] Cf. Suyūṭī, *Muzhir*, i, 248–9; ii, 355; Jāḥiz, *Bayān*, iii, 366.

[3] Ibn Nadīm, 9–10, 132; *Aghānī*, iv, 253; *Tahdhīb al-tahdhīb*, ii, 67; Ibn Sa'd, iv, 395; vii/2, 17; vi, 63; v, 216.

[4] Cf. *Aghānī*, vi, 94; iv, 257; Ibn 'Abd al-Barr, *al-Qaṣd*, 43.

al-'Alā' (d. 154/770) and Ḥammad al-Rāwiya (156/772) collected poetry, *akhbār* and genealogical data of the pre-Islamic Arabs primarily from tribal *rāwīs* and tribal monographs, and resorted to writing to preserve some of their work.[5] From this period we have also the first collections of *ḥadīth*, made in different provinces, and the first available works on the *Sīra*. All this indicates a general phase of cultural development, of which historical studies had a share. *Akhbārīs* and 'learned' *ruwāt* are our first historians.

Just as in the *Sīra* literature we have predecessors for Ibn Isḥāq, such as Zuhrī, on whom he largely depends, so we find that the *akhbārīs* drew largely from certain *ruwāt*. Thus out of over sixty *rāwīs* from whom Sayf b. 'Umar (as quoted in Ṭabarī) drew, he leans heavily on two, Talḥa b. al-A'lam and Muḥammad b. 'Abdallāh, from each of whom he took over a hundred reports.[6] These *rāwīs* were interested in events or public affairs, not just information relevant to a tribe. In this category come genealogists who went beyond the limits of one tribe. Still, with them, there remained the tribal *ruwāt*.

Akhbārīs were thus the first historians in the tribal line. They differ from the *ruwāt* of anecdotal traditions in their practice of collecting traditions relevant to a theme or event, and putting them in a coherent monograph (*kitāb*). Among these *akhbārīs* were Abū Mikhnaf (d. 157/774), 'Awāna b. al-Ḥakam (d. 147/764), Sayf b. 'Umar (d. 180/796), and finally their foremost representative, al-Madā'inī (d. 225/839).

These *akhbārīs* show an interest in the affairs of the *Umma*, though special attention is given to the affairs of Iraq. The concept of the unity and continuity of the experience of the *Umma* is noticeable. Besides, the continuity of Arab history is felt. Sayf linked the *Ridda* with the conquests; 'Awāna dealt with Islamic history during the first century—the Orthodox Caliphs, the *Ridda* and conquests, the civil war and the affairs of Iraq and Syria until 'Abd al-Malik; Abū Mikhnaf treated early Islamic history till Ṣiffīn, and then continued with the affairs of Iraq to the end of the Umayyad period; Madā'inī ranges through the whole field of Arab history—political, literary, social—starting with the *Jāhiliyya* and going to the beginning of the third century A.H.

Thus the *Umma*, not the tribe, is the focus of interest. Other ideas can be seen in their works. We notice the conflict between the idea of predestination in public affairs as propagated by the Umayyads, and the idea of free will and human responsibility as expressed by opposing parties. 'Awāna illustrates the Umayyad line: Yazīd attributes Umayyad power to God,[7] 'Uthmān predicted that authority would go to 'Abd al-Malik and his

[5] Cf. Ibn Sallām, *Ṭabaqāt*, 40; Suyūṭī, *Muzhir*, ii, 304; Ibn Sa'd, vii/2, 42; *Mukhtārāt Ibn al-Shajarī*, 123, 127, 136; *Aghānī*, iii, 322.

[6] Other examples, Ibn Abī Ṣāliḥ on biblical history in Ibn al-Kalbī; Abū al-Dhubāl and al-Mufaḍḍil al-Ḍabbī for Khurāsān in Madā'inī.

[7] Ṭabarī, ii, 378.

sons.[8] This is in contrast to the line of Abū Mikhnaf, especially when we consider his accounts of the revolt of al-Ḥusayn and the movement of the *Tawwābūn*.

The concept of state, with emphasis on the rights of the *imām* (from the Umayyad angle) and his claim to loyalty and obedience, versus the tribal or partisan attitude which puts other interests (provincial, tribal, etc.) above the state, is reflected in their works. Risings against the Umayyads are not condemned, even if not praised. Even when Mu'āwiya's stand against 'Alī is criticized (as by Naṣr b. Muzāḥim), it is done on party lines, rather than on the concept of state.[9] Yet the fragments preserved show great moderation. Those historians did not fall to the level of sheer partisanship and were not representative of one view only. It is possible that the process of selection from these works (especially in Ṭabarī and Balādhurī) eliminated some extreme traditions. But we may find the explanation in the importance attached to the tradition (*riwāya*) versus opinion, and to the discipline imposed by scholarly judgement.

Party, province and tribe had their influence. In Abū Mikhnaf we notice 'Alid sympathies,[10] Iraqi sympathies,[11] and some tribal glorification; thus, in his account of Ṣiffīn, tribal glories are clearly stressed. Sayf explains the role of tribes in the conquest of Iraq and underlines the role of Tamīn.[12] 'Awāna is considered 'Uthmānī in leanings. He clearly gives Umayyad traditions and occasionally inner stories.[13] Yet some accounts are broadly anti-Umayyad.[14]

Akhbārīs had to carry on a wide search for traditions. Thus they used family traditions, tribal traditions in their province, and a vast number of single reports. They had to supplement these traditions by those of other provinces with which events were linked, and thus brought in traditions of Syria, Medina, and Arabia. Abū Mikhnaf used traditions of the elders of tribes from Azd, Namīr, Muḥārib, and Tamīm as well as family traditions.[15] He quotes reports of participants in events and numerous individual reports.[16] His authorities for Ṣiffīn, the episode of Muslim b. 'Aqīl, and Karbalā' were in the main Kūfī; but they were supplemented by 'Alid, Syrian, and Medinese traditions.[17] Sayf b. 'Umar depends, especially for the conquests, on Kūfī traditions, supplemented by some Medinese and Syrian traditions. For the *Ridda* he relies on traditions from Kūfa, Arabia, and Medina. Among his Medinese authorities are Hishām b.

8 Balādhurī, *Ansāb*, v, 240.

9 Cf. Ṭabarī, ii, 3–4, where an unjust *imām* is preferred to no *imām*.

10 Cf. Ṭabarī, ii, 182, 186; i, 2337, 3276; ii, 307–8.

11 Cf. Ṭabarī, i, 3291–2, and especially ii, 145, when he quotes a *rāwī* saying 'I have seen people in Kūfa say, "the first degradation (*dhull*) which befell Kūfa was . . ."'

12 Cf. Ṭabarī, i, 2068–9, and the rôle of Qa'qā' al-Tamīmī.

13 Cf. Balādhurī, *Ansāb*, iv, 1, 31; Ṭabarī, ii, 13.

14 Ṭabarī, i, 1837; Balādhurī, *Ansāb*, v, 369.

15 Ṭabarī, i, 3261, 3302, 3303, 3309.

16 Cf. Ṭabarī, ii, 3202–3.

17 Cf. Ṭabarī, ii, 279, 410–14, 376, 479.

'Urwa and Mūsā b. 'Uqba. Many reports go back to participants in events.[18] 'Awāna uses family and Kalbī traditions, other tribal traditions, numerous odd reports and many Syrian and Umayyad traditions.[19] Besides, *akhbārīs* used official documents (letters and treaties) possibly from official *dīwāns* or from people who possessed them.[20]

An *akhbārī* could lean heavily on traditions of his province (e.g. Abū Mikhnaf) or his tribe (e.g. Sayf), but he could not disregard other opposing traditions.[21] By this time the method of the Traditionists was fairly widespread and influenced the *akhbārīs*. Thus their critical method was used in the scrutiny of reporters and in assessing the worth of traditions. For example, Sayf states, 'This story of Ubulla and its conquest is contrary to what the authors of *siyar* know and contrary to the account of the Traditions.'[22] Abū Mikhnaf in reference to a question about Karbalā' says, 'But what we heard from Mujāhid and Ṣaq'ab and other Traditions is in line with the consensus of Traditions. They say . . .'[23]

However, the stories of the *majālis* and relevant poetry found a place in their accounts. This is primarily the situation with Naṣr b. Muzāḥim, who quotes much forged poetry and follows clearly (in his *waq'at Ṣiffīn*) the lines of *majālis* stories which are a continuation of the *Ayyām* stories.[24] Traces can be seen in others, like Sayf b. 'Umar, Abū Mikhnaf[25] and 'Awāna. These *akhbārīs* wrote in direct, simple prose, giving at times a graphic and vivid account of events. In treating battles, poetry, oration, and dialogue are used. The narrative is usually continuous, and the flavour of the *Ayyām* style is occasionally felt.

Yet the *akhbārīs* represent a phase of transition from the early disregard of authorities to the strict citation of transmitters of the Traditionists, for they show much freedom and sometimes laxity in their chains of authorities. Thus we come across broken chains, or cases when only the first name of the *rāwī* is mentioned, or statements like—'it was reported', 'the elders say . . .', 'those who know report', 'a man told me . . .' During the second century one report is usually given on each point, and reports supplement each other to carry the story further. It is with Madā'inī that more than one report on the same point is given, and a more balanced and impartial presentation. Most of the sources were oral traditions, but some were probably written as is clear from expressions like *qāla* and *ḥaddathanī* referring to the same authority.

[18] Cf. Ṭabarī, i, 1786, 1797, 1931–6, 1947–8.
[19] Cf. Ṭabarī, ii, 785, 791–5; Balādhurī, *Ansāb*, v, 32–5, 140.
[20] Cf. Ṭabarī, i, 20, 28.
[21] Cf. Ṭabarī, ii, 182, 202, 323, for Abū Mikhnaf; Balādhurī, *Ansāb*, iv, 1, 31; v, 369; and Ṭabarī, i, 1833, for 'Awāna.
[22] Ṭabarī, i, 2025.
[23] Ṭabarī, ii, 378.
[24] Cf. Khaṭīb, xiii, 482–3; Ṭūsī, *Fihrist*, 171.
[25] Ṭabarī, i, 2071–3, 2058, 2102; ii, 3, 8–50.

It is fitting here to remark that philologists helped to evolve a more critical approach by their studies on poetry and their attempts to separate genuine from forged poetry. They also helped to collect and sift historical data, and thus introduced a method of internal criticism side by side with that of external criticism of authorities. Their line of writing was, however, similar to that of the *akhbārīs* in grouping their data round a topic or a theme and writing monographs.

The genealogists made a contribution to historical studies by giving the *ansāb* with some biographical data; this is especially true of Zubayrī. Here, social interests, tribal quarrels and tribal politics, gave the impetus. These studies provided for the tribal aristocracy—in a limited form—what the *ṭabaqāt* books did for Traditionists. The *Shu'ūbiyya* controversy and the impact of the *mawālī* gave an added impetus to the studies of genealogists and philologists, and led to an emphasis on the continuity of Arab cultural history. The source for genealogists and philologists was primarily poetry, coupled with tribal traditions related to poetry or documented with poetry. Thus their studies overlapped with, and were linked to, historical studies.

Genealogical studies were first limited to a tribe. Again during the second century, there appeared genealogists who collected tribal traditions from the *nassābs* of different tribes, and from poetry, especially that of the *naqā'iḍ*.[26] During the same period philologists and grammarians collected Arabic poetry from tribal books and from individual *rāwīs*. Starting from a limited interest in genealogy or grammar, some philologists and genealogists ranged over the whole field of Arab history.[27] Here again the movement was from no *isnād*, to an attempt to mention some authorities, and thence to a full development of the *isnād*. Hishām b. al-Kalbī relates on the authority of some 'people of the book', of a certain Ibn Abī Ṣāliḥ on biblical history, of translations, of records in Ḥīra and stories on the Persians and Arabs, and mainly of some *mashāyikh* of Kūfa, and of Abū Mikhnaf and 'Awāna on Islamic history. Abū 'Ubayda reports from his *shuyūkh*, Abū 'Amr. b. al-'Alā', Akhfash, 'Īsā b. 'Umar al-Thaqafī, Yūnus b. Ḥabīb, and from Hishām b. 'Urwa, Wakī' and a group of eloquent (*fuṣaḥā'*) bedouins.[28]

A certain historical conception emerges—that of the cultural continuity of Arab history and its bearing on contemporary questions, especially the claims of Arab aristocracy, the relation of Quraysh to other tribes, the Arabs' attitude to the *mawālī*, and questions of language and of the literary heritage. These broad questions extended the outlook of the genealogists

[26] e.g. Muḥammad b. al-Sā'ib al-Kalbī (d. 146/763) and Abu'l-Yaqẓān (d. 190/804).

[27] Cf. the works of Hishām b. Muḥammad al-Kalbī and Abū 'Ubayda.

[28] Suyūṭī, *Muzhir*, ii, 401–2; Khaṭīb, xiii, 252; Ibn Khallikān, i, 820; *Naqā'iḍ*, 30, 487; *Majāz al-Qur'ān*, i, 400.

and philologists to the history of other nations before Islam. Hishām b. al-Kalbī went to biblical history and to Persian history related to Arab history, while Abū 'Ubayda went to Persian traditions—among his books are *Akhbār al-Furs* and *Kitāb al-mawālī*. Political issues are reflected in them to a certain extent. Thus, Hishām b. al-Kalbī shows some pro-'Alid sympathies; Abū 'Ubayda, as seen in the *Naqā'iḍ* reveals an interest in exposing Arab vices and defects (which could not be accounted for by his being a *Khārijī*) and follows the *Shu'ūbī* line.[29]

By the beginning of the third century, historical studies reached a stage which led to the appearance of the great historians of that century. In their monographs, *akhbārīs*, philologists and genealogists, set the scope of historical studies and ranged over its whole field.

This established the concept of the unity of Islamic history, which was probably given a strict chronological sequence in al-Haytham b. 'Adī's work *Kitāb al-ta'rīkh 'alā l-sinīn*. They developed the genealogical line into a historical line as in the *Nasab Quraysh* of Zubayrī (233–6/844–50) and more clearly in scope and plan in the *Ta'rīkh al-ashrāf al-kabīr* of al-Haytham b. 'Adī. They expressed the idea of universal history (e.g. Hishām b. al-Kalbī) ranging over biblical, pre-Islamic Arab—both Northern and Southern—and Islamic history. In method, increased attention was given to the *isnād*, and the idea of reporting variant traditions was adopted by Madā'inī and Abū 'Ubayda. Besides, we notice in Madā'inī, Abū 'Ubayda, and Hishām b. al-Kalbī the tendency to utilize written material as well as oral traditions. These people used the works of the generation of Abū Mikhnaf, 'Awāna, Muḥammad b. al-Sā'ib al-Kalbī, and Abū 'Amr b. al-'Alā' as sources for their works.

The third century saw a new phase of cultural development. There was a great mass of traditions reported or recorded in different provinces. This was the period of 'travels for knowledge' initiated by *ḥadīth* scholars, to collect and correlate these traditions, and the resulting contacts led to reciprocal influences in method and approach. The *isnād* was now widely used and its rules more strictly applied. Furthermore, learned opinion was being formed about the value of previous works and the trustworthiness of their authors—a thing which made collection and criticism more practical.

The third-century historians, al-Balādhurī (d. 229/892), al-Ya'qūbī (d. 284/897), al-Dīnawarī (d. 282/897), Ibn Qutayba (d. 270/882), and al-Ṭabarī (d. 310/923) wrote continuous histories and not monographs. Their basic ideas were the unity of the experience of the *Umma*, and universal history. Al-Balādhurī represents the first idea, the rest the second. Their motives for writing differed. Al-Balādhurī wrote a history woven around the Arab aristocracy, thus indicating where the emphasis lay, and

[29] Cf. Ghannāwī, *Naqā'iḍ*, 146.

giving full emphasis to an Arab social idea. His *Futūḥ* expresses a central mission of Islam and meets a juristic and administrative need. Al-Ya'qūbī wrote a universal history with a Shi'ite (Ja'farī) touch, and gave pre-Islamic history a religious and cultural significance. Ibn Qutayba thought of secretaries (*kuttāb*) and their need for a comprehensive historical manual which would represent a synthesis of types—*Ayyām*, universal history, juristic needs. Al-Dīnawarī wanted to show the rôle of Iraq and Persia in his universal history, and found his justification in Sasanid and 'Abbasid times. Al-Ṭabarī wanted history to explain the will of God and to illustrate His revelation.

The critical approach of the Traditionists is more fully applied. Al-Ṭabarī is a strict Traditionist in approach as can be seen from his emphasis on chains of authorities and his abstention from criticism of the content. Ibn Qutayba, critical of his sources to the extent of going to the Old Testament to check Wahb b. Munabbih, takes what is well established in his sources. Al-Ya'qūbī is critical of his sources, especially for pre-Islam; he scrutinizes his authorities for the Islamic period, but contents himself with referring to them in the introduction as their chains of authorities are known. Al-Balādhurī follows a middle course, quoting previous historians by name, but dropping their *isnāds*, except where necessary. Al-Ṭabarī and al-Balādhurī both give different traditions bearing on the same point. There is less in them, and the others—even al-Ya'qūbī—that is partisan, and the correlation of previous authorities helps considerably to give a balanced view.

These historians added their wide researches—historical, geographical and literary—to the work of *akhbārīs*, and used oral and written material (after reading them to some *shaykh*), and sometimes documents and archives. They synthesized the lines of genealogists, *akhbārīs* and philologists, and benefited greatly from the school of Medina. They superseded the *akhbārīs* and definitely set the lines of Muslim historiography.

4. ISLAMIC BIOGRAPHICAL LITERATURE

SIR HAMILTON GIBB

University Professor and Jewett Professor of Arabic, Harvard University

It is probably a truism that every kind of literary production which is regularly cultivated in a society expresses some enduring element in both the conscious motivations and unconscious orientations of the society as a whole or of its public exponents.

The study of Arabic biographical literature cannot, therefore, be confined to a simple listing and analysis of the extant works of this kind, but must begin with questions about the motivations of this literature, and the evidence that it supplies or indicates as to changing or enduring social and intellectual attitudes or trends. What kinds of data may the historian expect to find in these works? What critical apparatus must he bring to their study and use?

(1) *Motivations*

In approaching this question, a starting-point is furnished by two remarkable facts. One is that the biographical dictionary is a wholly indigenous creation of the Islamic Community. The only analogous productions are the biographical sections of the Chinese dynastic histories, but these, as will appear later, are governed by entirely different principles, and any possibility of borrowing is excluded. The Syriac martyrologies likewise furnish no parallel or precedent. The second fact is that the composition of biographical dictionaries in Arabic developed simultaneously and in close association with historical composition. The early dictionaries themselves give no reasons for their composition, but plunge directly into their subjects. Further, these subjects themselves are in no instance limited to political personalities, nor are political figures and events given special attention. On the contrary (and here in marked contrast to the Chinese tradition), political history is entirely incidental to the main structure of the works. Thus it is clear that the conception that underlies the oldest biographical dictionaries is that the history of the Islamic Community is essentially the contribution of individual men and women to the building up and transmission of its specific culture; that it is these persons (rather than the political governors) who represent or reflect the active forces in Muslim society in their respective spheres; and that their individual contributions are worthy of being recorded for future generations.

Thus the earliest extant dictionary, that of Ibn Sa‘d, aims firstly to commemorate all those Companions of Muḥammad, however obscure otherwise, who took part in the battle of Badr, then the later *Muhājirs*, and finally those Followers who laid the foundations of Islamic learning and society in Arabia and the new provinces. Similarly inspired are the other early biographical works (almost all now lost), especially those on the *qāḍīs* of the capital cities. Although the conception of biography broadened out later, the communal (rather than political) function or moment remains the predominant factor in the selection and treatment of personalities. This is strikingly brought out by one of the most eminent of later biographers, al-Saḵẖāwī (9th/15h century): 'History as a technical term means the communication of time, whereby the circumstances are accurately registered of the birth of *transmitters and imāms*, and of their death, health, intelligence, bodily state, journeys, pilgrimages, powers of memory, accuracy, and reputation for trustworthiness or otherwise . . . *Subsidiary to this* is the record of contingent events and important occurrences relating to the rise of religious communities, the origination (and sequence) of religious obligations, caliphs, viziers, raids, battles, and so on.'[1]

(2) *Principles of Selection*

It follows therefore that the basic qualification for inclusion in the general run of biographical dictionaries is the contribution brought by the individual to the cultural tradition of the Muslim Community, in one or other of its aspects, and that the selection of the biographer is determined by the particular aspects or aspect of Islamic culture to which his concern is directed. And this latter in turn is determined as a rule by his own interests or discipline. Since the earliest organized disciplines in Islam were the religious and legal disciplines of *ḥadīth*-study, the earliest biographical works are oriented towards meeting their requirements both in general works and in the 'histories' of particular cities and provinces. As the practice of biography spread, corresponding limitations continued to be observed; while religious scholars continued to confine themselves to traditionists, jurists, and other religious classes, men of letters compiled dictionaries of poets and writers, administrative officials dictionaries of viziers and secretaries, scientists and philosophers dictionaries of their own kind. The first biographical dictionary of more general scope was apparently the History of Baḡẖdād of al-Ḵẖaṭīb al-Baḡẖdādī (5th/11th century), although the traditionalist interest still heavily predominates in this work. Not until the famous dictionary of Ibn Ḵẖallikān (7th/13th century) is the attempt made to include (if on a relatively small scale) a comprehensive selection of eminent figures in all fields of activity in all parts of the Islamic

---

[1] *I'lān*, 67; trans. F. Rosenthal, *Muslim Historiography*, pp. 204–5; cf. al-Kāfījī, *Muḵẖtaṣar*, ibid., pp. 188, 478: 'The fundamental objective of history is the accurate registration of mankind in an authoritative (or specific) manner.'

world.[2] The groundwork for this had, however, been laid earlier by the new type of chronicle history apparently introduced by Ibn al-Jawzī, which constituted in the main a chronological biographical dictionary, the *wafayāt* under each year occupying many times the space allotted to political events. Thenceforward almost all chroniclers adopted the same practice, with more or less attention given to political events or personalities; so that the 'universal history' became at the same time a 'universal biographical dictionary', the climax of this development being furnished by the immense History of Islam of al-Dhahabī (8th/14th century), in which political events and biographies are grouped in blocks of ten years.

Although therefore dictionaries of special classes (secretaries, grammarians, religious scholars, physicians, jurists, etc.) continued to be compiled, the biographical dictionary had by now developed into a comprehensive commemoration of all notabilities in all fields. After al-Dhahabī, it became a regular practice to group biographies by centuries (of *wafayāt*, i.e. death dates); this began with Ibn Ḥajar for the 8th/14th century, and was continued for successive centuries by al-Sakhāwī, al-Ghazzī, al-Muḥibbī, and al-Murādī, and by other regional compilers. Religious scholars undoubtedly predominate numerically in these works, but only alongside a catholic selection of political figures, sultans, viziers, officials, men of letters and poets, merchants, physicians, notable women and occasionally even persons noted for some special gift, as schoolmasters or chessplayers.

It is, however, a remarkable fact, which calls for explanation, that this type of biographical activity was almost exclusively confined to the Arabic provinces of Islam. Until the 19th century, few biographical dictionaries were compiled either in the Turkish areas or in Iran or India, and none at all which correspond to the Arabic 'centennial' series.

(3) *The Biographical Structure*

The passage quoted above from al-Sakhāwī defines the essential points of a biographical notice for the traditional scholars: who, when, where, intellectual powers, reputation. Physical facts are included, but only as being relative to the preceding, and are seldom mentioned otherwise. In keeping with this formula, the vast majority of biographical notices contain little more than shorter or longer outlines of the biographee's life (including in later works details of posts held), his teachers and pupils, traditions transmitted or books composed, and somewhat stereotyped

[2] 826 biographies in all; distributed as follows (some being duplicated): Caliphs, kings, governors, conquerors 145; Viziers 41; *Qāḍīs* 32; Jurists 161; Traditionists 87; Qur'anic expositors 21; Grammarians 95; Prosewriters and historians 94; Poets 147; Preachers and ascetics 42; Theologians 17; Philosophers and physicians 19; Musicians 3. (It is to be remembered that the writer deliberately omitted the first generation of Muslims.)

generalities on his character, with little interest in his personality as such. Many early works, indeed, abbreviate the formula still further, omitting dates and personal events, and after a bare statement of identity list only writings, or (as in Bayhaqī's *Ta'rīkh al-ḥukamā'*) only noteworthy sayings attributed to him.

At no period, however, did such bare schematic outlines constitute the entire repertory of biographical notices. From Ibn Sa'd to al-Murādī, all biographical dictionaries (and even al-Bayhaqī) include entries running into 20, 30, or even 50 pages. There is here an evident elaboration of the basic scheme, but not in the sense of a development in structure or method, or an improved technique of analysis or characterization. In many instances, the purpose of the lengthier entries is simply to transmit all information which the writer has been able to collect on the biographees; this is especially evident in Ibn Sa'd, *al-Aghānī*, al-Khaṭīb al-Baghdādī and the notices of saints in Abū Nu'aym's *Ḥilyat al-awliyā'*. There is no evidence of any attempt to create a literary, or even an historical, organization of these materials. The presentation remains throughout concrete and factual. In so far as anything more than mere collection is involved, the most that can be said is that the additional materials often add psychological depth indirectly by their implications. This is because the filling consists mainly of anecdotes relating to the individual, which present him in a variety of circumstances and attitudes; in the later biographical works it may, indeed, be surmised that they are consciously directed to this purpose without involving the writer in personal judgements. Ibn Ḥajar in particular excels in his ability to portray an individual by brief remarks of an anecdotal character (e.g. of a *qāḍī* in Aleppo): 'His speech was more abundant than his knowledge, and he was hot-tempered in discussion and given to shouting';[3] and of a teacher: 'He was most forbearing, especially in face of the rudeness of the students from the Maghrib and the Egyptian peasantry.'[4]

(4) *Sources of Biographical Notices*

Early biographical materials are obviously compiled from oral traditions, and for the most part presented as such, with chains of transmission. The same technique is continued into later centuries (e.g. by al-Iṣfahānī and al-Khaṭīb al-Baghdādī), although written sources gradually increases and later compilations (e.g. al-Dhahabī) clearly reproduce material from earlier works, with or without acknowledgement. The problem of critical analysis is usually, therefore, one of some difficulty, and has scarcely been attempted as yet. In the later 'centennial' dictionaries, there is some evidence that the biographer collected part of his materials by

[3] ii, 343. [4] ii, 313.

correspondence, as well as from personal acquaintance with his contemporaries, but other than written sources are only rarely indicated.

(5) *Value of the Biographical Works for Historical Studies*

To the historian of Islamic civilization in its broader aspects the dictionaries are obviously of capital importance, but with certain limitations. Agriculture and the industrial arts are as thinly represented as in *Who's Who*, although trade and economic activities are by no means neglected in the Mamluk and later dictionaries. Given the religious and literary interests of the great majority of biographers, it is evident that they provide the fullest and most complete detail for the religious and intellectual life of the Muslim Community throughout its history, including educational and (thanks to the biographies of *ḥukamā'*) scientific activities. Without these works, indeed, no detailed study of Islamic culture would be possible.

With the exceptions noted above, they supply also valuable data for social history and institutions, but in more sporadic and anecdotal fashion, and which have often to be combined with materials from other sources to become fully intelligible. In this respect, the earlier comprehensive works (Ibn Sa'd, *al-Aghānī*, *Ta'rīkh Baghdād*, and perhaps also Ibn 'Asākir) are of special value, both by reason of their wide fields of selection and discursiveness, and because of the relative paucity of other surviving materials. The biographical dictionaries also supply almost the sole materials for the social activities and status of women in Muslim communities.

In regard to political history, the value of these works is subject to wide variations. Where other sources are sparse, they help to fill lacunae; where the former are plentiful, they serve to add detail and precision, or for critical study. But since the narratives with a political interest are for the most part anecdotal and related to individual incidents, the question of sources and authenticity is in this field particularly acute. It is, in other words, unsafe to draw conclusions from the anecdotes of the biographical works, unless substantiating data can be adduced. On the other hand, if no bias can be demonstrated or suspected, the general judgements of the biographers on individual princes, governors or officials may be generally accepted.

5. THE HISTORIOGRAPHY OF THE SELJUQID PERIOD

CLAUDE CAHEN

Professor of the History of the Muslim Orient in the University of Paris

The Seljuqs, in spite of several useful partial studies, still await the comprehensive historian whom their role in Muslim history would seem to deserve. The indispensable preliminary assessment of the sources has itself so far been the subject of only incomplete soundings.[1] Short of being complete itself, the present report aims at least to assist in establishing certain data and directions of enquiry.

Neither the beginning nor the end of Seljuq rule marks a true break in the development of Muslim historical literature; the drawing of a specific picture of Seljuq historiography is therefore uncalled-for. What we more especially propose to do here—because it is at the same time the most indispensable to the historian and the least often carried out—is the systematic examination of the sources and of the documentary value of the works on which the modern historian must base his researches. For this reason it has seemed preferable, at the risk of leaving a few temporary gaps, to concentrate on the Seljuq domain proper, namely the Iraqi–Iranian territory from the middle of the eleventh to the end of the twelfth century A.D. There have been left on one side, therefore, as regards territorial extent, the too specific historical writings of Syria-Jazīra on the one hand, and of Asia Minor (even under the Seljuqs) on the other, and, as regards time, the previous history of the Seljuqs[2] as well as their epigons of Khwārizm.

As is to be expected of authors who composed their works during the heyday of the ʿAbbasid caliphate, or at least when the memory of this heyday and of the unity of Muslim was still alive, the first great monuments of Muslim historiography mostly include, as far as possible, the whole domain of Islam. Baghdād especially, although the historians who lived there had an understandable tendency to grant to it a pre-eminence, was the focus of this pan-Islamic conception of historiography, and it did not cease to be so even when the Buwayhids had made the Caliph their puppet and converted Iraq in fact into a separate principality. The great works of Thābit b. Sinān, Hilāl al-Ṣābī, and Miskawayh in fact date just from this Buwayhid period. However, in the regions which led a more or less separate life the idea of separate chronicles had been born: in Egypt and the West, in the Yemen, etc. Moreover, from the tenth century, and even

[1] Especially V. A. Ḥamdānī in an unpublished thesis (cf. *Abstracts of dissertations of the University of Oxford*, 1939). [2] Of which I have spoken in 'Le Maliknāmeh etc.', *Oriens*, ii (1949).

earlier in the original case of Mecca, the development of civic pride or autonomy in certain places had given birth to city histories. The idea of histories centred on dynasties could occur only when and where dynasties were encountered which were endowed with their own personalities independent of the countries where they held sway. Even the Buwayhids as such hardly had historians. Later on their religious quality produced some for the Zaydīs of the Yemen and the Fatimids; the Tulunids alone had had some *ratione personae*, so to speak, but only for a short time, for their rule had been brief. The West set apart, in the East the true dynastic history of which the tradition could pass over into the Seljuq period appeared under the Ghaznawids, both in Arabic (ʿUtbī) and in Persian (Bayhaqī), so that at the moment when the Seljuqs appeared on the scene three types of historiography: pan-Islamic, regional, and dynastic, and (in the territories where they settled) two languages, Arabic and Persian, were flourishing. For the moment it is not necessary to speak of certain other works of a more special or marginal character.

Strangely enough, it seems that the Great Seljuqs produced no historian during their lifetimes. Later on we shall discuss the sources from which the authors of dynastic histories composed a century after them may have gathered the, on the whole, rather meagre information on them. But for us, in any case, the essential sources for the history of Ṭughril Beg, Alp Arslan, and Malikshāh are to be found in the Baghdād historiography of a general character which carries on without great change that of the Buwayhid period.

The great enterprise with which most of the others are connected is the History of Hilāl al-Ṣābī,[3] of which the section covering approximately the three years 989–92 (which do not concern us) alone is preserved. It is to be assumed that he first wrote the history of the period going from Thābit b. Sinān's end to his own time, and carried it on subsequently to the entry of Ṭughril Beg into Baghdād in 447/1055. The importance of the work is well known despite the fact that it has not always been sufficiently stressed that, for the century which it covers, it is practically the sole source of all subsequent Baghdād historiography, if only indirectly. Sibṭ Ibn al-Jawzī tells us, however, that for the last fifteen years (433–47) he had been unable to find a manuscript in Syria.[4] It is a fact that general historiography on this period is rather thin; Ibn al-Athīr, whose accounts concern the activity of the Turkomans, then of the Seljuqs in western Iran, Kurdistan, and the Jazīra, is the one exception. It is not impossible that the reason may simply be that he, unlike the others, had access to a manuscript of Hilāl. It is not so well known that Hilāl had a son, Ghars al-Niʿma Muḥammad, who continued his father's work in the same spirit until 479/1086, and that his

[3] H. F. Amedroz, *The historical remains of Hilāl al-Ṣābī* (Leiden, 1904), reproduced in *The eclipse of the Abbasid Caliphate*, ed. Amedroz and Margoliouth, vol. iii (tr. vol. vi).

[4] H. F. Amedroz, *History of Damascus by Ibn al-Qalānisī*, p. 1, n. 2.

History is not less important for his time than Hilāl's for the previous century. It is true that this time absolutely nothing has come down to us directly of this History, and it even seems that the Mesopotamian historians did not have it at their disposal for long; in particular, it is unlikely that Ibn al-Athīr can have known it in spite of the abundance of his materials. One author only has preserved for us long extracts or analyses of it; rather paradoxically it is a thirteenth-century Syrian author, Sibṭ Ibn al-Jawzī, in his *Mir'āt al-zamān*, which is still unpublished for this period in spite of the great importance conferred upon it by the use of this source, unrecognized until now. It may be that the manuscript of Ghars al-Ni'ma, possibly unique, had found its way to the Syrian capital.

The History of Ghars al-Ni'ma Muḥammad, as it appears through the *Mir'āt* (of which, for these years, apart from the obituaries, it forms almost the sole source), consists first of an exact and intelligent diary of Baghdād political events and then of a fund of information, often without correspondence elsewhere, concerning the rest of the Muslim world from Egypt to Iran, passing sometimes even through Asia Minor. This information is based on the author's personal experience, on the accounts of persons of his acquaintance, on documents. As the heir to a great fortune[5] he had perhaps never followed a profession but had always been highly esteemed among the entourage of the Caliph al-Qā'im. As for his History, entitled *'Uyūn al-tawārīkh*, I have long had the intention of publishing the version by Sibṭ Ibn al-Jawzī, completing it by the few other discoverable quotations;[6] but there is a difficulty in the fact that the *Mir'āt* itself, for this period, has come down to us in two very different versions, between which, of course, comparison must be made.[7]

A comparison between works posterior to that of Ghars al-Ni'ma and his own work shows an undeniable relationship but, as has been stated already, it does not follow that the utilization is without error, or in all cases, direct. It seems that later authors generally contented themselves, whether or not of necessity, with summaries including additional matter or with works based on parallel information. The chief historian to be considered in this respect is probably Muḥammad b. 'Abd al-Malik al-Hamadhānī (d. 515/1121).[8] It is not always easy through the scattered information and quotations to reconstruct exactly what his work may have been; this again is almost wholly lost. It seems that it comprised, as far as

[5] His biography in Amedroz, *Hist. Rem.*, Preface, especially after Sibṭ Ibn al-Jawzī (slightly shortened); add Bundārī, Paris, Bibl. Nat. arabe 6152, 95 ro.

[6] Especially in the *Bughya* of Ibn al-'Adīm; also Ibn al-Qifṭī, ed. Lippert, p. 211. The interest of the *Mir'āt* has been recognized also by G. Makdisi who fortunately has agreed to share in the editing.

[7] *Revue des Etudes Islamiques*, iv (1936), 339–40.

[8] As for others, Simnānī, see my *Syrie du Nord* (Paris, 1940), p. 72, n. 1, adding that he is quoted by Sibṭ Ibn al-Jawzī for the end of the reign of Malikshāh; Ibn Bābā al-Qāshī, for whom see *infra*, n. 22; and Ibn Bannā', for whom *infra*, p. 77.

history is concerned, a relatively detailed continuation of Ṭabarī, of which a portion remains for the tenth century only (and paradoxically in a Maghribī manuscript),[9] then a more abridged general history (lost but for quotations) with the title *'Unwān al-siyar*, and lastly a History of the Viziers in continuation of that of Hilāl al-Ṣābī.[10] But during the lifetime of our Hamadhānī there were other Hamadhānīs, themselves more or less historians, and it is possible that their works have been confused, especially by Ḥājjī Khalīfa.[11] It is not impossible that a manuscript of the *'Unwān* may still be found one day, especially in Syria, since in the fifteenth century al-'Aynī (still unpublished) quotes it systematically. The hope for the later works is not so good, later authors quote them little but rather refer to 'the 'Irāqīs' comprehensively, apparently because the differences between several works derived from the same sources were slight. I am not in a position to assert that Muḥammad b. 'Abd al-Malik utilized Ghars al-Ni'ma, whom in any case he does not reproduce slavishly; but his information is drawn from the same source, and for the tenth century he quotes al-Ṣābī by name.

However that may be, it seems to be Muḥammad b. 'Abd al-Malik al-Hamadhānī who ends the series of the great Baghdād historians of pan-Islamic attitude. It is true that there were still in the 6th/12th century writers with pretensions to carry on the tradition, whom al-Zawzānī quotes:[12] al-Raghūnī until 527/1132, Ibn al-Ḥaddād until the eve of his death in 570/1174. Their works, still not found, seem to have been second-rate and practically confined to Iraq and the regions in immediate contact with it. This is henceforth the case with almost all Baghdād historiography which witnessed, truly enough, a revival of the caliphate but of the caliphate now as a regional principality much more than as a pan-Islamic institution. The only work which concerns us here is the *Kitāb al-muntaẓam* of the famous Ḥanbalī doctor Ibn al-Jawzī.[13] This History, which pretends to be universal, is in reality above all Baghdādī. It carries on the chronicles of the 5th/11th and 6th/12th centuries which we have just enumerated, after utilizing them and supplementing them by Ḥanbalī informants up to 573/1177. The *Muntaẓam* has enjoyed a reputation which certainly seems to us a little exaggerated, and has been constantly used by later

[9] Bibl. Nat. arabe 1469, now edited by Kan'ānī in *Mashriq*, 1955–8.

[10] An explicit quotation from the great History, Ibn Khallikān (De Slane), i, 464; from the *'Unwān* in the *Bughya*, Saray, ii, 61 ro, vi, 94 ro, *Historiens orientaux des Croisades*, iii, 706 and 729, and above all in 'Aynī, see *infra*. Quotations without title in Ibn Khall, iii, 231–2, 284, 289, Yāqūt, *Irshād*, v, 69–72, Sibṭ Ibn al-Jawzī in his biographies of Malikshāh and Niẓām al-Mulk, etc.

[11] In particular with Abū Shujā' Shihrawayh b. Shahriyār al-Hamadhānī, see F. Wüstenfeld, *Die Geschichtsschreiber der Araber*, p. 225, Yāqūt, *Irshād*, i, 94, and Sakhāwī quoted in Rosenthal, *Muslim historiography*, Index under the two Hamadhānīs.

[12] The abbreviator of Ibn al-Qifṭī. The passage, already cited by De Slane, Ibn Khall., i, 290, is also in Rosenthal, p. 73.

[13] Ed. Krenkow (Hyderabad), 5 vols. and Index, 1357–60/1938–41.

writers; but, however interesting it may often be for the history of Baghdād proper, it cannot stand as a general history. Even in regional history it has unevennesses of exposition which are surprising, and which are perhaps solely due to the author's habitual haste. Basically he was interested only in setting forth the lives of scholars. He seems to have originated the habit which became general after him of following the account of events for each year by more or less detailed obituaries, and so distributing in chronological order the material which is found in alphabetical order in the biographical dictionaries.

Before Ibn al-Jawzī there is no need to call attention further to anything except the historical section, which appears to be unpublished, of the *Tadhkīra* of Ibn Ḥamdūn. This was terminated in 553/1158[14] and gathers concisely information relating to the various eastern Muslim countries. After Ibn al-Jawzī a certain importance should probably be attached to another lost work, the continuation of the Abridgement of Ṭabarī composed about the end of the 6th/12th century by an 'Irāqī immigrant in Syria. Quotations from the writer, Abū Ghālib b. al-Ḥusayn al-Shaybānī, in the *Bughya* of Ibn al-'Adīm, scattered over this book's account of the 5th/11th and 5th/12th centuries, although centred on Syria, show him to be abundantly informed on the general activity of the sultan Alp Arslan.[15] Of another genre is the History of the Caliphs, distributed by reigns, composed some years after the *Tadhkīra* and probably partly based on it by another 'Irāqī exile, Muḥammad 'Imrānī.[16] It is not possible to prolong here the examination of works which would oblige us to go far outside the Seljuq domain.[17] Practically our knowledge of Iraqi-Iranian historiography in the 6th/12th century draws largely from the somewhat later *Kāmil* of Ibn al-Athīr, of which, apart from the specifically Seljuq sources which we shall deal with below, Ibn al-Jawzī, who is once quoted by name,[18] is by far not the sole provider of Mesopotamian documentation. It is possible that he used directly the *Dhayl* of Abū Ghālib, and also Ibn al-Ḥaddād, as his pupil Ibn Khallikān was occasionally to do again after him.[19] He refers several times to 'the 'Irāqīs' in opposition to the historians of other regions, which proves that in any case he followed several, but for the moment we must confess our inability to be more precise.

From the same point of view as the *Kāmil* a Syriac work (translated into Arabic by the author himself), the *Chronography* of Gregory Abu'l-Faraj

[14] *REI* (1936), p. 337. The Khanjī firm of Cairo printed something of the *Tadhkīra* in 1345/1927, but I have not been able to ascertain the contents.

[15] *Syrie du Nord*, p. 53; consider also Ibn al-Dahhān, ibid., p. 54.

[16] *REI*, loc. cit.; a copy of the Istanbul MS. (not identified in the catalogue) exists in the Bibl. Nat. arabe 4842.

[17] I permit myself to refer to my *Syrie*, pp. 48–9, 53, 54, and 71–2.

[18] Only in connection with his death, it is true (xii, 112); but textual similarities are very numerous.

[19] De Slane, ii, 138.

Bar-Hebraeus,[20] ought as an exception to be considered. Gregory, besides Syriac predecessors, had used Persian and Arab historians. Ibn al-Athīr appears as the principal of the latter, but for the history of the Great Seljuqs he had supplementary information, though certainly drawn for the most part from Baghdādī sources, especially those of the same family as Sibṭ Ibn al-Jawzī's.[21]

Several more or less general histories were composed also in Iran. In these Iran generally occupies a greater place. One or two authors had already written histories of the Muslim world conceived as a succession of dynasties.[22] In 520/1126 an anonymous author, writing possibly at the court of the Kākūyid princes of Yazd in Fārs, finished a work of this type in Persian. This *Mujmal al-tawārīkh* begins with the ancient kings of Persia. Its last pages, devoted to the Seljuqs up to this date, are probably related to the 'Irāqī sources, perhaps to 'Abd al-Malik al-Hamadhānī: for the earlier period the work names Hilāl al-Ṣābī.[23]

More important for the Seljuq period in Iran was apparently the *Mashārib al-tajārib* of the Khurāsānī 'Alī b. Zayd al-Bayhaqī known as Ibn Funduq, of which we have once again to lament the total loss. The title seems evidently to suggest a continuation of the *Tajārib al-umam* of Miskawayh (itself adapted from the chronicles of Thābit b. Sinān and Hilāl al-Ṣābī). When Ibn Funduq appears to inform us elsewhere[24] that he took the continuation from the Ghaznavid writer al-'Utbī, who stopped at 410/1019, that cannot mean that he began at this date, for we have an earlier quotation from the *Mashārib*.[25] The fact that Ibn Funduq had composed this work in Arabic in a country which was giving up this language and that, inversely, he probably lacked documentation on the Arab countries, which could have made certain of the preservation of the *Mashārib* if its contents had satisfied them, no doubt explains its disappearance. Nevertheless, one could possibly still become acquainted with it at the beginning of the Mongol period if the quotation made by Juvaynī[26] rests on direct acquaintance. Moreover, a manuscript may have reached the Arab countries in the 7th/13th century as it is a fact that not only Yāqūt[27] who had travelled in Iran, but also and above all Ibn al-Athīr[28] used it.

[20] Ed. and tr. Budge (1932), 2 vols.

[21] See for example my article 'La Campagne de Mantzikert', in *Byzantion* (1934), especially the last pages.

[22] For example Ibn Bābā al-Qāshī, who announced a Seljuq History which probably never saw the light (Hamdani, 'Some rare MSS. in Istanbul', *JRAS* (1938), pp. 562–3).

[23] Ed. Bahār (Tehran, 1936) (it does not contain the chapter on the Ghaznawids, particular to the Paris MS.).

[24] *Tārīkh-i-Bayhaq*, ed. Aḥmad Bahmanyār, p. 25, with the Preface by Muḥ. Qazwīnī.

[25] Yāqūt, *Irshād*, ii, 314, concerning the Buwayhid vizier Ibn 'Abbād.

[26] *Tārīkh-i jahān-gushā*, ii, 1.

[27] *Irshād*, loc. cit. and v, 124–6 (on the Seljuq vizier al-Kundurī).

[28] *Kāmil*, ed. Tornberg, xi, 249, but cf. *infra*.

The quotations given by these authors plus allusions in other works (this time preserved) of Ibn Funduq are all that we can exploit in an attempt to ascertain the character of the *Mas͟hārib*. We cannot discover if it was a true general history or in fact a regional one. The date when it was finished is obscure. In a first form, which consisted of four volumes, Yāqūt extracted from it the autobiography of Ibn Funduq which he has preserved for us and which stops at 549/1154;[29] but this autobiography and auto-bibliography mentions already among the works of the author his collection of biographies, *Tatimmat ṣīwān al-ḥikma*. Now, he alludes in this latter to the eighth volume of his *Mas͟hārib*;[30] thus the two works must have been carried on side by side. Ibn al-At͟hīr seems to father on Ibn Funduq an account of the history of K͟hwārizm which he introduces in 568/1172 but carries on till 595/1198. But this last date is practically impossible since Ibn Funduq by his own account was born in 499/1105, and in fact Yāqūt, according to an unknown source, gives the date of his death as 565/1169, and the last date of the History of Bayhaq, another extant work of Ibn Funduq which does not appear in Yāqūt's list, is 562/1166.[31] Can it be that Ibn al-At͟hīr knew the *Mas͟hārib* only through an intermediary of whom he failed correctly to delimit a quotation (which could even deal with facts previous to 568/1172 if he found it in a general account of the beginnings of the Khwarizmian dynasty), or did he allow his notes to become disordered? We shall come across this question again when we seek eventually to determine more generally the place of the *Mas͟hārib* among the sources of the *Kāmil*.

But however that may be, the *Mas͟hārib* itself came too late for the author to be able to refer to direct testimony on the subject of the first Seljuqs, and so we are faced with the problem of its own sources. The first histories of a general character to which Ibn Funduq alludes elsewhere are a continuation of 'Utbī's biography of Maḥmūd of G͟hazna by a certain Abu'l-Ḥasan Muḥammad b. Sulaymān and the famous vast History of Abu'l-Faḍl Muḥammad b. Ḥusayn al-Bayhaqī of which he had still been able to consult the volumes scattered between Sarak͟hs and Nīs͟hāpūr which today have only been rediscovered in part.[32] As from the middle of the 5th/11th century it certainly seems that apart from scattered notes in local histories Ibn Funduq no longer had the work of predecessors at his disposal, and had to make an effort to gather material himself. This effort could have been made easier by his long stay at Nīs͟hāpūr and his familiarity with highly placed personages at the court of Sultan Sanjar.

The only extant work in which the *Mas͟hārib* may have been extensively used is the *Kāmil* of Ibn al-At͟hīr. It would have had a considerable interest for the distinguished historian, for, much as we may admire on the one

[29] *Irs͟hād*, v, 208–12.
[30] *Tatimma*, ed. Muḥ. S͟hafī' (Lahore, 1935), p. 166.
[31] *Supra*, n. 24.
[32] *Tārīk͟h-i Bayhaq*, 19, 175.

hand the breadth of his documentary researches, nothing, on the other hand, indicates that he knew Persian, and so, in the Iranian field, he would have been considerably handicapped if he had had no Arabic texts at his disposal. His information on eastern Iran cannot all be due to such of his other sources as we know (see again below) and this information, which is specially abundant for the middle of the 6th/12th century, suddenly diminishes about 560/764 and that is an especially plausible date for the termination of the *Mashārib*. Though the local and fragmentary character of the accounts of events in the *Tārīkh-i Bayhaq* of Ibn Funduq prevents any definitive comparison, at least the background of general history is the same. On the other hand, the sole specific reference to the *Mashārib* in the *Kāmil* faces us, as we have seen, with a quasi-impossibility; and until the middle of the 6th/12th century events in eastern Iran, when they are not linked with those of western Iran, are after all treated by Ibn al-Athīr in a relatively summary fashion. It is true that Yāqūt, in connection with the vizier al-Kundurī and his relations with the poet Bākharzī, quotes from the *Mashārib* passages which are undoubtedly at the source of Ibn al-Athīr's corresponding account; but the comparison is not completely conclusive, for these accounts are also to be found in the commentaries on the *Dumyat al-qaṣr* of Bākharzī and also in the *Zubda*, of which we shall speak presently.[33] It may be that Ibn al-Athīr knew the *Mashārib*, complete or certain of its volumes, only through an intermediary, which would have to be determined, it is true. There is again for the events of *c.* 568–90/1193 concerning the Khwārizmshāh Töküsh a parallelism between Ibn al-Athīr and Juvaynī, and we have said that the latter could have been acquainted with the *Mashārib*; but the express quotation which he makes from it at the beginning of his History of the Khwārizmshāhs solely concerns the remote origins of the dynasty, and he also may have known it through an intermediary. It is possible that our two authors had a common intermediary which was presumably in Arabic. One among others could be al-Ma'mūnī's History of Khurāsān, which was later known to Ibn Khallikān; but it stopped at 570/1174.[34]

In any case we reach with the *Mashārib al-tajārib* the period when one after another three important histories special, now, to the Seljuq dynasty are composed. It is not of course totally out of the question that one had existed already at the beginning of the century, by Abū Ṭāhir al-Khātūnī, a well-known man of letters and high official of the Seljuqs at the end of the 5th/11th and beginning of the 6th/12th century. But the only testimony

[33] *Irshād*, v, 124–7; *Kāmil*, x, 20–1. The *Dumya*, an anthology of poetry, devotes a special section to al-Kundurī, who was the poet's patron and himself a poet on occasion.

[34] It went back to the Buwayhid period; Ibn Khall. (De Slane), ii, 334. The same author quotes it in connection with the death of Dubays, of whom he may have spoken apropos of the reign of Sanjar (i, 506) and in the life of Alp Arslan (iii). In Persian, see the historical chapter of the *Javāmi' al-'ulūm* of Fakhr al-Dīn Rāzī.

to this effect comes from Dawlatshāh[35] who wrote at the end of the 9th/15th century, and the quotations which he makes from it consist entirely of extracts from poets similar to those which he borrowed from an Anthology of the same author. 'Imād al-Dīn and Ẓahīr al-Dīn (see below) likewise testify to Abū Ṭāhir's poetic activity. They attribute to him several anecdotes or satires to accompany his verses but do not speak of a historical work in the ordinary sense.[36] One may even assert that it was either a negligible or non-existent work or at least that it remained unknown, since the information of later authors on the time of the Great Seljuqs is by and large strangely meagre (with the exception of 'Imād al-Dīn's borrowings from Iraqi sources, see below). Possibly Abū Ṭāhir had composed illustrative anecdotes forming the materials for memoirs around an anthology of verse by himself and his contemporaries; but this conjecture is the most that can be made, and is gratuitous at that.

In contrast, there are memoirs which, although lost in their original Persian form, are substantially preserved in the Arabic guise given to them by 'Imād al-Dīn al-Iṣfahānī:[37] those of the vizier Anūshirwān. They do not seem to have been either exclusively personal memoirs nor yet a true complete chronicle, but something in between, 'memoirs as a contribution to the history of their time'. The personal affairs and rivalries of the milieu of viziers and their associates rather, unfortunately, than their governmental functions seem to have constituted the essential part. It is for the reign of Malikshāh, where Anūshirwān remains nevertheless incomplete, that 'Imād al-Dīn introduces Anūshirwān; he names him for the last time in 522/1128, in spite of having said elsewhere that the work went up to 528/1133.[38] Anūshirwān's Memoirs do not seem to have been known to any other Persian or Arab author than 'Imād al-Dīn, and everything indicates that the latter, who belonged to the same circles, had in his hands a unique manuscript which had ceased to be useful and had disappeared because of the Arabic translation made by him in an Arab country.

The author of an insignificant Seljuq History of the Mongol period, 'Alī b. Ḥusayn, declares in his preface that he had found no predecessor other than an author stopping at the reign of Maḥmūd.[39] Since there is no question of 'Alī's dependence on Ẓahīr al-Dīn or Rāwandī (see below) for the whole of his work he has been accused of plain falsehood.[40] That is

[35] Ed. E. G. Browne, pp. 64, 76.

[36] Apart from lines of verse here and there (which do not coincide with those of Dawlatshāh), 'Imād al-Dīn quotes Abū Ṭāhir as the author of a satire against a vizier of the end of the 5th/11th century. Bundārī (ed. Houtsma), p. 88, and Ẓahīr al-Dīn, pp. 32 (=Rāwandī, p. 131), claims to have seen an anecdote about Malikshāh written in Abū Ṭāhir's own hand, which seems to exclude the possibility that he used some more general work than this.

[37] MS., Bibl. Nat. arabe 2145.

[38] Bundārī, p. 150, and Houtsma's Preface, p. xxx.

[39] *Al-'Urāda* etc., ed. K. Süssheim, p. 15.

[40] Muḥ. Qazwīnī in the Preface to his edition of Juvaynī, *Tārīkh-i jahān-gushā*, p. lxxv, reproduced by Muḥ. Iqbāl in that to his edition of Rāwandī, *Rāḥat al-ṣudūr*, p. xxxiv.

perhaps a little hasty. It is a fact that for the reign of Maḥmūd these three authors are strangely laconic as though there were in fact a break in their information. The reference could not be to the *Mujmal al-tawārīkh* even though 'Alī seems to say that the work included the reign of Maḥmūd, because in the *Mujmal* it is this very reign which is described with an exceptional abundance of detail. For the same reason the Memoirs of Anūshirwān cannot be taken into consideration either. Those of Abū Ṭāhir, if they existed, do not seem on the other hand to have been able to include the reign of Maḥmūd. At all events the work in question cannot be here either a very important one.

The first in date of the important Seljuq Histories to have come down to us and apparently the first to have been composed is that of 'Imād al-Dīn al-Iṣfahānī.[41] It is true that according to his own testimony[42] he did not put it into its final form until 579/1183, when he had already been in Syria for seventeen years; but the detailed history practically ceases at the moment when the author had to leave Iraq, and he states himself[43] that his being far away prevented him from doing more. This would have prevented him *a fortiori* from discovering records concerning the past, and it is difficult to believe that his own memory alone or the chronicles available in Syria could have sufficed to provide him with all the material for the detailed accounts by which he continues and completes the Memoirs of Anūshirwān which he translates. It must therefore be concluded that he had nursed the project of his History, taken notes for the composition of it, and acquired the manuscript of Anūshirwān before 562/1166. The *Nuṣrat al-fatra*, as this history is entitled, like everything else from the pen of 'Imād al-Dīn, is over-flowery in style, which explains why his compatriot al-Bundārī, likewise an immigrant in Syria, made in 623/1226 an edition which is simpler in style but faithful in substance.[44] But already the work had had a certain success, since it is found to be known to Ibn Abī Ṭayyi'[45] and to the author of the *Akhbār* of which we shall speak presently. It was also to be known to Ibn al-Athīr about the time when al-Bundārī was working.

The sources of 'Imād al-Dīn are rather complex. The nucleus of the book is formed by the Memoirs of Anūshirwān; but as he says himself, for the very period for which he translates them, he completes them and corrects them when necessary. On the other hand, it is evidently not Anūshirwān who furnished him with the history of the Seljuqs subsequent to his Memoirs, nor that of the first representatives of the dynasty. For

[41] See n. 37. [42] Bundārī, p. 136. [43] Bundārī, p. 904.

[44] Ed. Houtsma (*Recueil de textes, etc.*, ii). I once made a minute comparison of Bundārī with the original for the long account of the campaign of Manzikart (*supra*, n. 21) and several other passages, from which it becomes clear that Bundārī scrupulously preserved all the hard facts.

[45] Everything about the East quoted by Ibn al-Furāt from Ibn Abī Ṭayyi' is the equivalent of 'Imād al-Dīn without addition.

the latter the notes taken by 'Imad al-Dīn, his own experience, and the experience of his relatives who were all important personalities under the régime are probably a complete list of the sources of information of the *Nuṣra*. For the 5th/11th century the question is less simple because the author always abridges too much for exact textual comparisons to be often possible. But as a general rule the nature of his additions to Anūshirwān for the reign of Malikshāh and the content of his versions of the reigns of the first two Seljuqs likewise incline us, without it being possible to be more exact,[46] toward Baghdādī historiography, with which its general correspondence is undeniable. He had not necessarily read Ghars al-Ni'ma, but he had almost certainly read Hamadhānī.

The History of 'Imād al-Dīn is very nearly the sole source for the years 485/1092–547/1152 of a work which is otherwise independent of it and which has come down to us in the form of a unique manuscript with the rather strange double title of *Zubdat al-tawārīkh*, *Akhbār* (not preceded by *fī*) *al-umarā' wa'l-mulūk al-saljūqiyya*.[47] The end of the text as we have it was composed in 622/1225 but the real narrative stops at 590/1193, the date of death of the last Seljuq of Iran, Ṭughril, of whose entourage the author had known a member,[48] so that it is probable that the work was composed at the end of the 6th/12th century (we shall see a confirmation of this presently), and that the references to 622/1225 are due to a later copyist or editor. The work opens by an attribution (at least of the first sentences) to a certain *Sayyid* Ṣadr al-Dīn 'Alī b. Nāṣir, who is in fact named by Juvaynī[49] and Kamāl al-Dīn b. al-'Adīm,[50] as the author of a *Zubdat al-tawārīkh* devoted to the Seljuqs. However, an author who, in the text which we have, expresses himself in the first person, met during a journey to Khwārizm a merchant whose teachers (*shaykhs*) had taken part in the battle of Manzikart (464/1071).[51] This evidently excludes an author of 622/1225 and makes rather improbable an author of the 6th/12th century; moreover, the final author belongs evidently to the north-west of Iran (see below) whereas one is tempted to see in the traveller to Khwārizm an easterner responsible for the important information about Khurāsān in the 5th/11th century. But if there are two authors, which of them is 'Alī b. Nāṣir? Süssheim[52] once proposed to identify him with a *sayyid* of this name whom he found mentioned in the '*Umdat al-ṭālib fī ansāb āl Abī Ṭālib* and who must have been alive in the middle of the 6th/12th century. But Juwaynī still attributes explicitly to one 'Alī b. Nāṣir[53] an apparently

[46] And with the exclusion of the poetical borrowings from Abū Ṭāhir and others.

[47] Ed. Muḥ. Iqbāl (Lahore, 1933). [48] p. 191. [49] *T. jahān-gushā*, ii, 44.

[50] *Bughya*, Bibl. Nat. arabe 2138, 189 ro, quotation corresponding with Muḥ. Iqbāl's edition, p. 30 at head.

[51] p. 51.

[52] *Prolegomena zu einer Ausgabe der Seldschukgeschichte etc.* (Leipzig, 1911), 22 ff.

[53] See n. 49; cf. Ibn al-Athīr, xi, 210, and xii, 100, for the determination of the probable date.

slightly later paragraph (under the reign of Arslan, about 560/1164), which would place our author in north-west Iran. Some paragraphs, for example the one which is devoted to the horoscope of Sanjar, seem to have been composed soon after the latter's death.[54] What is more, the manuscript has as its title *Akhbār* etc., and it is the first sentence only of the text which introduces 'Alī as the author of a *Zubda*, coupled, perhaps by the copyist, with the *Akhbār*, which might mean that the author of the *Akhbār* refers us to that of the *Zubda*, 'Alī b. Nāṣir.[55]

The question of the composition of the *Akhbār* which we have is, however, more intricate still. From the death of Malikshāh (sporadically even earlier) to 547/1152 it is composed in fact almost entirely of borrowings (acknowledged) from 'Imād al-Dīn al-Iṣfahānī's *Nuṣrat al-fatra*, which was finished, as we have seen, in 579/1183. Thereafter there are two possible hypotheses: either the author of our *Akhbār* was acquainted with the *Nuṣra* and used it to compose a work which is the *Zubda*; or this latter was a distinct work and a later author combined them into one. Ibn al-Qifṭī and Ibn Ẓāfir, who, by virtue of being Egypto-Syrians, may well have been acquainted with 'Imād al-Dīn's work, had each composed at the beginning of the 7th/13th century, according to their friend and contemporary Yāqūt,[56] a Seljuq History which could hardly, in the region where they lived, be original. Of the first nothing is known;[57] but the second seems to lie behind Nuwayrī's account in the *Nihāya*, and Süssheim[58] remarks that a quotation given by Nuwayrī towards the end on the death of Sanjar[59] corresponds word for word with a sentence in our *Akhbār*. All the same I do not think that these *Akhbār* are the work of Ibn Ẓāfir; at any rate the work which later authors call the *Zubda* is explicitly attributed by Ibn al-'Adīm and Juvaynī to 'Alī, while neither the first of these nor Ibn Khallikān, who often use, on the one hand, other writings of Ibn Ẓāfir, and, on the other hand, the *Zubda*,[60] establishes a link between them. Besides, an examination of Nuwayrī seems to suggest that Ibn Ẓāfir's Seljuq History was arranged on the same plan as the other dynastic histories of his preserved in his work *Al-duwal al-munqaṭi'a*, which is not the case with the *Akhbār*. But to explain the parallelism pointed out by Süssheim it must be admitted that Ibn Ẓāfir employed possibly in combination with the *Nuṣra* a version of the *Zubda*, which was therefore in existence before

[54] pp. 64–5; see also p. 26 at foot.

[55] I pointed out, without insistence, in *Oriens* (art. cit., n. 2, p. 34), that Awfī, *Lubab al-albāb*, ed. E. G. Browne, ii, 142–3, eulogized a Khwarizmian History by an anonymous 'king of the *sayyids*, *ṣadr al-ajall*' Nīshāpūrī whose style was superior to that of 'Utbī (and so perhaps in Arabic?). The date seems to be very early.

[56] *Irshād*, v, 228, 484.

[57] Though there may have existed at Kazan a MS. bearing its name.

[58] Op. cit., n. 52, 22.

[59] Leiden MS. 2k, 16 vo=Muḥ. Iqbāl's ed., p. 124.

[60] This in the *Bughya* (see note 50) and in Ibn Khall. (De Slane), particularly i, 151, 612, and iii (life of Alp Arslan).

613/1216, the date of his death, but which did not necessarily include the narratives concerning western Iran in the second half of the 6th/12th century which are very briefly echoed in Nuwayrī.

Moreover, the text of our *Akhbār* suggests that it consists of a résumé of an original or originals.[61] That this résumé is the *Akhbār* and not the *Zubda* appears to be implied by the fact that the quotation found in Juvaynī does not appear in our *Akhbār* (the epitomizer, perhaps the introducer, of the *Nuṣra*). In fact the following facts become clear from the comparison. On the one hand, while parallelisms are frequent and clear for the 5th/11th century they are lacking for all that part of the 6th/12th century, the second half, which does not consist of an abridgement of 'Imād al-Dīn. It is true that for this period Ibn al-Athīr had other quite good sources of information at his disposal, but not so much as to make the *Zubda*, if he knew of it, quite useless. One thus has the impression that he was acquainted with a *Zubda* which, for his purpose, did not go usefully beyond the middle of the 6th/12th century, even though for some years it still gave sundry information such as the undated quotation in Juvaynī.

On the other hand, what do the parallelisms between Ibn al-Athīr and our *Zubda* for the 5th/11th century consist of? First, in the version from the *Maliknāma* of the origin of the Seljuqs until Dandānqān (432/1040). That Ibn al-Athīr did not use this *Maliknāma* directly is shown not only by the fact that he was apparently ignorant of Persian, but also by a passage which I have pointed out elsewhere,[62] where the interpretation which he gives of it is identical with that of the *Zubda* and contrary to that of Mīrkhwānd, who referred directly to the original. However, and in spite of the difficulties of comparison arising from the fact that Ibn al-Athīr combines various sources, it is difficult not to think that the text of our *Zubda* lacks details which are present in the *Kāmil* and inseparable from the *Maliknāma*. The impression is even clearer for the period following, and especially for the reign of Alp Arslan. There are considerable correspondences of form and matter but even here there are various additions in one or the other (but especially in Ibn al-Athīr) of which some can hardly be supposed to be drawn from other sources.

Of course for the 5th/11th century even the author of the original *Zubda* must have used earlier sources (for the first half of the 6th/12th century his information must have been scanty since the *Nuṣra* was substituted for them). First there is the *Maliknāma* which breaks off at Dandānqān; for the sequence of events the author of the *Zubda* takes little interest in facts outside Iran and completely ignores the activity of Ṭughril Beg before his entry into Baghdād (in which he resembles the other Persian Seljud historian of whom we shall speak presently). On the other hand, he is informed about Chaghri Beg or more precisely on Alp Arslan from the

[61] p. 100.

[62] *Oriens*, art. cit., n. 2, p. 42, n. 29.

time when he was still in Khurāsān in the reign of the latter. And, though one may be tempted to suppose that the valuable information in the *Akhbār* on the wars against the Georgians are the result of Āzarbāyjānī accounts gathered by the second author, it seems more probable that they form part of an ancient collection of materials on Alp Arslan. The chapter on the relations between Chaghri Beg and the Ghaznavids gives, however, the impression of being drawn from a Ghaznavid history. Must we suppose the introduction of the *Mashārib* as the passage already pointed out[63] about al-Kundurī and Bākharzī seems to invite us? Not necessarily, for the same reasons adduced for the *Kāmil*. At all events, as for the *Kāmil*, a utilization of the whole of the *Mashārib* seems to be out of the question if one wishes to take into account also the places where the author of the *Zubda* shows a lack of knowledge (to judge by the *Akhbār*). The place which the *'Amīd Khurāsān* Muḥammad b. Manṣūr al-Nasawī, a well-known personage, occupies in the *Akhbār* inclines one perhaps to look for the source of information particularly about Alp Arslan in his entourage. On Niẓām al-Mulk the author names a special anonymous work of *faḍā'il* composed by a client of the vizier and possibly used by later writers.[64]

As a very imprecise and provisional conclusion it may be supposed that about 560/1164 there was a *Zubdat al-tawārīkh* by 'Alī b. Nāṣir which was itself based on a combination of partial sources for the 5th/11th century, and less well informed, if it continued, for the 6th/12th century. About 600/1203 an Iranian from the north-west, probably not 'Alī, enlarged it by adding a history of the sultanates of Arslan and Ṭughril and the atabegs of Āzarbāyjān: his personal situation must have rendered him independent of any literary source. He himself or a third person who might, just conceivably, be Ibn Ẓāfir, introduced the *Nuṣra* into the original, but at the same time abridged, work. The date of 547/1152 which marks the interruption in the borrowing from the *Nuṣra* is perhaps that at which the second author began his work, but might also be the result of a possible third author. Thus the *Akhbār*, as we have it, is not in any case an original source except for the second half of the 6th/12th century, but for the 5th/11th century preserves for us, alongside Ibn al-Athīr, an extract from previous sources lost to us.

We have been brought back time after time to Ibn al-Athīr. The intelligent way in which this author recasts his sources, which he rarely names, makes it difficult to assess the precise value of his information. But since no author has gathered such a wide documentation it is the more urgent that a general critical study of the *Kāmil* should be attempted, at least for

[63] See n. 27 and 33.

[64] See n. 94 and 95 and *Akhbār*, p. 70. The few parallelisms between the two works pointed out by K. Süssheim are probably due to the use of such a source also by Hamadhānī.

the 5–6th/11–12th centuries. This ought perhaps to proceed as for a new edition.

There is however a family of works which remains distinct from all those which we have considered so far: those which are based upon the *Seljuqnāma* of Ẓahīr al-Dīn Nīs̲h̲āpūrī. The Histories which we have studied up till now were Arabic, or dependent, like the *Mujmal*, on Arabic sources, or have come down to us, like Anūs̲h̲irwān, through Arabic translations. Ẓahīr al-Dīn was a Persian writing in Persian. He knew none but Persian authors, and was himself known only by Persian authors. It was during the reign of that same Arslan in whose time ʿAlī b. Nāṣir was probably working that Ẓahīr al-Dīn Nīs̲h̲āpūrī, the sultan's preceptor, also began to compose his *Seljuqnāma*, which he could not complete until shortly after the accession of Ṭug̲h̲ril, Arslan's successor and the last of the Seljuqs of Iran.[65] It was long thought that the text of the *Seljuqnāma* proper was wholly lost and that it was consequently necessary to have recourse in its place to the version, overloaded with literary interpolations, made of it right at the beginning of the 7th/13th century by Rāwandī, another personage of the same milieu, in his *Rāḥat al-ṣudūr*.[66] Rāwandī, however, for lack of an Iranian Seljuq, had to dedicate his work, once it was finished, to Kayk̲h̲usraw I, a Seljuq of Rūm. But some time ago Ismāʿīl K̲h̲ān Afs̲h̲ār[67] showed that Ẓahīr al-Dīn's text seemed to be much more faithfully preserved as a part of the simple collection of chronicles constituted by Qās̲h̲ānī's *Ẓubdat al-tawārīk̲h̲* (beginning of the 8th/14th century). Recently the text has been published.[68]

There is no doubt that this publication, though in itself rather negligent,[69] restores to us the original of Ẓahīr al-Dīn much better than Rāwandī, to such an extent that henceforth Rāwandī is valuable to us only as a control except for the last years (reign of Ṭug̲h̲ril and immediate sequel to his death) which are an original contribution by the latter author. The more awkward style, the often more precise details, collation with the various Persian chronicles which are stated to be based on Ẓahīr al-Dīn—all prove in fact that we are dealing, if not certainly with an absolutely faithful copy of the original, then at least with a version which in general is very close to it. The slight reserve which, however, I introduced is due to the fact that here and there statements of detail are to be found in Rāwandī which seem to be too much a part of the narrative to be derived from any of the other sources which he had.[70] As a matter of fact he does

[65] See Muḥ. Iqbāl's Preface to his edition of the *Rāḥat al-ṣudūr*.

[66] Ed. Muḥ. Iqbāl in Gibb Mem. Ser.

[67] In the review *Mihri*, 1313/1934.

[68] By Gelāleh K̲h̲āwar, Tehran 1332/1953.

[69] Especially in the orthography and identification of the proper names; there is a useful index.

[70] For example, the name of Göher-Aīn, p. 119, as master of the slave who captured Romanus Diogenes, cf. Ẓahīr, p. 25; in the reign of Maliks̲h̲āh only Rāwandī gives the name (Sulaymān) of the K̲h̲ān vanquished by the Sultan in his second eastern campaign and fixes the number of

not recognize any sources outside a number of limited oral sources.[71] On the other hand—not to mention the first pages (Seljuq origins) where Rāwandī perhaps passes over certain words which he found difficult to understand—in the account of the battle of Manzikart the details of Ẓahīr al-Dīn's account are much more numerous than those of Rāwandī's, and one may ask why Rāwandī, for so famous an event, should have omitted them. These have, in places, a slightly suspect air[72] which brings them close to later Persian historiography, and one may consequently wonder whether they were not an interpolation in Qāshānī's manuscript by himself or a predecessor. The answer is uncertain, but the question must be asked.[73]

Before Rāwandī a certain 'Abd al-Ḥamīd Kirmānī had added an appendix to Ẓahīr al-Dīn which carried on the history up to the fall of Ṭughril. This text, preserved by Rashīd al-Dīn and not used by Rāwandī, is published by the editor at the end of Ẓahīr al-Dīn.

Henceforth we know Ẓahīr al-Dīn sufficiently surely in general to study his work in itself. What can his sources of information have been? It is certain that he had relatively poor sources at his disposal for the Seljuqs before his own lifetime, especially if we compare the impression left on men's minds by one such as Malikshāh, for example, with the very perfunctory chapter which he devotes to him, or if we consider the almost total emptiness of his account of the reign of Maḥmūd at the beginning of the 6th/12th century which was, however, full of complications. (This proves, by the way, his ignorance of Anūshirwān.) It may be that he desired purposely to centre his work on the sultans who were his direct masters, but it is difficult to avoid the impression that he lacked good sources. Nevertheless, whatever shortcomings they may have had, it

Seljuq soldiers at 46,000, rounded by the copyist of Ẓahīr al-Dīn to 50,000. The verse by Abū Ṭāhir quoted at the end of the reign is different, as though two different selections were made from an original combining them both, etc.

[71] See for example pp. 98, 102.

[72] The most delicate question is the enumeration, freely taken up again afterwards by Persian historiography, of a series of Turkoman chiefs at the battle of Manzikart: Artuq, Saltuq, Mangujak, Dānishmand, Chavli, and Chavuldur. Except for the last these are numbered again a little afterwards for the conquests made just after in Asia Minor. It is easily understood that the descendants of these families, become relatively powerful, should be eager for their ancestors to have taken part at Manzikart. But general literature is unaware of them and does not know most of them till twenty, not to say thirty or forty, years later. If it is true that at the time of Qāshānī the descendants of Artuq only still existed, and if one may if need be suppose that Rāwandī omitted the list of chiefs, some of whom had descendants reigning in his time, because they were more or less rivals of the Rūm Seljuq to whom he dedicated his work, nevertheless the name of Chavli is unknown in the Asia Minor of the time of the conquests, while the name Chavuldur, which in the *Dānishmandnāme* romance is attached to that of the historical chief Chaka, is the name of a tribe of which the texts say nothing then, whereas the growth of Turkoman influence in the Mongol period caused these names to be carefully gathered.

[73] It must be pointed out, in the reverse sense to the previous reservation, that the Khiṭāy are mentioned in the account of the reign of Sanjar as still masters of *Mā warā' al-nahr* at the time of the author, which cannot refer to the time of the Mongols. nor even of Rāwandī.

appears that he must all the same have had some for the 5th/11th century and the Great Seljuqs. It is remarkable that this man, who was personally attached to Arslan, had no inkling of the existence of the *Maliknāma*, of which the manuscript, as we have pointed out, cannot have been found at his court. In practice he knew the history of the Seljuqs before the empire only in so far as it is part of Ghaznavid history, and thus through a Ghaznavid source. As long as Rāwandī or other adaptors only were known one could ask whether the important place occupied in this account by Isrā'īl and Qutlumush, the ancestors of the Rūm Seljuqs, was not an addition by Rāwandī for the sake of his patron;[74] but the account goes back to Ẓahīr al-Dīn and is thus to be explained by the fact that it is placed in Ghaznavid territory, which would not be the case with accounts dealing with the other Seljuqs at the same period.[75] As for determining the Ghaznavid source used, I can state definitely only that it appears not to coincide with those used by the Arabic-using Iranians studied previously (though it is difficult to believe that writers using one or the other language in Iran did not each know the other, just as the author of the *Zubda* used the *Maliknāma*). More generally, though we have seen, until towards the middle of the 6th/12th century, Iranian authors profiting in works composed in Arabic from predecessors who wrote in both languages, and though, until the Mongol period, Persian translations of old Arabic works on Iranian history were made, as far as Seljuq history is concerned we have the impression that Ẓahīr al-Dīn and his epigons knew nothing of the Arabic group of sources, even the Iranian ones, and that, in short, there are two families of histories, each ignorant of the other, separated by a cleavage of language. Moreover, it appears to be out of the question that there was any important monument of Seljuq or eastern Iranian history between the end of Bayhaqī's History and the Mongol period. To be convinced of this one has but to consider the effort which the author of the *Ṭabaqāt-i Nāṣirī* had to make, and for what meagre results. Collections of anecdotes were all that was made, such as those which we have of Niẓāmī 'Arūḍī, Awfī, and Mubārakshāh, who themselves declare that they drew on no historical work, contrarily to what they acknowledge of previous authors.[76] It is not our task here to study non-Seljuq eastern-oriental historiography, but this general impression had to be given.

To return to Ẓahīr al-Dīn al-Nīshāpūrī: his work, compared with later

[74] Which I made the error of doing in the article 'Arslan b. Saldjuḳ' in *EI*², not yet having Ẓahīr al-Dīn at my disposal.

[75] Moreover, the author, like that of the *Zubda* (but not 'Imād al-Dīn nor the Baghdādīs), wishes to represent Sulaymān b. Qutlumush as regularly invested by Malikshāh, which is very improbable. For an opposite reason this affirmation is taken up again by the Seljuq or post-Seljuq Rūm historiography.

[76] Cf. especially Muḥ. Niẓām al-Dīn, *Introduction to the* Jāmi' al-ḥikāyāt *of Muḥammad Awfī* (London, 1929).

Iranian historiography, is characterized by relative soberness and accuracy. He or Rāwandī are directly or indirectly the essential and often the sole source of all the writers in Persian who, under the Mongols or the Timurids, from Rashīd al-Dīn and Mustawfī Qazwīnī, include a chapter on the Seljuqs in their universal histories. Even in Asia Minor, where the *Rāḥat al-ṣudūr*, though dedicated to Kaykhusraw, seems hardly to have attracted attention, Aqsarayī's introduction to his History of the Rūm Seljuqs (beginning of the 8th/14th century) [77] bears an evident relationship to Ẓahīr al-Dīn. The anonymous *Seljuqnāma*[78] composed about the same time seems, on the contrary, to be acquainted, directly or not, with the Baghdādī sources. To study this late historiography would be another subject.

To the general Histories of the Seljuqs must be added the one special to the autonomous line of Kirmān. This line found its chronicler in Afḍal al-Dīn Kirmānī, a high official of the last members of the dynasty and their immediate successors. His work is not extant directly, but it has proved possible to reconstitute a text which one may be assured is in agreement with the original[79] by a comparison between the history of Kirmān by Muḥammad b. Ibrāhīm (10th/16th century),[80] which copies it, and other works of which the chief is the *Jāmiʿ al-tawārīkh* of Ḥasan Yazdī (7th/13th century), which a scholar has recently thought of using for this purpose. It seems that the author composed first an account, entitled *ʿIqd al-ʿulā*, of the reign of Malik Dīnār, who inherited from the Seljuqs (583–602);[81] later he prefixed to it a history of the Seljuqs under the title of *Badāʾiʿ al-azmān fī waqāʾiʿ Kirmān*; he himself seemingly carried on the whole to 612/1215 by a *Risāla* recently rediscovered in a composite Arabic-Persian collection in the Vatican.[82] Later another writer wrote, under the title *Simṭ al-ʿulā*, the history of the Karakhiṭāy dynasty, which gained control of the country soon after and kept it as vassals of the Mongols.[83] The *Badāʾiʿ al-azmān*, which does not appear to have had any help from previous historiography, Baghdādī, Ghaznawid, or other, for the 5th/11th century, is meagrely, though usefully, documented for the period; but for the 6th/12th century it becomes really interesting.

With the history of Kirmān we broach the category of regional or local histories which we cannot study here, for each has its own problems which generally extend beyond the Seljuq period. But certain of them were composed in the Seljuq period and have a substantial importance for its history. We mention only those of Ibn Isfandiyār for the south Caspian

[77] Ed. Osman Turan (Ankara, 1943).

[78] Ed. Feridun Hafiz Uzluk (Ankara, 1952).

[79] Ed. Mahdī Bayānī (Tehran, 1326/1947). The editor has established that Afḍal al-Dīn, though in more abbreviated form, was also used, among others, by Qāshānī.

[80] Ed. Houtsma, *Recueil de textes etc.*, i.

[81] Ed. (Tehran, 1311/1932).

[82] Ed. ʿAbbās Iqbāl (Tehran, 1331/1952), whose preface provides an excellent exposé of the questions concerning Afḍal al-Dīn.

[83] Nāṣir al-Dīn Kirmānī, ed. ʿAbbās Iqbāl (Tehran, 1328/1949).

provinces (beg. 7th/13th century),[84] of Ibn Funduq (already named) for the town of Bayhaq,[85] and of an anonymous author who wrote about the beginning of the 6th/12th century and had a continuer in the Mongol period for Sīstān.[86] There is also much history in the chiefly geographical *Fārsnāma* of Ibn al-Bal<u>kh</u>ī (beg. 6th/12th century),[87] which is rather summarily supplemented in the 7th/13th century by the *<u>Sh</u>īrāznāma* of Ibn Zarkūb.[88] It has recently been pointed out that a History of Bāb al-Abwāb composed about 500/1106 and still known to Münejjim-ba<u>sh</u>ī in the 11th/17th century[89] should be of great interest. It is difficult to judge from meagre quotations of what the History of Khurāsān composed in 570/1174 by al-Ma'mūnī for the <u>Kh</u>w̱ārizm<u>sh</u>āh Tökü<u>sh</u>[90] consisted, or that of <u>Kh</u>w̱ārizm, most probably biographical, composed at the end of the same century by Abū Muḥammad Maḥmūd b. Muḥammad b. Arslan.[91] It is well known that the same word *ta'rī<u>kh</u>* is in fact used for biographical dictionaries, especially of towns, which general history, despite their rather minor interest, cannot ignore, but which we cannot study here. The historians of the Seljuq period seem to have availed themselves particularly of those of Ba<u>gh</u>dād (Sam'ānī and Ibn al-Najjār, continuing <u>Kh</u>aṭīb Ba<u>gh</u>dādī), and that of Nī<u>sh</u>āpūr.[92]

Other works of a semi- or para-historical kind must be simply mentioned here: the partially rediscovered Journal of the 6th/12th century Ba<u>gh</u>dādī Abū 'Alī b. al-Bannā';[93] Mas'ūd b. Nāmdār's account, varied by verse, letters, and documents, of his misadventures at Baylakān towards the end of the same century;[94] the *Siyāsatnāma* of Niẓām al-Mulk, naturally;[95] the Histories of Viziers, whether Persian[96] or even Arabic;[97] and all the historians have used the *Dīwāns* of poets who inversely sometimes include useful information in their commentaries. I need not concern myself with the *inshā'* documents which we are fortunate to possess for the Seljuq period, particularly for the kingdom of Sanjar.

[84] Ed. Tehran, 1952, and pruned translation by E. G. Browne, 1905.

[85] See n. 24.

[86] *Tārī<u>kh</u>-i Sīstān*, ed. Bahār (Tehran, 1936).

[87] Ed. Le Strange and Nicholson, *GMS* (1921).

[88] Ed. Bahmān Karīmī (Tehran, 1932).

[89] V. Minorsky, *Studies in Caucasian history* (1952).

[90] Above, n. 34.

[91] Abundantly quoted by all authors of biographical dictionaries.

[92] Cf. Ritter in *Oriens*, iii (1950).

[93] Ed. and tr. G. Makdisi, *BSOAS* (1956–7).

[94] Analysis by C. Cahen and V. Minorsky in *JA* (1949).

[95] To which should be added the late compilation, but which perhaps preserves some authentic old material (see n. 64) called *Waṣāyā* of Niẓām al-Mulk, where the *Zubda* of 'Alī b. Nāṣir seems to be used; on them cf. H. Bowen in *JRAS* (1931).

[96] For the Seljuq period these works seem to be based substantially on the *Nuṣra* of 'Imād al-Dīn, on the one hand, and on the anonymous Nāsā'im al-ashār (Ḥamdānī, in *JRAS* (1938), p. 563) of the beginning of the 8th/14th century, on the other hand. The information in this latter does not seem to be entirely derived from that in our chronicles. Another later History of Viziers (the *Ā<u>th</u>ār al-wuzarā'*, Ethé 347 of the Bodleian), knows in addition the (or a) treatise on the *faḍā'il* of Niẓām al-Mulk (*supra*, p. 72).

[97] Besides the already mentioned History of the Viziers by al-Hamad<u>h</u>ānī, let us mention, for the close of our period, that of al-Qādisī (elsewhere the continuator of Ibn al-Jawzī) at the beginning of the 7th/13th century. Ibn <u>Kh</u>allikān knew this work.

Moreover, I have only considered Muslim chronicles in this account. For the history of the western activities of the Seljuqs the Armenian, Syriac, and Greek chroniclers must of course be added to them. I have already spoken of Bar Hebraeus, who, because of his Syriac, Arabic, and Persian sources is to be partially assimilated to the Muslim authors. He was acquainted with the *Maliknāma* and Baghdādī sources which relate him partially to Sibṭ Ibn al-Jawzī (and thus perhaps to Ghars al-Niʿma) for the Great Seljuqs; for subsequent events such of his work as is not drawn from Michael the Syrian appears to come from Ibn al-Athīr. At all events, he was an author of the Mongol period who could work only as a compiler, unlike Michael the Syrian, Matthew of Edessa, or Anna Comnena, to mention only three especially illustrious writers of the various Christian confessions, but who all wrote outside the proper domain of the Iraqi-Iranian Seljuqs. There is, however, a Nestorian chronicle of Baghdad, that of Mari, continued by ʿAmr bar Sliba, which does belong to this domain[98] and to which I draw attention here because it has hardly ever been used and yet, without being of the first importance, contains useful points of detail on the period of the Great Seljuqs in particular.

The foregoing exposition is not, of course, even a contribution to the analysis of the general characteristics of the historical work of the Seljuq period. But it has become evident that it constituted an essential preface to it and that, for lack of time to do everything, an even incomplete research of this kind, still too often neglected in our discipline, was the best effort that I could make in view of our conference. It needs, of course, to be taken up again and completed, but I shall be happy if, whether in the Seljuq domain or others, it gives currency to the idea of an indispensable *Quellenforschung*. In the undertaking of this task we have at our disposal an important assistance in our colleague Rosenthal's *Muslim Historiography*; but historians (in the proper sense) hope that it may be completed and deepened in the direction which has just been indicated.

He who engages in the study of a branch of Arabic literature knows the preliminary services rendered by Brockelmann's *GAL*; he knows too how it has caused him to be misled subsequently. This last statement is nowhere perhaps more true than in respect of historiography. It was probably beyond the power of any one man to do better, and is consequently so to produce a new and revised edition; but at the least a few historians might perhaps pool their efforts to compile a more complete and less inaccurate list of the products of Arabic historiography. Storey is much less to be reproached for Persian historiography; nevertheless he takes only extant works into consideration and his *Survey* might thus be supplemented in this respect. Since the frontier between the two literatures is not always sealed the two projects might gain by being combined.

[98] Ed. Gismondi (Rome, 1896).

6. SOME NOTES ON ARABIC HISTORIOGRAPHY DURING THE ZENGID AND AYYUBID PERIODS (521/1127–648/1250)

M. HILMY M. AHMAD

Assistant Professor of History, Dar al-Ulum Faculty, Cairo University

(1) *Definition of the Period*

The expansion of Seljuqid influence and authority into Syria and Mesopotamia was a turning point in the history of this area both in its internal relations and in its relations with Egypt. Syria and Mesopotamia had been split into amirates and were subject to ambitious *amīrs* and governors, who, in the absence of a supreme authority, were involved in an unending struggle, military at times, against their opponents. The Fatimids of Egypt were still in possession of certain cities in Palestine, whilst the Byzantine forces were gaining strongholds previously under Muslim control. It was the Seljuqs, especially under Tutush (471–88/1079–95), who attempted to bring most of these scattered principalities under one control. After he had fallen in the battlefield, the work begun by Tutush was continued, although with less vigour, and with less success.[1] It was not till ʿImād al-Dīn Zengi, the *atabeg*, was appointed governor of Mosul, as a Seljuq vassal, that Syria and Mesopotamia began to enter upon a real phase of unification ending with the annexation of Egypt at the time of Nūr al-Dīn.

The significance of these attempts at unification, which ended successfully, can be viewed as follows:

(*a*) They brought Egypt, Syria, and Mesopotamia finally under one Sunnī control, at a time when the main Seljuq power in Iraq and Persia was declining, and at the mercy of family disputes.

(*b*) They introduced the Seljuq *iqṭāʿ* system—a system which was maintained during the Zengid and Ayyubid periods. Under this régime the government administration rested mainly in the hands of the army commanders.

(*c*) This régime, as has been practised in this vast area, was in need of popular support. This was obtained through the ʿ*ulamā*ʾ and by following up the policy of Niẓām al-Mulk, the vizier of the Seljuqs (d. 485/1092), who established the Niẓāmiyya school and thus created a class of ʿ*ulamā*ʾ who supported the Seljuq régime. The Niẓāmiyya school was a model to

[1] It was during this period of restlessness that the Crusaders succeeded in establishing their Latin principalities. Ṭughtegin, the founder of the Burid dynasty in Damascus (497/1104), also attempted a unification of sorts, going so far as to ally himself with the Fatimids of Egypt, in 501, and 506 A.H., against the Franks, in order to check the latter from gaining further positions.

be followed on a very wide scale in Syria and Egypt, especially during the times of Nūr al-Dīn and Saladin.[2]

(*d*) The *iqṭā*ʿ-holding commanders and the ʿ*ulamā*ʾ became the two pillars of the Zengid and Ayyubid governments. The ʿ*ulamā*ʾ in particular exploited their status in the government and at court, voicing the opinion of the populace strongly and successfully. They also had their say in military activities against the Crusaders and the Frankish settlements.[3]

(*e*) The centre of political and intellectual activities shifted from Iraq and Persia (in general) to Mosul, Damascus, Aleppo, and Cairo, the greater cities of the new united powers.

Thus it would seem clear and logical that the Zengid and Ayyubid periods should be considered as one epoch, and they will be so treated in this paper.

(2) *The Status of Historiography in this Period*

The centre of Arabic historiography had gravitated to the new centres of learning (Damascus, Aleppo, Mosul, and Cairo) as a result of radical political, social, and cultural changes. It is significant, however, that the study of history, as such, was not included in the curricula of the numerous *madrasas* established under this régime. This might well be explained if it is remembered that the *madrasa* was a Sunnī institution. It was an anti-Shīʿī reaction in Syria, Mesopotamia, and Egypt, especially after the fall of the Fatimid dynasty. This reaction was a contributory factor in the flourishing of learning and the increasing number of *madrasas*, a development which was not so marked in the east (Persia) although the *madrasas* originated there. This meant the revival of the old orthodox method of Islamic studies, and this meant going back to the Qurʾān and the *ḥadīth* as the fundamental basis for the knowledge and education. Independent judgement, or *ijtihād*, was not widely encouraged in these *madrasas*, since it might lead the student astray. Philosophy was officially banned because, according to the Sunnī view, it was the tool used by the Ismāʿīlīs to under-

[2] The first *madrasa* (school) in Damascus was established after 497/1103, during the time of Ṭughtegin; and the first in Aleppo was in 517/1123. Ibn Jubayr (d. 614/1217) mentions in his *Riḥla* that he saw about twenty *madrasas* in Damascus and five in Aleppo. Later, Ibn al-Shiḥna names fifty-four *madrasas* in Aleppo alone, all of which had been founded between 516/1122 and 665/1266. Ibn Shaddād, the author of *al-A*ʿ*lāq* visited Damascus in 631/1233 and stated that he found there six hundred and sixty mosques and ninety-three *madrasas*.

[3] When the army of Nūr al-Dīn in Egypt was about to split after the death of Shīrkūh, it was the *qāḍī* ʿĪsā al-Hakkārī who strove to keep it united under the command of Saladin. Similarly, whenever Saladin found defection within his army or from his kinsmen in command, it was al-Qāḍī al-Fāḍil who generally undertook to restore loyalty. Lastly, when al-Malik al-Kāmil of Egypt failed to obtain the support of his brother, al-Ashraf, of Mesopotamia, against the Crusaders, and al-Muʿaẓẓam of Damascus, another brother of al-Kāmil, was also unsuccessful on the same occasion, it was Sibṭ Ibn al-Jawzī who brought al-Ashraf at the head of a vast army to Egypt to co-operate in its defence. Examples of the influence of the ʿ*ulamā*ʾ during this period are numerous.

mine Islam. Other subjects, such as *fiqh*, Arabic grammar, and poetry, were either dependent on Qur'ān and *ḥadīth* or served to facilitate their study. The study of *fiqh* varied according to the four Sunnī juristic doctrines, but the Ḥanbalī doctrine received the least encouragement.[4]

But where was the place of *history* among these religious subjects? In answering this question Ibn al-Athīr states that some leading personalities of the '*ulamā*' of his time 'scorned history since it was merely stories and anecdotes'. He found it necessary to defend historical studies by pointing out the benefit of these studies 'in this life and the life hereafter'. Among his points: 'When the kings read in the history books about the biographies of just rulers and how they were highly esteemed by their subjects, they would try to follow their examples. And when they knew, through history, of the tyrants and how much they were scorned and hated, they would refrain from following their policy. Also the historian would attract the attention of those who listen to him when he would give examples from history in support of his arguments. Furthermore, it is through "history" that man could develop a good character and patience and scorn this mortal world with all its good promises and disturbing evils.'

Abū Shāma, another prominent historian of this period, admits that he evinced an interest in historical studies only after a prolonged study of religious and literary subjects. By such studies he aimed at 'the completion of his education through this subsidiary subject'. His approach to history was also of a religious nature. He writes: 'Hardly could one find one of the '*ulamā*' who did not contribute to historical studies. Al-Shāfi'ī himself studied the wars of pre-Islamic Arabia for twenty years.' Thus Abū Shāma found himself compelled to justify his interest in history through examples set by many of his predecessors in the circles of learning as well as through verses of the Qur'ān and the spirit of the *ḥadīth*.[5]

Yāqūt also points out that some of the '*ulamā*' would think it would have been better for him if he had paid attention to religious studies instead of devoting his efforts to the writing of his *Irshād*. He approves, to a certain extent, of this point of view, yet he remarks that human interests differ from man to man and if all men confined their studies to one subject, other subjects would diminish. Then he adds that his book contains the biographies of certain people who had been the source of all studies of Qur'ān

[4] The Ḥanafī school had been encouraged by Nūr al-Dīn whilst the Shāfi'ī became dominant during the time of the Ayyubids. An interesting example of anti-Hanbalism occurred when Zakī al-Dīn ibn Rawāḥa (d. 622/1225) established two *madrasas* in Damascus and Aleppo. One of his conditions in the *waqf* was that no Christian, Jew or Ḥanbalī should be allowed to enter these schools.

[5] It is worth mentioning that al-Maqrīzī in the *Khiṭaṭ* says: 'As to the subject of this book it is the science of history, through which religions were made known to the people, and the traditions of the prophets and messengers were preserved.'

and *ḥadīth*, and through their knowledge the sultanate and the vizierate could find guidance to the welfare of the people.

This was the official status accorded to history, among other subjects, both in *madrasas* and among the *'ulamā'* of this period. Yet historiography flourished widely, assuming many forms. Reasons for this may be found in the fact that some leading personalities of the Traditionists and of the jurisconsults took special interest in the writing of history. Mention can be made of Ibn 'Asākir, Ibn al-Athīr, Abū Shāma, and Ibn Khallikān as outstanding examples, although the majority of these historians were noted first and foremost during their lifetime, and later, for subjects other than history, mostly *fiqh* or *ḥadīth*. On the other hand, some of the *'ulamā'* who occupied official posts in the Zengid or Ayyubid period contributed to the writing of history by their compilations or by the documents prepared by them on official occasions. One need only cite al-Qāḍī al-Fāḍil, Ibn Shaddād, Kamāl al-Dīn, and Ibn Khallikān. In this way their contribution was of marked significance for historical writings.

Thus it could be asserted that historiography enjoyed semi-official support indirectly through this class of official *'ulamā'*, and through the patronage of certain sultans or *amīrs* and other persons in authority.[6]

(3) *Types of Historiography*

During the period in question historiography assumed broadly six forms:

(1) Universal history works beginning with the Creation; the chief examples of this kind were *al-Kāmil* of Ibn al-Athīr and *Mir'āt al zamān* of Sibṭ Ibn al-Jawzī.

(2) Local history,[7] a type favoured by the majority of the historians of this period. An explanation of this tendency would seem to be that for quite a long period there had been in Syria and Mesopotamia régimes of autonomous amīrs which were centres of conflict. As each amirate had often to defend itself against neighbouring aggressions there developed a regional consciousness .The Zengid and the Ayyubid forms of government which depended largely on the *iqṭā'* system did not discourage this regional feeling, on the contrary, during the Ayyubid period, after the death of Saladin, these régimes revived under the pressure of conflict among the Ayyubid princes.[8]

[6] For instance, Ibn 'Asākir began his history of Damascus, later putting it aside. After some time he learnt that Nūr al-Dīn was willing to see the book, and that encouraged him to finish it. Ibn al-Athīr produced the copy of *al-Kāmil* known to us after receiving orders from Badr al-Dīn Lu'lu' of Mosul.

[7] Although intended to be a kind of regional history, the contents of them ranged beyond defined areas.

[8] These conflicts motivated Abū Shāma to write *al-Rawḍatayn* recording the good deeds of Nūr al-Dīn and Saladin, in order that the *amīrs* of his time might find in these two sultans exemplary prototypes of the perfect ruler.

The local histories took several forms:

(*a*) Chronological works, such as *Dhayl ta'rīkh Dimashq*, by Ibn al-Qalānisī, and *al-Rawḍatayn* by Abū Shāma.

(*b*) Biographical works, such as *Ta'rīkh Dimashq* of Ibn 'Asākir and *Bughyat al-ṭalab* by Kamāl al-Dīn.

(*c*) A combination of biography and history proper, such as *al-Mudhayyal 'alā al-rawḍatayn* which Abū Shāma had composed in chronological order.

(3) The third form is the biographical works, either of a general nature such as *Irshād al-adīb* of Yāqūt and the *Wafāyat* of Ibn Khallikān, or of certain classes of people, such as *Usd al-ghāba*, a biographical dictionary of the Traditionists, compiled by Ibn al-Athīr, and '*Uyūn al-anbā'*, on the doctors, by Ibn Abī Uṣaybi'a.

(4) Monographs, on individuals, such as *al-Nawādir* of Ibn Shaddād on Saladin, or on certain dynasties, such as the *Mufarrij* of Ibn Wāṣil on the Ayyubids, and *al-Bāhir* of Ibn al-Athīr on the *atabegs* of Mosul.

(5) Autobiographies: the famous works of Usāma ibn Munqidh and *al-Nukat al-'aṣriyya* of 'Umāra al-Yamanī are good examples.

(6) An administrative manual, which was compiled by Ibn Mammātī, entitled *Qawānīn al-dawāwīn*.

(4) *Materials used by the Historians*

As Margoliouth pointed out: 'With us the natural seat of a book is some material such as paper; it may or may not be committed to memory. With the Arab the natural seat of a book is the memory; it may or may not be committed to writing.'[9] To some extent the oral (*samā'*) method was still in use during the Zengid and Ayyubid periods. Thus oral sources remained one of the main sources for the writing of history during this period. Ibn al-Athīr, for example, states in his history of the *atabegs* that he had derived most of the material for his book from hearsay evidence, and especially from his father, although, as he says, he compiled it some time after his father's death.

It was the custom for a student of history, or any other subject, to write out a copy of the historical work in which he was interested, and then read his copy out to a certain *shaykh* who was held to be a specialist on that particular work and who had already obtained a diploma (*ijāza*) on it. It was also the practice for an historian to lecture on his work which he had compiled, such lectures being attended by a number of the '*ulamā'*, whose approval of the contents, as given in the lectures, would be taken as a sign of the validity and accuracy of the work.[10] Such procedures, no

[9] *Lectures on Arabic Historians* (Calcutta, 1902), p. 3.

[10] Ibn al-Athīr gave several lectures on his book *al-Kāmil*, before publishing it in its final form. Abū Shāma also gave lectures on *al-Rawḍatayn*, and he states that leading personalities in the circle of the '*ulamā'* had been present.

doubt, were due to the predominating influence of the study of *ḥadīth*, in which the principal of the *isnād* was highly estimated. Ibn 'Asākir repeatedly advised his students to check the accuracy of the manuscripts through the *samā'* method. Thus when Ibn Shaddād wrote his biography of Saladin (*al-Nawādir*) he made it clear from the beginning that the first part of his book, i.e. up to the year 584 A.H., was compiled mainly from the evidence he had heard, at first-hand, from trustworthy persons. The second part was the result of his personal experiences which he had gained through his contact with Saladin.

Another important source of material was the official documents. These were used in two ways: Ibn al-Qalānisī must have made use of them in his chronicle of Damascus, since he had twice occupied the office of *ra'īs* in the city. Yet he rarely quotes documents. Ibn al-Athīr also must have had access to documents prepared by al-'Imād al-Kātib, the secretary of Saladin, since he had used the latter's works. Yet he rarely quotes these documents.

The other method of using documents is represented by quoting them verbatim. Al-'Imād al-Kātib quotes official documents prepared by himself, in his two books *al-Fatḥ* and *al-Barq*.[11] Ibn Abī Ṭayyi', of Aleppo, quotes the documents of both al-'Imād and al-Qāḍī al-Fāḍil, another secretary of Saladin. Abū Shāma quotes the documents written by these two secretaries as well as those of other officials. In *al-Rawḍatayn*, Abū Shāma's main work, there are more than two hundred documents, the greatest number to be found in one book of that period.[12]

In one case we come across a statement by an historian to the effect that he intentionally declined to use official documents, though he had access to them. It is in *Qawānīn al-dawāwīn* of Ibn Mammātī, when recording the different revenue districts in towns and villages of Egypt during the Ayyubid period. The reason he gives is official secrecy.[13]

It is thus evident that there was a significant tendency among the main historians of this period to consult actual documents where extant, adducing them as accurate and important material for their historical compilation.

(5) *Observations on Certain Works of Historiography*

(1) Ibn al-Qalānisī, Abū Ya'lā, Ḥamza b. Asad al-Tamīmī (d. 555/1160), the author of *Dhayl ta'rīkh Dimashq*, a chronicle of Damascus covering a period of a hundred and seven years, 448/1056–555/1160. The work, however, begins eighty-five years earlier, in 363/973, with extracts from

[11] There are 54 documents in *al-Fatḥ*.

[12] *Al-Barq* of al-'Imād is not included in this generalization since we have access to only two parts. The other five are lost.

[13] *Qawānīn al-dawāwīn*, ed. A. S. Atiya (Cairo, 1943), p. 84.

the history of Hilāl al-Ṣābī to which Ibn al-Qalānisī wrote his *Dhayl*. These extracts are mainly concerned with Damascus, except on a few occasions when they record the death of a caliph or an attack by Byzantine forces. In quoting these extracts Ibn al-Qalānisī does not keep strictly to the chronological order, but he groups the events under nineteen headings, the number of the governors who ruled in Damascus during these preceding eighty-five years.

On beginning his history with the year 448/1056, he adheres strictly to the chronological order, with the exception of the year 473/1080, which he entirely omits. The unit of this chronicle is the year, but under the heading of each year Ibn al-Qalānisī deals with the events piecemeal according to the date of their happenings. So one finds the records of certain events being interrupted by records of other events.[14] His records tend to be of increasing length from the year 497 when Ṭughtegin, the atabeg, assumed supreme control in Damascus. One reason for this is obvious since he was then able to record reliable and first-hand facts.

It has already been stated that Ibn al-Qalānisī rarely quoted official documents although he had occupied the office of *ra'īs* in Damascus on two occasions, the last being in 548/1153, seven years before his death. Yet it can be safely assumed that his records must have been based on archive material since he had access to it, at least during his term of office; and being an eyewitness of most of the events recorded in his book, his work has the value of documentary material.

(2) Al-Qāḍī al-Fāḍil, 'Abd al-Raḥīm b. 'Alī al-Baysānī (d. 596/1199). He is of great importance as an authority on the life of Saladin. Al-Qāḍī al-Fāḍil had worked his way up in administrative offices from the last years of the Fatimids in Egypt. He also served the Ayyubids before the foundation of their dynasty and became the right-hand man of Saladin as vizier, and even as his deputy in Egypt in the years 585/1189–588/1192. The documents compiled by him, and known as *Rasā'il*, furnished rich material for the historians of that period, among whom was his contemporary, al-'Imād al-Katib, another secretary of Saladin. Al-'Imād used these documents in his work *al-Barq al-shāmī*. Ibn Abī Ṭayyi' and later Abū Shāma depended on these documents when compiling their works.

In addition to these documents al-Qāḍī al-Fāḍil left his administrative historical work referred to, in later works, as *al-Mutajaddidāt* and *al-Muyāwamāt*. On this work, Ibn Khallikān states that he 'was told by an authority that al-Fāḍil left some works by himself comprising, in all, more than a hundred volumes.' Ibn Qāḍī Shuhba later adds: 'These volumes recorded the work of al-Qāḍī al-Fāḍil as a secretary to Saladin.' These records were produced 'in daily form' as Ḥājjī Khalīfa observes. In the

[14] Such was the case in most of the chronicles preceding that of Ibn al-Athīr.

Khiṭaṭ of al-Maqrīzī there are a number of quotations from works of al-Qāḍī al-Fāḍil called *Mutajaddidāt*, *Muyāwamāt* or *Mujalladāt*. Abū Shāma refers to the *Mujalladāt* as a work containing the *Rasā'il*, i.e. correspondence of al-Qāḍī al-Fāḍil.

Becker suggests[15] that al-Qāḍī al-Fāḍil's correspondence should be distinguished from another work called *Ta'līqāt*. This theory is based on an identical phrase with which al-Maqrīzī, on two occasions, introduced extracts from al-Qāḍī al-Fāḍil's work. It reads: 'Al-Fāḍil said in the commentary on *al-Mutajaddidāt* . . .' But Becker does not pursue the matter by examination of these extracts, along with others also quoted by al-Maqrīzī, which appear to back his suggestion.

First, the subject matter of the *Mutajaddidāt*, as quoted in the *Khiṭaṭ*, differs from that of the *Rasā'il*. The latter, as quotations by al-'Imād, Ibn Abī Ṭayyi' and Abū Shāma, and the manuscripts show, deal with occasional questions, political moves, missions to the caliphs, descriptions of battles and often their subject material is not interrelated. They are collections of self-contained themes. The *Mutajaddidāt* deals with questions which are not of an occasional nature.

Secondly, in the *Mutajaddidāt*, al-Qāḍī al-Fāḍil starts with the day of the week and the date. For example he says: 'On Tuesday, the fourteenth of Rajab . . .' but in each of his *Rasā'il* he gives a number of dates, and this is because it deals with a specified event and its developments. In some of the *Rasā'il* there is no mention of any date.

Thirdly, the British Museum manuscript shows that each of the *Rasā'il* can stand as a separate unit, but the *Mutajaddidāt* is in the form of a continuous journal.

Moreover the words: *Mutajaddidāt*, *Ta'līqāt*, *Muyāwamāt*, never appear in *al-Rawḍatayn* of Abū Shāma, where the word *Rasā'il* is in frequent use. That is because Abū Shāma was interested in the *Rasā'il* which corroborated his records, since they were of an official nature.

It can be concluded that the *Mutajaddidāt* and *Muyāwamāt* are two alternative names for the historical work written, in daily form, by al-Qāḍī al-Fāḍil. This work must be distinguished from the *Rasā'il* which was used extensively by al-'Imād, Ibn Abī Ṭayyi' and Abū Shāma.[16]

(3) Al-'Imād al-Kātib, Muḥammad b. Muḥammad al-Iṣfahānī (d. 597/1201). He wrote two works on the history of Syria and on Saladin. The first, *al-Barq al-shāmī*, deals with the years 562/1166–589/1193, covering the period which he spent in the domains of Nūr al-Dīn and Saladin. This gives the book the value of a historical record of events narrated by an eyewitness. The second, *al-Fatḥ al-qussī fi'l-fatḥ al-qudsī*, covers the years

[15] *Beiträge zur Geschichte Ägyptens under dem Islam*, i (Strassburg, 1902), pp. 24–5.

[16] Of the *Rasā'il*, there are manuscripts in the British Museum, Cambridge University Library, Leyden and in Konya at the Yūsuf Agha Library.

583/1187–589/1193, i.e. from the year in which Jerusalem was conquered by Saladin till his death. Al-'Imād joined the service of Saladin in 570/1174, yet he started *al-Fatḥ* with the year 583/1187. He explains why he chose this date: 'It is the second Hijra of Islam, but this time to Jerusalem. This Hijra is the more important of the two and the more lasting . . . It can justly be regarded as the beginning of a new era, since it marks a turning point in the course of Islam . . .' *Al-Fatḥ* is also a first-hand record of the most eventful and critical period of the rule of Saladin.

The documents included in these two books add to their value as sources for sound and accurate historical material despite the ornate and flowery style which is a detracting feature. Ibn al-Athīr, Ibn Abī Ṭayyi', Abū Shāma and Ibn Wāṣil made great use of these two works to the extent that the reader of history might well neglect the original works unless he has special interest in their colourful literary language. Both *al-Barq* and *al-Fatḥ* follow a year-by-year order in dealing with events, and little attention is paid to the recording of obituaries except in the case of a prince, an administrator or a distinguished *'ālim*.

Al-'Imād wrote another book dealing with the history of the Seljuqs: sultans, viziers, and administrators. Again the ornate and bombastic style reduced its value as an historical work during his time, and a synopsis of it was made by Fatḥ b. 'Alī al-Bundārī[17] who had also summarized *al-Barq al-shāmī*.

(4) Ibn Shaddād, the *qāḍī* Bahā' al-Dīn Yūsuf b. Rāfi' (d. 632/1234), the author of *al-Nawādir al-sulṭāniyya*, a monograph on Saladin. Ibn Shaddād is an important authority on the life of Saladin, although he accompanied him for only five years (584/1188–589/1193). *Al-Nawādir* is a short work compared with those of al'Imād al-Kātib, but the clear simple language makes it a valuable contribution dealing with bare facts. It falls into two parts, the first outlining the life of Saladin and his virtues (e.g. justice, generosity, and observation of religious practices), each in a small chapter beginning with a verse of the Qur'ān or a *ḥadīth*.[18] The second part forms the main body of the work, recording the current of events which took place from the time of Shīrkūh's expeditions into Egypt up to the death of Saladin, in 589/1193.

From the time he joined the service of Saladin in 584/1188, he accompanied his master everywhere on his travels and even in the battlefield into the front lines. For this period he is thus able to render a full and accurate eyewitness account. As to the years of which he cannot supply first-hand information he claims that he derives his material from the most reliable

[17] Al-Bundārī started on this synopsis, entitled *Zubdat al-nuṣra* in 623/1226 for al-Mu'aẓẓam 'Īsā, of Damascus. The original was entitled *Nuṣrat al-fatra*.

[18] Ibn Shaddād was a *ḥāfiẓ*. He collected Traditions dealing with the *Jihād* in a special book for Saladin. He also used to lecture to Saladin, on the battlefield, on *ḥadīth*.

authority. Yet he, sometimes, declines to shoulder the responsibility of the records, saying: 'So I was informed by some people because I was not present when this took place.'

On a few occasions Ibn Sẖaddād's records for the early years of Saladin's life are inaccurate. Historians like Abū Sẖāma and Ibn Kẖallikān could correct his narratives adducing other authorities.[19]

Throughout the work one finds that, with four exceptions, Ibn Sẖaddād does not quote documents. This might be explained by the fact that he did not hold any secretarial office, and, unlike al-Qāḍī al-Fāḍil and al-'Imād, whose main work in the court of Saladin was correspondence, he had no responsibility for official dispatches.

(5) Ibn al-Aẖtīr, 'Alī b. Muḥammad, 'Izz al-Dīn Abu'l-Ḥasan (d. 630/ 1233), the author of *al-Kāmil fi'l-ta'rīkẖ*. Biographies of him tell of his contribution to Islamic studies, citing his two works *Usd al-gẖāba* and *al-Lubāb*, both being classified biographical dictionaries of the Prophet's Companions and of the Traditionists. His two historical works *al-Kāmil* and *al-Bāhir* are not ranked as high as his two dictionaries although they enjoyed a good reputation.

In *Usd al-gẖāba* he completely depended on earlier works which he thoroughly studied and then reproduced in one book omitting repetitions and the long chains of *isnād*. Yet he devoted a chapter to the summary of those chains, pointing out that he did so in order to avoid repetition. The biographies were strictly arranged in alphabetical order. The aim of this book was to collect into one large book the materials which were to be found in different books.

Al-Lubāb is a recension of the great work of al-Sam'ānī (d. 562/1167) called *Kitāb al-ansāb*. Al-Sam'ānī was highly respected among the Traditionists, so that Ibn al-Aẖtīr took special care when revising his text. He stated that he preserved the views of al-Sam'ānī even when he was sure that al-Sam'ānī had been mistaken. In certain instances, however, he corrected the records of al-Sam'ānī although he hesitated for a long time, fearing that he would be accused of wishing to undermine the work of that great author. Ibn al-Aẖtīr's contribution again rests in the omission of repetition and the reduction of the *isnād* to the shortest form. Al-Sam'ānī repeated certain biographies, a fact which Ibn al-Aẖtīr attributed to the disorder in which the original work was produced and, in some cases, to unawareness on the part of the author.[20]

The works which gained Ibn al-Aẖtīr his fame as an historian were his universal history named *al-Kāmil*, and his local history *al-Bāhir fī ta'rīkẖ*

---

[19] For example, compare the records of Ibn Sẖaddād, Abū Sẖāma and Ibn Kẖallikān on the date of Sẖīrkūh's first expedition into Egypt.

[20] A study of al-Sam'ānī's work shows that the author did not revise his work and that he used to supplement it from time to time.

atābakāt al-Mawṣil. He states, in *al-Kāmil,* that he noticed that the historical books of his predecessors were, in general, inadequate, 'some dealing with the East, others with the West. Facts were overlaid in many of them through their repetition, ornate style, or through long chains of *isnād* to be cited: and so many important events had been intentionally passed over or omitted through prejudice.' So he decided on a 'comprehensive work which would avoid the shortcomings hitherto inherent in such histories'. Thus *al-Kāmil* was planned to contain a great amount of historical information, dealing with all localities, in chronological order. The unit of this chronological record is the year, and the events taking place within the limits of one year are classified and dealt with seriatim, and are thus treated as a continued sequence often comprising a single chapter. In these records the author draws upon previous works, al-Ṭabarī occupying a favourite position in the first three centuries.

For the period 477/1084–607/1210 Ibn al-Athīr gives us two records, one in *al-Kāmil* in continuation of the universal work, and the other in his history of the atabegs, which covers only these hundred and thirty years. There is a great similarity in the recording of this period in the two works. In some instances, however, one finds marked differences, in the order of events, in the actual text or in the parts added in one or other of the two works in recording a certain event. *Al-Kāmil* was compiled before *al-Bāhir,* yet Ibn al-Athīr did not publish it until after the year 619/1222, i.e. about eleven years, at least, after the publication of *al-Bāhir.*[21] The reason, as understood from Ibn al-Athīr, was that *al-Kāmil* was a master work and it therefore required time for revision before publication. He put it aside for 'a long period', although he had been requested by friends and students to give lectures on it, which he did for a short time. Then he received a 'command' from him 'whose orders could not be disobeyed' to publish the book in its final form. It was al-Malik al-Raḥīm Badr al-Dīn Lu'lu' who so requested publication.[22] Our historian thus pushed forward the completion of the final copy.

The total period of *al-Bāhir* and the corresponding part of *al-Kāmil* extends over a hundred and thirty years, of only a quarter of which Ibn al-Athīr could have been eyewitness, although he lived through fifty-two years of this period.[23] He was of course in a position to have first-hand knowledge of the history of the region at that time, especially since he

[21] Ibn al-Athīr also says, in *al-Bāhir,* that he had the idea of compiling a history of his native town, in acknowledgment of the kindness which the atabegs showed his family and himself. The accession of al-Qāhir Mas'ūd, a minor, in 607/1210, prompted him to write this history in order that the new atabeg might acquaint himself with history of his lineage and might follow the example set by them of good administration and sound policy.

[22] Lu'lu' did not take the title of al-Malik al-Raḥīm until 619/1222, when he was proclaimed the atabeg of Mosul.

[23] He was born in 555/1160.

travelled among the different cities in that area. But what were his sources for the preceding period? The only one to whom he repeatedly refers, especially in *al-Bāhir*, is his father, who, he says, acquainted him with most of the facts. He mentions him in phrases such as: 'My father told me . . .' or 'So my father told me', and occasionally he adds: 'and I have also found that written in the books of history'. Yet he does not name these books. It is also important here to state that he says that he could not recount all that his father had told him owing to the fact that he wrote from memory after his father's death. It even seems that Ibn al-Athīr intentionally omits the mention of the sources in his works, a conclusion which can be drawn from both *al-Kāmil* and *al-Bāhir*, because he sometimes writes: 'The most competent of the genealogists of his time told me . . .', or 'a trustworthy person told me . . .', or 'I was told by a man who is learned in histories of genealogies, and he is the one who has the greatest knowledge of them, that . . .' without naming these authorities whose records, according to such statements, must have been of great value. This attitude of Ibn al-Athīr towards his authorities could be understood if one considers it along with his attitude to the long chains of *isnād* which he intentionally omitted when writing *Usd al-ghāba* and *al-Lubāb*. He made it his practice to read the sources, compare them, set the events in different order and reproduce them. This could be regarded as an attempt on the part of Ibn al-Athīr to free himself from the Traditionist method followed by his favourite historian, al-Ṭabarī, and by his contemporary Ibn 'Asākir. But when comparing his records with those of his sources it can be demonstrated that, on some occasions, he distorts the accounts when reproducing them. This is certainly the case when using the works of al-'Imād al-Kātib on the life of Saladin, surely because Ibn al-Athīr was not sympathetic to the Ayyubids in general. On one occasion, at least, we find him partial to Nūr al-Dīn, and a later historian, who also had special admiration for Nūr al-Dīn, rejects the record of Ibn al-Athīr, basing his rejection on a document which must have been at the disposal of Ibn al-Athīr.[24]

This attitude of Ibn al-Athīr made Abū Shāma refrain from using his works extensively when recording for the life of Saladin.

(6) Yaḥyā b. Abī Ṭayyi' (d. *c.* 630/1232), a Shī'ī native of Aleppo. He is an important source of historical information, as can be gathered from the frequent quotations from his works by later historians, particularly

[24] When recording some pious endowments established by Nūr al-Dīn, Ibn al-Athīr mentions the Bīmāristān of Damascus saying: 'Nūr al-Dīn did not limit the use of this Bīmāristān to the poor, but gave the right of benefiting from it to all Muslims, rich and poor alike.' Abū Shāma rejected this account saying: 'I read the document on this *waqf* and found no reference to this, but it is only what the common people say . . . He (i.e. Nūr al-Dīn) allowed the rare medicines to be given to whoever needs them, poor or rich, and so this intention should not be misinterpreted.'

Abū Shāma and Ibn al-Furāt. There is a similarity between him and al-Qāḍī al-Fāḍil in that the works of both have been lost and that both of them are known through other historians.

Ibn Abī Ṭayyi' received his education in Aleppo under the supervision of his father who was a carpenter and an eminent Shī'ī.[25] Yāqūt, as quoted by al-Ṣafadī, states that Yaḥyā did not follow his father's career, and that he took to writing as a means of earning his living. He wrote several books on grammar, philology, commentaries on the Qur'ān, government administration, rhetoric, biography and history, and even botany. His historical works are ten in number, according to Yāqūt. They are: a history of the Prophet and his Companions, a history of Aleppo entitled *Ma'ādin al-dhahab*, an appendix to this history of Aleppo, a history of the kings of Aleppo, a history of Syria, a history of Saladin, a history of al-Ẓāhir (the son of Saladin), a history of Egypt, a short history of North Africa (*al-Maghrib*), and a universal history called *Ḥawādith al-zamān*.[26] He also wrote two biographical dictionaries, *Ta'rīkh al-'ulamā'* and *Ta'rīkh ruwāt al-Shī'a*.

Ibn Abī Ṭayyi''s sources of information are his father, who appears to have been an eyewitness of some events, especially during the period of Nūr al-Dīn, and the works of the *qāḍī* Ibn Shaddād and al-'Imād al Kātib. He also quoted the documents of al-Qāḍī al-Fāḍil and al-'Imād. The fact that he acknowledges the value of documents in writing history, and the significance of relying on eye-witness accounts, entitles him to be considered as a reliable historian, the more so since extensive use is made of his works by later historians, especially Abū Shāma, Ibn Khallikān, and Ibn al-Furāt.[27]

(7) Sibṭ Ibn al-Jawzī, Yūsuf b. Qizughlū, Shams al-Dīn, Abu'l-Muẓaffar (d. 654/1257). His father was a slave of Ibn Ḥubayra, the vizier of Baghdād, who freed him and arranged for his marriage to the daughter of the learned Shaykh Ibn al-Jawzī. Hence he was better known by the name Sibṭ (i.e. the grandson of) Ibn al-Jawzī. He worked his way up in the court of the Ayyubids till he became the most favoured '*ālim* in the court of al-Mu'aẓẓam 'Īsā, of Damascus (d. 624/1226). Through this, Sibṭ Ibn al-Jawzī abandoned his Ḥanbalī belief and embraced the Ḥanafī doctrine, the one which al-Mu'aẓẓam strongly supported. This action of Sibṭ Ibn al-Jawzī was condemned by the scholars of his time, and he was not able to make a satisfactory rebuttal. Yet one finds several references in his

[25] The father was once exiled from Aleppo, in 543/1148, during the time of Nūr al-Dīn, on the grounds of his Shi'ite activities.

[26] Ḥājjī Khalīfa names only six of them: *Ma'ādin al-dhahab, Kanz al-muwaḥḥidin fī sīrat Ṣalāḥ al-Dīn, 'Uqūd al-jawāhir fī sīrat al-Malik al-ẓāhir, Ḥawādith al-zamān, Mukhtaṣar ta'rīkh al-Maghrib*, and *Ta'rīkh Miṣr*.

[27] On Ibn Abī Ṭayyi' see C. Cahen, 'Une Chronique Chiite . . .', *Comptes Rendus de l'Acad. des Inscriptions et des Belles Lettres* (1935), pp. 258–69.

Mir'āt al-zamān to the great respect shown him by his students and by Damascenes attending his religious lectures.

The main work of Sibṭ Ibn al-Jawzī, the *Mir'āt al-zamān*, is a universal history, beginning with the Creation and ending in 654/1257, the year of his death. The portion dealing with the Zengid and Ayyubid periods relies largely on first-hand information derived from contemporaries, most of whom have already been mentioned, such as Ibn al-Qalānisī, al-'Imād, and Ibn Shaddād. Another important source was his grandfather Abu'l-Faraj ibn al-Jawzī (d. 597/1200), especially for material concerning Iraq and Persia. Being born in 581/1185, he was able to give first-hand information about events which he had witnessed, first in Iraq, where he had studied, and later in Syria, especially after he had strengthened his relations with al-Mu'aẓẓam of Damascus. So his work became a source of material for Abū Shāma, who used it, to some extent, in his appendix to *al-Rawḍatayn*, up to the year 626/1228.

Sibṭ Ibn al-Jawzī does not use documents on a large scale, although he uses the works of al-'Imād. His main interest, however, was the biographies of the *'ulamā'* rather than the political history as such. So his book consists of a blending of biographical accounts with purely historical records; in this he follows the example of his grandfather.

(8) Abū Shāma, 'Abd al-Raḥmān b. Ismā'īl, al-Maqdisī (d. 665/1268), the Traditionist, jurist, grammarian and historian. He was not, however, especially distinguished as a historian, and the biographers do not lay special stress on his historical writings. Like so many of his contemporaries he wrote several books on varied subjects, among which seven deal with history. These are: *al-Rawḍatayn*, a history of Nūr al-Dīn and Saladin's periods, the *'Uyūn*, a summary of *al-Rawḍatayn*, an appendix to it entitled *al-Mudhayyal 'alā al-Rawḍatayn*, two synopses of *Ta'rīkh Ibn 'Asākir*, one in fifteen parts, the other in five, *Kashf ḥāl banī 'Ubayd* (i.e. the disclosure of the secret of Banī 'Ubayd, a refutation of the claims of the Fatimid dynasty) and *al-Sīra al-'alā'iyya*, a biography of 'Alā' al-Dīn of Khwārizm. Of all these books only three are extant, *al-Rawḍatayn*, the *'Uyūn*, and the *Mudhayyal*. There is one part of one of his synopses of *Ta'rīkh Ibn 'Asākir* in manuscript form in Berlin. According to Abū Shāma two more works were begun but were not completed when his autobiography was written in 659/1260. These are a summary of *Ta'rīkh Baghdād* and a history of Mecca, Medina, and Jerusalem.

When Abū Shāma first decided to write history he chose 'the greatest work written in the method of the Traditionists', the history of Ibn 'Asākir, 'abridged it, rectified, adding to it useful material from other works'. This method influenced him when writing *al-Rawḍatayn*, making it a rule to cite each author that he quotes. It was this traditionist approach, too, which made him quote verbatim, thus introducing the stilted style of al-ʿImād, whose works Abū Shāma reduces, only in size, to the minimum without omitting or distorting any fact. He naturally does not content himself with one account only, but supports it, and enlarges or explains by adducing quotations from other available relevant sources.

His aims in writing history differ from one book to another. First, he wished to induce kings to follow a course of conduct which would lead to the prosperity of the people and not to the realization of their own ambitions. Later he noticed that the kings persisted in their quarrelling, with consequent harm to their people and the prolonging of their sufferings. So he abandoned his ideal aim of preserving prosperity in an Islamic body politic. He wrote history thereafter to 'remind himself of his relatives, friends, and acquaintances who were dying in great number, and to prepare his soul for its inevitable destiny'.

The most important of Abū Shāma's historical works is the history of Nūr al-Dīn and Saladin entitled *al-Rawḍatayn*. This work opens with a short account of the *atabegs* of Mosul, the ancestors of Nūr al-Dīn, laying special stress on the activities of ʿImād al-Dīn Zengi, Nūr al-Dīn's father. This account is given in short chapters until within the year 541/1146 when Zengi was assassinated and succeeded by his two sons, Ghāzī in Mosul and Nūr al-Dīn in Aleppo. Thereafter Abū Shāma records the history of Nūr al-Dīn, and after his death in 569/1174, of Saladin, in chronological order, beginning with the year 542 and terminating with Saladin's death in 589/1193.

Abū Shāma based his choice of sources on two principles—the contemporary and the local. The earliest of his authorities was Ibn al-Qalānisī who died in 555/1160, whilst the last was the *qāḍī* Ibn Shaddād who lived till 632/1234. As for authorities on localities, Ibn al-Athīr was a native of Mosul, so his history of the *atabegs* would be the most reliable source for that region. The same case applies to Ibn Abī Ṭayyi' of Aleppo and Ibn al-Qalānisī, the Damascene. Al-Qāḍī al-Fāḍil, al-ʿImād and Ibn Shaddād could be quoted for different localities, since, in most cases, they accompanied Saladin as his secretaries.

Being so careful in choosing his sources, he does not attempt to comment on them or assess their accuracy. This is certainly allowable because he may have felt that to be beyond his discriminatory powers, since he did not witness the events, nor was he personally involved in the matters he relates.[28] In the *Mudhayyal*, which covers the years 590/1193–665/1266, of most of which he was contemporary, being born in 599/1203, he relies on Sibṭ Ibn al-Jawzī as well as some of his own professors and friends, and his own observation. The *Mudhayyal*, however, is a combination of political and biographical accounts, mostly centred in, and around Damascus.

[28] Except on a very few occasions when he comments on certain records relying in this comment on a document or on other accurate accounts.

An examination of Abū Shāma's major work shows that it was based on important works which he selected and the accuracy of which he accepted. These sources, although local and limited in period, contribute as a group to the understanding of the history of this period. Now Abū Shāma's contribution is very important since he studied these works and reproduced them in a concise, accurate, and highly reliable work. One needs to consult the sources of Abū Shāma when seeking particular detailed accounts of certain localities which are not within the theme of *al-Rawḍatayn*. But for these subjects which fall within this theme it is always advisable that *al-Rawḍatayn* should be consulted, because its author furnished several reliable accounts, some of which can rarely be found elsewhere, such as those of al-Qāḍī al-Fāḍil. The great number of official documents which Abū Shāma includes, selected and detailed as they are, make it worthy of acceptance.

(9) Ibn Wāṣil, Jamāl al-Dīn, Muḥammad b. Sālim (d. 697/1298), the author of *Mufarrij al-kurūb fī akhbār Banī Ayyūb*, a history of the Ayyubids. Like Abū Shāma, Ibn Wāṣil begins his book with a short account of the history of the atabegs, especially of 'Imād al-Dīn Zengi. This particular way of introducing the history of the Ayyubids shows how much Ibn Wāṣil was influenced by Abū Shāma. Yet certain differences can be found between *al-Rawḍatayn* and the *Mufarrij* in dealing with this introductory part. *Al-Rawḍatayn* tends to give more detailed and lengthy records than does the *Mufarrij*, and most of the poetry included in *al-Rawḍatayn* is omitted in the *Mufarrij*. This is readily understood when one realizes that *al-Rawḍatayn* was planned as a history of two personalities only, Nūr al-Dīn the atabeg being one of them. The *Mufarrij*, on the other hand, is the history of the dynasty of the Ayyubids, who were not atabegs.

The authorities cited by Ibn Wāṣil in the first part of the book, i.e. till the death of Saladin, are also those of Abū Shāma. It is clearly noticeable that this part of the *Mufarrij* follows the order of *al-Rawḍatayn*, and even the wording of the records. On examination it can be shown that Ibn Wāṣil depended to a great extent on Abū Shāma in many of his records. For instance, the accounts given in the *Mufarrij* about the recapture of Edessa by Nūr al-Dīn, in 541/1146, are obviously taken from *al-Rawḍatayn*. In these accounts Abū Shāma omits certain parts, when quoting Ibn al-Athīr, and Ibn Wāṣil omits exactly the same parts.[29] When recording the year 564/1168 Abū Shāma quotes Ibn al-Athīr and Ibn Shaddād on the unwillingness of Saladin to participate in the expedition launched against Egypt, until Nūr al-Dīn ordered him to do so. Ibn Wāṣil quotes the two records in the order in which they are given in *al-Rawḍatayn* and in the same manner. When Abū Shāma becomes less dependent on Ibn

[29] Abū Shāma uses Ibn al-Athīr and Ibn al-Qalānisī for these accounts, whilst Ibn Wāṣil is satisfied with the accounts of Ibn-al-Athīr as they are given in *al-Rawḍatayn*.

al-Athīr and relies on Ibn Shaddād and al-'Imād, Ibn Wāṣil shows great dependence on Abū Shāma and quotes him frequently. It is certain that Ibn Wāṣil used Ibn al-Athīr extensively and directly, but even in this case it is noticeable, in the main, that he deals with the points already dealt with by Abū Shāma, and in the majority of the instances in the very same order. The year 577/1181, in which al-Ṣāliḥ Ismā'īl of Aleppo died, could be regarded as a turning point in Ibn Wāṣil's attitude to his sources. Up to this year, in many cases, he uses the sources of Abū Shāma, especially Ibn al-Athīr. But after this year, it can be definitely shown that he depends entirely on Abū Shāma.

As for the latter part of the *Mufarrij*, i.e. after the death of Saladin in 589/1193, Ibn Wāṣil derives his material from other sources and from personal observation and experience, being born at the turn of the century, in 604/1207, and able to travel frequently between different regions subject to the Ayyubids. Thus this part covers most of the period which Abū Shāma declined to deal with extensively although he was also an eyewitness.

(10) Ibn Mammātī, al-As'ad b. al-Muhadhdhab (d. 606/1209), a chief of the Ayyubid departments of war and finance for Saladin and his son al-'Azīz. He was descended from a Coptic family in Upper Egypt. A number of his ancestors had occupied similar positions for the Fatimids of Egypt. When Shīrkūh seized control of the country, as vizier for the last Fatimid caliph, al-Muhadhdhab adopted Islam, along with his sons, thus retaining his office as chief of the war department.[30]

The family of Ibn Mammātī were, therefore, experts in financial and administrative affairs in Egypt, having been in charge of these matters since Badr al-Jamālī assumed office (in 466/1073) as vizier for al-Mustanṣir, the Fatimid caliph, till Ibn Mammātī had to flee to Aleppo, after the death of al-'Azīz of Egypt in 595/1198. This service amounts to nearly one hundred and forty successive years. Thus, since al-As'ad compiled his work *Qawānīn al-dawāwīn*, an administrative history and survey of Egypt, during his term of office, it can certainly be said to rank as the most reliable work of its kind. The dependability of this work would also seem to be assured by the attitude of the author towards what he calls state secrets (*asrar al-dawla*). These, he says, cannot be published, and are therefore excluded from consideration.[31]

In this connection it should be taken into consideration that he wrote his work for his sultan, al-'Azīz 'Uthmān, to serve as a guide for state officials. In fact, he gives two reasons for writing the book: first, that an official loyal to his state should endeavour during his lifetime to serve his

[30] He embraced Islam as a matter of expediency, since some of his envious colleagues sought to influence Shīrkūh against him. It is also said that the then vizier of Egypt was Saladin, as Shīrkūh had died.

[31] *Qawānīn al-dawāwīn*, p. 84.

sultans, not withholding the benefit of his experience and knowledge, but making this experience useful to the state by recording it. Secondly, to facilitate the task of the *kuttāb*, i.e. government officials, by setting forth necessary details of administrative duties and by explaining the rules of this administration especially in matters concerning *iqṭā'*, revenue, taxation, agricultural products and so forth.

Ibn Mammātī divided his work into fifteen sections, each of which is divided into subsections. They cover four main aspects: First, a detailed description of the regions and terrain of Egypt (e.g. villages, estates, canals). Second, the government departments, their several activities, and the duty of certain officials concerned. Third, a survey of agricultural lands, classifying them according to fertility, irrigation, products, seasons, horticulture, and so forth. Fourthly and lastly, he deals with the agricultural year as regulated by the Coptic calendar, adding geometrical and mathematical problems and land survey methods.

According to al-Maqrīzī, and as explained by Professor A. S. Atiya, the work was originally in four large volumes all of which have been lost. The version preserved in the different manuscripts and finally published is only a summary of the great work, dealing with ten of the original fifteen chapters.

The significance of the work, as has already been mentioned, is that it is a result of a hundred and forty years of family experience in dealing with purely administrative and financial matters. The fact that the author was a member of a Coptic family, purely Egyptian, adds to the value of the work.

In conclusion the following points may be mentioned.

1. Historical studies did not receive positive encouragement from the body of learning in schools, since the curricula of the latter were concentrated on Qur'anic and Traditionist studies. Yet historiography nevertheless flourished since certain *'ulamā'* found some religious justification for their personal interest in history. Moreover, certain leading *'ulamā'* occupied official government posts and were thus involved in political and military affairs. Such persons contributed much to the writing of history, and in two ways; first, through documents which they compiled during their term of office, and second, by the documentary material which they left in their actual historical works.

2. Through this semi-official encouragement and because of prevailing circumstances, historiography became both prolific and colourful. The writing of general chronicles, local histories, monographs, biographies, and autobiographies received great attention during this period. A veritable cavalcade can be found covering the whole period and supplying first-hand historical information through contemporary eyewitness, beginning with

Ibn al-Qalānisī and ending with Ibn Wāṣil. On the administrative side of history we have that important work of Ibn Mammātī which could be regarded as the earliest of its kind on Muslim Egypt. Although this work deals only with Egypt, it can help to form a similar idea about Syria, since both Egypt and Syria were Ayyubid dominions, and because the book was written soon after the death of Saladin.

3. Historians during this period acknowledged the value of documents, and thus a number of these were used to support certain accounts, to give more details, to correct, and even furnish new material.

4. Even poetry was used, occasionally, by certain historians, as documentary material since it gave dates and details of certain events, and examples of this can be found in *al-Rawḍatayn* of Abū Shāma.

5. During this period some historians attempted to free themselves from the Traditionist method (e.g. Ibn al-Athīr who intentionally deserted the *isnād* method, and Sibṭ Ibn al-Jawzī who combined different accounts of al-ʿImād and Ibn Shaddād in summarized records).

6. Some historians attempted successfully the systematic approach by selecting the sources which have a local and a contemporary value, when writing about events which they themselves did not witness.

7. THE ARABIC HISTORIOGRAPHY OF THE CRUSADES

FRANCESCO GABRIELI

Professor of Arabic Language and Literature in the University of Rome

The concept of the Crusades as an historical phenomenon in itself with its own characteristics, which might be treated separately, either in a monograph or within the framework of a general periodization of history, is one alien to Muslim historiography. The events which took place in Syria, Egypt and Mesopotamia between the end of our eleventh century and the end of the thirteenth by the fact of the Frankish invasion and the Muslim resistance, have never been the object of a special and at the same time comprehensive treatise on the part of the chroniclers and the Muslim historians, except in a few instances (as in the *Fatḥ al-qussī* of 'Imād al-Dīn) where the unity is not given by the events themselves but by the personality of a champion of Islam whose exploits the author wishes to relate. In general, the wars with the Crusaders were for the Muslim historians one element among several others, a thread in the cloth of their history, although naturally this thread at certain times had a very special importance and development. The Muslims never reached the point, one would say, of regarding the Christian attack in the West as anything fundamentally different from the other wars against the Infidels, whether they were the Franks or Byzantines: in Syria itself in the course of the tenth century and before, in Andalus throughout the Spanish Reconquista, in Sicily against the Normans. Even the well-known passage of Ibn al-Athīr, where he compares the First Crusade with the Christian offensives in Spain and Sicily, although it shows the breadth of the Mesopotamian historian's vision, proves to us that he did not perceive what distinguished the Crusades from the other wars between Christians and Islam in the Middle Ages, nor realize the special characteristics of the Latin settlement in the Levant.

The cause of this mistake on the part of Islam in the evaluation of an historical phenomenon of which it was first the victim, then the bitter adversary and finally the victor, can be found in our opinion in the indifference, caused by a sense of superiority and contempt, which the Muslims always showed, except on a few occasions, for the western world, its history and culture throughout the Middle Ages, in contrast with the profound interest they demonstrated in the ancient cultures and civilizations of the Orient.[1] This contrast in attitude comes out very well even if the Arab historiography of the Crusades is compared with Muslim historio-

[1] Cf. B. Lewis, 'The Muslim Discovery of Europe', *BSOAS* (1957), xx, 409–16.

graphy in general (and in this instance particularly Persian) on the Mongols, who, coming from the other end of the world, inundated the *dār al-Islām* in the same century. But while in regard to the latter (of whose first invasion the same Ibn al-Athīr in a celebrated page has clearly underlined the extraordinary and terrible character) the Muslim historians soon tried to get to know and to explain origins, customs, traditions and institutions, however remote from their own civilization, nothing comparable is found for the Franks who were established for two centuries on Islamic soil. We can scarcely glean any details on them even in a writer as perceptive and curious as Usāma, who spoke of them as 'things seen' without attaching any importance to them or making any effort at systematic research. For the rest, while not forgetting the sum of distress, sacrifices and blood demanded from Islam in its conflict against the Crusaders, it is tempting to compare the Muslim attitude towards them with that of the desert camel towards the tick lodged in his side which climbed and slid, as the poet says, the length of the smooth surface and finally fell off after having caused much annoyance to its unwilling host without his deigning to show any interest beyond a flick of the tail.

A history of the Crusades, even, of course, from the opposite point of view, thus cannot be found among the Muslim (i.e. almost entirely Arab) historians of the period, but only pieces of this history, more or less developed and followed up, contained in other treatises, embedded in other schemes and fitted, so to say, into the historical patterns proper to medieval Muslim culture which were self-sufficient in themselves and scorned to venture beyond. It was, of course, the task of the chroniclers to inform us, among the happenings in a town, region, or section of the Muslim world the events of which they were cataloguing, of the arrival there of the Franks, and the history, now monotonous, now dramatic, of the events which followed—sieges, battles, pillage, murders, truces more or less observed, ransoms, hostages. But who were these Franks, what urged them on, where did they come from, how did they differ from the Byzantines who were the only invaders Syria had known till then? In general there is almost complete silence on this point: the Franks arrived like famine, earthquake or epidemic, and were accepted as a scourge of God; and Syrians tried to make the best of it by arms or cunning. Such, for example, is the beginning of the History of the Crusades in the oldest Muslim historian who deals with it, the Damascus chronicler Ibn al-Qalānisī; and other twelfth-century chroniclers are even more concise. The entry on the scene of the Franks remained thus *ex abrupto*, even if the framework of the local and regional chronicles expanded into the great 'universal' histories in which the thirteenth and fourteenth centuries are so rich, and where the fact 'wars with the Franks' is an item, so to say, drowned in the flood of events which the author catalogues in the different theatres of history, within the framework of a chronological arrangement by years. We have already noted as an honourable exception the picture drawn by Ibn al-Athīr at the beginning of the First Crusade. The subject is more directly and fully approached by the dynastic histories and biographies, where they treat of princely families and individuals who devoted their lives to the holy war against the infidel invaders; such, as we have already said, were the works on Saladin, by 'Imād al-Dīn and Ibn Shaddād or the *Kitāb al-Rawḍatayn* of Abū Shāma; or, for the Mamluk period, the histories of Ibn Wāṣil and Ibn 'Abd al-Ẓāhir. It is with the *disjecta membra* of all these authors, none of whom thought of looking precisely into relations with the Franks for the guiding line of his exposition, that we can reconstruct from the fragments a Muslim history of the Crusades. This reservation made, there is no doubt that the relative materials in the historical literature in Arabic are imposing in quantity and sometimes excellent in quality. Rosenthal's learned book on Muslim historiography, which deals above all with its literary typology, is rather disappointing, and a better picture, exhaustive in its day, of the material for the Crusades from the Arab side was traced nearly twenty years ago by Claude Cahen in his great book on Northern Syria and the Principality of Antioch.[2] The war and the troubled times which followed the book's publication do not seem to us to have greatly altered this summing-up as far as the finding of new texts or the publication of unpublished ones is concerned. Suffice it to point out here the publication in progress of *Mufarrij al-kurūb* of Ibn Wāṣil,[3] one of Cahen's most urgent desiderata; that of the *Zubdat al-ḥalab* of Ibn al-'Adīm[4] and the Egyptian edition of the *Nujūm* of Ibn Taghrī Birdī, which includes the period of the taking of Acre by al-Ashraf, not included in the editions of Juynboll-Matthes and Popper.[5] Supposing that the editions of Ibn Wāṣil and Ibn al-'Adīm do not stop as soon as they have begun, I think the unpublished author most urgently in need of publication is the Egyptian Ibn 'Abd al-Ẓāhir, with his Life of Qalā'ūn (identified by Cahen with the anonymous *Tashrīf al-ayyām wa'l-'uṣūr*) and that of al-Ashraf of which the extract published by Moberg is only a fragment.[6] Much of Ibn 'Abd al-Ẓāhir has passed, it is true, into the later chroniclers (such as Maqrīzī, Ibn al-Furāt, and Ibn Taghrī Birdī), but an edition of the original text is no less desirable than that of the *Barq al-shāmī* of 'Imād al-Dīn (in the part preserved at Oxford to which Gibb has drawn attention) although this has been used by Ibn

[2] Cl. Cahen, *La Syrie du Nord à l'époque des Croisades et la principauté franque d'Antioche* (Paris, 1940).

[3] Ed. M. Shayyal, I, Cairo 1953 (to the death of Nūr al-Dīn); II (1957) (the age of Saladin); III (1961) (The Ayyubids).

[4] Ed. Sami Dahan, I–II (Damascus, 1951, 1954).

[5] Ed. Cairo, Dār al-kutub al-miṣriyya, VIII (1939).

[6] Part of the life of Baybars by the same Ibn 'Abd al-Ẓāhir has been published by F. Sadeque, *Baybars the first of Egypt* (Dacca-Oxford, 1956). An edition of the complete text has been prepared by Dr. A. A. Khowaitir (London Ph.D. thesis, 1960), and is to be published.

al-Athīr and Abū Shāma. Clearly it would also be desirable to have good new editions of many authors known up to now in out-of-date editions (starting with Ibn al-Athīr himself of whom Tornberg's edition is far from satisfactory), but finally it is undeniable, with a few exceptions, that the most important texts are now available to orientalists interested in history to throw light 'from the other side' on the history of the Crusades. The historians ought now to base their work on that of the philologist editors, in dealing with the 'oriental' version of the Crusades not only simply as a curiosity but as a means of analysing the Western sources and using them critically to present the most complete picture possible of events and to contribute to the illumination of problems which are still debatable.

The two last general histories of the Crusades, those of Grousset and Runciman, have not failed to use as far as they could the oriental sources, when they were available to them in translation, above all in the *Recueil des Historiens des Croisades*. There is no space here to discuss the merits and defects of these great works which however both suffer from having only this *indirect* contact with Muslim historiography, and from the recognized defects of the intermediary (the *Recueil*, largely the work of Barbier de Meynard),[7] through which they had access to this historiography. Neither the political nationalism of Grousset nor the philo-Byzantinism of Runciman are the best means of getting the greatest profit possible from the use of Muslim sources, which they seem to have treated as a purely technical tool of verification, without arriving at a deeper insight into the spirit of their authors, and into the Muslim vision and interpretation of events. A technical approach, as well as a feeling for these oriental sources, is only possible for historians who are also orientalists, who can read the original texts, and can not only check the facts, but also reassess and judge the ideas and feelings which gave birth to these facts or colour them; who develop, in a word, in listening to the Muslims, a Muslim spirit whose testimony is added to the file of evidence compiled by their modern historian's consciousness.

The direct contribution of orientalists to a modern history of the Crusades is one of the merits of the last great enterprise in this field, the Philadelphia *History of the Crusades*, set on foot by the late La Monte and edited now by Setton, of which the first volume (the only one which has yet appeared)[8] counts among its contributors specialists like H. A. R. Gibb, and, in spite of the inconvenience of dividing the subject matter among several authors, gives us at last a first-hand analysis of oriental history combined with the direct experience and *Einfühlung* necessary. Also to

[7] 'Recueil des Historiens des Croisades', *Historiens Orientaux* (Paris, 1872–1906). A small anthology in Italian, *Storici arabi delle Crociate* (Turin, 1957), has been collected by the present author.

[8] *History of the Crusades*, i, *The first hundred years* (Philadelphia, 1955).

Gibb, and to his English pupil and colleague, B. Lewis, as well as to Cahen in France, goes the merit in the last decades of very thorough specialized studies in the Arabic historiography of the Crusades, and in the many episodes of this history; from the *Notes on the Arabic Materials for the History of the Early Crusades* by Gibb, which was inspired by Grousset's first volume, to his more recent analysis of the Arabic sources for the life of Saladin and, in particular, of the work of 'Imād al-Dīn, right up to the researches of Lewis on the sources for the history of the Assassins in Syria.[9]

Taking account of these studies we shall examine very rapidly some of the most outstanding figures of the Arab historiography of the Crusades, trying to determine their physiognomy as it seems to us, in the relative critical literature and by direct examination of their works; to attempt finally a general appreciation of the value and limits of this historiography of which we can only mention here the most significant representatives.

Ibn al-Qalānisī is at the moment the most ancient Arabic source, unknown in the nineteenth century, for the history of the first two Crusades and the Frankish penetration in Syria.[10] This worthy citizen of Damascus, who gave his Chronicle no other title than that of *Dhayl* or Continuation of the work of an earlier chronicler, expanded his interests beyond his town of birth and embraced all the events touching Upper Syria and Mesopotamia and the neighbouring territory as far as Baghdād on one side and Cairo on the other. The Crusades are only, as we have said, one element in the narrative, although an element of the first importance. The Muslim resistance movement with which he deals is that of the Damascus *atabeg* Ṭughtegin, to whose descendants, the feeble Burids, the chronicler remained faithfully devoted. His municipal patriotism makes him by contrast look with a disapproving eye at the conduct of Zengi and the Zengids whom he saw finally triumph with Nūr al-Dīn at Damascus, and the salient point of his contrast, the alliance of 1140 of the Damascenes with the Franks against Zengi is clearly related by Ibn al-Qalānisī. A striking feature of his chronicle is the unevenness of the style, usually simple and uncomplicated, but rising to the cadences of rhythmic prose when the dignity of the subject matter demands it. Happily for us, this is not the case for events in Damascus itself of which Ibn al-Qalānisī was an eyewitness, and the page on the siege of 1148 in the Second Crusade remains a precious first-hand document of this event which no literary embellishment

[9] H. A. R. Gibb, 'Notes on the Arabic materials for the history of the early Crusades', *BSOAS* (1935), vii, 739–54; 'The Arabic Sources for the life of Saladin', *Speculum* (1950), xxv, 58–72; 'The achievement of Saladin', *Bulletin of the John Rylands Library* (1952), xxxv, 44–60; 'Al-Barq al-Shāmī: The History of Saladin by the Kātib 'Imād al-dīn al-Iṣfahānī', *WZKM* (1953), lii, 93–115. B. Lewis, 'The Sources for the history of the Syrian Assassins', *Speculum* (1952), xxvii, 475–89; 'Saladin and the Assassins', *BSOAS* (1953), xv, 239–45; 'Three biographies from Kamāl ad-Dīn', *Mélanges Fuad Koprülü* (Istanbul, 1953), pp. 325–44.

[10] Ed. Amedroz (Leiden, 1908). Partial translation by Gibb, *The Damascus Chronicle of the Crusades* (London, 1932), and R. Le Tourneau, *Damas de 1075 à 1154* (Damascus, 1952).

spoils. To sum up, Ibn Qalānisī is the most informed and reliable Arabic source for the whole of the earlier period of the Crusades.

Before the publication of this text, the key work for this period, as well as for the following era of Saladin, and in general for oriental history up to about 1230, had long been considered to be the *Kāmil* of Ibn al-Athīr who had the advantage of being early known to European orientalists in the mediocre edition of Tornberg (Leiden, 1853–64). There can be no question here of a general appreciation of this great work of oriental historiography, but for what concerns the middle period of the Crusades the value of Ibn al-Athīr has been considerably reduced by Gibb's studies, to the advantage of Ibn al-Qalānisī for the first half of the twelfth century, and of 'Imād al-Dīn for the second. The Mesopotamian was only too clearly a passionate partisan of the Zengid dynasty of the *atabegs* of Mosul, to whom the Damascene Ibn al-Qalānisī was hostile, and this bias is reflected in Ibn al-Athīr by a continued hostility against Saladin that all the fine achievements of this great champion of Islam cannot overcome. But besides this, which makes Ibn al-Athīr the *advocatus diaboli* in all that concerns the great Ayyubid (often *against*, but sometimes *to the advantage* of historical truth), the analysis of Gibb has shown the not always faithful and informed use which he makes of his sources, his errors of chronology, his manipulations of texts, so that we arrive at the conclusion that the greatest caution must be shown in the use of Ibn al-Athīr for the history of the Crusades, and that the authors already cited, and others also, are greatly to be preferred to him. For our part, while subscribing to the judgement of the eminent English historian of Islam on all questions of detail, we should like to observe discreetly that the same defects which make Ibn al-Athīr a bad chronicler confirm his value and character as an historian who does not confine himself to relating the events but aspires to explain them, who researches into the immediate and remote causes (liable to self-deception in this research though he is), and brings to his history, with his 'prejudices', his judgements which, though debatable, are not inconsiderable in an historical literature which often is marred by a total lack of critical spirit. Alone among his precursors and contemporaries Ibn al-Athīr tried to incorporate the phenomenon of the Crusades in the great antagonism between Christianity and Islam (it is less important that certain particular characteristics of the Latin exploits overseas escaped him), and he knew how to fit it into place in his universal history, which again proves his sense of proportion, his capacity for synthesis, although hampered by his annalistic treatment (but he knew at least on one occasion to depart from it in his account of the Fifth Crusade), and, last but not least, his mastery and good taste as a writer. After the researches of Gibb he can no longer be considered as a primary source for the early history of the Crusades, or even for the age of Saladin, overwhelmed or contradicted as he is by other sources such as Bahā' al-Dīn and 'Imād al-Dīn. He remains nonetheless a real historian, perhaps the only real historian of Islam in the earlier Middle Ages, and no one who looks at the major figures of the historians of the Crusades can ignore him.

The value of Ibn Shaddād as an honest and conscientious biographer of Saladin and chronicler of his exploits from 1188 has no need of being stressed here, since a critic as severe as Gibb has already recognized it. If we may make one literary observation here on his behalf it is to say that his *Nawādir sulṭāniyya*, besides its importance for the events related, presents us with a specimen of royal biography (an ideal sovereign admittedly, but the original helped him to provide the model), based on a study of character, not on a collection of anecdotes only, which is without parallel in the historical literature of early Islam.[11] Something of the human grandeur of his hero is certainly missing in Bahā' al-Dīn's biography, and his portrait of Saladin remains somewhat dull for our taste because of the exclusive part given to religious piety. But one would not ask a twelfth-century Muslim *qāḍī* to be a Lytton Strachey and, in sum, the portrait that he gives of Saladin as absorbed with and motivated by a high religious ideal, is matched exactly by the judgement of his most recent historian, the same Gibb whom we have often mentioned.

The same English scholar, while depreciating Ibn al-Athīr, has reassessed the position of another source which has been practically neglected till now, that of the Kātib 'Imād al-Dīn al-Iṣfahānī. His historical work, comprising the *Fatḥ*[12] and the unpublished *Barq*, repels the West (and sometimes Orientals themselves as the example of Abū Shāma shows) by the intolerable artificiality of his style. Gibb has shown that under these rhetorical trappings is hidden an excellent first-hand source, a faithful witness, intelligent and informed of the successes and reverses of Saladin, free from prejudice as well as flattery, to such an extent that he judges the work of 'Imād al-Dīn the foremost and best source for the career of the Ayyubid sultan. This poses the task, still largely remaining to be done, of a complete exploitation of the *Fatḥ*, which up to now nobody has been bold enough to translate and analyse except in part,[13] and of a study, which Gibb himself has outlined, of the surviving part of the *Barq*, important for the period before 1187, Saladin's year of triumph. Nevertheless the obscurities and turgidity of style make the use of this source difficult, and the historical *facts* contained in the *Fatḥ* (the only part of the Kātib's work with which I am familiar) could be contained in a fifth of the book

[11] Text and translation in *Recueil des historiens des Croisades*, iii.

[12] Ed. Landberg (Leiden, 1888).

[13] J. Kraemer, *Der Sturz des Königreichs Jerusalem (583/1187) in der Darstellung des 'Imād al-dīn al-Kātib al-Iṣfahānī* (Wiesbaden, 1952). A complete translation of the *Fatḥ* is announced by H. Massé.

if the hotchpotch of words and the plays on words were rejected. This is just what the compilation of Abū Shāma (*Kitāb al-rawḍatayn*)[14] aimed at, blending extracts from 'Imād al-Dīn, stripped of their verbiage, with those of Bahā' al-Dīn, Ibn al-Athīr, and the lost Shi'ite historian of Saladin, Ibn Abī Ṭayyi'. This does not enable us to dispense with the originals, when we have them, because many important details have been lost in the process of compilation.

Saladin and his time have attracted up to now the maximum of interest and learned research in the field of the history of the Crusades. From the start of the thirteenth century, the analysis of sources and detailed studies which we can use for the preceding period are lacking, and we have rather to manage with modern reconstruction based on eclectic rather than critical principles. None of the Arabic historians of the thirteenth century such as Sibṭ Ibn al-Jawzī and Ibn Wāṣil has been the subject of studies and systematic appreciation, although it is established that these two authors are sources of primary value for the Ayyubid and Mamluk period (adding for the latter Ibn 'Abd al-Ẓāhir). Sibṭ Ibn al-Jawzī and Ibn Wāṣil have left us up to now the most interesting details on the relations between the Ayyubids and the Hohenstaufen, on the 'diplomatic' Crusade of Frederick II and the cession to him of Jerusalem by al-Kāmil, one of the most singular and still ill-examined events of this period.[15] Then Ibn Wāṣil (known until now in later compilations which used him) informs us of the Fifth Crusade, the narration of which ends the great work of Ibn al-Athīr, and in some precious personal memories inform us of the relations of the first Mamluks of Egypt with the last Swabian princes in Southern Italy.[16] But, as we have remarked, this source has hardly been touched on. Then lastly, largely unpublished, is Ibn 'Abd al-Ẓāhir, the historian of the first great Mamluks, used by the compilers of the fifteenth century (Ibn al-Furāt and Maqrīzī, the first of whom has preserved something of Ibn Abī Ṭayyi' and the second much of Ibn Wāṣil), and above all valuable for the text of diplomatic and chancery documents (letters and treaties), which he has transmitted to us. The last agony of the Latin states of Outremer has still never been exhaustively studied with the help of these Muslim sources, if one leaves out Cahen's monograph on the Principality of Antioch. Even the last bloody act of the drama, the fall of Acre, taken by storm by the Sultan al-Ashraf in 690/1291 (of which Abu'l-Fidā' was an eyewitness and Abu'l-Maḥāsin reproduces an earlier source), has not

[14] Ed. Cairo 1287/1870, new edition Muḥ. Ḥilmī, i (Cairo, 1957).

[15] A facsimile edition of the *Mir'āt al-zamān* of Sibṭ, for this period, was published by Jewett (Chicago, 1907). The same text was printed in Hyderabad in two volumes (1951–2). On Frederick II and al-Kāmil, H. L. Gottschalk, 'Al-ambaratur/Imperator', *Der Islam* (1957), xxxiii, 30–6, and *Al-Malik al-Kāmil von Egypten und seine Zeit* (Wiesbaden, 1958).

[16] Cf. F. Gabrieli, 'Le ambascerie di Baibars a Manfredi', in *Saggi orientali* (Cattanisetta, 1960), pp. 99–106; H. L. Gottschalk, 'Der Untergang der Hohenstaufen', *WZKM* (1957), liii, 267–82.

yet, that I know of, provoked a comparison between the eastern and western sources that describe them, and the chronological questions that they give rise to.

The exact amount that these later Egyptian chroniclers owe to their predecessors for the events of the thirteenth century, and the appreciation of the part of each of these for our knowledge of the final period of the Crusades, is one of the most urgent tasks that Western historical research poses for the Arabist.

Although this Muslim historiography is only *incidentally* a historiography of the Crusades, it is possible to try and establish its value and limits in relation to the period and theme we are discussing. It is an elementary truth and almost a tautology that it presents us with the oriental vision, the other side of the hill, of the events which we know generally from Latin and Romance sources, with the reversal of value this entails. It is most remarkable that this reversal bears more on the understanding of facts than on the facts themselves, and that the systematic distortions of the truth that we have known, unfortunately, in the religious wars of our time are not the practice of these early historians. The average level of truthfulness of these oriental sources is, in our opinion, quite high, while bearing in mind the religious zeal, the national *'aṣabiyya* (Arab, but often also Turkish, although expressed in Arabic), and the laudatory and courtly spirit which inspires some of these authors. It has already been seen that the greatest champion of Islam, Saladin, had enemies, more or less dissimulated, among the historians of his time, and in his own circle biographers devoted but devoid of servile flattery, which is not the rule, it is true, in Muslim court historiography. The chroniclers of the first period of the Crusades, for their part, do not hide from themselves, or conceal, the Muslim weaknesses and disagreements which allowed the Franks to enter Syria (there is even a sincere comment of Ibn al-'Adīm on the heartbreaking attitude of the local *amīrs* who welcomed the success of the Franks because of their rivalries and particular interests), and Saladin himself (or al-Qāḍī al-Fāḍil in his name) did not hesitate in one of his appeals to arms to underline the tenacity, the spirit of sacrifice and what we should call the idealism of the enemy. This objectivity and relative broadness of spirit seems to diminish in the historians of the later epoch, writing under the uncivilized and despotic Mamluks, but by this time the balance was already weighted in favour of the Muslims, and apologia of the Sultan's victories could quite well be reconciled with the truth.

More than the bias, undeniable but hardly ever ending in bad faith, the limitation of this oriental historiography at the time of the Crusades seems to us to be general to medieval Muslim (and perhaps not only Muslim) historiography of the Middle Ages. Interest is limited to strictly pragmatic and dynastic history, caring little for economic and social factors, quicker to seize the exterior aspects of phenomena than to shed light on their genesis and development; hence the well-known predilection of these authors for details and anecdotes, which often adorn their pages to the detriment of real historical value, and the absence in contrast of that which is taken for granted in themselves and ignored in the enemy: institutions, customs, law and economics. One rarely finds, scattered here and there by chance in Muslim authors, allusions to the social and legal structure and to the religious and cultural life of the Infidel, unless it is to note the example where they did homage to the superior civilization of the Muslims by learning their language and initiating themselves into their culture. All this adds up to the feeling of superiority and disdain for the stranger that we have already pointed out among the Muslims, which after the stormy contact of the Crusades could only harden and develop up to modern times. The example of William of Tyre, who learnt Arabic and wrote from Arabic sources his lost history of the Orient, remains without parallel on the other side. Islam turned in on itself and took all the heavy consequences of this. But the rich and substantial section of its historiography that was dedicated to the events of the two centuries of the Crusades appears to an unbiassed judge to be of no less value than the best Western historiography of this period, and sometimes clearly better.

8. THE ORIGIN AND DEVELOPMENT OF THE LOCAL HISTORIES OF SYRIA

SAMI DAHAN

Member of the Arab Academy, Damascus

Already at the time of the Arab conquest of Syria in the seventh century A.D., we find the Arabs extremely attached to the new region which had become their base and point of departure for the Asian and African world. They had sayings attributed to the Prophet showing that Syria was to be the paradise of Islam and the centre from which the new religion was to spread. Every town in Syria received its share of this sense of sacredness, thus encouraging the inhabitants of each to regard their town as the finest in Islam. This was not peculiar to Syria, applying to all Muslim towns, but it was particularly marked in Syria and the veneration of Aleppo and Damascus, not to mention Palestine, was widely practised and recognized. The Companions of the Prophet who lived and died in Syria added to the sense of sacredness attaching to it. Patriotic fervour mingled with deep religious feeling to endear Syrian towns to their inhabitants. Historians were the first to reflect these feelings and, once Islam had been established there, they began to recall the *ḥadīths* about Syria and enumerate the tombs of the Companions which were scattered throughout the country. Thus was local history born, encouraged, as has been stated, by religious feelings, a feeling for glory in battle and perhaps by victories over such infidels as the Byzantines (*al-Rūm*).

In this way Arab historians came to describe monuments in Syria, attributing Muslim qualities to them which made them sacred and venerable. Citadels, walls, wells, chasms, roads and even ancient houses all acquired a religious quality which would stave off evil. It is therefore easy to understand why local history, by bringing religious considerations to the fore, should in consequence have become a local history of islamized places. When mosques appeared on the scene they occupied an extremely important place for historians. A clear description of each of them indicated the exact position of its four sides. The teachers in the mosques represent Muslim law, and are presented in the guise of Muslim great men, preachers and guides of the Muslim peoples. It will be seen that in this area local history was concerned with recalling religious feeling and the memory of those men, caliphs and kings, who defended Islam. We shall now consider these local histories century by century.

Arabic sources relate that Muʿāwiya, the first Umayyad caliph, was the first to be concerned with these popular feelings. He called upon Yemenite scholars to recount the past glories of the Arabs. 'Abīd b. Sharya al-Jurhumī, who died in A.H. 70, was among the scholars summoned to Syria to write a general history. His book entitled *Kitāb al-mulūk wa-akhbār al-māḍīn* was to win popularity and repute but is no longer extant. It was the Caliph Mu'āwiya, then, who sowed the first seeds of Arab history-writing in Syria, but this history, as we have seen, was a general history of the Arabs. It was not until the second century that Arab local history came into being.

Local History

Under Yazīd I, the son of Mu'āwiya, scholars kept up the tradition and sought to continue their oral lessons in the Syrian mosques, in order to teach their listeners about the glorious past of the Arabs in Syria. Some works on such historic events as the conquest and the war in Syria were in fact written, but we do not know much about them. Al-Awzā'ī (d. A.H. 157) is said to have written a book on the history of Syria, but we know nothing about it. According to al-Dhahabī (a Damascus historian of the seventh century H.), al-Walīd b. Muslim, an Umayyad himself, wrote several historical works which have not survived. During the same period Persian histories are said to have been translated for the benefit of Caliph Hishām b. 'Abd al-Malik, to show the Persian influence on the beginnings of Arab history in Syria, and serve as a model to Arab historians.

At the end of the first century of Islam, Syrian historians had to leave their country and accompany the court to the new capital at Baghdād. They all left, along with scientists and men of letters, to settle and earn a living there. During the 2nd/8th century not a single historian in Syria is known who was working on the history of his country.

It was not until the 3rd/9th century that Syria again produced historians like Muḥammad b. 'Ā'idh who wrote a work on the conquests in Syria. Abū Mushir b. 'Abd al-A'lā worked on the genealogy of the Syrians. Abū Zur'a of Damascus (d. A.D. 894) wrote a history about the biographies of famous men in Syria, which has proved useful to many historians needing to speak of that country, such as al-Khaṭīb al-Baghdādī, Yāqūt al-Rūmī and al-Dhahabī. A manuscript of his work has been preserved in the Fātiḥ library at Istanbul (No. 4210) relating the lives of the caliphs, *qāḍīs* and scholars of Syria. Aḥmad b. al-Mu'allā (d. A.D. 899) wrote a history of Damascus, which has been largely reproduced by Ibn 'Asākir and Ibn Jubayr. Al-Qushayrī of Ḥarrān wrote the history of the Syrian town of al-Raqqa, the manuscript of which has been preserved. He names the Companions of the Prophet buried there.

In the 4th/10th century a number of Syrian historians devoted themselves to the history of their country. Dionysius the Jacobite Patriarch (or the author of the work attributed to him), Maḥbūb the son of Constantine of Manbij, and the historian and geographer al-Maqdisī provided a rich store of information on the local history of Syria.

It is essential to make clear at this point that the majority of Syrian historians of this era tended to write on the towns of Syria, especially the two big towns of Aleppo and Damascus. They were of course inspired by the love of these charming riverside cities surrounded by gardens, which had once been the home of their forefathers. There was also their important geographical position at the crossroads between Persia, Byzantium and the Mediterranean. Thus, from the ninth century onwards, historians writing on Syrian towns combined history and geography to such a degree that it would be difficult to separate them or distinguish between them. Alongside historical facts on the conquests and wars in Syria, we find descriptions of Syrian monuments and dates relating to them. Sir Hamilton Gibb quite rightly points out: 'From the middle of the fourth century, however, the distinction between general and provincial history becomes difficult to maintain.' For not only did they combine history and geography, they also quoted from annals on all the countries of Islam; but they still offer important information on Syria.

In the 5th/11th century several historians wrote on the cities and districts of Syria works constructed as annals, *ṭabaqāt*, or descriptions of monuments.

In the 6th/12th century Syrian historians made great efforts to tackle the local history of their country. It was of course the century of the Crusades, a century therefore in which the Arab lands played a conspicuous role. Professor Cahen has emphasized the importance of this in his book on the period, where he states: 'Less personal than similar works by Franks, Arabic historiography is generally more copious, this being particularly true of Syria.' He goes on to remark: 'But histories often consists simply of copies of a previous work agumented by minute additions and there is very little ratio between the total Arabic contribution of original material and the total amount of ink put to paper.' Nevertheless, historians of this era were for the most part eyewitnesses of the Crusades and have handed down information and accounts that complete our knowledge of the European invasions.

We shall therefore enlarge somewhat on the authors of this period and their valuable works, which can be divided into three categories: (1) according to regions, (2) according to categories of people, (3) universal histories. Mention will only be made here of the histories according to regions, first Aleppo then Damascus. For, as has already been stated, the authors of these saw in their work the nationalist or patriotic task of praising their country through Islam. To retrace their country's past, they reviewed the centuries of glory when Arabs drove their enemies before them. They were forced to consider, summarize, and collate earlier sources. This work of compilation was in some measure successful, embracing lost documents and sources.

Local Histories of Aleppo

The 11th- and 12th-century chronicles of Aleppo, or rather of North Syria, have been lost and we have scarcely any trace of them today. But they are known through later histories which drew a good deal of their data from them. Here are a few brief indications concerning the chroniclers: Ibn Zurayq al-Tanūkhī al-Ma'arrī, born at Ma'arra in 442/1051, wrote a chronicle of the Turkish conquest and Frankish invasion. His work is lost but is reproduced in several places by Ibn al-'Adīm and others. Ibn Abī Jarāda was the author of a book on the sovereigns of Aleppo, passages from which are to be found in later works. Al-Atāribī of Aleppo wrote a treatise on the history of the Frankish conquest, some pages of which are quoted by Ibn al-'Adīm. He is especially interesting because he lived close to the Norman lord of the region of Atārib. He died in 542/1147. Al-'Aẓīmī, a schoolmaster born in Aleppo in 483/1090, undertook a history of Aleppo and a world history. Only the second is extant, and contains valuable information at the end.

It is worth considering Kamāl al-Dīn b. al-'Adīm a little more closely, for he is the most important of the historians of his region, and more particularly of his birthplace, on which he wrote a voluminous local history. Of a great family of Iraqi origin, his grandfather settled in Baṣra, where he became the first member of an aristocratic family. One of Ibn al-'Adīm's ancestors had come and settled in Syria in 200/815 to escape the plague which had struck Iraq. His rich descendants had been able to buy a village not far from Aleppo; later they lived in Aleppo itself where a number of them became writers, *qāḍīs*, poets, and courtiers in the service of the Mirdasid and subsequently Nurid and Ayyubid dynasties. They were famous at the time. The historian's father was a grand *qāḍī* under Nūr al-Dīn, 'Izz al-Dīn, 'Imād al-Dīn, and Saladin. His son 'Umar was born in Aleppo in 588/1192 and had a thorough education. From his earliest childhood he travelled in the Arab countries, Jerusalem, Damascus, Iraq, and Ḥijāz, whence came his taste for travel and history. When he was twenty-eight he joined the galaxy of great teachers in the schools of Aleppo. Later he entered the service of the Ayyubids al-Malik al-'Azīz and al-Malik al-Nāṣir as a minister (*wazīr*). In that capacity he was able to make a number of official journeys to Egypt and Iraq as his sovereign's ambassador, and was able to meet the great scholars of the day. Contemporary historians quote his journeys and praise him highly. These missions obviously influenced the author by giving him the opportunity of seeing the Muslim world for himself such as he was subsequently to describe it. When the Mongols attacked Syria in 658/1260 and sacked his home town, he fled with al-Malik al-Nāṣir to Barza near Damascus. Hūlāgū recalled him to Syria, and offered him the post of grand *qāḍī*, but he preferred to make for Gaza and thence Egypt. He did not stay long in Egypt, returning home as soon as the invaders left. When he saw his town destroyed he went back to Cairo, died there in 660/1262 and was buried at the foot of al-Muqaṭṭam.

Historical sources speak of Ibn al-ʿAdīm as a great poet and writer, emphasizing his wide knowledge in all branches of historical and legal matters. What concerns us here is his historical work on Aleppo. He composed a vast history of his birthplace, first of all in the form of a biographical dictionary entitled *Bug͟hyat al-ṭalab fī taʾrīk͟h Ḥalab*. He conceived it along the broadest lines: an account of all the famous men of Aleppo, all those who were born there and all those who had been there, even for a few hours. It is only natural that such an ambitious work should run into several tens of volumes. It could be that the structure of the dictionary was based on al-K͟hatīb's history of Bag͟hdād or Ibn ʿAsākir's history of Damascus. Ibn al-ʿAdīm's dictionary begins with the historical topography of Aleppo and its surroundings, thus of the whole of North Syria. Then come the biographies in alphabetical order and of differing length, according to the sources he had at his disposal. His sources are for the most part no longer accessible to us, since he used manuscripts and documents which have since been lost. Besides words reported directly from the lips of famous men, whom he knew because of his high office and his important contacts in the places he visited, he was able to read inscriptions on monuments and refer to coins. He hardly ever quotes a report, a discovery or a source without specifying the time and the library or the lips which vouchsafed them. He often repeats: 'I have heard', 'seen', 'read', 'having been present', as would a historian of our own time. For centuries his dictionary remained a historical document on Aleppo of the utmost value. Historians quoted it as a primary authority, and boasted of having read it.

Unfortunately we have not all its volumes complete. One single historian in the 10th/16th century, al-Sak͟hāwī (d. A.H. 902), has described the number of volumes which he personally had seen. In his *Iʿlām* he records that he saw an autograph copy in nine volumes at the home of his friend Ibn al-Sābiq al-Ḥamawī. That same copy is extant today, just as it was described by al-Sak͟hāwī, in the Istanbul libraries. Several European scholars have consulted it there, including our erstwhile colleague Jean Sauvaget, Professor Claude Cahen and Professor Bernard Lewis, to quote but the most recent. For my own part, in order to study this inexhaustible mine of information, I was able while in Istanbul to photograph it in its entirety. It runs into ten volumes, each of 300 pages. It stops at the letter *zayn* but this copy is the author's draft, containing empty spaces in a number of places. The author was waiting for the right moment to fill them in or complete them. But that time never came.

As from the 7th/13th-century historians of Aleppo undertook sequels to this dictionary. One should mention the following: Ibn S̲h̲addād (d. A.H. 684) in his book *al-A'lāq* speaks of the monuments of Aleppo and the facts they recorded. Ibn K̲h̲atīb al-Nāṣiriyya (d. 843/1439), wrote his work entitled *al-Durr al-muntak̲h̲ab* on the famous men of Aleppo, bringing their biographies up to date. Sibṭ Ibn al-'Ajamī (d. A.H. 884), follows Ibn al-'Adīm in his work *Kunūz al-D̲h̲ahab* and brings him up to date. Ibn al-S̲h̲iḥna (d. 890/1485), summarized previous works, and contributed indispensable material for the history of Aleppo. A considerable part of his work, as also of the previous one, was translated by Jean Sauvaget (publications of the French Institute in Damascus). Ibn al-Ḥanbalī (d. A.H. 971) also brought biographies up to date. Ibn Mīro and certain more modern writers like Ṭabbāk̲h̲ and al-G̲h̲azzī undertook to continue and complete the biographies.

Ibn al-'Adīm himself used his dictionary to write a chronicle of Aleppo called *Zubdat al-Ḥalab*, which is a chronological presentation of material gathered for the dictionary. The chronicle ends in the year 641/1243, when Ibn al-'Adīm was in the middle of diplomatic missions and no longer had the time to work at it. It has the great virtue of bringing all sources together, recording various opinions on historical events and placing them before us in chronological order or according to political states. This work is an intelligent historical exposition of the politics and wars of the Arab states reigning in North Syria, written in a clear, precise style. It contains such information in such detail as is rarely found elsewhere. Important states like that of the Mirdasids in Aleppo are treated fully in this work.

I was able to edit two-thirds of this work in two volumes at Damascus. The third part records facts of which the author was an eyewitness. He is the supreme historian of the Crusades, for in treating them he rises to the peak of historical science, by reason of his impartiality and rich documentation. He gives a true story of this important period when friction and contact left traces that are still with us today.

Local Histories of Damascus

The town of Damascus also attracted the attention of a number of historians, who wrote local histories of considerable importance on the subject. They began by composing works in praise of the holy town for, as was stated earlier, it was the Paradise of the Faithful and was to be the refuge of Christians after Christ's Second Coming.

The following works on the religious significance of Damascus may be added to those mentioned earlier: al-Rabaʿī (d. 444/1052), wrote a work on the religious qualities of the town and its superiority over others. Abu'l-Fatḥ al-Kātib (d. 400/1067), deals with the same subject, adding poetic and literary matter which emphasizes the picturesque quality of the town and the charm of its beauty spots. Al-Armanāzī (d. 509/1115), a native of Armanāz near Aleppo, wrote a history of Damascus and another of Tyre. His works have been lost, but reproduced by Yāqūt. Al-Khawlānī, *qāḍī* of Damascus (d. 365/975), composed a history of Dārayya, a village near Damascus, listing the Companions of the Prophet who lived and were buried there. Al-Akfānī of Damascus (d. 542/1130), wrote a sequel to al-Khawlānī's history of Dārayya.

Ibn al-Qalānisī of Damascus (d. 551/1180), wrote a history covering the years 444–555 H. Arranged in annals it gives historical facts which occurred under the Fatimids and Seljuqs. It gives a clear and precise picture of life in Damascus, its society, its wars with Egypt, its revolutions and *coups d'état*. It was edited in 1908 by H. F. Amedroz after the Oxford manuscript, and in part translated into English by H. A. R. Gibb (London, 1932). A part of it has since been translated into French by R. Le Tourneau (Damascus, 1952). It is the only extant detailed chronicle on the period from the Turkish invasion to Saladin. It follows the same pattern as Ibn al-Athīr's history, but the author gives it a personal note by referring to archives he had consulted. He was born about 465/1073, the son of a great Damascus family, and after studies in theology and literature followed an administrative career and became head of the chancery.

Ibn ʿAsākir (ʿAlī b. al-Ḥusayn Abu'l-Qāsim), born at Damascus in 499/1105, studied widely throughout the Muslim world, in Baghdād and Persia, then became a teacher in the town of his birth at the Nūriyya *madrasa* and died at Damascus in 571/1175. His main work is the history of Damascus in eighty volumes. He opens with the topography of the town and continues with a kind of dictionary of famous men of Damascus. It is conceived along the same lines as the work of the historian al-Khaṭīb al-Baghdādī. Abū Shāma (d. 665/1266) made a summary of it in fifteen volumes which have been lost. This colossal work is the best source book on the history of Damascus from the earliest times, supplying copious details on its intellectual, commercial and historical life. It gives the development of the town and biographies of famous men from all over Syria, for it includes visitors to Damascus: kings, princes, and scholars in all branches of learning known at that time. Only a few volumes of this great local history of Damascus have been published. Ibn ʿAsākir's son, al-Qāsim b. ʿAsākir (d. 600/1203), wrote a sequel to his father's work which is now for the most part lost.

Al-Maqdisī (al-Ḍiyā' Muḥammad), a Ḥanbalī (d. 643/1245), composed a history of Damascus mentioning the town's religious qualities. Of this, only the second volume is extant in the Ẓāhiriyya of Damascus. Another al-Maqdisī (Ibn 'Abd al-Dā'im), a great Damascus scholar (d. 668/1269), selected certain chapters of Ibn 'Asākir's history of Damascus which have been preserved to this day. Al-Irbilī (Al-Ḥasan b. Aḥmad b. Zufar) (d. 726/1326) originally from Irbil in Iraq, settled in Damascus and composed a history of it containing descriptions of schools, mosques and baths. A part of this work still exists in the Ẓāhiriyya of Damascus. Ibn Shākir al-Kutubī (Muḥammad) (d. 764/1336), wrote an historical introduction to the town of Damascus. Ibn Kathīr al-Qurashī (Ismā'īl), born at Baṣra near Damascus, studied in Damascus and died in 774/1333. His work *al-Bidāya wa'l-nihāya* contains extremely useful information on the city. Ibn Rajab al-Dimashqī ('Abd al-Raḥmān), a Ḥanbalī scholar (d. 795/1392), wrote on the religious qualities of Damascus. Ibn Ḥajjī (Aḥmad), born in the neighbourhood of Damascus, completed advanced studies in jurisprudence, became *qāḍī* of Damascus and died 816/1413. His work on the Damascus schools is known to us through later writers. He dealt with the teachers and founders of the *waqfs* of these schools. Ibn 'Abd al-Hādī (Yūsuf), a Ḥanbalī scholar (died in Damascus 909/1503), wrote several works on Damascus, its mosques, *khāns*, baths, and *sūqs*, as also on the topographical history of al-Ṣāliḥiyya, an important suburb of Damascus. His works of varying lengths are all extremely important for the history of the town. Al-Nu'aymī ('Abd al-Qādir), a Shāfi'ī scholar and historian of Damascus, died in the town of his birth, 927/1521. He wrote a voluminous work on the Damascus schools, giving biographies of all the famous men who taught there. It also deals with the mosques, convents, and a large part of the town's topography. There are several works from his pen on the *qāḍīs* and famous men of the Syrian capital. Ibn Ṭūlūn (Muḥammad b. 'Alī) was born in al-Ṣāliḥiyya, Damascus, and died in Damascus 953/1546. A great historian of his town, he contributed several works on Damascus and its environs such as al-Mizza, al-Ghūṭa, the citadel of Damascus and al-Ṣāliḥiyya, as well as on the famous men from these parts.

Local Histories of the Jazīra

The Jazīra was part of the Syrian theatre where the wars between Muslims and Franks were fought over a very long period. As has already been stated, it was North Syria that played an important part during the Crusades, whilst Southern Syria, apart from Palestine, was devastated by the wars against the Egyptians, and often subjected to their rule.

There were not many historians of the Jazīra and those known to us through sources are very few. Ibn al-Azraq (Aḥmad b. Yūsuf al-Fāriqī), a member of the great Mayyāfāriqīn family, was born 510/1116, engaged as a young man in commerce and was sent on missions on behalf of his

Ortoqid prince, Timurtash. He was later administrator of the *waqfs* for the province, then for Mayyāfāriqīn. He travelled several times through the Jazīra, Iraq, and Georgia, and in Syria. He died in 572/1176. He composed an extremely interesting chronicle on his birthplace, based on contemporary archives and oral accounts he had heard personally. It contains the local history of Diyār Bakr and Mayyāfāriqīn with accounts and facts that are of primary importance concerning Syria and Mesopotamia at that time.

Ibn Shaddād (Muḥammad b. Ibrāhīm), born at Aleppo in 613/1216, studied there and devoted himself to history and correspondence. His scholarship and knowledge brought him into contact with the princes of his time. He acted as ambassador on various diplomatic missions, to Ḥarrān when he was twenty-seven, and to Hūlāgū in 656/1258. He accompanied the rulers on their travels. When the Mongol invasion was about to swamp Aleppo he went to Cairo, where he remained the object of respect and consideration until his death in 684/1285. His importance in the present context lies in his account of the Jazīra, the best ancient Arabic source on the region.

Thus were local histories in Syria created and developed over the centuries, until European scholarship was assimilated into our methods and systems of history-writing.

Conclusion

The object of this rapid and incomplete survey of some of the local histories on Syria, restricted here to Damascus, Aleppo, and the Jazīra, was to present the best material for a detailed study of the subject. This material is of vast interest and considerable value.

No overall study of the majority of these sources has been undertaken. The greater part of these local histories remain unexplored, and are still waiting for a determined and patient editor to produce critical editions of them, because they will serve as a starting point for thorough studies of these regions, and help in drawing up historical and geographic maps of all the areas indicated, century by century. We agree that this task will be arduous but one day it will have to be undertaken, if we are to trace the development of Syrian towns over the centuries, as did the late Jean Sauvaget for Aleppo in his doctoral thesis *Alep, Essai sur le développment d'une grande ville syrienne, des origines au milieu du XIXe siècle* (Paris, 1941).

The towns of Syria deserve special attention because of their links with the West, particularly during the Crusades. We should complete our knowledge of these wars on Syrian soil by reference to local Arab sources, which as yet have not been fully used or drawn on. Professor Claude Cahen has set a good example of such a study in his book on North Syria at the time of the Crusades. Professor Marius Canard has provided a model for scholars in his work on the history of the Hamdanid dynasty in the Jazīra and Syria, drawing on literary, political, and historical material. Both of these scholars used a great number of local Syrian historical sources, but they concentrated their research within a fixed period.

It still remains to continue research and study by collating sources and documents on all Arab periods, in order to form some overall judgement about the towns of Syria over the centuries. No less than the documents, the towns themselves deserve our attention, for many of their monuments are still with us and can complement written sources on the areas we have mentioned.

It has no doubt been apparent that this rapid survey deals not with histories but historians; it gives an outline of their lives, not the number of pages or summaries of the contents of their books. It would take whole pages to consider a single work in this way and our object was not to deal exclusively with one work. Finally, it should be pointed out that these historians were amateurs, not professionals. They make no revelation of their religious or political leanings, only the quality of their minds and scholarship; whence their value and importance. Let there be no doubt that the Arab historians of Syria made their contribution to the glorious history of their country and fulfilled the learned and sacred task that falls to the great historians of the world. They are therefore worthy of the attention of great European scholars and may expect vast studies and critical editions in the near future as a recompense for their own efforts, which were far from being unfruitful.

9. THE ORIGIN AND DEVELOPMENT OF HISTORIOGRAPHY IN MUSLIM SPAIN

CHARLES PELLAT

Professor of Arab Language and Civilization in the University of Paris

From an overall examination of the vast historical achievement of the Arabs, it is possible to say that after an initial period of trial and error it reached its first peak with al-Ṭabarī, whose monumental work was to serve as a basis for histories conventionally and incorrectly called universal; later historians who were to reach other peaks took all al-Ṭabarī's data, which they summarized, completed on particular points and continued up to their own time; or else simply wrote histories limited in time (dynastic history, for example), in space (history of a town or district), according to subject matter (political and military history, literary and scientific history or the history of important people), or using various methods of exposition (chronological or alphabetical order). It would not be difficult to set out in terms of these categories a general framework, in which the appropriate works of historians on each region of the Muslim world and each broad section of history could be placed, thus making it possible to grasp immediately and systematically the main characteristics and dominant tendencies of local historiography, bearing in mind that on the whole the conception and execution of historical works in Arabic are extremely homogeneous, offering only the slightest differences.

This paper does not attempt to reproduce the kind of picture of Arab historiography in Spain drawn up according to the method indicated above; nevertheless for the sake of clarity a preliminary outline is given, based largely on the *Ensayo bio-bibliográfico* of Pons Boygues, which despite its age is extremely useful and still remains the starting point of research into Andalusian historiography.

Dealing with a region of the Muslim world which was conquered a century after the emergence of Islam and lay at a distance, moreover, from the great centres of intellectual activity, one cannot expect to find in Spain a vivid reflection of the questions which preoccupied the earliest Eastern scholars; nevertheless, in spite of the distance, numerous and frequent travels enabled the Andalusains to keep up to date with the results of Eastern activity and to bring back to their own country the fruit of the lessons they had learned. Their store of information, however, remained fragmentary, new doctrines and literary models only reaching Spain and having any influence there after some considerable delay; not until rather later did the Andalusians add a personal and local note to what they had brought from the East. These general considerations seem broadly to apply to historiography.

The earliest Andalusian 'historian' we can trace was a famous *faqīh*, 'Abd al-Malik b. Ḥabīb (d. 238/852), who after a visit to the East became the propagator of Mālikī doctrines in Spain; if there is nothing astonishing in his having written a biography of the Prophet and a history of Quraysh, it is rather more curious that he should have given us a part at least of a world history dealing with events from the creation of the world to the Umayyads, which, particularly in the parts on the conquest of Spain, is a tissue of fables. It seems therefore that at the beginning of the 3rd/9th century, conditions favouring the birth of true historiography were not yet in existence. In fact it was probably with the Rāzīs, Aḥmad b. Muḥammad b. Mūsā (d. 344/955) and his son 'Īsā b. Aḥmad, that the first historical works worthy of the name appeared; the latter of these two points out, in a passage quoted in Ibn Ḥayyān's *Muqtabis*, that history 'was not a branch of learning cultivated by the Andalusians. [His father Aḥmad] collected data from old people and transmitters of reports, which he collated and organized into a history. He was thus the first to codify the rules of historical composition in Spain. His work brought him closer to the sovereign and earned himself and his son a greater measure of royal favour. Together they endowed the Andalusians with a science they had not hitherto practised with success.'[1] 'Īsā b. Aḥmad, who gives us such valuable information on the beginnings of historiography, was himself official historiographer to al-Ḥakam II (350–66/961–76) and E. Lévi-Provençal considers the annalistic form of the 3rd–4th/9th–10th centuries, such as it appears from Ibn Ḥayyān, as 'court historiography, centred on the person of the sovereign, essentially subjective, deliberately leaving out anything that might undermine the prestige of the dynasty'.[2]

Official, then, and centred on the Umayyad dynasty to begin with (although chronicles more limited in time and space were written during the same period, as Ibn Ḥazm makes clear in his famous *Risāla*),[3] Arab historiography in Spain broadened out and acquired greater independence as from the 5th/11th century but, as might have been expected in such a highly individual region of the Muslim world, it retained its local character, being above all a history of Muslim Spain.

That does not mean that no Andalusian scholar showed any interest in the East or other regions of the Islamic Empire. Not counting a number of

[1] E. Lévi-Provençal, *Histoire de l'Espagne musulmane*, iii, 504. [2] Ibid., iii, 505.

[3] Translated by Ch. Pellat in *al-Andalus* (1954/1); these chronicles, now lost, deal chiefly with rebels against Umayyad authority; as they are quoted straight after Aḥmad al-Rāzī's, Brockel, mann wrongly attributes them (S I 231) to that author.

works by Andalusians who had temporarily or permanently left the homeland (such as the history of Ifrīqiya by Muḥammad b. Yūsuf al-Warrāq (d. 362/973)), we find in Spain itself works clearly belonging to the tradition of Eastern historiography: several biographies of the Prophet of which the most important is probably the one by the famous Abū ʿUmar b. ʿAbd al-Barr (d. 463/1070), another of whose biographical works, the *Kitāb al-īstīʿāb fī maʿrifat al-Aṣḥāb*, was considered by Ibn Ḥazm in spite of the meagre accounts it gives, as superior to any other compilation of the same order; information on ancient Arabia is included in such *adab* works as the *ʿIqd* of Ibn ʿAbd Rabbih (d. 328/940) and in universal histories. Ibn Saʿīd (d. 673/1274) even devoted a volume to the subject. The history of various Muslim countries in the East is the subject of some ten works mainly by Ibn Saʿīd, Ibn Ḥayyān (d. 469/1076) and Lisān al-Dīn Ibn al-Khaṭīb (d. 776/1374). Major works on genealogy could not of course overlook the East: Ibn Ḥazm contributed a *Jamhara* of exceptional importance in this field.

All these works were of course compilations, whose sole value lies in the bulk of secondhand information they give and their skill of presentation. They are moreover closely rivalled by Eastern books, which could have satisfied the curiosity of many Andalusians, not greatly inclined to take an interest in anything not directly concerning them. The same observation applies to universal history, which was closely dependent on al-Ṭabarī. ʿArīb b. Saʿd (d. 370/980), later imitated by other writers, summarized it and continued it up to his own time, reserving the fullest treatment for Spain; this pattern was probably followed in some half-dozen books, including the one by Muḥammad b. Aḥmad al-Shāṭibī (d. 850/1446) who, no doubt foreseeing the approaching end of Arab domination in Spain, completed a kind of 'historical stocktaking'. But within this context the work of Ṣāʿid of Toledo (d. 462/1069) deserves special emphasis; his *Jawāmiʿ akhbār al-umam min al-ʿArab waʾl-ʿAjam* is now lost, but his *Ṭabaqāt al-umam* constitutes a compendium of universal history, where nations are grouped in two categories according to whether or not they cultivated the sciences. The first category includes the Indians, Persians, Chaldeans, Greeks, *Rūm*, Egyptians, Arabs, and Jews; each of these forms the subject of a chapter, setting forth the state of Arab knowledge of these peoples in the 5th/11th century.

We do of course find a good number of compilations in the rich production of historical writing on al-Andalus, but it is in these that we have our best chance of discovering original features; a definite conclusion is, however, not possible since we are often faced with titles which are equally likely to fall short of their promise or to disguise interesting innovations. Within the framework of the history of al-Andalus, it is best therefore to try to distinguish categories broad enough to limit the margin of error arising from the loss of the majority of texts.

(1) *General Chronicle of al-Andalus.* Apart from the writers of universal histories, about ten authors have dealt with this. After the Rāzīs, Ibn al-Qūṭiyya (d. 367/977) wrote a *Ta'rīkh fatḥ al-Andalus* going from the conquest to the reign of 'Abd al-Raḥmān III; although it could not really be called an official history, Ibn al-Qūṭiyya's work suffers from the necessity of not displeasing the Umayyads. In the following century, this obstacle to the historian's freedom was removed with the fall of the Umayyads, and authors adopted a more critical attitude to the past, tending towards greater truthfulness and less dissimulation. Ibn Mufarrij al-Ma'āfirī al-Qubbashī (d. after 430/1039) wrote a history of al-Andalus of which the *Crónica anónima de 'Abd al-Raḥmān III al-Nāṣir*[4] could well be a fragment. The leading historian and the most prolific one of this period was Ibn Ḥayyān (d. 469/1076); the sixty volumes of his *Matīn* are lost but a part of his *Muqtabis* has been preserved. E. Lévi-Provençal attached the greatest importance to this chronicle, considering Ibn Ḥayyān an able historian; his *Muqtabis*, where he records, according to a strict plan, the names of important persons and details of the events of the reign, is characterized by greater historical veracity. After him come a number of names of lesser importance, until we reach Lisān al-Dīn Ibn al-Khaṭīb (d. 776/1374) who, by the fullness of the information he gives and his astonishing output, dominates the whole of Andalusian historiography and literature during the latter part of Arab domination.

(2) *Dynastic History.* The historic destiny of Muslim Spain, first subjected to the Umayyads then split up into a host of principalities, which neither the Almoravids nor the Almohads were able permanently to reunite, was bound to give rise to a flowering of dynastic history, which often merges into the history of the capital cities. The majority of the chronicles quoted so far, although constructed within a broader framework, were centred on the Umayyads and can be considered as belonging to dynastic history; we may also include the works of Mu'āwiya b. Hishām (4th/10th century), which Ibn Ḥayyān used and those of Ibn Ḥazm (d. 456/1063). Already the 'Amirids had inspired three chronicles (one by Ibn Ḥayyān) and under the *Mulūk al-ṭawā'if* régimes each dynast was anxious to have the deeds of his family recorded. We have barely any trace of the whole of this writing, however, except through later compilations (the *Memoirs* of 'Abd Allāh will be mentioned later). As for the following period, J. Bosch Vilá in his history of the Almoravids was only able to draw on a few extracts from Ibn al-Ṣayrafī (d. 570/1174), the Andalusian chronicler of the dynasty; similarly, A. Huici Miranda, when writing the history of the

[4] Translation and edition by E. Lévi-Provençal and E. García Gómez (Madrid–Granada, 1950).

Almohads, only found at his disposal one volume of *al-Mann bi'l-imāma* by Ibn Ṣāḥib al-Ṣalāt, the Andalusian historian of the Moroccan dynasty; all their other sources are Maghribī, as are the most detailed works we still have on the Umayyads and other periods of Andalusian history ('Abd al-Wāḥid al-Marrākushī, Ibn 'Idhārī, Ibn Khaldūn, al-Maqqarī, etc.).[5] On the other hand, we are better informed on the kingdom of Granada, the strong personality of Lisān al-Dīn Ibn al-Khaṭīb having no doubt contributed to the partial preservation of his historical work.

The loss of numerous texts on the history of particular towns—Badajoz by al-A'lam al-Baṭalyawsī (d. 646/1248), Malaga by Ibn 'Askar (d. 636/1238), Almeria by Ibn al-Ḥājj (d. 774/1372), and Ibn Khātima (d. 770/1369), Seville by Ibn al-Shāt (d. 723/1323), etc.—deprives us of any standard of assessment, leaving us unable to determine the method used by their authors, but it is very probable that they were collections of biographies of important people in the towns in question; they can therefore, for the most part, be included definitely in the immediately following category.

(3) *Biographical Writings.* To write a general or dynastic chronicle, even in the form of annals, it is necessary to have a certain historic sense and that synthesizing approach which is known often to be lacking in the Arabs, whose punctilious love of detail finds free scope in a genre which only entails classifying, in chronological or even simply alphabetical order, entries following a standard pattern and supplied with information taken from earlier works or collected personally. This biographical form, widely cultivated in all parts of the Muslim world, was particularly fashionable in Spain where several such collections have by a happy chance been discovered and published.

Although in biographical writing history is only seen through the persons who made it, the sequence of time was broadly respected once the chronological method of classes or *ṭabaqāt* was adopted; that was the case in Spain with the classes of scholars (al-Khushanī, d. 360/970, Ibn al-Dabbāgh, d. 546/1151), grammarians (al-Zubaydī, d. 379/989, Ibn Khazraj, d. 478/1085), *qurrā'* (Abū 'Amr al-Dānī, d. 444/1052), poets ('Uthmān b. Rabī'a, d. 310/922), *kuttāb* (Aqushtīn, d. 307/919, Sakan b. Sa'īd, d. 457/1066), physicians (Ibn Juljul, d. after 384/994; and also classes of physicians of antiquity and the East), etc. Judging solely from the titles of works, it seems that this form of biographical collection was soon abandoned in favour of alphabetical classification; the same applies, if I am not mistaken, to the biographical chronicle, which respects the sequence of time and of which a typical Spanish example is the history of the *qāḍīs* by al-Khushanī.

[5] Throughout this paper only historical works by Andalusians have been considered. One should be careful, however, not to dissociate them too sharply from the rest of Maghribī historiography, nor to forget that the history of Muslim Spain was not written in the peninsula only.

The alphabetical method, easier to apply, separated biographical writing somewhat from history in the proper sense; it was, however, as widely used in Spain as in the East. What is most striking, when examining this genre in al-Andalus, is the great continuity in the biographers who, while putting into their dictionaries people of every kind, both Andalusians and foreigners (provided they came to Spain), continued, corrected and completed each other. For instance the *Jadwat al-muqtabis* which al-Ḥumaydī (d. 488/1095) composed in Baghdād from inadequate material, was carried on by al-Ḍabbī (d. 599/1202); a still better example: the *Ta'rīkh 'ulamā' al-Andalus* by Ibn al-Faraḍī (d. 403/1013), who, notwithstanding his predecessors, may be considered the creator of the genre, gave rise to a *Kitāb al-ṣila* by Ibn Bashkuwāl (d. 578/1182), which was completed by two or three contemporary writers, particularly Ibn al-Abbār (d. 658/1260) in a *Takmila li-kitāb al-ṣila* (which contains a catalogue of his numerous sources), then Ibn al-Zubayr (d. 708/1308) in his *Ṣilat al-ṣila*, which was in turn continued by Ibn al-Khaṭīb.

Besides these general collections, one should not overlook a host of biographical works, sometimes dealing with the scholars or important people in a given town—Ibn 'Abd al-Barr (d. 338/949) on Cordova, Qāsim b. Sa'dān (d. 347/958) on Reyyo, Abū Isḥāq al-Bājī (d. 350/961) on Beja, Ibn al-Khaṭīb on Granada, etc.; at other times dealing with groups of individuals belonging to the same profession. This second category has already been mentioned in connection with collections divided into *ṭabaqāt*, and the lack of sufficient data on this type of writing makes it impossible to enumerate other works, for we do not know the method of presentation used. We can simply note that there are few hagiographic collections; as far as I am aware, only two have been found whose authors were Ibn al-Ṭaylasān (d. 642/1244) and Ibn al-Ḥājj (d. 774/1372). As a curiosity we may also mention the biographies of famous women by Sulaymān b. Najāḥ (d. 496/1001). Several monographs on isolated individuals could also be added, but for the present we shall only draw attention to the Memoirs of King 'Abd Allāh b. Buluggīn al-Zīrī (d. *c.* 483/1090) which are interesting not only for their historical value but also because they represent a genre rarely cultivated in Arabic literature.

Another genre of a rather special character and one that was to be equally fashionable in Morocco was that of the *fahrasa* (or *barnāmaj*),[6] a list of teachers and of works studied under their supervision, which most scholars set their heart on leaving to posterity; these catalogues supplied material on which biographers drew heavily, and it is through their use that the monotonous enumeration of the subject's teachers found their way into individual biographies. The earliest *fahrasas* go back to the 5th/

[6] On this class of writings, see 'Abd al-'Azīz al-Ahwānī in *Revue de l'Institut des manuscrits arabes* (1955), I/1, 91–120.

11th century and it is probable that earlier ones existed, but the most important of those that have been preserved is the one by Ibn Khayr al-Ishbīlī (d. 575/1179), giving in particular a detailed catalogue of works known in Spain in his time.

(4) *Verse Chronicles.* Another feature of Andalusian historiography is the abundance of verse chronicles or historical *arājīz*; in a good many cases we seem to be dealing not with didactic or mnemotechnic poems, but on the contrary with original compositions, nearer to the historical poem than to the epic. Ten or so poets practised this form, from Ghazāl (d. 250/864) down to Ibn al-Khaṭīb (d. 776/1374) and including Ibn ʿAbd Rabbih (d. 328/940), Ibn Zaydūn (d. 463/1070), Ibn ʿAbdūn (d. 529/1134) and others of less importance.

Arab historiography in Spain, as can be seen from this brief survey, and above all from Pons Boygues' catalogue of over three hundred authors of widely differing quality, was copious, rich, and varied. All genres favoured by the Arabs have their place in it for various reasons, but what above all and quite rightly interests historians is the history of al-Andalus; it is presented in general or dynastic chronicles, or else in these biographical collections which, for many scholars, constitute History.[7]

Until the 4th/10th century Spain, still culturally dependent on the East, produced no original work; if it may be assumed that historical traditions relating particularly to the conquest were recorded quite early and were drawn on by later historians, we must, nevertheless, await the discovery of works at present inaccessible to assess the range of that activity. Without breaking the links joining them to the East, about the time of the inauguration of the Umayyad caliphate (316/929) the Andalusians gradually became conscious of their individuality and, with their natural pride making itself felt, of their superiority; that feeling emerged in the 'defence and glorification' of Muslim Spain presented objectively by Ibn Ḥazm and more subjectively by al-Shaqundī (d. 629/1231) in his famous *Risāla*. There is therefore nothing surprising in the Andalusians, anxious to leave a written record of their country's history and encouraged in that direction by the great masters of the day, starting enthusiastically to gather together and make use of all possible material, once the Rāzīs had set the example.

Although I have undertaken no special research into the social background and intellectual formation of historians, it is possible to state that they all had a fundamentally Islamic culture; many biographers were *fuqahā'* or *qāḍīs*, whilst the chroniclers seemed generally more disposed towards a broader literary culture. A number of them, amongst the earliest at least, were official historiographers and if their successors enjoyed greater freedom and in some cases, when away from Spain, wrote the history of a

[7] Cf. E. Lévi-Provençal, *Chorfa*, p. 45: *ajall min al-ta'rīkh tarājimu'l-kibār.*

dynasty which had not treated them according to their deserts, nevertheless the person or family of the reigning prince remained the favourite subject of many chroniclers—not, however, that they were incapable of being fairly objective, or were willing to remain silent about court intrigues and minor scandals.

Techniques of composition show some degree of uniformity; in certain chronicles facts are classified by reign, but the annalistic form was used very frequently, events then being recorded year by year and month by month. In biographies the author states the date of his subject's birth and death, a list of his teachers, the journeys he made 'in search of knowledge', the works he wrote and the offices he occupied: poems and anecdotes are often quoted.

If a good many historical works are reliable and some authors show evidence of critical ability, the cause of historical events is rarely sought after, and historical sense is often lacking in these writers, whose works offer only a documentary interest. Once established, the tradition was maintained and respected punctiliously (as we have seen from the biographers) no one ever dreaming of departing from it: Spain was the central preoccupation, but only Muslim Spain[8] was the object of scholars' researches, the Muslim element alone having the right to be considered as part of history, and then only if it belonged to the military or intellectual aristocracy. The rest of the population did not count and the only Christians to earn a mention were those encountered on the field of battle.[9] Not before Ibn Ḥazm came on the scene are we reminded of the presence of Christians and Jews on Spanish soil under Muslim domination, and then in a general history of religious ideas which was to remain an isolated incident in Arabic literature.

[8] The 'pre-Islamic' period of Spanish history is dealt with, but briefly and in a traditional manner without, it appears, giving rise to any original studies.

[9] Interest in Christendom seems to have been more marked amongst geographers than amongst historians proper.

10. THE EVOLUTION OF PERSIAN HISTORIOGRAPHY

BERTOLD SPULER

Professor of Islamic Studies in the University of Hamburg

The following remarks on the evolution of Persian historiography ought not to be considered as a history but rather as an outline of some ideas based on the supposition that the names of the authors and the main facts are known.

It is a well-known fact to all specialists in Persian historiography that hardly any work written in Persian exists which deals with the history of Persia until the beginning of the Mongol period (thirteenth century). Works on the first centuries of islamized Persia, i.e. the period between about 642 and 1255, must be based on sources in foreign languages, in the first place Arabic.

When we try to explain this fact, in my opinion, some factors are to be considered. First: historiography seems to have been of no great importance to pre-Islamic Iranians. We know of no real historical work of this period. The well-known inscriptions of Behistūn (*Bīsutūn*) and other places of Iran relate the deeds of the various kings in a kind of public reports; we may suppose that the official record books mentioned in the Book of Daniel were of a similar nature and, in addition, contained simple lists of facts and dates, together with copies of official notices and letters in order to help state functionaries in their office work.

In later periods, especially during the reign of the Sasanids (third to seventh centuries), legends originated covering the whole of the known Persian history, but omitting most important events and presenting historical events as actions of a few principal figures, heroes and their wives, representing the mythical self-appreciation of the leading classes of this people. These legends present just as little actual history as, for instance, the *Nibelungenlied* and the *Chanson de Roland*. Thus, we must state that apparently no real historiography existed in pre-Islamic Persia. This statement is substantiated by the fact that neither among the writings of the post-Islamic Zoroastrian communities in Persia, nor among the Parsees in India (i.e. the Zoroastrian refugees of 717), does a real historical work, either of pre-Islamic or of later origin, exist.

Therefore, we must assume that there was no prototype of Persian historiography when the Arabs conquered the Iranian highlands. On the other hand, the Arabs had a kind of historical tradition even before the beginning of Islam, the so-called *Ayyām al-ʿArab* or 'Battle-days of the

Arabs', which described in real detail campaigns between two or more tribes and the heroic deeds of their leaders. To be sure, this kind of historiography also was to a very high degree mythological, like that in the Iranian books of the kings; but their proximity to life, their interest in the feeling of the masses and their sense of real and possible detail (without legendary exaggeration) made them suitable as the nucleus for real historical reports.

More important appears to me the fact that Islam as a religion was based not only on a holy book, but also on the utterances and the deeds of the Prophet. Forming a highly important normative rule in the life of the Muslims, these utterances and deeds had to be gathered and critically examined. It is a well-known fact that from this examination originated the *ḥadīth*-science with its auxiliary sciences: *Sīra*, *Ṭabaqāt*, and eventually general historiography in the sense of a description of the deeds of God with his selected people; general history as the history of the salvation of God's holy community: the Muslims.

We need not enter into details of this evolution. We must only underline that there was an historiographical prototype in the Arabic language but none in Persian. This appears to me an important reason for the fact that nearly all Iranians interested in history wrote—and had to write—their works in Arabic: al-Ṭabarī, al-Dīnawarī, al-Bīrūnī, and others.

They adopted the prototype of Arabic historiography to such an extent that al-Ṭabarī has been declared by Renan, Nöldeke and Kowalski to be an example of the Semitic kind of history-writing in aphorisms—Ṭabarī, an Iranian from Ṭabaristān!

Besides, I suppose a second reason of the early Muslim historians to write their works in Arabic was their desire to make and to strengthen their contact with the whole Arabic (i.e. the whole Islamic) world. The influence of Arabic in the Muslim world with its richly developed culture was so great that it would have been really unwise to write history in any other language than Arabic.

It would have been unwise to write Persian history in any other language than Arabic for those interested in all-Islamic relations; among them Arabic was used in the same way as Latin in Europe during the Middle Ages. But were all Iranians really interested in contacts with the Muslim world? The answer must be: No, by no means. We are well aware of the fact that many members of the Persian élite adopted Islam very early: they realized that only by doing so could they preserve their social standards; indeed, they preserved them as well as the Bosniaks during the fourteenth century by becoming Muslims. Thus they were able to maintain their social feeling. We may take that as an additional proof of the predominantly economic reasons for their conversion. This social feeling may be perceived nowhere as clearly as in the legends of the old kings and their heroes. This type of literature survived the invasion of Islam because of the fact that there still existed a class living according to this historical tradition, regarding the social features described in the literature as their own ideals. This class of the so-called *Dihqāns* was by no means interested in the history of Islamic Persia: they read or—more often—listened to the recitations of the book of the kings with the description of the heroic deeds of their alleged ancestors, who felt, spoke, and acted in the same way as they did. It was useless to describe the history of Islamic Persia to them, even in Persian.

In contrast to the situation between Latin and various vernacular languages in Europe, Persian was a highly developed language with a well-regulated chancery tradition. I am convinced that Persian was neglected in historical and other scientific works, not because it was unsuitable but rather because of social reasons, as mentioned earlier.

But times changed, and Iranian dynasties began to rule considerable parts of Iran. There were three types of such dynasties: several, as the Ziyarids and the not yet islamized princes of Māzandarān (North Iran), were representatives of a Sasanid restoration or a real Zoroastrian tradition: all above-mentioned facts can be applied to them. A second type was represented by the Zaydī rulers in Gīlān and the Saffarids: they belonged not to the official Sunnī denomination of the Caliphs, but to Shī'ī or syncretistic sects. These communities had an enormous influence on the masses of the Iranian people; to them and to the mystic (Ṣūfī) communities a good many conversions to Islam with a religious (and not a social) motivation must be ascribed. This fact has been described and proved by quotations of sources in some of my publications, and I do not wish to enter into further details on this point now. In any case, these Shī'ī communities, heterodox as they were from the point of view of the government, were not interested in the official conception of Islamic history. For them theological meanings which did not reflect the doctrine of the Caliphs, were more important than the real historical evolution.

It was the third type of dynasties which became important for the development of the historiography using Persian for its utterances. Among them the Samanids in North-East Persia (Khurāsān) and Transoxania (ninth and tenth centuries) are the most important. They were definitely orthodox Sunnīs and feigned therefore to be only governors for the Caliphs: in reality they were independent rulers. They acknowledged the official religion and the governmental theory of the Caliphate; based on their political and military force in their provinces, they could support the foreign mission of Islam too. Along the borders of the whole of the Islamic world lived—in Persia as well as elsewhere—communities of 'frontier fighters', the *Muṭawwi'ūn* and the *Ghāzīs*. Sunnīs as they mostly were, they were backed by the Sunnī rulers—in Persia by the Samanids. In addition to the Indus valley, the Turkish tribes of Central Asia became the target of these missionaries. Since about 960, i.e. about 1,000 years ago, the Turks were peacefully islamized. In this way the Sunna became the denomination of nearly all Turks, and Turks belonged to its most zealous followers.

Although the Samanids in their administrative offices used exclusively Arabic, they had a sense of the importance of Persian as a cultural language of Islam, and they patronized the newly developing—neo-Persian—poetry. The beginning of linguistically Persian historiography belongs to this cultural evolution as well as to the necessity of making subjects acquainted with the Islamic conception of the State. Among other measures, they strove to attain this objective by publishing a mostly abridged Persian version of al-Ṭabarī's *Ta'rīkh al-rusul wa'l-mulūk*: the work of a Persian, Sunnī author, who at the same time was one of the most authoritative exegetes of the Qur'ān, a scholar whose historical work was orthodox, and strongly interested in Persian events and the relations between Persia and the Caliphate. This translation showed to the Sunnī Persians, faithful to the Caliphs, their standpoint within the Islamic Oecumene in a quite positive manner. For the Samanids, the translation of Ṭabarī into Persian was not only a cultural but also a political act. As described by Ṭabarī, the fate of the Persian nation was destined to be ranged among the faithful Sunnī subjects of the Caliph.

Immediately after the translation of Ṭabarī's work into Persian (about 963), Turkish dynasties became the rulers of most of the Persian provinces. Being zealous Sunnīs, as described, they became the cultural heirs of the Iranian Samanids: the greatest of the Ghaznawids, Maḥmūd, was Firdawsī's protector as well as the real promoter of (Sunnī) Islam in the Indus valley.

Nevertheless, a new era began in the Asian parts of the Near East with the predominance of the Turkish peoples in the eleventh century, in politics as well as in the 'mood of the times' (according to G. von Grunebaum's term). The periods of internal peace, secured by the Ghaznawids, the Seljuqs, and the Khwārizmshāhs in wide areas of Western Asia, were characterized by Sunnī orthodoxy and anti-European feeling as a consequence of the Crusades and the suppression, or at least repression, of the Hellenistic (i.e. Western) influence in philosophy, theology, and sciences.

One of the most important proofs of the greatness and the profundity of Persian culture is the rapidity with which the Turks adapted themselves to it and became its ardent followers. For the Turks, Persia was the ideal of life: the Arabic world, the Arabic language always took the second place for them. The Turks completed the victory of Persian as the second cultural language of the Islamic world. In the meantime, a good many special Arabic terms had been introduced into it. They encouraged the use of

Persian more than former Iranian dynasties ever had done. For them Ṭabarī's translated history became the main source of their historical information: the numerous copies and adaptations of this work, later even Turkish translations, prove its popularity. Evidently this work was sufficient for their interest: as new converts to Islam they neglected their own pre-Islamic history which—to be sure—was only very slightly known. The neglect of their heathen ancestors in Bal'amī's translation of Ṭabarī's work obviously did not hurt them. In this way Persian authors seem not to have been encouraged in publishing new Persian contributions to the field of historiography: the production of Persian historical descriptions is extremely slight under Seljuq and Khwarizmian rule.

On the other hand, the class of the *dihqāns* had extensively survived the Turkish conquest: their ideals were still alive, and Firdawsī's poem became very soon the 'Bible', the 'historical canon', i.e. the guide to the way of life of this class. Its incomparable flavour enchanted the whole nation and made its heroes personalities who seemed to be the real representatives of Persian nature. Thus, the *Shāhnāma* really became soon after its composition the national epos of the Persians. Both works, the translation of Ṭabarī and the *Shāhnāma*, co-existed during the eleventh and twelfth centuries as representatives of the two really enduring aspects of Persian way of life.

The Seljuqs, eager as they were to adopt Persian culture, tried to consign to oblivion even their 'Turanian' origin and to convert themselves into 'Iranians'—if we use Firdawsī's terminology. And, indeed, the second and even more the third generation of the Seljuq princes called their children not only by Turkish, but at the same time by Iranian, by Firdawsian names. All these Kay Kāvūs and Kayqubād, these Tahamtan and Rustam and Zāl were Turkish by origin (and their second name, such as Kilij Arslan and so on, often pointed it out very clearly), but Iranians by culture and (Asia Minor excepted to a certain degree) even as to their language.

To be sure they did not continue the old line of the *dihqān*-tradition, inasmuch as Firdawsī was perhaps the ideal of military glory, but not of the whole of their way of life. For they had adopted Islam not only for social, but for really religious reasons. Inasmuch as Firdawsī glorified the Zoroastrian past of Iran, the Seljuqs were his stubborn opponents. The Iranian literature of their period was allowed to describe pre-Islamic facts and epochs, as Niẓāmī did; but it was not allowed to be anti-Islamic or neglect Islamic views. Thus, a synthesis between the classical, nearly wholly Indo-European Persian, and the Arabic language of the religion and the sciences was effected during the eleventh and twelfth centuries by introducing many Arabic loan-words: it seems that this was the psychological price Persian had to pay in order to be accepted as an Islamic cultural language.

During these two centuries, a kind of symbiosis between the Turkish rulers and a substantially unshaken *dihqān*-society allowed the continuation of the old traditions among certain circles of the Persian people. The historiography produced an increasing number of translations from Arabic originals, particularly of narratives on Iranian conditions of life. But without the real interest of the governing class, the historiography written primarily in Persian, was relatively rare.

The great change came not earlier than after the Mongol invasion about 1220 and again about 1256. Particularly the first of these two campaigns was really disastrous for the Persian nation, especially for the population of Transoxania and Khurāsān. From then on, the majority of the old *dihqān*-families who were primarily situated in these regions, was annihilated or at least scattered and deprived of their possessions. Since the Mongol invasion, this class lost its dominating influence in Persian society, its ideals vanished, and Firdawsī ceased to be a guide-book for the social and even ideological way of life; since this time, people have appreciated him only with regard to his poetical aspect.

The social structure of the Iranian people changed for some centuries: it was no longer the descendants of the old families (even where they survived and kept their official duties) but the Turkish *begs* who were the real leaders of the nation.

Whereas the Seljuqs had embraced Islam before conquering Persia, and whereas they always remained its convinced followers, the Mongols invaded Iran (and the other countries they subjugated) as heathens or as Nestorian Christians. They kept for some decades their national and cultural traditions: for nearly a century they were proud of their origin and were by no means eager to be regarded as Iranians. On the contrary, they wished to see their own and their ancestors' glory described in the language of their subjects. In a period in which the reading of Arabic books was no longer popular in Iran, Persian was the only possible language for the composition of such books, so much the more as the Mongol rulers of Iran, the Īl-Khāns, mastered this idiom very soon.

To this 'challenge' there came within one generation a quite overwhelming 'response' of Persian historiography—if we use the terminology of Arnold Toynbee's much discussed work. Several ministers of the Mongols published historical descriptions of the Ilkhanid period and of Mongolian 'prehistory': Juvaynī used a highly complicated style which grew out of the language of the chanceries; Rashīd al-Dīn, formerly a physician and a convert from Judaism, therefore evidently not too familiar with the linguistic traditions of Muslim civil servants, wrote in a very clear and plain style which approached in a high degree the popular speech of his century as it was intermingled with Mongol terms.

Both inherited the historiographical manner of the Arabs as it was developed till the thirteenth century, Ibn al-Athīr's work being the best example of this Arabic style. But they surpassed this example by the depth of their historical understanding, by their consideration of social and economic factors in the evolution of mankind and by a pragmatical arrangement of their works, Rashīd al-Dīn, moreover, by the breadth of his historical view that included China and India as well as the history of the Mongolian tribes before Chingiz-Khān and the evolution of Europe, according to Martinus Polonus's then well-known synopsis.

Unfortunately, rhetoric became an influential factor in Persian historiography in the beginning of the fourteenth century. Vaṣṣāf, a historian of deep insight into the historical evolution, thought it necessary to embellish his important contribution by rhetorical phrases, so that even the Persians themselves need a dictionary for reading this book; therefore the Persian lithographs add always a list of rare words to it.

Vaṣṣāf's example influenced Persian historiography for centuries. It is as important a historical source as it is complicated with regard to the style for European and modern Iranian readers. The style overwhelmed the sense for the historical facts. The enjoyment of this style, possible only for a very small class of well-trained scholars and men of letters, obscured the true purpose of historiography for many centuries and turned this literature—despite its high value as source—into a surrogate of modern European historical fiction: the style, the arrangement of facts, was often more important than the historical truth.

It lasted for several centuries until the Persian historiography overcame this trend. In the meantime it had adopted the ideology of the Arabic descriptions which regarded world history as the history of the salvation of God's own people—the Muslims—by His revelation. This ideology answered to the now wholly Islamized, later on Shi'itized Persian nation; consequently this trend of the Persian historiography remained dominant until the irruption of modern European secularized thinking. With this statement we are transgressing the threshold of the present time which we do not intend to describe in this paper.

11. JUVAYNĪ AND RASHĪD AL-DĪN AS SOURCES ON THE HISTORY OF THE MONGOLS

J. A. BOYLE

Reader in Persian Studies in the University of Manchester

It is difficult to think of two historians more dissimilar, whether in style or in their approach to their subject, than Juvaynī and Rashīd al-Dīn. Juvaynī is a master of that ornate and elaborate prose which was already in his day the normal vehicle of historical writing; Rashīd al-Dīn has no literary pretensions whatsoever and uses the plainest and most straightforward language, probably dictating his work, as Niẓām al-Mulk before him. Juvaynī, his feet firmly planted in the pre-Mongol past, is still concerned with justifying, as much to himself as to his readers, the terrible calamities that had overtaken Islam; Rashīd al-Dīn, writing at a time when these calamities were dim and distant memories, accepts the *Pax Mongolica* as the natural order of things.[1]

Nevertheless, as sources on the history of the Mongols, the two historians are generally assumed to be in broad agreement, Juvaynī being simply the older and Rashīd al-Dīn the fuller authority. Such an assumption is not borne out by a detailed comparison of the two authors. It is true that in certain parts of his history, notably in the account of the campaign in the West, Rashīd al-Dīn follows Juvaynī almost word for word, but even here there are, as we shall see, interpolations from a Far Eastern source, and it is incorrect to assert with Barthold[2] that this part of his work is based 'exclusively' upon Juvaynī.

The impression that the two authorities are in general harmony is partly due to the reliance of historians of the Mongols on the work of d'Ohsson, who does not always make it clear which authority he is quoting. It is this uncertainty that has led Grousset[3] to attribute to Juvaynī and Rashīd al-Dīn jointly and Martin[4] to Juvaynī alone, a death-bed speech of Chingiz-Khān which is actually taken from Rashīd al-Dīn and is inconsistent with the facts as given by Juvaynī. According to the latter there were present at the Conqueror's bedside not only Chaghatai, Ögedei, and Tolui, but also the comparatively obscure Kölgen, who afterwards met his death in Russia, and two sons not mentioned in the extant Far

[1] For a detailed comparison of the two historians see Minorsky, 'Caucasica III: the Alān Capital Magas and the Mongol Campaigns', *BSOAS* (1952), xiv/2, 221–2.

[2] *Turkestan down to the Mongol invasion*, p. 45.

[3] *L'Empire Mongol*, pp. 277–8.

[4] *The rise of Chingis Khan and his conquest of North China*, pp. 302–3.

Eastern sources who, according to Rashīd al-Dīn, had died in their childhood. In Rashīd al-Dīn's version of the death-bed scene only Ögedei and Tolui were present and in his speech Chingiz-Khān specifically refers to the absence of Chaghatai; and this is the speech now ascribed to Juvaynī, who had caused all of Chingiz-Khān's sons to be present, even two, who, according to Rashīd al-Dīn, were long since dead![5]

There are in fact many points of disagreement between the two historians and the explanation can only be that they drew their information on the Mongols from different sources. In the case of Rashīd al-Dīn this source is well known and indeed is specified by Rashīd al-Dīn himself. It is the *Altan debter* or 'Golden book', which 'was always preserved in the treasury of the Khān in the hands of the oldest amīrs'. Rashīd al-Dīn had not direct access to this official chronicle of the Mongols, which was regarded as sacred; it was interpreted to him orally by Bolad Chingsang, 'Bolad the *ch'êng-hsiang* or Minister', the representative of the Great Khān at the Persian Court, as also by the Īl-Khān Ghazan himself, who as an authority on the Mongol traditions was second to Bolad alone.[6] The Mongol original of the *Altan debter* has not come down to us, but a Chinese version survives in the *Shêng-wu ch'in-chêng lu* or 'Description of the Personal Campaigns of the Holy Warrior (Chingiz-Khān)', written some time before 1285;[7] it was also utilized in the *Yüan shih*, the history of the Mongol dynasty in China, composed in 1369.

In the early part of his history the *Altan debter* is Rashīd al-Dīn's sole source. In his account of the campaign in the West, whilst for the most part simply reproducing Juvaynī, he makes frequent use of the Mongol work and even adopts its faulty chronology, in accordance with which the events of the campaign take place a year later than in reality. The following comparisons give some idea of his indebtedness to the Mongol source:

1. *Siege of Gurganj*

Juvaynī	Rashīd al-Dīn
Represents Jochi as sending reinforcements from Jand.[8]	Follows Juvaynī almost word for word in his account of the siege but causes Jochi to take part in person.[9] (In this he is in agreement not only

[5] See Juvaynī, *The history of the World-Conqueror*, transl. J. A. Boyle, pp. 180–2.

[6] Barthold, op. cit., pp. 44–5.

[7] See Hambis's Introduction to his and Pelliot's edition and translation of this work (*Histoire des campagnes de Gengis Khan*), pp. xii–xiii. Only vol. i has so far appeared. There are also partial translations of the *Shêng-wu ch'in-chêng lu* by Bretschneider, *Mediaeval researches from Eastern Asiatic sources*, i, 291–4, and Haenisch, 'Die letzten Feldzüge Cinggis Han's und sein Tod nach der ostasiatischen Überlieferung', *Asia Major* (1933), ix.

[8] *The history of the World-Conqueror*, p. 124.

[9] *Sbornik letopisei*, i, 2, transl. O. I. Smirnova, pp. 214–17.

with the Far Eastern sources but also with the contemporary Moslem authorities.)

2. *Toqochar*

Juvaynī

Does not mention this Mongol general unless he is to be identified with Toghachar, the son-in-law of Chingiz-Khān, who fell before Nīshāpūr.[10]

Rashīd al-Dīn

Represents him as being sent, in the wake of Sübetei and Jebe, in pursuit of Sultan Muḥammad Khwārizm-Shāh and as disobeying Chingiz-Khān's command not to plunder in the territories of Khān Malik, i.e. Amīn al-Mulk, the *malik* of Harāt who had submitted to the Mongols.[11] (Neither Juvaynī nor Nasawī mentions Amīn al-Mulk's submission, a circumstance which throws grave doubt on the whole episode.)

3. *Bala of the Jalayir*

Juvaynī

Mentions only Dörbei Doqshin (and not Bala) as being sent across the Indus in pursuit of Sultan Jalāl al-Dīn.[12]

Rashīd al-Dīn

Places Bala and Dörbei Doqshin in joint command of the expedition, thus harmonizing Juvaynī's account with the Far Eastern version of the episode in which mention is made of Bala only.[13]

4. *Chingiz-Khān on the Indus*

Juvaynī

Says only that after the defeat of Sultan Jalāl al-Dīn he 'proceeded along the banks of the river'.[14]

Rashīd al-Dīn

Adds the information (also in the *Shêng-wu ch'in-chêng lu*) that he marched *upstream* whilst sending Ögedei *downstream*.[15]

[10] Op. cit., pp. 174–5 and n. 11.

[11] Op. cit., p. 218.

[12] Op. cit., pp. 141–2 and 413.

[13] Op. cit., pp. 255–6. See also Boyle, '*Iru* and *Maru* in the *Secret History of the Mongols*', *HJAS*, 17 (1954), pp. 406–9.

[14] Op. cit., p. 135.

[15] Op. cit., p. 225, Haenisch, op. cit., p. 529.

Juvaynī's sources appear to have been purely oral, at any rate for the earlier history of the Mongols. Some of his data however are also to be found in the *Secret history of the Mongols*, which in such cases must be considered the ultimate authority for his information. Already Barthold[16] had drawn attention to an image which Juvaynī seemed to have borrowed from this source. The following appear to be further instances of information derived, perhaps at second or third hand, from the *Secret history*:

(1) Juvaynī's account of the death of the shaman Teb-Tengri (not recorded by Rashīd al-Dīn) is in broad agreement with the more detailed account in the Mongol source.[17]

(2) The story of Chingiz-Khān and the bundle of arrows is also to be found in the *Secret history* but is there related of his mythical ancestress Alan Qo'a.[18]

(3) Juvaynī agrees with the *Secret history* in making Tarbai (Darbai) the envoy of the ïdï-qut or ruler of the Uighur to Chingiz-Khān—not *vice-versa* as in Rashīd al-Dīn.[19]

(4) According to the *Secret history* the election of Ögedei to the Khanate took place in the spring of 1228 (not 1229 as in Rashīd al-Dīn), and with this Juvaynī appears to be in agreement.[20]

Juvaynī's apparent use of the *Secret history of the Mongols* is of particular interest in view of the probability that the work may have been reduced to writing about a year before his visit to Mongolia. The *Secret history* was completed, according to the statement in the last paragraph (§ 282), 'at Köde'e Aral on the Kerulen in the seventh month of the Year of the Rat, at the time of the assembly for the great *quriltai*'. Since the chronicle terminates in Ögedei's lifetime the Year of the Rat has usually been taken to be the year in the cycle corresponding to 1240. There are, however, as Grousset has pointed out,[21] certain indications of a later date. In § 255 Chingiz-Khān is represented as prophesying that should the descendants of Ögedei prove incapable of reigning, the Empire would have to pass to the descendants of another of his sons. And in § 281 Ögedei is made to subject himself to a searching of conscience which has very much of the appearance of a posthumous judgement on that prince, who died on 11 December 1241. These considerations led Grousset to pose the question (answered in the negative by Pelliot) whether this work might not have been completed during the next Year of the Rat, i.e. 1252, when Chingiz-Khān's 'prophecy' had been fulfilled and the Khanate had passed to another branch of the family. A further argument, not mentioned by Grousset, in favour of the later date is the circumstance that the work was

[16] Op. cit., p. 41 and n. 3.
[17] Op. cit., p. 39 and n. 17.
[18] Op. cit., p. 41 and n. 7.
[19] Op. cit., p. 45 and n. 9.
[20] Op. cit., p. 187 and n. 26.
[21] In his Introduction to Vladimirtsov, *Gengis-Khan*, transl. Michel Carsow, pp. v–vi.

completed at the time of the 'great *quriltai*'. There is no record of such an assembly of the Mongol princes in or about 1240, whereas if we assume the later date for the completion of the *Secret history* the reference is clearly to the *quriltai* at which Möngke was elevated to the Khanate. This actually took place a year earlier, in 1251, but the *Secret history* is never very accurate in its chronology. If we accept the later date, for which there is also other evidence,[22] we can the more readily understand how Juvaynī, who was resident in Mongolia in 1252–3, had some kind of indirect access to a work which at that time represented the official point of view. It may have been interpreted to him by those same 'trustworthy Mongols' who supplied him with the details about Teb-Tengri.[23]

Thus the lack of agreement between Juvaynī and Rashīd al-Dīn as historians of the Mongols is accounted for by their following different traditions. One of Juvaynī's sources appears to be the *Secret history of the Mongols*, which, as Hambis says, is to be regarded not as a single historical work but rather as a collection of historical texts, 'assemblage d'ailleurs assez peu homogène, où l'on rencontre des généalogies et des pièces épiques allitérées'.[24] If, as seems likely, it was composed in 1251 or 1252, it is also to be regarded as a sort of political pamphlet written to justify the change in the line of the dynasty. Rashīd al-Dīn's information, on the other hand, is based on what was in his time 'the official history of the imperial family'.[25] The earlier part of his work appears to be a literal translation of the lost *Altan debter*; and, as we have seen, his account of the campaign in the West, though for the most part based on Juvaynī, also contains details from the Mongol source. Had this source survived in its original form the value of Rashīd al-Dīn as an authority on the rise of the Mongol Empire would have been very considerably reduced; the importance of Juvaynī's work, founded on contemporary Muslim sources and on personal investigations on the spot, would have been unaffected.

[22] There appear for instance to be references to the conspiracy against Möngke.
[23] *The history of the World-Conqueror*, p. 39. [24] Op. cit., p. xiii. [25] Ibid., p. xv.

12. THE PERSIAN HISTORIAN BAYHAQĪ

MUJTABA MINOVI

Iranian Culture Attaché, Ankara

The *Tārīkh-i Bayhaqī* is unique amongst Persian historical works in many respects. The author, Abu'l-Faḍl Muḥammad b. al-Ḥusayn al-Bayhaqī, a native of Bayhaq of old times, the present-day Sabzavār, was one of the civil servants in the court of the Ghaznavid rulers, Maḥmūd, Mas'ūd, Mawdūd, and 'Abd al-Rashīd. When (during the reign of Maḥmūd and Mas'ūd) Abū Naṣr Mushkān was chief of the Office of Correspondence in the Court of the king, Bayhaqī was his trusted and close associate, and in addition to what he saw, read, and wrote in his official capacity as the copyist-in-chief of the important letters, especially those addressed to courts of other kings, he heard privately from Abū Naṣr, and later on from Aḥmad b. Muḥammad b. 'Abd al-Ṣamad, the Chief Minister to Mawdūd, accounts of conversations that took place in private between important persons and happenings that were held back from the public. It appears that, long before he began to write his history, he had conceived the idea and had been making notes in the calendars and separate pieces of paper, collecting copies of documents in Arabic and Persian that came to his hands, and treasuring all the material necessary for such a history as he wrote.

We know very little about his private life, because he does not give accounts of what happened to him personally except as an indication that at such-and-such a happening he was present and a witness, and because he is mentioned in two or three books on biographies of famous men of letters without much information given. It appears that he was born in 385/995 or 386/996 and was educated in Bayhaq and Nīshāpūr. At the age of sixteen he saw in Nīshāpūr the celebrations connected with betrothal of Sultan Maḥmūd's daughter to Manūchihr b. Qābūs of Gurgān in 402/1011 (p. 209).[1] He says that when he was young, and living in Nīshāpūr, he had heard many stories about Sultan Mas'ūd's deeds, prowess, and courage, and his private life in his youth.

It is not known at what age and when he entered the service of the court, but it may be assumed that it was about 406/1015 when he was twenty. In the year 426/1034 he accompanied Sultan Mas'ūd and his army and retinue to Gurgān and Māzandarān; and in 431/1040 he was

[1] Reference is given in brackets to the pages of the *Tārīkh-i Bayhaqī*, ed. Dr. A. Fayyāz (Tehran, 1324 H.S.).

with them at the battle of Dandāngān, and saw the army being defeated, uprooted, and dispersed, and the king in flight. After the death of Abū Naṣr Moshkān in the year 431/1039 Abū Sahl Zūzanī was appointed the Chief of the Office of Correspondence, and the Sultan had said that if Abu'l-Faḍl were not so young, he would have appointed him to that office. Abu'l-Faḍl at this time was forty-five or forty-six years old. Once, when Zūzanī was sent on a mission, Abu'l-Faḍl was appointed his deputy by Zūzanī himself with the consent of the king.

After the accession of Sultan 'Abd al-Rashīd (441/1049) he was for some time holder of this office, but was involved in the court intrigues of the subsequent period and was arrested, his property confiscated and himself put in prison. It is also reported that he was put in gaol for failing to pay the matrimony portion to a wife of his, and he was transferred from the gaol to the castle prison after Ṭughril killed 'Abd al-Rashīd in the year 444/1053. He accepted no post after he was set free, but retired to Ghaznin and, from the year 448/1056 was engaged in writing his history. References are made to the years 450, 451, and 455 in the history, and his death reported, rather doubtfully, to have taken place in 470/1077.

His intention to write the history of the Ghaznavid kings goes back to the time when he was still in service of the court. He says, for instance, that in the year 432, 'I asked the Minister Aḥmad-i 'Abd al-Ṣamad to tell me more minutely, and truthfully, the happenings connected with killing of Munjūq, the commander of the garrison army dispatched by Sultan Maḥmūd to Khwārizm; for I had been wanting to write this History, and I clung to whatever detail I could learn from any source.'

Abu'l-Faḍl is not particularly proud of his own work, for two reasons: first, that there are other great men in the capital of Ghaznavid kings better fitted then myself with what is necessary for writing this History, and because they have other and more important work to do, and have no time for a work such as this, I am doing what I can do about it; second, that some people, unnamed throughout but referred to several times, had intentionally destroyed the greater part of documents, copies of official letters and notes he had taken for his book, and therefore he had to be content with what was left and what he remembered. A few sources became available while he was busy writing the book, such as: a long account of the life of Mas'ūd in his youth written in 451/1059 by Abū Sa'īd 'Abd al-Ghaffār, who had been a companion of Mas'ūd's for a great many years and with whom Bayhaqī was acquainted from 421/1030 onwards; a history of Khwārizm by the famous scholar and scientist Abū Rayḥān al-Bīrūnī; and what he heard from Sharīf Abu'l-Muẓaffar in the year 450/1058.

The portion of the *Tārīkh-i Bayhaqī* that now exists, and has been printed four times, deals with the years 421 to 432, i.e. from immediately after the death of Maḥmūd down to the moment Mas'ūd decided, after his defeat at the hands of the Seljuq tribe, to raid India. This portion comprises vols. 6–9 and parts of vols. 5 and 10. The rest of the book is lost and no trace of it has been found in any of the libraries so far examined. Yet, that he had written more than what exists is certain, for long passages from the lost parts are found in various books.[2] There are chapters even in the extant portion that deal with the history of earlier Ghaznavid rulers, but these are digressions intentionally brought in here and there in order to make the history more enjoyable. In fact, this is one of the main features of Bayhaqī's History: long stories, historical accounts, *qaṣīdas* and shorter poems in Arabic and Persian and such, interpolated in the course of the history of Mas'ūd's reign. As much as the author is trustworthy in describing happenings of his own time of which he was a witness, he is unreliable in accounts he has read or heard of happenings belonging to earlier periods, such as the time of Kisra, Hārūn, al-Ma'mūn, and even Samanid rulers. Evidently he did not immediately before putting such stories down consult a book, or the book, in which the story was recorded. But as to the history of the reign of Sultan Mas'ūd, his sources were, as I said before, the calendars of the years concerned upon which he had day by day noted whatever had happened, and copies of documents that passed through his hands, and the notes he was making of what he heard from eyewitnesses; all these in addition to what he had treasured in his memory.

He is passionately interested in his work, and intelligent enough to be objective. His history is a very lively one. Every page of it contains some very interesting account, maybe of some political intrigue, some administrative circumstance, some social or economic information, some diplomatic incident, or secret event. In point of style and language also is his book very interesting: it is full of special words, terms, expressions and turns of phrase that make his writing lively and set a model for composition in an accurate and sparing language. These words enrich the Persian vocabulary and help us better to understand other books written in those centuries.

His judgement upon the acts and deeds of men with whose doings he deals are very fair. He does not forget good sides of anyone even though he were his own enemy, and even when he is stating for a fact bad actions and condemnable conducts of a person, he leaves the final judgement upon him with God.

[2] Most of these passages have been collected and published by Sa'īd Nafīsī.

13. PERSIAN BIOGRAPHICAL LITERATURE

ANN K. S. LAMBTON

Professor of Persian in the University of London

In this paper I shall confine my remarks mainly to works written in Persian concerning the geographical area of Persia and Iraq, thus excluding, for the most part, both Persian works written in India or Turkey and works written in Arabic by Persians, though I shall make an exception in the case of works written in Arabic with a clearly local Persian bias. The works which I shall mention range in time from the 4th/10th century to the 13th/19th century inclusive; but only those nineteenth-century works which can be regarded as being in the main line of medieval tradition will be discussed.

Biographical literature in Persian is perhaps more limited in scope than its Arabic counterpart; there is nothing in Persian comparable, for example, to the biographical dictionary of Ibn Khallikān, the *wafāyāt* in the history of Ibn al-Jawzī, or the History of Islam of al-Dhahabī. On the other hand there is an astonishing continuity in the cultivation of certain forms of biographical literature in Persia; and if we accept with Sir Hamilton Gibb 'that every kind of literary production which is regularly cultivated in a society expresses some enduring element in both the conscious motivations and unconscious orientations of the society as a whole or of its public exponents', it may be possible to draw from this fact certain conclusions with regard to the characteristics and intellectual attitudes of Persian society. It is the purpose of this paper to suggest what these may be.

Persian biographical material falls into the following categories: (i) biographical dictionaries; (ii) biographical material in local histories; (iii) biographical material in geographical dictionaries; (iv) biographical details in chronicles and dynastic histories; (v) biographies of individuals; (vi) biographies of families or tribes; and (vii) autobiographies. I shall not list or analyse all the works which fall into these various categories, but merely refer to some by way of example.

(1) *Biographical Dictionaries*

Sir Hamilton Gibb in his paper entitled 'Islamic Biographical Literature' has suggested that the conception underlying the oldest Arabic biographical dictionaries is 'that the history of the Islamic Community is essentially the contribution of men and women to the building up and transmission of its specific culture; that it is these persons (rather than the political governors) who represent or reflect the active forces in Muslim society in their respective spheres; and that their individual contributions are worthy of being recorded for future generations.' This is also true of much Persian biographical literature; but this is not to say that the authors of biographical dictionaries necessarily thought of these works as 'history', since this, from the 3rd/9th century at least, was typically embodied in the chronicle.

The biographical dictionaries in Persian are seldom universal or general. They tend rather to be limited to particular classes or groups. The most numerous biographies are those of Shīʿī divines, *sayyids*, Ṣūfīs, and poets. Other classes figure less frequently. That Persian biographical dictionaries are seldom universal may perhaps be due to the special circumstances of Persia within the larger Islamic world, the memory of the old Persian state having to some extent survived the Muslim conquest so that the conception of a 'national' empire existed beside that of universal Islam. Again, that a large number of biographical dictionaries should be devoted to Shīʿīs of one sort or another (in Persia as elsewhere) is not surprising; even before Shiʿism became the majority rite in Persia under the Safavids Shiʿism was endemic in Persia, and consequently biographies of Shīʿī were always at least as common as those of Sunnī *ʿulamā'*. The saints (*awliyā'*) are also the subject of numerous biographical dictionaries such as the *Taẕkirat al-awliyā'* of Muḥammad b. Ibrāhīm Farīd al-Dīn ʿAṭṭār (b. 513/1119–20), and the *Nafahāt al-uns* of Jāmī (written in 881/1476). The latter contains more or less chronologically arranged notices of 567 male saints, 34 female saints, and 13 Ṣūfī poets, and is a modernized recension of ʿAbdallāh Anṣārī's *Ṭabaqāt*, which was an enlarged version of Muḥammad b. al-Ḥusayn al-Sulamī's *Ṭabaqāt al-Ṣūfiyya*. Various Ṣūfī orders, in particular the Naqshbandī order, are also frequent subjects of biographical dictionaries. Many of these works on saints and Ṣūfīs belong to hagiographical rather than biographical literature.

This tendency to devote biographical dictionaries to special classes, which is not by any means limited to Persia among Islamic countries, is to some extent a reflexion of the corporate nature of medieval Islamic society. In the classification of the philosophers four orders are customarily found: (i) men of the pen, among whom were included the religious classes, scribes, learned men of different kinds, and poets; (ii) men of the sword; (iii) merchants and artisans, and (iv) husbandmen. As has been indicated above, there is no dearth of biographical dictionaries on the religious classes, but it is a striking fact that there are almost none on members of the bureaucracy. A notable exception is the *Dastūr al-vuzarā of* Khwāndamīr (who died probably in 942/1535–6). The comparative paucity of such works supports the view that what is regarded as important is the contribution of the individual Muslim and not that of the state (or its officials). On the other hand biographical dictionaries of poets are especially popular in Persia. These, however, though they often contain brief notices of the lives of the poets, specimens of whose works they record, and the rulers under whom these poets lived, have no pretensions to be considered as historical writings; their interest, if any, to the historian is the witness they bear to the special literary bent of the Persian people and the place of the poet in society. The second class of the philosophers, the men of the sword, also receive scant mention in the biographical dictionaries; this may perhaps be partially explained by the fact that in so far as they rose to eminence their deeds were recorded in the chronicles and the dynastic histories. The third class, comprising the merchants and artisans, is virtually ignored in the biographical dictionaries and for that matter in the *wafāyāt* of the histories; very occasionally mention of them is made in the local histories. The fourth class, the cultivators, is, perhaps naturally, entirely ignored in Persian biographical writing.

Persian biographical dictionaries would seem to conform more or less to the pattern of their prototypes in Arabic. In the notices, which tend to be fairly short, some or all of the following items are usually given: dates of birth and death; the names of those under whom the subject studied; the titles of his works, or some of them; the journeys he undertook; *obiter dicta*; and, more occasionally, the political events in which he took part. The biographer like the historian, was concerned to record rather than to recreate and so details of the personal characteristics and 'private' lives of those listed are rare. Another reason for this lack of detail is perhaps that the individual himself was of little importance except as a contributor to the building up and transmission of Islamic culture. Hence the main relevant facts were when and where he lived, his position in the line of transmission (i.e. from whom he obtained his knowledge), and what he wrote. His journeys were also relevant since they were likely to have been undertaken in pursuit of religious knowledge or in the course of the pilgrimage. His character and private life except in so far as they aided (or impeded) his positive contribution to Islamic culture and its transmission were irrelevant; this is probably why when personal characteristics are related they concern in the main piety, learning, and stock Islamic virtues such as beneficence and justice. The above remarks as to the content of the individual biographies are also broadly true of the biographical materials in categories (ii), (iii), and (iv) below.

(2) *Biographical Material in Local Histories*

Although the chief interest of the Muslim was centred on the Islamic community, his loyalty was also accorded to his local town or province. The towns were in many cases virtually semi-autonomous units, which in times of trouble and disorder might act independently, often under the leadership of the local *qāḍī* or *shaykh*. These local communities formed reservoirs on which Persia could draw to replenish herself after periods of disaster. Often they were closely knit and in many periods played an important role in the transmission of Islamic civilization. Such circumstances account for the cultivation of local histories, which in many cases consist mainly of biographical material. Some, such as the *Maḥāsin Iṣfahān* of Māfarrūkhī (written in Arabic in 421/1030) and its various Persian recensions, contain notices of the famous men who ruled, visited, or lived in the locality; others, such as the *Shīrāznāma* of Ibn Zarkūb (finished in 744/1343–4), are confined mainly to mention of religious classes; while in others the biographical material is limited to a special class or family, as, for example, the *Tārīkh-i Qumm* (originally written in Arabic by Ḥasan b. Muḥammad b. Ḥasan Qummī in 378/988–9 and translated into Persian by Ḥasan b. 'Alī b. Ḥasan b. 'Abd al-Malik al-Qummī in 825/1422), which has chapters on the *sayyids* who came to Qumm and the Arab settlers in Qumm belonging to the family of Mālik b. 'Āmir al-Ash'arī. Some writers, as for example Junayd al-Shīrāzī in the *Shadd al-izār* (written in 791/1389), confine themselves to the biographies of those buried in a particular locality. In addition to the local history proper the general histories also sometimes contain special sections on the native town or province of the author. Ḥamdallāh Mustawfī, for example, gives an account (with some interesting details) in the *Tārīkh-i guzīda* (completed in 730/1329–30) of the principal families of Qazwīn.

As in the case of the biographical dictionaries of the Shī'ī divines, saints, and Ṣūfīs, there is an extraordinary persistence in the cultivation of local history in Persia. Typical examples are the *Tārīkh-i Bayhaq* of Ibn Funduq (composed in 563/1167–8), the *Jāmi'-i Mufīdī* of Muḥammad Mufīd (completed in 1090/1679), and the *Tārīkh-i Tabrīz* of Nādir Mīrzā (written *c.* 1302/1884–5). Their structure is broadly similar; it is however a notable fact that the arrangement of the last-named is rather more haphazard than that of the first two. Ibn Funduq in the *Tārīkh-i Bayhaq* after some introductory material, including a discussion on the science of history, and a brief geographical description of Bayhaq, proceeds to 'Mention of the ancient and noble families in this district.' The order of, and the space given to, the various entries is interesting. First come the *sayyid* families of Bayhaq (eleven pages of printed text); then the Tahirids (only half a page), followed by the Saffarids (one and a quarter pages), the Samanids (two and a half pages), the Ghaznavids (one page), and the Seljuqs (one and a half pages). Having thus disposed of 'rulers', Ibn Funduq describes in varying detail local families, including his own and that of Niẓām al-Mulk. The next chapter, which occupies most of the remainder of the book, is entitled 'Mention of the *'ulamā'*, *imāms*, and learned men who came from this area or settled in it'. The next and final section includes some further biographical information and miscellaneous items.

The *Jāmi'-i Mufīdī*, in so far as the biographical material is concerned (and it is considerable), reflects the corporate nature of contemporary Persian society. This material refers in sections to the following classes: *sayyids*, *wazīrs*, *kalāntars*, *mustawfīs*, *mīnbāshīs* and *yūzbāshīs*, '*ulamā'* and *fuḍalā*, *qāẓīs*, *muḥtasibs*, *wā'iẓīn*, *khaṭībs*, astrologers, calligraphers, physicians, poets, men of rank and wealth, ascetics, geometers, and artists; in addition there are biographical notices on the *imāmzādas* and *shaykhs* of Yazd, and their disciples. An account of the author's own life is also included in the work.

Biographical material is scattered haphazard through the *Tārīkh-i Tabrīz*. For example, the section on *qanāts* contains biographical details of their founders; similarly under the list of the city quarters biographical details of their *kadkhudās* are supplied. Various classes, '*ulamā'*, men of letters, governors, and *sayyids* are separately listed; but details of individuals turn up here and there throughout the book.

(3) *Biographial Material in Geographical Dictionaries*

These are not really concerned with geography as such but are rather a combination of the biographical dictionary and the local history; in them the biographical material is arranged under towns and countries usually with some description of the geography of the town or district in question. Two well-known but rather dissimilar examples of this type of work are the *Haft iqlīm* of Amīn b. Aḥmad Rāzī (completed 1003/1593–4) and the *Majālis al-mu'minīn* of Nūrallāh Shushtarī (finished in 1010/1602). The former contains mention of some 1,560 poets, saints, '*ulamā'*, and others. The latter comprises twelve sections dealing with the following subjects: places with Shī'ī associations; some Shī'ī tribes and families; Shī'ī contemporaries of the Prophet (*sic*); Shī'īs of the next generation (*tābi'īn*); Shī'ī scholars of the succeeding generations; Ṣūfīs; philosophers; Shī'ī rulers and Shī'ī dynasties; *amīrs* and military leaders, etc., *wazīrs* and calligraphers; Arab poets; and Persian poets.

(4) *Biographical Material in Chronicles and Dynastic Histories*

Some but not by any means all Persian histories include biographical material, in the form of *wafāyāt*, at the end of each year, or reign, or in the form of appendices on the learned and famous men of the period with which the author is dealing. In the choice of biographical material in this category there is a strong bias, as in the categories already mentioned, towards the religious classes. In so far as the general histories are concerned, some account of the lives of rulers and officials is given in the body of the work and it is perhaps natural that the majority of those recorded in the *wafāyāt* or in appendices should belong to other classes. This, however, does not account for the overwhelming preponderance given to the religious classes in the biographical dictionaries mentioned above or for the greater importance given to them in relation to other classes of the population (excluding rulers and officials) in the *wafāyāt* and local histories. Sir Hamilton Gibb has pointed out one of the reasons, namely that the selection of the biographer was 'determined as a rule by his own interests or discipline'. Since the earliest organized disciplines in Islam were the religious and legal disciplines of *ḥadīth*-study, the earliest biographical works are oriented towards meeting their requirements both in general works and in the "histories" of particular cities and provinces.' The pattern once set, the general tendency was to follow it. Moreover, the *madrasas* enjoyed, in medieval Persia, a monopoly in education, and the education given in them, whether to members of the religious classes, men of letters, or government officials, was an education in the religious sciences. Also it was probably among the religious classes that biographical information about their predecessors was best preserved and consequently both the training of the writers and the material most easily available reinforced the influence exerted by the example of the early biographers. The fundamental reason, however, for the tendency to concentrate on the religious classes is in all probability to be found in the Muslim attitude to history, which was determined by the assumption that God's cause triumphs in Islam. The importance of any single event or individual was on this account inevitably measured by the extent to which the event or person contributed to the building up and preservation of the Islamic community. Ostensibly, at least, the religious classes played a more important rôle in this than any other class, and so, there are more notices of them than of other classes in the biographical literature.

Although there is a considerable amount of biographical material to be gleaned from the Persian chronicles and dynastic histories, the *wafāyāt* do not in general form an important part of the Persian chronicles. Bundārī in his History of the Seljuqs of Iraq (which is based partly on the work of Anūshirwān b. Khālid, whose death is variously recorded as taking place in 532/1137–8, 533/1138–9, and 534/1139–40, and 'Imād al-Dīn's translation and additions to this) gives a few details at the end of each year or group of years of those who had died during that period; the notices are confined mainly to important members of the religious classes and officials of the bureaucracy. If these notices formed part of the work of Anūshirwān b. Khālid they are one of the earliest examples of Persian *wafāyāt*. They are, however, extremely brief. The Mongol chronicles for the most part do not contain *wafāyāt* as such. The *Tārīkh-i guzīda* has a special chapter containing biographical details of some members of the religious classes. The distribution is as follows: 13 *imāms* and *mujtahids*, 10 readers of the

Qur'ān, 7 traditionalists, 287 *shaykhs* (some without any biographical details), a considerable number of *rāwīs* (without any biographical details), 105 *'ulamā'* of various sorts including physicians, philosophers, and astrologers; the only other class to be included is that of the poets, of whom 4 Arabic and 63 Persian are mentioned. Significant, too, of the relative importance attached to the various classes is the order in which Ḥamdallāh Mustawfī lists men who visited Qazvīn: first are the Companions of the Prophet, then the Followers of the Companions, then imams and caliphs, then *shaykhs* and *'ulamā'*, then rulers and *wazīrs*, and lastly *khāqāns* and *amīrs*.

The Timurid chronicle, the *Maṭla'-i Sa'dayn*, has no *wafāyāt*. The *Mujmal*, a chronicle extending from 1–845/622–1442, by Faṣīḥī of Khwāf, who was a finance official under Shāhrukh and Bāysunqur, includes, on the other hand, the deaths of eminent persons under each year; a large proportion of them are poets and men of letters of Khurāsān and Transoxania.[1] Khwāndamīr in his *Ḥabīb al-siyar*, a general history extending to 930/1524, includes a certain amount of biographical material arranged at the end of each reign; the vast majority of entries are of *sayyids*, *'ulamā'*, *fuḍalā'*, and *shaykhs*. The Safavid chronicle, the *Aḥsan al-tavārīkh*, which extends from 807/1405 to 985/1577–8, but of which only the portion from 900/1494 to 985/1577–8 has been printed, includes at the end of some threequarters of the years in the printed text a list of those who died during the year. These lists contain a fair proportion of *amīrs* and officials but the majority are members of the religious classes, especially *qāżīs*. The details given are meagre and seldom does any picture emerge of the persons whose death is being recorded. Occasionally, however, there is some indication of personal rivalries and intrigues, as for example in the case of the notices on Amīr Jamāl al-Dīn Muḥammad of Astarābād and Amīr Ni'matallāh, a *sayyid* of Ḥilla, under the years 931/1524–5 and 940/1533–4 respectively.

The biographical material in the *Tārīkh-i 'ālam ārā-yi 'Abbāsī* of Iskandar Beg (completed in 1038/1628–9) is of a somewhat different order and perhaps shows that the author is concerned with the state as it existed in fact (a most unusual phenomenon) and not with the Islamic community. In the biographical material included there is no overwhelming bias towards the religious classes; on the contrary a balance is preserved between the military classes, the religious classes, and the bureaucracy, which would seem to correspond, in some measure, to the actual distribution of power in the state. There are two groups of biographical material in the *'Ālam ārā*, one at the end of the reign of Shah Ṭahmāsp and the other at the end of the reign of Shah 'Abbās. In the former brief mention is made of the great *amīrs* (i.e. the Turkoman tribal leaders), military officails,

[1] See E. G. Browne, *Literary history*, iii, 426–8.

sayyids, *shaykhs*, and *'ulamā'*, *wazīrs*, *mustawfīs* and members of the bureaucracy, physicians, calligraphers, artists, and poets of the period. In the section at the end of the reign of Shah 'Abbās, among those dealt with are the great *amīrs*, *ṣadrs* (who were officials of the religious hierarchy), *wazīrs*, *mustawfīs*, and members of the bureaucracy of the period. The principles of selection underlying the work of Iskandar Beg, whether conscious or unconscious, are clearly different from those followed by earlier writers; in general only those whose work was important in the light of the state appear to have been included and the information given concerns rather appointments and dismissals than births and deaths.[2] It is tempting to see in this change of emphasis, if indeed it is such, a reflexion of the change in the theory regarding the rôle and position of the ruler which had been gradually evolving over a long period but had become more clearly marked under the Safavids. For many centuries the ruler had been regarded as the Shadow of God upon earth, but beside this there had survived —albeit in an attenuated form—the conception of the ruler as the shepherd of his people, who were a 'trust from God' and for whom he was responsible to God. Under the Safavids the conception of the ruler as the Shadow of God upon earth was reinforced by Shī'ī absolutism and the Safavid shah, as the representative of the Hidden Imām, if not himself the perfect man, was at least closer to the possession of absolute truth than any of his fellows. In such circumstances the only function left to the 'community' was the privilege of praying for the well-being of the shah. From this it follows that the main attention in biographical notices was likely to be devoted to officials of the state and not representatives of the 'community'. It is difficult, however, to judge whether the biographical sections of the *'Ālam ārā* represent a new trend among the writers of histories, because few of the general or dynastic histories of this period or that immediately following contain *wafāyāt* or biographical material.[3]

(5) *Biographies of Individuals*

The most common type is that of the *shaykh* of a religious order. Such works like the biographical dictionaries of the saints and Ṣūfīs are often largely anecdotal and tend to concentrate on the exercise of miraculous powers by the *shaykh*. An early example of this type of work is the *Asrār al-tawḥīd fī maqāmāt al-Shaykh Abī Sa'īd*, probably written in 547/1178–9, which throws considerable light on the life and times of Shaykh Abū Sa'īd b. Abi'l Khayr (357/440/968–1048–9). A later example is the *Ṣafvat al-ṣafā*, a recension by Abu'l Fatḥ al-Ḥusaynī of an earlier work by

[2] The inclusion in the first list of physicians and artists, etc., can be explained in that the former contributed to the health of the monarch, and the latter to his glory.

[3] In Muḥammad Yūsuf's *Dhayl-i tārīkh-i 'ālam ārā-yi 'Abbāsī*, which deals with the reign of Shah Ṣafī (1038–52/1629–42) there are brief notices at the end of the work of the officials of the period.

Ibn Bazzāz (written probably about 750/1349–50). It is a lengthy work concerned mainly with the alleged supernatural powers, prophetic utterances, and miracles of Shaykh Ṣafī al-Dīn, the founder of the Safavid order, and his *murīds*.[4]

(6) *Biographies of Families or Tribes*

These are comparatively rare. In the case of the latter the resemblance is to the dynastic history rather than to the biographical dictionary. One of the earliest family histories in Persian is the *Tārīkh-i Barāmika*, which is thought to belong to the fourth or fifth century of the Hijra. It consists mainly of anecdotes about eminent members of the family rather than a detailed account of their lives.

(7) *Autobiographies*

Autobiographies earlier than those of the twentieth century (which are not considered in this paper, diverging as they do from the medieval tradition) are few and relatively unimportant in that they seldom provide the historian with a detailed picture of the life and times of the author. Among them are the autobiography of Shaykh Muḥammad ʿAlī Hazīn of Iṣfahān, entitled *Tārīkh-i aḥvāl bi-tazkirat-i ḥāl-i khwud*, the *Rūznama* of Mīrzā Muḥammad, *kalāntar* of Fārs, being his 'recollections' which he began to write in 1200/1785–6, and the *Tajribat al-aḥrār va-tasliyat al-abrār* of ʿAbd al-Razzāq Beg Maftūn b. Najaf Qulī Khān Dunbulī (d. 1243/1827–8), which consists mainly of personal memoirs. Shah Ṭahmāsp (930–84/1824–76) also wrote an autobiography; but it does not bear comparison with, for example, the *Bābur Nāme*.

The motives of those who compiled the biographical material mentioned above were not as a rule very different from those of the historians. Both were Muslims and took for granted the social and political order under which they lived. Ideally the function of the state was to create conditions in which the good life could be lived, and histories were in some measure composed in order to illustrate this view; the biographies were written rather in order to record the lives of those who lived, or most nearly lived, the good life. Moreover since the culmination of history was God's revelation to the Prophet Muḥammad and His triumph manifest in the life of the Islamic community, it followed that the main emphasis in biographical literature was laid on those Muslims who might be regarded as the special repositories of divine wisdom because of their pursuit of knowledge, i.e. the *ʿulamāʾ*, or because of their special relationship to the Prophet, i.e.

[4] In the view of Aḥmad Kasravī the disciples of the Safavid family have made alterations in the copies of this work which have come down to us (*Nizhād va tabār-i Ṣafaviyya* in *Āyanda* (1927/8), ii, 361, quoted by R. M. Savory in a thesis for the degree of Ph.D. (London, 1958), entitled *The development of the early Ṣafavid state*).

the *sayyids*. The work of the biographer was thus largely one of *pietas*. Both he and the historian were concerned with the relation of fact (or what they conceived to be fact); but their relation of it was conditioned by their view of the world as Muslims. It is perhaps worth emphasizing that there could be for the Muslim no question of 'church' and 'state'. He was not conscious of belonging to more than one society. His orientation was thus towards a 'religious' interpretation of history. This is illustrated by the *Tārīkh-i guzīda* of Ḥamdallāh Mustawfī. In Chapter V on *Imāms*, Readers, *Shaykhs*, and '*Ulamā*' (which follows the chronicle proper) the following statement is found: 'They (the '*ulamā*') hold in the faith of Islam the rank of prophets (*anbiyā*') in other religions. Mention of the prophets has been made in the section on prophets [at the beginning of the book]; mention of them (the '*ulamā*') shall be at the end [of the book] so that its beginning and end shall be illumined by mention of the people of religion.'[5] He also relates, on the authority of the great *shaykhs* of Merv, that in Islamic times there would always be 300 of the saints (*awliyā*') of God on earth, 40 of whom would attain to high, 7 to higher, and 1 to supreme rank, the latter being the *quṭb* or Pole of the Day, God's proof to his creatures and the Pivot of the World. Whenever one of these died one from the next rank below succeeded him so that the hierarchy remained unbroken.[6] It was the belief in the '*ulamā*' as the heirs of the Prophet and the, at least in Persia, widely held belief in the existence of a hierarchy of saints, which assured for the religious classes a dominant position in the biographical literature of Persia.

The purpose of the biographer, like that of the historian, also included admonition and edification. Muḥammad b. Maḥmūd Āmulī states in the *Nafā'is al-funūn* (composed in 735/1334–5) that the value of history and biography lay not in the collection of stories and traditions but in admonition and warning, so that wise men might not set their hearts on this world but might concern themselves with the acquisition of eternal happiness.[7] This motive, common enough among the historians, however, is relatively rare among the biographers, who seem to be more commonly actuated by the wish to edify. This is particularly the case with the writers of the biographies of saints and Ṣūfīs, which are often less concerned with bare facts than with anecdotes illustrating the miraculous gifts of those about whom they are writing. Thus, 'Aṭṭār in his preface to the *Tazkirat al-awliyā*' mentions among the motives which had induced him to compose the work the following: the wish to remedy the existing state of affairs when the best men were bad and holy men had been forgotten; and the belief that the sayings of the saints disposed men to renounce the world, meditate on the future life, love God, and set about preparing for their last journey. He was also actuated by the hope that those who read the work

[5] Ed. E. G. Browne, Persian text, p. 755. [6] Ibid., pp. 796–7. [7] Lith. (Tehran), ii, 211.

would bless the author and thus, possibly, secure his welfare beyond the grave and that the influence of the saints would bring him happiness before he died and their intercession pardon hereafter.[8]

The writers of the biographical notices in local histories, in addition to being influenced by some of the motives mentioned above, were also, indeed perhaps mainly, inspired by local patriotism; here, too, the element of *pietas* comes in. The writers of many of the biographical works, however, were simply popularizers (and as such drew freely with or without acknowledgement on the works of their predecessors); they wrote to instruct, edify, and divert. Works such as the *Haft iqlīm* and the *Tazkiras* of the poets belong to this class. Those who wrote autobiographies did so for a variety of reasons. Some, like Mīrzā Muḥammad, the *kalāntar* of Fārs, wrote for personal amusement or diversion; others perhaps merely desired to record the events in which they had personally participated.

Of the various categories of biographical literature discussed above, none are peculiar to Persia; their characteristics are all shared to a greater or less degree by similar writings in other parts of the Islamic world. Two forms are, however, more characteristic than others of Persian biographical literature: the biographical dictionary of the religious sect or order and the local history with its main emphasis on the biography of local families and officials. I would suggest that this is not fortuitous, but that it derives from the fact that two of the most marked tendencies in Persian medieval life were the *pīr-murīd* relationship and provincial particularism. The value of these two categories of biographical literature to the historian is, clearly, not uniform. The writers of the first tend to be highly uncritical and much of their material is anecdotal and of little value to the historian, though even the most uncritical narrative may throw light on contemporary conditions or fill in lacunae. The information in the local histories, on the other hand, in spite of their limited scope, is often invaluable for the historian of Islamic civilization. For the rest Persian biographical literature, like its Arabic counterpart, except where the writers are merely popularizers, supplements our information from other sources and supplies valuable data for social and administrative history.

[8] Ed. R. A. Nicholson, Preface, pp. 13–15.

14. THE RISE OF OTTOMAN HISTORIOGRAPHY

HALIL INALCIK

Professor of History in the University of Ankara

There appear to have been good reasons why Ottoman historiography first produced its general works early in the fifteenth century after the collapse of Bāyezīd's empire and then upon the death of Meḥemmed the Conqueror at the end of the same century. Th. Seif has already pointed out that various *Tevārīkh-i āl-i 'Osmān* were written towards the end of the fifteenth century as a result of the consciousness of having established a great empire. The attempt to correlate the phases of Ottoman historiography with the development of Ottoman history itself can shed new light upon various problems.

I

With the first serious studies on Ottoman sources after the First World War it was thought that the oldest accounts of Ottoman history must be a *menāqibnāme* by Yakhshī Faqīh and Aḥmedī's chapter on the Ottomans in his *Iskendernāme*. Yakhshī Faqīh's work, the *Menāqib-i āl-i 'Osmān*, which deals with the period up to the time of Bāyezīd the Thunderbolt, is mentioned only by 'Āshîqpasha-zāde (Ashpz.). He had met Yakhshī Faqīh in Geyve in 1413. The latter had been granted land by Meḥemmed I whom he seems to have supported in his struggle for the Sultanate. The bitter criticism in Ashpz. against Chandarlî 'Alī Pasha who sided with Emīr Süleymān apparently comes from Yakhshī Faqīh. It seems that he composed his work under Meḥemmed I. Fr. Giese rightly pointed out that for the first century of Ottoman history Ashpz. and the anonymous *Tevārīkh-i āl-i 'Osmān* must have used a common source which appears to be Yakhshī Faqīh. Giese further suggested that this source can be reconstructed from these and Neshrī who, Giese thought, had included a good text of Ashpz. When Uruj's chronicle was discovered it was immediately seen that it is connected with the same source. Fr. Babinger, its editor, was of the opinion that it was composed in the Conqueror's time and the anonymous *Tevārīkh* was nothing but a new version of it. But in the first place the history of Uruj was dedicated to Bāyezīd II as is seen in the introduction of the Manisa manuscript. Secondly, Uruj and the anonymous *Tevārīkh* are independent versions of the original source in Ashpz. (Compare, for instance, the battle of Koyun-ḥiṣārî in three texts). Their relationship on the basis of a common source can be established from the emergence of 'Os̱mān Ghāzī up to the suppression of Muṣṭafā, the rebellious brother of Murād II in 1422. Now it seems that the common source was Yakhshī Faqīh's work with a continuation to 1422. Let us have a closer look at our chronicles.

In the first chapters the following theme is common to the three sources: An Oghuz group immigrated into Anatolia under Süleymān-shāh who was drowned in the Euphrates. His son Ertoghrul and his brothers moved back to Sürmeli-Chukur. (Three brothers are named in Neshrī and Kemāl Pashz., and only two in Ashpz., Uruj, and the anonymous *Tevārīkh*), 'Alā' al-Dīn, the Seljuqid ruler, granted to Ertoghrul and his followers the area of Sögüd-Tomalich-daghi̊ and Ermeni-beli. This theme is enlarged in Uruj and the anonymous *Tevārīkh* with additions from different sources, but from Tursun Faqīh's *khuṭba* in the name of 'Os̱mān Ghāzī onwards our three texts agree much more closely. Here only the anonymous *Tevārīkh* contain an original account of the fight at Yalak-ova between 'Os̱mān's forces and the emperor's army which was sent to relieve Nicaea. Incidentally, it is this battle not that of Koyun-ḥiṣāri̊ that agrees with the account of the battle at Baphaeon described by Pachymeres. Baphaeon is mistakenly associated with Koyun-ḥiṣāri̊ by Hammer and by all who wrote after him. There is a version of the same account in Neshrī which is linked with 'Os̱mān's receiving the symbols of princely power as a reward for this success. 'Os̱mān's victory over the forces sent by 'the *tekvur* of Konstantin' under his son in Uruj may be another variant of the same account. It would have been most surprising if there had been no mention in the Ottoman sources of this event which induced Pachymeres to mention 'Os̱mān in his history for the first time. In fact it is mentioned by Uruj and the anonymous *Tevārīkh*, but it is not mentioned by Ashpz.

The famous story of the dragon and the dervish in connection with the siege of Nicaea is found only in the anonymous *Tevārīkh* and is a widely scattered folk-tale which is also found in the *Saltuqnāme*. Uruj inserted a story about Bābā Ilyās citing his source as the *menāqibnāme* by Elvān Chelebī. Besides these additions from *menāqibnāmes* Uruj and the anonymous *Tevārīkh* give two accounts of the battle of Maritza against the Serbs, one corresponding to that of Ashpz. the other completely different. Uruj's account of the battle against Mircea in 1395 is completely original and agrees with what we now know from a Turkish document about it.[1] No mention is made of this important event in Ashpz. while a second account of it is found in the Bodleian Rūḥī, Neshrī and Bihishtī apparently from the same source. On the other hand Ashpz. has whole chapters which Uruj and the anonymous *Tevārīkh* lack altogether, such as those on Orkhan's operations in the Sakarya valley. Ashpz.'s further additions from his oral sources are not included, of course, in the other two texts. Relating to

[1] See *Proceedings of the X. International Congress of the Byzantinists* (Istanbul, 1957), pp. 220–2.

Bāyezīd's time we find a greater number of additions. Only the anonymous *Tevārīkh* contains a detailed account of Timur's capture of Sivas and his treatment of Bāyezīd in captivity as well as the stories about Sulṭān Aḥmed the Jelayirid. These stories are repeated by 'Ālī[2] nearly two hundred years later who said he obtained them from Hamzavī. On the other hand in the anonymous *Tevārīkh* the verse portions of these stories appear to come from the same source. It is safe to say that the important additions on this period in the anonymous *Tevārīkh* must have come from a separate source.

The statement on Bāyezīd's treatment of the corrupt *qāḍīs* and the clown is found jointly in our three texts with the difference that the anonymous *Tevārīkh* and Uruj reproduce the original source more fully. In general the anonymous *Tevārīkh* is more detailed in the parts criticizing the administration than the other sources.

Uruj and Ashpz. make the same mistakes when they spell the name of the battlefield of Marj Dābiq as *Majnūn Ṭabaq* while the anonymous *Tevārīkh* gives the correct form. I think this is another indication that Uruj cannot be considered as a source for the anonymous *Tevārīkh*.

To sum up Ashpz., Uruj and the anonymous *Tevārīkh* use each in his own fashion a common source from the emergence of 'Os̱mān up to 1422. In general Ashpz.'s version is the most detailed, although Uruj appears to give in a few places a fuller treatment of the original text. All three of them add to the common source new information from different sources such as oral traditions and *menāqibnāmes*. However, the anonymous *Tevārīkh* must have also used a rhymed work from 1402 up to 1424, probably Hamzavī's. For this reason all these texts must be considered as separate sources. Kemāl Pashz. and Neshrī both of which may be connected with the Ashpz. source group should be considered also separate versions because even in the statements obviously from the common source both of them contain details which cannot be found in any other. On the other hand individual copies of all these chronicles may be as important as different texts because their authors made revisions at various dates with additions or abridgements. For example, the Cambridge manuscript of Uruj concludes with the events in 899 H. But according to the introduction in the Manisa manuscript this copy is a revision, which brings the events up to 906 H. and in it we find detailed additions, for instance on the tribes in the Chukur-ova which came with Süleymān-shāh, allegedly grandfather of 'Os̱mān. This addition was made apparently in view of the current struggle against the Mamluks to get the upper hand in this region. There is no doubt that Ashpz. also made such new revisions with continuations. Therefore, Professor Wittek's theory of a more detailed Ashpz. text than those we possess today is still valid even when we recognize many additions made by Neshrī in Ashpz.'s text as coming from Rūḥī's source and the calendars.

[2] Vol. v, p. 94.

Here is a summary of what we have said on the earliest texts connected with the so-called Yakhshī Faqīh.

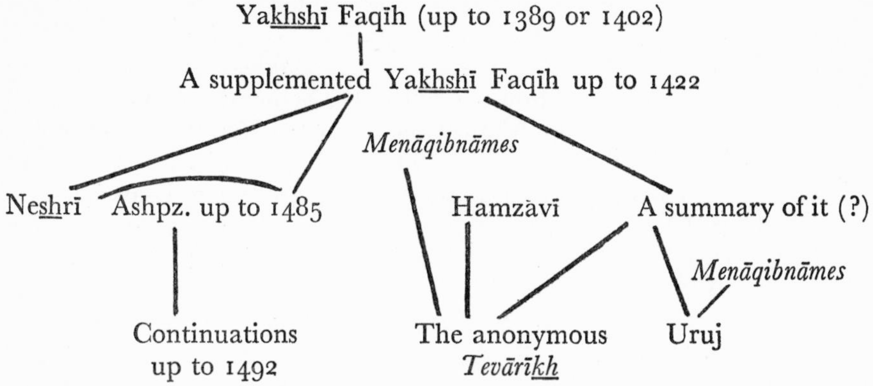

It is to be observed that the first compilation originated in the period of struggle for the existence of the Ottoman state after the fateful defeat in 1402. One can easily see in this historical account the effort to explain the disaster as God's punishment for the sins committed under Bāyezīd I. He and his *vezir* 'Alī Pasha are accused of encroaching upon the *Sherī'at* (*Sharī'a*) and introducing innovations in the government. When the chronicle describes 'Osmān Ghāzī as having no gold and silver in his possession at his death and as rejecting new taxation on dealings in the bazaar as a violation of the *Sherī'at*, our source appears to intend to criticize his own period by setting the first Ottoman ruler as an ideal example. The emphasis put on the respect shown by the first Ottoman rulers for the dervishes by granting them generous plots of land can also be interpreted as a denunciation of Bāyezīd's policy of abolishing the rights on the *mulk* and *waqf* lands. Thus this work on the first century of Ottoman history bears the marks of the great disappointment at the collapse of Bāyezīd's empire. The Ottomans then felt the need to have a general outlook on their historical existence and at the same time sought a historical basis for their future claims. The soft and conciliatory policy of Meḥemmed I and Murād II in contrast to Bāyezīd's impetuous government seems also to be reflected in these reactionary views. Timur's successors regarded any new action on the part of the Ottomans altering the situation set up by Timur in Central Anatolia as a violation of the status quo, and sent threatening words to Murād II on account of his operations against the Karamanids. What is more, the Timurids were trying to keep the Ottomans as their vassals at least legally. Now what we find in the Ottoman chronicles as well as in Murād's letter to Shāhrukh is that in order to continue their *ghazā* obligations in Rumeli the Ottomans claimed, as leaders of the *ghazā*, that they had to repulse the Karamanid attacks from the rear. The genealogies in the chronicles which link them to the Oghuz tradition seem to have been forged simply to make the Ottomans appear the equals of the Khāns in the East, so that they could escape the vassalage of the Timurids and claim supremacy over the Turkish principalities in Anatolia. Bāyezīd I had already claimed the title of *Sulṭān al-Rūm* which would make him the heir of the Seljuqids over all Anatolia. Our chronicle put these words in the mouth of 'Osmān: 'If Allah gave the Seljuqid Sultan the Sultanate, the same Allah gave me the Khanate by reason of *ghazā*. If he says that he is of the Seljuqid house I say I descend from Gökālp.'[3] Yazïjï-zāde of the time of Murād II added similar statements in his *Tārīkh-i āl-i Seljuq* which later were taken over by Rūḥī or his source. Another tradition in our chronicle made 'Osmān the legal heir of the last Seljuqid Sultan. That all these claims were added in the sources in the period after Bāyezīd I is well demonstrated by Professor Wittek.

In brief our original source is shaped under the strong influence of the ideas current in the Ottoman state in the first decades of the fifteenth century, and thus represents a particular outlook on Ottoman history which the future historians, Ottoman or Western, found ready for their use without understanding much of its true meaning. The compiler of this chronicle appears to have used as his material *menāqibnāmes* and *ghazavātnāmes* written on individual events and persons.

After 1422, however, Ashpz. on the one hand and the anonymous *Tevārīkh* and Uruj on the other follow completely different sources. Ashpz. often adds his own personal experiences and oral information to the *menāqibnāmes* which he says he summarized in his work. At the end of Murād II's reign he says: 'I, 'Āshiqī Dervīsh Aḥmed, have seen and known all the *ghazās* that this Sultan made as well as the circumstances which occurred to him and his utterances and actions, but I wrote them in summary in this *menāqibnāme*.' As for the anonymous *Tevārīkh* and Uruj they follow essentially a common source from 1422 to 1484. Significantly enough Uruj gives two different accounts of Muṣṭafā's rebellion in 1422, the first of them is apparently the same as in the anonymous *Tevārīkh* and Ashpz. The anonymous *Tevārīkh* shifts to the new source with the usual formula of '*Rāvīler shöyle eydürler kim*', on the events after 1422. The common source of Uruj and the anonymous *Tevārīkh* for the period after this date seems to be the calendars which we shall deal with presently. But let us first examine *menāqibnāmes*, apparently original sources of Ottoman historiography in the first period.

The origin of this religio-heroic literature was sought on the one hand in the popular Turkish epics, on the other in the Islamic tradition of *maghāzī*, *siyar*, and *menāqib-i-evliyā* literature. F. Köprülü suggested that

[3] Ashpz. Giese ed., p. 20.

the achievements of the Anatolian Turks in the Rumeli *ghazā* areas gave birth to a third cycle of these popular epics after those represented by *Baṭṭālnāmes* and *Dānishmendnāmes*. In his opinion the third cycle is exemplified by the *Saltuqnāme* which is a collection of the popular *menāqib*, religio-epic tales, the *ghazā* and islamizing activities of the famous saint Sarï Saltuq in Rumeli.

In Ashpz., the anonymous *Tevārīkh*, and Uruj we find actually two kinds of *menāqibnāme*; one consists of typical folk-tales as in the case of 'Osmān Ghāzī's dream about the future of his house, and Murād I's miraculous deeds; the other consists of *menāqibnāmes* or *ghazavātnāmes* of real historical information. The typical examples of the latter are the detailed accounts of the first battle of Kossovo and of Meḥemmed I's activities between 1402 and 1415 in the Bodleian Rūḥī and Neshrī. The story of the capture of Bursa in Ashpz. can be considered as the same type of *menāqibnāme*. As an original example of this type we now possess a separate *ghazavātnāme*, *ghazavāt-i Murād Khān* on the battle of Varna in 1444. Though a *menāqibnāme* of a later period this detailed book gives a good idea of this kind of *menāqibnāmes*. The epic of Ghāzī Umur in Enverī's *Düstūrnāme* can be also classified as belonging to this type of *menāqibnāme* or *ghazavātnāme*. Incidentally, our texts use both terms indiscriminately, a fact which is quite normal if we consider that in the Ottoman frontier lands dervishes and *ghāzīs* often became identical. In any case written about individual events or persons, about sultans or famous frontier *begs*, these historical *menāqibnāmes* appear in general to give detailed and quite reliable historical information.

In a society imbued with the *ghazā* spirit *menāqibnāmes* were usually intended to be read aloud in public gatherings, in the army or in the bazaars where we find, as one *qāḍī* record of Bursa reports, merchants equipping soldiers at their own expense. Reflecting popular feelings in simple language, the genre of *menāqibnāme* survived in many *ghazavātnāmes* as well as in such popular works as Ashpz. and the anonymous *Tevārīkh* in the following centuries. Actually Ashpz. addresses his listeners, 'Hey Ghāzīler' and concludes as follows: 'Whoever reads or listens to these *menāqib* of the house of 'Osmān and sends prayers for their souls, may God grant him heavenly bliss.'

As for the calendars which became the main source of Uruj and the anonymous *Tevārīkh* and which were found in astrological works entitled *jedāvil al-taqvīm*, *jedvel al-ikhtiyārāt* or *aḥkām ve-ikhtiyārāt*, they belong to an early branch of Muslim astronomy. As a basis for their predictions of the future, astrologers of the early centuries of Islam included in their works chronological lists on important events, political or natural. Referring to the scheme proposed by the Ikhwān al-Ṣafā for astrological works in the tenth century, Fr. Rosenthal considers them to be very close to an annalistic history. It seems that the Anatolian Turks were interested in this *'ilm* quite early. We have an original copy of Zayn al-Münejjim b. Süleymān al-Konevī's *Jedvel al-ikhtiyārāt* written in Sīvās late in the summer 1371 which contains a chronological list on the Sejuqids and the Ilkhanids. The subsequent notes made on the cover of the manuscript referring to such events as the meeting of Bāyezīd Beg, Tāj al-Dīn Beg and Ḥājji Shād-geldi on Chal-dagh on 6 Muḥarrem 780, are very interesting because they show how astrologers recorded their chronological data on the spot. The significance of the numerous Ottoman works on *aḥkām ve-ikhtiyārāt* many of which contain chronological lists has been realized only recently.[4] The oldest Ottoman works that have survived belong to the years of 849 and 851 H. and are obviously based on earlier works. It seems that at the beginning of each new year a calendar with *aḥkām ve-ikhtiyārāt* was drawn up for the Sultan's use. In fact there exists another calendar for the year of 856 H. in which the chronological lists in the above-mentioned texts were summarized. Thus the *münejjims* in the court can be regarded as the first *vaq'anuvīs*.

Now let me give you an example of how Uruj and the anonymous *Tevārīkh* drew their information from these calendars. In the calendar of 849 H. we read as follows: 'It is four years since the castle and the city of Novabiri and some of its territory were taken from the unbelievers by Shihāb al-Dīn Pasha, Beglerbegi of Rumeli, and some places by Isḥāq Beg, Beg of Uj-eli, in the time of Murād Khān.' In the anonymous *Tevārīkh* we read: 'It was in the year of 843 H. that Sultan Murād fell upon Belgrade but could not take it and then came back and conquered the castle of Novaberda and Shihāb al-Dīn Pasha, Beglerbegi of Rumeli, and Isḥāq Beg, beg of Uj, conquered some of its territory.' And in Uruj is as follows: 'In the year of 843 H. Shihāb al-Dīn Pasha took the castle of Novaberda and its territory on this side, Isḥāq Beg, *beg* of Uj, was along with him.' Lastly Neshrī gives the same record this way: 'In the year of 844 the castle of Novabiri with some provinces of the unbelievers were taken by Shihāb al-Dīn and some castles by Isḥāq Beg, *beg* of Uj.' It is noticed that Uruj copies out its source fairly well but the anonymous *Tevārīkh* leaves the honour of the capture of Novobrdo for the Sultan. The calendars must have used a chronicle for the first Ottoman rulers since it is unlikely that any calendar was written in this early period. In fact the calendars give very little information until the last years of Murād I. The chronicle that they may have used seems to be the same as that used by Karamānī Meḥemmed in 1480. Important contemporary events were usually related in some detail as was the case with the battle of Varna in the calendar of 849 H. This statement of one page is reduced to a few lines in the calendar of 856 H. But it is to be noted that Uruj's

[4] See my *Fatih Devri* (Ankara, 1954), i.

description of this battle is much more detailed than even that of the *taqvīm* of 849. Apparently Uruj as well as the anonymous *Tevārīkh* made use of *ghazavātnāmes* for the great events such as the battles of Varna or Kossovo and one can see breaks in the chronological records of *taqvīms* whenever *ghazavātnāmes* are used. Our texts contain peculiarly abundant records taken from *taqvīms* concerning earthquakes, astronomical phenomena, fires and pests. The calendars, the anonymous *Tevārīkh* and especially Uruj are incomparably better in chronology than later compilations such as Neshrī. One important characteristic of Uruj is that he gives the names of pashas in the Dīvān every time there is change. For instance, that Meḥemmed Pasha was the first vizier in 832 is reported only in Uruj, a fact also confirmed by his *vaqfiyyes*. For these details the Manisa and Paris manuscripts of Uruj are better than those published by Babinger. Also Uruj is much more detailed in its chronological parts up to the first years of Bāyezīd II than the anonymous. It is most likely that the latter used a *taqvīm* or *taqvīms* of recent date with the data much summarized. For the first period of Bāyazīd II's reign up to 891 H. the anonymous *Tevārīkh* appears to use a more detailed *taqvīm* than Uruj, while from 891 onwards they both follow one *taqvīm* which contains the precise dates for all the important events. We hope that a systematic investigation in our library collections may bring to light the original calendars used by Uruj and the anonymous *Tevārīkh*. At the moment we can draw this diagram:

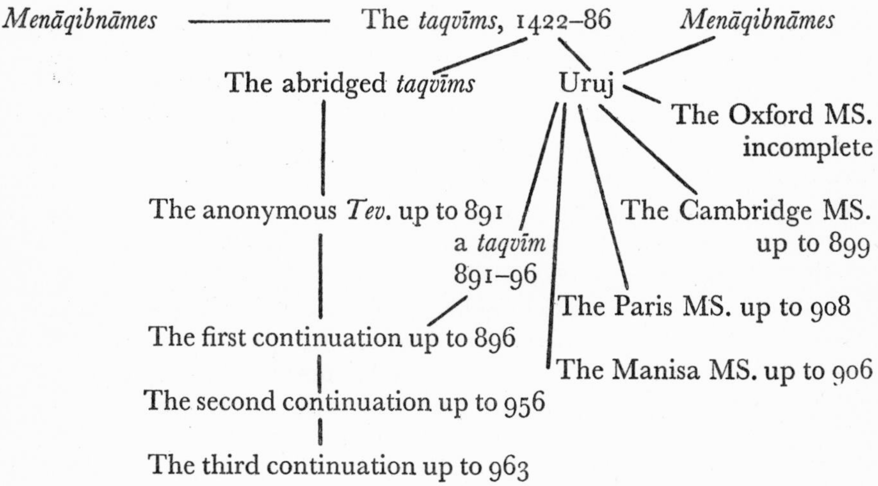

II

It was thought that, along with Yakhshī Faqīh, Aḥmedī's *Dāsitān-i Tevārīkh-i mulūk-i āl-i ʿOsmān* in his *Iskendernāme* was the second oldest account for the first century of Ottoman history, and we know that this *dāsitān* was dedicated to Süleymān I (1403–10). Here we shall try to show that Aḥmedī's source is the same one as that used by Shükrullāh, Karamānī Meḥemmed Pasha, Meḥemmed Konevī, Rūḥī, Sarija Kemāl, and Neshrī. Rūḥī and Neshrī reproduce the information more completely than the others. Thus these texts altogether represent a second group of sources as distinct from the group of Ashpz., Uruj, and the anonymous *Tevārīkh*. Neshrī tried to unite these two different groups selecting the statement on a given event from one of these sources and arranging his selection chronologically, apparently without making any important change in the statement itself. But the Bodleian manuscript of Rūḥī seems to copy out the statements without insertions or omissions such as are made by Neshrī, so that it contains the original source more completely. For example, in the chapter *Ḥikāyet-i murūr-i Süleymān Pasha ilā Rumeli* Neshrī follows the common source with Rūhī up to '*Karasi vilāyeti timariydi, hemen feth olundughu gibi ana vermishdi*' and then with the word *al-qiṣṣa* he changes over to the Ashpz. text. In this section the remainder of the account given by Rūḥī is left out by Neshrī, but in one place he adds with the expression '*derler ki*' the names of the two castles conquered by Süleymān Pasha as *Ödküklük* and *Eksamilye* as alternatives to the names *Jimbini* and *Aya Shilonya* given by Ashpz. But in their statement from the common source Neshrī gives a more detailed text than the Bodleian Rūḥī. We find *Ödküklük* and *Eksamilye* in Shükrullāh, Meḥemmed Konevī, Sarija Kemāl, Karamānī Meḥemmed, but not in Aḥmedī, whose work, though the oldest, is the shortest recension of the common source. In this second group of sources which differ from each other only by their additions or omissions, there is a completely different tradition about the origin of the Ottomans and their immigration into Anatolia. Characteristic points in this tradition are as follows: Akhlat is mentioned as the first settlement area of an Oghuz group of 340 immigrant families, the genealogy is recorded as Ertoghrul, son of Gündüz Alp, son of Gök Alp, son of Sarkuk-Alp, son of Kopuk-Alp. This group had finally settled down in Karajadagh near Ankara. 'Alā' al-Dīn, the Seljuqid ruler, came to Sulṭān-öyügü and made Ertoghrul a *ghāzī* chief there. The Bodleian Rūḥī seems to combine this tradition with that of Ashpz., while Neshrī mostly gives both traditions side by side. Rūḥī also adds the interesting account of Yazijizāde of the election of 'Osmān by the Oghuz tribes in the *Uj* (frontier zone) as well as of the general conditions in Anatolia at that time. In Karamānī we find Akhlat and the Kopuk-Alp genealogy but no figure, in the *Selāṭīnnāme* by Sarija Kemāl only the number of the immigrants as 1340. Aḥmedī, the earliest version of the source, contains only the statement on 'Alā' al-Dīn as in all the other texts.

To show the degree of their relationship to the original source the following example is interesting. Aḥmedī mentions a certain S͟heyk͟h Efendi without giving his name. S͟hükrullāh gives the name as Ramaẕān, but Rūḥī, Sarîja Kemāl, and Nes͟hrī make it clear that S͟heyk͟h Ramaẕān was appointed *qāḍī'asker* by Bāyezīd I. On the biography of Ramaẕān *S͟haqā'iq-i nu'māniyye* takes over the same information from them. The punishment of the corrupt *qāḍīs* by Bāyezīd I is mentioned by Aḥmedī S͟hükrullāh, Rūḥī; an account is also given by the Ashpz. group but from another source.

We can conclude that Aḥmedī's source was used by others separately and more fully. This source must have come down to the conquest of Malatiya in 1399. Now it is clear that we have various versions of it made in the fifteenth century: Aḥmedī towards 1410, S͟hükrullāh in 1456–59, Karamānī Meḥemmed and Meḥemmed Konevī towards 1480, Rūḥī, Nes͟hrī, and Sarîja Kemāl around 1490. As a separate and apparently older source than that contained in the first group of chronicles, it is undoubtedly most important for a critical study of the first century of Ottoman history. For example, we can now state positively that in Bāyezīd I's time there was a radical reform of the *qāḍīs*, an event which in the form in which it occurs in the Ashpz.-Yak͟hs͟hī Faqīh tradition has the appearance of a legend. The archaic character of the Aḥmedī-Rūḥī tradition is shown by its emphasis on the *g͟hazā*, its more modest genealogy for the Ottoman house, the eminent place devoted to Süleymān Pasha, brother of Murād I, and the fact that it mentions such names as Sinān Pasha and *qāḍī'asker* S͟heyk͟h Ramaẕān who were unknown to Ashpz.

It appears that S͟hükrullāh, Rūḥī, and Nes͟hrī used a text which had copied Aḥmedī's source more faithfully than Aḥmedī himself and had continued it up to the end of Meḥemmed I's time. In fact S͟hükrullāh, Rūḥī, and Nes͟hrī are closely related to each other up to 1421. The section covering the period 1399 to 1420 in these texts shows again a completely different character from the Ashpz.-Uruj tradition. It deals with the uprising of the Ṣūfīs in Karaburun, the disorders in the Amasya and Tokat region caused by the Karakoyunlu intervention, the fortification of the three castles of Sak͟chi, Yeni-Sale and Yergögi on the Danube, and the capture of Severin. The first group of chronicles lack these points completely.

Rūḥī makes two long additions to his source, one concerning Murād's expedition into Karaman-eli and the battle of Kossovo, the other concerning Meḥemmed I's struggle for supremacy during the period of civil war. As we have said these must have been taken from two different *menāqib-nāmes*. We find these additions in Nes͟hrī too, the first one with more detail than Rūḥī and the second identical in both texts.

For Murād II's time Rūḥī is an independent source with original data except for the second reign of this sultan from 1446 to 1451 where he appears to use the same source as Ashpz. Probably this was a separate *menāqibnāme*. This is the only part where the two texts agree. Ashpz. gives the common source in more detail except on Meḥemmed II's expedition into Karamān-eli in 1451. The demonstration of the Janissaries against the Sultan during this expedition is related only by Rūḥī. S̲h̲ükrullāh gives a very superficial outline of Murād II's time and Meḥemmed Konevī seems simply to copy it. For the reign of Meḥemmed the Conqueror, Konevī appears to use a calendar which makes him very close to Uruj and the anonymous *Tevārīk̲h̲*. That Karamānī did not use S̲h̲ükrullāh directly as a source can be seen by comparing their treatment of the reign of Murād II. For the conqueror's time Karamānī seems to have made use of a calendar. As for Rūḥī he gives an original text on the reigns of Meḥemmed II and Bāyezīd II up to the conquest of Akkerman and Kili in 1484 (he distinguishes two expeditions of the Conqueror into Serbia in 1454 and 1455, mentions the wounding of Maḥmūd Pasha during the expedition against Trebizond and the dispatch of Aḥmed Bikrījī by Uzun Ḥasan to make peace).

A completely original work on the Conqueror's reign is Tursun Beg's *Tārīk̲h̲-i Ebu'l-Fetḥ* which is based on his own personal experiences. As for the *S̲h̲āhnāmes* written under the Conqueror we shall deal with these later.

Here is a diagram of what we have said on the second group of sources.

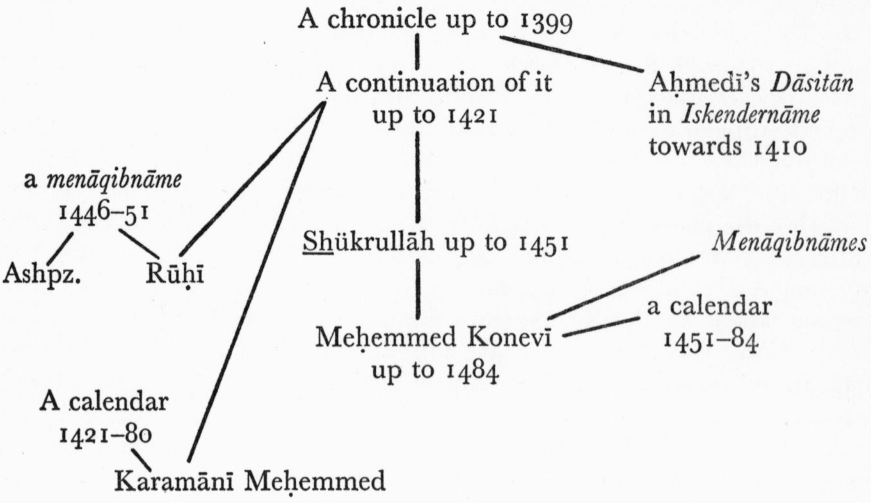

III

Tārīk̲h̲-K̲h̲wāns, history-readers and popular poets reading *menāqib-nāmes* were present in the courts of the Seljuqid Sultans and Türkmen *begs* in Anatolia. The Ottomans continued the tradition. It seems that historical works in the form of *ghazavātnāmes* were written to be read aloud to the Sultan in his retreat to satisfy his pride and literary taste.

As the time went by the court and upper classes were interested in more sophisticated types of *menāqibnāmes* and *ghazavātnāmes* written in high literary style and mostly in Persian. Aḥmedī's *Dāsitān* in Turkish can be regarded as one of the first examples of it. Around 1456 Kāshifī, a Persian poet, wrote his *ghazānāme-i Rūm*, a versified work in Persian glorifying the Conqueror's *ghazās*. It was dedicated to the sultan; as a historical source it contains quite a lot of original information. Under Meḥemmed II this kind of literature which is shown under the general name of *shāhnāme* seems to have flourished. A number of Persian poets who then invaded the Ottoman capital were in keen competition not only with the Ottoman writers but also with each other to attract the Sultan's favours. Following Kāshifī, Ḥamīdī, Mu'ālī, Shehdī are the names which have survived as the authors of such works during this period. In Laṭīfī's *tezkere* it reads: 'Thirty poets were granted salaries and yearly pensions (by the Conqueror) who were putting in rhyme his history or writing poems in his praise.' Mu'ālī's *khünkārnāme* which was discovered recently at the Topkapı-Sarayı, but Ḥamīdī's and Shehdī's works are missing. It is safe to say that *shāhnāme*-writing as an early type of court historiography was established in the middle of the fifteenth century. Its main function was to glorify in a high literary form the exploits of the reigning Sultan, but occasionally *shāhnāme* writers composed also general histories of the Ottoman house. For their own time they produced generally original works based on first-hand information. Still linked with the old *menāqibnāme* tradition special *ghazavātnāmes* were composed for famous chiefs of *ghazā*. *Ghazavātnāme-i Mikhāl-oghlu 'Alī Beg* by Sūzī Chelebī was recently published by A. S. Levend. *Ghazavāt-i Dāvūd Pasha* by Khayr al-Dīn Chelebī, no copy of which has been found, was actually borrowed by Kemāl Pasha-zāde in his *Tevārīkh* at the end of the seventh volume. The genre of the old popular *menāqibnāmes* seemed also to continue in the court on the one hand with the *qiṣṣa-khwāns* who were ranked below the *shāhnāme*-writers, and on the other hand with the appointment of *münshīs* who were famous stylists to compose *Tevārīkh-i āl-i 'Osmān* on the model of fashionable Persian historiography. Under Bāyezīd II who desired that the history of his house be written in Turkish, we find written in the *shāhnāme* style Qivāmī's *Fetḥnāme* on the Conqueror's *ghazās*, Kemāl's *Selāṭīnnāme*, a general history of the Ottomans, the *Quṭbnāme* by Firdevsī on the naval expedition for Mytilene, and the *ghazavātnāme* by Ṣafāyī on the exploits of Kemāl Re'īs. Qivāmī's work was recently published by Babinger and the manuscript copies of others are now known.[5] In the following centuries the genre of *shāhnāme* continued with numerous works some of which had

[5] See A. S. Levend, *Gazavatnameler* (Ankara, 1956).

real artistic value in calligraphy, miniature and illumination. It is noteworthy that some of the *s͟hāhnāme*-writers were versed not only in these but in astrology too. *Sūrnāmes* describing royal wedding festivities can be considered as a branch of *s͟hāhnāme* genre.

IV

Was it just a coincidence that many of the general histories of the Ottoman house were composed in Bāyezīd II's time and that most of them concluded with the events of 1484–85? Ashpz., Rūḥī, the first composition of the anonymous *Tevārīk͟h*, the Menzel manuscript of Nes͟hrī, Meḥemmed Konevī, Qivāmī, Sarīja Kemāl, Tursun Beg end their work with the events of 1484 or 1485. For this unusual activity in producing compilations on the general history of the Ottomans at that time the first and foremost reason was no doubt Bāyezīd II's desire to see such works written, and the '*ulemā*' of his time responded to it. Bāyezīd II then wanted to use this means for shaping public opinion in his favour. Bāyezīd represented a reactionary policy in all political, social, and legal fields in contrast to the Conqueror, while Jem Sulṭān, still alive, was regarded as the symbol of the previous régime. In all the above-mentioned works Bāyezīd is demonstrated primarily as a just and law-abiding ruler with the mission of consolidating the large conquests which his predecessor had made (see especially the introductions in Tursun Beg, Kemāl Pshz., and Idrīs). Gedik Aḥmed who was an idol of the Janissaries and had seized actually all the power in the state was executed in 1482 and his father-in-law Isḥāq Pasha was dismissed from the grand vizierate the following year. The Janissaries became restless and Gedik Aḥmed's previous opposition to the policy of concessions to Christendom was shared naturally by all the *g͟hāzī* elements. It was under these conditions that Dāvūd Pasha, famous for his *g͟hazā* achievements in Bosnia, was chosen as grand vizier and the Sultan felt bound to lead the army himself into Moldavia, where the Conqueror had previously failed. In order to influence public opinion the victory won there should have been propagated as widely as possible. Commenting on the victory in Moldavia Meḥemmed Konevī said emphatically as follows: 'None of his ancestors was able to take these two strongholds', and Tursun Beg emphasizes that Sultan Meḥemmed was not able to lay siege to Kili.[6] If the Ashpz. text is read in the light of Bāyezīd's reactionary policy its controversial character would become evident throughout. It can be added that in Nes͟hrī Gedik Aḥmed is blamed for his ill advice to Bāyezīd during the battle of Otluk-beli in 1473, while Ibrāhīm C͟handarlī is praised for his efforts, all this being simply an addition to the original source by Nes͟hrī himself. Also Dāvūd Pasha's rôle

[6] *TOEM* edition, p. 186.

in the Conqueror's time is often exaggerated in most of these works. A careful study of their introduction is revealing indeed. In Rūḥī we read: 'Sultan Bāyezīd said: "Histories of the prophets are regarded as the best and most preferable, and thus, the '*Ulemā*' prefer to write this kind of histories, but the history of the Ottoman Sultans who are the most distinguished and honourable among others has not yet been the subject of a compilation written in a language for everybody's profit. It is desirable that it should have been." This statement of the Sultan made me decide to collect the histories [of the Ottomans] in Turkish which are circulating in the Ottoman dominions.' Neshrī makes a similar statement in his preface: 'I found that many works are written on the other '*ilms* but that those on history still remain scattered especially in Turkish.' Sultan Bāyezīd's insistence on such a history in a Turkish simple enough to be understood by everybody is significant.

The works written in the first years of Bāyezīd and directly connected with the victory in Moldavia are most important for Ottoman historiography, because it was these compilations that became the basis of all that is written later on the first two centuries of the Ottoman history and their original sources are now mostly unavailable for us. Ashpz. obviously made several revisions of his work with continuations and the last one seems to have been made in 1484–85. Meḥemmed Konevī started writing under Meḥemmed the Conqueror and completed his work under Bāyezīd II. An official record testifies that Mevlānā Rūḥī was given awards by Bāyezīd towards 1503. Sarija Kemāl completed his *Selāṭinnāme* in June 1490. As to Neshrī's work Professor Taeschner finds, in view of the Menzel manuscript, 1485 as *terminus post quem* and 1495 as *terminus ante quem* for the date of its composition. Statements in Bihishtī, Uruj, and the anonymous *Tevārīkh* are clear enough to show that all are written under Bāyezīd II.

An attempt has been made in the preceding pages to find out what kind of sources were used in these compilations, and we concluded that in their greatest part Ashpz. on the one hand, Rūḥī on the other, give us two different traditions in their most detailed form. Neshrī is, indeed, the oldest compilation which seeks to combine the two traditions from Ashpz. and Rūḥī. But it is again a question whether Neshrī used a source common to Rūḥī or a detailed copy of Rūḥī, because Neshrī relates the same accounts as in the Bodleian Rūḥī but often with more details even on the events as late as 1484. It is to be recalled that Neshrī also utilized calendars which were a source for Uruj, the anonymous *Tevārīkh*, and Konevī too. Now it is possible to draw a list showing which parts in Neshrī come from which sources. He appears to add very little personal information.

Not only did reaction to the Conqueror's policies characterize the compilations made under Bāyezīd II, but also the consciousness of having established a universal Muslim empire in competition for supremacy with the Mamluk and Persian states in the East required a new evaluation of Ottoman history at that time. In the previous outlines of world history, for example in Shükrullāh's and Enverī's works, Ottoman history occupied a modest place as a continuation of Islamic history, and the Ottoman Sultans were presented as *ghāzīs* on the frontiers of the Muslim world. But now Bāyezīd II claimed to be *Ashraf al-Salāṭīn*, the most distinguished and honoured of the Muslim rulers, and one of these compilers said that except for the Prophet himself and his four immediate successors no other Muslim ruler had more achievements than the Ottoman sultans. It must be remembered that it was then that the Ottomans had entered a long war against the Mamluks for South Anatolia and wished to show themselves superior to their opponents in every respect. The Ottomans still emphasized their *ghazā* mission but claimed that it had the most significant place in Islam. Around 1502 Kemāl Pasha-zāde said in the introduction of his work: 'The Sultan remarked that if the histories and stories and anecdotes were not written down and thus the glories and the achievements of the great rulers were not perpetuated for the ages to come, they would be forgotten. He, therefore, asked that his achievements and those of his ancestors should be recorded. And in order to be useful for the distinguished as well as for ordinary people it should be composed in a clear style in Turkish and I was appointed by him to do this.'

About the same time Idrīs Bidlīsī, a famous Persian *münshī*, was ordered by the Sultan to write a great history in Persian worthy of the Ottoman house. Idrīs himself relates it as follows: 'Sulṭān Bāyezīd ordered that a history of this great dynasty from its beginning in the year of 710 up to the present year of 908 should be written in a style favoured by the distinguished as well as by ordinary people with the correction and elucidation of the accounts concerning this dynasty. It is true that there are in Turkish a number of works on the subject but their stories lack elegance in style and truth on the events.'

The *Shaqā'iq*[7] makes it clear that the *Qāḍī'asker* Mu'ayyad-zāde had suggested to Bāyezīd II that as Molla Idrīs was asked to write a history of the Ottoman house in Persian, it was suitable or perhaps necessary to have a work in Turkish on the same subject and this could be accomplished only if Mevlānā Kemāl Pshzd. agreed to do it. It is clear that, unsatisfied with the current histories of his house, Bāyezīd II gave orders for two great *münshīs* of his time, Idrīs in Persian, Ibn Kemāl in Turkish, to write this history again. They tackled the task in a similar plan devoting a separate book to each Ottoman Sultan. With his most elaborate work, *Hasht bihisht*, Idrīs composed Ottoman history in the most sophisticated form of Persian historiography. Later Khoja Sa'd al-Dīn took this work as a model for his *Tāj al-tevārīkh* in Turkish, which became a classic. It seems that

[7] Turkish translation by Mejdī, p. 384.

Idrīs followed mainly the Rūḥī tradition. We find in Idrīs some of the personal accounts of Tursun Beg too. Idrīs gives some original information on the events concerning Central and Eastern Anatolia. The description of the Ottoman court and government in a separate chapter gives this work a unique place among Ottoman chronicles. The Turkish counterpart of *Hasht bihisht* is Ibn Kemāl's *Tevārīkh-i āli-ʻOsmān*, the largest and the most important compilation in this period. It is also an important literary work reflecting the desire to create a high Turkish prose competing with Persian. Ibn Kemāl apparently used a detailed copy of Neshrī and added Karamānī's account for the first period. For the Conqueror's time he followed principally Tursun Beg and Neshrī, and there are indications that he is also familiar with Rūḥī or his source and a detailed copy of Uruj like the Paris or Manisa manuscripts. As was said above, his work contains here Khayr al-Dīn Chelebī's *Ghazavāt-i Dāvūd Pasha*. Moreover Ibn Kemāl added many important details from his personal knowledge as well as from contacts with others. He shows great skill in selecting his sources on individual events and utilizing them. He can be regarded as the greatest of all the Ottoman historians including Khoja Saʻd al-Dīn, ʻĀlī, Naʻīmā, and Jevdet Pasha.

15. THE BEGINNINGS OF OTTOMAN HISTORIOGRAPHY

V. L. MÉNAGE

Lecturer in Turkish, School of Oriental and African Studies, London

By the beginning of the 10th/16th century nearly all branches of Ottoman literature had succumbed to Persian influence: the models had been studied and the language developed to the point where writers could aspire to producing works which in elaboration and subtlety would vie with those of the poets and prose-writers of Persia. In historiography, the turning-point is represented by the works of Idrīs Bidlīsī and Kemālpasha-zāde. The first demonstrated that Ottoman history could be recorded in Persian as elegantly and grandiloquently as the history of other dynasties had been, the second showed that the Turkish language was now an adequate vehicle for the same rhetorical devices.

As for the historical texts of the preceding century, their attraction as literature lies in the direct and robust style in which most of them are written—a style which did not disappear with the change of taste but was submerged, continuing in use in popular literature but despised by the artistic historian who wrote for the court and for learned circles and for whom the mode of expression often became an end in itself.

The importance of these early texts for the historian is patent, but they are of interest also to the student of historiography, for they are the raw material on which later writers relied, directly or at one or more removes, for the history of the first two centuries of the Ottoman state. A high proportion of these texts has survived, so that it is possible to trace the various threads—of legend, tradition, chronicle, and panegyric—as they are woven together by successive compilers and finally embroidered in the artistic histories.

The change of style had this great advantage for the modern historian that a text written in ornate prose tended to be more faithfully transmitted. A rhyme-word or a punning epithet often prevented the deformation even of an unfamiliar proper name, and the copyist of such a text, feeling that to interpolate or to modify would be to spoil the artistry, hesitated to tamper with it. The copyist of the earlier, more popular, histories felt no such reverence: he felt at liberty to 'correct', expand, abridge or continue model, so that it is often impossible to decide whether a given manuscript represents the author's original work, a later redaction by the author (for many texts were worked over by their authors more than once), or a new redaction by a copyist, who, by the extent of his additions, deserves to rank as an author in his own right. This fact alone—not to speak of the deterioration in a text produced by the normal hazards of transmission—makes it very difficult to edit such works, and in spite of the efforts of modern scholars we have no entirely satisfactory edition of any fifteenth-century history. The growing practice of publishing such texts in the form of a facsimile of a single manuscript has more to commend it than cheapness: the reader may well receive sounder guidance from the one manuscript than from an edition whose readings are a hotch-potch from different recensions.

The following survey does not pretend to be exhaustive: it does not include all the works that are known to exist nor even all that are published; and some writers are omitted (notably Yazîjî-oghlu 'Alī and Tursun Beg) who, while they did not write general histories of the Ottomans, exerted an important influence on their successors. It is no more than a general sketch of the character of some of the fifteenth-century histories and of the methods of their authors.

Aḥmedī, the first writer to be considered, is not a historian but a poet. He was born in Anatolia in about 1330 and studied in Egypt, where he became versed in all branches of Moslem learning. He lived for a long time at Kutahya, the seat of the ruler of Germiyān, one of the strongest and most cultured of the successor-states of the Seljuq sultanate of Rūm, but at some stage, most probably in about 1380 when part of Germiyān was incorporated in the Ottoman dominions, attached himself to the rising Ottoman House. After Timur's withdrawal from Anatolia he enjoyed the patronage of Emīr Süleymān at his court at Adrianople, and certainly survived into the reign of Meḥemmed I. His great work is the *Iskendernāme*, a long *mes̱nevī* poem of something over 8,000 couplets, in which he used the events of the Alexander Legend as pegs on which to hang a series of discourses on philosophy, theology, medicine, and history. (Hammer describes the poem very appropriately as being the work at once of a Lucan and of a Lucretius.) About a quarter of the whole poem consists of an account of world history, from the time of the legendary Kayūmarth. Aḥmedī has ingeniously worked this in by the device of making Alexander ask his tutor Aristotle to relate to him the history of the world down to their own time, and the account is then continued in the form of a prophecy of what is going to happen afterwards. In some manuscripts this prophetic section ends with the sack of Baghdād by Hūlāgū; in others it is continued to Aḥmedī's own time, the last chapter, some 340 couplets, telling the story of the Ottomans from Ertoghrul to Emīr Süleymān, with whose praises it ends.

The poem was extremely popular, thanks to its simple pedestrian style and its tone of pious didacticism, and numerous manuscripts, representing several recensions, exist. It is clear that the poem was worked over more than once by the poet himself for his successive patrons, modifying the dedication and bringing the historical section up to date, but it would be a very laborious—and perhaps superfluous—task to establish the successive stages of revision. The chapter on Ottoman history as we have it must have been introduced when Aḥmedī came under Emīr Süleymān's patronage. The style in which it is written suggests that behind the verses there lay a bald prose chronicle, which Aḥmedī has versified and adorned with various digressions. It is not easy to decide at what point this source ended: it was probably about the middle of the reign of Bāyezīd I, for there is no mention in Aḥmedī's text of Bāyezīd's resounding victory at Nicopolis, and only a brief and uncircumstantial mention of Timur's invasion.

No historical work has survived from the next forty years or so, though chronicles compiled during this period (and perhaps containing fragments of the chronicle which Aḥmedī used) have been incorporated in later works. The next source after Aḥmedī, and the earliest source to survive in its original form, consists of a group of short texts which may conveniently be called 'Royal Calendars', for the three that are known[1] were certainly composed for the Palace. The two earliest appear in almanacs written in 848/1444 and 850/1446 for Murād II. The almanacs begin with chronological lists of the Prophets from Adam, of the Caliphs, and of the main events of the Seljuq, Ottoman and Karamān dynasties; then follow astronomical and astrological sections, with prognostications for the current year, rules for the interpretation of dreams, etc. The third almanac, with similar contents, was written for Meḥemmed II one year before the capture of Constantinople. The Calendar sections are short and pithy, but contain here and there important details: the third Calendar, for example, makes it quite clear that the pretender 'Düzme' Muṣṭafā, who challenged Murād II's claim to the throne, was recognized to be in fact the son of Bāyezīd I who had disappeared after the battle of Ankara.

As important as their content is the evidence they provide of how these early records were kept. Events are dated not by the Hijra year in which they occurred but as having happened so many years before the almanac was drawn up, each year's entry being cast in the form 'Since . . . is . . . years' (*—eldenberü . . . yildur*). The first entries in the Ottoman section are very short, recording only the birth and accession of the sultans and the noteworthy conquests, but the entries for recent years are very much fuller, each year containing several events, some related in fair detail,

[1] Now five. Besides the two *taqvīms* of the time of Murād II (MSS. in Paris and Oxford) published by O. Turan (Ankara, 1954) and that of 856/1452 (MS. Topkapu Sarayi, Bağdat Köşkü 309) first used by H. Inalcık (in his *Fatih devri üzerinde tetkikler ve vesikalar* (Ankara, 1954), i) and now published in full by Ç. N. Atsız in *Istanbul Enstitüsü Dergisi*, iii, there is the Nur-i Osmaniye MS. 3080, a *taqvīm* belonging to the year 858 and very closely related textually to the Bağdat Köşkü *taqvīm*. A MS. in the Chester Beatty Library (No. 402) contains a short Ottoman *taqvīm* which seems to be earlier than any of these but much less detailed (cf. *A catalogue of the Turkish manuscripts and miniatures*, V. Minorsky (Dublin, 1958), p. 3).

others being noted only as the 'affair' (*vāqi'a*) of so-and-so. At this stage major events in other Moslem states are included as well. The contents of the three calendars so far known are very similar (though not identical), and it is clear that each year a new almanac was prepared by the court astrologer, the old one either being stored away or disposed of outside the palace. In principle, all the compiler had to do was to copy out the old calendar, adding one to the figure ending each entry, and append a final paragraph for the previous year's happenings, which would end '. . . is one year ago'. It should therefore be a simple matter to tabulate the events listed in the calendars, make the appropriate subtractions from the years to which the almanacs belong, and arrive at a consistent set of dates in Hijra years. In fact, of course, it is not so easy: each compiler has forgotten to add a year here and there and the discrepancies have accumulated, so that even the entries for recent years are often difficult to reconcile.

Apart from their intrinsic value, these Royal Calendars and other popular calendars, originally computed in the same fashion by 'relative' dates, are of importance for the historian, since they have been incorporated in later literary sources, usually being taken over verbatim, but occasionally influencing the compiler to re-cast his material to make it agree with their chronology. Thus the dates given in these later works must be accepted only with reserve, for apart from the probability of an error in the chronology of the calendar-source we have to reckon with the possibility of a further error being introduced by the copyist or compiler who re-computed the figures into Hijra years.

This consideration applies particularly to the popular anonymous chronicles, of which very many manuscripts exist in European and Turkish libraries, usually bearing the simple title *Tevārīkh-i āl-i 'Os̱mān*, and which, in spite of great variety in their contents, are all ultimately related. These chronicles all begin at about the same point, with the migration of Süleymānshāh to Rūm, but are brought down to different points: one group of manuscripts, whose text contains indications that it received its present form in the reign of Bāyezīd II, relates events down to about 900/1494, another group has a continuation down to about 957/1550, while a few manuscripts are extended into the 11th/17th century. Nevertheless the nucleus of this chronicle must be a much earlier text, composed apparently in the first years of the reign of Murād II. This nucleus is written in a fairly discursive style: it is a collection of tales, many of which are legendary in tone. Several dates are included, but all the same it is a story-book rather than a dry chronicle. Then, with the accession of Murād II, there comes an abrupt change of style: the events of the next twenty years or so are recorded in a series of short, pithy entries, very similar in style to the entries in the Royal Calendars except that the anonymous chronicles conclude each year's entry with a Hijra date. However there are traces in the text that in this annalistic section the system of relative dating had been used first: the entry for 836, for example, concludes with the anacolouthon 'Since the Muslims suffered defeat/in the year 836.' The source incorporated here was clearly a calendar similar in form to (but quite different in content from) the Royal Calendars. With the description of the battle of Varna the text becomes more detailed, but thereafter reverts to that of a concise annalistic record, with only a few major events related in detail.

The problem of the recensions of these anonymous chronicles is very complex. The version edited under Bāyezīd II presents a fuller text than the corresponding passages of the version continued and re-edited under Süleymān, the former containing not only extra tales but also lengthy quotations from Aḥmedī's *Iskendernāme*. When F. Giese edited the chronicles from fourteen manuscripts he had to decide whether the Bāyezīd II version was the original text and the Süleymān version an abridgement of this to which a continuation had been added, or whether the Bāyezīd II version was an expansion of an originally concise text, which has survived only in the later version. He chose the first alternative. Unfortunately the discovery of manuscripts of a text closely related to these chronicles suggested that Giese had made the wrong choice, and that the manuscript which he chose as the basis of his edition is a worked-over version of an earlier text that is preserved more faithfully in the later redaction. But thanks to Giese's exhaustive critical apparatus it is possible to reconstruct the other text in detail.

The text which partly clarified and partly still further confused the question of the relations of these chronicles has been published from two manuscripts in the Bodleian and the Cambridge University Libraries. Apart from slight but often significant variations in detail, it differs from the anonymous texts mainly in having a prologue in which is named the author or compiler, Uruj b. 'Ādil. The Oxford text seems to be better and fuller, but it is incomplete, breaking off with the events of 872/1467–8, whereas the Cambridge text ends with the events of 899/1494. The importance of Uruj's chronicle is that he gives, broadly speaking, the text of the Süleymān version without the continuation, i.e. the text which Giese had regarded as an abridgement of the Bāyezīd II version. Moreover, this chronicle contains indications that it had been composed originally in the reign of Meḥemmed II and was therefore closer to the basic text from which all Giese's manuscripts derived. Nevertheless, perhaps too much stress has been laid on the fact that the Oxford manuscript breaks off short at 872: there seems no reason to doubt that both manuscripts originally came down to 899, and that Uruj (of whom nothing at all is known) was working in the reign of Bāyezīd II, recasting and amplifying the anonymous material. Two manuscripts in the Bibliothèque Nationale have texts very close to that of Uruj, but are continued to the year 908. In fact, it is probable that several more such texts remain to be identified and described. All this chronicle material was regarded as common property, and each copyist or redactor (the terms are, in this connection, often synonymous) felt himself at liberty to alter or expand as he wished. The sifting of historical truth from such texts requires great caution and care.

Three histories from the reign of Meḥemmed II have survived, none of them extensive. Only the third is specifically a history of the Ottomans, the other two being—like Aḥmedī's work—universal histories to which the authors have added sections on the Ottoman house to bring the story down to their own day. They are very different in style, one being written in fairly straightforward Persian prose, the second in very pedestrian Turkish verse, and the third in elaborate Arabic prose.

S͟hükrullāh, the author of the first, was born towards the end of the reign of Murād I and entered the service of the Ottomans at the age of twenty-two. He was a member of the *'ulemā'* and was employed by Murād II on various diplomatic missions. He wrote his history, the *Behjet al-tevārīk͟h*, in retirement at Bursa in 861–3/1465–8, and presented it to the Grand Vizier Maḥmūd Pasha. Only the last of the thirteen chapters deals with the Ottomans. In spite of its enormous scope, his history is quite a short book and much of it consists only of lists of rulers, together with the dates of their accessions and deaths and calculations of the lengths of their reigns. In his preface S͟hükrullāh gives a long list of the authorities he used, but makes no mention of a source for his information on the Ottoman period. The Ottoman chapter contains a fairly full account up to the accession of Murād II, but from that point on there is very little factual detail. The main characteristics of S͟hükrullāh's history are his interest in chronology, and in recounting the virtues and pious foundations of the sultans.

Of Enverī nothing is known except that he accompanied Maḥmūd Pasha on various campaigns and that he finished his universal history, the *Düstūrnāme*, in 869/1465. It is divided into twenty-two short 'books', of which the first seventeen consist in the main of a versified translation of Bayḍāwī's *Niẓām al-tevārīk͟h*. Book 18 tells the story of the exploits of Umur Beg of Aydîn, and book 19 the history of the Ottomans from the legendary beginnings of the dynasty to the accession of Meḥemmed II. Book 20 is devoted to the reign of Meḥemmed II (to 868); book 21, covering very similar ground, recounts the victories of Enverī's patron, Maḥmūd Pasha, and book 22 enumerates Maḥmūd Pasha's pious works. According to Enverī, the composition of the whole work did not take more than a month, which indicates that for the Ottoman sections as well he was doing little more than to versify a text which he had before him. From the style of his account it is clear that he was relying largely on a calendar of the same genre as those already described, but he adds, from his own experience, details on some campaigns in which he had taken part.

The Grand Vizier Karamānī Meḥemmed Pasha, who was killed in the riots in Istanbul immediately after the death of Meḥemmed II, has left a short history in Arabic prose. It is in two parts, the first recounting the history of the Ottomans to the death of Murād II, the second the events of the reign of Meḥemmed II. Much of this history too seems to be a recasting into Arabic of a simple calendar to which many chronograms and some ornate passages of *saj'* have been added.

All the histories so far mentioned show that they are basically compilations from popular tales and calendars, the style, however elaborate, failing to conceal the transitions from a catalogue of names and dates to a story and back again. Again, three of these writers—Aḥmedī, S͟hükrullāh, and Enverī—treat Ottoman history merely as an appendix to a universal history. The first work to survive that is a coherent whole, devoted exclusively to the Ottomans and recognizably marked with the stamp of a personality, is that of 'Ās͟hîqpas͟ha-zāde. A descendant of the mystic poet 'Ās͟hîq Pasha, as his name shows, he was born in about 1400 and probably lived to be a centenarian, so that his life spans nearly the whole of the century under consideration. Throughout the reign of Murād II and in the first years of that of Meḥemmed II he was in Rūmeli taking part with the *g͟hāzī* leaders in raids on Christian territories and in the great campaigns. He wrote his history towards the end of his life while living in retirement in Istanbul.

After such a long and active life he was well qualified to write of what he had seen and heard, and his experiences, coupled with his gift for narration, make his book very lively and vigorous. It is evidently composed to be read aloud: much of it is cast in direct speech, and many of the short chapters have at the end an exchange of question and answer, when we are to imagine one of the circle of listeners interposing a question or an objection and the author clearing it up before reading on. It is very much a popular history, the author, no respecter of persons, making no attempt to hide his prejudices; the sultans are usually above reproach, but statesmen and generals receive scathing criticism when he thinks they deserve it. The second half of 'Ās͟hîqpas͟ha-zāde's history must derive from his own experiences or from first-hand accounts that he had received from his comrades-in-arms. Though he says that he settled down to write his book at the age of eighty-six, he must have been compiling it for a long time before that, revising and expanding as the years went by. The first half of the book contains much material which agrees almost verbatim with what has been referred to above as the 'nucleus' of the Anonymous Chronicles, the agreement between the texts stopping at the point where the nucleus seems to have ended. Now 'Ās͟hîqpas͟ha-zāde relates that once when he was a lad he lay ill in the house of Yakhshī Faqīh, the son of Orkhān's *imām* Isḥāq Faqīh, and that it is on the authority of Yakhshī Faqīh that he recounts the tales (*menāqib*) of the Ottoman House up to the time of Bāyezīd I. This statement has induced some commentators to believe that it is the matter common to the Anonymous Chronicles and to 'Āshïqpasha-zāde which derives from Yakhshī Faqīh. More probably the converse is true: the common material derives from a written source that reached to about 1420, and some or all of the matter peculiar to 'Āshïqpasha-zāde represents the stories he had received from Yakhshī Faqīh some years earlier. In any case it is noteworthy that a text of the end of the fifteenth century contains stories and traditions of the time of Orkhān, over 150 years earlier, which are related at only two removes from the contemporary observer.

Of Neshrī, who was writing shortly after 'Āshïqpasha-zāde, practically nothing is known. He is said to have been a *müderris* at Bursa and to have died there in the reign of Selīm I. The one definite fact, which we have on his own authority, is that he was in the Ottoman camp when Meḥemmed II died; he gives a vivid picture of the consternation among the ministers and the disorders in Istanbul which followed. The history which we have is only the sixth and last book of a universal history, the *Jihānnümā*, which Neshrī composed. This last book he presented, as a separate work, to Bāyezīd II. It is in three sections, on the descendants of Oghuz Khān, on the Seljuqs, and on the Ottomans, this last being by far the longest. A few cross-references in the text give some clues to the contents of the first five books, which, however, are not known to exist.

The great interest of Neshrī's Ottoman history is that though he nowhere names a written source it is possible to identify three sources that he used and by comparing these sources with his text to see the way he went to work. His main source is 'Āshïqpasha-zāde's history, chapter after chapter following that text with a very close verbal correspondence; a word or a phrase is modified here and there, the verses with which 'Āshïqpasha-zāde diversified his text are omitted or paraphrased into prose, the 'questions and answers' are smoothed into narrative, and all the autobiographical references are omitted, but the vigour and directness of the original are not smothered. The most striking change that Neshrī makes is that he frequently softens or omits 'Āshïqpasha-zāde's forthright judgements on public men: to 'Āshïqpasha-zāde the Chandarlï family, for example, who were for nearly a century at the head of affairs, are anathema, but Neshrī tones down the criticisms; he is writing for a more sedate public and seeking a patron in Bāyezīd II, with whom Ibrāhīm, the last distinguished member of the Chandarlï family, was in high favour.

Another source used by Neshrī was one of the Royal Calendars, the text that he used being closest to, but not identical with, that of the third calendar noted (that of 856). 'Āshîqpasha-zāde's chapters usually end with a date, and Neshrī's usual practice is to append to the chapter the material which his calendar contained for that year. In some points of detail, notably that of the genuineness of the pretender Muṣṭafā, Neshrī modifies 'Āshîqpasha-zāde's text to make it accord with the testimony of the calendar.

The third source used by Neshrī was very close to the text of an Ottoman history in Turkish of which a manuscript is preserved in the Bodleian Library[2] and which was composed for Bāyezīd II by an anonymous *kātib*—possibly the Shevqī who is mentioned in books of biography. The preface of this history is written in the most elaborate style of *inshā'*, but the history itself is a straightforward and direct narrative. Neshrī has drawn extensively on this text to supplement 'Āshîqpasha-zāde's account: he has taken from it not only his long relation of the civil wars after the battle of Ankara and several scattered chapters, but also odd sentences, phrases, and even single names, which he has very skilfully woven into 'Āshîqpasha-zāde's text. For his account of the reign of Bāyezīd I he has gone beyond mere compilation: he has completely rearranged 'Āshîqpasha-zāde's narrative to make it accord with the chronology of events as related in the Bodleian text, and done it so carefully that only the closest analysis reveals discrepancies. But while admiring the ingenuity with which he has reconciled the often divergent chronologies of his three sources one must admit that he has probably done great violence to historical reality, a fault that is the more serious in that his history served as a main source for many later historians.

Yet for all his faults of method Neshrī is a true historian, for he possessed the historian's fundamental virtue, the desire to establish the truth of events. It is doubtful whether the same can be said of Idrīs Bidlīsī, whose *Hasht bihisht*, modelled on the histories of Vaṣṣāf and Juvaynī, was written at the command of Bāyezīd II avowedly in order to glorify the deeds of the Ottoman House. Here and there, it is true, Idrīs has preserved information which he culled from earlier sources now lost, but it is probable that a thorough analysis of the contents of his history (a task long overdue) would show that it has been much overrated as a historical source, and that when the rhetoric is stripped off the basic narrative is little more than a repetition of the story told by Neshrī, with some additional distortions caused by attempts to harmonize conflicting traditions.

The importance as a historian of Idrīs's contemporary Kemālpasha-zāde is only now being recognized, for it is only recently that manuscripts

[2] Marsh 313. This text is usually attributed to Rūḥī, with whose history it has much in common, but it stops at an earlier point (889/1484) and seems to be rather Rūḥī's main source than his own work.

of the bulk of his history have been identified. He wrote in Turkish, but in the same ornate style as Idrīs and in emulation of Idrīs's *Hasht bihisht*, the first eight books of his very lengthy and detailed history being composed at the command of Bāyezīd II. He was a man of affairs, who had begun his life as a soldier and then turned to theology, rising to be *Sheykh al-Islām* under Süleymān the Great. To judge from the content of his book on the reign of Meḥemmed II, recently published in facsimile and transcription, he brings to Ottoman historiography an entirely new outlook, in that he endeavours to narrate the happenings of the past not as a string of unconnected incidents, which for all their differences of style is the method of the Anonymous Chronicles, 'Āshiqpasha-zāde, Neshrī, and even Idrīs, but as a chain of related events. He is very much concerned to establish the causes of events, looking further than the *casus belli* and referring the reader back to earlier episodes which have produced the situation next to be described. He is not content, as are nearly all his predecessors, to lump the Christian powers together as the 'accursed infidel', but introduces each new theme with a short description of the land that is to be the scene of action.[3] He shows discrimination in selecting his sources, and relies to a great extent on the accounts of eyewitnesses, among whom figure several of the great men of his day. In short, he shows the attitude of a statesman endeavouring to see a pattern in events and looking for guidance in future policy.

The claim that their works have a practical value for statesmen and rulers is of course regularly made, especially by the theologian-historians such as Shükrullāh and Neshrī who, while writing for learned circles in general, are also seeking the patronage of the great. For them history has two merits: it is the handmaid of theology; and it is the guide which will assist rulers in their duty of just government. The novelty of Kemālpasha-zāde's work is that in fact it could conceivably serve the second end, which some of his predecessors so glibly and unrealistically profess to have in view.

The real motives which prompted the historians of the fifteenth century to write are less openly expressed but perhaps more sincerely felt. The first is piety, a motive exemplified in the well-known passage in Aḥmedī's *Iskendernāme* where, after speaking of the misdeeds and tyranny of the Mongols, he turns with relief to recount the deeds of the Ottoman *begs*, who were 'good Muslims and just', and who had the peculiar merit of ceaselessly carrying on the *jihād*. This theme runs through all the later histories. The fact that many campaigns are directed against Muslim states is irrelevant, for these fellow-Muslims are regarded as hindering the

[3] This characteristic at least he borrowed from Tursun Beg's *Tārīkh-i Ebu'l-Feth*. It remains to be seen how far the other books of Kemālpasha-zāde's history (the publication of which has been undertaken by the Türk Tarih Kurumu) show the same penetration.

ghazā, either by petty raids into Ottoman territory or by alliances with the Christian enemy; hence the Sultan is obliged to suppress them in order that the mighty work in Europe can go forward without interruption. And just as the battle with the infidel is God's work and the sultans and warriors who have engaged in it have acquired sanctity, so the recording of their deeds is a holy work, and the author is as entitled as they to a *fātiḥa* for the repose of his soul.

Closely allied with this motive is the frank desire to entertain. Uruj in his preface emphasizes in the same spirit as Aḥmedī the virtues of the Ottoman rulers, but begins by pointing out that the stories of these sultans need to be recorded to take their place with 'the stories of saints, the *shāhnāmes*, the tales of wonders, and the stories of Afrāsiyāb and Rustem'; and one redaction of the Anonymous Chronicles is announced in the introduction as containing 'the annals of the Ottoman house, and also wonderful tales of what happened in the past'. It is indeed an anachronism for us to classify such works rigidly as 'historical texts': they form part of the popular literature of amusement and edification of the day. The value of even such an apparently sterile record as the Anonymous Chronicles is well expressed in words used of a very similar text, the *Anglo-Saxon Chronicle*: the primitive use of the chronicle form 'was to *characterize* the receding series of years, each by a mark and sign of its own, so that the years might not be confused in the retrospect of those who had lived and acted in them. . . . To posterity they present merely a name or two, as of a battlefield and a victor, but to the men of the day they suggested a thousand particulars, which they in their comrade-life were in the habit of recollecting and putting together. That which to us seems a lean and barren sentence was to them the text for a winter evening's entertainment.'[4]

In conclusion, it is worthwhile to recall that the historical tradition recorded in the fifteenth-century texts considered here has for long been known and used in Europe. Hieronymus Beck brought to Vienna in 1551 a manuscript of the later version of the Anonymous Chronicles (with the continuation to 956/1549), of which a German translation by J. Gaudier was printed in Frankfort in 1567 and a Latin translation by Hans Loewenklau (Leunclavius) in 1588. Leunclavius was an extremely able translator, and not only was the manuscript which he used (and which has since disappeared) very much older than the surviving manuscripts, but there are signs that though it belonged to the later recension it preserved here and there characteristics of an even earlier version than any represented in our texts. Leunclavius's *Historiae Musulmanae Turcorum* (Frankfort, 1591) is a compilation from two Turkish texts, one being another recension of the Anonymous Chronicles, the other a compilation containing the greater

[4] Charles Plummer, quoted in *The Anglo-Saxon chronicle*, tr. G. N. Garmonsway (Everyman series, London, 1953), p. xviii.

part of the Ottoman section of Neshrī's history. Comparison of the relevant parts of the *Historiae* with the recently published texts of Neshrī shows that the manuscript represented there belonged to the earliest recension of Neshrī's work, and was free of many of the errors which later copyist-redactors have introduced. In fact the non-Orientalist student of today is little better provided with translations of the fifteenth-century Ottoman texts than was Knolles as he worked on his *Generall historie of the Turkes* in 1600.

16. THE USE BY MUSLIM HISTORIANS OF NON-MUSLIM SOURCES

BERNARD LEWIS

Professor of the History of the Near and Middle East in the University of London

Herodotus, the father of history, wrote of the 'great and wonderful actions' of both Greeks and Barbarians, and pursued his study into the past of alien lands and remote times. Though excluded by the hierophantic mysteries from access to oriental writings, he tried to make good the deficiency by travel and personal enquiry in Eastern lands. Some fifteen centuries later another European, William, Archbishop of Tyre in the states of Outremer, wrote a history of the Islamic Empires. He too sought his information from oriental sources, and, better placed than Herodotus, was even able to read them in the original.[1]

These first European students of oriental history were, however, exceptional. Herodotus, though acclaimed as the father of history, was not accorded the respect of classical historians, most of whom preferred to follow the precept and practice of Thucydides, and limit their concern to the deeds of their contemporaries and compatriots. The medieval European chroniclers were for the most part content to follow their example, and it is no accident that while William of Tyre's history of the Crusaders in the East—the *Historia rerum in partibus transmarinis gestarum*—was widely read and even translated into French, his *Gesta orientalium principum* has not, as far as is known, survived in a single manuscript. It was not until the Renaissance had awakened a new European curiosity and the Discoveries had whetted it with the sight of remote and alien peoples, that European historians began to show interest in other lands and societies, and to seek out and pass on information and opinions about them.[2] This universal historical curiosity is still a distinguishing, almost an exclusive, characteristic of Europe and her daughters. Oriental societies study their own history;

[1] 'Accessit praeterea domini Almarici regis (cujus anima sancta requie perfruatur) illustris memoriae, et inclyptae in Domino recordationis jussio, non facile negligenda, et instantia multiplex, quae ad id ipsum nos maxime impulit, cujus etiam rogatu, ipso Arabica exemplaria ministrante, aliam Historiam a tempore seductoris Mahumeth, usque in hunc annum, qui est nobis ab Incarnatione Domini 1184, per annos quingentos septuaginta decurrentem conscripsimus: auctorem maxime secutivirum venerabilem Seith, filium Patricii, Alexandrinum patriarcham.' William of Tyre, Prologue.

[2] Cf. A. Momigliano, 'The Place of Herodotus in the History of Historiography', *History* (1958), xliii, 1–13, for an illuminating discussion of these questions.

perforce they also study the history of the West which has influenced or dominated them. They still show little interest in one another.[3]

The medieval Muslim, like the citizens of most other societies that have appeared among men, was profoundly convinced of the finality, completeness, and essential self-sufficiency of his civilization. Islam was the one true faith, beyond which there were only unbelievers—the Muslim equivalent of the Greek term barbarians. The Islamic state was the one divinely ordained order, beyond which there were only tyranny and anarchy. Universal history was the history of the Islamic community, outside which were lands and peoples whose only interest was as the settings and objects of Muslim action.

These lesser breeds were not unknown to Muslim historiography. Sometimes there were intrepid travellers who ventured among them. With many there were the normal exchanges of commerce, war, and diplomacy. From some there were acknowledged borrowings of useful knowledge and crafts. But none of these led to any interest in the history of the infidel peoples. To fight the Greeks it was necessary to have political and military intelligence; to learn from the Greeks it was useful to have philosophic and scientific training. For neither was there any need to enquire into the history of the Greek past. For centuries the Muslim Caliphate stood face to face with the Byzantine Empire—the House of War *par excellence* of medieval Islam. The Muslim chroniclers have much to say of the war on the frontiers; the Muslim geographers have ample information, probably drawn ultimately from secret service files, on the topography, administration, and strength of the enemy Empire, and even of the scandals of its court and capital. But at no time did they attempt to consult Greek historical sources, or to deal in a connected form with the history of the Greek Empire.

Still more striking is the case of the Crusades. For two centuries the Muslims of the Middle East were in intimate if hostile contact with groups of Franks established among them—yet at no time do they seem to have developed the least interest in them. As Professor Gabrieli has pointed out,[4] the Muslims, unlike the Christians, did not regard the Crusades as something separate and distinctive, nor did they single out the Crusaders from the long series of infidel enemies whom from time to time they fought. The chroniclers report in detail the smallest skirmishes between Muslim and Frankish troops—but they have little to say about the internal affairs of the Frankish states in the Levant, and even less about their countries of origin. The omission is the more remarkable in that the geographers and cosmographers have some information, mostly derived from

[3] It is noteworthy that the first efforts to develop Sanskrit and Chinese studies in the Middle East were made in Ankara and Jerusalem.

[4] See above, p. 98 ff.

western Muslim sources, about the Franks and their countries. Yet with one or two minor exceptions, the historians of Islam made no attempt to relate their narrative of the Syrian wars to this information, to trace the invaders back to their countries of origin, or to enquire into the mighty yet invisible movement that had launched them.[5]

The Crusades opened the way to closer diplomatic and commercial relations between the Muslim and Christian states of the Mediterranean. These are reflected in the manuals of civil service usage of the Mamluk period. In the encyclopaedic bureaucratic vade-mecum of Qalqashandī, and similar works, we find lists of the European sovereigns with whom the Sultans of Egypt had corresponded, with the correct names, titles, and forms of address for each, and some allusions to earlier exchanges of letters or embassies. We find nothing about the history of those countries.

All this does not mean that Muslim historians never concerned themselves with non-Muslim history. For the Muslim, the Islamic revelation is not a beginning but a completion, the final link in a chain of revelation—and the Islamic community is thus no new creation, but a revival and improvement of something that had existed long before. The history of Islam therefore did not begin with Muḥammad; it included the history of the earlier prophets and their missions, and something also of the peoples to whom they were sent. This earlier history is chiefly biblical and Arabian, within a framework defined by the historical allusions in the Qur'ān. The development of this history, and the use made of biblical sources and of Jewish and Christian informants, are discussed in Professor Rosenthal's paper. The Prophet also speaks of Caesar and of Chosroes, and here too some historical elaboration was permissible—was even required for the explanation of the sacred tradition. For this too information was to hand—Persian converts to Islam, with memories of and access to Persian historical writings, Eastern Christians with knowledge of the histories of the pagan and Christian Roman Empires. Through them some accounts of Persian and Roman history found their way into the Arabic language, and, together with the Judaeo-Christian biblical material, became part of the common stock of Muslim universal history.

This stock, acquired in the early days when the Islamic community was still malleable and receptive, received few later accretions. It appears chiefly in the general introductory matter, leading up to the establishment of the Islamic oecumene; it is interesting to note that it is not normally supplemented by any discussion of the conditions in any specific country prior to the Islamic conquest. The Islamic community as a whole has

[5] A possible exception is the account (*sīra*) 'of the European Christians who in those years had come to the Muslim countries', mentioned by Ibn Muyassar (p. 70) and cited by F. Rosenthal, *A History of Muslim historiography* (Leiden, 1952), p. 55. It is however symptomatic of the general lack of interest that this work has not survived even in quotation. See further, B. Lewis, 'The Muslim Discovery of Europe', *BSOAS* (1957), xx, 409–16.

some earlier history; the individual Islamic countries begin theirs with the advent of Islam.[6]

The external interests of Islamic historiography were thus limited to the prehistory of the Islamic community itself, and were moreover confined to the earlier period. With few and rare exceptions, they did not extend to the history of alien peoples or cultures, or even to the pre-Islamic history of the peoples and countries brought into Islam. In other words, Muslim historians were concerned only with their own civilization and its immediate ancestors—and in this they resembled the historians of most other human communities, including, until comparatively recent times, our own.

There were some exceptions. The universal curiosity of Masʿūdī led him even to Frankish history, and enabled him to give a list of the Frankish kings from Clovis to Louis IV, based, he tells us, on a book prepared by a Frankish bishop for the Andalusian Caliph al-Ḥakam in 328/939.[7] The transcendent genius of al-Bīrūnī carried him across the impenetrable religious barrier of an alien script, to study Sanskrit and learn something of India—though his interests were philosophical and scientific rather than historical. These were however few and unrepresentative; even as great a historian as Ibn Khaldūn, in his universal history, does not go north of Spain or east of Persia.[8] Within that area he tried very hard to deal with non-Muslim as well as Muslim history, and made use of such non-Islamic sources as were available to him—as Orosius on Rome and Josippon on the Jews.[9] But he did not go beyond the limits of his own civilization and its known and recognizable predecessors—like the authors of most of the so-called universal histories written in Europe until very recently.

The first genuine universal history of Islam—probably in the world—is that of Rashīd al-Dīn. The Mongol conquests, by uniting for the first time under one dynasty the civilizations of South-West Asia and the Far East, created new opportunities for social and cultural contacts between societies previously separated by political and religious barriers. At the same time they opened the door to new contacts with Europe, as a number of Europeans availed themselves of the opportunity offered by the presence of non-Muslim rulers in the Middle East to explore the overland routes to China.

[6] The Persian sagas of the mythical emperors of ancient Iran, and the Egyptian legends woven around the broken, massive remnants of the Pharaohs, threw into relief the lack of real historical knowledge about the pre-Islamic past.

[7] *Murūj*, iii, 66–7, 69–72. See also B. Lewis, Masʿūdī on the Kings of the 'Franks,' *Al-Masʿūdī Millenary Commemoration Volume* (Aligarh, 1960), pp. 7–10.

[8] Ibn Khaldūn does indeed discuss the Mongols at some length, but this is preliminary to an account of their invasion of the lands of Islam. Cf. W. J. Fischel, 'Ibn Khaldūn's Sources for the History of Jenghiz Khān and the Tatars', *JAOS* (1956), 76, pp. 91–9.

[9] Cf. G. Levi Della Vida, 'La Traduzione araba delle storie di Orosio', *Al-Andalus* (1954), xix, 257–93; W. J. Fischel, 'Ibn Khaldūn and Josippon', *Homenaje a Millas-Vallicrosa* (Barcelona, 1954), i, 587–98; idem, 'Ibn Khaldūn: on the Bible, Judaism and the Jews', *Ignace Goldziher Memorial Volume II* (Jerusalem, 1956), pp. 147–71.

The *Jāmi' al-tavārīkh*—a universal history prepared by Rashīd al-Dīn for the Mongol Ghāzān Khān—is a product of these new contacts. To carry out his task, he assembled a team of collaborators, including two Chinese scholars, a Buddhist hermit from Kashmir, a Mongol specialist on tribal tradition, and a Frankish traveller, probably a monk who had come as envoy from the Papal Curia. Through him Rashīd al-Dīn made the acquaintance of a European chronicle which has recently been identified as that of the thirteenth-century chronicler Martin of Troppau, also known as Martin Polonus. From this source, brought up to date by his informant, Rashīd al-Dīn was able to include a brief chronicle of the Holy Roman Emperors as far as Albert I and the Popes as far as Benedict XI. Both are correctly described as living at that time.[10]

Rashīd al-Dīn's venture into occidental and oriental scholarship, made possible by the brief interlude of Mongol power, found few imitators. His account of European history, the first since Mas'ūdī's king-list, was the last until the sixteenth century, when the Ottoman need for political intelligence about Europe began to grow into an interest—albeit still a faint and disdainful one—in European history.

In the Saxon Landbibliothek in Dresden, there is a Turkish manuscript containing a history of France from the legendary Faramund to the year 1560. It was made by order of Ferīdūn Bey—compiler of the famous *Munshe'āt-i Selāṭīn* and Reis Efendi from 1570 to 1573—and was the work of two men, the *terjumān* Ḥasan b. Ḥamza and the *kātib* 'Alī b. Sinān. The book was completed in 980/1572.[11]

This work may well have been the first translation of a European historical work into Turkish. It was followed by an account of the discovery of the New World, adapted from European sources, which reflected the growing Turkish concern at the vast expansion of Western maritime power.[12]

During the seventeenth century several other Turkish historians show signs of an interest in European history and an acquaintance with European sources. Ibrāhīm Mülhemī (d. 1650) is said to have written a *Tārīkh-i Mulūk-i Rūm ve-Ifranj*, of which unfortunately no copy appears to have survived.[13] His more famous contemporary Ḥājjī Khalīfa (d. 1657) was also interested in Europe. Ḥājjī Khalīfa's researches into European geography are well known, and followed a line of enquiry opened, for practical reasons, by Ottoman map-makers and navigators in the previous

[10] K. Jahn, 'Les légendes de l'Occident chez Raşīd al-Din', *Mélanges Fuad Köprülü* (Istanbul, 1953), pp. 255–7; idem, *Histoire universelle de Raşid al-Din . . . I. Histoire des Francs* (Leiden, 1951).

[11] Cf. F. Babinger, *Geschichtsschreiber der Osmanen . . .* (Leipzig, 1927), p. 107.

[12] The *Tā'rīkh al-Hind al-Gharbī*, written *c.* 1580 for Murād III, and printed at the Müteferriqa press in 1142/1729. The same interest is reflected in other Turkish writings, notably in the geographical section of 'Ālī's *Künh al-akhbār*.

[13] Babinger, p. 170.

century. Ḥājjī Khalīfa incorporated European material in his world geography, the *Jihānnümā*, and, with the assistance of a French priest, converted to Islam and known as Sheykh Meḥmed Ikhlāsī, prepared a Turkish version of the Atlas Minor of Mercator and Hondius. Probably with the help of this same Frenchman, Ḥājjī Khalīfa also prepared a Turkish translation of a history of the Franks—*Tārīkh-i Firengī*. Mordtmann, who believed this work to be lost, guessed that it was a translation of the Byzantine history of Chalcocondyles.[14] At least one copy, however, was preserved in private possession in Turkey, and parts of it were actually published, in serial form, in the newspaper *Taṣvīr-i Efkār*, in 1279/1862–3.[15] According to the preamble with which the editors of the journal introduced these excerpts, the work deals with European history, and is translated from the chronicle of the German historian Johann Carion (1499–1537). This work, which ended in 1532, was revised and in fact rewritten by Philip Melanchthon (1497–1560), and continued by Caspar Peucer or Beutzer (1525–1602); it was translated into French by Simon Goulart (1543–1628).[16] It is possible that it was one of these latter versions that formed the basis of Ḥājjī Khalīfa's Turkish text. The choice of a Lutheran work, much used in Protestant propaganda, would seem to suggest that Ḥājjī Khalīfa's French collaborator, though described as a priest, had a Protestant and not a Catholic background.

Of quite a different character was the use made of European sources by another Ottoman historian of the early seventeenth century, Ibrāhīm-i Pechevī (1572–1650). Pechevī was not concerned with universal history; stilll-ess was he interested in writing or translating the history of the infidel kings. His concern, like that of most Ottoman historians, was with the history of the Empire of which he was a subject, and more especially of the wars fought by the Ottoman armies in Europe. His history covers the events of the years 1520–1639. For the later period he relied to a large extent on his own knowledge or on the reports of old soldiers; for the earlier period he seems to have made use of the writings of his predecessors in Ottoman historiography. But in addition to those Pechevī had the revolutionary idea of consulting the historians of the enemy. He was interested above all in military history, and seems to have been fascinated by the stories of the great battles fought by the Ottoman Sultans and other Muslim rulers, dwelling with loving attention on every detail. But sometimes the Muslim chronicles were sadly lacking in details—and so Pechevī had recourse to the accounts written by the enemy. 'In our country', he

[14] EI[1] s.v. Ḥādjdjī Khalīfa, followed by Babinger, p. 200.

[15] Adnan Adıvar, *La Science chez les Turcs Ottomans* (Paris, 1939), p. 118, repeated with some modification in idem, *Osmanlı Türklerinde ilim* (Istanbul, 1943), p. 129. For the best and most recent discussion see Orhan Şaik Gökyay, in *Kâtib Çelebi, hayatı ve eserleri hakkında incelemeler* (Ankara, 1957), pp. 54–6.

[16] My thanks are due to Professor A. T. Hatto for this information.

says, 'there are men without number able to read and write Hungarian.'[17] It was therefore a simple matter to have Hungarian chronicles read to him and to translate some of them into Turkish.[18] A number of passages, Pechevī says, he thought fit to incorporate in his own chronicle. These include an account of the battle of Mohacs, and other narratives of the wars in Hungary. Though Pechevī does not name his Hungarian sources, two of them have been identified by Kraelitz as Kaspar Heltai and N. v. Istvanfy, whose histories were published in 1575 and 1623 respectively.[19]

Pečevī was not, as has sometimes been stated, the first Ottoman historian to use Western sources. He does however seem to have been the first to compare foreign accounts with native accounts of the same events, and to weave them into a single narrative. In this he can have had but few predecessors anywhere. He certainly had few successors.

Meanwhile, however, the more general interest in Western history continued. An outstanding historian of the late seventeenth century was Ḥuseyn Hezārfenn (d. 1691), most of whose works are unfortunately still unpublished. Like Ḥājjī Khalīfa, whom he cites with admiration, he was a man of wide-ranging curiosity, and seems to have been especially interested in the geography and history of remote countries, as well as in the earlier history of his own. To an extent rare if not unique among Muslims of his day, he sought the acquaintance of European scholars and men of letters, not a few of whom visited Istanbul. He is known to have been acquainted with Count Ferdinand Marsigli and Antoine Galland. It seems likely that he also knew Prince Demetrius Cantemir and Pétis de la Croix. It was no doubt through the good offices of these and other European friends that Ḥuseyn Hezārfenn was able to gain access to the contents of European books, and incorporate them in his own works.

The most important of these, for our purpose, is his *Tenqīḥ al-tevārīkh*, completed in 1673. This is divided into nine parts, of which the sixth, seventh, eighth, and ninth deal with history outside the Islamic oecumene and its accepted predecessors. Part 6 deals with Greek and Roman history, including some account of the Greek philosophers; part 7 with the history of Constantinople since its foundation, including the Byzantine period; part 8 with Asia—China, the Philippines, the East Indies, India, and Ceylon; part 9 with the discovery of America. Oddly enough, Ḥuseyn Hezārfenn does not seem to have included Europe in his survey, but his accounts of both Asia and America are based almost entirely on European sources, probably on French travel literature. His accounts of Greek,

[17] *Tārīkh-i Pechevī*, i, 106.

[18] 'Okuttuk ve ničesin türkīye terjüme ettik.' The implication would seem to be that Pechevi had the chronicles read to him and then himself turned some of these into written Turkish prose —a procedure reminiscent of the Toledo school of translators. I owe this observation to Professor P. Wittek.

[19] F. v. Kraelitz, 'Der Osmanische Historiker Ibrâhîm Pečewi', *Der Islam* (1918), viii, 252–60.

Roman, and Byzantine history are also based on European works—probably the first time that these were used to augment the meagre stock of Islamic knowledge of classical antiquity.[20]

With the work of Aḥmed b. Luṭfallah, known as Münejjimbashî (d. 1702), we return to universal history in the grand manner. His great *Jāmiʿ al-duwal*—the title is an obvious echo of Rashīd al-Dīn's *Jāmiʿ al-tavārīkh*—is a universal history of mankind from Adam to the year 1083/1672, based, so the author tells us, on some seventy sources. The Arabic original of the work is still unpublished, but a Turkish translation, prepared under the direction of the poet Nedīm, has been printed.[21] The bulk of the work, as one would expect, is concerned with Islamic history. A large part of the first volume, is, however, devoted to the history of the pre-Islamic and non-Islamic states. The former, as is usual, included the Persians and Arabians on the one hand, and the Israelites and Egyptians on the other, discussed on more or less traditional lines. Münejjimbashî's ancient history, however, goes beyond the common Islamic stock. His accounts of the Romans and of the Jews clearly derive from Roman and Jewish sources, already in part available to him in the adaptation of Ibn Khaldūn. Münejjimbashî has however much fuller information than Ibn Khaldūn, and is able to deal with such peoples as the Assyrians and Babylonians, the Seleucids and the Ptolemies, previously barely unknown to Islamic historiography. For these a European source must have been used. This becomes certain when we come to Münejjimbashî's chapter on Europe, which includes sections on the divisions of the 'Frankish' peoples and on the kings of France, of Germany, of Spain, and of England. The source of these would appear to have been the Turkish translation of the chronicle of Johann Carion, though, since Münejjimbashî continues his narrative down to the reigns of Louis XIII of France, the Emperor Leopold in Germany, and Charles I of England, he must have had later supplementary material at his disposal. He reports the English civil war and the execution of King Charles. 'After him the people of England (Anglia) did not appoint another king over them; we have no further information about their affairs.' (i, 682).

Münejjimbashî's outside interests were not limited to Europe. For his account of the kings of Armenia, he tells us he made use of translations of Armenian chronicles (i. 652). For the ancient history of the Jews, he had recourse to Hebrew sources, made available to him by Jewish informants

[20] The MSS. are listed in Babinger, pp. 229–30. I was able to consult one belonging to the Hunterian Museum in Glasgow (cf. *JRAS* (1906), pp. 602 ff.). It was made at the French Embassy in Constantinople, by the Dragoman Francis Salibi, and was at one time the property of Pétis de la Croix.

[21] On Münejjimbashî see Babinger, pp. 234–5, and Brockelmann, *GAL* II, 443, and *S* II, 637. The Turkish version, entitled *Ṣaḥā'if al-akhbār*, was published, in 3 volumes, in Istanbul in 1285/1868–9. References are to the Turkish edition.

(i. 684). From his accounts of his dealings with these informants, and of his painstaking attempts to verify and compare material in languages unknown to him, we may get some idea of the far-ranging curiosity and meticulous scholarship of Münejjimbashî. Even China and Hindu India are included in the history, though here Münejjimbashî's information is meagre and poor.

During the eighteenth century the nature of Ottoman interest in Europe underwent a radical change. The peace-treaty of Carlowitz, signed 26 January 1699, marked the end of an epoch and the beginning of another. For a long time the growing internal crisis of Islamic civilization had been masked by the imposing military façade of the Ottoman Empire, protecting the Muslim heartlands both from foreign attack and from self-realization at home.

Now this façade was, for the first time, dangerously shaken. There had been unsuccessful campaigns and inconclusive wars before now. But the disastrous retreat that followed the second Ottoman failure at Vienna, in 1683, was the first clear and unmistakable defeat. At Carlowitz the Ottoman Sultan, for the first time since the foundation of the Empire, was compelled to accept terms dictated by a victorious infidel enemy.

A Turkish document, written shortly before the treaty of Passarowitz (1718), records an imaginary conversation between a Christian and an Ottoman officer, in which they discuss the military and political situation. The purpose of the writer seems to have been to prepare Ottoman ruling circles to accept defeat, by depicting as darkly as possible the unfavourable situation of the Empire. The conversation also makes a comparison between the Austrian and Ottoman armies, to the great disadvantage of the latter, and would appear to embody a plea for military reform.[22]

The impact of military defeat, and the resulting desire to seek out and make use of the talisman that had brought victory to the enemy, opened a new phase in the relations between Islam and the Western world—one which, with some important modifications, has continued until today. The new interest was at first limited to the weapons and military science of Europe, but it was inevitable that it should be extended at least to as much of European culture as seemed necessary for their effective application. In 1721, when the famous Yirmi Sekiz Meḥmed Sa'īd Efendi was sent as ambassador to Paris, his instructions were 'to make a thorough study of the means of civilization and education, and report on those capable of application' in Turkey.[23] One of these 'means of civilization' was printing, the establishment of which among the Turks owed much to the initiative and enthusiasm of the ambassador's son, Sa'īd Chelebi. Closely associated with him in this work was Ibrāhīm Müteferriqa, a Hungarian convert to Islam.

[22] Faik Reşit Unat, 'Ahmet III devrinde bir Islahat Takriri', *Tarih vesikaları* (1941), i, 107.
[23] Cited by Selim Nüzhet Gerçek, *Türk Matbaacılığı* (Istanbul, 1939), i, 44.

The first book appeared in February 1729. By the time the press was closed in 1742, seventeen books had been printed, most of them dealing with history, geography, and language. They included an account by Meḥmed Sa'īd Efendi of his embassy to France, a treatise by Ibrāhīm Müteferriqa on the science of tactics as applied in European armies, and a translation of a European account of the wars in Persia. Editions of earlier works included the sixteenth-century history of the discovery of the new world—*Tārīkh al-Hind al-Gharbī*—and part of the geographical treatise of Ḥājjī Khalīfa.

The new interest in Europe was primarily concerned with military matters. But once the barrier separating the two civilizations had been breached, it was no longer possible to keep a strict control over the traffic passing through. An interest in military science on the one hand, and a need for political and military intelligence on the other, led to an interest in recent European history which, desultory and sporadic at first, became more urgent as the realization spread that the very survival of the Empire might depend on an accurate understanding of European developments.

Besides the books printed at the Müteferriqa press, a small number of manuscripts in Istanbul collections testify to this new interest in European history. A manuscript of 1135/1722, entitled *Nemche Tārīkhi*, gives an outline history of Austria from 800 to 1662 A.D., and was translated from the German by the interpreter 'Osmān b. Aḥmed. Of rather a different kind is a survey of the historical conditions of the states of Europe—*Avrupa devletlerinin ba'ẓī aḥvāl-i tārīkhiyyesi*. This report, dated 1146/1733–4, was made by the famous Aḥmed Pasha Bonneval, a French nobleman who joined the Ottoman service and was converted to Islam. It discusses events in Austria, Hungary, Spain, and France, and was translated into Turkish from the author's presumably French original. An outline survey of the major dynasties—the *Fihris-i Düvel* of 'Abd al-Raḥmān Münīf Efendi (d. 1742)—includes the pagan and Christian Roman emperors, the Byzantine emperors, the kings of France in Paris, and the kings of Austria in Vienna. Towards the end of the century a survey of European affairs—*Ijmāl-i aḥvāl-i Avrupa*—discuss Prussia under Frederick William II and France in the revolutionary period, and in 1799 an unknown Greek author called Kosmo Komidas prepared, in Turkish, a handlist of reigning European sovereigns, with their dates of birth and accession, their capitals, titles, heirs, and other useful information.[24]

These works, or others of the same kind, became known to Ottoman historians, and some of the information they contained found its way into

[24] For descriptions of these works see *Istabul Kütüphaneleri tarih-coğrafya yazmaları katalogları*. 1. *Türkçe tarih yazmaları* fasc. 1, *Umumi tarihler* (Istanbul, 1943), and fasc. 3, *Arab tarihi, Iran tarihi, Diğer milletler tarihleri* (Istanbul, 1945). On 'Osmān b. Aḥmed see R. F. Kreutel and Otto Spies, *Leben und Abenteuer des Dolmetschers Osman Aga* (Bonn, 1954), especially p. xxv.

the main stream of Ottoman historiography. The first of the Imperial Historiographers who himself learnt a Western language and made use of Western sources was ʿAṭāʿullah Meḥmed, known as S͟hānīzāde (1769–1826). By education one of the ʿ*Ulemā*ʾ, he was a man of encyclopaedic knowledge, and became Imperial Historiographer in 1819. He seems to have learnt several European languages, and made a study of European medicine and other sciences. His major work was a Turkish translation, probably made from an Italian version, of an Austrian medical textbook. He also made a translation, in 1220/1805, of the Instructions of Frederick the Great to his commanders—*Viṣāyānāme-i seferiyye*. It was therefore natural that, when called upon to write the history of the Empire for the years 1808–20, he should make some use of European sources.

The vast, swift campaigns of the Revolutionary and Napoleonic wars drove the lessons of the new warfare deep into the lands of Islam, while the new, secular ideas of the Revolution, untainted in Muslim eyes with any recognizably Christian origin, could for the first time penetrate the barrier that had hitherto excluded every movement of ideas from Europe, and thus provide the Muslim peoples, in their new liberalism and nationalism, with the ideological foundations of Westernization.

In the first half of the nineteenth century there were two main centres of westernizing reform in the Middle East—Turkey and Egypt. In both of them the preparation and publication of translations of Western books played an important part. In Egypt under Muḥammad ʿAlī Pasha there was an organized, state-sponsored programme of translation, for the like of which we must go back to medieval times. Between 1822 and 1842 243 books were printed at the Būlāq press, the greater part of them translations. Of these, rather more than half were in Turkish, most of the remainder in Arabic. Under Muḥammad ʿAlī's rule Turkish was still the language of the ruling élite in Egypt, and we are therefore not surprised to find that works on military and naval subjects are almost all in Turkish. The same is to a large extent true of pure and applied mathematics, which were chiefly needed for military purposes. Works on medicine, veterinary science, agriculture, and grammar, on the other hand, are mostly in Arabic. History would seem to have been regarded as a matter for the Turkish-speaking rulers, since the few historical books issued from the press in the early period are all in Turkish. The first was a translation of Castera's *Histoire de l'impératrice Catherine II de Russie*, translated by the Greek Yakovaki Argyropoulo, and published in 1244/1829. It was reprinted in Istanbul in 1287/1870. Another early translation was an extract from the *Mémorial de Sainte Hélène*, published in 1247/1832 under the title *Tārīk͟h-i Napolyon Bonapart*. It is also known as *Napolyon sergüzes͟hti*. Then came versions of Botta's *Histoire d'Italie* and of the memoirs of the Duc de Rovigo, both published in 1249/1834. These four books complete the historical translations from Western languages in the early period, though there were also one or two translations from Arabic into Turkish. Thereafter there was an interval of several years until the next historical translation appeared—a version of Voltaire's *Histoire de Charles XII*, published in 1257/1841. This time it was in Arabic, as were also a number of subsequent translations of historical works by Voltaire, Robertson, and others.[25]

In Turkey the movement began more slowly. The translations made in Egypt seem to have been known and studied, but it was not until the middle of the century that translations of European historical writings begin to appear in Istanbul. In 1866 a Turkish translation appeared, by Aḥmed Ḥilmī, of an English *Universal history*—probably the first world history in modern Turkish literature. Thereafter the translation movement developed quickly, especially in Turkey and Egypt, and rapidly altered the world picture as it appeared to Muslim students and readers.[26]

[25] On the productions of the Būlāq press see A. Perron, 'Lettre à M. Mohl sur les écoles et l'imprimerie du pacha d'Egypte', *J.A.*, 4th series (1843), ii, 5–23; J. H. Dunne, 'Printing and Translation under Muḥammad 'Ali', *JRAS* (1940), pp. 325–49. The most recent and most detailed study is that of Professor Jamāl al-Dīn al-Shayyāl, *Ta'rīkh al-tarjama wa'l-ḥaraka al-thaqāfiyya fī 'aṣr Muḥammad 'Alī* (Cairo, 1951), with full lists of publications. See also below, pp. 403 ff.

[26] See further B. Lewis, 'History-writing and National Revival in Turkey', *MEA* (1953), iv, 218–27, and Dr. Kuran's paper, below, pp. 422 ff.

17. THE UTILITY OF OTTOMAN FETḤNĀMES

G. L. LEWIS

Senior Lecturer in Islamic Studies in the University of Oxford

Fetḥnāme is defined as an account of a victory, whereas *ghazānāme* is an account of a single action, and *ghazavātnāme* an account of a series of actions. The description of a victorious battle is a *ẓafernāme*. The terms were confused, however, *ghazavātnāme* being applied to what are properly termed *fetḥnāme* or *ẓafernāme*, while descriptions of battles were latterly known as *ẓafernāme*.[1] In its usual acceptance, *fetḥnāme* is an official report of a victory.

As sources for the military details of the victories they describe, the *fetḥnāmes* of the Ottoman Empire are as unreliable as the publicity handouts of any other belligerent, ancient or modern. There is, for example, a specimen *fetḥnāme* on the battle of Chaldirān in the *Kitāb laṭā'if al-inshā'*,[2] which tells how Sultan Selīm defeated 'the profligate crew who are called Ṣūfī, though there is nothing Ṣūfī about them except the *ṣūf*'. No details of the battle are given; we are simply told that 'eventually the Sacred Ones, who sit at the foot of the Throne, came hand in hand down the Milky Way . . . whereupon the enemy became irresolute . . . and were scattered like locusts over the lands and climes.'

Genuine *fetḥnāmes* are not usually so scant of fact as this, but often they are not much more informative. The most remarkable incident in Meḥemmed III's conquest of the fortress of Eger (Egri) in October 1596 was the massacre of the entire garrison after they had surrendered on a promise of quarter. The cynical justification was that there was a popular song current among the Ottoman frontier-troops, whose words may be freely translated:

'With you, you Eger worms,
We'll never come to terms.'[3]

So the garrison should have had more sense than to expect the promise to be kept. In the *fetḥnāme*, however, there is no mention of the surrender, the massacre, or its justification.[4]

One is, of course, building on shaky foundations when using the *Munshe'āt* of Ferīdūn as source-material. Besides his occasional blunders

[1] A. S. Levend, *Gazavat nameler* (Ankara, T.T.K., 1956), p. 1.

[2] Bodley MS. Sale 1, dated 1062/1652.

[3] 'Yoḳdur sizünle viremüz
'Egrili gidi Egrili.'

[4] Ferīdūn Bey, *Mejmū'a-i munshe'āt al-selāṭīn* (Istanbul, 1265), ii, 2–3.

and omissions, it is well known that he was capable of deliberate forgery when he wished to fill a gap in his collection.[5] Na'īmā[6] states that the Nis̲h̲ānjï Lām 'Alī C̲h̲elebi was dismissed for his exaggeration of Jag̲h̲ala-zāde Sinān Pasha's services, in the *fetḥnāmes* of Eger and of the *ṭābūr*. Ferīdūn's text of the *fetḥnāme* of Eger mentions no individual by name (though of course his may represent a revised second edition), and he does not give the *fetḥnāme* of the *ṭābūr* at all.

Nevertheless, despite Ferīdūn's shortcomings, we can give him credit for knowing what a *fetḥnāme* was for. In what he describes as the *fetḥnāme* from Sultan Ork̲h̲ān to the Jānīk K̲h̲ān on the occasion of the Ottoman conquest of Nicaea, the hope is expressed that the news will be spread abroad, 'so that the friends of the *dawla* may be gladdened, and the enemies of the faith and religion of the Prophet may be dispirited'.[7]

The primary function of the *fetḥnāme* was propaganda. A brief examination of some of the *fetḥnāmes* of C̲h̲aldirān will illustrate this.[8]

To his son and successor Süleymān, Selīm writes:

> 'As the worker of corruption, the Zindīq and heretic called "the son of Ardebīl" had made dissension and corruption his undergarment, unbelief and heresy his outer garment, the afflicting of the servants of God his boast, and the devastation of lands his adornment, I set out for the east to seek him, solely in order to aid the distressed and to succour the oppressed, to revive the ceremonies of the Faith and restore the ordinances of the perspicuous Law . . . I consulted the *S̲h̲eyk̲h̲s* and '*Ulemā*' who declared him an infidel and gave a *fetvā* saying that he should be slain. Consequently it became my high purpose to erase the impure blot of his existence from the page of time, with the claws of the knife and the tempered blade.'

We are then told how the Sultan wrote to the Shah, inviting him to mend his ways and become a Muslim, but there was no reply. The Army then came to Tabrīz, and thence to 'a plain called C̲h̲aldirān'. There the Shah, judging that his men had no power to resist the Ottomans, 'clothed them in armour from head to foot'. Little detail of the engagement is given; we are told that the struggle was protracted and many commanders fell on both sides, and eventually the enemy took to flight. 'It was confirmed that he himself was wounded. We are now making for Tabrīz and, God willing, shall gain a total victory.'

The *fetḥnāme* to the K̲h̲ān of the Crimea is much the same. In neither is there any mention of the Persian lack of firearms or of the clever tactical

[5] See the series of articles by Mükrimin Halil in *TOEM*, Nos. 77–9 and 81, which demonstrate the spuriousness of documents purporting to belong to the reigns of 'Os̲mān I, Ork̲h̲ān, and Murād I.

[6] *Tārīk̲h̲* (Istanbul, 1283), i, 173. [7] *Muns̲h̲e'āt*, i, 67. [8] Ibid., pp. 386–96.

use Selīm made of his. The inference is that the Ottomans wished their victory to be ascribed to their superior valour and the justice of their cause, and that they therefore projected the unsportingness of which they felt they had been guilty in using the new weapon, on to the Persians, by drawing attention to their unsporting use of full armour.

On the other hand, in the *fetḥnāmes* to the '*begs* of the eastern lands, the *emīrs* of the Kurds, and the chiefs of the tribes' and to the notables of Tabrīz, the Persians' use of armour is not mentioned, presumably because these people, unlike the citizens of Istanbul and the Crimea, would know very well that the advantage of the Persian armour was more than offset by the Ottoman cannon.

The content of these two latter *fetḥnāmes* is not only propaganda but an announcement of the next steps to be taken. The *begs*, *emīrs*, and chiefs are given a perfunctory apologia and description of the battle, and then come their instructions:

> 'Ismā'īl, the godless worker of corruption, met me and, by the grace of God, was routed in the twinkling of an eye. As it is not known where he has gone, in order that you may not lose this opportunity of demonstrating your sincerity and subordination to my throne, I have sent this order which must be obeyed: on its arrival, have it written on numerous pieces of paper and circulate it . . . and inform me where this Redhead is, and what is his state of health.'

The *fetḥname* to the notables of Tabrīz is very terse: the leader of the damned, the marshal of the cohorts of devils, has been routed; we are on our way to Tabrīz, and if anyone doesn't behave himself his blood is on his own head.

To Shah Rustem, ruler of Lūristān, Selīm says, more ingenuously than convincingly:

> 'The object of removing that heretic and extirpating that worker of corruption is nothing else but to extol the Word of God and to set in order the affairs of all the people of the Empire and the Faith.'

An apparent divergence from the usual purpose of *fetḥnāmes* is afforded by the document Ferīdūn describes as the *fetḥnāme* to the Sevündük Khān (ruler of the region round Erzurum and formerly a Safavid supporter), in which the precariousness of the Ottoman position is not concealed. It is clear, however, from the wording that this is not a *fetḥnāme*:[9]

> 'When the good news of the victory, and of the flight of Ismā'īl, was reported, to rejoice and delight and gladden those who . . . hold the trains of the Ottoman State, a note was appended saying that the Army

[9] Ibid., pp. 393–4.

would winter in those parts, and ordering provisions to be collected . . . This was followed by a *hükm-ü sherīf* to the same effect. But as the region round Tabrīz, where the Army was then encamped, was all unsafe, because of the evil and sedition of that cruel tyrant, and it was difficult to provide food and shelter for so vast an army, it seemed impossible to winter there, and it was necessary to withdraw. It should be possible next year to deal with him; weak and defeated as he is we cannot give up . . . In view of your hereditary and acquired devotion to the Porte, you will arrange for foodstuffs sufficient for the entire Army to be brought to Shüregel, Choban Köprüsü and Erzurum, together with the owners, so that they can sell them.'

Ferīdūn gives the text of three *fethnāmes* for the capture of the fortress of Kemākh and the defeat of 'Alā' al-Dawla Dhu'l-Qadr in the battle of Turnadāgh (May–June 1515).[10] These are addressed to Prince Süleymān, Mengli Girey, and Ghūrī. The first two do not differ materially, except that in the second the strength of the fortress is emphasized; Süleymān did not need impressing as much as the Tatar Khān: 'The height of the fortress was unimaginable; the depth of the ditch was inconceivable. Yet my victorious Army paid no heed . . .' There is a touch of unconscious humour in what we may unfairly term a description of Janissary marksmanship: 'They discharged their muskets all together, and sent their bullets flying far past the constellation of Orion.'

The third of this group is reported to have left Ghūrī speechless, and no doubt this effect was partially due to the document's being accompanied by the head of 'Alā' al-Dawla, who, like Ghūrī, had had an understanding with the Safavids. It begins with praises to God, 'Destroyer of him who sheds the blood of mankind unjustly and tyrannically', and blessings on the Prophet 'who summoned mankind to the straight path, when before they had been tumbling down the abyss of ignorance and the precipice of error, and aiding the Recusants [*rafaḍa*] and the impious rebels'. After this odd but effective anachronism, Ghūrī is addressed in the politest terms:

> 'Aide of the *Ghāzīs* and the Monotheists, Helper of the Commander of the Faithful, in the enumeration of whose qualities the minds of the sagacious fall short, and the recounting of whose virtues wearies the tongues of the eloquent, who adorns with his power and his excellence the throne of Cairo, and cements with the ranks of his hosts the structure of the Sultanate.'

Then comes the *matn*, the menace of which is intensified by the simplicity of its language:

[10] Ibid., pp. 409–13.

'Among the victories of two months of the present year . . . was that at the beginning of Spring we went with our victorious Army, first of all to the fortress of Kemākh, on Thursday 5 Rabī' I . . . and by the afternoon the fair breeze of victory and conquest blew . . . Then we purposed to go against the land of the Dhu'l-Qadr. On Tuesday, the 22nd of the same month, my Grand Vizier Sinān Pasha went out against the enemy . . . On Wednesday 1 Jumādā I there came a messenger from him announcing that the enemy had been routed, and bringing the head of 'Alā' al-Dawla, with the heads of his sons and his commanders, approximately fifty, "like unto the heads of devils". We have sent, out of pure joy and good cheer, the head of that God-forsaken prince to the Court of Cairo . . . that it may also be the cause of happiness to you.'

There follows a request that the good news may be proclaimed 'in the lands and cities of the Monotheists'. 'Next year we have resolved to subjugate the eastern lands and eliminate such of the red-headed Recusants as have survived the sword . . . We hope that you will not heed their appeals . . . and that you will return our envoy safely.'

A year later, Ghūrī has ceased to be the 'Helper of the Commander of the Faithful'. In the *fetḥnāme* on Marj Dābiq[11] he is 'the doomed to destruction, the forsaken of God'. 'The Army of Islam was victorious, and the Circassian hordes were defeated'—a perfect example of the identification of the *Umma* with the *Dawla*.

The purpose of this brief paper is to suggest that a fruitful line of enquiry may be to seek in *fetḥnāmes* not so much accurate reports of events as clues to the *persona* of the Ottoman Empire (to use Jung's term for the figure we make of ourselves in our imaginations for the purposes of behaviour), and a picture of how the Empire wanted to be regarded by its friends and by its enemies.

[11] Ibid., pp. 427–30.

18. THE HISTORIOGRAPHY OF OTTOMAN-SAFAVID RELATIONS IN THE SIXTEENTH AND SEVENTEENTH CENTURIES

J. R. WALSH

Lecturer in Turkish in the University of Edinburgh

Historiography is as much the result as it is the record of events, and should, therefore, be expected to react variously to the circumstances in which it is produced, in accordance with the temper of its times. In its prejudices and its assumptions, in its omissions no less than in its contents, it is the reflection of the inconstant human situation, and even where it is least informative its supplies us with data which no explicit statement could convincingly express, and which, perhaps, are as valuable to the understanding of the past as the dates and the deeds. From this it would follow that no single piece of historical writing can be fully appreciated except in relation to its literary tradition, the nature and degree of differentiation from which establishes its individuality and exposes its character. For, ultimately, any appraisal of historiography must regard it as a literary form, appreciating that its distinction among the other branches of literature is almost wholly due to the fact that its conventional materials have an unbroken continuity by which its development may be measured and which, moreover, may usually be observed from several angles through the historical writings of other peoples. Every such work, therefore, however inadequate and inaccurate it may be in detail, is itself a historical fact of singular importance, and is best understood when considered with its fellows in their mutual complementary relationship throughout a total situation rather than being merely confronted with them on the particulars.

However acceptable this statement may be as a general principle applying to all historiography, it has an undeniable relevance to Persian and Ottoman historical writing, much of which is of an almost wholly recreational nature. A society which does not paint pictures or carve images does not invent stories, and so the folk-tales and romances of Islam are all either pre-Islamic or borrowed from other peoples, and, like the looted portraits and statues, defaced of their specifically human features. That human need for diversion which in other societies is satisfied by the mythopeic faculty found its response in Islam in history, which, from an ancillary to the sacred and serious sciences of *ḥadīth* and *tafsīr*, developed among the Persians, and thence the Turks, into a distinct literary genre, and, indeed, the only dignified vehicle for 'creative' writing in prose.[1] Like any other literary medium, it therefore became subject to rigid conventions, which were imposed on it more by the temperament of its audience than the demands of its materials. The extravagant elegance of Idrīs Bidlīsī's *Hasht bihisht*, written in Persian and modelled, we are told, on such histories as the *Jihān-gushā* of Juvaynī,[2] grows out of the Oriental notion of useless luxury as an appurtenance of majesty, while, at the other extreme, Neshrī's *Jihānnümā* is the bare story told at the level of general intelligibility. But the contrast is wholly literary, and in conception, attitude and matter there is little to distinguish the two; and just as much Turkish folk-poetry is but simplified *dīvān* literature,[3] so, too, are those histories of a patently popular nature, such as the Anonymous, Uruj, 'Ashîqpasha-zāde, and Rūḥī, all imitations of court productions.[4] In all may be seen the same preoccupation with events in themselves, and these events are invariably given an individual human motivation. The paradox here is that the individuals are rarely presented as personalities, but rather remain obscured behind the tired formulae of praise or blame; a paradox which is even more striking in the biographical literature, where the impression prevails that man is to be regarded as the sum of his experiences and appointments. One need hardly point out the essentially Islamic origins of these characteristics, and it should only be noted that the static nature of Muslim society did not allow for their development even among peoples of different race and in different circumstances. With his work bound by such conventions and traditions, and limited by the understanding and and expectations of his patrons, the personality of the historian himself, to

[1] Cf. Ahmed Hamdi Tanpınar, *Ondokuzuncu asır Türk edebiyatı tarihi* (Istanbul, 1942), p. 62. In the introduction to the *Hasht bihisht*, 9a, Idrīs Bidlīsī describes history as a branch of the science of *muḥāḍarāt*, which is, in general, le savoir-dire of polite society but, in particular, the art of the anecdote. (Cf. Tashköprüzāde, *Miftāḥ al-sa'āda* (Hyderabad, 1328), i, 182.)

[2] Op. cit., 4b. Three other histories are mentioned: that of Vaṣṣāf, the *Tārīkh-i Mu'īnī*, and the *Ẓafernāme* of Sheref al-Dīn 'Alī Yezdī. This passage is incorrectly quoted in Mehmed Şükrü, 'Das Hešt Bihišt des Idrīs Bitlīsī', *Der Islam* xix (1930–31), 143.

[3] This remark can, apparently, be generalized to most literatures; cf. W. R. Halliday, *Folklore studies, ancient and modern* (London, 1924), Preface, pp. x–xi.

[4] Originally those of the Seljuk courts; for among the Ottomans, the popular histories antecede the more stylized works and are, in fact, the latter's only source for the origins and early reigns of the dynasty. But they were not regarded seriously; the *Hasht bihisht* was commissioned because the existing histories were couched in the crude vernacular and written in the style of fables (op. cit., 4b) and, indeed, Rūḥī does begin his work by recalling the prophecy of the legendary Dede Ḳorḳut (Ḳorḳut Ata) that the *khanlïk* from Oghuz Khān will pass down in the line of Ḳayî, from whom the Ottomans are supposed to descend. Idrīs, whose dependence on 'Āshîqpasha-zāde has been shown by M. Şükrü (op. cit., pp. 142–8), never mentions him as a source; while Sa'd al-Dīn (i, 8) does not find them worthy of mention and says that he wrote his work because most of the existing histories were in Persian (i.e. Idrīs and Lārī's *Mir'āt al-advār*), though he does throughout generally acknowledge his popular sources. The inter-relation of these early chronicles has been studied by P. Wittek, 'Zum Quellen-problem des altesten osmanischen Chroniken (mit Auszügen aus Nešrī)', *MOG* (1921–22), i, 77–150; cf. also, F. Taeschner's introduction to Neshrī's *Jihānnüma* (Leipzig, 1951), vol. i.

the degree that it can be detected through the maze of contrivance, is one of our chief human contacts with the problems and anxieties of the period.[5]

It is lack of such human data as would afford a purchase to the imaginative grasp that has immobilized much of the historical writing about the Islamic East: in the sources, events are invariably self-contained, and rarely escape from a narrative context which literary considerations have made selective and artificial to the point of abstraction; matters of social, economic or institutional import, where found at all, are merely incidental, and so sporadic that inferences therefrom must be limited by reservations of such variety as to render them valueless; interpretation is confined to drawing a moral or confirming revealed truth. However, by regarding these historians as literary personalities—which, indeed, is how they intended they should be regarded[6]—it is possible to sense something of the mood of their times; for the sum of the psychological differences between, for example, such roughly contemporary historians as Kemālpas̲h̲a-zāde, Sa'd al-Dīn Efendi, 'Ālī, K̲h̲oja Nis̲h̲ānjî, and Kara C̲h̲elebī-zāde 'Abd al-'Azīz Efendi is equally as great as the points of similarity in their materials, and, when taken into the total account, suggests, however imperfectly, the spiritual ambience in which they lived and wrote. Moreover, it is only by such contrasts in the actual practice of historiography that we can form an impression of the historical conceptions of each age; the self-conscious, and usually apologetic, statements on the purposes and benefits of history which are an inseparable part of the introduction in all these works are for the most part the perfunctory elaboration of platitudes and rarely show any evidence of independent thought.[7]

[5] It is only in this sense that it would be valuable to have, for example, an edition of the *Has̲h̲t bihis̲h̲t*, which, despite Babinger (*GOW*, p. 47), is rarely more than an otiose reworking of familiar materials. That the work was highly esteemed is undeniable, and its praise often inspired an extravagance of language no less than its own (e.g. Jelāl-zāde Nis̲h̲ānjî, *Ma'āṣir-i Selīm K̲h̲ān*, p. 119b); but its defects were also noted, and the 'glowing eulogy' of the work which Rieu attributes to Sa'd al-Dīn (*Cat. Pers. MSS in Brit. Mus.*, i, 217a) is in reality the extreme to which adverse criticism could go without allowing the impression that he found it difficult to understand. (Sa'd al-Dīn, op. cit.)

[6] 'Ālī, for example, never tires of pointing out his literary attainments; cf. Ibnü'l-Emīn Maḥmūd Kemāl's criticism of this trait in his introduction to the *Menāqib-i hünerverān* (Istanbul, 1926), p. 103. Tanis̲h̲ b. Mīr Muḥammed states the attitude almost blatantly in his introduction to the *S̲h̲arafnāme-i S̲h̲āhī*, where he says that since a young man it has been his ambition *ki dar fann-i tārīk̲h̲ kitābī ins̲h̲ā sāzad va dar ān ṣan'at-î badī' -āyīn dar g̲h̲āyat-i takalluf va tazyīn har gūne suk̲h̲an pardāzad* (Brit. Mus., Or. 3497, 5b; India Office, Ethé 574 (*'Abdullāhnāme*) 3b). Despite frequent disclaimers, the attitude persists among the *Vaḳā'i'-nüvīsān*, and at the end of the eighteenth century, Vāṣif Ef. rather proudly (and with much justice) says that because of the *münāsebet-i lafẓiyye ve ma'neviyye* of his earlier history the critics of the age referred to it not as the *Tārīk̲h̲-i Vāṣif* but as the *Tārīk̲h̲-i Vaṣṣāf* (*Tārīk̲h̲*: 1203–09, Millet, *'Alī Emīrī*, 608, 7b). Similar vauntings of his literary ability are to be found at the end of the printed section of his work (Istanbul, 1219), ii, 314. On the limitations of these official histories, cf. Jevdet Pasha, *Tārīk̲h̲* (*Tertīb-i jedīd*, Istanbul, 1302), i, 4.

[7] And for this reason the work of F. Rosenthal, *Muslim historiography* (Leiden, 1952), being based on such statements, is as misleading as would be Māwardī as a source for Islamic administration, or Abū Yūsuf for Islamic taxation.

Such historical works cannot be treated individually; as our reaction to them is conditioned by our awareness of the complex of which they form a part, this must also influence our judgement of their authenticity. That besetting evil of all Islamic historical literature, the mechanical repetition, verbatim or in paraphrase, of earlier works, is endemic in the Ottoman historians of this period.[8] While sincere writers, such as 'Ālī and Pec̲h̲evī, can employ their sources with discrimination, adding quite as much in interpretation or comment as they take in fact, the majority, of which Kātib C̲h̲elebī in his *Fez̲leke* may serve as a prominent example, are little more than servile copyists. So common was the latter practice that it finally came to be regarded as normal, and Na'īmā can actually praise the *Fez̲leke*, though he must have recognized that, apart from some personal reminiscences, most of it was largely transcribed or boiled down from S̲h̲āriḥ al-Menār-zāde and 'Aṭā'ī (Na'īmā, i, 6). But eliminating these plagiarists, there is still left a considerable body of authentic material of sufficient character and literary integrity to warrant their being regarded as representative of the historical mood; and where method is often makeshift and facts are always discretionary, it is in the degree that they express the feeling of events that they have their chief value as a presentation of the past.

The presumption, therefore, is that, despite the numerous factors tending to absorb them into a conventional pattern, the authentic Ottoman and Persian historians of the sixteenth and seventeenth centuries will show each a discernibly individual response to the affairs and activities of their times, and that, for all the arbitrariness it may seem to imply, the tone as well as the content of their works should be given consideration in the formation of our historical judgements. Such an approach to the sources would seem to be particularly useful in the study of the course of Ottoman-Safavid relations in these centuries; for the issue behind all the duly recorded revolts and repressions, campaigns, and embassies is nothing less than the spiritual and political hegemony of the Islamic world, an objective that towards the end of the sixteenth century takes on an urgency born of the increasing awareness that Islam had reached the limits of its expansion and that its security and survival depended largely on the moral unity it could present to Christian Europe. Nowhere, probably, will an explicit statement of these ends be found and, no doubt, they were at no time ever

[8] Cf. the remarks of Jemāl al-Dīn Efendi, *Āyīne-i ẓurefā* (Istanbul, 1314), p. 5. Contemporary Safavid histories are so few that the observation hardly applies there; and, moreover, the production of these two centuries is so dominated by the '*Ālam-ārā* of Iskandar Beg that comparisons among them seem grotesquely disproportionate, the latter being one of the greatest of all Islamic historical works and, indeed, perfect within the limitations of its traditions. It is to be regretted that we still do not have a reliable edition of this work; the recent two volume edition, with its valuable index by Iraj Afs̲h̲ār, merely reproduces the imperfect lithograph of 1314, and the readings must still be controlled by a manuscript.

consciously formulated into policy;[9] it is only through the shifting metabolism of the histories that the historical trend emerges as palpable, human reality. This, unfortunately, is the very aspect of the works which defies objective description and even eludes translation; it is, in fact, the total subjective response to the sources which colours the view and shapes the theory of history of all who use such materials in their study of the past.

Like all historical periods, that of the Ottoman-Safavid struggle is highly artificial, valid only in that it allows us to isolate one phase of a problem the origins of which are to be sought long before the rise of Shah Ismā'īl in the East, and, indeed, even before the establishment of the Ottoman state. With the conquest of Constantinople in 1453, the Ottomans first began to regard their presence in Europe as something more than a protracted intrusion, for conquest in all eastern experience had always demanded the seizure of the visible symbols of rule and the destruction of its acknowledged head. Hitherto they had been an Asiatic power with outposts in hostile territory, and nothing is more expressive of this feeling than that the dead of the Ottoman line are almost always brought to Bursa for burial.[10] But now they were the successors—and, by right of conquest, the legitimate successors—to the Emperor, assuming the problems and responsibilities of Empire as well as imperial prerogatives and presumptions. Although an Islamic state, the frontiers of the Orthodox Church are made its natural boundaries; and, unable to expand on the religious plane, all conquests outside these lines, as in Hungary, Wallachia, and Moldavia, could not be absorbed, but had to be given an indeterminate tributary status. But there was also another force limiting its expansion in Europe—the idea of Europe itself, which the implications of the fall of Constantinople and the contrasting presence of an unyielding alien faith had made the geographical expression of Latin Christianity, soon to find political expression in Hapsburg ambitions. The Ottoman response to this moral barrier was to strengthen its own spiritual foundations, by importing and subsidizing the traditional culture and scholarship of Islam, by displaying lavishly the conspicuous piety of mosques, schools, and hospitals, and by re-asserting its identity with the Asiatic homelands of the faith.

However, with the decline of Mediterranean commerce as a result of Portuguese navigation around the Cape and, later, the rapid growth of

[9] This must not be taken to mean that there existed no policy-making body in the Empire: the consistency in the conduct of affairs throughout this period would indicate the influence of a responsible corps of advisers operating behind the caprices and inanities of the throne, the harem and the divan.

[10] This attitude towards the royal dead is reminiscent of ancestor-worship in Islam, and among the Ottomans the visitation of the royal *türbes* was one of the first ceremonies of a new sultan. The desecration of the tombs of a conquered dynasty is mentioned as early as the 'Abbasid revolution, and instances are met with down to late Safavid times. On the anxiety of certain of the Shahs to conceal their places of burial, cf. *Yādigār*, III/2, p. 9 ff.

Atlantic trade, these lands of the Islamic Middle East were becoming progressively eccentric to world economic developments; reduced to an almost wholly consuming region, they are henceforth little more than a marketing terminal in the Mediterranean system, productively withdrawing further and further into uncomplementary local and parochial economies. The strategic Ottoman hinterlands of Anatolia were particularly sensitive to these changes, suffering as well the consequences of the stagnation of Black Sea trade due to the abandonment of the Central Asiatic caravan routes; the regionalism which the geographical physiognomy of the land had encouraged throughout all periods of its history manifests itself now in sporadic, incoherent revolt. It is wrong to regard these various local insurrections as being provoked by Safavid propagandists; that they are presented as such by the Ottomans arises from the concern to give their repressive measures against Muslims the allure of counter-heretical activity. Safavid proselytism in the area was at best disorganized and erratic, undertaken on the initiative of local *shaykhs* whose religious views are rarely susceptible of definition. In fact, it must be recognized that the rôle of religion and the dervish orders in these disturbances has been given an attention out of all proportion to the realities of the situation.[11] It should also be remembered that the Turkish *begs* and tribal chiefs in Anatolia were not in the same condition of dependence as those in the Balkans, whose very survival in the face of a powerful adversary was due only to the support, active or potential, of the Ottomans. Although their exposed and vulnerable position forced them into a co-operation quite unnatural to their traditions and inclinations, they were still little more than small, isolated groups in hostile territory; and it could have been nothing but the threat of Ottoman retaliation that prevented the Christians from destroying them piecemeal. In Anatolia, on the other hand, there was no such menace, and here the Turkish tribal elements could maintain their natural independence of each other and of the central power; though the petty amirates were gradually absorbed, that instinctive separatism which had formerly atomized the Seljuq state of Rūm into ineffectual *begliks* was too ingrained in these pastoral peoples ever to respond easily to coercion or argument, especially when to the East lay an assured and inviting haven.

Safavid Shiʿism was political in nature, representing the last and most successful bid for power of those Caspian regions which had always resisted

[11] Missionary significance must not be attached to correspondence between the Shah and his sympathizers in Ottoman territory, such as the letters which were intercepted by Süleymān during the campaign of 955, addressed to certain 'heretics' in Amasya (Kara Chelebi-zāde, *Süleymānnāme*, p. 150); the Ottomans, too, were certainly in touch with their own sympathizers among the Shah's subjects. Cf. Taʿlīqī-zāde, *Tebrīziyye* (Top Kapı Sarayı, Revān Köşkü, 1299), f. 24a, where the author records a conversation which he had with the *aʿyān-ỉ Tebrīz* after the city was taken by ʿOsmān Pasha in 933, in which he says how gracious it was of the Sultan that *maḥż-ỉ mekārim-i Khidīvānelerinden size khafīyeten mektūb-ỉ saʿādet-maṣḥūblarỉn irsāl idüb istidʿā-yỉ istiqbāl-i ʿasker-i iḳbāl-rehber buyuralar.*

the central authority of Islam;[12] in adopting Shah Ismāʿīl and providing him with an ʿAlid genealogy, they sought to win to their cause those regions of Āẕarbāyjān where the prestige of the family among the Turkish tribal elements would assure them additional military support in their bid for power. What Shiʿite tendencies may previously have been shown by the Ardabīl dervishes are probably little more than sufistic syncretism, and the Kizilbash Turks, far from being devoted fanatics, behave always with complete religious indifference: their tribal identity is never allowed to disappear into that of the state, and the interests of the tribe are the only paramount ideal which they are ever seen to serve. This will hold true also of those tribes which took part in the Anatolian insurrections,[13] and which, when defeated, could only turn eastward where they would be welcomed and absorbed into the Safavid armies. For having succeeded in their venture, the Safavids had now inherited the traditional Iranian military responsibility of maintaining the Oxus frontier against the unrelenting pressure of the Central Asiatic ferment. Policy demanded that they should foster peace with the Ottomans, as indeed they consistently seek to do;[14] always it is the Ottomans who are the aggressors, and only a sense of insecurity in Europe and a fear of separation from the Islamic matrix could have impelled them to persist in these profitless and inconclusive campaigns in the untenable regions of Āẕarbāyjān and along the Euphrates.[15]

In the Ottoman Empire war was a state enterprise, the staple export, the proceeds of which redressed the disastrous trading balance and assured what economic stability there was; and only war in Europe could promise such returns. It was this Ottoman preoccupation with its European frontier that led the Asiatic provinces to regard it as a foreign power, and to look towards the east for protection from the systematic exploitation to which

[12] In a recent study on the personalities associated with the rise of Shah Ismāʿīl, Jean Aubin has shown the important part played also by the Iranian aristocracy of ʿIrāq-i ʿAjem in the direction of the affairs of the early state. Cf. ʿEtudes Safavides, Iʾ, *Journal of the Economic and Social History of the Orient* (1959), ii, 37–81.

[13] Ulama Beg Tekkelü will serve as an example. Having fled to the Shah after the defeat of Shāh Kulī, he was made *amīr* of Āẕarbāyjān; in 937 he revolted against the Shah out of disappointment in not receiving a preferment (Ḥasan Rūmlū, text, 237; transl., 109) and again came over with his troops to the Ottoman side, for whom he captured Bitlīs from the rebel Kurdish leader, Sheref Khān. (ʿĀlī, *Künh*, 27th event of the reign of Süleymān; Kara Chelebī-zāde, 114; Pechevī, i, 175; Jelāl-zāde Nishānjī, *Ṭabaqāt*, 180b, who doubts the sincerity of his return to Sunnism.)

[14] And the Ottomans must have been quite aware of this. Cf. ʿĀlī, *Künh* (8th event of the reign of Süleymān), where he says of Shah Ṭahmāsp: *rāh-i mudārātī meslūk ve serkeshlik maʿāyibini metrūk kīlmak üzre deprendi*; *fī nefsi ʾl-emr ekser-i eyyām ve leyāli bu shehryār-i ʿālem-medāruñ ʿatebe-i ʿulyāsīna daʿvā-yi khulūṣ üzre güzerān eyledi.*

[15] And once even into Khuzistān; in 991, when in an attempt to engage the Safavids on a wider front and compel them to dissipate their forces, Elvend-oghlī ʿAlī Pasha led a campaign against the ʿAlī Allāhī Arabs of Shushter and Dizfūl. That such was the purpose of the campaign is stated by Niyāzī, f. 6b.

they were subjected in the interests of Istanbul. That many of these revolts had dervish leadership can be attributed to the superstitious reverence which allowed them a franchise and an immunity denied to others, as well as to the confidence they enjoyed among all sections of the people; but in most cases they must be regarded as but the articulate figureheads of deep-seated discontents amongst the sedentary as well as the tribal elements.

In the sixteenth century, Western Europe, and notably Spain, France, and England, witnessed the evolution of the national state conceived in terms of confessional unity, and this is strikingly paralleled by developments in the Islamic East. Shiʿism, as previously Zoroastrianism, was made the principle on which the Iranian peoples could establish their national unity within their traditional frontiers, excluding even the non-Iranian peoples already present therein. It is for this reason that the Ḳizilbash tribes, even when they try to conform, are never absorbed, and their foreign presence is a persistent irritant in the internal order of the state down to the reign of Shah ʿAbbās I, when they are definitely relegated to their proper status.[16] The familiar paradox of this Persian state being ruled by a dynasty of Turkish origin has concealed the extent to which the latter was made the instrument of a policy formed and directed by others, and which it later came to regard as its own; to see more than this in it is to confuse national aspirations with military objectives.

The Ottomans, on the other hand, had no such national basis, precedent or memory of unity and were compelled to operate within a concept of empire defined only by Islam. It is not mere rodomontade when, in his letters to foreign princes, the Sultan describes the extent of his dominions as embracing practically the whole Muslim world; this was recognized to be the area of political possibility, the formal integrity of which was to balance the growing dynamism of Christian Europe, and in this oecumenical area only Safavid Persia was prominently discordant. Hence the series of fruitless wars which in the histories are usually supplied with some trifling reason out of all proportion to their expense in men, money, and materials, but which may be seen as a result of the innate insecurity of the Ottoman Empire.

II

Probably the most notable contrast between the Persian and Ottoman histories of this period is in the terms and tone they use in speaking of one another. The Persian historians generally show a becoming respect for their western neighbour whom they regard as a bastion of Islam against

[16] It would be interesting to study whether the persecution of the Ṣūfīs by the Safavids and the polemic waged against them by the Shīʿa doctors was, in fact, but the projection of this activity against the Turkish tribal elements onto a doctrinal plane.

infidel Europe,[17] and they accept the occasional campaigns against their own territories as something quite natural between military states with ill-defined boundaries. However fierce the engagements may be, they are never churlish in defeat or gloating in victory. In fact, the Ottomans, unlike the Uzbeks of Transoxania, were never considered a serious menace, and after the misadventure of Shah Ismā'īl at Chaldirān it became policy not to confront them in battle, but to wait to the end of the campaigning season when they would be obliged to return to their own territories and leave their conquests to be painlessly reclaimed.[18] But whether Ottoman, Uzbek or Mogol, and whether hostile or friendly, their relations with their neighbours are always very much secondary to the intense preoccupation with the internal conflicts out of which the new state was slowly and laboriously developing.[19] Attention is unwaveringly fixed on the court and the events of which it is the centre, and throughout the entire two centuries under consideration factionalism and intrigue are the major themes of all their narratives, an attitude similar to that which begins to be observed in the Ottoman histories after the first quarter of the seventeenth century.

The latter, on the other hand, are unrestrained, often to the point of scurrility, in the opprobrium of the Shah and his adherents, and the shibboleths appear unfailingly whenever the opportunity affords.[20] Quite apart from the arguments which are urged in support of persisting in these

[17] Ḥasan Rūmlu and Iskandar Beg always speak of their victories over the Christians in terms of the greatest satisfaction, and it is usually only their failure to respect treaties that occasions reproach. Even the insane Sultan Muṣṭafā is accorded the due courtesies (cf. the report in Iskandar Beg that he was opposed to war against Persia, p. 652), which contrasts strikingly with the apocryphal story in Solakzāde that Shah Ismā'īl's mother, the daughter of Uzun Ḥasan, was mad (p. 315). Sām Mīrzā in the *Tohfe* (Tehran, 1314) includes Selīm I and Süleymān among the poets of the age (p. 19).

[18] For this reason, the Ottomans always taunt Ṭahmāsp with being a cowardly hermaphrodite. Knowing that they could not hold their conquests in Safavid territories, they made it a practice to despoil and destroy the regions through which they passed, taking the people slaves. Cf., for example, Luṭfī Pasha, p. 455, on Süleymān's campaign of 961, and 'Ālī, *Nuṣretnāme*, 8a–10a, for the *fetvās* delivered by the *muftīs*, sanctioning such activity against heretical Muslims. In Ta'līqīzāde, *Tebrīziyye*, 20b, there occurs the verse:

Rāfiḍī kushtan be-dil nārad malāl
Māl-i shī'ī hast bar sunnī ḥalāl

Iskandar Beg, more in sorrow than in rancour, reproaches Murād III with enslaving Muslims and selling them to Jews and Christians, and he mistakenly believes that no previous sultan had done this (p. 345).

[19] There is an unmistakable note of apology in the chapter-heading of Iskandar Beg for the year 1033: *Ẕikr-i vaqā'i'-i Rūm ki chūn mevqūf 'aley-i maqṣad ast az īrād-i ān chāre nīst* (p. 713).

[20] But the attitude towards the Safavids can be frequently contradictory: Selānīkī, after describing in great detail the cordial reception of Shah Ṭahmāsp's ambassador in 975, ends the passage with an abrupt reversion to the usual upbraiding of their creed and their practices, and prays that God will deliver their lands into the hands of the Ottomans to be peopled with Sunnīs (pp. 88–95). The scathing epithet becomes an almost inseparable part of the names of the Shahs, and even in our own century, 'Alī Emīrī refers to Ismā'īl as *Şāh-i gümrāh* (*Tārīkh ve Edebiyāt Mejmū'asi*), No. 2 (Istanbul, 1334), p. 24.

costly campaigns, the very passion of the invective shows the struggle to have been regarded as a war of religion. Accusations of licentiousness, atrocities against the Sunnis and desecration of Qur'āns, mosques and other pious objects abound, usually based on hearsay and without any attempt at substantiation, and, in the absence of any more immediate reason, are frequently offered as adequate motives for launching an attack against Safavid territory.

The impression is inescapable that neither side had very much information about the other, and naturally for contemporary events each side had to rely on the accounts of travellers, ambassadors, and merchants.[21] Kātib Chelebī, in the *Kashf al-ẓunūn* (Istanbul, 1941–43), knows of the *Ṣafvat al-ṣafā* (ii, 1079) only through mention by Khwāndamīr in the *Ḥabīb al-siyar*, and the latter he criticizes for devoting too much space to Shah Ismā'īl (i, 629). Ghaffāri's *Nusakh-i jihān-ārā* (i, 622), Qāsimī's *Shāhnāme* (ii, 1026) and the *Lubb al-tavārīkh* by Mīr Yaḥyā (ii, 1547) appear to be the only other Persian historical works dealing with the early history of the Safavids to which he had access. The Ottomans know practically nothing of Persian activities except on their own frontiers. In none of the Persian histories is there any mention of written Ottoman sources, though the genealogy going back to Kara Khān through Oghuz which is given by Ḥasan Rūmlu for Sultan Selīm II (text, 459; trans., 199) must have been derived from one of the early Ottoman histories. Likewise, the account given by Iskandar Beg for the reasons behind the revolt of Shāhzāde Bāyezīd in 966 and his war with Shāhzāde Selīm seems to reflect an Ottoman version (p. 76). Iskandar Beg, too, frequently attributes his remarks on the Ottomans to rumour or current report.

The blasphemies and outrages with which the Ottomans charge the Safavids are in all probability deduced from the behaviour of the tribal elements in Anatolia during the so-called 'dervish revolts';[22] such excesses were quite in character for these groups whose conceptions of Islam were even at this time little removed from their ancestral shamanism. Essentially these insurrections were in the nature of migrations to the more congenial atmosphere of the Safavid territories, where the tribes could expect to play an active part in the Kizilbash armies and attain a position no longer

[21] And how unreliable such information could be may be seen from the report which Süleymān Pasha sent to the Grand Vizier at the beginning of the campaign of 940. Cf. M. Tayyib Gökbilgin, 'Ibrahim Paşa'nın Irak Fütuhatı', *Türk Tarih Kurumu Belleten* (1957), xxi, 463.

[22] Some of the documents for the Shāh Kulī rising in 917 have been published by Çağatay Uluçay, 'Yavuz Sultan Selim nasıl padişah oldu?', *Istanbul Üniversitesi Edebiyat Fakültesi Tarih Dergisi* (1954), vi, 53–90; (1954), vii, 117–42. From these it is clear that the movement was also, in part, a revolt of the *sipāhīs* of Anatolia. Cf. Sa'd al-Dīn, ii, 163, and Isḥāq Chelebī, *Selīmnāme*, 23a. Similar local dissatisfaction underlay the revolts of 932–3, the most important of which was that of Sheykh Qalender, a descendant of Ḥājjī Bektash. Cf. 'Ālī, *Künh* (15th and 16th events of the reign of Süleymān); Pechevī, i, 120–2; Kara Chelebī-zāde, *Süleymānnāme*, p. 98.

possible in the military aristocracy of the Ottoman Empire.[23] That the Safavids welcomed the support of such contingents and, at times, even encouraged their migration,[24] must not be taken to mean that it was their sectarian propaganda which produced the dissatisfactions underlying the risings; these can be seen developing as far back as the invasion of Timur at the end of the fourteenth century, and, indeed, even further. In their inability to perceive the pattern of events, the Ottoman historians can find no connection between the invasion of Timur, the revolt of Simawna Qāḍīsi-oghlî, the wars of succession between Bāyezīd II and Sultan Jem and, later, that between Selīm I and Sultan Aḥmed; each event and its agent is specific, and as the presence of Safavid *shaykhs* is to be the adequate explanation for any tribal disturbance, their doctrine had to be shown as hideous in order to justify the mercilessness of their repression.[25]

The doctrines of the sect are invariably attributed to Shah Ismā'īl, rather than to the Ardabīl *shaykhs*. 'Ālī (*Nuṣretnāme*, 5b) says that he selected at will innovations and practices from each of the seventy-one heretical sects of Islam to form this new creed; and Abu'l-Faḍl b. Idrīs Bidlīsī, in the *Selīmnāme*, refers to the Kîzîlbash as Ismā'īlīs: *refaḍa-i Ismā'īliyye* (51a), *müntesibān ve-mürīdān-i Ismā'īliyye* (64a). The anonymous account of Süleymān's campaign of 955, entitled the *Jāmi' al-jevāhir*, can still speak of Ṭahmāsp as the son of 'Sheykh' Ismā'īl (13b). Only in 'Āshîqpasha-zāde is Sheykh Ḥayder given any particular mention (p. 267), but here, too, it is his son who is presented as the centre of veneration of the Ṣūfīs, and in the *Anonymous*, the refugees of the Shāh Kulî revolt are said on reaching Tabrīz to have fallen down in worship before him. Safavid claims to 'Alid descent are seldom alluded to: one of the *fetvās* in the *Nuṣretnāme* describes how, when Ismā'īl compelled the *sādāt*

[23] Busbecq, writing in 1555, says that the fortress of Amasya is maintained as a stronghold 'seu contra Asiae populos imperio Turcarum non nimis aequos (ut dicam postea) seu contra Persam, etc.' *Epistolae* (Lipsiae, 1589), p. 106; and he later relates an anecdote to illustrate that 'populi illi Asiatici religionem imperiumque Othomannorum gravate ferant', ibid., p. 120.

[24] Ḥasan Rūmlu says quite clearly that Shāh Kulî's rising in 917 was a migration to Āẕarbāyjān (text, 125; trans., 57), and the following year Nūr 'Alī Khalīfe Rūmlu is said to have been sent to Rūm merely 'to collect' supporters from this disturbed region (text, 134; trans., 62). Shah Ismā'īl's need of recruits from this quarter is given as the reason for his violation of Ottoman territory in 908 (Sa'd al-Dīn, ii, 126); and that there was never any intention of hostilities against his mighty neighbour in this can be judged from the words 'Āshîqpasha-zāde attributes to him: *Ben ḳandan sizüñ vilāyetüñüze 'asker chekmek ḳandan* (p. 269). Cf., also Luṭfī Pasha, p. 201, where, however, this event is placed in the year 913. Subsequent treaties of peace will include provisions to prevent such migrations into one another's territories, e.g. Iskandar Beg, p. 78. 'Ālī, *Nuṣretnāme*, 7b, considers it one of the offences of Ismā'īl II which justified the campaign of Lala Muṣṭafā Pasha in 985, that he accepted into his territories certain Kurdish tribes from Shehrzōr and Vān.

[25] In preparation for his Persian campaign of 920, Selīm I is reported to have had 40,000 of his Anatolian subjects suspected of sympathy with the Shah executed or imprisoned. (Sa'd al-Dīn, ii, 247; 'Ālī, *Künh*, 238b). The rites and rituals of the Safavids were conceived as being similar to the *dhikr* of the dervish *tekkes*. Ta'līqī-zāde, *Tebrīziyye*, 21b, says that the mosque of Uzun Ḥasan in Tabrīz, on the capture of that city by the Ottomans in 933, once again heard the recital of the Qur'ān and *sadā-yi ozan yerine nidā-yi eẕān oḳunub*, etc.

of Meshhed to include him in the *Bahr al-ansāb*, they gave him a genealogy from a *seyyid* whose line was known to have died out. Yet the conclusion of the *fetvā* seems to allow the possibility of the claim being true, for it attempts to show that even allowing such descent their conduct would put them in the same class as infidels.[26]

No doubt the earlier respect shown by the Ottomans to the Ardabīl Ṣūfīs[27] made it necessary to ascribe all such heretical deviations to Ismā'īl. This reverence was a survival of the early tribal days of the state when, in composition and ideals, it was wholly Turkish, and when the Islam such as preached by the dervishes afforded a moral core to a society the elements of which had no natural cohesion and were only brought into co-operation by the rich rewards which the conquests in Europe promised. When gradually the concept of empire evolves and an effort is made to assume the responsibilities which this implied, the independent and arrogant tribal aristocracy had to be replaced by one of the Sultan's own creation selected from among the subject peoples.[28] Moreover, the organization and good order of this empire demanded the adoption of Islam at its most civilized expression, with all its heritage of law and administration, and so the dichotomy between Ottoman and tribal Turk resolves itself into a contest between the *medrese* and the *tekke*, a contest weighed heavily in favour of the former by the influence of the throne.[29] The ambition was to keep this disenfranchized element contained in Anatolia, and hence arose the polarization of this region towards the east, where the young Safavid state was rising to power with the military support of just such elements. In his letter to Bāyezīd II, Ismā'īl mentions the special devotion of Rūm to his family (Ferīdūn Beg, i, 345), and in the journal of Selīm's campaign in 920, it is implied that Shah Ismā'īl entered the battle of Chaldirān, expecting many of the Sultan's troops to desert to his side (Ferīdūn Beg, i, 461).

While the Ottomans did not want this tribal element intimately involved in the operation of their own state, they dared not lose them to the Safavids, in whose armies they would certainly be turned against their former masters. It was this that made necessary the campaign of 920: the polarization had to be neutralized by inflicting a signal defeat on the

[26] The *fetvās* issued for the campaign of 1135 concentrate on the persecution of Sunnism in Ṣafavid territories, but in general tone and language they bear a striking similarity to these earlier ones. Cf. Küchük Chelebī-zāde, *Tārīkh* (ed. 1282), pp. 64–6.

[27] Cf. the correspondence between Bāyezīd I and Shah Ismā'īl in Ferīdūn Beg, i, 345–47. Here Bāyezīd shows himself to be aware of the economic significance to Anatolia of these eastward migrations.

[28] Cf. the explanation of such processes in Ibn Khaldūn, *Muqaddima* (trans. de Slane), i, 319.

[29] The well-known incident in the biography of Kemālpasha-zāde on his decision to enter the learned profession after seeing Luṭfī Ef., a mere *müderris* in Filibe, accorded greater honour than Evrenos-oghlî Aḥmed Beg by the Grand Vizier Ibrāhīm Pasha, is an example of this attitude. Cf. Tashköprüzāde, *Shaqā'iq al-nu'mānīye*, trans. Mejdī (Istanbul, 1269), p. 381.

Shah, discrediting him in the eyes of all who might look expectantly to that quarter. Selīm's greatest anxiety was that the latter might refuse to give battle (Ferīdūn Beg, op. cit.), as indeed he would had he not counted on the disloyalty of the Ottoman troops. But, of course, this victory did nothing towards the solution of the basic problem of Anatolian unrest, and merely provided the precedents and the ideologies for similar fruitless attempts throughout the following century. It is probable that the same sense of insecurity *vis-à-vis* Europe which was mentioned earlier forced the Ottomans to maintain this struggle with the Safavids on the religious plane and blinded them to the more immediate social and economic causes of their troubles. 'Why', asks Murād III, 'were things so cheap and everyone so prosperous in the old days when justice ['*adālet*, and, certainly, here by metonymy for Islam[30]] was not so widespread, while now hardship increases daily and things are forever going wrong?' (Ferīdūn Beg, ii, 576). Quite apart from its economic *naïveté*, the question betrays the assumption that Islam should be the solvent for all difficulties, and this assumption explains the new series of eastern campaigns begun in his reign, those campaigns which foreign observers attributed merely to opportunism and the Sultan's vanity and which the practical Sokollu Meḥmed Pasha tried his best to prevent.[31] The problem is still that which exercised Selīm and Süleymān, but over half a century of ideological warfare had so identified this with the *ghazā-yi akbar* that victory in the latter was seen as the only final and comprehensive solution; motives need no longer be stated nor occasions awaited; an oppressive complacency informs all the histories.

After the reign of Meḥemmed III, however, when in Persia Safavid policy towards the Turkish tribes assumes much the same features as that of the Ottomans towards the end of the fifteenth century, it slowly begins to be appreciated that the incessant insurrections in Anatolia can no longer be reasonably attributed to instigation from the outside, and where formerly in the histories figured fanatical sectarians led by their *shaykhs* we now find bandits and outlaws (*eshqiyā, jelālīler*) serving some military

[30] For example, cf. Ferīdūn Beg, ii, 12: *Nūr-ī haqq-bīn ve yakīn ile rūshen olan khired-i 'āqibet-bīn ḳatīnda ẓāhir ve müstebīndur ki khavākīn-i dīndār ve selāṭīn-i sherī'at-shi'ār her bār ki ṣafḥa-ī eknāf ve eṭrāf-ī diyārī shirk-i ve khāshāk-ī ilḥād ve fesāddan tīgh-i ābdār ile taṭhīr ve pāk ideler iqtiżā-yī jibillet-i 'ādilāne üzre sāḥat-ī memlekete dakhī envār-ī 'adālet ile müstenīr ve tābnāk itmek lāzim ve müteḥattimdür.*

[31] R. Knolles, *The Generall historie of the Turkes* (London, 1621), p. 925; G. T. Minadoi (in P. Bizaro, *Rerum Persicarum historia* (Frankfurt, 1601)), p. 523. The statement of Giovanni Micheli (in E. Alberi, *Relazione degli Ambasciatori Veneti al Senato*, III/2, p. 259) is representative: '. . . la causa di questo guerra non è stata l'antica ed invecchiata dissensione di fede, come forse è stato per multo tempo creduto, ma solo un desiderio ambizioso di Amurat, re dei Turchi, di aggrandire i confini del suo regno; il quale desiderio non nacque tanto in lui contro Persia, che contro ogni altra nazione dell'Europa non potesse ancora nascere.' On the attitude of Ṣoḳollu, cf. Pechevī, ii, 36; Ḥasan Beg-zāde states baldly that the campaign was opportunist, seeking to profit from the disorders which followed the murder of Ismā'īl II and the accession of the blind Muḥammed Khudābanda (f. 45a), and both Pechevī, op. cit., and 'Ālī (10th event of the reign of Murād III) would seem to concur.

adventurer. The instability of the eastern frontier comes to be regarded as normal, and the reversals suffered at the hands of the Safavids inspires a new respect for the Shah and an ungracious acceptance of the political realities of the age. The treaty of Qaṣr-i Shīrīn in 1049 confirms the utter exhaustion of both sides, and the final realization by the Ottomans that they had forgotten the purpose of the warfare on this front which had survived for over three quarters of a century on slogans born of the illusion of an Islamic *oikumene*. Already in 1038, Shāriḥ al-Menār-zāde Aḥmed Efendi, in a very appreciative obituary, even palliates the Shiʿism of Shah ʿAbbās I, implying that it was not so much a religious conviction as compliance with the traditions of the dynasty and the prejudices of his people.[32]

But historical aspect is quite as artificial as historical period, and to present the events of these two centuries entirely in terms of religio-political activity would be as partial as a wholly economic or military interpretation. It is, however, an aspect in which the historical literature, more than all the archives, can be of unique service, and it is probably only through these works that we can ever form our impressions of the spiritual life of the age, basing our judgements on values which are ultimately literary. A historiography is best described by the conceptions to which it gives rise, and, indeed, one can say nothing of other than bibliographical interest about any historiography until one has already formed from it a conception of the age to which it belongs. Such has been the approach of the present paper. Ottoman history, today inhibited in all its utterances by anticipation of the disclosures of the archives, will at no time be able to dispense with this material, without which the documents and statistics are as lifeless as the hands that wrote them; for, however much the facts may approach the ideals of mass-observation, it should still be the concern of every conscientious historian that the bias of his statements be as accurate and as well-founded as their basis.

[32] I am assuming that the accounts in Kātib Chelebī, *Fezleke*, ii, 112, and Naʿīmā, ii, 448, both go back to this common source. Cf. also the honorific forms of address prescribed to be used in letters to Shah ʿAbbās in Ferīdūn Beg, i, 8 (Nos. 1, 2 and 10).

WORKS MENTIONED IN THE TEXT

'Ālī, *Künhü'l akhbār*, 4th *rükn* (Sulaymaniye, As'ad Ef., 2162).

— *Nuṣretnāme* (Sulaymaniye, As'ad Ef., 2433).

'Āshīqpasha-zāde, *Tevārīkh-i āl-i 'Osmān*, ed. 'Alī Beg (Istanbul, 1332).

Anonymous, *Die Altosmanische Chronik*, ed. F. Giese (Leipzig, 1929).

Jāmi' al-javāhir (Millet, Rashīd Ef., 655).

Jelāl-zāde Nishānjī, *Ṭabaqāt al-mamālīk* (British Museum, Add. 7855).

— *Ma'āṣir-i Selīm Khān* (British Museum, Add. 7848).

Ferīdūn Beg, *Münshe'āt al-selāṭīn* (Istanbul, 1275).

Ḥasan Rūmlu, *Aḥsan al-tavārīkh*, ed. and trans. by C. N. Seddon (Baroda, 1931–4).

Ḥasan Beg-zāde, *Tārīkh*, 926–1032 A.H. (Nuruosmaniye, 3134).

Iskandar Beg, *'Ālam-ārā-yi 'Abbāsī* (Tehran, 1313–14).

Idrīs Bidlīsī, *Hasht bihisht* (British Museum, Add. 7646, 7647).

Idrīs Bidlīsī and Abu'l-Faḍl, *Selīmnāme* (British Museum, Add. 24960).

Isḥāq Chelebī, *Selīmnāme* (Bibliothèque Nationale, MSS. turcs, AF, 141).

Kātib Chelebī, *Fezleke* (Istanbul, 1286–7).

Kara Chelebī-zāde, *Süleymānnāme* (Bulaq, 1248).

Luṭfī Pasha, *Tevārīkh-i āl-i 'Osmān*, ed. 'Alī Beg (Istanbul, 1341).

Niyāzī, *Ẓafernāme-i 'Alī Pasha* (Millet, 'Alī Emīrī, 369).

Na'īmā, *Tārīkh*, 6 vols. (Istanbul, 1280).

Pechevī, *Tārīkh* (Istanbul, 1283).

Rūḥī, *Tārīkh-i āl-i 'Osmān* (Bodleian, Marsh, 313).

Selānīkī, *Tārīkh* (Istanbul, 1281).

Sa'd al-Dīn Ef., *Tāj al-tevārīkh* (Istanbul, 1279).

Ta'līqī-zāde Meḥmed Chelebī, *Tebrīziyye* (Top Kapı Sarayı, Revān Köşkü, 1299).

19. THE TRADITIONAL HISTORIOGRAPHY OF THE MARONITES

K. S. SALIBI

Associate Professor of History in the American University of Beirut

> The changes of time perplex the mind of man. None would have told of past ages but for the written annals:
> Those are the annals that tell the story of our homeland and of those who dwelt before us in the Mountain of Lebanon.
>
> IBN AL-QILĀʿĪ

Maronite historiography has a twofold interest for the student of Middle Eastern history. While serving as an important source on the history of Lebanon since the twelfth century, it also reflects the internal development of the Maronite community, its evolving relations with Rome, and its gradual integration in the Lebanese polity. Despite the fact that most of the works of the Maronite historians have appeared in print, modern Lebanese scholarship has paid little attention to the critical treatment of these works and, while tending to use them as absolute standards of reference, has left their reliability almost unquestioned.[1]

Indeed, Lebanese historiography, of which Maronite historiography forms a major part, provides the main body of source material for the history of Lebanon from the twelfth century through the nineteenth. For the Ottoman period, Lebanese histories and chronicles may be considerably supplemented by the works of European and Ottoman travellers and observers, and by materials found or as yet undiscovered in the European and Ottoman archives; but this is certainly not the case for the Crusader and Mamluk periods. In fact, what is found in non-Lebanese sources about the history of Lebanon in the later Middle Ages substantiates facts found in the Lebanese sources, but adds little to them. To the Arab chroniclers of the Zengid, Ayyubid, and Mamluk periods, Lebanon was important only as a border province of Muslim Syria, with an unruly heretical and infidel population, which was vulnerable to attack from the sea and by the coastal route. They, therefore, devoted little attention to its internal history. Eastern Christian chroniclers rarely mentioned Lebanon, although a large proportion of its inhabitants were Christians of the various Eastern communions. Even the Crusader chroniclers and historians, who seem to have been greatly impressed by the qualities of the Maronites as fighters and

[1] I have attempted a critical treatment of some Maronite histories in my *Maronite historians of mediaeval Lebanon* (Beirut, 1959) where I study the works of three Maronite historians: Jibrā'īl b. al-Qilāʿī, Isṭifān al-Duwayhī, and Ṭannūs al-Shidyāq. Georg Graf has surveyed Maronite historiographic literature in his *Geschichte der christlichen arabischen Literatur* (Rome, 1944–53): cited as Graf.

by their devotion to the Frankish cause, wrote of them only in general terms, virtually ignoring the internal history of a country which fell under Frankish rule for the greater part of the twelfth and thirteenth centuries. A number of pilgrims and missionaries who visited the Holy Land during and after the Crusader period dwelt at some length on the religious condition of the Maronites and contributed some information of relevance to the history of Lebanon at the time; but the later pilgrims and missionaries tended to repeat what earlier travellers had noted and did not always record their own observations. The Lebanese histories which deal with the pre-Ottoman period hold, therefore, a unique position and are indispensable to the historian of medieval Lebanon.

This paper is concerned with the traditional historiography of the Maronites: an important section of Lebanese historiography which includes the works of Maronite historians who lived and wrote in Lebanon and who attempted to survey or interpret the history of their community and of Mount Lebanon. It will not deal with local histories or narratives of particular events, subjects worthy of study on their own, or with the works of Maronite scholars who lived and wrote in Europe. Nevertheless, a brief general note on the history of Maronite historiography may be of use as a background to the subject.

Little is known about Maronite historical writing before the fifteenth century. It is likely that some Maronite history was written during the Crusader period, a period of basic importance in the history of the Maronite community; but whatever may have been written is now lost. One may suppose that the triumphant Uniate Maronite church of the fifteenth century destroyed the older literature in an effort to wipe out the memory of pre-Uniate times and the violent dissensions which divided the Maronites over the cause of union for four centuries.[2] In his *Geschichte der christlichen arabischen Literatur*, Georg Graf lists only two Maronite histories written before the fifteenth century: a Church history written in the thirteenth century by the monk Yuḥannā (Yuḥannā al-Rāhib al-Mārūnī) and an early fourteenth-century history of the monastery of Mār Shallīṭā Maqbis (1194–1307) by Tādrus, archbishop of Ḥamāh—a brief historical sketch which must have formed part of a larger work.[3]

[2] The union of the Maronite church with Rome, far from being a single event, was a process which started in the twelfth century, soon after the coming of the Franks to Syria, and which continued through the thirteenth, fourteenth and fifteenth centuries, causing considerable and often bloody dissension among the Maronites, until an effective basic union was established in the early sixteenth. I have dealt with this subject at length in an article, 'The Maronite church in the Middle Ages and its union with Rome', *Oriens Christianus*, 42 (1958), pp. 92–104. The emphasis laid by later Maronite historians on the fictitious perpetual orthodoxy of their church suggests that older Maronite literature had been destroyed in an effort to do away with all evidence pointing to the original heresy of the church.

[3] Graf, ii, 100–1. The latter work was published by Būlus Qar'alī (Paul Carali) as an appendix to *Ḥurūb al-muqaddamīn, 1075–1450* (Bayt Shabāb, 1937), pp. 85–8.

The earliest Maronite historian a number of whose works is still available is Jibrā'īl b. al-Qilā'ī (d. 1516), the first known representative of the traditional school of Maronite historiography. Ilyās of M'ād, a contemporary of Ibn al-Qilā'ī, seems to have been a chronicler of some importance; but his work has been lost and is known only through reference by later writers. The sixteenth and seventeenth centuries saw little development in Maronite historiography. Ibn al-Qilā'ī wrote his history in vernacular verse (*zajal*), and the more important Maronite writers of this period imitated him in this respect; some followed him also in dealing with Maronite history as a whole and in his manner, while others dealt with particular events only. A few minor works in prose dealing with Maronite history were also written; and genealogical tables of Lebanese families were drawn up by the priest Jirjis Mārūn.[4] Latinized Maronites like Gabriel Sionita (d. 1648), Abraham Ecchellensis (d. 1664), and Faustus Naironus (d. 1712), who lived and wrote in Europe, tried to explore the origins of the Maronites; and the last published his *Dissertatio de origine, nomine, ac religione Maronitarum* at Rome in 1679. Maronite historiography, however, was first given coherence by the patriarch Isṭifān al-Duwayhī (1629–1704), rightly called the Father of Maronite History. He was the first Maronite to attempt a serious history of his community from its origins to his own day.

Maronite historians from Ibn al-Qilā'ī to Duwayhī were mostly clerics who had received their education and training in Rome. With the exception of Duwayhī, whose historiographic field of interest was large, they were concerned mainly with the history of the Maronite church and community. The clerical tradition in Maronite historiography was carried on by a number of historians who followed Duwayhī, like Jibrā'īl Jirmānus Farḥāt (1670–1732) and Arsāniyus Arūtīn (1707–86), both of whom wrote on the history of Maronite monasticism, and by Yūsūf Mārūn al-Duwayhī (d. 1780), Isṭifān 'Awwād al-Sim'ānī (1711–82), his contemporary Anṭūn Qayyāla,[5] Yūsuf al-Dibs (1832–1907), and Yūsuf Daryān (d. 1920).[6] With the beginning of the nineteenth century Maronite historians appeared who were not only laymen, but who were interested in non-ecclesiastical aspects of Maronite history and in the general history of Mount Lebanon. Anṭūniyūs Abū Khaṭṭār al-'Ayntūrīnī (d. 1821), Ḥaydar Aḥmad Shihāb (1760–1835), and Ṭannūs al-Shidyāq (*c.* 1794–1861), for instance, dealt mainly with the political history of feudal Lebanon. The historians who followed in this lay tradition have left little that is worthy of serious

[4] For full reference on the Maronite historiography of the sixteenth and early seventeenth centuries see Graf, iii, 333–61 *passim*.

[5] The writings of Sim'ānī and Qayyāla in defence of Maronite perpetual orthodoxy were published together in Afrām al-Dayrānī, *Kitāb al-muḥāmāt 'an al-Mawārina wa-qiddīsīhim*, n.p. (1899).

[6] The most learned living representative of this tradition is Mgr. Pierre Dib, Maronite archbishop of Cairo, who writes in French.

attention, except for some valuable sketches and narratives of local or family history or of particular events.

The traditional historiography of the Maronites seems to have come into being as an expression of Maronite national pride. As a small, closely-knit community surrounded by enemies and enjoying marked unpopularity among the other Christian communions of the East, the Maronites tended to be deeply interested in their own history,[7] taking pride in having retained their identity through centuries of vicissitude. The Maronite church is, perhaps, the smallest of the communions of Eastern Christendom; and, although not the oldest, it was among the first to begin a tradition of attachment to and finally of union with Rome. Centralized and strongly localized on the almost inaccessible northern slopes of Mount Lebanon, it was never subject to the direct political authority of Islam to the same extent as the other Eastern churches. The Maronites, through centuries of Muslim rule in Syria, remained comparatively free from Muslim tutelage. Their awareness of these facts has, no doubt, contributed to that intense national pride which inspired and was expressed in their historical writing.

While this intense consciousness of national identity seems to have been the driving force behind the traditional historiography of the Maronites, giving it distinctive colour, the development of this historiography has certainly been conditioned by the circumstances which surrounded the development of the Maronite community.

Throughout their history, the Maronites have been on the defensive both as a community and as a church. The dominant trait of their political history has been resistance to Muslim rule. The immigration of Jacobites and Melchites into Mount Lebanon as a result of sporadic persecutions, particularly during the fourteenth and fifteenth centuries, was also strongly resisted by the Maronites, who were wary of absorption by the wealthier and better-organized immigrants and disinclined to share their sparse cultivable land with strangers. The tone of the religious history of the Maronites has been no less defensive. Starting with the fifteenth century, the Maronite church has been constantly trying to establish its superiority over the other Uniate churches by emphasizing its original and unbroken orthodoxy and union with Rome in the face of valid and invalid contrary accusations by Uniate and Western Catholic writers alike. Despite the devotion of the Maronites to Roman Catholicism, the hesitancy of Rome to give clear and formal recognition to their claim of perpetual orthodoxy has been the cause of a constant underlying tension.[8] The basically polemi-

[7] Graf (iii, 306) considers the Maronites to have produced the best historiography among the Eastern Christian communities.

[8] Rome has never recognized Yūḥannā Mārūn, the semi-legendary founder of the Maronite church in Lebanon, as a saint, since he is suspected to have been a Monothelete heretic; neither has Rome recognized any other Maronite saint.

cal nature of Maronite historiography is a reflection of all this. Maronite historians wrote in defence of their community, stressing its importance, and refuting real or imagined disparagement. In most cases, their aim was not so much to establish its history as to vindicate its claims.

Likewise, the involvement of the Maronites in the history of Mount Lebanon was reflected in the gradual widening of the field of interest of Maronite historiography. Until the Ottoman conquest the Maronites were secluded from the Druzes. Maronite northern Lebanon, included in the Frankish county and later the Mamluk *mamlaka* of Tripoli, shared little with Druze southern Lebanon, which formed part of the Latin kingdom of Jerusalem and later of the *mamlaka* of Damascus. The establishment of Ma'nid hegemony over the whole of Mount Lebanon during the late sixteenth and early seventeenth century brought the Maronites and the Druzes, along with the other Lebanese communities, into close political association. The *mutaṣarrifiyya* organization of the late nineteenth century preserved the unity of Mount Lebanon until it was integrated in Greater Lebanon under the French Mandate. Thus, whereas pre-Ottoman and early Ottoman Maronite histories are exclusively concerned with the internal affairs of the Maronite community and its ecclesiastical problems, later Maronite historians become increasingly conscious of the other Lebanese communities, particularly the Druzes, and their interest is gradually widened to include the whole of Mount Lebanon as a unit.

The isolation of the Maronite historiographic tradition has also contributed to its peculiar development in various ways. Though Duwayhī and his successors were not unacquainted with the general history of the area of which Lebanon formed part, they never had a clear understanding of the relationship of Maronite and Lebanese history to the history of Muslim Syria and of Islam. The tendency to exaggerate the intimate history of the community at the expense of its setting is certainly an outstanding trait of Maronite historical writing. The Umayyad, 'Abbasid, and Fatimid caliphates, the Seljuq sultanate and its successor states, the Frankish states in Syria, the Mamluk Empire, and even the Ottoman Empire are entities never clearly understood or defined by Maronite historians. This is especially true of the earlier historians: Ibn al-Qilā'ī related the history of the Maronites under Frankish and Mamluk rule without making the least distinction between Maronites and Franks, and he referred to the Mamluks simply as 'the Muslims'. Another outcome of this historiographic isolation was the tendency among later Maronite historians to depend exclusively on their predecessors, to repeat them, and to accept and build on their often untenable conclusions. In addition, because of its seclusion, the Maronite historiographic tradition remained unexposed to criticism, which accounts for its most serious defects. Although the traditional Maronite historians were often men of considerable learning who had studied in Rome and received the benefits of Western scholarly discipline, they wrote in Lebanon for their own limited people. Consequently, Maronite historiography tends to be naïvely dogmatic in its assertions and denials of historical facts; its errors, repeated and magnified over the generations, have continued almost unchecked.

The clerical tradition in Maronite historiography was born in the throes of internecine dissensions over the question of union with Rome. It was first developed during the last decade of the fifteenth century and the first decade of the sixteenth by the poet-priest Ibn al-Qilāʿī, in whose days the Maronite dissenters, led by a number of feudal lords and some clergy and supported by Jacobite immigrants, were making a last stand against union.

Ibn al-Qilāʿī, an ardent pro-Roman, wrote the history of his people to demonstrate the advantages of union with Rome. Born in northern Lebanon towards the middle of the fifteenth century, he joined the Franciscan order in Jerusalem at an early age and was sent to Italy in 1470, where he took orders and remained for twenty-three years, studying in Rome and in other Italian cities.[9] He returned to Lebanon in 1493 a dull and unimaginative pedant,[10] and served as Roman missionary to his own people, leading a Crusade against the Maronite dissenters. In 1507 he was appointed Maronite bishop of Cyprus, a diocese which included some Lebanese districts, and died in that post, in Nicosia, in the year of the Ottoman conquest of Syria.

In an attempt to educate his people in Roman orthodoxy and to reconcile the diffident among them to union with Rome, Ibn al-Qilāʿī popularized Catholic dogma and Maronite church history in vernacular poetry. An abundance of verse, prosaic in conception and didactic in temper, remains to testify to the vigorous campaign waged by Ibn al-Qilāʿī against the opponents of union. He also wrote in prose, and translated into Arabic a number of Latin works on theology, church discipline, and ritual to instruct the Maronite clergy in the Catholic faith; all this in addition to numerous letters to clergy and notables, rebuking dissenters, warning the fickle, and instructing the faithful.[11]

In his history of the Maronites and the Maronite church, Ibn al-Qilāʿī did not try to convey to his readers a factual picture of the Maronite past, but rather to preach a sermon. By means of historical material which, in many cases, he distorted and mixed with legend, he sought to prove to his

[9] Ibn al-Qilāʿī, with two companions about whom very little is known, travelled to Italy and studied there before the establishment of the Maronite College of Rome in 1584. They are the first Maronites known to have studied in Italy.

[10] Although Ibn al-Qilāʿī lived in Italy in the heyday of the Italian Renaissance, he seems to have remained completely unimpressed by that great cultural movement.

[11] In his original and translated prose works, as in his letters, Ibn al-Qilāʿī wrote in classical Arabic, a language of which he had an imperfect knowledge. Apart from his incorrect orthography, his syntax and his idiom are foreign to Arabic, recalling both the Lebanese colloquial, with its Syriac affinities, and medieval Latin.

people that the Roman faith was the orthodox faith, that the Maronites were orthodox by origin, and that the preservation of their 'original' union with Rome was not only beneficial but absolutely necessary. Ibn al-Qilā'ī tried to make the Uniate cause attractive and to ward off conservative objections by pointing out that orthodoxy and union with Rome were no innovations but the original state of the Maronite church since it was first founded in Lebanon by Yuḥannā Mārūn.[12] He also tried to show that the Maronites were happiest when in full concord with the Mother Church, and that calamity invariably followed their lapses into heresy: such lapses, he explained, having always been due to Jacobite or Melchite influence. Thus he explains the fall of Frankish Tripoli to the Mamluks and the resultant subjection of the Maronites to Muslim rule as divine retribution for the lapse into heresy of a Maronite prince, Sālim of Bsharrī.

Ibn al-Qilā'ī's main historical work is a long poem in the Lebanese vernacular entitled *Madīḥa 'alā Jabal Lubnān* (Panegyric on Mount Lebanon).[13] In this miniature epic, he related the struggle of the free Maronites of Mount Lebanon against the successive Muslim invasions, introducing his favourite theme regarding Maronite orthodoxy and union with Rome at frequent intervals to demonstrate their advantages and, likewise, the disadvantage of schism and heresy. In many places the chronology of events is incorrect, and there are several clumsy anachronisms, quite apart from the fact that there seems to be no distinction in the poem between authentic history and the poet's invention or repetition of popular traditions. Nevertheless, the *Madīḥa* is rich in local colour and is one of the few known sources for the history of the Maronites under Crusader and Mamluk rule. Another history in verse, entitled *Tabkīt kull man zāgh 'an al-īmān* (Rebuke of everyone who has strayed from the faith),[14] deals with events contemporary with Ibn al-Qilā'ī, and others in which Ibn al-Qilā'ī himself played part. A third work which is partly historiographic in content is a letter addressed to Sham'ūn, the Maronite patriarch, and dated 6 November 1494.[15] The letter cites the occasions on which the Maronites renewed their allegiance to Rome, and is otherwise concerned with Roman ritual.

Ibn al-Qilā'ī's concern as a historian was limited to the Maronite church and community, and he only made incidental reference to other Lebanese communities. He gave few dates and the chronology of most of

[12] See above, n. 8.

[13] Published by Būlus Qar'alī (Paul Carali), with notes and appendices, as *Ḥurūb al-muqaddamīn, 1075–1450* (Bayt Shabāb, 1937). In this published edition the poem consists of 294 quatrains. Qara'lī's notes, helpful at times, are more often misleading.

[14] Published by Ibrāhīm Ḥarfūsh in *al-Manāra* (1931), ii, 748–58, 805–13 and 901–7, from the unique Bkerke manuscript. The seven pages missing from the manuscript have been replaced in this edition by a paraphrase of the lost verses made by Duwayhī.

[15] Published by Ibrāhīm Ḥarfūsh in *al-Manāra* (1932), iii, 99–106, 176–83 and 260–3.

the events mentioned has to be conjectured. For his sources, he used the papal correspondence with the Maronite patriarchs preserved in the Vatican (of which he made inaccurate Arabic translations), and possibly some Maronite archive material available at the time. He also referred in his history to 'annals' (*tawārīkh*) which must have existed at the time and which are now lost. Some of these *tawārīkh* may have been mere scholia found on copies of the Gospels and other religious works, such as those used later by Duwayhī.

Ibn al-Qilā'ī's history was little more than Roman propaganda with historical and pseudo-historical notes. Nevertheless he is an outstanding figure in the history of Maronite historiography. He set the tone of the clerical tradition in Maronite historical writing, and the later historians referred to him as an authority. He was the first exponent of the theory of the perpetual orthodoxy of the Maronites, the dominant theme of later Maronite polemics; and his vernacular poetic style in writing popular history was imitated by Maronite historians who followed. Among his imitators were the archbishop Ilyās b. Ḥannā al-Duwayhī (d. 1659: uncle of the patriarch Isṭifān)[16] and the patriarch Yūsuf al-'Āqūrī (d. 1648):[17] the former left a history of the Maronite community in verse, similar in structure to that of Ibn al-Qilā'ī, and the latter a *zajaliyya* on the wars between the Maronites and the Melchites at the end of the seventh century.

It was not before the late seventeenth century that the next great exponent of the clerical tradition appeared: the Maronite patriarch Isṭifān al-Duwayhī. The grandson of a priest and the nephew of an archbishop, Duwayhī was destined for the church, and was sent to the Maronite College in Rome at the early age of twelve to study for the priesthood. Duwayhī showed exceptional merit as a student; and, upon his graduation in 1655, he was selected by the College of Propaganda as a missionary and sent back to serve in his native Lebanon. In 1668, after thirteen years of devoted service to his church in Lebanon and in Aleppo, he was appointed bishop of Cyprus; and two years later, in 1670, he was elected Maronite patriarch.

Duwayhī was not only an able church administrator who won for himself the posthumous title *al-Kabīr* (the Great), but a tireless scholar and seeker of knowledge. A man of keen intelligence polished by a thorough education, he was well suited by natural ability and training to establish the facts of Maronite history from the fragmentary and often semi-legendary information available. He began collecting material when he was a student in Rome; and he made good use of his time during his travels in Lebanon and in the region of Aleppo, before his appointment

[16] G. Graf, op. cit., p. 335. His work has not been published.

[17] Ibid., p. 339–40. A section of his *zajaliyya* on the wars between the Maronites and the Greeks is quoted in Duwayhī, *Ta'rīkh al-ṭā'ifa al-mārūniyya* (Beirut, 1890), p. 82.

as patriarch, by examining histories, chronicles, and church books for information and scholia relevant to the history of his people. The body of information collected by Duwayhī on Maronite history is considerable; and the sources he used, which are all acknowledged and often quoted, are of wide variety. Among these sources are the works of earlier Maronite historians and writers: Ibn al-Qilā'ī (to whom he makes frequent reference and whom he quotes abundantly), Jibrā'īl al-Adnītī,[18] Gabriel Sionita, Abraham Ecchellensis, Tūmā al-Kafarṭābī,[19] and Ilyās of M'ād, not to mention the fragments of old Maronite histories mentioned and quoted by Duwayhī, often from a Syriac original. Of the Crusader chronicles he acknowledged the use of the works of William of Tyre and Jacques de Vitry, and referred also to the writings of such pilgrims and travellers as Burchard of Mount Sion and others. He also used the Vatican archives and collected valuable material from Maronite scholia and inscriptions. Furthermore, he used the works of the better-known Arabic historians, such as Ibn al-Athīr and Abu'l-Fidā', and depended on the history of the Druze Ibn Sibāṭ in writing about non-Maronite Lebanon.[20] Another Arabic historian occasionally quoted by Duwayhī was Ibn al-Ḥarīrī, whose history is currently being published.[21]

Following the example of Ibn al-Qilā'ī, Duwayhī set out to prove the perpetual orthodoxy of the Maronites by refuting all evidence pointing to their Monothelite origin and all charges made against their unbroken union with Rome since the twelfth century. His best known work, *Ta'rīkh al-ṭā'ifa al-mārūniyya* (History of the Maronite community),[22] was written for this purpose. Whereas Ibn al-Qilā'ī had set forth the claim of Maronite perpetual orthodoxy to attract dissident Maronites to the cause of union, Duwayhī, in whose days the union had become unquestionably estab-

[18] Jibrā'īl al-Adnītī who, according to Duwayhī, discussed the origin of the Maronites in the introduction to *The Book of the Syriac Mass*, is not listed by Graf, neither have I been able to trace any of his works.

[19] Tūmā al-Kafarṭābī (G. Graf, op. cit., ii, 98–100), Maronite bishop of Kafarṭāb, a Syrian town to the south of Aleppo, is the author of a book of theological polemics, *Al-maqālāt al-'ashr* (The ten theses), in which he championed the Monothelite view (published by Philip al-Samarānī in *al-Manāra* (1936), vii, 347 ff.). Tūmā lived at the turn of the eleventh and twelfth centuries, before the union of the Maronite church with Rome; and his treatise on Monothelitism, seemingly the only surviving work of pre-uniate Maronite literature, is a constant embarrassment to the proponents of the theory of Maronite perpetual orthodoxy.

[20] The history of Ṣāliḥ b. Yaḥyā, the Buḥturid Druze prince (d. 1436), did not become known to Maronite historians until the end of the nineteenth century. Ibn Sibāṭ (d. 1520), who was in the service of the Buḥturid family, used Ṣāliḥ b. Yaḥyā's history in writing his *Ta'rīkh* (MS. of volume ii only, is in the Library of the American University of Beirut); and it was through him that Maronite historians became acquainted with the history of Druze Lebanon in the late Middle Ages.

[21] Aḥmad b. 'Alī b. Aḥmad b. al-Ḥarīrī, author of *Muntakhab al-zamān fī ta'rīkh al-khulafā' wa'l-'ulamā' wa'l-a'yān* (written in 926 A.H./1520 A.D.), see Brockelmann, SII, p. 406. I. A. Khalifé, S.J., is undertaking its publication.

[22] Published by Rashīd al-Khūrī al-Shartūnī (Beirut, 1890).

lished, defended the claim to promote Maronite pride in their perpetual orthodoxy and to silence charges against it by Western and Eastern Christian writers. Thus, while the history of Ibn al-Qilāʿī is unscholarly and propagandist in colour, that of Duwayhī is written in the ponderous style of dignified polemics. Besides, while the former used unestablished and often legendary material to substantiate his sermon on the necessity of union with Rome, the latter made a serious attempt to examine his data and establish his facts, although he followed the usual practice of polemics in being more critical of unfavourable than of favourable evidence. In a chronological listing of the Maronite patriarchs entitled *Silsilat baṭārikat al-ṭā'ifa al-mārūniyya,*[23] he tried to establish the names and dates of the patriarchs who preceded him in the Maronite see of Antioch since the days of Yūḥannā Mārūn: a basic contribution to later studies on Maronite history.

Duwayhī was successful in proving the unbroken official union of the Maronite church with Rome since the twelfth century, a fact undisputed by modern historians. The body of material he used in his arguments, which in themselves reveal remarkable acumen, is certainly impressive. On the other hand, his refutation of the original Monothelitism of the Maronites is unsound, and even naïve at times, being based on the untenable postulate of Ibn al-Qilāʿī. According to Duwayhī, Yūḥannā Mārūn was of Frankish descent[24] and, far from being a heretic, he was actually a keen defender of Roman orthodoxy against the Monothelite claims of the Byzantine emperors and their heretical patriarchs. Summoning a mass of spurious evidence, Duwayhī makes Yūḥannā Mārūn travel to Rome and receive his appointment to the patriarchal see of Antioch from the Pope himself: an appointment which, owing to persecution at the hands of Emperor Justinian II, did not become effective except in Mount Lebanon, where the true orthodox patriarch sought refuge. It is surprising that a careful scholar like Duwayhī should have written and believed such apocrypha.

The attitude of the traditional Maronite historians towards the question of perpetual orthodoxy has not changed much since Duwayhī. Later Maronite historians like Simʿānī, Qayyāla, Dibs,[25] Daryān,[26] and Dib[27]

[23] Published by R. K. Shartūnī in *al-Mashriq* (1898), i, 247–52, 308–13, 347–53, and 390–6. The chronology of the Maronite patriarchs was later improved by Ṭubiyyā al-ʿAnaysī in *Silsila ta'rīkhiyya li-baṭārikat Anṭākiya al-mawārina* (Rome, 1927).

[24] Compare with the theory of the descent of the Druzes of Lebanon from the Frankish Comte de Dreux, also developed in the seventeenth century.

[25] Yūsuf al-Dibs (Joseph Debs), *Al-jāmiʿ al-mufaṣṣal fī ta'rīkh al-Mawārina al-mu'aṣṣal* (Beirut, 1905), in Arabic. Also *Perpetuelle orthodoxie des Maronites* (Arras, 1896), in French.

[26] Yūsuf Daryān, *Lubāb al-barāhīn al-jaliyya ʿan ḥaqīqat amr al-ṭā'ifa al-mārūniyya* (Beirut, 1911).

[27] Pierre Dib, *L'église maronite*; tome I: *L'église maronite jusqu'a la fin du Moyen Age* (Paris, 1930). Also article 'Maronites' in *Dictionnaire de théologie catholique.* Dib notices the weaknesses of Duwayhī's arguments and tries to establish Maronite perpetual orthodoxy on other grounds, with little more success.

modelled their polemics on those of Duwayhī, commenting or expanding on his thesis. Few of those historians approached his standard of scholarship; and his dominant influence over the clerical tradition has prevented original departures.

Duwayhī's interest was not limited to the religious history of his community. In *Ta'rīkh al-ṭā'ifa al-mārūniyya* he explores the secular origin of the Maronites and postulates their descent from the Mardaites. This claim does not entirely lack evidence,[28] and Duwayhī gathered considerable data in its favour; but his assertion of the Mardaite origin of the Maronites has been disputed on various grounds worthy of consideration, and the claim remains controversial.[29] Duwayhī identified the original Maronites, who supposedly entered Mount Lebanon under the leadership of Yūḥannā Mārūn in the late seventh century, with the Mardaites of the Amanus and Taurus regions who raided Umayyad Syria and penetrated into Mount Lebanon twice between A.D. 666 and 689. He even considered Yūḥannā Mārūn to have been the uncle of Ibrāhīm, the presumed original Mardaite *amīr* of Mount Lebanon. Later Maronite historians, like Dibs and Daryān,[30] accepted the Duwayhī thesis with no attempt at criticism or improvement.

Living in an age when the Maronites and Druzes of Mount Lebanon had started to share a common political history, Duwayhī did not remain uninterested in the history of the Druzes, to which he devoted considerable attention. Duwayhī, besides, was a well-travelled and well-read scholar who had visited various parts of Syria and become acquainted with the better-known Arabic chronicles and histories; and he seems to have been impressed by the fact that the history of his community and that of Mount Lebanon were inseparable from the general history of Muslim Syria. This impression is reflected in his history. In a chronicle entitled *Ta'rīkh al-muslimīn* (History of the Muslims) or *Ta'rīkh al-azmina* (History of the times),[31] which covers the history of Muslim Syria from the Hijra to his own day, Duwayhī lays particular stress on the history of the Druzes and the Maronites of Lebanon in the context of the general history of the region of which Mount Lebanon forms part. Duwayhī did not explain the interrelationship between the history of the Maronites, that of the Druzes, and that of Muslim Syria; but the fact that he massed information on all three subjects in chronicle form reflects a novel trend in Maronite historiography of which he was the first representative.

[28] Henri Lammens, 'Mardaites', in *The Encyclopaedia of Islam*[1], iii, 272–3.

[29] Duwayhī, op. cit., pp. 68–70.

[30] Y. Dibs, op. cit.,; Y. Daryān, *Nabdha ta'rīkhiyya fī aṣl al-ṭā'ifa al-mārūniyya wa'stiqlāliha bi-Jabal Lubnān min qadīm al-dahr ḥatta'l-ān* (Beirut, 1916). The latter's position is not clear, since he argues for the Phoenician origin of the Maronites while accepting their Mardaite origin.

[31] Published by Ferdinand Tawtal, S.J., as volume xliv of *al-Mashriq*, under the title *Ta'rīkh al-azmina, 1095–1699 A.D.* (Beirut, 1951). Some manuscripts of the history begin with the year of the Hijra (A.D. 622), while others begin with the First Crusade.

In the late eighteenth and early nineteenth century, Anṭūniyūs al-ʿAynṭūrīnī and Ḥaydar Aḥmad Shihāb, both of whom were laymen, followed the new trend set by Duwayhī. The former was an important feudal *shaykh* in northern Lebanon (district of ʿAynṭūrīn) whose political ambitions brought about his arrest, torture, and execution at the orders of Bashīr II Shihāb, the governing *amīr*. His *Mukhtaṣar taʾrīkh Jabal Lubnān* (Compendium of the history of Mount Lebanon)[32] is a medley of genealogies and sketches dealing mainly with feudal Mount Lebanon, with some concentration on Maronite church history. ʿAynṭūrīnī introduced his medley with a review of biblical, classical, and Islamic history, beginning with Adam, and inserted further notes on the general history of Syria to explain special circumstances. His contemporary, Ḥaydar Aḥmad Shihāb, a member of the ruling dynasty of the Shihābs and a cousin of Bashīr II, wrote a chronicle similar to that of Duwayhī, dealing with the general history of Syria with particular emphasis on Mount Lebanon.[33] Both ʿAynṭūrīnī and Shihāb used a variety of sources, including earlier Maronite and Druze histories, genealogies, and written traditions; and both relied a great deal on Duwayhī. Shihāb, the better-read of the two, used a number of Arabic chronicles, and noted the more important events in European history.[34]

The lay tradition in Maronite historiography, started by Duwayhī and developed by ʿAynṭūrīnī and Shihāb, received its first mature expression in the work of Ṭannūs al-Shidyāq, the first Maronite (and Lebanese) historian to deal with Mount Lebanon as a unit. His history, *Akhbār al-aʿyān fī Jabal Lubnān* (Annals of the notables of Lebanon)[35] is not a chronicle, although its historical sections are related in chronological order: it is a systematic survey of the component parts of feudal Lebanon.

Shidyāq was neither ecclesiastic nor feudal lord. His ancestors and his kinsmen had been clerks and household tutors in the service of Lebanese feudal families since the early seventeenth century.[36] Apart from some private tutoring and a year's stay at the college of ʿAyn Waraqa, the well-

[32] Published with introduction and notes by Ighnāṭiyus Ṭannūs al-Khūrī (Beirut, 1953). Graf, iii, 477–8, lists ʿAynṭūrīnī among the Maronite clerical writers. ʿAynṭūrīnī was not a cleric. He held the honorary title of *shammās* (deacon) by virtue of his being a leading *shaykh*, in accordance with an old Maronite custom.

[33] Printed in Cairo (1900–1) under the title *Taʾrīkh al-amīr Ḥaydar al-Shihābī*. The chronicle is in three parts: the first, entitled *al-Ghurar al-ḥisān fī taʾrīkh ḥawādith al-zamān*, covers the period 622–1697; the second, entitled *Nuzhat al-zamān fī taʾrīkh Jabal Lubnān*, deals with the period 1697–1800; the third, entitled *al-Rawḍ al-naḍīr fī wilāyat al-amīr Bashīr Qāsim al-kabīr*, brings the chronicle to 1841 (continued after his death).

[34] Occasionally he mentions details in European history which reflect a good knowledge of the subject. Thus, under the year 956 A.H./1549 A.D., he mentions the printing of the first Book of Common Prayer in England 'by order of Edward VI', and its approval by Parliament. See op. cit., i, 612.

[35] Printed under the joint supervision of its author and Buṭrus al-Bustānī, the pioneer Lebanese scholar of the nineteenth century, at the American Press, Beirut, 1855–9.

[36] The Shidyāqs, like the Yāzijīs and some other families, formed a secretarial aristocracy in Mount Lebanon, and had the right to the title of *shaykh*.

known Maronite college of his day, Shidyāq was self-taught. He entered the clerical service of the Shihābs as early as 1810, when he was scarcely sixteen, and continued to serve various members of the family as clerk or household tutor for many years, while earning an additional living as a merchant.

As a servant of the Shihābs, Shidyāq was well versed in the political intrigues of his day, especially as he was used occasionally as agent and spy. His attachment to the ruling family and his relations with other feudal families enhanced his interest in the history of the feudal régime in Mount Lebanon. Shidyāq confessed that he had no interest in the 'history of churches and monks', which he thought unimportant. He laid all emphasis on the history of 'lay leaders and notables': the old Lebanese feudal families whose history was, to a large extent, the history of Mount Lebanon.[37]

The first five chapters of *Akhbār al-a'yān* are devoted to the natural and political geography of Mount Lebanon, and give valuable details on the feudal divisions of the country in the early nineteenth century. In the second part of the book, Shidyāq traces the genealogies of twenty-three Lebanese families: nine Maronite (including the Mardaite dynasty presumed by Duwayhī),[38] eight Druze, and six Muslim (both Sunnī and Shī'ī). The third and last part of *Akhbār al-a'yān* traces the history of Mount Lebanon under the successive feudal dynasties from the Arab conquest of Syria to the author's own day.

Shidyāq was a tidy compiler; but, unlike Duwayhī, he was no scholar. His work is a well-classified but uncritical compilation of historical facts; and, in parts, it is hopelessly confused in the details. He acknowledged the use of a number of sources, which include the works of Ibn al-Qilā'ī, Duwayhī, Ibn Sibāṭ, and Shihāb. Shidyāq, besides, had access to family genealogies, some of which may not have been genuine; and his contacts with the Lebanese notables made it possible for him to depend on oral accounts and traditions. For contemporary events, he depended on personal observations, and possibly on eyewitness accounts as well.[39] His history, with all its defects, is an invaluable source for the history of feudal Lebanon, particularly for the period of Shihābī rule, and it certainly deserves a critical edition.

The traditional historiography of the Maronites, from Ibn al-Qilā'ī to Shidyāq, had evolved with the times. Its scope had widened with the

[37] The quotations are taken from Shidyāq's introduction to his abridgement of Duwayhī's *Ta'rīkh al-azmina*, found in manuscript in a private collection.

[38] A list of the 'Mardaite' rulers of northern Lebanon was made earlier by Yūsuf Mārūn al-Duwayhī. See Duwayhī, *Ta'rīkh al-ṭā'ifa al-mārūniyya*, pp. 279–80. Shidyāq seems to have relied on this list.

[39] Shidyāq lists his sources at the beginning of his *Akhbār al-a'yān*. He acknowledged the use of family genealogies and of oral accounts, as well as of personal memoranda.

increased coherence of the Maronite community, after its full union with Rome, and its gradual involvement in the affairs of Mount Lebanon. The establishment of the Maronite College in Rome in 1584 and the training received by Maronite clergy provided the clerical tradition in Maronite historiography with able scholars like Duwayhī. The spread of lay education in Mount Lebanon by graduates of the College, beginning with the late eighteenth century, produced the Maronite lay historians of the early nineteenth century. Although they did not equal the clerical historians in scholarship, their broad secular outlook was an improvement on the narrower field of interest of the older historiography.

The clerical historians who followed Duwayhī lacked originality, and contributed little towards the improvement of the clerical tradition. Their unwavering stand with regard to the perpetual orthodoxy of their church and community limited the possibilities of their scholarship. Likewise, the lay historians who followed Shidyāq brought little improvement to the lay tradition. The spread of education through Catholic and Protestant mission schools and colleges beginning with the nineteenth century, and the twentieth-century educational developments in Lebanon, do not seem to have had much effect on Maronite historical writing except for the development of the monograph and the alarming increase in non-specialized scholarship.

The apologetic trend in the traditional historiography of the Maronites continues to embarrass Maronite scholarship. The Maronite historians of today, no less than their predecessors, continue to write in defence of their community and to exaggerate its importance. Conflicting trends in modern Lebanese politics have added fervour to the polemical tradition; and historiographic themes like the Mardaite origin of the Maronites, the unity of feudal Mount Lebanon, and the Phoenician origin of Lebanese history have been used by Maronite writers to rebut Pan-Arab claims. Fresh departures cannot be expected in Maronite historiography as long as contemporary Maronite historians fail to make a thorough revaluation of their traditional historiography in the light of modern scholarship.

20. HISTORIANS OF LEBANON

A. H. HOURANI

Lecturer in the Modern History of the Near East in the University of Oxford

In the last three hundred years the history of Lebanon has been recorded in detail by a series of Lebanese writers of varying skill, but almost all with some historical sense: that is to say, with some awareness of the sequence of cause and effect and the importance of basing their statements upon evidence. There is perhaps no other region of the Arab East of which this is equally true; most of our knowledge of seventeenth- and eighteenth-century Egypt is based on a single chronicle, our knowledge of Damascus, Aleppo, and Baghdad at that period is incomplete, and in the mountains of Kurdistan political processes not dissimilar to those of Lebanon found few local writers to record them. There are two reasons for this flowering of Lebanese historiography: first, the development of a literate class, with a good knowledge of Arabic and some of the intellectual interests of the modern age, and secondly the existence of an intelligible and unified subject-matter—not only an historical process to be explained but a thesis to be defended.

The first important group of modern Lebanese historians were Maronite and other Uniate priests educated in the seminaries of Rome, and their specific subject was the religious community to which they belonged. The special concern of the Maronites was to defend against other Catholic writers the claim of their Church always to have been steadfastly Catholic and never to have accepted the Monothelete heresy, the imputation of which, even after a thousand years, seemed to them a libel not to be endured. But they were writing at a time when the religious group was also the political community, and they celebrated not only the way in which their ancestors had defended the faith but also that in which they had preserved their autonomy in the valleys of northern Lebanon against the Muslim rulers of the surrounding lands, and established there a separate if fragile political existence. These two lines of thought converged in the work of the Patriarch Isṭifān al-Duwayhī (1630–1704), the greatest of the Maronite clerical historians. He wrote a number of historical works: a list of the Maronite Patriarchs, a history of the Maronite community, and a general history, the *Ta'rīkh al-azmina*.[1] Of these the last is the most impor-

[1] *Silsilat baṭārikat al-ṭā'ifa al-mārūniyya*, ed. Rashīd al-Shartūnī (Beirut, 1898, second ed. enlarged 1902). *Ta'rīkh al-ṭā'ifa al-mārūniyya*, ed. Rashīd al-Shartūnī (Beirut, 1890). *Ta'rīkh al-azmina*: partly included in the above, but ed. in full by F. Tawtal (Beirut, 1951).

tant. In form a general history, starting in some manuscripts in 622 and in others with the first Crusade and ending in 1699, it concentrates mainly on the history of Lebanon and its relations with the successive rulers of the surrounding regions, Crusaders, Mamluks, and Ottomans. It is particularly full and important for the last two centuries. Duwayhī was more like a modern historian than his predecessors. He based his work on as wide a collection of sources as possible, and even mentioned them. In his own manuscript copy of the *Ta'rīkh* he mentioned some of the earlier historians whose work he used: Ibn Sibāṭ for the Tanūkhīs, Ṣafadī for Fakhr al-Dīn, William of Tyre for the Crusades. He gathered material also from Maronite churchbooks and the archives of the Vatican. He made some effort to weigh the value of his sources, although his critical sense broke down when dealing with the early history of the Maronites. Moreover, he had more than an antiquarian's interest in facts for their own sake. Behind his work lies a historical vision; he is concerned with the Maronites not simply as one political group interacting with others, but as the bearers of certain doctrines and of a culture which has grown out of them. The Jacobites who infiltrated into Lebanon in the fifteenth century were, in his view, as much the enemies of the Maronites as were the Mamluk armies all around.

Duwayhī and similar writers did not write history for its own sake alone. Their interest in the Maronite church and its past was one expression only of the new movement of Catholic thought and devotion among the eastern Uniate priesthood. Even within the sphere of history, Maronites looked beyond themselves and their interest embraced the whole of Arabic history and culture, and the history and literature of all Eastern Christendom. Among the great number of Maronite scholars of this time, the family of Assemani were the most famous. A family of priests and scholars, trained in the Maronite College at Rome, they wrote more in Latin for the learned world of Europe than in Arabic for their own people, but they wrote mainly about the thought and life of the Eastern Christendom from which they sprang. The greatest of them, Joseph Assemani, Prefect of the Vatican Library (1687–1768), made, in the four volumes of the *Bibliotheca Orientalis*, a survey of the ecclesiastical literature of Maronites, Nestorians and Jacobites.[2] His nephew, Joseph Aloysius, wrote a history of the Chaldean and Nestorian Patriarchs,[3] and a third member of the family, Simon, wrote a learned thesis on the influence of Arabic on modern European literature.[4]

[2] 4 vol. (Rome, 1719–28).

[3] *De catholicis sea patriarchis Chaldaeorum et Nestorianorum commentarius historico-chronologicus* (Rome, 1775).

[4] *Se gli Arabi ebbero alcune influenza sull' origine della poesia moderna in Europa* (Padua, 1807).

II

When Duwayhī wrote local history, he wrote mainly about northern Lebanon, and indeed for most of the period which he covered north and south were not politically united. The south was ruled mainly by chiefly families of the Druzes, while the north was ruled partly by indigenous Maronite *muqaddams*, and partly by Muslim lords placed there by the Mamluks or the Ottomans to watch over a population whose loyalty could be doubted. But during the late sixteenth and early seventeenth centuries the whole mountain was unified by one of the great Druze families, that of Maʿn. From the time of Fakhr al-Dīn II (1586–1635) for over two hundred years, Lebanon was a hereditary princedom. The prince was drawn from the family of Maʿn until 1697, and then from the Muslim Shihābs from 1697 to 1841. In principle he derived his rights from the Ottoman Governors of Ṣaydā and Tripoli, who gave him annual investiture as chief tax-farmer for the whole mountain; but in fact he was virtually autonomous, and governed through a hierarchy of great families, Druze, Maronite, and to a lesser extent Muslim, to whom he delegated powers of tax-collection and who had the rights of land-ownership. Within this framework there developed a political life which has continued, to some extent, until today: the ruler struggling to maintain his autonomy against encroachments from outside and his authority against the powers and ambitions of the great families; loose associations of great families, Druzes and Maronites alike, competing with each other for land and political influence; religious tolerance masking a religious tension that could be brought to the surface by great political or social changes; a Christian intellectual ascendancy balanced by the political and social predominance of the Druzes; ceaseless efforts by the Turkish rulers of Syria to impose their control, and intervention by France and later by other European powers. The development of this political structure gave a new focus to historiography, and in the eighteenth century there appeared a new class intimately involved in the new political structure and capable of writing its history: families of Christian scholars and writers, mainly laymen but educated in the mission schools and Uniate seminaries, learning the sciences of the Arabic language from Muslim scholars and, because of this knowledge of Arabic, useful to the local rulers as clerks and men of affairs. Towards the end of the century, this group of literati began to produce a new sort of history: more exclusively secular and political, and concerned primarily with the struggle for political power, trying not simply to describe but to explain the formation and application of policy, and consciously or not seeing the political process from the point of view of the master whom they served.

Works of this type had indeed been written earlier; Ibn Sibāṭ[5] and Ṣāliḥ b. Yaḥyā[6] had written the history of the Tanūkhī rulers of the Gharb district, and Aḥmad al-Khālidī al-Ṣafadī that of Fakhr al-Dīn.[7] But in the eighteenth century they increased in number and scope. Since the south was the political centre of Lebanon and the scene of the struggle for power, it was there that most of these works were written, and we know more of what was happening in the south than in the north in this period. (There are exceptions to this: for example, Anṭūniyūs Abū Khaṭṭār al-'Ayntūrīnī, himself one of the *shaykhs* of the northern district of Bsharrī and grandfather of the Maronite national hero Yūsuf Bey Karam. His history[8] is particularly strong on the origins of Lebanese families, Maronite church history, and the political history of the northern districts; he gives valuable details, for example, about the expulsion of the Shī'ī family of Ḥamāda from the Maronite north. When he deals with general Lebanese history he is interesting because, unlike most of the other historians of his day, he supports the losing side in the political struggles of the time; he is on the side of the sons of Amīr Yūsuf against Amīr Bashīr, by whom in fact he was put to death in 1821.)

Among this group of works written by Christian scribes in the service of Druze or Muslim rulers of the south, we may mention those written by members of the Ṣabbāgh family about the ruler whom they served, Ẓāhir al-'Umar, who built a petty state in northern Palestine and southern Lebanon and founded the prosperity of Acre; there is a life of him by 'Abbūd Ṣabbāgh,[9] and another by Mīkhā'īl,[10] who served in Napoleon's administration in Egypt, fled with the French army to France in 1801, and worked there with the Orientalists of his day until his death in 1816. Of greater interest is Ibrāhīm al-'Awra's history of the rule of Sulaymān Pasha, who succeeded Jazzār as governor of Ṣaydā.[11] 'Awra was a clerk in the *Dīwān* of the provincial government of Ṣaydā (of which the capital had by now been moved to Acre), and a member of a family of clerks. He had been close enough to the centre of affairs to know how decisions were made, and he gives an interesting description of the provincial ruling group founded by Jazzār, which ruled until the Egyptian conquest of 1831: how it was formed, the balance of Mamluk and local, religious and secular, Muslim, Christian, and Jewish elements in its composition, the procedure used by officials and the way in which they were paid, the financial and

[5] Ḥamza b. Aḥmad b. Sibāṭ al-Gharbī: *Ta'rīkh*, MS. in American University of Beirut, 956.6 I 13.

[6] *Kitāb ta'rīkh Bayrūt wa-umarā' al-buḥturiyyīn*, ed. L. Cheikho (Beirut, 1927).

[7] Ed. by F. E. Bustānī and A. Rustum under the title *Lubnān fī 'ahd al-amīr Fakhr al-Dīn* (Beirut, 1936).

[8] *Kitāb mukhtaṣar ta'rīkh jabal Lubnān*, ed. Fr. I. T. al-Khūrī in *al-Mashriq*, vols. 46–7 (1952–3).

[9] *al-Rawḍ al-zāhir fī ta'rīkh Ḍāhir*. Extracts are published in the following work.

[10] *Ta'rīkh al-shaykh Ḍāhir al-'Umar al-Zaydānī*, ed. Fr. C. Bāshā (Harissa, 1927–8).

[11] *Ta'rīkh wilāyat Sulaymān bāshā al-'ādil*, ed. Fr. C. Bāshā (Ṣaydā, 1936).

other relations between the province and the central government in Istanbul. 'Awra wrote the book about half a century later (he says that he finished it in 1853), but he has recaptured vividly the events and atmosphere of his youth, and his is one of the few works of Lebanese history in which we can hear the voices of men talking.

The majority of these works of secular history were written by priests or clerks in the service of the Shihāb princes or devoted to their interests. Around the Shīhābs, and in particular around Bashīr II (1788–1840), the last but one and the greatest of them, there gathered almost all the men of letters of the day, who found in the service of the Prince work worthy of their talents (just as, later, the educated Lebanese were to find work in the service of the Khedive and the British in Egypt, and of the British in the Sudan). For this group of men, the writing of history was only one aspect of a multiple literary activity; the clerkly families produced not only the historians of their age, but the fathers of the poetic and linguistic movement of nineteenth-century Lebanon.

Among the outstanding figures of this group was a Greek Catholic monk, Ḥanāniyyā al-Munayyir (1756–1832?). He wrote a history of his own religious order, the Shwayrites,[12] a book on the doctrines of the Druzes which was used by Guys and praised by de Sacy, and a general history of Lebanon, or rather of the Shihāb family and the Shūf district which was the centre of their power. This last, *al-Durr al-mawṣūf fī ta'rīkh al-Shūf*,[13] is a political history from 1697 to 1807, based partly on general tradition, partly on his own observations, and partly on diaries and other documents of his own order of monks. Written in a clear and correct style and said to have been revised by the famous writer Shaykh Nāṣīf al-Yāzijī, it is for the most part a straight narrative, but it is not difficult to see that the author's sympathies are with Bashīr, in his struggle against the encroachments of Jazzār and against the internal opposition led by his kinsmen, the sons of Amīr Yūsuf.

The most important member of the group, however, was neither a priest nor an official, but a member of the ruling family itself. The Amīr Ḥaydar Aḥmad Shihāb (1761–1835) was a cousin of Bashīr II. Unlike Bashīr, whose religious allegiance remained in doubt throughout his life, although he died and was buried as a Catholic, Ḥaydar belonged to that section of the Shihāb family which had abandoned Islam and become openly Maronite during the second half of the eighteenth century. Bashīr employed him on confidential political tasks of some importance, but the greater part of his time was given to pious and learned works, and to gathering around himself a group of scholars and with their help writing the history of Lebanon and of his family. Entitled *al-Ghurar al-ḥisān fī*

[12] *Ta'rīkh al-rahbāna al-ḥannawiyya al-mulaqqaba bi'l-shuwayriyya*, in work cited, p. 232, n. 16.
[13] Ed. Fr. I. Sarkīs in *al-Mashriq*, vols. 48–51 (1954–7).

akhbār abnā' al-zamān, it is divided into three parts, each of which was given a separate title by later copyists, but not apparently by the author himself. The first part runs from 622 to the end of the Ma'nī dynasty in 1697, the second from 1697 to 1818, and the third from 1819 to 1827. Ḥaydar appears also to have written a shorter work late in life, dealing specifically with Amīr Bashīr and carrying the story almost down to the historian's death.[14]

In accordance with the custom of his own age, Ḥaydar does not refer to his sources in the course of the work, but it is possible to form some idea of them from internal and external evidence alike. For the first part he used the general Islamic histories, in particular al-Ṭabarī, some European sources (William of Tyre and Baronius), and the earlier histories of Lebanon. For the second and third parts also he relied on previous chronicles, but on much else besides. He had at his disposal a large number of official documents—Ottoman firmans, and correspondence between Bashīr and Turkish officials—and some of them he quotes in full. Bashīr's financial and general administration was carefully documented in accordance with strict rules of procedure, and a large proportion of the documents must have come within Ḥaydar's view in the course of his official work. Most important of all perhaps were his own observations and those of others with whom he was in contact. In a rural community where literacy is rare, where horizons are limited and the supremacy of custom makes it important to remember exactly what happened, a detailed and precise collective memory may go back for several generations. Born in 1761, Ḥaydar would have been able to draw on recollections going back practically to the beginning of the eighteenth century.

The main subject of his book is the policy of the Shihāb princes, and the later part of it is dominated by the figure of Bashīr. Since Ḥaydar was a member of the ruling family, his history is written not from the point of view of the 'civil service', but from that of the men who made policy and took decisions. The narrative is only rarely suspended for an explanation of motives, but it is clear that Ḥaydar had the political culture, the understanding of the aims, methods, and limits of political action, which ruling families develop and transmit. It is clear too that in all the disputes with which he deals he is on the side of his family, and of Bashīr. He stands with the Shihābs against Jazzār, with Bashīr against Amīr Yūsuf, and with Bashīr also against the challenge of the great Druze family of Jumblāṭ.

[14] All three parts of *al-Ghurar al-ḥisān* were published in an unsatisfactory edition by N. Mughabghab (Cairo, 1900). Fr. P. Carali published, in *al-Majalla al-sūriyya* (later *al-Majalla al-batriyārkiyya*), vols. ii–vii (1927–32), an anonymous history of Bashīr II which may incorporate Ḥaydar's shorter work. A. Rustum and F. E. Bustānī published a definitive edition of Parts II and III of *al-Ghurar al-ḥisān*, under the title *Lubnān fī 'ahd al-umarā' al-shihābiyyīn* (Beirut, 1933). They follow the author's own MS.; where it ends, in 1827, they add the narrative for the years 1828–32 from the work published by P. Carali.

He gives also a certain amount of economic and social history (his occasional price-lists might be of interest to an economic historian), and some general history of Syria, although of Damascus and northern Palestine rather than more distant parts. In the early part there are occasional references to European history, and in Part II there is a long account of the French expedition to Egypt, prefaced by a shorter account of the French Revolution—the deposition and execution of Louis XVI, and the rise of Bonaparte. This occupies almost a quarter of Part II—130 pages of the most recent edition. That so much space should be given to the French occupation of Egypt was due primarily to the large amount of material available. Ḥaydar's account is based indeed on a detailed history of the French occupation written by Nīqūlā Turk, a poet and member of Bashīr's court, who was sent by Bashīr to Egypt to report on the French occupation, and who later wrote what he had learnt and seen in a connected work of which two different versions exist.[15] But Ḥaydar was a self-conscious historian who selected and emphasized his material with a view to what was important; if he decided to use all Nīqūlā Turk's material, it must have been because the Revolution and the expedition to Egypt seemed to him events of quite unusual significance.

We have some information about the way in which Ḥaydar wrote his book. He had a 'workshop' of writers producing material and drafts. They included most of the prominent writers of the time: Fāris and As'ad al-Shidyāq, Buṭrus Karāma, Nīqūlā Turk and Nāṣīf al-Yāzijī. Some of the material produced by them may have been incorporated without change, but for the most part Ḥaydar himself wrote the definitive version and gave the work its final shape. It is this method of composition which explains why the book exists in more than one form. There are numerous manuscripts of it, some ending earlier than others, and they appear to fall into two distinct groups: those based upon the author's own version, and those derived from a copy made and freely amended by Nāṣīf al-Yāzijī. For the same reason, there exist a number of other works clearly based on the same material and having some connection with the main history, some of them ascribed to Ḥaydar himself, others anonymous or ascribed to one of his helpers. They include a history of Aḥmad Pasha al-Jazzār[16] recently edited and attributed by its editors to Ḥaydar, and a small work on the political geography and administrative procedure of Lebanon under Bashīr.[17]

Of those who worked closely with Ḥaydar and had access to the same

[15] A. Desgranges, *Histoire de l'expédition des Français en Egypte par Nakoula el-Turk* (Paris, 1839). Nicolas Turk, *Chronique d'Egypte*, 1798–1804, ed. and trans. G. Wiet (Cairo, 1950).

[16] Amīr Ḥaydar Aḥmad Shihāb: *Ta'rīkh Aḥmad bāshā al-Jazzār*, ed. A. Chibli and I. A. Khalifé (Beirut, 1955).

[17] Published several times in Arabic and European languages. The fullest version is that published by Fr. C. Bāshā in *al-Masarra*, vol. 22 (1936).

material, one was to become a prominent historian in his own right. Ṭannūs al-Shidyāq (1791–1861), the brother of Fāris and As'ad, published in 1859, with some assistance from Buṭrus Bustānī, a large book on the noble families of Lebanon: *Akhbār al-a'yān fī jabal Lubnān*.[18] It is divided into three parts, dealing respectively with the geography of Lebanon, the genealogy and history of its great families, and its recent political history. In the preface, the author gives a list of the sources he has used: they include the earlier chronicles, the personal reminiscences of Druze *shaykhs* and others, a few official documents, and his own memoranda, kept, he tells us, since 1820. Those parts of the narrative where he covers the same ground as Ḥaydar add little, but for later events—the last years of Bashīr, the Egyptian occupation and the growth of tension in the 1840's and 1850's—the work is of importance. It gives details about the origin and rise of families which can scarcely be found elsewhere (although sometimes we may suspect him of being too generous in conceding the claims of powerful families to ancient origin); moreover, its very conception is original. His specific subject is not, as with Ḥaydar, a ruler or a ruling family, it is a community, Lebanon itself—the title of the book is itself significant—and he sees Lebanon not simply as a territory unified and ruled by one princely family, but as a whole structure of families each with its own sphere of authority, and all intricately balanced and connected with one another. Those families may be Druze, Maronite, Sunnī or Shī'ī Muslim, but their authority derives from territorial power rather than religious allegiance, and their common interests give to Lebanon a unity which transcends religious difference. Ṭannūs al-Shidyāq has thus contributed something essential to our understanding of feudal Lebanon.

III

Feudal Lebanon disappeared in the convulsions of the generation which stretched from 1831 to 1860. In order to impose disarmament and conscription in obedience to the commands of Ibrāhīm Pasha, Bashīr began to play off Christians against Druzes; when Ibrāhīm was forced to evacuate Syria, Bashīr was deposed, and under a weak successor the Shihāb princes soon lost their authority and their throne. The Turks began to intervene more and more in order to destroy the autonomy of Lebanon as they had destroyed that of other regions of the Empire; the struggle of Britain and France for influence led the first to establish a relationship with a section of the Druzes, while the second strengthened her old relationship with the Maronites; and the growth of the Maronite community in population, wealth, culture, and solidarity, made them less willing to accept the traditional social leadership of the mainly Druze nobility. It was a combination

[18] Beirut, 1859. There is a recent reprint.

of these factors which led to the civil war of 1860 and caused it to take on the character of a religious conflict. After the war and the intervention of the Powers, Lebanon was made into an autonomous Sanjaq of the Empire, under the protection of the Powers and with a political structure laid down in an Organic Law (1861 and 1864) and based on the religious communities. Half a century later, in 1920, the Sanjaq was enlarged and made into the State of Greater Lebanon, which by the Constitution of 1926 was turned into a Republic based on the same principle of equal co-operation between distinct religious communities. These developments gave rise to a third genre of history in addition to the other two.

It is true, these two other genres still continued. Much sectarian history was written; it was still mostly Maronite, and concerned to defend the 'perpetual orthodoxy' of the Maronites and their rôle in preserving and spreading Catholic faith in the East. The works of Mgr. Derian (Daryān),[19] Afrām al-Dayrānī,[20] Mgr. Dib,[21] and Fr. Raphael[22] are in the direct line of descent from those of Duwayhī, although Mgr. Dib at least brought to the defence of the Maronites the authority of a fully-trained Church historian and theologian. There still continued to be something defensive about this Maronite writing; next to the accusation of heresy, what they most resented was the failure of the Church to recognize the Maronite popular saints, and there is an element of communal pride in the new cult of Mār Sharbal, whose tomb has become a centre of pilgrimage. How sensitive the Maronites are about their distant past was shown when the Vicomte Philippe de Ṭarāzī published a work (*Aṣdaq mā kān 'an ta'rīkh Lubnān*)[23] to prove that the Jacobites, not the Maronites, were the original inhabitants of Lebanon; this produced a sharp (and convincing) rebuttal from a Maronite scholar, Fr. P. Carali (Būlus Qar'alī).[24] Other religious communities were also interested in their own past, and particularly the Greek Catholics, the most cultivated and self-conscious of the Arabic-speaking Christian sects; Frs. C. Bāshā[25] and Shammās[26] wrote voluminously on their history, and we should mention also H. Zayyāt, who in a number of works of profound scholarship cast light on several aspects of the history of Christianity under Muslim rule.[27] Shaykh 'Ārif al-Zayn wrote on the history of the Shī'ī Muslims in southern Lebanon.[28] That nothing

[19] *Lubāb al-barāhīn al-jaliyya 'an ḥaqīqat amr al-ṭā'ifa al-māruniyya* (Beirut, 1911).

[20] *Kitāb al-muḥāmāt 'an al-Mawārina wa-qiddīsīhim* (Beirut, 1899).

[21] 'Maronite (Eglise)' in *Dictionnaire de Théologie Catholique*, vol. x, part I (Paris, 1928).

[22] *Le Rôle des Maronites dans le retour des Eglises Orientales* (Beirut, 1935); Arabic version, Aleppo (1936).

[23] 2 vols. (Beirut, 1948).

[24] *al-Mawārina fī Lubnān* (Jounieh, 1949).

[25] *Ta'rīkh ṭā'ifat al-Rūm al-malikiyya* (Ṣaydā, part I 1938, part II 1939–45).

[26] Yūsuf Shammās: *Khulāṣat ta'rīkh al-kanīsa al-malikiyya*, 3 vols. (Ṣaydā, 1947–52).

[27] They include: *al-Ṣalīb fi'l-Islām* (Harissa, 1935); *al-Rūm al-malikiyyūn fi'l-Islām* (Harissa, 1953).

[28] *Mukhtaṣar ta'rīkh al-Shī'a* (Ṣaydā, 1914).

should have been written about the Sunnīs or the Orthodox in Lebanon is not surprising, since for them Lebanon had never been a significant entity, still less the centre of their culture or political life. But the absence of Druze historiography (except for the work of Sulaymān Abū 'Izz al-Dīn)[29] is more difficult to explain.

There still persisted too the tradition of writing histories of powerful families, towns and districts, like 'Ārif al-Zayn's history of Ṣaydā;[30] Manṣūr Ṭannūs al-Ḥattūnī's history of the Kasrawān district[31] (important for the social disturbances of Kasrawān in the 1850's, the precursor of the civil war of 1860); Nawfal Nawfal al-Ṭarabulsī's *Kashf al-lithām*,[32] which, almost alone among Lebanese histories, seems to have made use of the Turkish historians; and the chronicle of Mīkhā'īl al-Dimashqī dealing with events in Syria from 1782 to 1841, and written by a government official whose identity is uncertain.[33] Of this type of local historian, perhaps the most important is 'Īsā Iskandar Ma'lūf, who wrote the history of his own town, Zahle,[34] and spent most of his life collecting materials for a vast history of Lebanese and Near Eastern families. He seems to have made some sort of a draft of it, but it was never published as a whole, and probably never completed in publishable form. Some parts of it however were finished and issued separately: a history of the Yāzijī family,[35] and a longer work on the Ma'lūfs themselves—*Dawānī'l-quṭūf fī ta'rīkh banī Ma'lūf*[36]—which is far more than its name implies. The Ma'lūfs are a large and scattered family, and on to the peg of family history the author has been able to hang a number of learned disquisitions; for example, the family came originally from Ḥawrān, and this makes it possible to write at length about the history of Ḥawrān. What gives importance to all Ma'lūf's work is his complete mastery of his sources. He had himself sought out, studied and in some instances copied the manuscripts of the older chronicles, and had a unique, almost textual knowledge of them; he had examined the muniments of monasteries and recorded local traditions stretching back to the eighteenth century. His history of Zahle throws a flood of light on to the growth of the new middle class of the market towns, whose refusal to fit into the feudal structure was one of the causes of the civil war of 1860.

[29] *Ibrāhīm bāshā fī Sūriyya* (Beirut, 1929). [30] Ṣaydā, 1913.

[31] *Nabdha ta'rīkhiyya fi'l-muqāṭa'a al-kasrawāniyya* (n.d., n.p.; probably Beirut, 1884. There is a recent reprint).

[32] *Kashf al-lithām 'an muḥayya al-ḥukūma wa'l-aḥkām*, MS. in American University of Beirut, unclassified. The author was writing it in 1883.

[33] *Ta'rīkh ḥawādith al-Shām wa-Lubnān*, ed. L. Ma'lūf (Beirut, 1912).

[34] *Ta'rīkh madīnat Zaḥla* (Zahle, 1912).

[35] *al-Ghurar al-ta'rīkhiyya fi'l-usra al-yāzijiyya*, 2 vols. (Ṣaydā, 1945). [36] Beirut, 1907–8.

IV

The third type of history which grew up beside these two was fertilized by a new problem. More than ever before there now existed a separate entity called Lebanon; its existence was enshrined in international documents and placed under the protection of the Powers. A new sort of political consciousness grew up, and this gave rise to a new idea, the idea of a community with a continuous historical tradition and worth preserving. Why it should exist, and how it could be preserved, were questions which produced a new sort of historical writing, with a specific purpose—not to defend a church or glorify a prince, but to mould the consciousness of a people.

The historical thought which this writing expressed revolved around two images, one of Lebanon happy and united, and the other of Lebanon in collapse. Much writing was devoted to the periods of happiness and prosperity, and to pointing the moral of them: the need for religious toleration, and for a strong executive power which would hold the balance between the different communities and create ties of common interest between them. This involved the study and analysis of the institution of the princedom, which had given Lebanon its unity and special character, and in particular of the two greatest princes, Fakhr al-Dīn in the seventeenth century and Bashīr in the nineteenth. The basic source for the history of the former, the chronicle of al-Ṣafadī, was published in 1936;[37] and at about the same time Fr. P. Carali published two volumes based on documents in the Medicean Archives of Florence (where Fakhr al-Dīn spent a period of exile), and the Archives of the Vatican and Propaganda in Rome.[38] He prefaced the documents with a long analysis of Fakhr al-Dīn's character and policy, presenting him as a far-sighted patriot who laid the foundation of Lebanese autonomy. Already in 1934 ʿĪsā Iskandar Maʿlūf had written a book in praise of the Maʿnī prince who 'strove with all his might for the independence, expansion and civilization of his country',[39] and other have followed since. It was less necessary to commemorate the achievements of Bashīr, because they are still very much alive in the collective memory of the mountain-villages. But he has been much studied; there is a recent analysis of his policy by Asad Rustum.[40] Since his own time he has attracted the attention of many European writers. Their work lies outside our scope, but we should refer to the three volumes of Colonel Churchill,[41] member of a cadet branch of the great

[37] See p. 229, n. 7 above.

[38] Vol. i: P. Carali, *Fakhr al-Din II . . . al Corte di Toscana* (Rome, 1936). Vol. ii, containing Arabic introduction and sources: *Fakhr al-Dīn al-Maʿnī al-thānī* (Rome and Harissa, 1938).

[39] *Ta'rīkh al-amīr Fakhr al-Dīn al-Maʿnī al-thānī* (Jounieh, 1934).

[40] *Bashīr bayn al-sulṭān wa'l-ʿazīz*, Vol. i (Beirut, 1956); Vol. ii (Beirut, 1957).

[41] C. Churchill, *Mount Lebanon*, 3 vols. (London, 1853).

English family, who acquired, in the course of a long residence in Lebanon, and through very close relations with the S̲h̲ihābs (with whom indeed he was connected by marriage) and the Druze nobility, a knowledge of Lebanon so intimate that he may almost be regarded as a Lebanese historiographer. His account of the Druze religion is taken largely from de Sacy, and the older history is based partly at least on Ḥaydar. But he claimed to have seen manuscript records still in the possession of the great Druze and Christian families, and his account of the reign of Bas̲h̲īr is based upon personal knowledge.

Through such works as these the image has been projected of the Ma'nī and S̲h̲ihābī princes as creators and symbolic embodiments of free Lebanon, but in recent years there has been an attempt by writers of socialist views to create another image, of 'popular' Lebanon struggling against its feudal bonds. Two revolts against heavy taxation in Bas̲h̲īr's reign (the '*āmmiya* of Antelias and Lahfad) have been regarded as early expressions of the popular will; more plausibly, attention has been directed to the revolt of the Maronite peasants of Kasrawān against their lords of the K̲h̲āzin family (also Maronites), and the establishment of a 'peasant republic' in 1857. Yūsuf Yazbak has published a contemporary chronicle of this event, with tendentious notes.[42]

The image of collapse has been provided by the period between 1840 and 1860, and in particular by the civil war and massacres of 1860. Here too the moral has not been far to seek; the need for mutual toleration, and the danger of foreign intervention making use of communal disputes. Events so unusual and tragic stirred many pens, and a number of the numerous reports by eyewitnesses have been published. Since most of them are written by Christians, a special interest attaches to the one published Druze memoir, that narrated by Ḥusayn Abū S̲h̲aqrā to Yūsuf of the same family.[43] Of all these reports, perhaps the most reliable is that of Mīkhā'īl Mis̲h̲āqa (1800–88), *al-Jawāb 'alā 'qtirāḥ al-aḥbāb*.[44] Himself a Christian, but a former servant of Bas̲h̲īr and with the outlook of one who serves and respects authority, Mis̲h̲āqa gives an unbiased analysis of the causes of the outburst, and does not hesitate to blame the Christians for lack of respect for the traditional authority of the nobility. Here also a work by Colonel Churchill should be mentioned; his *Druzes and Maronites*

---

[42] Anṭūn Ḍāhir al-'Aqīqī: *T̲h̲awra wa-fitna fī Lubnān*, ed. Yūsuf Yazbak (Beirut, 1938). English translation by Malcolm H. Kerr, *Lebanon in the last years of feudalism, 1840–1868* (Beirut, 1959).

[43] *al-Ḥarakāt fī Lubnān*, told by Ḥusayn Abū S̲h̲aqrā to Yūsuf Abū S̲h̲aqrā, ed. 'Ārif Abū S̲h̲aqrā (Beirut, n.d.).

[44] An unsatisfactory edition of this was published under the title *Mas̲h̲had al-a'yān bi-ḥawādit̲h̲ Sūriya wa-Lubnān*, ed. M. K. 'Abduh and A. H. S̲h̲ak̲h̲ās̲h̲īrī (Cairo, 1908). There is a better edition by A. Rustum and S. Abū S̲h̲aqrā, *Muntak̲h̲abāt min al-jawāb 'ala 'qtirāḥ al-aḥbāb* (Beirut, 1955). This, however, stops at the year 1841. Manuscripts of the complete work, including the later sections, are numerous; there is one in the library of the American University of Beirut.

under Turkish Rule[45] is the most vivid and comprehensive account of these events, although perhaps excessively harsh in its view of the Maronite Patriarch.

V

Within these two poles there has moved a great deal of historical thought: attempts to show, by historical analysis, why Lebanon should exist and how it can survive. Down to 1914, when Lebanon was an autonomous Ottoman Sanjaq with a Christian majority and under the protection of the Powers, the answer to such questions was fairly simple. It was given, for example, by M. Jouplain (the pseudonym of a Maronite, B. Noujaim) in his *La Question du Liban.*[46] This work was partly an analysis of the political structure and international position of autonomous Lebanon, partly a detailed history of the years of crisis from 1831 to 1861, based upon documents published by the British and French Governments, and by De Testa in his *Recueil des Traités de la Porte Ottomane*. From his analysis there emerges a clear conception of Lebanon. For him, Lebanon formed part of Syria, but a quite distinctive part. There was a Lebanese nation, with a continuous history since ancient times. It had at times been englobed by great empires, and most recently by the Ottoman Empire, but it had never been absorbed. Since 1861 its existence had been formally recognized, but within boundaries smaller than its natural limits. It was essentially a Christian nation, and looked to France to intervene in order to secure its natural frontiers.

Because Lebanon was still a province within an undivided Empire, because its desire to be free from the Empire found echoes in other provinces and because the new Lebanese historiography, like the new national consciousness, was linked with a flowering of culture in Arabic, it was possible for Lebanese writers to see the same principles embodied in a larger whole. The idea of 'Syria' as a whole served as an alternative focus of political loyalty and historical thought. Among the histories of 'Syria' in this broad sense produced by Lebanese, we may mention that of Jirjī Yannī,[47] an Orthodox Christian of Greek origin, which is important for the history of Tripoli; and the vast history of Syria by the Maronite Archbishop Yūsuf al-Dibs (1833–1907).[48] In form a general history of Syria from the earliest times until his own day, with 'Syria' as the explicit subject and with much general Islamic history and history of Arab culture, it tends in the later period to mean 'Lebanon' when it says 'Syria', and is particularly detailed and useful on Maronite ecclesiastical history, for the

[45] London, 1862.
[46] Paris, 1908.
[47] *Ta'rīkh Sūriya* (Beirut, 1881).
[48] *Ta'rīkh Sūriyya*, 8 vols. (Beirut, 1893–1905). The material on the Maronites is separately published also in *al-Jāmi' al-mufaṣṣal fī ta'rīkh al-Mawārina al-mu'aṣṣal* (Beirut, 1905).

author had much knowledge of Church literature and documents. The book is typical of a genre of history which became current at this time: its general framework and, in particular, its earlier sections are drawn from European sources, but when it comes to the recent history of Lebanon it changes its character and becomes local history of the traditional sort and based on the local sources.

We may mention, in this connection, another work written by a European so long resident in Lebanon, and so fully identifying himself with its problems, that it may be regarded as belonging to the Lebanese tradition of historical writing: Father H. Lammens's *La Syrie—Précis Historique.*[49] Here once more 'Syria' as a natural unit is the subject, but Lebanon is conceived of as having a separate existence inside it. Lammens did not indeed emphasize the existence of something called 'Syria' as an alternative to the idea of 'Lebanon', but as an alternative to that of 'the Arabs'. In his view, the Syrians, and *a fortiori* the Lebanese, were not Arab, and most Maronite writers of his age would probably have agreed with him. But there was a group of writers who, while accepting the existence of a separate entity called 'Syria', would have regarded it as part of a larger whole. The revival of Arabic culture in Lebanon induced some of the historians to look beyond the narrow confines of their mountain. Fr. L. Cheikho (Shaykhū) wrote much on Arabic literature,[50] Vicomte Philippe de Ṭarāzī published several volumes on the history of Arabic journalism,[51] and Jurjī Zaydān (1861–1914), in a prolific life as a journalist, published histories of Arabic literature, Islamic civilization and Egypt, a volume of nineteenth-century biographies, and a score of historical novels, modelled on the Waverley novels but nearer to Henty than to Scott, which have done much to arouse, and not in Lebanon alone, a romantic image of the Arab past.[52]

VI

Since Lebanon became a State, first under French Mandate and then with sovereign independence, there has continued to be an equivocation between the idea of Lebanon and the idea of some larger whole. Most of those who have written about Lebanese history have accepted the thesis of Ṭannūs al-Shidyāq, that there has long existed an entity called 'Lebanon', not simply a religious group nor the estate of a ruling family, but a society; and their problem has not been whether it exists, but what have been, and what should be, its relations with the surrounding world. We can dis-

[49] 2 vols. (Beirut, 1921).

[50] Including *al-Ādāb al-'arabiyya fi'l-qarn al-tāsi' 'ashar*, 2 vols. (2nd ed. revised, Beirut, 1924–6).

[51] *Ta'rīkh al-ṣaḥāfa al-'arabiyya*, 4 vols. (Beirut, 1913–33).

[52] *Ta'rīkh ādāb al-lugha al-'arabiyya*, 3 vols. (Cairo, 1911). *Ta'rīkh al-tamaddun al-islāmī*, 5 vols. (Cairo, 1902–6). *Ta'rikh Miṣr al-ḥadīth*, 2 vols. (Cairo, 1911). *Mashāhīr al-sharq*, 2 vols. (Cairo, 1907).

tinguish among recent historians those who lay more emphasis on the separateness of Lebanon and those who emphasize its links with the surrounding world; roughly corresponding with this distinction is another, between those for whom the significance of Lebanon is that it has been a free Christian enclave in a Muslim world, and those who see in it above all a multiple society where men of different faiths have been able to live side by side in peace. But the distinction is no more than one of emphasis; for most historians Lebanon is both a land of asylum and a place of meeting. Among those who lay their stress on the former, we may mention Michel Chebli, who has published a life of Fakhr al-Dīn followed by a work on Lebanon under the princes who succeeded him.[53] It is devoted to the glory of the princes who gave Lebanon a good public administration and unity in tolerance; but it is devoted no less to the flowering of Christian culture in Lebanon of the seventeenth and eighteenth centuries. The author had a close connection with the theorist of Lebanese separatism, Michel Chiha, who himself pointed the moral of the book in his preface:

> 'L'histoire des Chehab est l'histoire d'une résistance. C'est l'histoire d'une communauté nationale, faite de communautés confessionelles établies sur une montagne maritime qui leur sert d'inviolable refuge et unies pour le défense et la préservation de leurs libertés spirituelles et temporelles.'[54]

It is significant of the development of modern Lebanon that an historian coming from one of the non-Christian communities should be able to point a similar moral, although his stress is less on the need for Christians to preserve their spiritual liberty than on the need of those who have different beliefs to live together in peace. In 1955 Adel Ismail published the first volume (in French) of a *Histoire du Liban du XVIIe Siècle à nos Jours.*[55] Planned to cover the modern history of Lebanon in six volumes, it will be the most ambitious survey of the subject. This first volume deals with Lebanon in the time of Fakhr al-Dīn. M. Ismail follows the example of Fr. Carali in going beyond the little group of classical chronicles (Duwayhī, Ṣafadī, Shihāb, Shidyāq) on which almost all subsequent work has been based, and trying to find a more secure base in contemporary documents. Whereas Fr. Carali used Italian sources, Ismail has made exhaustive use of French documents: the Archives Nationales, those of the Ministry of Foreign Affairs, and the important commercial archives of Marseilles. He

[53] *Fakhr al-Din II Maan, Prince du Liban* (Beirut, 1946). *Une Histoire du Liban à l'Epoque des Emirs, 1635–1841* (Beirut, 1955). Among other works written broadly from a Lebanese nationalist point of view, note: A. Rustum and F. E. Bustānī, *Ta'rīkh Lubnān* (Beirut, 1939); and Yūsuf Mizhir, *Ta'rīkh Lubnān al-'āmm*, 2 vols. (n.d., n.p.).

[54] *Histoire du Liban*, Preface, p. 11.

[55] Vol. i: *Le Liban au temps de Fakhr al-Din II (1590–1633)* (Paris, 1955). There has now appeared also vol. iv: *Redressement et déclin du féodalisme libanais* (Beirut, 1958).

is thus able to give a fuller survey of social and economic life than has usually been attempted. On the administration of Fakhr al-Dīn he does not add much to Carali; but there is a comprehensive view of Fakhr al-Dīn's foreign policy. Indeed the importance of the Ma'nī prince is clearly brought out, as the man who first gave Lebanon a separate foreign policy. Not in this respect alone, Ismail regards Fakhr al-Dīn as the creator of the modern Lebanese nation. He goes further than older writers, and further perhaps than the evidence warrants, in regarding Fakhr al-Dīn as a conscious nationalist with an articulate grasp of the modern idea of a nation. He had a

> '. . . conception moderne de la "nation". . . . Tout en restant druse, il sut être musulman, chrétien, maronite, capucin, ou jésuite. . . . De cette Macédoine de confessions et de rites qu'était le Liban, il fit naître une nation et une patrie dans un Empire ou l'idée de Patrie était inconnue.'[56]

That Chebli, Ismail, and others who have written Lebanese history in modern times should be in some sense Lebanese nationalists is not surprising; had Lebanon not been a significant entity for them they would scarcely have cared to write about it. Side by side with them there have been other writers who have devoted themselves to a broader subject. The late nineteenth-century concept of 'Syria' has fallen into the background, banished (although perhaps not for ever) by the march of events, but the concept of 'the Arabs' has become more definite. The works of Philip K. Hitti on Arab history are too well-known to need comment; written in America for an English-speaking audience, they scarcely fall within our scope. His recent work, *Lebanon in History*,[57] is almost the first attempt to treat the whole history of Lebanon from the dawn of history until today, and to place it in the context of Near Eastern history. The chapters on modern history represent one more exploitation of the chronicles, more careful and controlled than that of his predecessors although not different in essence; but there is more on the period from 1861 to 1914, and on the social and intellectual changes of the nineteenth century, than can be found elsewhere.

The history of the Arab national movement, *The Arab Awakening*, has been written by a historian of Lebanese origin, George Antonius.[58] Subsequent historians, working on one or other aspect of the subject, have differed from his interpretation,[59] and Miss Sylvia G. Haim has cast doubt on his integrity as a historian.[60] But the most of which he can be

[56] pp. 167–8. [57] London, 1957. [58] London, 1958.

[59] E. Kedourie: *Britain and the Middle East* (London, 1956). Z. N. Zeine: *Arab-Turkish relations and the emergence of Arab nationalism* (Beirut, 1958); also Zeine: *The struggle for Arab independence* (Beirut, 1960).

[60] ' "The Arab Awakening", A Source for the Historian?' in *Die Welt des Islams*, N.S. vol. ii, No. 4 (1935).

legitimately accused is that he rarely quoted his sources or explained why, when they conflicted, he preferred one of them to another; and that he laid too much emphasis on the points which he regarded as important. He gives too much importance to the rôle of the Lebanese Christians, and the American mission-schools in Lebanon, in the formation of Arab nationalism. He regards them indeed as having created the movement; later, 'the ideas which had originally been sown by Christians were . . . finding an increasingly receptive soil among the Moslems'.[61] He says nothing about the influence of the 'Islamic modernists' of Egypt, although Jamāl al-Dīn is briefly mentioned; and while the Syrian members of the Ottoman official and officer class are mentioned as those who became the leaders of the secret societies, the impression is given that they derived their ideas from the Lebanese Christians, not from the professional schools and political atmosphere of Istanbul, and the tradition of their own families. Antonius's very conception of Arab nationalism, as a secular link binding together adherents of different religions, is Lebanese. The first political problem of Lebanon is how to create such a link; in the other Arab countries, where the Christians form a minority, it may be an important problem but it is not the first of all. It is true, Antonius is in no sense a Lebanese nationalist. When talking of Lebanon under the French Mandate, his point of view is that of the Arab nationalists of Damascus, who took it for granted that

> 'the play of natural forces was bound in time to "expose" the artificiality of the present frontiers; and that the day would come when the Lebanese themselves would seek a modification, if not the total abolition, of the barriers'.[62]

But in this he was typical of the Orthodox Christians of Lebanon of his generation; they felt the attraction of the Lebanese idea far less than the Catholics, and their allegiance was given to the idea of Syria or of the Arabs.

VII

Appendix—the Publication of Sources

We wish here to draw attention to one of the cardinal virtues of the Lebanese school of historians: their care to base their work on primary sources, and their concern to make those sources available. This quality can be seen as far back as the time of Duwayhī and Ḥaydar Shihāb; both of them went to some trouble to collect all the materials they could, and Ḥaydar frequently quoted the text of official documents. But of course

[61] p. 95. [62] p. 385.

they lived before the principles of modern historical enquiry had been made clear, and it is to later writers that we owe the painstaking collection and publication of texts and documents. Before 1914 three important collections were published. Philippe and Farīd Khāzin published three volumes of diplomatic documents dealing with the policy of the Great Powers in regard to Syria and Lebanon from 1840 to 1910;[63] they were mostly drawn from British and French official publications and from De Testa, although some had not previously been published. T. Anaissi collected important ecclesiastical documents in his *Bullarium Maronitarum*;[64] and Father A. Rabbath published six fascicles of *Documents inédits pour servir à l'histoire du Christianisme en Orient.*[65] Very few of his documents had been published before; they were drawn mainly from the archives of the Society of Jesus, and also from those of the French Ministry of Foreign Affairs, the Vatican, the eastern patriarchates and bishoprics, and from papers in the Bibliothèque Nationale in Paris. Covering the period of the development of modern Catholic missions, from the sixteenth to the nineteenth century, they deal above all with the splendours and miseries of the missionaries, their struggles with the Orthodox hierarchy, their persecution by the Ottoman authorities and the protection given them by the Ambassadors and consuls of France.

In the years since the First World War the chronicles of Lebanon have been published or republished in improved editions, mainly through the efforts of a few individuals. Fr. P. Carali published, among others, the early chronicle of Ibn al-Qilāʿī[66] and Ḥaydar's shorter work on Bashīr II; his book of Italian documents on Fakhr al-Dīn has already been referred to,[67] and we may also mention his book on the Syrians in Egypt,[68] based on Church registers. Fr. C. Bāshā edited the chronicles of Mīkhāʾīl Ṣabbāgh[69] and Ibrāhīm al-ʿAwra;[70] the first-named was part of a series of *Documents inédits pour servir à l'Histoire des Patriarches Melkites*. A. Rustum and F. E. Bustānī published, under the auspices of the Lebanese Directorate (subsequently Ministry) of Education and the Fine Arts, al-Ṣafadī's history of Fakhr al-Dīn,[71] and the second and third parts of Ḥaydar's chronicle.[72] These were intended to be the first two in a series which should include all the basic Arabic sources for the history of Lebanon. The Second World War intervened and the series went no further, but in the last few years more

[63] *Majmūʿat al-muḥarrarāt al-sīyāsiyya wa'l-mufawwaḍāt al-duwaliyya ʿan Sūriya wa-Lubnān*, 3 vols. (Jounieh, 1910–11).

[64] Rome, 1911.

[65] 2 vols. 6 fascicles (Fasc. I–V, Paris, 1905–11; Fasc. VI, ed. F. Tournebize, Beirut, 1921).

[66] *Ḥurūb al-muqaddamīn* (Bayt Shabāb, 1937).

[67] See p. 236, n. 38 above.

[68] *al-Sūriyyūn fī Miṣr*, vol. i (Cairo, 1928).

[69] See p. 229, n. 10 above.

[70] See p. 229, n. 11 above.

[71] See p. 229, n. 7 above.

[72] See p. 231, n. 14 above.

official series have been started, one by the Lebanese University[73] and one by the Department of Antiquities in the Ministry of Education.[74]

Much of the work of publishing chronicles, biographies, and memoirs was done by periodicals, some of them comparatively short-lived, like *al-Manāra*,[75] *al-Masarra*,[76] *al-Majalla al-sūriyya*,[77] and its continuation *al-Majalla al-batriyārkiyya*,[78] and the recently established *Awrāq lubnāniyya*,[79] others with a longer history and a solid reputation. Two have been particularly important: Shaykh ʻĀrif al-Zayn's *al-ʻIrfān*,[80] which has published much work on Shīʻī doctrine and antiquities in the last half-century, and the Jesuit periodical *al-Mashriq*[81] which has naturally laid most emphasis on Christian Lebanon and Eastern Christendom in general. In the last few years it has printed a new and complete edition of Duwayhī's *Ta'rīkh al-azmina*,[82] and the chronicles of ʻAyntūrīnī[83] and Munayyir.[84] With these, the publication of the important chronicles is virtually complete, except for the work of Ibn Sibāṭ.

There has been a tendency among Lebanese historians to base their work simply upon what previous historians have written, and in particular upon the four or five major chronicles. In recent years, however, the importance of going beyond chronicles to official and other documents has been more fully recognized. Some types of document are comparatively scarce in Lebanese historiography; for example, the memoirs, diaries and private letters which are so important a source for modern European political history. Official documents, however, exist in abundance, and the first man to collect them systematically was A. Rustum, who has published two large collections dealing with the history of Lebanon and Syria under Ibrāhīm Pasha (1831–41). The first is a collection of Arabic sources,[85] drawn from family papers and the archives of the religious courts (the only important archives for the Ottoman period which seem to exist in the Arab provincial towns); of particular importance are the long extracts from the register of the *majlis* set up by Ibrāhīm Pasha in Aleppo, which throw a flood of light in Ibrāhīm's methods of administration and on the social and economic life of Syria at that time. The second work is a calendar of papers in the Egyptian archives relating to Syria:[86] an exhaustive list with text or full summaries of the more important documents. These two works will be of fundamental importance for anyone who wishes to write the history of Syria and Lebanon during these crucial years. It is a pity that Professor Rustum himself has not yet had an opportunity to write the

[73] *Manshūrāt al-jāmiʻa al-lubnāniyya, qism al-dirāsāt al-ta'rīkhiyya.*
[74] *Mudīriyyat al-āthār, nuṣūṣ wa-wathā'iq ta'rīkhiyya.*
[75] Jounieh, 1930–50. [76] Harissa, 1910–. [77] Cairo, 1926–9.
[78] Jounieh then Beirut, 1930–. [79] Ḥadath, 1956–. [80] Ṣaydā, 1909. [81] Beirut, 1898.
[82] See p. 226, n. 1 above. [83] See p. 229, n. 8 above. [84] See p. 230, n. 13 above.
[85] *al-Uṣūl al-ʻarabiyya li-ta'rīkh Sūriyya fī ʻahd Muḥammad ʻAlī bāshā*, 5 vols. in 4 (Beirut, 1930–3).
[86] *al-Maḥfūẓāt al-malikiyya al-miṣriyya*, 4 vols. (Beirut, 1940–3).

work of synthesis for which he is uniquely qualified. He has, however, published several short works on specific points.[87]

It is partly due to his efforts, and partly to those of the Director of Antiquities (Amīr Maurice Shihāb, himself a member of the former ruling family) that the National Archives of Lebanon have been created in the last few years. The basis of these are two collections of family papers; those of the Khāzins, the Maronite lords of Kasrawān, and those of the Muslim Bayhums, one of the leading merchant families of Beirut. Recently, there have come to light, in the palace of Bteddin, a large number of documents of the period of Bashīr II, and others from that of the autonomous Sanjaq (1861–1915). Microfilms have been made of all important documents dealing with Lebanon in the French archives, and it is hoped to do the same for the British and Ottoman archives. All these papers are now being arranged and classified, and some of them are already available to historians.[88] They will provide the necessary foundation for the history of one of the two poles of Lebanese life, the government in its successive forms—the princedom, the autonomous Sanjaq, the independent Republic. There is another pole, the Maronite Patriarchate; its archives are well-preserved but have only been spasmodically open to scholars, and perhaps they too will some day become readily available.

[87] They include: *The Royal Archives of Egypt and the Origins of the Egyptian Expedition to Egypt, 1831–1841* (Beirut, 1936); *The Royal Archives of Egypt and the Disturbances in Palestine, 1834* (Beirut, 1938); *Bashīr bayn al-sulṭān wa'l-'azīz, 1804–41*, vol. i (1956), vol. ii (1957).

[88] For a partial exploration of the Archives, cf. Dominique Chevallier, 'Aux origines des troubles agraires libanais en 1858', in *Annales* (Jan.–Mar. 1959), i, 35–64.

21. SYRIAC CHRONICLES AS SOURCE MATERIAL FOR THE HISTORY OF ISLAMIC PEOPLES

J. B. SEGAL

Professor of Semitic Languages in the University of London

Sixty years ago William Wright wrote of Syriac literature in the following terms:

> 'We must own . . . that the literature of Syria is, on the whole, not an attractive one . . . The characteristic of the Syrians is a certain mediocrity. They shone neither in war, nor in the arts, nor in science. They altogether lacked the poetic fire of the older . . . Hebrews and of the Arabs. . . . Yet to the Syrians belongs the merit of having passed the lore of ancient Greece to the Arabs, and therefore, as a matter of history, their literature must always possess a certain amount of interest in the eyes of the modern student. . . . And even Syria's humble chroniclers . . . deserve their meed of praise, seeing that, without their guidance, we should have known far less than we now know about the history of two important branches of the Eastern Church, besides losing much interesting information as to the political events of the periods with which their annals are occupied.

So far William Wright. No one will deny the substance of his remarks. These Syriac writers were indeed lacking in imagination; and they were, for the most part, lacking in the humour that is a sensible by-product of imagination.

And yet Wright has done less than justice to the work of the Syriac chroniclers. To the student of history this very mediocrity of the Syrians and their homely respectability—for all the writers whom I shall mention are men who played a solid part in the affairs of their own times—is of advantage, rather than a defect. It is our best guarantee of the trustworthiness of their narrative. Our Syriac chroniclers were simple men, but they were men of good sense and integrity. They were all, it is true, devout, even doctrinaire, sons of the Church, and they make all the affairs of human kind conform to a certain larger pattern drawn by the guiding hand of Providence. But they tell their story without guile or affectation, without conceit and without cynicism. Carlyle wrote that 'the merit of originality is not novelty; it is sincerity'; these Syriac chroniclers were sincere men.

Let me define briefly the scope of the Syriac chronicles. By Syriac I mean that branch of the Aramaic language that was written and spoken by the peoples of Syria, Mesopotamia, and the adjacent regions during the first thirteen centuries of the Christian era. Syriac, it should be noted, was not confined to Syria itself. On the contrary, at the time of its widest diffusion it was in common use from the Mediterranean seaboard in the west to the province of Adiabene in the east, from Lake Van and the Armenian highlands in the north to the borders of Galilee in the south. From the third century until the emergence of Islam, this area was predominantly Christian; and when, with the spread of Islam, the Christians became a minority, they remained nevertheless a close-knit and numerous community. The Syriac chronicles were (as I have already observed) Christian both in content and expression. They are profoundly coloured by the Bible and the Church Fathers. Most of them were composed in Mesopotamia, and several at or near Edessa, which had special sanctity as the first city of this region—indeed, the first kingdom in the world—to adopt Christianity as its official religion. At Edessa was spoken and written that form of the language which was a model throughout the Syriac world.

There is one striking feature common to the native Christians of Mesopotamia during the thousand years—from the third to the thirteenth centuries—over which these chronicles extend. They never took a direct part in governing their own affairs, nor did they ever seek to do so. Theirs was a helpless fatalism that was the product of their circumstances. During the first four centuries of this period they were divided between the great Aryan empires of Byzantium in the west and Persia in the east. The frontiers of the two powers marched between the Euphrates and the Tigris; and the countryside was ravaged by constant warfare in which the Christian peasantry had little interest. The political division of Mesopotamia induced also religious division, for a schism in the Syrian church in the fifth century gave the Persian Christians ecclesiastical independence of their brothers in the west. Only with the emergence of Islam was the barrier—this Iron Curtain of antiquity—removed, and Mesopotamia resumed its natural homogeneity of race and tradition. But the Christians had now become a dwindling minority, without effective power in the government of their country.

I make no apology for this brief digression. The value of these Syriac chronicles lies precisely in the picture that they present of the society in which they were composed, the background upon which were superimposed the lines of policies and action of the rulers of armies and of states.

II

The origins of Syriac historical writing may be sought in the numerous works of the early Church, narratives designed to arouse and intensify

Christian loyalties. Among them we have the legendary account of the arrival of the first Christian missions at Edessa and the exploits of the righteous Emperor Constantine and his successors. Others again are martyrologies, and their number is legion.[1] But of these the great majority may be dismissed as fanciful; the extraction of fact from their fiction is not a profitable task for the serious historian.

There is, however, another genre of literary composition—older than Christianity in Mesopotamia—which I prefer to regard as the lineal ancestor of the Syriac chronicles. I refer to the city archives; and the compilation of archives in some of the cities of Mesopotamia may well go back to at least the early Seleucid period. Only the records of Edessa have survived in Syriac, unhappily in a fragmentary condition.[2] The earliest entry belongs to the year A.D. 180. But the most extensive entry—and this we may term the earliest Syriac chronicle—is a description of the floods of Edessa in A.D. 201, whose vivid details clearly postulate its composition by an eyewitness. I cannot quote more than the opening lines:

> 'The springs of water that come forth from the great palace of king Abhgar became abundant and rose; and, as on a previous occasion, it grew full and overflowed on all sides . . .
>
> . . . And the courtyards and porticos and houses of the king began to be filled with water. And when our lord Abhgar the king saw this, he went up to a safe place on a hill overlooking this palace where the craftsmen of the royal works lived and dwelt.'

This is fine straightforward narrative, and it is the prototype of all that follows. Our next chronicle—the so-called Chronicle of 'Joshua the Stylite'—was composed after an interval of almost three centuries.[3] We know nothing of the writer. His chronicle opens in about A.D. 395–6 and ends in 506; and from its freshness and clarity we may assume that it was compiled at Edessa at that time. It is written with simplicity, honesty, and vitality, and the sequence of its dates is remarkably accurate.

We are given an account of the wars between the empires of Byzantium and Persia, and that slow attrition of their power that was to render them an easy prey to the Arabs a century and a half later. There are graphic descriptions of the methods of siege warfare, of ambushes and weapons. We hear the rumblings of the great hordes on the outskirts of western Asia. The Huns swept over Mesopotamia and even Syria, leaving behind a trail of devastation. Frequently foreign mercenaries took service in the armies of one or the other of the empires, attracted by the prospect of loot rather than by the meagre pay. So in 502, a force of Persians, Arabs, and Huns under al-Nu'mān ibn al-Aswad raided the fields of Harran and Edessa. Here is 'Joshua's' famous account of the Gothic detachments of the Byzantine army who were quartered on the citizens of Edessa:

> Those too who came to our aid under the name of deliverers, both when coming down and when going up, plundered us almost as much as enemies. Many poor people they turned out of their beds and slept in them, whilst their owners lay on the ground in cold weather. Others they drove out of their own houses and went in and dwelt in them. The cattle of some they carried off by force as if it were spoil of war; the clothes of others they stripped off their persons and took away. Some they beat violently for a mere trifle; with others they quarrelled in the streets and reviled for a small cause . . . Many they fell upon in the highways . . . From old women, widows and the poor, they took oil, wood, salt and other things for their own expenses; and they kept them from their own work to wait upon them. In short, they harassed everyone, both great and small, and there was not a person who did not suffer some harm from them.

But it was the nomads who were an ever-present terror to the inhabitants of the cities and villages of northern Mesopotamia. These are not, it should be observed, the people called *'Arab* or *'Arbaye* in the Syriac of that period. The latter dwelt in the steppe country—principally between Āmid and Thannurios—that lay beyond the villages. They were semi-sedentary, and the authorities sought to hasten the process of their evolution to settled farmers. It was the Scenite, or tent-dwelling, Arabs—the *Ṭayyaye*, as they were commonly called—who defied all the conventions of established society. The roads and peaceful villages were at their mercy. The story of the prince of al-Ḥīra who sacrificed four hundred captive virgins to the moon-goddess al-'Uzzā passed from mouth to mouth. True, Christianity had begun to temper the lawlessness of the Beduin, but usually their hands were against all men. 'Joshua' writes that they

> crossed the Tigris, and plundered and took captive and destroyed all that they found in Persian territory. Thy Holiness,

he continues, addressing his correspondent,

> must be well aware of this, that to the Ṭayyaye on both sides the war was a source of much profit, and they wrought their will upon both kingdoms.

We observe the homeliness and directness of style of the writer. Like all our Syriac chroniclers—even those who, by virtue of their office, were the greatest prelates of the Syrian church—'Joshua' shows sympathy and understanding of the common people, whose desire was to live in quiet and comfort. He tells us the prices of wheat and barley and vegetables and wine; he writes of good and bad harvests, of taxation and of popular rejoicings—even of the spring festival of Edessa which had obvious pagan significance and of which he himself heartily disapproved.

Of more severe character is the history of John of Ephesus, who lived from 516 to about 587.[4] A native of Āmid, John resided most of his life at Constantinople and was intimately associated there with the Emperors and the leading personalities of the capital. He travelled widely, carried out a great proselytizing campaign in Asia Minor, and was one of the promoters of the Byzantine expedition to Nubia. He himself declares, somewhat ponderously, that he

> was no stranger to the conflict (of events) . . . but one of those marshalled in the battle who . . . endured those sufferings and patiently bore the pain of persecution and imprisonment . . .

For John was a leading member of the Monophysite church which was regarded by most Byzantines as dangerously schismatic. He was in an exceptional position to describe the 'narrowness and bigotry . . . the want of self-restraint, injustice and cruelty' which were a commonplace of that period.

The accident of John's Monophysitism brought him into close relation with Christian Arabs who were members of the same sect. We read, for example, that when a large body of Christians were imprisoned by the Persians at Antioch, two Christian Arabs succeeded in escaping from the city and made their way to Constantinople; there John brought them to the notice of the court. And when Tiberius, fearful of the religious schisms that tore his empire, invited al-Mundhir ibn al-Ḥārith to his capital and sought to effect a reconciliation with that Christian Arab king, John was himself a delegate at the conference. We find in the pages of John's chronicle a vivid picture of al-Mundhir and of his renown throughout the empire both as warrior and statesman.

Another acquaintance of John's shed a strange light on the Arab history of this time. One of the few representatives of the Monophysite church in Persian territory was Simeon of Beth Arsham, a rude and bitter disputant. He made frequent journeys to Persia, eluding his Nestorian enemies with the ingenuity of a Scarlet Pimpernel. It was while on a visit to al-Ḥīra in 524 that Simeon met the envoys of the Jewish king, Dhū Nuwās. He records in the pages of John's chronicle the despatch of Dhū Nuwās to the prince of al-Ḥīra, his account of the attack on Najrān and of the massacre of its Christians—an event which had far-reaching repercussions throughout the Arab world.

We should pay tribute to John's honesty as historian. To the king of Persia, the hated enemy of Christian Byzantium, he gives generous praise:

> As the facts themselves prove, he was a prudent and wise man, and all his lifetime he assiduously devoted himself to the perusal of philosophical works . . . It appears also that the war between Persia and the

> (Byzantines) was a cause of great grief to him, and that he would readily have submitted to much for the purpose of re-establishing peace.

And how many chroniclers of this period would prefix their account of distant happenings with this warning—as did John in his outline of events Persia?

> (These are) events which we neither saw nor learned of our own knowledge, nor can we testify to their truth ourselves, inasmuch as we were far away from the countries in which they occurred.

John wrote, in addition to his chronicle, the biographies of the Christian recluses and ascetics who were his contemporaries in the region of his early upbringing, Āmid.[5] Here is material for the student of pre-Islamic Mesopotamia. It is an account of pious, ignorant folk, glorying in their poverty and self-abnegation. To the cynic their torments may border on the masochistic, but it was these men and women who inspired the Beduins of their time to feats of devotion in prayer, fasting, and continence. The brutal directness of Monophysite doctrine appealed to the nomad Arab more than the compromise of the Nestorians; and this was the portent of a more passionate proselytizing movement that was to burst out from the desert scarcely two generations later.

The chronicles of which I have written are the work of Syrians of western, that is, Byzantine, Mesopotamia. The Syrians of Persian Mesopotamia produced, during this period, only biographies of saints and church leaders that are stilted and tendentious. But we may note three, composed in the sixth century, that are not without value—the Chronicle of Meshiḥazekha (with precious information on the rise of the Sasanid dynasty), the History of Karka de Bheth Slokh (with topographical data on pre-Islamic Persia), and the recently published History of Barḥadbeshabba.[6]

III

At the death of John of Ephesus, the prophet Muḥammad was probably seventeen or eighteen years old; and the world was soon to change more swiftly than any man could have foreseen at the time. We have, unfortunately, no detailed contemporary account of the Arab invasion in Syriac; indeed, one biography of this time passed over the campaigns of Heraclius and of the Arabs in no more than a few words.[7] When the curtain rises again, Moslem domination is securely established.

In the Islamic period these Syriac chroniclers are no longer to be relied upon for a record of the major events of their times. They had, it is true, always been remote from the direction of affairs. But now, with the exception of a few individuals, they lived the separate life of a minority community, isolated from the courts of kings and princes by political inferiority, passive and uninterested—even disillusioned—spectators of the passage of events. For a Christian it was safer to have little communication with the temporal power. In 765, for example, the Patriarch George, traduced by his enemies, was seized and whipped before the Caliph al-Manṣūr. When the Caliph harshly demanded why he had not applied for the royal diploma confirming his office in the Church, he replied mildly, 'I did not wish to disturb anyone.' Yet the Christians, however aloof they remained from the wars and intrigues of Moslem rulers, were nevertheless affected by those problems that affect the common folk in every land and in every age. From our Syriac chronicles we derive useful information on the social and economic condition of the ordinary people. And we obtain an illuminating picture of the problems that confronted a religious minority under Moslem rule. We must, of course, apply to these later chronicles a different slide-rule of historical reliability. In the pre-Islamic era the views of Syriac chroniclers are of interest even when they describe occurrences before their time, for they might well be repeating trustworthy traditions handed down by their predecessors. The later chroniclers can do no more than confirm facts established by Arab historians; where their views differ from those of Arab historians, they may be preferred only where they describe events which they themselves witnessed or which took place near to their own lifetime.

To one point I particularly draw attention. In these chronicles are passages that are critical—even severely critical—of the existing régime. Did the Moslem authorities give remarkable latitude to these non-Moslem writers; or did the latter feel free to write as they pleased in the strange tongue of Syriac? Whichever hypothesis we accept, the value of these records is considerably enhanced.

I have already shown that Syriac history—as we understand the term history—is a product of western, not of eastern, Mesopotamia. That this is the outcome of long tradition, and not an accident of literary survival, is demonstrated by the record of the Islamic era. Mesopotamia was no longer divided into two areas of different cultures, one under the aegis of Greek-speaking Byzantium, the other under that of Persia. Yet even when both regions were under the common rule of Islam, the writings of east Mesopotamian authors—Denḥa, Isho'denaḥ, Thomas of Marga, and the anonymous biographers of martyrs and saints—are no more than an uncritical medley of fact and pious fiction. Only two exceptions must be noted. The first is the anonymous chronicle which gives an account of events in Persia from the dethronement of Hormizd IV in 590 up to 670; its value is great because it must have been composed not much later than 680, probably by a Nestorian monk. The second is the Chronography of Elias, Metropolitan of Nisibis in the eleventh century; this, however, is little more than a bare list of events and dates.[8]

Those west Mesopotamian chronicles that are extant, on the other hand, although few in number, maintain the breadth and integrity of earlier Syriac histories. First in chronological order is the chronicle incorrectly ascribed to the Patriarch Dionysius of Tell Mahre.[9] It ends in the year 774. It is a somewhat tedious narrative, full of lengthy quotations from Scripture, of apostrophes to Heaven against the wrongdoing of man, and of vapid moralizing. Yet it gives us a picture of eighth-century Mesopotamia:

> All the land . . . was remarkable for its vines, its fields, its numerous cattle. There was not a single poor man in a village who did not have a field, donkeys and goats. There was no place more or less cultivable which was not sown or planted with vine-trees; even in the mountains wherever the plough could pass was planted with vines . . . The land was filled with shepherds out of the abundance of pasturage.

But, our author exclaims, the land is filled also with injustice. He writes bitterly of factious strife within the Church, of civil unrest, of revolt against authority and the carnage which followed. He inveighs against the exactions of governors and their minions, against expropriations, the branding of men's bodies to ensure full payment of the capitation tax, the constant interference with the liberty of the individual—even the fisherman, he declares, is not allowed to fish in the river without a licence. Tax officials overestimate the tithes:

> The fields had been inscribed as well filled, even though not more than five measures had been harvested. The Arabs endured more cruel trials than the Syrians.

Then the tax-collectors

> fall upon them with blows and torments of all kinds. In theory they had to take the tenth part; in fact, the Arabs could not collect what was demanded of them even when they had sold all that they possessed. They tried to persuade them to take according to the laws established by Muḥammad . . . and by the first kings, to take from each one according to what he had, grain from him who had grain, cattle from him who had cattle. But they did not agree and cried to them, 'Get away. Sell your goods and give us gold.'

Of great interest is the autobiography of this patriarch Dionysius (to whom the chronicle which we have just described is wrongly attributed).[10] Dionysius had quietly practised the study of history in a monastery before he was—against his will—consecrated as Monophysite patriarch in 816. Throughout his career he struggled tirelessly on behalf of his community, against schism from within and oppression from without. He travelled to

Mosul, to Baghdad, even to Egypt, to seek the intervention of the authorities. His autobiography—he was a shrewd observer of men—depicts the helplessness of minorities and their dependence upon the goodwill of individuals rather than upon the written articles of law. Here are the disdainful words to Dionysius of the Caliph al-Ma'mūn:

> You trouble and disturb us much, you Christians, and particularly you others, the Jacobites—even though we ignore the complaints you present before us, one against the other. Go away for now, and come back some other day.

And in his account of his visits to Egypt we have this graphic picture of a Christian community there.

> Our city is surrounded by water, and we have neither crops nor any other resources; we cannot keep flocks; the water that we drink comes from afar and we buy it at four *zuze* a pitcher; our work consists in the wool which our womenfolk spin and which we weave; the price which we receive from the cloth-merchants is one-half *zuz* a day. And since our work does not provide sufficient bread for our mouths—when we are taxed we are obliged to pay five dinars (that is, thirty *zuze*) each—we are beaten and thrown into prison; we are forced to give our sons and daughters as security, to work as slaves, two years for a single dinar . . .

Dionysius reported their plight to the ruler of Egypt, and he

> gave order that they should pay tribute according to the law of al-Jazīra—48 *zuze* from the wealthy, 24 from the middle class, and 12 from the poor—when the capitation tax was collected.

Another chronicle treats of the history of Edessa and its environs during the first half of the twelfth century.[11] It is a fine account, recalling in its virility of style the chronicle of 'Joshua the Stylite' some seven centuries earlier. The wealth of intimate detail and the familiarity of the author with the topography of Edessa show that he must have been contemporary to those events and probably an eyewitness of some; perhaps he was Basilius, the Syrian metropolitan of the city at the time. We read of the exchange of knightly courtesies between the Moslem governor of Mosul and his captive, the Crusader Joscelyn. But such generosity alternated with acts of shocking cruelty. There are vivid scenes of the terror and destruction at Edessa and nearby towns during their tenure by the Crusaders, of the capture of Edessa by Zengi in 1144—which aroused the zeal of Bernard of Clairvaux and a new host of Crusaders—and its recapture by Nūr al-Dīn two years later. A more pleasing incident was the visit of Zengi to the city in 1145:

> The metropolitans, priests, deacons, and all the Christians went out to meet him on one hand, and the Moslems who had gathered from all quarters on the other. He greeted the Christians with joy, kissed the Gospel, saluted the metropolitan, and asked after his health. He said that he had come for their sake to supply what they lacked . . . He visited our Syrian churches, examined their beauty, ordered two great bells to be given them and hung on them, as was the custom in the time of the Franks . . . He told the metropolitan to be zealous in guarding the town, and not to betray his government.

This account is incorporated in a chronicle whose author was present at the fall of Jerusalem to Saladin in 1187; his history was continued to the year 1234.[12] Better known, and of more importance, is the contemporary historical work of the Patriarch Michael, usually called Michael the Syrian.[13] He became head of the Monophysite church in 1166 and held that position for thirty years. He was a militant priest with a passion for polemics, and a disciplinarian who was unpopular even among his own adherents. His chronicle is frequently a platform for doctrinal argument—but, for all this, it is invaluable. It is set out in three columns; one deals with secular events, a second with religious affairs, while the third contains miscellaneous anecdotes and matters of local or personal interest. To us the third column, with its record of harvests and droughts, building and conflagrations, is often the most illuminating. The rulers and petty chieftains of Mesopotamia cared little for the welfare of the ordinary people, those simple townsfolk and peasants who formed the bulk of Michael's flock. And for those among them who were Christian the story was the same as in previous centuries, their fortunes precariously subject to the whims of foreign mercenaries and their Moslem overlords. In the fighting between Kurds and Turkomans each party vented its spite upon the local Christians. Nūr al-Dīn had a reputation for piety and charity among Muslims; the Christians saw him otherwise. When he came to Mosul, Michael tells us, he

> multiplied tribute from the Christians, increased the capitation tax, and established the law that they must be girded with a girdle, and must not permit the hair of their heads to grow—so that they might be recognized and derided by the Arabs. He also decreed that the Jews must carry a piece of red material on their shoulders that they might be recognized.

When a new Caliph ascended the throne in 1170, the vizier Ibn al-Baladī was put to death. Since, declares Michael,

> the vizier who had been slain was the enemy of Christians, the new Caliph took it upon himself to love the Christians from hatred of the vizier.

But Nūr al-Dīn remained the arch-enemy of the Christians. They placed great hope in Amalric I, and it was with dismay that they learned of his death in 1174. In such circumstances not even Michael could condemn as immoral the bribes offered to Muslim governors for the release of Christians who had fallen into their power.

Michael was an outspoken advocate of his flock and of his rights as its leader. To Sayf al-Dīn al-Ghāzī who proposed to nominate a rival priest as patriarch, he declared boldly:

> If you wish to change what has been done by the kings your predecessors, know that you are in opposition not only with me, but with the prophets Moses, Christ and Muḥammad; for you destroy . . . the will of God . . . But for me the loss of my head is a little thing . . . Here I freely give my head; bid them cut it, for I shall not transgress the precept of the law.

In 1181 Michael was summoned by Qilij Arslan to Melitene. He went in trepidation. But the sultan received him with honour and courtesy; the Patriarch conversed with him and was heard (he assures us)

> with pleasure . . . in such wise that tears flowed from (the sultan's) eyes.

Michael had occasion to visit his congregation throughout Mesopotamia and Syria, and he received representations also from Monophysites in Egypt. Three times he visited Jerusalem, then in the hands of the Franks, and he obtained diplomas from both Amalric I and Baldwin IV. His comments on the three principal power groups in western Asia at this period —the Turks, the Franks, and the Greeks (of Byzantium)—are concerned in the first place with religious freedom, but they are of wider interest.

> In the years of which we shall now write, calm and tranquillity reigned in our Orthodox Church for this reason . . . The cruel Greeks were confined beyond the seas . . . The Franks who at this time occupied the places of Palestine and also of Syria, and who had pontiffs in their churches, did not raise difficulties in the matter of faith . . . but considered as Christian anyone who adored the Cross without enquiry or examination. For their part, the Turks who occupied most of the country in which the Christians dwelt, who had no notion of the sacred mysteries and therefore considered Christianity an error, were not in the habit of informing themselves on professions of faith or of persecuting anyone for his profession of faith, as did the Greeks, a wicked and heretical people.

With Bar Hebraeus we come to the last of our Syriac chroniclers. He completed the history of the region from the death of Michael the Syrian down to the year of his own death in 1286. His Syriac chronicle—I do not discuss his Arabic chronicle here—is in two parts, one dealing with secular, the other (in two sections) with ecclesiastical, events.[14] The arrival of the Mongols had changed the political scene. Bar Hebraeus reports the new conditions competently, and more particularly events at Melitene, his birthplace. He was himself present as metropolitan when Aleppo was captured by the Mongols in 1259–60. He was acquainted with princes and princesses of the Mongol court. The fortunes of the Christians followed an unpredictable course. On the one hand, Arabs combined with Christians to defend Melitene against Tatar attack in 1243 and again in 1256. So, too, in the Mongol assault on Baghdād in 1258, the wealthy Arabs of the city entrusted their property to the safe-keeping of the Catholicus. On the other hand, Christian monasteries were sacked by the soldiery and the Kurdish tribesmen, and Christian townspeople were attacked by Moslem mobs at Baghdād, Mosul, and Arbil.

The Christian community was certainly in a strange situation at this period. Mongol princes were not ill-disposed towards them; some even professed the Christian faith, and Christians held high rank at court. Bar Hebraeus declares that

> the Church acquired stability and protection in every place,

and he calls Kublai Khān

> the just and wise king, and friend of the Christians; he honoured the men of books, and the learned men, and the physicians of all nations.

Indeed, the commander of the Egyptian forces slaughtered all the Christians of a certain town

> because it had been said to him, The Tatars are made strong by these Christians whenever they pass over into Syria.

Yet this association gave no security to the Christians from the Tatars themselves. Bar Hebraeus writes of the Tatars in the same campaign that they

> in their greed also killed many of the Christians, and they made captives of them and looted, even though the king of kings had commanded that they were not to harm the Christians.

Bar Hebraeus's chronicle, for all its competence, is unsatisfying. He gives us none of the personal touches which his career and personal contacts lead us to expect. His loyalties are sectarian and narrow, and he seems lacking in the standards of honour and integrity by which earlier chroniclers were distinguished. For the cruelty and treachery of the Christian Mongol general Sandagha (that 'splendid young man') there is no reproach. Yet we should perhaps not judge Bar Hebraeus harshly. To him the writing of this chronicle was little more than an exercise in Syriac composition, part of his general endeavour to revive interest in the ancient language. The experiment was foredoomed to failure, for the renaissance of Syriac was beyond the power even of Bar Hebraeus's erudition and industry. It is symbolic that the inscription over the grave of Bar Hebraeus is written in Karshuni—the script is Syriac but the language is Arabic.

SELECT BIBLIOGRAPHY

I. *General*

A. Baumstark, *Geschichte der syrischen Literatur* (1922).
J. Labourt, *Christianisme dans l'empire perse* (1904).
W. Wright, *Short history of Syriac literature* (1894).

II. *Individual Works* (in the order in which they are referred to in the paper)

1. W. Cureton, *Ancient Syriac documents* (1864).
G. Phillips, *Doctrine of Addai* (1876).
R. Gottheil, *Selections from the Syriac Julian romance* (1906).
F. C. Burkitt, *Euphemia and the Goth . . .* (1919).
P. Bedjan, *Acta martyrum et sanctorum* (1890–7).
2. 'Chronicon Edessenum', *Chronica minora*, i (*Corpus Scr. Christ. Or.*, vol. 1), ed. I. Guidi (1955), 1 ff.
3. *Chronicon anonymum pseudo-Dionysianum vulgo dictum* (*CSCO*, vol. 91) ed. J.-B. Chabot (1953), 235 ff.; Wright, *Chronicle of Joshua the Stylite* (1882).
4. *Johanni Ephesini historiae ecclesiasticae pars tertia* (*CSCO*, vol. 105), ed. E. W. Brooks (1952).
5. John of Ephesus, *Lives of the Eastern saints* (*Patrologia Orientalis*, xvii. 1, xviii. 4, xix. 2), ed. Brooks (1923–5).
6. A. Mingana, *Sources syriaques* (1908), i.
C. E. Sachau, *Chronik von Arbela* (1915).
G. Hoffmann, *Auszüge aus syrische Akten persischer Märtyren* (1880).
Histoire de Barḥadbešabba 'Arbaïa (*Patr. Or.*, ix. 5, xxiii. 2), ed. F. Nau (1913–32).
7. *Histoire de Marouta* (*Patr. Or.*, iii. 1), ed. Nau (1905).
8. Th. Nöldeke, *Die von Guidi herausgegebene Syrische Chronik* (1893).
Eliae metropolitae Nisibeni opus chronologicum (*CSCO*, vol. 63), ed. Brooks (1954).
9. *Chronicon anonymum pseudo-Dionysianum vulgo dictum* (*CSCO*, vol. 104), ed. Chabot (1952), pp. 145 ff.
Chabot, *Chronique de Denys de Tell-Mahre* (1895).
10. Michael the Syrian, *Chronicle*, Book XII, ch. ix ff. (Chabot, *Chronique de Michel le Syrien*, 1905–10, fol. 498 ff.)
11. *Anonymi auctoris chronicon ad A.D. 1234 pertinens*, ii (*CSCO*, vol. 82), ed. Chabot (1953), pp. 51 ff.
A. S. Tritton, H. A. R. Gibb, 'First and Second Crusades from an Anonymous Syriac Chronicle', *Journal of the Royal Asiatic Society* (1933), 69, 273.
12. *Anonymi auctoris chronicon ad A.D. 1234 pertinens* (*CSCO*, vols. 81–2).
13. Michael the Syrian, *Chronicle*, Book XVIII, ch. ix ff. (Chabot, *Chronique de Michel le Syrien*, fol. 666 ff.)
14. E. A. W. Budge, *Chronography of Bar Hebraeus* (1932).
J. B. Abbeloos, T. J. Lamy, *Gregorii Barhebraei Chronicon ecclesiasticum* (1872–7).

22. ARMENIAN HISTORIOGRAPHY

C. J. F. DOWSETT

Lecturer in Armenian, School of Oriental and African Studies, London

At no time in its long history has Armenia played a leading rôle in world affairs. Its frontiers have, except perhaps for a brief period under Tigran the Great, been narrow, and for most of its history it has been a small, heterodox Christian people in many ways isolated from its neighbours. In outlook as well as content a nation's historiography is conditioned by the nation's history, and one will search the Armenian authors in vain for the broad, human view of the world characteristic of a Thucydides or Ibn Khaldūn. On the other hand, historiography is a principal genre in Armenian literature, which is not the case with the literatures of the much greater powers of India and Persia. Indeed, when one considers that Armenia's geographical position afforded its inhabitants a close-up view of major world events such as the fall of Sasanid Persia, the rise of the Arabs, the Seljuq conquests, and the invasions of Tīmūr, one may perhaps be glad that the affairs of this world were thought worthy of record by the writers of Armenia. The facts contained in their pages are thus often of first importance; their interpretation was however frequently impaired by the prejudices of a people too closely and usually too painfully involved in the political convulsions of the world around them to be wholly objective.

Whereas in the Cilician period of Armenian literature works were composed by laymen—e.g. the two Hethums, king of Armenia and prince of Korikos respectively—historical writing in Armenia Major, to the general characteristics of which the following pages will be confined, was primarily in the hands of the clergy. Of the principal historians only Faustus Biwzandatzi appears to have been a layman, a circumstance which may have been responsible for some passages in his history being thought by some of his early readers, as will be seen below, not quite proper or even wholly absurd. Among the other historians, John of Draskhanakert was a catholicos, Stephen Ōrbēlean an archbishop, Sebēos and Ukhtanēs bishops, and Eliseus Vardapet, Lazarus of Pharp, Vardan Areweltzi and Kirakos of Gandja monks. The clergy was the most literate section of Armenian society, and before the invention of the Armenian alphabet at the beginning of the fifth century and for some time afterwards, conversant with Greek and Syriac. The author of the history in the name of Moses of Khoren complains of 'the ignorance of our kings and other ancestors and their lack of intelligence', and this judgement was probably valid for the nobles of his own time (seventh century?). The limitations of the priest as historian, however, are manifest; there is scarcely one Armenian writer who would fail to explain the various disasters which overtook his country as God's chastisement for the sins of the people, or victories and periods of prosperity as due to the goodness of the Lord. A narrow outlook, however, is not the monopoly of clerical historians, and one is at any rate fortunate that many of the priestly writers of Armenia were close to the court and sometimes involved in the events they describe. Eliseus, for example, claims at least to have been an eyewitness of the war against Yazdigird II in 451, while at the end of the ninth century John Catholicos played an active political rôle as adviser to the king and intercessor between quarrelling nobles, and himself suffered imprisonment at the hands of the Arab governor. So little is known of the lives of the historians in general, however, that no satisfactory survey can be made of their social origins. Lazarus of Pharp, so he tells us, was brought up with prince Vahan Mamikonean in the palace of Ashushay, *bdeashkh* of Georgia, and was on friendly terms with the lords Nerseh and Hrahat Kamsarakan. The aristocratic origins of Thomas Artsruni, Shapuh Bagratuni, John Mamikonean, and Stephen Ōrbēlean are evident from their noble surnames. Three historians are traditionally considered to have been foreigners. The preface to the history of Agathangełos presents the author as 'a certain Agathangełos from the city of Rome, versed in (his) native arts and in Roman and Greek literature and not ignorant of the writer's craft'. Faustus is said to be a Byzantine by Lazarus of Pharp, while the fictitious or fraudulent Zenob Glak is traditionally considered to have been a Syrian.

The Armenians took their models for historical writing partly from the Greeks. 'If there are writers of many nationalities,' says Moses of Khoren, 'above all Persians and Chaldeans, in whom the affairs of our nation are recorded, let no-one be surprised that we mention only the Greek historians. I do not hesitate to name Greece the mother and nurse of wisdom.' The Greek authors mentioned by Moses are, however, minor ones like Alexander Polyhistor, Polycrates, Euagoras, Olympius of Ani, Ariston of Pella, etc., although he does briefly refer to Herodotus in one passage (ii, 2); he does not consult writers like Xenophon and Strabo, who had something to say concerning Armenia. The reverence in which some writers held the Greeks is illustrated by the passage in Lazarus of Pharp treating of suspected interpolations in Faustus which do not 'conform to what is expected of a learned Byzantine'. After the foundation of Constantinople as capital, says Lazarus, 'streams of knowledge flowed abundantly from the city, since scholars from all regions of Greece hastened thither, and down to the present day these streams of knowledge have continued to spread to all regions. How could a man like Faustus, educated in such a city, possibly put into his history matter offensive to his readers?' Syriac works also had perhaps some influence on Armenian literature. Moses of Khoren pretends that a considerable part of his history is the work of Mar Abas Katina and Bardesanes, but there is nowhere any reference to a clearly genuine ancient Syriac history which might have influenced the historical writing of the Armenians. Moses of Khoren also mentions the existence of Persian historians, but it is not known of whom he was thinking.

Mere chronological lists of events like the works of Samuel of Ani and Mkhithar of Ayrivanq are called *zhamanakagruthiwnq*, a calque on Gk. *chronographia*. These are of no interest for the present paper, although they are of importance as sources: as Moses of Khoren puts it, 'there is no true history without chronicles'. Also calqued on the Greek is the little-used word for historiography, *patmagruthiwn*; the Armenian translation of Gregory of Nyssa's *Creation of Man* contains the phrase 'Historiography is the art of relating much by little.' The usual word for 'history', *patmuthiwn*, connected with the verb *patmel* 'to relate', covers many different forms of writing. The works of Agathangełos and Koriwn are biographical and hagiographical. Authors of so-called universal histories which begin with Adam include Moses of Khoren, Vardan Areweltzi, Moses of Kałankatuq, Stephen of Taron called Asołik, and John Catholicos. Other writers, for instance, Lazarus of Pharp, Faustus Biwzandatzi, Zenob Glak, and Łewond, restrict themselves to a particular period, usually claimed to be contemporary. Eliseus and Sebēos deal with a particular event, Moses of Kałankatuq and Djuanshēr with a particular region, and Thomas Artsruni and Stephen Ōrbēlean with a particular family. Such histories were often commissioned by a sponsor, and in many cases one can detect his influence upon the outlook of the author. According to them, Eliseus wrote his history at the request of a priest of noble birth, David Mamikonean, and Lazarus of Pharp at that of the *marzpan* of Armenia, Vahan Mamikonean; their descriptions of the valour of the Mamikoneans in defence of their country, however, owe as much to historical fact as to hired bias, for the Mamikoneans were the most active princely family in the period with which their histories are concerned. The Bagratunis, the later rivals of the Mamikoneans, were the sponsors of three histories. Łewond the Priest wrote his History of the Caliphs at the request of Shapuh Bagratuni (whose own history, referred to by John Catholicos, Asołik, Ukhtanēs, Kirakos, etc., is now lost), and his bias is quite obvious. He openly takes sides in the struggle between Gregory Mamikonean and Ashot Bagratuni in the middle of the eighth century: when the latter, appointed governor of Armenia by Marwān II, attempts to make common cause with the Arabs during a revolt of the nobles led by Gregory and is captured and blinded by him, Łewond calls the Mamikonean an 'Armenian traitor' and his allies 'deceitful nobles'. Moses of Khoren, accepting the commission of a sponsor he claims to be the *marzpan* Sahak Bagratuni (*c.* 480), tells him that he will 'bequeath this book to your memory and that of future generations of your family; for you are of ancient, valorous and fertile stock, not only by virtue of useful counsel but also of very great and numerous and glorious feats which we shall record in this history'. John Catholicos does not give the name of the sponsor of his history, but indicates that he wrote it 'at royal command', that is, probably at that of Ashot I (885–90) or Smbat I Bagratuni (890–914). The Bagratunis at this time had no rivals for the leadership of Armenia, and John's support is to be expected. Loyalty, however, is a source of bias in a historian, and seems sometimes to have affected John's judgement. When Ashot (the future Ashot I of 885) is in 862 created prince of princes by the Arab governor, John writes that 'all the princes decreed that his family should be considered a royal family, recognizing that it merited special distinction and was worthy of being raised to the dignity of a royal family, remaining apart from all the other princely families'; it is possible that the historian has here anticipated the coronation of twenty years later. Thomas Artsruni was commissioned to write the history of his family, the third great noble house of Armenia, by his kinsman Gregory, prince of Vaspurakan. The very scheme of his book entails a high degree of bias, for the Artsrunis are constantly brought to the fore and made to overshadow other noble families who played just as important a rôle at the time. Thomas does not, however, gloss over the faults of past members of his family, and he gives the fullest account, for example, of the deeds of the traitor Meruzhan Artsruni during the reign of Arshak II; the adage he quotes in connection with Meruzhan's death at the hands of the generalissimo Smbat Bagratuni, however, does not flatter the latter's family: 'foxes have often thought to be king, but the dogs have prevented them'. Despite such examples of bias, there was some feeling (rarely acted upon, one feels) in Armenian historians that a sponsor should be portrayed with all his warts. Agathangełos, relating that he was commissioned by Trdat II to write his history, says that he was ordered 'not to tell false stories about his valour or pleasantly-worded fables in excess of the king's merits, but to describe things as they happened in the course of the changing fortunes of war'; in fact, of course, Trdat's pre-Christian misdeeds are used as contrast to his piety after his conversion. Some histories were commissioned by catholicoi: Joseph I (441–52) commissioned that of Koriwn, Nersēs III (640–61) that of John Mamikonean, while St. Gregory the Illuminator is traditionally but wrongly considered to have commissioned that of Zenob Glak.

What was it that attracted the Armenian historians and their sponsors to historical writing? One of the principal factors was patriotism. 'Though we are but a tiny plot of land,' writes Moses of Khoren, 'a people few in number, our borders narrow, a country weak and often subject to other nations, still have there been many deeds of valour performed in this country of ours worthy of written record.' In the case of writers like Thomas Artsruni, Stephen Ōrbēlean, Moses of Kałankatuq, John Mamikonean, etc., it was more a question of family or regional rather than national pride. There was usually also a clear didactive motive for the composition of Armenian histories. Eliseus states that he has written his history 'not to satisfy the need of the soul for an abundance of terrestrial knowledge, but in order that one might meditate upon Divine Providence, which announces the invisible by the visible'; he does not hesitate to point to the moral of the tale he tells: 'as some good historians say, "Concord is the mother of good and discord the progenitor of evil." ' Lazarus of Pharp, who treats more objectively of those events related by Koriwn and Eliseus, is also not without his moral purpose: 'many brave men, hearing of the deeds of others who performed feats of valour before them, leave behind them a famous name for their own and their nation's glory, while the indolent and cowardly, looking into themselves and hearing the reproaches of others, thus spurred on to seek virtue, may endeavour to improve their ways.' Aristakēs of Lastivert, writing of the collapse of Armenia before the Seljuq invasions, says that he has recorded what happened 'in order that you might know that sin was responsible for all that happened to us and that, seeing them [the Seljuqs] among us, you might fear the countenance of the Lord, prevent the infliction of punishment by confession and repentance, and thus oppose them.' As Eliseus wrote his prose epic on an historical theme to impress upon his fellows the need to unite behind Christ against the heathen Sassanians, so Aristakēs composed his historical jeremiads that his people might do likewise in order to repel the Seljuqs; their work, therefore, like that of Łewond, has a political motive. Thomas Artsruni's aims are open and unconcealed: 'we shall,' he says, 'from the few brief remnants of memorials in previous historians, throw light upon the affairs and domains of the native lords of the Artsruni family, with names and places and dates, in order that their valour and virtue may be clear to all.' Other Armenian historians are more concerned with history as a collection of pretty stories. 'As the heavens are bright with stars and the earth with flowers,' exclaims Moses of Kałankatuq, 'so are the works of historians adorned by divers events . . . Oh, what wonderful stories are those which I have prepared to publish for the attention of the world far and near! The accounts of earlier ages . . . cannot compare!'

The majority of Armenian historians are aware that history should be objective and scientific, although, the tenor of many a book changing after the preface, their works do not always conform to their intentions. Most of them have a definite scheme in mind and pursue it more or less methodically. Eliseus' introduction, for example, systematically exposes the division of his work into seven chapters corresponding to the seven phases into which he analyses the Armenian war of 451. John Catholicos has no doubts about how to write a history: 'one must not restrict oneself to a narrative which would be a succession of truncated facts; one must compose a history which, based upon irrefutable data, shall be irreproachable both in subject-matter and style.' One is frequently aware of a sense of the eternality of history and the realization that a historian forms a single link in an unending chain. Lazarus of Pharp considers his work a continuation of that of Agathangełos and Faustus, while John Mamikonean, whose own history was commissioned as a continuation of that attributed to Zenob Glak, beseeches future generations of monks to 'add to this book that which was done in their own days in this house, for so we found it prescribed by our predecessors'. Faustus mentions that certain events described in his book have been 'written about by others', but adds that he has nevertheless included them for the sake of a proper sequence of events; 'for part of our history concerns first things, and part latter things, and that which happened in between has been written by others; but in order that our history shall not resemble a broken bridge, we have indicated [these intermediate events], like as it were a brick placed into the construction of a wall for the sake of the completeness of the whole.' Thomas Artsruni says that previous writers composed their histories 'in order that those who came after them might be encouraged to undertake the same studies and discovery of meanings [N.B.], that the more skilled and studious of men might pursue their researches with less labour'.

The exact sources upon which the Armenian historians drew for the composition of their works are for the most part unknown. Moses of Khoren, in his attack upon the ancient Armenians who, it seemed to him, were 'ignorant, unintelligent and barbarous', will not accept as an excuse for the lack of histories the absence of an Armenian alphabet before the fifth century, stating that 'there are Persian and Greek documents still extant in Armenia in numerous registers concerning the affairs of each village, each canton and even each house, and innumerable books of legends, above all those concerning the genealogy of our own nobility'. Moses' own claim to have consulted the archives of Edessa must be treated with scepticism, but it is possible that there existed in Syriac information concerning Armenia now lost to us. Thomas Artsruni, while complaining of the difficulty of tracing the history of his family owing to the passage of time and the loss of archives in Armenia, mentions among his sources 'ancient historical books and many historical narrative tales', but he gives no names. John Catholicos mentions 'foreign chronologists who have related the history of our race with the greatest care', but he, too, fails to be more specific. Stephen Ōrbēlean, in an exposé of a method which could be that of a modern historian, quotes as his sources the ancient and modern histories of Armenia, church inscriptions, old archives, and the testimony of informed persons, and promises to satisfy himself concerning their authenticity and to reject all nonsense. The Armenians drew by preference upon the scriptures and the works of Christian writers whom Thomas Artsruni calls 'studious and highly intelligent men, who were like nurses to those of us who follow them and who gave us wholesome and substantial nourishment and led the studious and God-fearing to mature wisdom.' All the historians profess to treat their sources with circumspection. Lazarus of Pharp is confident that the 'discriminating mind can distinguish between the words of learned men and the chatter of fools'. It is usually pagan authors who suffer the most abuse. Moses of Khoren, the Armenian Herodotus, considers it superfluous to repeat 'the fables of profane authors', although he makes an exception in the case of some events and personages referred to by the scriptures and concerning which he is willing to use 'heathen accounts, although from these we shall take only that which we think to be reliable'. *Quellenkritik* is not a modern phenomenon, and some writers manifest a great distrust of the sources, even the Armenian ones, at their disposal, especially where they do not accord with their own preconceptions. On occasions they may suspect that the text at their disposal has been tampered with in the past. Lazarus of Pharp, for example, referring to the presence of untoward things in the text of Faustus, considers them interpolations by ignorant and impudent Greeks and Syrians. Whereas Lazarus finds too much in his sources, Thomas does not find enough: he attributes the absence of any mention of an Artsruni hero from the account of the Armenian War of 451 to the malice of a certain Nestorian who, ordered by prince Nershapuh Artsruni from his domains, spitefully removed the passages relating to the Artsrunis from Eliseus' manuscript. Most writers pretend to be impervious to old tales and legends. 'Mere stories', says John Catholicos, 'are too feeble to entertain the mind'; he will have nothing to do with 'uncertain traditions culled from the mouths of old men'.

The feeling that rhetoric is not desirable in a historical work is stronger in some writers than in others; few are free from occasional outbursts. Koriwn denies that he has had recourse to 'deceptive eloquence'. Conscious that a certain prince might be thought worthy of even greater praise than that which he has lavished upon him, Thomas seeks to be excused 'since this is the time for history and not eulogy'; he leaves the latter to 'more capable and intelligent men'. Style was nevertheless considered to be of some importance, although not intended to interfere with historical fact. Lazarus of Pharp considered the writing of history a task in which 'the aptness of words and arrangements made in accordance with the dictates of science are essential; one must not expand one's account with things which did not occur merely for the sake of useless word-spinning, nor curtail one's account of things which did occur for lack of zeal; the whole must be presented judiciously and with moderation'. Unfortunately for historical accuracy, a purple passage from one author might be applied to different circumstances by another: Thomas Artsruni's description of al-Mutawakkil, for example, is borrowed from Eliseus' description of Yazdigird II. Perhaps the common Armenian method of clarifying the motives and attitudes of historical personages by means of invented letters is due more to reasons of style than to a desire to deceive by forgery.

Owing to the special nature of their religious convictions and national ambitions, the Armenians looked upon none of their neighbours with any marked degree of sympathy. After Armenia's conversion to Christianity, Sasanid Persia became its arch-enemy, and the events of 628 and 637 remain unlamented in Armenian sources. Peoples like the Khazars were considered beneath contempt as human beings—Moses of Kałankatuq refers to their 'customary northern dull-witted stupidity'—although they had often to be reckoned with politically. The Byzantines, who were the object of admiration on the part of certain Armenian historians and to whom the country usually turned, with little success, in its hours of need, were, after the schism between the two churches at the beginning of the sixth century, like the Georgians, 'cursed dyophysites' and 'heretical Chalcedonians'. One cannot say, however, that the Armenian writers, all men with a message, overflattered their own compatriots. After all, it was their sins which brought foreign invasion upon them. It was also realized by some—and the realization was expressed with a view to achieving Armenian unity—that the well-nigh perpetual internal turmoil in which first one Armenian faction and then the other prevailed could drive their neighbours to distraction: Sebēos, for example, puts part of the blame for the division of Armenia between Byzantium and Persia in 590 upon his fellow countrymen by the reproduction, or more likely the invention, of a a letter from Maurice to Chosroes in which the Armenians are called 'a devious and disobedient people who cause only trouble between [them]'.

As one might expect, the Armenian historians had little good to say of the religion of Muḥammad and their Arab conquerors, and their outlook was prejudiced often to the point of absurdity. The Arabs for them were 'sons of Belial', 'accursed Hagarites' with 'natural propensities towards evil-doing'. Moses of Kałankatuq, who could phrase a nice insult, calls them 'a foolish, infidel, self-indulgent race'. Armenian sources contain a number of slanderous rumours concerning the character of the prophet; the same Moses, for example, accuses him of killing his teacher Baḥīrā. It is clear that the Armenians' knowledge of Islam, at the period with with which we are dealing, was exceedingly poor and unworthy of serious writers. Thomas Artsruni considers the Qur'ān the work of Salmān al-Fārsī with insane interpolations by the illiterate Muḥammad, while Vardan Areweltzi gives a quite fantastic account of the genesis of the *Sūrat al-baqara* and a burlesque version and explanation of the pilgrimage to Mecca. One cannot expect the Armenians to have had any love for the invaders and overlords of their country, and there are many passages devoted to stories of atrocities and forced conversions to Islam. It is perhaps only fair to say that the Armenian writers were by no means always happy about the behaviour of their own princes and troops. The caliphs are rarely flattered. Hārūn al-Rashīd was a 'greedy and avaricious man' according to Łewond; according to Moses of Kałankatuq he 'brought such excessive oppression upon Armenia that many cantons went over to the Greeks', a tell-tale remark which shows that the Armenians preferred, in the normal course of events, Arab suzerainty to Greek absorption. There is sometimes agreement between Arab and Armenian sources concerning a caliph's character. Al-Manṣūr is said by Łewond to have died 'exhausted by his love of silver, a defect common to all his race', and Thomas Artsruni knows that the Arabs themselves called him *Abu'l-dawāniq* [Arm. *Abdlang* for **Abldang*]. Łewond has some rare praise for his successor al-Mahdī, whom he calls 'nobler and more virtuous than his father . . . He opened up the treasury kept by his father under lock and key, distributed gifts to the army, and abolished the tariffs on his frontiers in order to provide merchants with greater liberty and to benefit the poor . . . Although he increased the yoke of taxation, the country was relieved of its wretched situation by an increase in the production of silver, for many silver mines were opened up in Armenia in his day.' According to their own account, taxation weighed heavily upon the Armenians. Hārūn al-Rashīd's governor Sulaymān, 'the wickedest and most deceitful of them all', employed a Greek to collect double the normal amount of taxes from the Armenians. 'He had', says Łewond, 'a leaden seal affixed to everyone's neck as a receipt for many *zuz*, thus reducing the people to abject poverty. No one was master of his own possessions.' But few can look with equanimity upon the tax-collector.

Islam and the Arabs, then, are not treated with any objectivity and impartiality by the Armenian historians, and the pages devoted to them are, historiographically speaking, poor. It was clearly beyond the power of the Armenian priest-historians to view the growth of Islam without prejudice, or even panic.

The Armenian historians were naturally preoccupied with events in their own country, and in this sphere they reveal themselves to be appreciative of many of the political, social, and economic factors governing its internal affairs. Relations between Church and State, King and barons, the rivalry between the various noble families and opposing political factions, the economic effects of foreign invasions, the founding of social institutions like schools and hospitals, all claim their attention. They rarely showed the breadth of vision more common in historians of great powers, but they were not blind to the importance of world events, and show that although it may prefer a more spacious plot, history, like philosophy, may still flourish in a tub.

PART II

EUROPEAN (INCLUDING RUSSIAN) HISTORICAL WRITING ON THE NEAR AND MIDDLE EAST FROM THE MIDDLE AGES TO THE PRESENT DAY

23. BYZANTINE HISTORIANS AND THE OTTOMAN TURKS

SIR STEVEN RUNCIMAN

One of the few branches of literature in which the Byzantine Greeks excelled was historiography. Byzantium produced a creditable number of serious historians. They had their faults. Most of them had strong political, racial, and religious prejudices. The need to justify their friends and themselves was usually greater than their dispassionate love of truth. They were apt to be careless about matters which did not hold their interest. Each of them saw himself as the reincarnation of Thucydides; and the consequent selfconsciousness of their style, combined too often with the usual medieval taste for flowery writing, makes much of their work very arduous reading. But they did have a sense of style and of form. They believed that history should contain some sort of moral philosophy; they were interested in the sequence of cause and effect; and they knew that it was important to use reliable sources and sometimes to quote them. On an average they were considerably superior to their historian contemporaries.

Amongst their weaknesses is a certain lack of interest in foreign affairs. Their eyes were fixed on Constantinople, the seat of the government and of the Imperial and Patriarchal Courts on which their intrigues were centred. Foreigners were seldom noticed unless their armies penetrated into the heart of the Empire or unless the Emperor's adventures over the frontiers led to his death or a Palace revolution. The Byzantines were not as a whole ill-informed about their neighbours, as Constantine VII's diplomatic manual, the *De administrando imperio*, shows. But the polished historian felt that the barbarians had little place in his work. He is apt to apologize for introducing barbarian names; which, indeed, he usually transliterates into an almost unrecognizable form. There was a fashion, from the tenth century onwards, for giving foreign peoples some classical name. The Bulgarians are apt to appear as Moesians, the Russians as Scythians, the Turks, rather confusingly, as Persians. Whole periods of Byzantine foreign history are very scrappily treated. A consecutive study of the wars between Byzantium and the Arabs must depend far more on Arabic than on Greek sources.

The Turkish invasions from the eleventh century onwards created new foreign problems that could not be thus ignored. Thenceforward Byzantine historians were forced to take note of the Turks and to study something of their history. It is, indeed, to Byzantine writers that we must go for much of our information about the Seljuqs of Rūm and their fellows. For instance, we would know nothing about the remarkable adventurer, the amīr Chaka of Smyrna, if it were not for Anna Comnena's history (though it must be admitted that some of her information about him is contradictory). The emergence of the Ottoman dynasty brought the Turks into a closer and more urgent relationship with Byzantium; and inevitably the Byzantine writers give more and more attention to their formidable neighbours and future conquerors.

It has been calculated that if we include the century after the conquest of Constantinople there are close on forty Greek authors or collections of documents which contain information about the Ottoman Turks. Many of these are chronicles of the Turkish Sultans written in Greek in the sixteenth century, of which the most important is a History of the Turks from 1373 to 1512, only extant in one unpublished manuscript (Vatican-Barberini 111), which contains information not found elseswhere, for example about the Nicopolis and Varna campaigns. There is also a group of chronicles based on the so-called *Ekthesis chronike* (of which the original manuscript ends in 1517) which includes a later version by Malaxos and Dorotheos of Monemvasia and a verse version by Hierax. This group is useful for some precise chronological details. There are one or two Patriarchal chronicles, interesting for their evidence about the Conqueror's establishment of the Greek *millet*; and there are a number of chronicles based on earlier histories, especially on the work of Laonicos Chalcocondyles.

It would take too long to list these minor works. There are, however, seven major historians of the fourteenth and fifteenth centuries who make a serious contribution to Ottoman history. First is George Pachymer, who was born in Nicaea in 1242 and died in Constantinople in 1310, shortly after having completed a history that covers the period from 1261 to 1308. Next is John Cantacuzenos, who usurped the Imperial throne in 1341, was eventually crowned in 1347 and forced to abdicate in 1355. He retired to Mount Athos and there wrote a history of his times, from 1320 to 1356. Contemporary with him with Nicephoros Gregoras, who was born in Paphlagonia in 1295 and died in 1359 or 1360, having written, amongst many other works, a history of Byzantium from 1204 to 1359. Then there is a gap, till we come to the four Byzantine historians of the Fall of Constantinople. These are George Phrantzes, who was born in Constantinople in 1401 and died in 1478 in Corfu, where he had written a history dealing with the period from 1258 to 1477—there also exists a shorter version beginning at 1413;—Ducas (whose Christian name is unknown, as are the dates of his birth and death), a Greek from Western Anatolia, whose History covers the years from 1204 to 1462: Laonicos Chalcocondyles, who was born in Athens in 1432 and died in Crete in 1490 and whose History stretches from the Creation, and in more detail from the late thirteenth century, to 1478; and Hermodoros Michael Critobulos, who was born on Imbros in about the year 1405 and died on Mount Athos after 1470 and who wrote a history of the reign of Sultan Meḥemmed II, from 1451 to 1467.

All these seven historians are of major importance for early Ottoman history. The earliest of them, Pachymer, was the contemporary of 'Os̲mān. He is not an easy writer to read. His style is verbose and he loves neo-Classicisms; for example, he calls the months by their Attic names, and the Turks the Persians; and his main interests were domestic, especially theological. But he wanted to give a full picture of the careers of the Emperors Michael VIII and Andronicus II. He was therefore obliged to take note of the situation among the Turks. He made a serious attempt to disentangle the various local Turkish dynasties. His story of the career of 'Os̲mān (whom he calls Atman) is factual and reliable. Though his evidence is restricted to the occasions on which the Turks impinged on Byzantine politics, it is useful and indeed more indispensable than most Turkish historians are ready to admit.

Our next historian, the Emperor John Cantacuzenos, was the man who was actually responsible for the Turks' first settlement in Europe. It was no doubt inevitable that the Turks would soon cross into Thrace; but John definitely invited them in order to have their help in a civil war. During all the period covered by his History John was the most prominent political figure in Byzantium; and though he wrote in retirement, he seems to have kept copious notes. His book is an apologia; and the facts are interpreted in a manner to justify himself and his friends and discredit his enemies. But the facts themselves seem reliable. In consequence he provides an invaluable account of all the military and diplomatic relations between Byzantium and the Turks which occurred in his time. He seems to have thought the Turks less dangerous to the Empire than the Serbians, and to have had no strong feelings against them and their religion. Amongst his other works is a Defence of Christianity, against Islam, written for a Turkish friend who had become a convert to Christianity, in which he tried honestly to understand the Muslim point of view.

John's story is confirmed by the History and supplemented by the many letters written by Nicephoros Gregoras, who took an opposing view of politics. He has a little less to tell us about the Ottoman Turks, though like Pachymer, he tries to straighten out in his mind the various Turkish states still extant in Anatolia. But he seems to have regarded them as the chief danger for the Empire. He disliked them. When he tells of John marrying his daughter to Orkhān as the price of the Sultan's alliance, he refers to it as a wholly shameful thing, whereas John himself glosses it over as a splendid affair and dilates upon his daughter's loyalty to Christianity. With the two accounts to check each other we have a full account of

Orkhān's reign, at least as regards his relations with the various Christian powers. It is all the more valuable because of the lack of many good Turkish sources on the period.

For the second half of the fourteenth century we are dependent on the Byzantine side on Phrantzes, Ducas, and Chalcocondyles. All three of them, writing after the Ottoman Conquest, were interested in Ottoman history; and all three had some experience of the Sultan's Court before the Conquest. But while they are reliable on Byzantine affairs, where they had been able to consult the city records up to the Conquest, for early Ottoman affairs they accepted the legends current in their time about the dynasty, giving it an exalted origin and various legendary accretions of doubtful credibility. Indeed, Chalcocondyles can be blamed more than anyone else for a fanciful account of Ottoman origins which was accepted in the West for many centuries.

Phrantzes belonged to the Byzantine nobility and was married to a connection of the Imperial family. As a young man he was patronized by the Emperor Manuel II, and he became the most intimate friend of Manuel's son, Constantine, the last Emperor. He represented each of them on different occasions at the Sultan's Court, going once also as special envoy of the Empress Helena, Manuel's wife, to Sultan Murād II, with whom she claimed kinship, apparently because she was related to Despina of Serbia, his grandfather's favourite wife. Phrantzes learnt at the Turkish Court how to use Turkish titles; and the long account that he inserts on early Turkish history is derived, he says, partly from written sources but mainly from what 'wise men'—presumably the Sultan's elder courtiers—told him. He reproduces roughly the same legends as Chalcocondyles. He shows, however, considerable ignorance about the Qur'ān and the Prophet. For the events of his own lifetime Phrantzes is a valuable guide, because of his close connection with the Imperial family. Alone of the Byzantine historians he was present at the siege and fall of Constantinople. He escaped from the city alive and was able to ransom his wife; but his two children were captured and put to death by the Turks. His account of the last years and the end of the Empire is that of an honest well-informed and intelligent eyewitness, but is coloured by a bitter hatred of the Turks.

The historian Ducas was also of good family. His grandfather had been involved in a conspiracy in 1341 and had fled to the court of the *amīr* of Aydîn; and it seems likely that Ducas was born and grew up in Turkish-controlled territory, as his grandfather refused to return when he could to Europe, believing that the Turks would soon conquer the whole Balkan peninsula, so he might just as well stay in Asia. Ducas seems to have spent some time in Smyrna, and his geographical knowledge gives especial value to his account of the Turkish wars in that district in the fourteenth century. Ducas nowhere attempts to give a consecutive history of the Turks, but he often describes Turkish institutions. In particular he gives the first full account of the organization of the Corps of Janissaries. His literary style might almost be called journalese; it is straightforward and readable, though not always elegant. He had his prejudices. He regarded the Turks as the great enemy, and he was not fair to the Greeks who did not share his view that an alliance with the West must be sought, whatever the religious price. Otherwise, as far as we can judge, he is a remarkably careful and reliable historian.

Chalcocondyles conceived of his work more as a history of the growing Turkish Empire than of Byzantium. He, like Ducas, did not like the Turks and believed that Byzantium should have allied itself with the West; but he was not a bigot and he had wide interests. Though the Turks form his main theme he makes lively if inaccurate digressions into western European history, and, in a not unsuccessful imitation of Herodotus, shows some skill in arranging his narrative so that it is never dull, though his style, too obviously based on Thucydides, is selfconscious and unattractive. As a historian his importance is that he is the first to attempt a history of the Turks. For early Ottoman history he seems to have known the same legends as Phrantzes, probably derived, similarly, from traditions current at the time at the Turkish Court, which was anxious to give the dynasty a grander origin than it actually possessed. He seems to have been the first extant historian to pretend that 'Os̱mān was the great-grandson of Duzalp, chief of the Og̱ẖuz nation, also to tell of the dream that turned Ertog̱ẖrul into a good Muslim. These stories appear in more or less the same form in the Ottoman writers of the sixteenth century. We obviously cannot regard him as a trustworthy source on early Ottoman history, especially as his chronology is sometimes vague and even inconsistent; but he does probably reproduce fairly accurately what the Turks of the fifteenth century had begun to believe about their past. His descriptions of the Ottoman financial and military organization of his time can be taken as reliable.

Critobulos is of a lesser stature than the other three. Like Chalcocondyles he determinedly copied the style of Thucydides, inventing long orations to put into his characters' mouths; but his language is even more forced. His importance is that he belonged to the party among the Greeks who saw that Ottoman dominion had come to stay and who believed in adjusting themselves as best as possible to altered circumstances. He clearly intended that his work should give pleasure to the Conquering Sultan, who features throughout as a gallant and gracious monarch, well disposed to his Christian subjects. In his account of the siege and fall of the City he is moved by the courage of the Greeks, but suggests that it was misplaced and wasted. But as a historian he is careless and inaccurate. He is useful because of some of the details that he is able to provide about the Siege from the Turkish viewpoint; and his account of the Sultan's campaigns after 1453 is of value. But it is above all as a representative of anti-Western Greeks that he is of interest.

Among minor Byzantine historical works of the time there is an account by John Cananos of Murād II's siege of Constantinople in 1422. It is a straightforward narrative written in popular language by a simple and rather superstitious man, whose main theme is that the Holy Virgin would not allow the City to fall to the infidel. More sophisticated—and written in grander and less readable language—is the account by John Anagnostes of the Turkish capture of Thessalonica in 1430. Historically it is a sober and reliable narrative of the events leading up to the fall of the town.

A large number of Byzantine orations and letters of the period have survived, which give some idea of the atmosphere of the Empire faced as it was by the growing encroachment of the Turks. The funeral oration over Andronicus II, made by Theodore Metoechites in 1328, is of interest as being the first definite statement by a Byzantine statesman of the seriousness of the Turkish menace. The more important letter-writers who make constant references to the Turks are Demetrios Cydones and Nicephoros Gregoras in the fourteenth century and the Emperor Manuel II at the turn of the century; and there are letters written just after 1453 which throw a light on the fate of the Greeks who survived the siege, as, for example, some of the humanist Filelfo who writes from Florence to relate the difficulties that he had to rescue his wife's relatives from captivity. He found it necessary to send off a laudatory ode to the Sultan. References to the Turks also occur in various controversial works dealing with political and theological matters within Byzantium. For example the philosopher Plethon illustrates an argument by referring to a detail (actually inaccurate) of Ottoman genealogy; and it is indeed possible that his political theories were influenced by his personal acquaintance with the organization of the *futuwwa*. But it must be confessed that none of these references add substantially to our historical knowledge.

The contributions of the Byzantines to Ottoman historiography lies in the works of these seven last great Byzantine historians. Early Ottoman history is not very well served by its Turkish sources. In spite of the work of distinguished modern Turcologists there are still obscure and controversial patches. These Greek historians, if used with proper caution, can each of them throw some light on it all. It must, however, be added that each of them, with the exception of Chalcocondyles and, to a lesser extent, of Critobulos, is badly in need of a new edition. The manuscripts of the other six have not been adequately collated, and in the only published editions, in the Migne *Patrologia* and the Bonn series, they are provided with Latin translations of remarkable inaccuracy; and, such are the ways of historians, the inaccuracies have far too often been copied and perpetuated by scholars who have not troubled to study the original Greek.

24. RENAISSANCE HISTORICAL LITERATURE IN RELATION TO THE NEAR AND MIDDLE EAST (WITH SPECIAL REFERENCE TO PAOLO GIOVIO)

V. J. PARRY

Lecturer in the History of the Near and Middle East, School of Oriental and African Studies, London

The Renaissance—here understood to embrace the fifteenth and sixteenth centuries—has bequeathed to us an extensive and varied historical literature relating to the lands and peoples of the Near and Middle East. An attempt to review this literature in detail would tend, within the dimensions of this present paper, to become a tedious catalogue of names and titles. It will be more convenient therefore to indicate some of the main categories of material, with the obvious proviso, however, that the classification given below is not intended to delimit in full, but merely to illustrate our field of inquiry:[1]

(*a*) the reports of ambassadors—e.g., of Contarini or of Busbecq.

(*b*) the narratives of men who had been members of an ambassadorial retinue—e.g., of Dernschwam, Pigafetta and Wratislaw.

(*c*) the reports of captives of war who had remained long in the service of the Ottoman Sultan—e.g., of Schiltberger and of Angiolello.

(*d*) the '*Ordo Portae*' type of literature, which describes the political, religious, and social institutions of the Ottoman empire—e.g., the writings of Iacopo de Promontorio de Campis, of the anonymous Ragusinus and of Menavino.

(*e*) the collections of letters, reports, documents, etc.—e.g., of Reusner or in publications like the '*Tesoro Politico*'.

(*f*) the pamphlets and periodical literature—e.g., the *Zeitungen* which were issued twice a year at the Frankfurt Fairs and contained the latest news, intelligence reports, captured correspondence, lists of casualties, etc., received from couriers, government officials, soldiers, and even from 'war correspondents' at the Hungarian front.

(*g*) the first-hand accounts of particular events or episodes—e.g., of Coriolano Cippico or of the anonymous Italian who, in 1538, served with the Ottoman fleet sent against the Portuguese at Diu in western India.

[1] There is no single, comprehensive study of Renaissance historical literature. Notes on some of the better-known authors will be found, however, in (*a*) E. Fueter, *Geschichte der neueren Historiographie*, (München, Leipzig, 1911), and (*b*) B. R. Reynolds, 'Latin Historiography: A Survey 1400–1600', in *Studies in the Renaissance* (Publications of the Renaissance Society of America) (New York, 1955), ii, 7–66. Cf. also the bibliographical indications given in F. Chabod, *Machiavelli and the Renaissance* (London, 1958), pp. 242–4.

(*h*) the histories of specific wars, battles, sieges, etc., written at second-hand, but on the basis of authentic, and often eyewitness, material—e.g., of Bizarus and of Minadoi.

(*i*) the more general histories devoted partly or wholly to the lands and peoples of the Near and Middle East—e.g., of Giovio and of Knolles.

(*j*) the literature of political comment and analysis—e.g., of such authors as Busbecq, Folieta, Tarducci, and Soranzo.

(*k*) the literature of pilgrimage and travel—e.g., the narratives of men as diverse in origin and character as Fabri, von Harff, de Breves, and Sanderson.[2]

[2] Cf. in relation to the authors and works mentioned in the above classification: (i) *Il Viaggio del Magnifico M. Ambrosio Contarini Ambasciadore della Illustrissima Signoria di Venetia al Gran Signore Ussuncassan Re di Persia nell'anno MCCCCLXXIII*, in G. B. Ramusio, *Delle Navigationi et Viaggi* vol. ii; (Venice, 1559), (ii) C. T. Forster and F. H. B. Daniell, *The Life and Letters of Ogier Ghiselin de Busbecq* (London, 1881); (iii) *Hans Dernschwam's Tagebuch einer Reise nach Konstantinopel und Kleinasien (1553–1555)*, ed. F. Babinger (München, Leipzig, 1923); (iv) M. A. Pigafetta, *Itinerario a Costantinopoli* (London, 1585)—text also to be found in *Starine na sviet izdaje Jugo-slavenska Akademija Znanosti i Umjetnosti*, Knjiga XXII (Zagreb, 1890) pp. 70–194; (v) A. H. Wratislaw, *The Adventures of Baron Wratislaw of Mitrowitz* (London, 1862); (vi) *The Bondage and Travels of Johann Schiltberger (1396–1427)*, Hakluyt Society (London, 1879) (see also the edition of V. Langmantel in the *Bibliothek des Literarischen Vereins in Stuttgart* (Tübingen, 1885), vol. clxxii, based on the Nuremberg MS.); (vii) *Breve Narratione della Vita et Fatti del Signor Ussuncassano, fatta per Giovanni Maria Angiolello*, in G. B. Ramusio, op. cit., No. (i) above (Venice, 1559), vol. ii; (viii) F. Babinger, *Die Aufzeichnungen des Genuesen Iacopo de Promontorio-de Campis über den Osmanenstaat um 1475*, in *Bayerische Akademie der Wissenschaften*: *Sitzungsberichte* (*Phil.-Hist. Klasse*), Jahrgang 1956, Heft 8 (München, 1957); (ix) *Catalogus Librorum Bibliothecae Tigurinae* (Zürich, 1809), vi, 398: *De Origine, Ordine et Militari Disciplina Magni Turcae domi forisque habita Libellus* (Ragusini cujusdam, ed. Conradus Adelman ab Adelmansfelden), s.l. et a. (text reprinted in T. Bibliander, *Machumetis Sarracenorum Principis Vita ac Doctrina, quae . . . et Alcoranum dicitur* (Basle, 1543, 1550), iii, 100–6); (x) *I Costumi et la Vita de Turchi di Gio. Antonio Menavino* (Florence, 1551); (xi) N. Reusner, *Epistolarum Turcicarum Libri XIV* (Frankfurt am Main, 1598–1600); (xii) *Thesoro Politico . . . in cui si contengono Relationi, Istruttioni, Trattati, et varij Discorsi, pertinenti alla . . . Ragion di Stato* (Pts. I and II: Milan, 1600–1; Pt. III: Tournon, 1605); (xiii) F. Stieve, *Ueber die ältesten halbjährigen Zeitungen oder Messrelationen* (*Bayerische Akademie der Wissenschaften*: *Abhandlungen, Hist. Classe*, Bd. XVI (München, 1883), pp. 177–265); (xiv) M. A. H. Fitzler, *Die Entstehung der sogenannten Fuggerzeitungen in der Wiener Nationalbibliothek* (*Veröffentlichungen des Wiener Hofkammerarchivs*, (1937), vol. ii); (xv) B. Kertbeny, *Ungarn betreffende deutsche Erstlingsdrucke, 1454–1600* (Budapest, 1880); (xvi) C. Cippico, *De Petri Mocenici Imperatoris Gestis Libri Tres* (Basle, 1544) (also in K. Sathas, *Documents Inédits relatifs à l'Histoire de la Grèce au Moyen Age* (Paris, 1888), vii, 262–302); (xvii) *Viaggio et Impresa che fece Solyman Bassà . . . per racquistar la Città di Diu in India* (printed in A. Manuzio, *Viaggi fatti da Vinetia alla Tana, in Persia, in India, et in Costantinopoli* (Venice, 1543), fol. 159r–180r); (xviii) P. Bizarus, *Cyprium Bellum* (Basle, 1573) (in effect, a translation of G. Sozomeno, *Narratione della Guerra di Nicosia* (Bologna, 1571), and of N. Martinengo, *Relatione di tutto il successo di Famagosta* (Venice, 1572)); (xix) G. T. Minadoi, *Historia della Guerra fra Turchi et Persiani* (Venice, 1588, 1594); (xx) P. Giovio, *Historiarum Sui Temporis Libri XLV* (Florence, 1550–2; Paris, 1558–60); (xxi) R. Knolles, *The Generall Historie of the Turkes . . . Together with The Lives and Conquests of the Othoman Kings and Emperours* (London, 1603, 1610); (xxii) The *De Re Militari contra Turcam instituenda Consilium* of A. Busbequius (Leipzig, 1595); (xxiii) the *De Causis Magnitudinis Imperii Turcici*, of U. Folieta (Leipzig, 1595); (xxiv) the *Turco Vincible in Ungaria*, of A. Tarducci (Ferrara, 1597); (xxv) the *Ottomanno*, of L. Soranzo (Ferrara, 1599); (xxvi) F. Fabri, *Evagatorium in Terrae Sanctae, Arabiae et Egypti peregrinationem*, ed. C. D. Hassler, in the *Bibliothek des Literarischen Vereins in Stuttgart* (Stuttgart, 1843), vols. ii–iv; (xxvii) *The Pilgrimage of Arnold von Harff, 1496–1499* (Hakluyt Society: London, 1946); (xxviii) *Relation des Voyages de M. de Breves,*

It is a notable fact that, in all this wealth of material, there are few works which can be described as general histories of the Arab lands or of Persia.[3] Information about the earlier centuries of Muslim rule in these countries could be obtained at this time only from the Byzantine historians and the Latin chronicles of the Crusades, i.e., from sources inadequate in their data and often difficult of access, most of them remaining as yet in manuscript form.[4] Moreover, with the fall of the Mamluk Sultanate in 1516–17, there was left in the Arab world no Muslim state capable of acting as an effective counterpoise to the dominance of the Turks and thus of arousing the sustained and, as it were, separate attention of the Christians. Events in Egypt and Syria came therefore, after 1517, to be regarded not so much in their own right as within the broad context of Ottoman affairs. Persia, it is true, continued to be a strong and independent state. The belief that in the armies, first of the Ak Koyunlu, and later of the Safavids there might be found an apt instrument to hinder the Ottoman advance against Christendom became engrained in the political consciousness of Europe. This attitude of mind led the men of the Renaissance to interest themselves above all in the various wars which broke out between the Ottoman empire and Persia during the fifteenth and sixteenth centuries, i.e., to write about Persia as a declared foe of the Turks rather than as an object of interest in itself. Difficulties of communication also constituted yet another restrictive influence. The Portuguese alone of the Christian nations had a direct, close and continuous contact with Persia before 1600. It was not until the relative isolation of Persia had been overcome in the period following the arrival of the English and the Dutch in the Indian Ocean that a more intimate and detailed knowledge of the Safavid régime could be made available in Europe.[5]

tant en Grece, Terre-Saincte, et Aegypte, qu'aux Royaumes de Tunis et Arger. Le tout recueilly par le Sieur Du Castel (Paris, 1628, 1630); (xxix) *The Travels of John Sanderson in the Levant, 1584–1602* (Hakluyt Society: London, 1931).

[3] Cf. (*a*) N. Zeno, *Trattato dell'Origine et Costumi degli Arabi*, in F. Sansovino, *Historia Universale dell'Origine et Imperio de' Turchi* (Venice, 1560–61, 1568, 1573, 1582, 1600); (*b*) C. Augustinus Curio, *Sarracenicae Historiae Libri Tres* (Basle, 1567, 1568 and Frankfurt am Main, 1596); and (*c*) P. Bizarus, *Rerum Persicarum Historia* (Antwerp, 1583; Frankfurt am Main, 1601).

[4] Cf. E. Gerland, *Das Studium der byzantinischen Geschichte vom Humanismus bis zur Jetztzeit* (*Texte und Forschungen zur byzantinisch-neugriechischen Philologie*, No. 12: Athens, 1934). It should also be noted that some of the Latin chronicles relating to the Crusades were in fact available at this time in printed form: e.g., the *Historia Belli Sacri*, of William of Tyre, ed. H. Pantaleon (Basle, 1564) and the *Chronicon Hierosolymitanum*, ed. R. Reineccius (Helmaestadii, 1584). On the growth of Arabic studies in general, see J. Fück, 'Die arabischen Studien in Europa vom 12. bis in den Anfang des 19. Jahrhunderts', in *Beiträge zur Arabistik, Semitistik und Islamwissenschaft*, edd. R. Hartmann and H. Scheel (Leipzig, 1944), and also K. H. Dannenfeldt, 'The Renaissance Humanists and the Knowledge of Arabic' (*Studies in the Renaissance* (cf. note 1 above) (New York, 1955), ii, 96–117).

[5] It is not fortuitous that the most detailed Western sources relating to Safavid Persia appeared only after 1600: e.g., the *Journal du Voyage du Chevalier Chardin en Perse* (London, 1686; first complete edition, Amsterdam, 1711).

The case was far different in regard to the Turks. There existed a close and constant intercourse between the Christian states and the Ottoman Empire. Ambassadors and their retinues, sailors, and merchants came more and more frequently from Europe to the Porte and to the markets of the Levant. Ottoman armies, long since entrenched on Balkan soil, now battered at the gates leading into the German and Italian lands. The old ideal of a Christendom which should unite, irrespective of race and language, all nations professing the true faith was not yet dead in Europe. The call to arms against the Infidel was an appeal that continued to bring numerous volunteers, both Protestant and Catholic, to serve on the Hungarian front.[6] Resistance to the Turk could still be described in 1594 as a conflict fought 'pro aris et focis, pro patria et religione'.[7] The Ottomans were, to the Christians of this time, 'the greatest terrour of the World',[8] overshadowing in peace and war alike the entire horizon in the East. Almost all that Renaissance Europe knew about the Islamic lands came to it coloured and filtered through an Ottoman medium. Muslim was now a term synonymous with Turk. Even the Qur'ān had been transformed into the *Alcoranum Turcicum*, so marked and pervasive was the impact of the Ottomans on the Christian mind.[9] It is not surprising therefore to find that in the literature of the Renaissance far more attention was given to the Turks than to the Arabs or the Persians.

The literature of the Renaissance devoted to the lands and peoples of the Near and Middle East consists, in large degree, of memoirs relating to particular episodes or events, political commentaries, travel-accounts, and the like, i.e., of works which cannot be regarded as true histories in the fullest sense of the phrase, but are rather the raw material of the genuine historian. Amongst the authors relevant to our present theme there are few who wrote with an amplitude of range, of vision and design sufficient, in our modern view, to raise them from the rank of mere annalist to the more honourable status of historiographer. It will not be inappropriate therefore to concentrate our attention on one such author, whose main work deals at great length with Muslim affairs and also illustrates well some of the more notable characteristics of Renaissance historiography.

Paolo Giovio (1483–1552) studied at Pavia and Padua, went later to Rome and there won the favour of Pope Leo X. He remained in the papal service during the pontificates of Adrian VI, Clement VII, and Paul III,

[6] See, e.g., S. Schardius, *Historicum Opus* (Basle, 1574), iv, 2301: 'Fuere et ex Anglica nobilitate qui suis sumptibus hanc militiam sequerentur' (a reference to English noblemen who, at their own expense, followed the Imperialist forces during the campaign of Szigetvár in 1566).

[7] Cf. *Briefe und Acten zur Geschichte des Dreissig-Jährigen Krieges in den Zeiten des vorwaltenden Einflusses der Wittelsbacher, IV*: F. Stieve, *Die Politik Baierns (1591–1607)*, Erste Hälfte (München, 1878), p. 198, n. 2.

[8] Cf. R. Knolles, op. cit., n. 2, No. (xxi) above: Induction to the Christian Reader, (ii).

[9] Cf., e.g., Knolles, op. cit. (1603): Induction to the Christian Reader, (vi), where the author names amongst his sources the '*Alcoranum Turcicum*'.

was made Bishop of Nocera dei Pagani in 1528 and spent the last years of his life at Florence under the protection of the Medici prince Cosimo I.[10] Three books of Giovio must be mentioned here: (i) *Commentario delle cose de' Turchi*;[11] (ii) *Elogia Virorum bellica virtute Illustrium*;[12] and (iii) *Historiarum Sui Temporis Libri* XLV,[13] which, since it is the magnum opus of Giovio, will be hereafter the object of our special attention.

Few historians have been submitted to censure and praise in such varied measure as Paolo Giovio. Criticism, whether hostile or favourable, has rested to a large degree, however, on the *Historia* and, within this work, on the account given of events in western Europe. The numerous pages in the *Historia* which treat of Muslim affairs have received little notice. Adverse comment was directed against the *Historia* soon after its first appearance in 1550–52. The Florentine Donato Giannotti considered it to have been written 'per buffoneria'.[14] Jean Bodin, too, helped to bring it into disrepute, arguing that Giovio wrote much about the Persians, the Abyssinians, and the Turks which he could not know to be true, since he gave credence to mere rumour; Bodin also declared that Giovio, refusing to limit himself to those things which he could have known well, preferred to treat of matters beyond his competence and, in addition, committed the crime of prostituting his labour for base and material ends, thus acquiring unmerited rewards far greater than those which fell to other historians who set down nothing but the simple truth.[15] Credulous and venal—such, in substance, was the verdict on Giovio of some amongst his near

[10] On the career and works of Giovio, see (*a*) G. Sanesi, 'Alcune Osservazioni e Notizie intorno a Tre Storici Minori del Cinquecento (Giovio, Nerli, Segni)', in *Archivio Storico Italiano*, ser. V, (Florence, 1899), xxiii, 260–88; (*b*) E. Fueter, op. cit., note 1 above, pp. 51–5; (*c*) A. Morel-Fatio, *Historiographie de Charles Quint* (Paris, 1913), pp. 105–22; (*d*) L. Rovelli, *L'Opera Storica ed Artistica di Paolo Giovio Comasco Vescovo di Nocera* (Como, 1928); (*e*) C. Panigada, *Le Vite del Gran Capitano e del Marchese di Pescara* (Bari, 1931), pp. 477 ff.; (*f*) B. Croce, *Scritti di Storia Letteraria e Politica, vol. XXV*: *Conversazioni Critiche*, ser. III (Bari, 1932), pp. 296–308 ('Intorno a Paolo Giovio'); idem, *Scritti di Storia Letteraria e Politica, vol. XXXVI*: *Poeti e Scrittori del Pieno e del Tardo Rinascimento* (Bari, 1945), ii, 27–55 ('La Grandiosa Aneddotica Storica di Paolo Giovio'); (*g*) F. Chabod, 'Paolo Giovio', in *Periodico della Società Storica Comense* (1954), vol. xxxviii—an article not available to me for consultation.

[11] First published at Venice in 1531.

[12] First published at Florence in 1551. An edition illustrated with portraits appeared at Basle in 1575.

[13] Cf. note 2, No. (xx) above. The title will be abbreviated hereafter in these notes to *H.S.T.*, reference being made throughout to the Paris edition of 1558–60.

[14] Cf. G. Sanesi, op. cit., note 10 above, p. 262.

[15] Cf. J. Bodin, *Methodus ad Facilem Historiarum Cognitionem* (Paris, 1566), pp. 62–4 *passim*: '. . . refert multa de Persarum, Abissinorum ac Turcarum imperio: quae utrum vera sint, ne ipse quidem scire potuit, cum rumoribus fidem habuerit. . . . Quae igitur verissime scribere potuit, noluit puta res in Italia gestas, quae voluit, non potuit . . . hoc tamen acerbius est ac indignius, quod cum historiam venalem prostituisset, uberiores tulit mendacij fructus, quam quis alius vera scribendo . . .' (cf. J. Bodin, *Method for the Easy Comprehension of History*, trans. B. Reynolds (*Records of Civilization*: *Sources and Studies*, No. XXXVII) (New York, 1945), pp. 61 ff., *passim.*).

contemporaries. There is reason, however, to regard this condemnation as suspect: Giovio had not been afraid to criticize the actions of Florence and of France—and his chief detractors seem in fact to have been Florentine or French in origin and allegiance. It will be enough to mention here, as a counterpoise to these adverse comments, the view of a more recent historian, Leopold von Ranke, who, having examined much of the *Historia* in some detail, found that Giovio had not falsified his facts for venal purposes and that his work, though deficient in power of analysis, contained none the less a rich store of good information.[16]

Giovio tells us that he resolved to write the *Historia* because he might thus be able to perpetuate his name through the composition of a work which would be remembered and praised long after his own death—indeed, it was his sincere hope that some foretoken of such an enduring renown would be vouchsafed to him in his lifetime.[17] He does not describe in full the criteria that he followed in his choice and treatment of historical data, but contents himself with the general assertion that, being the friend of kings, popes, and captains famous in war, he has gathered from conversation with them those things which are set down, without favour as without hatred, in the *Historia*.[18] Much information might be gleaned about the methods of Giovio from his large correspondence, and also about the means through which he acquired his knowledge of Muslim affairs. His letters remain, however, uncollected and unedited, although it should be noted that a considerable number of them have been printed here and there at various times since his death.[19]

The influence of classical models is evident in the work of Giovio. It has been suggested in a recent article[20] that two diverse conceptions of history are discernible in the literature of Greece and Rome. The task of the historian, as exemplified by Thucydides, is to record and analyse events contemporaneous with himself, largely political and military in character, and originating within the society to which he belongs. His task, as illustrated by Herodotus, has a much less restricted scope, embracing the

[16] Cf. L. von Ranke, *Zur Kritik neuerer Geschichtsschreiber* (Leipzig, 1874), pp. 73, 76, 78.

[17] Cf. Giovio, *H.S.T.* (1558–60), Praefatio to Tome I ('. . . nihil beatius esse potest, quam nominis famam immortalibus invicti animi monumentis ad non incertam spem sempiternae laudis extendisse . . .') and Praefatio to Tome II ('. . . in hac vita aliquam mihi aeternitatis spem hoc tanto atque utilissimo labore percipiendam arbitrarer: quam mihi obventuram opto speroque. . . .').

[18] Cf. Giovio, *H.S.T.* (1558–60), Praefatio to Tome I ('. . . Maximorum autem regnum atque pontificum, insigniumque bello ducum familiaritatem ac amicitiam promeriti, ex eorum ore haec hausimus, quae amore vel odio nusquam distracti, fideli literarum memoriae mandavimus. . . .').

[19] Cf. (*a*) G. G. Ferrero, 'Per una nuova edizione delle lettere di Paolo Giovio', in *Giornale Storico della Letteratura Italiana* (Turin, 1939), cxiii, 225–55; and (*b*) idem, 'Politica e Vita Morale del '500 nelle lettere di Paolo Giovio', in *Memorie della Reale Accademia delle Scienze di Torino*, ser. 2, vol. 70, Pt. 2 (*Classe di Scienze Morali, Storiche e Filologiche*) (Turin, 1942), pp. 57–102.

[20] A. Momigliano, 'The Place of Herodotus in Historiography', in *History* (London, 1958), xliii, No. 147, 1–13.

history of the past and, with an emphasis on cultural and sociological phenomena, of states and peoples geographically remote from his own world. The divergent ideas of Thucydides and Herodotus, as outlined above, are to be seen, not dissociated but combined together, in the work of Giovio, and in such a manner as to determine some of its more notable and characteristic features. The *Historia* does in fact describe the great occurrences of his time (sui temporis), above all in the Christendom to which he belonged and with a special concern for the fields of politics and war.[21] It also deals, however, with a world of which Giovio had no direct and personal experience, i.e., with the contemporaneous affairs and, to some extent, the customs and traditions of the Muslim peoples in the Near and Middle East and in North Africa.

The influence of the Greek and Latin historians is also visible perhaps in the large, though not exclusive rôle that Giovio gives to oral evidence and, most certainly, in the rhetorical speeches which he attributes to various personalities prominent in his narrative.[22] It can be discerned, too, in occasional peculiarities of style: e.g., the Turks are sometimes called 'barbari' and the sultan 'tyrannus'—terms that do not reflect here a spirit of mere derogation arising from religious or cultural prejudice, but seem rather to retain some of the sense and flavour attached to them in the classical usage.[23]

Giovio does not seek, in the *Historia*, to vaunt the excellence of the Christian over the Muslim cause. He was convinced, however, of the need for united resistance to the danger which threatened Christendom from the East and deplored the madness of the Christian princes who, preoccupied with their wars and bitter rivalries, had failed to crush the power of the Ottomans, when it might still have been overcome, and had thus allowed it so to increase that in his own time it bade fair to win dominion over the entire world.[24] The fact that so much of the *Historia* is devoted to the Turks can be regarded as a sure indication of how imminent and real he felt the danger to be, and also as a sign of his respect and even admiration for the Ottoman achievement.[25]

[21] Cf. the articles of Croce listed in note 10 above: 'Paolo Giovio', p. 305, and 'Aneddotica', p. 38; also Ferrero, op. cit., note 19 (*b*) above, p. 63.

[22] Cf., e.g., *H.S.T.* (1558–60), Tome I, 143v–144r and 147v–148r (speeches attributed to Sultan Bāyezīd II and to his son Ḳorḳud).

[23] It should be noted that books 5–10 in Tome I and books 19–24 in Tome II of the *Historia Sui Temporis* are missing. Giovio has left us, however, epitomes of them—epitomes which he perhaps wrote (cf. Fueter, op. cit., note 1 above, p. 51) in conscious imitation of the summaries that replace for us the lost books of the *Historiae ab Urbe Condita* of the Roman historian Livius.

[24] Cf. Giovio, *H.S.T.* (1558–60), Tome II, 115r–v: '. . . nostrorum temporum conditionem deflere, Christianorumque principum insaniam detestari lubet, qui dum inter se bello aut odio dissident, ita Ottomannis parcunt, ut qui toties superari delerique potuerint, non immerito adaucta in immensum potentia, ad totius orbis imperium aspirent . . .'

[25] The folios of the *Historia Sui Temporis* that relate to Muslim affairs can be summarized thus: (*a*) Tome I: 1v–2r (general remarks on the East), 25r–26r (Jem Sulṭān in Christian hands),

There are long passages in the *Historia* which describe the origin and growth of tension between the Ottomans and the Safavids, the revolt of Shāh Kulī in 1511, and the great conflict begun in 1514. Giovio mentions here and there some of his sources of information: an Armenian named 'Cassinus', a letter from the Grand Master of the Knights of Rhodes to Pope Leo X, men who were present at the battle of Chaldirān in 1514, the reports of merchants and of certain Persians and Armenians.[26] He refers in the Commentario to men deserving of trust who witnessed the battle of Chaldirān, and in the Elogia to the Armenian Patriarch, who was well acquainted with Shah Ismā'īl.[27]

Giovio had read the 'relazioni' of various ambassadors, e.g., of '. . . Catarinus Zenus, Iosaphates Barbarus, et Ambrosius Contarenus

86v and 87v–88r (the Ottoman-Venetian war of 1499–1503), 132v–144v (rise of Shah Ismā'īl in Persia after 1499, troubles inside the Ottoman empire during the years 1511–12), 145r–163r (war between the Ottomans and the Persians, 1514–16), 194v–208v (Ottoman conquest of Syria, 1516), 209r–223r (Ottoman conquest of Egypt, 1517), 230v–231r, 232r, 233r, 235r–236r (the first years of the reign of Sultan Süleymān (1520–66): campaigns of Belgrade, Rhodes and Mohács); (*b*) Tome II: 61v–70r (Ottoman campaign against Vienna, 1529), 100r–103r, 103v–106r, 107r–109v, 110v–111r (Ottoman campaign of Güns, 1532), 114v–119r, 121r–123r (fall of Coron to Andrea Doria, 1532), 126r–128v (Ottoman recapture of Coron, 1533), 130v–133v (affairs of Transylvania, 1534), 134r–151v (Khayr al-Dīn Barbarossa, Ottoman campaign against Persia, 1533–1536), 151v–167r (expedition of the Emperor Charles V against Tunis), 182v–198v (Ottoman naval campaign against Diu in India, 1538; the Ottoman-Venetian war, 1537–40; the battle of Eszék, 1537), 205r–205v, 208r–215r (the sea campaigns in the Mediterranean and in the Indian Ocean, 1537–40), 239v–246v, 247v–254v (events in Hungary, 1540–1541), 255r–266r (Ottoman campaign in Hungary, 1541), 266v–276v (expedition of the Emperor Charles V against Algiers, 1541), 284r–286v (diplomatic relations between the Ottoman empire and France), 288r–296r (events in Hungary, 1541–43), 300r–301r (Khayr al-Dīn Barbarossa), 304r–312r (Ottoman campaign in Hungary, 1543), 317v–320r, 321v–326r (Khayr al-Dīn Barbarossa at Nice, affairs in North Africa, 1543–4), 337r–340v (the war at sea in the Mediterranean). The *Historia Sui Temporis*, measured in its full extent, embraces the years 1494–1547. It will be of some interest to note here that Giovio, because of his marked interest in Ottoman affairs, was accused of receiving gifts from Sultan Süleymān and from the Grand Vizier Rustem Pasha and, in compliance with their wishes, of so praising 'il valore, le forze, la prudenza, et ogn'altra virtù de' Turchi' as to make the Christians despair of success in their efforts to stem the tide of Ottoman conquest: '. . . che ancor da Solimano, et da Rusten Bassà egli havea doni per mezo del Capitan Polino, et di Mons. d'Aramon, Ambasciatori presso al Turco per il Re di Francia, et che però si veggia in quelle sue istorie essere stato cosi soverchiamente profuso nelle minutissime narrationi de' fatti Turcheschi, et così (com'essi dicono) affettatamente prender per tutto occasione di lodar tanto il valore, le forze, la prudenza, et ogn'altra virtù de' Turchi, che quasi ne venga in un certo modo a mettere in disperatione i Cristiani di potersi a lungo andare difender da essi che non occupino tutta la Cristianità . . .' (cf. *Istorie del suo Tempo di Mons. Paolo Giovio . . . tradotta per M. Lodovico Domenichi* (Venice, 1560): *Sopplimento di Girolamo Ruscelli nell'Istorie di Monsignor Giovio*, 1, and also 5–6 (arguments in defence of Giovio)).

[26] Cf. Giovio, *H.S.T.* (1558–60), Tome I, 154r–v ('. . . Cassinus natione Armenius qui huic bello interfuit . . . nobis indicavit . . .'), 156r ('. . . scripsit ad Leonem pontificem Fabritius Carrectus Rhodiae militiae magister, ad quem omnia haec diligentissime perferebantur . . .'), 156v)'. . . retulere qui huic praelio interfuerunt . . .'), 159v (' . . . non fabulosa . . . sed certa et explorata undique mercatoribus ac variis legationum commentariis illustrata . . .') and 222v ('. . . nos autem quum a Persis Armenisque hominibus talia quaereremus . . .').

[27] Cf. Giovio, *Commentario* (Venice, 1540), 20r ('. . . ho odito dire da uomini degni di fede quali si trovorno in questa battaglia . . .') and *Elogia* (Florence, 1551), 227 ('. . . tradunt autem Persae (ut ab Armenio Patriarcha qui Hismaelis familiaris fuit audivimus . . .) . . .').

legati in Armenia cum Ussumcassane . . .' and, in addition, the 'commentaria' of Giovanni Maria Angiolello, who, as an ex-captive of war returned to his native land after some years spent in the service of the Ottoman Sultan, recounted 'in Turchesco, et in Italiano' the campaign of Meḥemmed Fātiḥ against Uzun Ḥasan, the Ak Koyunlu master of Persia.[28] He was acquainted moreover with Donado da Lezze, the presumed author of a valuable *Historia Turchesca* incorporating material obtained, as it would seem, from Angiolello himself.[29] It must remain, in the absence of more detailed research, a matter of conjecture whether or not Giovio, through da Lezze, met and talked with Angiolello. There is, however, reason to believe that he came into personal contact with another Italian who had served under the Ottomans. Giovio declares in the *Historia* that 'Antonius Utrius Ligur' ('Giovanni Antonio da Utri Genovese' in the Italian translation of the *Historia*), one of the pages of Bāyezīd (1481–1512) and author of certain '*Commentaria*' relating to Ottoman affairs, gave him information about the death of the Sultan.[30] The author here mentioned is in fact

[28] Cf. Giovio, *H.S.T.* (1558–60), Tome I, 136v ('. . . Catarinus Zenus, Iosaphates Barbarus, et Ambrosius Contarenus legati in Armenia cum Ussumcassane . . . Ii enim diversa via totum Orientem pervagati, officiorum suorum ac itinerum commentarios posteris reliquerunt . . .'); *Commentario* (1540), 9r (Sultan Meḥemmed II (1451–81) '. . . fece gran careze a Gio. Maria Vicentino schiavo di Mustafa suo primogenito, il quale havea scritto in Turchesco, et in Italiano la vittoria havuta contra Usuncassano Re di Persia, qual noi havemo letta . . .'); and *Elogia* (1551), 149 ('. . . nam et commentaria rerum ab ipso gestarum a Liberto eius conscripta legimus . . .'). The 'relazioni' of the three ambassadors 'in Armenia' can be found in Manuzio, op. cit., note 2 above, No. (xvii) (this collection does not include the narrative of Zeno) and in Ramusio, op. cit., note 2 above, No. (i), vol. ii. The second volume of Ramusio also contains the *Breve Narratione della Vita et Fatti del Signor Ussuncassano, fatta per Giovanni Maria Angiolello*. Giovio seems to have been well acquainted with the historical literature available in his own time to a scholar interested in Muslim affairs—e.g., with such authors as William of Tyre and Marinus Barletius (cf. Giovio, *Elogia* (1551), 26 and 130), Sagundino, Pius II and Callimachus (cf. Giovio, *Commentario* (1540), 6v and 8r) and also Blondus Foroliviensis, Sabellicus and Paulus Aemilius (cf. Rovelli, op. cit., note 10 above, 74 ff.).

[29] Cf. Giovio, *Elogia* (1551), 29 ('. . . nobis communicavit Donatus Lectius patritii ordinis Venetus, diu in Cypro, Syriaque gestis Magistratibus, historiae et omnis antiquitatis studio clarus . . .'). See also *Historia Turchesca* (1300–1514), ed. I. Ursu (Bucarest, 1909) and, on Donado da Lezze himself, I Ursu, 'Uno Sconosciuto Storico Veneziano', in *Nuovo Archivio Veneto*, nuova serie, vol. xix (Venice, 1910), Parte I, 5–24. Da Lezze, in a letter of September 1514 mentions that he had received advice from Angiolello in regard to Ottoman affairs (cf. M. Sanuto, *Diarii*, edd. F. Stefani, G. Berchet and N. Barozzi, vol. xix (Venice, 1887), col. 57). Information also came to da Lezze from 'il vescovo di Armenia, nominato Davit' (cf. Sanuto, op. cit., vol. xv (Venice, 1886), col. 438 and vol. xx (Venice, 1887), cols. 245 and 268). Ursu ('Uno Sconosciuto Storico', 17) suggests that Giovio had access to the *Historia Turchesca* of da Lezze 'nell'originale stesso' and that his *Commentario* is in fact an abridged version of that chronicle. Cf., on Angiolello, (*a*) J. Reinhard, *Essai sur G. M. Angiolello* (Angers, 1913); (*b*) N. di Lenna, 'Ricerche intorno allo storico G. Maria Angiolello', in *Archivio Veneto-Tridentino*, vol. v (Venice, 1924), 1–56; (*c*) G. Weil, 'Ein unbekannter türkischer Transkriptionstext aus dem Jahre 1489', in *Oriens*, vol. vi (Leiden, 1953), 239–65; and (*d*) G. Weil, 'Ein verschollener Wiegendruck von Gio. Maria Angiolello', in the *Festschrift für Rudolf Tschudi*: *Westöstliche Abhandlungen*, ed. F. Meier (Wiesbaden, 1954), 304–14.

[30] Cf. Giovio, *H.S.T.* (1558–60), Tome I, 149r–v ('. . . Antonius Utrius Ligur a cubiculo Baiazetis, qui de his rebus commentaria ad Leonem pontificem conscripsit, referebat nobis . . .')

Giovanni Antonio Menavino, who wrote a well-known treatise printed at Florence in 1551 under the title *I Costumi et la Vita de Turchi.*[31] Among the informants of Giovio can also be numbered soldiers like Gian Giacomo Trivulzio and Giovanni Paulo Manfrone and scholars acquainted with the Ottoman milieu, e.g., Ioannes Lascaris.[32]

Giovio describes at some length the Ottoman conquest of Syria and Egypt (1516–17). He was able to consult men who had been at the battle of Raydāniyya in 1517 and also the Venetian 'Luigi Mozenigo', ambassador to the victorious Selīm I (1512–20) at Cairo.[33] Giovio notes, too, that Selīm I, before marching into Syria, had sent as ambassadors to the Mamluk Sultan Qānṣūh al-Ghūrī (1501–16) a soldier 'Iachis', and a 'Cadilescher', the latter of whom wrote an account of the ensuing war, which Giovio himself read in Italian.[34] This translation, made in 1517, came from the governor of Genoa to Gian Giacomo Trivulzio, and thence to Donado da Lezze, through the good offices of Caroldo, 'ducal secretario' to Trivulzio.[35]

The *Historia* contains various remarks indicating how and where Giovio acquired information about the Hungarian campaigns of Sultan Süleymān Qānūnī (1520–66). There are references to men who described from their own experience what the Sultan did at Buda in 1526 after the battle of Mohács; to a letter which Süleymān sent in 1532 from Güns to the Archduke Ferdinand of Austria and which Giovio saw at Vienna in that

and Domenichi, op. cit., note 25 above, Tome I, 353 ('. . . Giovanni Antonio da Utri Genovese paggio di Baiazet, il quale di queste cose scrisse alcuni commentari a Papa Leone, mi diceva . . .').

[31] A Latin translation of this work can be found in Tome I of P. Lonicerus, *Chronica Turcica* (Frankfurt am Main, 1578, 1584). Menavino is described on the title-page of the Florence edition (1551) as 'Genovese da Vultri'. Rovelli, op. cit., note 10 above, 73, refers to him as 'Antonio di Vetri'.

[32] Cf. Giovio, *Commentario* (1540), 11r and 11 v; also Giovio, *H.S.T.* (1558–60), Tome I, 143v.

[33] Cf. Giovio, *H.S.T.* (1558–60), Tome I, 207v ('. . . narrant qui huic praelio interfuere . . .'); also Giovio, *Commentario* (1540), 25v ('. . . mi diceva . . . Luigi Mozenigo . . . che essendo lui al Cayro Ambasciadore, appresso a Soltan Selim, et havendo molto ben praticato che nullo huomo era par ad esso in virtù, iustitia, humanità, et grandezza d'animo, et che non haveva punto del Barbaro . . .'). See in addition *Commentario* (1540), 26r: a reference to what Giovio had heard about Sultan Selīm.

[34] Cf. Giovio, *H.S.T.* (1558–60), Tome I, 197r (' . . . ad Campsonem legatos cum muneribus mittit. Cuius legationis principem locum obtinebant Iachis vir militaris et Cadilescher maiore sacerdotio et sacrarum literarum cognitione insignis. Hic postea huius belli commentaria conscripsit, quae nos Italico sermone donata perlegimus . . .'). The 'commentaria' here mentioned can be read in (*a*) Ramusio, op. cit., note 2, No. (i) above, vol. ii: *Breve Narratione . . . fatta per Giovanni Maria Angiolello*, chaps. XX–XXIII and (*b*) Sanuto, op. cit., note 29 above, vol. xxv (Venice, 1889), cols. 651–69 (Ramusio gives a somewhat shortened version of the Sanuto text). The Italian translation refers to the ambassadors of Sultan Selīm as a 'Cadi Lascher' and a certain 'Zachaia Bassa'. H. Jansky, 'Die Eroberung Syriens durch Sultan Selim I' (in *Mitteilungen zur osmanischen Geschichte*, vol. ii (Hannover, 1926), 173–241), 190 names the two Ottoman ambassadors as the 'Heeresrichter von Rumelien', 'Zirekzade Maulana Rukn eddin' and 'Karağa Paşa' (cf. also Ibn Iyās, *Badā'i' al-Zuhūr*, vol. iii (Būlāq, A.H. 1312), 40, and M. Sureyyā, *Sijill-i 'Osmānī*, vol. ii (Istanbul, A.H. 1311), 416).

[35] Cf. Ursu, 'Uno Sconosciuto Storico', op. cit., note 29 above, 19, note 4.

same year; to 'Nicolizza', i.e., Nikolas Jurischitz, who had offered a most stubborn and brilliant resistance to the Ottoman assault on Güns and later recounted to Giovio the story of the siege; to men who fought at the disastrous battle of Eszék in 1537 and, being ransomed from the Ottomans, gave to Giovio the data on which he based some portion, and perhaps the whole, of his own long and vivid narrative of the event; and, finally, to informants who had heard the Sultan himself speak about certain affairs relating to Transylvania.[36] Giovio also mentions elsewhere that he obtained an account of the siege of Strigonia (Gran) in 1543 from four renegades, Spanish and Majorcan, who had fled out of the Ottoman lines before the fortress.[37]

Giovio was able to learn much about the war at sea and in North Africa from men who had served under the famous Khayr al-Dīn, known to the Christians as Barbarossa. He refers to a Spaniard, 'Franciscus e Medelino Hispaniae oppido' and to 'Vincentius Catareus', a eunuch of Dalmatian origin who had received the Muslim name and status of 'Giafferagas'.[38] Further information came to Giovio from captives of war who described for him the character and abilities of the corsair Sinān the Jew; from the Emperor Charles V, who himself related to Giovio the events of the campaign against Tunis in 1535; from the Muslim prince 'Muleasses' whom the Emperor sought to maintain as a vassal at Tunis; and also from the Genoese admiral Andrea Doria and the captains who had fought under his command at the battle of Prevesa in 1538.[39]

[36] Cf. Giovio, *H.S.T.* (1558–60), Tome II, 62v ('. . . sicuti nos ab his qui interfuerunt accepimus . . .'), 104v ('. . . ut literas ad Ferdinandum Caesaremque deferrent: eas nos tum vidimus in oblongo et perangusto dentatae chartae volumine aureis atque caeruleis literis Arabice scriptas, obsignatasque aureo sigillo, et saculo purpureo inclusas . . .'), 105v ('. . . a quo demum obsidione liberato, Viennae eam rem longa percunctatione didicimus . . .'), 198r ('. . . sicuti nonnulli viri nobiles, et in his Laurentius Streytpergus et Dietmarus Losenstainus retulerunt, qui redempti reducesque . . . reversi sunt . . .') and 294v ('. . . Solymanus in hanc sententiam gravissime respondit, sicuti ab his qui sermoni interfuerunt didicimus . . .'). Further indications can be found in *H.S.T.* (1558–60), Tome II, 104v and 106r (references to information derived from captives of war) and in Giovio, *Commentario* (1540), 30r ('. . . ho inteso da huomini degni di fede che spesso dice (i.e., Sultan Süleymān) che a lui tocca di raggione l'Imperio di Roma, et di tutto Ponente per esser legittimo successore di Costantino . . .').

[37] Cf. Ferrero, op. cit., note 19 (*b*) above, 82 ('. . . . son venuti qua quattro renegati spagnoli e maiorchini fugiti dal campo turchesco da Strigonia, quali mi hano reso il conto verissimamente . . .'—a letter to the Cardinal Farnese, dated 28 August 1543, and now preserved in the State Archives of Parma).

[38] Cf. Giovio, *H.S.T.* (1558–60), Tome II, 164r ('. . . in his fuere Franciscus e Medelino Hispaniae oppido, et Vincentius Catareus Dalmata, defectae virilitatis eunuchus. Hic Giafferagas vocabatur. Illum a pueritia educatum, et Arabicas edoctum literas, Hariadenus in deliciis habuerat, et Memim appellabat . . .') and 165v ('. . . Medelinum autem et Giafferem . . . Barbarussae alumnos . . . a quibus postea multa de Barbarussae consiliis arcanisque moribus didicimus . . .'). V. Cian, 'Gioviana' (in *Giornale Storico della Letteratura Italiana*, vol. xvii (Turin, 1891), 277–357), 337 quotes from a letter of the Florentine Marco Bracci, who visited Giovio at Rome in 1546 and found him engaged in the task of answering a number of letters, amongst them 'una di Barbarossa'.

[39] Cf. Giovio, *H.S.T.* (1558–60): (*a*) Sinān the Jew: Tome II, 156r ('. . . haec in primo

The modern historian, well aware that oral evidence is often unreliable, will wonder how Giovio was able to distinguish between the true and the false in the stories told to him. There is indeed ample justification for the attitude of another Italian, G. T. Minadoi, who, impatient of the discrepancies to be found in the reports that reached him from the Levant, declined to continue his own work beyond the point where his personal knowledge of affairs in the East came to an end.[40] Giovio can claim, however, and with some justice, to have used the utmost care and diligence in gathering from princes, soldiers, ambassadors, and other conditions of men 'verissima notitia de le cose'.[41] As a member of the Papal Court at Rome he could, and did encounter people who had witnessed or were well informed about the great events of the age. Moreover, his large correspondence brought him additional news of a varied and often accurate character. It would be wrong, therefore, to approach his work in a spirit of excessive scepticism. An example drawn from the *Historia* will serve to illustrate this remark. Giovio, in describing the campaigns of Sultan Selīm I, argues that the Persian and the Mamluk horsemen surpassed in skill and valour the Ottoman *sipāhīs*, that the use of cannon and of the arquebus was a despicable and unchivalrous mode of warfare and that firearms constituted the decisive factor in the brilliant success of the Ottomans. The parallelism, in attitude and sentiment, between his own words and similar expressions in the Muslim chronicles which deal with these same events is so close as to suggest that Giovio,

congressu dicta fuisse ab his qui sermoni interfuerunt, didicimus . . .') and 338r ('. . . prudentia vero aequitateque iudicii facile superior, vel ipso captivorum testimonio, qui eum Barbarussa, uti saepe iracundo atque acerbissimo, mitiorem dominum experti fuissent . . .'); (*b*) the Emperor Charles V: Tome II, 162r ('. . . audivi ego postea a Caesare quum apud Neapolim mihi scripturo totius partae victoriae seriem enarraret . . .'); (*c*) 'Muleasses': Tome I, 216v ('. . . haec nobis scribentibus Muleasses rex Tunetanus . . . enarravit . . .') and Tome II, 138v ('. . . operaepretium erit paucis enarrare quae de Muleassis imperio moribusque Poenorum didicimus; nam multa digna cognitu quae diu solis mercatoribus comperta fuere, nobis scribentibus, victoria Caesaris aperuit . . .'), 165v ('. . . rex ipse postea me audiente . . . disserebat . . .'), 322r ('. . . sed ego postea ab ipso Muleasse regno pulso orbatoque luminibus didici . . .'), 325v ('. . . caeterum Muleasses . . . ut ipse aiebat . . .') and 326r ('. . . ab eo demum narrante multa literarum memoriae digna, de recentibus bellis, Punicisque rebus, et institutis didicimus . . .' and '. . . memorabant autem familiares eius . . .'); and (*d*) 'Auria', i.e., Andrea Doria: Tome II, 159v ('. . . ego postea ab ipso Auria accepi . . .'), 209v ('. . . Auria, sicuti haec eum postea narrantem audivi . . .') and 210r ('. . . uti postea confirmatione maiorum minorumque ducum, qui aderant, didicimus . . .'). Cf. also Giovio, *Elogia* (1551), 315 (on 'Muleasses': '. . . nobis ex eius humanitate perdiscere licuit, quae ad historiae nostrae fidem pertinebant . . .') and Giovio, *H.S.T.* (1558–60), Tome II, 320r (the opinion of the Marchese del Vasto on the military skill of the Ottomans). On the account, given in Giovio, of the Tunis campaign in 1535, cf. Morel-Fatio, op. cit., note 10 above, 108, 113–14 and G. Voigt, 'Die Geschichtsschreibung über den Zug Karls V gegen Tunis' (*Abhandlungen der Königlichen Sächsischen Gesellschaft der Wissenschaften*, vol. xvi (Leipzig, 1874), 161–243), 193 ff., 215 ff., 231–8.

[40] Cf. Minadoi, op. cit., note 2 above, No. (xix) (Venice, 1594), 364–5 ('. . . quanto a noi, stanchi delle diversitadi con cui udiamo gli avisi di Levante, non habbiamo havuto core di scrivere li successi dell'anno LXXXVII . . .').

[41] Cf. Giovio, *Commentario* (1540), Preface addressed to the Emperor Charles V.

at least in this case, was able to consult accurate sources of information.[42]

It has been said of Giovio that he was the first great journalist in the field of historical writing.[43] Another view is to the effect that he was a man interested above all in the wars of his own time and in the political circumstances which gave rise to them, a man little concerned with the institutions and internal affairs of the peoples about whom he wrote, and one who lacked, moreover, the breadth of vision and the deep insight into events that mark the great historian.[44] Attention has also been drawn, and in somewhat more favourable terms, to his awareness of how enlarged the horizon of international relations had become in his time and to his frequent use of chorographical and topographical data in order to make his narrative more clear and comprehensible.[45] The orientalist, bearing in mind the general tenor of these comments, will perhaps remain disinclined to regard Giovio as an author of importance. Such an attitude would be quite erroneous, if it did not recognize that the *Historia* contains, even at the lowest estimate, much material which can be used with advantage to complement the Muslim sources. A final verdict on Giovio is, however, not yet feasible in the absence of such desiderata as a collected edition of his letters and a critical analysis of those pages in the *Historia* which relate to the Near and Middle East.

There is little need to underline further the qualities that make Giovio an instructive example of the Renaissance historiographer. It will be, nevertheless, not unfitting to take leave of him with a last quotation illustrating that indefatigable zeal for first-hand knowledge which seems to have been so dominant in his character: he gives, in a letter written at Pisa during the final year of his life, a brief but vivid picture of himself with his room full of Moors from the ships in the harbour, so that he might acquire better information—'. . . io mi trovo spesso la camera piena di Mori, cima d'huomini, di quelli che stanno qui su le galee, per miglior informatione . . .'.[46]

[42] Cf. the references listed in *BSOAS*, vol. xxi (1958), 188–90 (a review of D. Ayalon, *Gunpowder and Firearms in the Mamluk Kingdom* (London, 1956).

[43] Cf. Fueter, op. cit., notes 1 and 10 above, 53 ff.

[44] Cf. the articles of Croce listed in note 10 above: 'Paolo Giovio', 304–5, and 'Aneddotica', 30, 31, 33, 38 ff.

[45] Cf. Ferrero, op. cit., note 19 (*b*) above, 63.

[46] Cf. *Lettere Facete et Piacevoli, raccolte per M. Dionigi Atanagi* (Venice, 1582), 88 (a letter dated 'il 18. di Gennaio, 1552').

25. THE TREATMENT OF ARAB HISTORY BY PRIDEAUX, OCKLEY AND SALE

P. M. HOLT

Reader in the History of the Near and Middle East in the University of London

Until the last years of the seventeenth century, writings upon the history of the Arabs had been, in England as in Europe generally, academic in their purpose and nature. As I have indicated in an earlier paper,[1] the study of Arab history was not in that period a specialized discipline; oriental studies had developed as ancillaries to Old Testament studies and ecclesiastical history and polemics. Few scholars were primarily interested in Arabic; still fewer made any significant investigations of Arab history. In comparison with his contemporaries, Pococke made an outstanding contribution to historical knowledge, and in his writings he displays the temperament of an historian—a notable achievement as will appear by contrast with some of his successors. Nevertheless Pococke's work was limited both in its scope and its impact. He produced no organized body of history: his publications consisted of the text and translation of two late Christian Arabic chronicles, and the erudite notes, not confined to history but ranging over the whole field of Arab antiquities and Muslim religion, which he appended to his *Specimen Historiae Arabum*. Translations and notes were alike in Latin, addressed to an academic audience rather than to the educated public at large. During the last twenty-eight years of Pococke's long life (1604–91), he was preoccupied with Hebrew and the writing of commentaries on the Minor Prophets. He made no further contributions to the study of Muslim history.

Humphrey Prideaux

Humphrey Prideaux,[2] born in 1648 in Cornwall, was a pupil at Westminster School under the celebrated Dr. Busby. This was of some importance, since Dr. Busby, who has lived on in popular fame as a flogging headmaster, was keenly interested in contemporary orientalism, and added Hebrew, Aramaic, and Arabic to the normal classical curriculum of his school.[3] In 1668 Prideaux went to Christ Church, Oxford, where in 1679

[1] P. M. Holt, 'The study of Arabic historians in seventeenth century England: the background and the work of Edward Pococke', *BSOAS* (1957), xix/3, 444–55.

[2] *Dictionary of National Biography*, xlvi, 352–4: article by Rev. Alexander Gordon.

[3] *The Diary of John Evelyn*, Everyman Edition (London, 1945), i, 357, entry of 13 May 1661: 'I heard and saw such exercises at the election of scholars at Westminster School to be sent to the

he became a lecturer in Hebrew. He left Oxford in 1686, when James II appointed a Roman Catholic as dean of Christ Church. The remainder of his life was spent in East Anglia. He had already been appointed a canon of Norwich in 1681; from 1688 to 1694 he was archdeacon of Suffolk, and from 1702 until his death in 1724 he was dean of Norwich. When Pococke died in 1691, Prideaux was offered the chair of Hebrew at Oxford, which he declined, and in 1697 he published his most famous work, *The true nature of imposture fully display'd in the life of Mahomet. With a discourse annex'd for the vindication of Christianity from this charge. Offered to the consideration of the Deists of the present age.* The book won an immediate success; there were two editions in 1697 and others subsequently, while a French translation was published in 1698.

The full title of Prideaux's work announces its polemical purpose and its appearance was closely connected with the theological controversies of the late seventeenth centuries. Prideaux had originally intended to publish a much larger work entitled *The History of the Ruin of the Eastern Church*, covering the period 602 to 936, from which he hoped to illustrate by example the dangers of theological disputes. The controversies of the Eastern church, Prideaux believed, 'wearied the Patience and Long-Suffering of God', so that 'he raised up the *Saracens* to be the Instruments of his Wrath, . . . who taking Advantage of the Weakness of Power, and the Distractions of Counsels, which these Divisions had caused among them, soon over-ran with a terrible Devastation all the *Eastern* Provinces of the *Roman* Empire.'[4] Prideaux saw in this a terrible warning to the sects in England after the Revolution of 1688: 'Have we not Reason to fear, that God may in the same Manner raise up some *Mahomet* against us for our utter Confusion . . . And by what the *Socinian*, the *Quaker*, and the *Deist* begin to advance in this Land, we may have Reason to fear, that Wrath hath some Time since gone forth from the Lord for the Punishment of these our Iniquities and Gainsayings, and that the Plague is already begun among us.'[5]

Prideaux's composition of this tract for the times was, however, abruptly suspended on the outbreak of the Trinitarian Controversy.[6] He feared that

University in Latin, Greek, Hebrew and Arabic, in themes and extemporary verses, as wonderfully astonished me in such youths, with such readiness and wit, some of them not above twelve, or thirteen years of age.' Letter from Edmund Castell to Samuel Clarke in 1667, Baker MSS., Cambridge University Library, Mm. 1. 47, p. 347: 'I also send you some papers from Dr. Busby, who . . . desires the cast of your eye, and your most exact censure, alteration, and emendation of the Hebrew, Chaldee, Arabique . . . Papers, which he sends to you, as also that you would, with his service, present them to Dr. Pococke . . . Our request is, that he would also be pleased to do the like with you, to read, censure, etc. with as much severity as may be.'

[4] Prideaux, *Life of Mahomet*, 8th edition (London, 1723), 'To the Reader', pp. vii, viii.

[5] Ibid., pp. xi–xii.

[6] For the Trinitarian Controversy, see E. M. Wilbur, *A History of Unitarianism in Transylvania, England, and America* (Harvard University Press, Cambridge, Mass., 1952), pp. 226–31.

his account of the dissensions in the Eastern Church might unintentionally provide fresh ammunition for those prowling enemies of the Establishment, 'the *Atheist*, the *Deist*, and the *Socinian*'. He therefore selected the passages of his work which dealt with the life of Muḥammad and published them in the form we have today.[7]

Prideaux may have had the intention of refuting an earlier work on the life of Muḥammad and the early history of Islam, which had been circulating for some years in manuscript. Its author, Henry Stubbs (alternatively Stubbes or Stubbe), who died in 1676, had also studied at Westminster under Busby, and had graduated at Oxford. He had served in the Parliamentary army during the Civil War. In later life he practised medicine. His book, which was not printed until 1911,[8] existed in several different rescensions[9] and is notable for its sympathetic attitude towards Islam. In essence it is an anti-Trinitarian tract, of some interest since it appears to be uninfluenced by Socinian doctrine and thus lies outside the main current of seventeenth-century Unitarian theology.[10] For his materials concerning Islam, Stubbs depended upon the translations and writings of Hottinger, Erpenius, Pococke, and others, and upon the accounts of travellers.

Prideaux's book is therefore a two-handed engine of controversy: not only is it intended to expose the errors of Islam (a traditional exercise of Christian apologists), but more immediately to point the contrast between the origins of Islam and Christianity, and thereby to constitute a defence of Christianity against contemporary Deism. For the Deists were Prideaux's particular obsession. As a controversialist, he does them less than justice, seeing in them merely followers of a fashionable belief that Christianity is an imposture.[11] Their one merit is that they, 'seeming to retain the common Principles of Natural Religion and Reason, allow a sufficient Foundation whereon to be discoursed with'. The atheist and the epicurean deist (who denies God's providence), by contrast 'do leave no Room for any Argument but that of the Whip and the Lash, to convince them of those impious Absurdities, and therefore deserve not by any other Method to be dealt with'.[12]

[7] Prideaux, pp. xiii–xiv.

[8] Henry Stubbe, *An account of the rise and progress of Mahometanism with the life of Mahomet and a vindication of him and his religion from the calumnies of the Christians* (London, 1911). The publication was subsidized from Muslim sources. Second edition, edited with an Introduction and Appendix, by Hafiz Maḥmud Khan Shariani (Lahore, 1954). I am obliged to Professor Fück for drawing my attention to this work.

[9] The manuscripts are listed in the Introduction to the second edition of the printed text. They include the following in the British Museum: (i) Sloane 1709, 1786: two fragments of a single manuscript; (ii) Harley 1876, 6189: two complete manuscripts.

[10] Stubbe is not mentioned in either of the two standard histories of Unitarianism, H. J. McLachlan, *Socinianism in seventeenth century England* (O.U.P., London, 1951); E. M. Wilbur, *op. cit.*

[11] For the Deists, see G. R. Cragg, *From Puritanism to the Age of Reason* (Cambridge, 1950), pp. 136–55.

[12] Prideaux, p. xv.

Prideaux's book consists of two parts; the first, entitled 'The Life of Mahomet' occupies 125 pages. The pagination continues for the second part, shortly entitled 'A Letter to the Deists, etc.', which has however a separate title-page. The final section (pp. 235–60) contains 'An Account of the Authors quoted in this Book.' I am not here concerned with the 'Letter to the Deists' which is, as it were, the sermon for which the preceding 'Life of Mahomet' is the text.

Prideaux's sources, and his use of them, are of some interest. He is anxious to present his biography as a well-documented work, so that he 'may not be thought to draw this Life of *Mahomet*, with Design to set forth his Imposture in the foulest Colours the better to make it serve (his) present purpose'. In his 'Account', Prideaux lists thirty-six Arabic authors or works, and makes a great display of their names in his footnotes. Upon examination, however, it becomes clear that his knowledge of them was derived at secondhand, from translations or quotations in the works of orientalists.

Three major works which he used were the printed editions (with Latin translations) of al-Makīn by Erpenius, Bar Hebraeus by Pococke, and Eutychius, also by Pococke.[13] For the Qur'ān, he appears to have relied chiefly on the twelfth-century Latin translation of Robert the Englishman, which had been printed by Bibliander in 1543.[14] He strongly criticizes this version as 'an absurd Epitome of it, . . . whereby the Sense of the Original is so ill represented, that no one can by the one scarce anywhere understand what is truly meant by the other'. Although a printed Arabic Qur'ān had recently become available[15] and is mentioned by Prideaux, he seems to have been unable to use it, since he says, 'Had he [the editor] added a *Latin Version*, he would have made it much more useful.' Prideaux also speaks of du Ryer's French translation[16] (of which he remarks 'it must be said that it is done as well as can be expected from one who was only a Merchant') and the faulty English version made from this by Alexander Ross.[17] Another important translation used by Prideaux was that erroneously called *Geographia nubiensis*, an abridgement of al-Idrīsī's great geography, *Nuzhat al-mushtāq*. The translation was made into Latin by the Maronites, Sionita and Hesronita, and was published in 1619.

Prideaux appears to have known the great majority of his Arabic authorities only through citations and references in Christian writers. Pococke

[13] (*a*) Thomas Erpenius, *Historia Saracenica* (Leiden, 1625). (*b*) Edward Pococke, *Historia compendiosa dynastiarum* (Oxford, 1663). (*c*) Edward Pococke, *Contextio gemmarum* (Oxford, 1658–9).

[14] See J. Fück, *Die arabischen Studien in Europa bis in den Anfang des 20. Jahrhunderts* (Leipzig, 1955), pp. 3–9.

[15] Abraham Hinckelmann, *Al-Coranus s. lex Islamica Muhammedis . . .* (Hamburg, 1694). See Fück, pp. 94–5.

[16] André du Ryer, *L'Alcoran de Mahomet* (1647).

[17] Alexander Ross, *The Alcoran of Mahomet* (London, 1649).

above all provided a mine of information in his *Specimen historiae Arabum.*[18] A comparison of Prideaux's bibliographical notes with those appended by Pococke to his Specimen (pp. 359–89) indicates the extent of his dependence. In few of his notices does he add anything to Pococke's account of the authors; he is mostly content to translate, perhaps to curtail, Pococke's paragraphs, and to convert the *hijriyya* to Christian years. An impressive array of Arabic authorities in a footnote usually implies the incorporation of material from Pococke's notes in the *Specimen.* In a few cases he draws upon other seventeenth-century orientalists, particularly the *Historia orientalis* of the Swiss scholar, Hottinger;[19] and the *Historia Arabum* of the Maronite, Abraham Echellensis.[20]

Side by side with this information, drawn, albeit at secondhand, from Arabic authors, Prideaux uses the writings of anti-Muslim controversialists. Two of these, 'Disputatio Christiani contra Saracenum de Lege Mahometis', reputedly translated from Arabic into Latin early in the twelfth century, and 'Confutatio Legis Saracenicae' composed by Richard, a Dominican, in the thirteenth century, were printed with Bibliander's Qur'ān. Another, which Prideaux particularly esteemed, was *De Confusione Sectae Mahometanae*, written by Joannes Andreas, a Muslim converted at Valencia in 1487. The edition used by Prideaux was a reprint, published at Utrecht in 1656, of a Latin translation made from an Italian rendering of the Spanish original.[21] Prideaux states that the works of Richard and Joannes Andreas' are the best of any that have been formerly published by the Western Writers on this Argument, and best accord with what the *Mahometans* themselves teach of their Religion'.[22]

Prideaux uses his sources with little discrimination. Material from Muslim writers and Christian controversialists are treated as equally valid, and with the aid of his footnotes it would be a possible, if unprofitable, exercise to disentangle information derived from each of the two groups of sources. The resultant biography is an unskilful combination of Muslim tradition and Christian legend, inspired by a sour animosity towards its subject. Yet it marks a real if limited advance, when compared with accounts of Muḥammad's life current earlier in the century, such as that given in Sandys's *Journey*[23] or the one appended by Alexander Ross to his translation of the Koran. These are almost wholly legendary. In Prideaux's work there is at least a historical framework although much overlaid by legendary material (both Christian and Muslim) and distorted by polemical bias.

[18] Edward Pococke, *Specimen historiae Arabum* (Oxford, 1650).

[19] J. H. Hottinger, *Historia orientalis* (Zürich, 1651 and 1660).

[20] Abraham Echellensis, *Historia Arabum*; supplement to *Chronicon orientale* (Paris, 1651).

[21] Prideaux, p. 257.

[22] Ibid., p. 259.

[23] George Sandys, *A Relation of a Journey begun An. Dom.* 1610, fifth edition (London, 1652), pp. 41–2.

Simon Ockley

A much more solid contribution to historical knowledge was the work produced by the Cambridge scholar, Simon Ockley, which is generally known as *The History of the Saracens*. Ockley was born at Exeter in 1678.[24] In 1693 he entered Queens' College, Cambridge, and in 1705, having taken holy orders, he became vicar of Swavesey in Cambridgeshire, where he died in 1720. In 1711 he was appointed to the Sir Thomas Adams chair of Arabic at Cambridge. His *History* was prepared and written in circumstances of great hardship. The first volume, entitled *The Conquest of Syria, Persia, and Aegypt, by the Saracens*, was published in London in 1708. The second volume, to which the title *The History of the Saracens* was first given, appeared ten years later. The whole was reissued with this title in 1757 at the suggestion of Dr. Long, then Master of Pembroke College, Cambridge, and Long is believed to be the author of a life of the Prophet prefixed to this edition. There was a reprint of the 1757 edition by Bohn in 1847.

Ockley's *History* is a landmark in two respects. It is the first attempt to write a continuous history of the Arabs in English, and it is based very largely on then unpublished manuscript sources. Chronologically the scope of the work is curious. The first volume begins with the election of Abū Bakr to the caliphate, and deals very fully with his reign and that of 'Umar. The volume ends with a short account of the reign of 'Uthmān. As the original title indicates, Ockley concerns himself principally with the wars of conquest and deals at great length with the Syrian campaigns. The second volume covers the period from the caliphate of 'Alī to that of 'Abd al-Malik (A.H. 35–86).

The omission of any account of the life of the Prophet is explained by the current popularity of Prideaux's book. In the Introduction to his second volume, Ockley sounds a faint note of criticism:

> 'I mention the *Life of* MAHOMET because it is the foundation of all our History; and though what hath been written of it by the Reverend and Learned Dr. *Prideaux* is sufficient to give a general *Idea* of the Man and his Pretensions, and admirably accomodated to his principal Design of showing the nature of an Imposture; yet there are a great many very useful Memoirs of him left behind, which would tend very much to the Illustration of the succeeding History, as well as the Customs of those Times wherein he flourished.'[25]

[24] See the article on Ockley by S. Lane-Poole in *DNB*, xli, 362–5; also the 'Memoir of Ockley' prefixed to the edition of *The History of the Saracens* by Bohn (London, 1847); and A. J. Arberry, *The Cambridge School of Arabic* (Cambridge, 1948), pp. 13–16. A detailed study of Ockley as an Orientalist has been made by Dr. A. M. A. H. Kararah in her (unpublished) thesis, 'Simon Ockley: his contributions to Arabic studies and influence on western thought (Cambridge, Ph.D. thesis, 1955). I am obliged to Professor Arberry for drawing my attention to this work. An abstract of it appears in *Abstracts of dissertations . . . in the University of Cambridge . . . 1955–1956* (Cambridge, 1957), pp. 185–6.

[25] Ockley, *History of the Saracens* (Cambridge, 1757), ii, p. xxxv.

The abrupt termination of the *History* with the death of 'Abd al-Malik is sufficiently explained by the troubles and distractions which beset Ockley in his daily life. The penury of his later years is mentioned in his Introduction to the second volume. 'I was forced,' he says, 'to take the Advantage of the Slumbers of my Cares, that never slept when I was awake; and if they did not incessantly interrupt my Studies, were sure to succeed them with no less constancy than Night doth the Day.'[26] As is well known, the second volume of the *History* was introduced to the world from Cambridge Castle, where Ockley was imprisoned for a debt of £200.

Ockley's difficulties were increased by the necessity of seeking his manuscript materials in the Bodleian Library. The oriental resources of the Cambridge university library were at that time inferior to those of Oxford, which by the end of the seventeenth century had acquired the great manuscript collections of Laud, Pococke, and Huntington.[27] Ockley began by making a draft from the printed histories available to him, al-Makīn, Bar Hebraeus, and Eutychius. On his first visit to the Bodleian, he came upon what he believed to be an authentic history of the conquest of Syria, the *Futūḥ al-Shām* of the pseudo-Wāqidī. It was from this manuscript[28] that he drew the bulk of his material for the first volume of his history: in the original work of 891 pages, 21 to 115, 131 to 237, and 265 to 342 are closely based on the *Futūḥ*. No other author was used extensively by Ockley for this first volume, but his marginal references show an acquaintance with manuscripts of Abu'l-Fidā''s *al-Mukhtaṣar fī akhbār al-bashar*, Ibn Duqmāq's *al-Jawhar al-thamīn fī sīrat al-khulafā' wa'l-salāṭīn*, Ibn 'Abd Rabbih's *al-'Iqd*, and two works on Jerusalem, one by Muḥammad b. Ibrāhīm al-Suyūṭī, the other entitled *al-Uns al-jalīl bi-ta'rīkh al-Quds wa'l-Khalīl*.[29]

Ockley's second volume deals with the political history of the caliphate after the death of 'Uthmān, and in writing this part he was not dependent mainly on a single source, as in his first volume. Once again he had recourse to the Bodleian. He spent on this occasion five months in Oxford,

[26] Ibid., p. xxxix.

[27] See Holt, 'Study of Arabic Historians', pp. 450–1.

[28] J. Uri, *Bibliothecae Bodleianae codicum manuscriptorum orientalium catalogus* (Oxford, 1787), p. 150, No. DCLV, MS. Laud. A. 118. Ockley also mentions another MS. of the pseudo-Wāqidi, MS. Pocock. 326; Uri, 154, DCLXXXIV.

[29] The MSS. are described in Uri's *Catalogus*: (1) Abu'l-Fidā', *al-Mukhtaṣar*; MS. Pocock. 303; Uri, p. 155, No. DCLXXXVI. The MS. contains the first part of the work, going to A.H. 454. Ockley's marginal reference (p. 9) numbers the MS. Pocock. 330. (2) Ibrāhīm b. Muḥammad b. Duqmāq, *al-Jawhar*; MS. Laud. B. 129; Uri, 148, DCXLVIII. Ockley's marginal reference (p. 8) numbers the MS. Laud. 806.11. (3) Aḥmad b. Muḥammad b. 'Abd Rabbih, *al-'Iqd*; MS. Huntington. 554; Uri, 172, DCCLXXXII. (4) Muḥammad b. Ibrāhīm b. Muḥammad al-Suyūṭī, *Itḥāf al-akhiṣṣā' bi-faḍā'il al-masjid al-aqṣā*; MS. Huntington. 510; Uri, 179, DCCCXXI. (5) Muḥyi'l-Dīn b. 'Abd al-Rahmān, *al-Uns*; MS. Pocock. 362; Uri, 154, DCLXXX. Anonymous in Ockley, who calls the work *The History of the Holy Land*, or *The History of Jerusalem*.

(his first volume had entailed two visits, each of less than six weeks), and was permitted by Bodley's Librarian to take the books he needed out of the library—a favour which was in breach of the statutes and had not been accorded to King Charles I! Ockley's marginal references and a table prefixed to Volume II show that he made use of manuscripts of Abu'l-Fidā' Ibn al-Athīr, and al-Ṭabarī, as well as of an anonymous historian which he greatly valued.[30] In addition he obtained a good deal of information, especially about 'Alī, from d'Herbelot's *Bibliothèque orientale*,[31] a pioneer encyclopaedic dictionary of orientalism, first published in 1697. Ockley's acquaintance with the Persian writers was acquired through d'Herbelot. With this exception, Ockley makes little use of secondary sources.

It will be clear from the foregoing that Ockley, unlike Prideaux, was a scholarly historian who based his work upon an investigation of original sources. His discrimination was not faultless, although it must be borne in mind that his most serious error, the acceptance of the *Futūḥ al-Shām* as a genuine work of al-Wāqidī, was not revealed until the nineteenth century. On the whole his instinct was sounder than that of Pococke, in his preference for early over later sources, and Muslim rather than Christian writers. Lacking the criteria which historical scholarship has assembled in the last two centuries, he is content to paint a full picture rather than to investigate the accuracy of details. His limitations in this respect appear in the remarks he makes on the author of *Futūḥ al-Shām*, whom he believes, from internal evidence, to have lived 'above two hundred years after the Matter of Fact which he relates'. He continues:

[30] (1) For Abu'l-Fidā', *vid. supra*, p. 10, n. 4(1). (2) Ibn al-Athīr, *al-Kāmil*; MSS. Pocock. 137 and 103; Uri, 156, DCXCIV and DCXCVI. These two MSS. cover the years A.H. 7–61 and 76–130. (3) Ockley's use of al-Ṭabarī is a matter of some complexity. (*a*) After giving up the Arabic version for lost, he states (*History*, ii, pp. xxxix–xl) that he 'luckily found a Piece of it in *Folio* amongst Archbishop *Laud's* Manuscripts.' He cites this in his table of MSS. Authors as 'The Second Volume of *Altabari's* Great History' and numbers it (Laud's MSS.) Num N, 55, 124. There is no Laudian historical folio MS. with such a number in Uri's *Catalogus* (which gives the older numbers) and the only Laudian MS. bearing the name of al-Ṭabarī is Laud. A. 124, al-Makīn, *Mukhtaṣar ta'rīkh al-imām Abū* (sic) *Ja'far Muḥammad b. Jarīr al-Ṭabarī*; Uri, 160, DCCXV. Ockley may have had the second part of al-Makīn's compendium in mind. It is perhaps relevant to note that another MS., with a similar number, Marsh. 124; Uri, 161, DCCXXII, is in fact described as the second part of al-Ṭabarī. The Marsh MSS. were a bequest to the Bodleian in 1713 and so would be available to Ockley for his second volume. (*b*) Ockley also lists as Laud. 161. A. (for Laud. A. 161; Uri, 149, DCL) 'An Imperfect Historian (and therefore Anonymous) . . . of singular Use in this History.' This, which is also marked on the MS. itself as Laud. 265, was identified by de Goeje as a portion of al-Ṭabarī covering the years A.H. 61–82. It is described in his communication in *ZDMG* (1862), 16, pp. 759–62, and in Guidi's note printed in the 'Introductio', pp. lv–lvi, to de Goeje's edition of *Annales quos scripsit . . . At-Tabari* (Leiden, 1901). (*c*) A fragment of al-Ṭabarī, so identified in Uri, covering the years A.H. 77–79, forms part of MS. Huntington, 198; Uri, 159, DCCXI, which seems to have been missed by Ockley. It may be noted in passing that the Uri references of MSS. Huntington, 198 and Marsh, 124, are transposed in de Goeje's communication cited above. (4) The other fragment listed as anonymous by Ockley is MS. Huntington, 495; Uri, 185, DCCCLVII, covering the early Umayyad period.

[31] Fück, pp. 98–100.

And if so, 'tis the same thing as if he had lived six hundred years after. For that Author that lives 1000 years after any Matter of Fact, is as much a Witness of it, as he that lives but at 200 years Distance. They are both of them oblig'd to take upon Trust, and if there be no Loss of good Authors during that Interval; he that writes latest is as credible an Historian as the first.[32]

One technical virtue of the historian he displays to the full; in the second volume especially he is meticulous in his dating. Each volume has a chronological table prefaced, while the second has marginal date-headings to each page. Where the chronology of his sources is obscure or confused, he draws attention to the discrepancies.[33]

The scholarly character of Ockley's work appears in his attitude towards the people with whom he deals. He does not fail to follow common form by stigmatizing Muḥammad, in his first line, as 'the great Impostor'; he describes the Arab conquests as 'that grievous Calamity', but the body of his work is totally lacking in the virulence which Prideaux displays. There is an echo of Prideaux in the 'Preface' to Ockley's first volume, where he speaks of the desirability of a knowledge of Arab history,

Not only because they have had as great Men, and perform'd as considerable Actions, as any other Nation under Heaven; but, what is of more concern to us Christians, because they were the first Ruin of the Eastern Church.[34]

The impression which one gains from reading Ockley is, however, that he is much more interested in the great men and considerable actions of the Arabs than in the ruin of the Eastern Church. Indeed, he tells us that his original purpose was 'to take in the whole Series of the Affairs of the Christians during the Period; but upon second Thoughts it appeared to me to be foreign to my Purpose'.[35] This transfer of interest, from the study of Arab history as ancillary to that of ecclesiastical history, to Arab history as in itself a subject of valid enquiry, is perhaps the most important aspect of Ockley's work.

George Sale

George Sale (?1697–1736)[36] was the first notable English Arabist who was not in holy orders. His father was a London merchant. He himself was a student of the Inner Temple in 1720, and subsequently practised as a solicitor. His interest in Arabic having been aroused, he received tuition from a Syrian Christian, Dadichi, who was in London in 1723. He may

[32] Ockley, *History*, i, p. xx.
[33] E.g., *History*, i, 159, 371; ii, 77–8, 296.
[34] *History*, i, p. ix.
[35] *History*, ii, p. v.
[36] See *DNB*, L, 179–81; article by H. Thomson Lyon.

also have been taught by another Syrian, Negri,[37] who was also in London about this time and was commissioned by the Society for the Promotion of Christian Knowledge to produce an Arabic version of the Psalter and the New Testament. Sale was a corrector of the Arabic New Testament, and from 1726 to 1734 he was closely associated with the S.P.C.K., which he served in his legal capacity. Meanwhile he was working on a translation of the Qur'ān, the publication of which, in 1734, is a landmark in the history of Qur'anic studies. Not only was his translation far more accurate than its only English predecessor, the seventeenth-century version by Ross, but it was annotated from the Muslim commentators (particularly al-Bayḍāwī and al-Suyūṭī) and other sources, and preceded by a long 'Preliminary Discourse' which forms a compendium of the information then available on the origins, doctrines, practices, and sects of Islam. The enlightened and objective attitude displayed by Sale may have been responsible for his gradual dissociation from the activities of the S.P.C.K. after 1734. Sale died in 1736, leaving his wife and family in financial difficulties. His collection of manuscripts ultimately passed to the Bodleian.

The purpose of the present account is not to give an appreciation of Sale's translation, which has been done by Professor Fück,[38] nor to analyse in general his sources of information. Over thirty years ago, Denison Ross indicated the dependence of Sale upon Marracci,[39] while in 1931 C. A. Nallino showed that Marracci himself quoted a considerable number of Arabic authors at secondhand, mainly from Pococke's *Specimen Historiae Arabum*.[40] I shall confine myself to the first two sections of the Preliminary Discourse, the subject-matter of which is specifically historical, and examine briefly their sources and outlook.

The first of these sections deals with the Jāhiliyya, the second with the career of the Prophet. Taken together they supersede Prideaux. The insufficiency of Prideaux's work, in spite of its popularity, had appeared almost at once. Its publication nearly coincided with that of d'Herbelot's *Bibliothèque orientale* (1697) and Marracci's *Alcorani textus universus*, with its Latin translation (1698).[41] The next important relevant publication was in 1723, when Gagnier published at Oxford the text of Abu'l-Fidā' dealing with the life of the Prophet. This was the first Muslim Arabic account of Muḥammad to be printed *in extenso* and it was accompanied by a Latin

[37] See Fück, pp. 95–7, for Negri and Dadichi.

[38] Fück, pp. 104–5.

[39] E. Denison Ross, 'Ludovico Marracci' in *BSOS* (1921), ii, 118–23; cf. also his 'Introduction' to the Warne edition of Sale (1921) in which he says, 'I have therefore been forced to the conclusion that with the exception of al-Baidhawi, Sale's sources were all consulted at second hand; . . . so much had been achieved by Marracci that Sale's work might also have been performed with a knowledge of Latin alone, as far as regards the quotations from Arabic authors.'

[40] C. A. Nallino, 'Le fonti arabe manoscritte di Ludovico Marracci sul Corano' (1932), reprinted in *Raccolta di Scritti* (1950), ii, 90–134.

[41] Marracci's polemical *Prodromus ad refutationem Alcorani* had been separately published in 1691,

translation.[42] The change of intellectual climate in western Europe in the later seventeenth and early eighteenth centuries was however producing a new attitude towards Islam and its Prophet, which rendered the tone of Prideaux as outdated as his sources were insufficient. Indicative of this is a French *Vie de Mahomet* by Count Henri de Boulainvilliers (1658–1722),[43] published posthumously in London in 1730.[44] Like Prideaux, Boulainvilliers uses the origins of Islam as the vehicle of his own theological prejudices, which are markedly anticlerical but these lead him to look with sympathy on his subject. He rejects the traditional axioms of Christian polemic with Muslims,

> that there is not any rational inducement in all that they believe or practise; insomuch that common sense must be discarded in order to embrace their system,

and

> that *Mahomet* was so coarse and barbarous an impostor, that he is not a man, who does not or cannot perceive plainly his cheat and corruption.

Boulainvilliers still assumes the superiority of Christianity but there is no acerbity in his tone; 'with respect to the essential doctrines of religion, all that [Muḥammad] has laid down is true; but he has not laid down all that is true; and that is the whole difference between our religion and his.'

La Vie de Mahomet, again like Prideaux's book, is not a work of scholarship. The author admits that he does not understand Arabic and is indebted to d'Herbelot's *Bibliothèque* and to translations. Factually his book is sounder than Prideaux's which he criticizes, but there are some errors and a good deal of embroidery. Boulainvilliers left his work incomplete, at A.H. 5, and the English publisher invited Gagnier to write the closing section. According to Gagnier, the negotiations broke down and the sequel as we have it is anonymous.[45] In 1732, Gagnier in fact came out with his own *Vie de Mahomet*,[46] a work of serious scholarship. He makes his attitude perfectly clear in a lengthy 'Préface: où l'on réfute les Paradoxes avancés

[42] J. Gagnier, *Ismael Abul-Feda, de vita et rebus gestis Mohammedis* . . . (Oxford, 1723). For Gagnier, a French cleric who became an Anglican clergyman, settled at Oxford and became Lord Almoner's Professor of Arabic, see the article by G. Goodwin in *DNB*, xx, 358–9.

[43] Boulainvilliers's primary interest was in his own illustrious ancestry, which impressed other French genealogists less than himself. This led him to write on the history and antiquities of France.

[44] Fück, p. 103 and n. 269ª. An English translation (the translator is anonymous) was published in the following year: *The Life of Mahomet, Translated from the French Original by The Count of Boulainvilliers* . . . (London, printed for W. Hinchliffe, 1731). The quotations that follow are taken from this translation, p. 243.

[45] The author of the article on Gagnier in *DNB* states that he was in fact responsible for the anonymous continuation. This would seem to be disproved by Gagnier's own words in his 'Préface' and his stringent denunciations of Boulainvilliers's work.

[46] J. Gagnier, *Vie de Mahomet*, 2 vols. (Amsterdam, 1732).

par Mr. le Comte de Boulainvilliers, dans sa Vie de Mahomet.' He criticizes particularly the favourable picture which Boulainvilliers gives of the Prophet, and the style of the work, which, he says, is romance rather than history.

Sale's account should be seen in connection with these two recent biographies. In the first section of his Preliminary Discourse he deals with five main topics: the geography of Arabia; the Arab tribes; the history of the Jāhiliyya; the pre-Islamic religions of Arabia; and the culture of the Arabs. His account of the geography is based partly on Greek and partly on Arabic sources, notably al-Idrīsī (known through Pococke and the *Geographia Nubiensis*), Bar Hebraeus and Abu'l-Fidā', a fragment of whose *Taqwīm al-buldān* had been printed by Gagnier at Oxford in 1726–7. Pococke's notes in the *Specimen* and those of Golius to his edition of al-Farghānī[47] also contributed information. It is interesting to note that Sale also used the *Account* of Joseph Pitts, the first Englishman known to have visited Mecca.[48]

In the remainder of this section a very great deal of information is derived from or through Pococke's *Specimen*. This is clear from Sale's footnotes, but these conceal the full extent of his borrowing since sometimes they cite only the author used by Pococke. A comparison of Sale's text with that of Pococke makes it clear, however, that the English account is often little more than a translation or synopsis of passages of the *Specimen*. This is particularly obvious in Sale's account of the pre-Islamic religions of Arabia, where Sale's footnote references to *al-Mustaṭraf*, al-Shahrastānī, al-Jannābī, al-Bayḍāwī, al-Jawharī, and *Naẓm al-durr* can, with two dubious exceptions, be traced back to the *Specimen*. Sale's other sources show an acquaintance with the printed, rather than the manuscript, material available at the time; d'Herbelot's *Bibliothèque orientale*, Gagnier's texts of Abu'l-Fidā', al-Makīn, and Bar Hebraeus. He mentions Prideaux's *Life of Mahomet* five times, once to correct an error, and has one reference to the first volume of Ockley's *History*.

The second edition of Sale's Preliminary Discourse falls into two parts. First he describes the condition of Christianity, Judaism and the Persian empire on the eve of the Muslim conquests. Here he naturally draws little information from Arabic sources: apart from a reference to the Qur'ān and one to Pococke's account of Mazdakism, which is derived from Abu'l-Fidā' and al-Shahrastānī, he cites only the two Christian Arabic writers, al-Makīn and Bar Hebraeus. They are mentioned on a single point only; for the rest he depends largely on Byzantine and modern sources. He refers

[47] Fück, p. 82 and n. 224. This source, which was used by others besides Sale, is commonly referred to as 'Golius ad Alfraganum'.

[48] Joseph Pitts, *A faithful account of the religion and manners of the Mahometans* . . . (London, third edition, 1731). Partially reprinted and edited by Sir William Foster, *The Red Sea and adjacent countries* (London, Hakluyt Society, Series II, C, 1949).

to Prideaux, Ockley, and Boulainvilliers when describing the errors and schisms of Christendom, and follows his predecessors by saying that the Arabs 'seem to have been raised up on purpose by GOD, to be a scourge to the *Christian* Church, for not living answerably to that most holy religion which they had received'.[49] But his pages, unlike those of Prideaux, are not imbued with a sense of warning and retribution; the theory of a divine judgement is unemotionally stated and probably not very seriously entertained.

Sale's principal source for the career of the Prophet was Gagnier's edition of Abu'l-Fidā', to which there are numerous references in his footnotes. On two points he corrects Boulainvilliers's narrative, and in the course of ten references to Prideaux he makes seven critical comments of greater or less importance. Characteristic of the difference in outlook between the two writers is Sale's remark, 'I cannot possibly subscribe to the assertion of a late learned writer [i.e. Prideaux, op. cit., 76], that he made that nation exchange their idolatry for another religion altogether as bad.'[50] Sale's dependence upon late sources and lack of historical criteria for evaluating his material caused him some difficulties. Like his predecessors, he accepted the story of the *Mi'rāj* as an authentic part of the Prophet's teaching. To Prideaux this had been an outstanding piece of evidence in support of his view of Islam. Sale finds it awkward since, as he says, 'I do not find that *Mohammed* himself ever expected so great a regard should be paid to his sayings, as his followers have since done; and . . . he all along disclaimed any power of performing miracles.'[51] He does not, however, conclude that the story may be a later accretion but says, rather lamely, that it seems 'to have been a fetch of policy to raise his reputation'.

The picture of early Arabia and the origins of Islam which is drawn by Sale is therefore still seriously at fault by modern standards of historical writing. Sale's range of sources was more limited and his Arabic scholarship perhaps less profound than appeared to his contemporaries. Nevertheless his work was of great importance. His freedom from religious prejudice (in which respect he compares favourably with many of his nineteenth and twentieth century successors), his obvious conviction that Arabic writers were the best source of Arab history, and Muslim commentators the fittest to expound the Qur'ān, marks an enormous advance on the hodgepodge of 'authorities' advanced by Prideaux. His work complements that of Ockley and for over a century the two played a leading part in creating the notion of the Prophet and the Arabs held by educated Englishmen.

[49] G. Sale, *The Koran, commonly called the Alcoran of Mohammed* (London, 1764), i, 47.
[50] Ibid., p. 51.
[51] Ibid., p. 61.

26. ISLAM AS AN HISTORICAL PROBLEM IN EUROPEAN HISTORIOGRAPHY SINCE 1800

J. W. FÜCK

Professor of Semitic Philology and Islamic Studies, Martin Luther University, Halle

The literature of Islamic history which has appeared during the last century and a half in European languages outside America and the Soviet Union is so extensive and varied that a mere survey would be far beyond the scope of a short paper. It is equally impossible to mention in a short compass the great strides which have been made in Islamic historical research since 1800. It may however be worth while to give a general survey of the changes which the picture of Islam and its history has undergone in Western historiography since 1800; at the same time we may try to ascertain the trends and motives which have influenced European Orientalists and non-Orientalist historians in the presentation and interpretation of Islamic history. In this study I shall limit myself to the literature of the history of Arab Islam, not considering the vast and predominantly politically-inspired literature of the so-called Eastern Question and the history of Persia and Turkey.

The attitude which a European historian of the last century would adopt towards Islam was normally determined in part by the conceptions and views of Islam formed by previous centuries. Even after 1800 there are still traces of the religious antithesis which determined the European judgement of Muḥammad and his works, and which found its pithiest expression in the slogans concerning Muḥammad 'the false prophet' or 'the antichrist', and Islam as a heresy 'spread by fire and sword'. Every historian of Christian outlook must naturally regard Islam from a Christian viewpoint, but even where no Christian standards were applied, the dualism of church and state in the Christian West could lead a student to misunderstand Islamic institutions.

In sharp contrast to this medieval point of view the Enlightenment viewed the East with frank curiosity and saw in it that background for strange happenings with which we have been familiar, since our childhood, from the *Thousand and one nights*. This picture of the 'unchanging' East was taken up by the Romantic movement and its influence also lasted on into the nineteenth century. Thus it was that the Moorish period of Islam in the Iberian peninsula was for long regarded in the transfiguring light of Romanticism, and the *Historia de la dominacion de los Arabes en España*, by José Antonio Conde, published in 1820 and translated also into French and English, held the field until, in the middle of the nineteenth century, R. Dozy led the advance of a critical study of history into this sphere. The same was true of the conception of the age of the Crusades, as is witnessed by the romantic enthusiasm for the Middle Ages which fills J. F. Michaud's *Histoire des Croisades* (1812–22).

In the meantime the Romantic image of the Orient inevitably faded as the economic and political penetration of the Ottoman Empire by the European great powers continued, giving rise to a steady increase in knowledge of the true conditions prevailing there. Napoleon's Egyptian campaign of 1798 marked a decisive turning point in this connection. It made the Muslims conscious of the superiority of a modern European state, and ushered in the period of Islamic modernism. It was only the rivalry between the Great Powers that enabled the Ottoman Empire to survive, and the 'Eastern Question' consisted mainly of the repeated disputes to which the break-up of the Ottoman Empire gave rise. Europe's two principal attitudes towards Islam were now joined by a third, based on the conviction that the prevailing superiority of Europe over the Orient was axiomatic and absolute. This attitude set the tone for virtually all European presentations of Islamic history right up to the First World War.

Contacts with the Orient, which had become increasingly close since 1800, had the further result that increasing quantities of material for a history of Islam found their way to Europe. Simultaneously oriental studies since the French Revolution had been breaking free of the bonds of theology, and the study of the Arabic language was placed on a solid grammatical and philological footing by Silvestre de Sacy. When the critical study of history appeared in the field demanding that by a critical analysis of the sources each event should be understood in its uniqueness before any attempt were made to evaluate its significance as a link in the historical development, Orientalists were not entirely unprepared to apply this method to Islamic history.

The first fruits of the critical analysis of historical sources were borne in the study of the dawn of Islam. Abraham Geiger, in his prize essay written in 1833, attempted to answer the question: 'What did Muḥammad adopt from Judaism?' and gave rise to a series of theories, all of which dealt with the contacts between Islam and the older monotheistic religions from the one-sided point of view which assumed that Muḥammad's teachings were derived entirely either from Judaism or from Christianity; it was not until 1930 that these theories were supplanted by a line of research which recognized the originality of the Arab Prophet.

The study of Muḥammad's life, on the other hand, benefited in the main from increased source material (Ibn Hiṣẖām, parts of Wāqidī, Ibn Sa'd and Ṭabarī, together with the biographies of the Prophet's Companions, commentaries on the Qur'ān and collections of Traditions). In their treatment of this material the various biographers followed their own ways. Aloys Sprenger, for instance, inspired by the study of Ibn Khaldūn, attempted in his work *Das Leben und die Lehre des Mohammad* (1861–65) to establish the general laws governing the origin of Islam, and interpreted it in purely rational terms as a creation of the spirit of the times—in contrast with the Romantic movement's idealistic philosophy of history and with Carlyle's hero worship. He may have considerably underestimated Muḥammad's religious motives and the part which he played, but he did not misunderstand the significance of Islam in world history and the profound influence of Islamic culture on the European Middle Ages; he even perceived that contemporary Islam would renew itself under the influence of Europe. On the other hand the Scottish writer Sir William Muir, although drawing the material for his *Life of Mahomet and history of Islam* (1856–61) from the same sources as Sprenger and reproducing it with sober objectivity, was convinced (as an orthodox Christian) that Muḥammad had been an instrument of the devil; he also assessed Islam's cultural significance differently, as he was hopeful that a time would come when the Muslims would be converted to Christianity.

Gustav Weil, in his *Geschichte der Chalifen* (1846–51) and *Geschichte des Abbasidenchalifats in Egypten* (1860–2) gave a comprehensive survey of Islamic history from 632 to 1517, based on indigenous sources. But the size of the undertaking and the wealth of the material (never completely sifted from a philological aspect either then or since) prevented him from going beyond a rather dry reproduction of the events recorded in the source material.

Sir William Muir, who has already been mentioned, gave a no less full and sober account of the same period—based on al-Ṭabarī's and Ibn al-Athīr's chronicles and Weil's History of the Caliphs—in his works *The Caliphate, its rise, decline and fall* (1891) and *The Mameluke or Slave dynasty of Egypt, 1260–1517 A.D.* (1896). Both books reveal in discreet fashion the author's Christian standpoint, and both enjoyed wide popularity in the English-speaking world.

The method of a critical study of historical sources was first applied to the Moorish period by the Leiden Orientalist R. Dozy, an anticlerical liberal historian and a competent philologist into the bargain. In his work *Recherches sur l'histoire politique et littéraire de l'Espagne pendant le moyen-âge* (1849) he refuted the efforts of his predecessors with trenchant criticism; subsequently, in his *Histoire des Musulmans d'Espagne* (1861) he drew a picture of Moorish Spain in the years from 711 to 1110 which won approval even in Spain and held the field unopposed until, from the turn of the century, Spanish Arabists and Hispanists began to criticize many of his opinions and conclusions (on the rôle of the Mozarabes, the spread of the national romance language, the character of the Cid etc.).

Michele Amari, the investigator of Muslim Sicily, was a historian to an even greater degree than Dozy. He studied Arabic solely in order that he might himself be able to read the Arab sources of the history of his native land in the original, and he made use of documents, inscriptions and coins in addition to literary texts. He had grown up in the spirit of the Risorgimento, was a determined adversary of political catholicism, and brought a generous understanding to the study of Islam, whose influence on European civilization he rated high. Nor did he share the opinion of those who prophesied an early end for Islam.

The historians mentioned hitherto had brought the political history of Islam into the foreground, or at least to a large extent taken it into consideration. For the Austrian diplomat A. von Kremer, on the other hand, only the civilization of Islam was of interest. His idealistic philosophy of history followed Ibn Khaldūn in considering the state as a sociological phenomenon, coming into existence, growing and decaying according to its own laws. In the ideas of the individual he found the forces which operate in politics, constitution, administration and legislation, in religion and in culture. He traced the growth of a civilization back to a clash of opposing ideas, and he attributed the decay of civilization (as it could be observed in the contemporary Islamic world) to the lack of conflicting ideas. In his *Geschichte der herrschenden Ideen des Islams, Gottesbegriff, Prophetie und Staatsidee* (1868) and still more in his *Kulturgeschichte des Orients under den Chalifen* (1875–77) he drew a picture of the culture and civilization of medieval Islam at the time of its widest sway, a picture which was rich in delicate observations and stimulating opinions.

The works considered so far were valuable as regards particular periods, but they were quite inadequate to give anything approaching a complete picture of the history of Islam over twelve centuries and three continents. This fact became apparent when August Müller attempted to present the political history of Islam for the general reader in W. Oncken's *Allgemeine Geschichte in Einzeldarstellungen*. Müller soon discovered that only a quarter of his field was adequately covered by the work of his predecessors. His attempt to pad out the gaps inevitably produced an unsatisfactory result.

But the non-Orientalist historians also had cause in the course of their work to devote attention to Islam or at least to its armed conflicts with the West. Having no access to the Arab sources they were restricted to the very limited number of previous publications in which the few Arabists had presented the results of their studies to a wider circle of readers. It thus happened that, right up to the present day, the treatment of Islam by non-Orientalists (through no fault of their own) bears no relation to the current state of Islamic research and is largely based on outdated material; moreover, this lack shows up all the more clearly the trends and motives which are displayed in these narratives.

L. von Ranke, for instance, one of the fathers of the critical study of history, in his *Weltgeschichte* (1881–88) treated Islam as the great antagonist of Christian Europe, whose attack was foiled by the resistance of the Germanic-Romance peoples, and who later fought off the attacks of the latter during the Crusades. His study of Venice's relations had given Ranke a deep insight into the state of the Ottoman Empire in the sixteenth and seventeenth centuries, and as a historian he was only concerned to 'establish the facts as they had occurred'. But his outlook on life, deeply coloured by Protestantism, made him see in the critically assembled details the operation of certain ideas characteristic of each epoch, and thus, in looking back on the decay of power of the Ottoman Empire he came to the conclusion that the fall of Constantinople had only been a Pyrrhic victory for Islam, as its followers had been unable to break the bonds of the Middle Ages and develop into free nations.

Jacob Burckhardt, one of the first to become aware of the problem of decadence, never saw eye to eye with Ranke in other matters, but he shared the latter's unfavourable opinion of Islam. The *Historische Fragmente*, edited from his unpublished papers and based on his lectures in Basel between 1844 and 1893 give clear expression to his dislike of Muḥammad. He first admits that Muḥammad was personally honest, but later concludes that he occasionally lied. He plasters Islam with derogatory adjectives such as 'wretched' and 'bare' and declares that any spirituality which it possesses has been acquired later from other sources. From the ban on portraits he deduces that Islam is hostile to all fine arts. On the other hand he freely admits that the Muslims have an unrivalled mainstay in their religion and that they are completely immune against proselytization. But, whereas he normally concludes that great achievements must arise from great causes, in the case of Islam he only sees a victory for triviality. Finally it is worth noting his opinion (an opinion which conflicts with the views prevailing at the time) that Islam saved the life of Byzantium, that Byzantium only succumbed to Islam after it had been weakened by the West, and that by this victory Islam saved Europe from the Mongol peril.

An even lower opinion of Islam was held by writers who attempted to explain the superiority of the West on racial grounds. Count Gobineau, in his *Essai sur l'inégalité des races humaines* (1853–55) harked back to the work of earlier French scientists and historians in asserting that races differ in mental qualities and that any superior race which mixes with an inferior race must perish. Gobineau also originated the opinion, frequently repeated in popular works, that the Shīʿa had been a reaction of the Indo-European Persians against the Sunnism of the Semitic Arabs. Although this theory was disproved by Wellhausen it continued to find supporters right into the present century, amongst them Carra de Vaux, the author of *Les penseurs de l'Islam*.

Ernest Renan held views similar to those of Gobineau, though less extreme. He attributed to the Arabs, for instance, as indeed to the Semites in general, a particular inclination towards religion, but would not credit them with any talent for philosophy or rational science. He did not deny the fact that for half a millennium (approximately 775–1250 A.D.) the Orient had been in the van of scientific advance, but he attributed this achievement to the non-Arab savants in the Islamic countries, whose activities orthodox Arab Islam had not at that time been strong enough to suppress; once Islamic orthodoxy had attained supreme power in the thirteenth century it had rendered all independent thinking impossible and thus brought about that state of backwardness which had prevailed ever since in Islamic countries. An immediate reply to Renan was given by Jamāl al-Dīn al-Afghānī, who was living at the time in Paris, to the effect that the Muslims ought not to be deprived of the hope of an advance in civilization similar to that already achieved by the Christian nations of Europe; he also rebutted Renan's assertion that only non-Arabs had contributed to Islamic civilization. But Renan regarded the fact that his critic belonged to an Indo-European nation as a confirmation of his racial theory.

There were, of course, many historians who followed the anticlerical tradition of the Enlightenment and the political beliefs of Liberalism in recognizing the cultural superiority of Islam over the Christian West in the Middle Ages. Among the exponents of this viewpoint may be mentioned the Königsberg historian Hans Prutz in his *Kulturgeschichte der Kreuzzüge* (1883); he went so far as to claim that only by contact with the world of Islam and its civilization had the West learned how to emancipate itself from the thraldom of the Church and its one-sided romanist educational ideals; the experiences of the Crusades, he maintained, had contained the germ of the Reformation and Renaissance, of Humanism and the creation of nation-states.

That such a high estimation of Islam was not incompatible with the racial theory is shown by the example of Gustave Le Bon. His training was scientific, he was a doctor by profession, and he was particularly concerned with social psychology. He belonged to the school of thought which held that there were mental differences between the races, but he regarded humanity with the unprejudiced eye of the natural scientist who observes the differences but does not evaluate them and who believes in the survival of the fittest. In his book *La civilisation des Arabes* (1884) he drew a picture of Islamic civilization which only incidentally touched on military and political history. He had a very high idea of the fruitfulness and originality of the Islamic peoples in the scientific and artistic fields, and he admitted frankly that the universities of the West had lived for 500 years on the books of their Arab neighbours. He rejected the medieval accusation that

Islam had been spread by fire and sword, and took the opposite position of praising the tolerance with which the Arabs had treated the subject races in the territories incorporated in the Arab empire. Not surprisingly his book found widespread approval in the Islamic world and was frequently quoted by Muslim modernists. It was even translated into Urdu by A. Bilgrami.

In his wide-ranging survey of Islamic civilization Le Bon had not neglected the centuries of decadence and the condition of the contemporary Islamic world. But the spokesmen of oriental studies in the universities of Europe, under the banner of critical historical research, turned their attention increasingly to an exclusive study of the origins of Islam and to its medieval prime. The exemplary editorial work of the Dutch school was devoted primarily to texts from the most brilliant period of the Baghdād caliphate. The Leiden edition of Ṭabarī (1879–1901) and the portions of the Berlin edition of Ibn Sa'd dealing with the biography of the Prophet provided rich material on the early history of Islam and gave an insight into the trends and motives of its earliest historians. The Leiden edition of Ṭabarī led to Wellhausen's pioneer work on the political history of Islam up to the fall of the Arab Empire in A.D. 750, a work in which the sifting of documentary sources and the psychological analysis of trends in power-politics form a complete unity. Wellhausen's historical criticism had its origins in his admiration for the nation-state. On the other hand he had no sympathy for the 'Abbasid dynasty. In a lecture (see G. v. Below, *Vierteljahresschrift f. Sozial-und Wirtschaftsgeschichte 1922*, p. 235) he gave it as his well-considered opinion that any comparison between the medieval civilization of Islam and the West (other than in the technical field) must inevitably favour the latter, and that this opinion applied especially to the political sphere. He mentioned incidentally that the renowned Caliphs could certainly not stand up to comparison with the great rulers of the Christian West such as the German Emperors.

Wellhausen's low opinion of the Eastern peoples was shared by Th. Nöldeke. Nöldeke had grown up in the tradition of neo-humanism, with its idolization of Graeco-Roman antiquity, and his interest in the interplay of relations between the Classical world and the Orient led him to the field of Persian studies. Of Ṭabarī's Chronicle, he edited the section dealing with the history of the Persians and Arabs at the time of the Sasanids, and he was the only one of the collaborators in this work to make his section of the text accessible to non-Orientalists in a translation. This task led him to write his *Aufsätze sur persischen Geschichte* (1887) in the Preface to which he admitted that his judgement of the Eastern races—and of the Persians in particular—was not over-favourable. 'My studies as an Orientalist,' he continued, 'have been the very means of increasing my philhellenism, and I think that the same experience will befall anyone who makes a serious but open-minded attempt to acquaint himself with the nature of the Eastern peoples.' He found Islamic modernism equally uninviting; Ameer Ali's book *The Spirit of Islam*, which created such a furore in 1891 seemed to him somewhat shallow and he felt that one should neither attach importance to books of this nature nor expect that they could achieve any practical result. (See his letter to C. H. Becker in the latter's *Islamstudien*, ii, 520.)

The critical method which Dozy had already applied to the Moorish period found a notable disciple in Spain in the person of Francesco Codera y Zaidin; he undertook the editing of source-books, established Spanish–Arabic numismatics on a systematic basis, and published monographs dealing with many problems of the Moorish period in Spain. Spanish-Arabic studies derive their special character from Spain's exceptional position as the only European country confronted by the problem of assessing the nature and value of a period of Muslim domination lasting eight hundred years. According to Codera's pupil and successor Julian Ribera y Taragó, Christian Spain had a great civilizing mission to perform in the Moorish period as mediator between Europe and the Orient. He put forward the theory that the Andalusian love lyrics forming the basis of the Arabic *zajals* contain the key to the understanding of Provençal Troubadour poetry, a theory which created no less of a sensation than that of his pupil and successor Miguel Asín Palacios: *La escatologia musulmana en la Divina Comedia* (1919). Both theories gave rise to a lively discussion which has lingered on into the present day and which shows how strongly European medievalists react when Arabic studies touch on basic questions of the history of Western thought.

In the field of Islamic studies Ignaz Goldziher applied the same methods of the study of history. Like A. v. Kremer he ignored the political aspect and devoted himself principally to the influence exerted on the development of Islamic thought by religious ideas. Brought up in the liberal atmosphere of Jewish emancipation he rejected both racial theory and the widely-held view that Islam was incapable of further development. His works gave due consideration to contemporary Islam and to the pronouncements of modernism.

With the rise of sociology, the study of contemporary affairs acquired an accepted position within the general field of Islamic studies; this process began in France, soon spreading to other countries which had political and economic interests in the Islamic Orient. It must be admitted, however, that even experts frequently misunderstood the strength of the forces which were moving in modernism and eastern nationalism, or they were inclined to overestimate the part to be played by their own country in a forthcoming reorganization in the Near East.

An exception among Orientalists was provided by Leone Caetani, who showed the penetrating vision of the born historian in correctly assessing the power-relationship between Europe and the Orient. In his youth he had shown his talent for historical research by his decision to produce in the *Annali dell'Islam* a philologically accurate translation of the complete source-material of the history of the Islamic peoples from A.D. 612 to 1517, both from printed and manuscript authorities, and to form from it a unified picture. If this tremendous undertaking, which was far beyond the powers of one individual, had been carried out, Orientalists would have had a complete index to the sources of the history of medieval Islam; moreover, non-Orientalist historians would have been able to read these documents in a reliable translation and to compare their own opinions with Caetani's synthesis. But an impressive torso is formed by the material actually produced—the account of the days of the Prophet and of the four Orthodox Caliphs, and the enumeration, in calendar form, of events down to the beginning of the 'Abbasid caliphate (144 A.H.). In the third volume of his *Studi di storia orientale* he drew a picture of Muḥammad as a statesman, stressing the political and economic factors at the expense (it must be admitted) of the religious motives. His deep insight into the interplay of relations between Occident and Orient led him to condemn colonialism, and when Italy annexed Tripolitania and Cyrenaica he issued a warning, in an essay, *La fonction de l'Islam dans l'évolution de la civilisation* (1912), against all attempts to europeanize the eastern peoples; in a stimulating study of the century-old conflict between East and West he defended the right of the Muslims to lead an independent life in accordance with their own traditions.

The consequences for Europe of the First World War, and the changes which took place in the Islamic countries, were so profound that the ideas of Islam prevailing in Europe had of necessity to be revised. Islamic studies at the European universities reflected this change in their paying attention (to a greater or lesser extent) to the contemporary Islamic world, its literature and its current problems. This shift of emphasis accorded with the changed line of development in Islamic studies, but the alterations which the picture of Islam underwent in the public mind outside Orientalist circles were more fundamental and often came near to constituting a break with previous conceptions. In conclusion, among the attempts to consider Islam in a new historical perspective, mention may be made to those of H. G. Wells, Spengler, and Toynbee.

H. G. Wells, in his *Outline of History* keeps closest to the old conceptions of Islam, fitting it into a system which treats human history as a historico-genetic unity and ends in the Utopia of a world government formed by the intellectual aristocracy of the future.

Fundamentally different is the philosophy of history portrayed by Oswald Spengler in his *Untergang des Abendlandes*. He does not recognize a separate Islamic civilization. Under the influence of a tendency (widespread at that time in German Islamic research) to derive Islamic civilization from oriental Hellenism, he combines the later Classical age, Hellenism, Judaism, early Christianity, and Iranianism with the first centuries of Islam—i.e., the period from approximately 300 B.C. to approximately A.D. 1000—as a single epoch of high civilization; for lack of a better name he designates it as 'Arabic' or 'Magian', and places it alongside the civilizations of ancient Egypt, ancient Babylon, ancient China, together with those of Antiquity (the Apollonic-Dionysian civilization) and of the West (the Faustian civilization). Spengler accuses the Oriental specialists of paying too much attention to linguistic frontiers and of failing to recognize that 'Magian life-feeling' (*Lebensgefühl*) which is found in all religions of this epoch, whether their outer form be Greek, Aramaic, Iranian or Arabic. Spengler attributes to this *Lebensgefühl* a special picture of the world. To the 'Magian' man the world is a cave, its top being the sky, its bottom the earth; the former is the home of the *pneuma* (the spirit) the latter of the *psyche* (the soul). Man is left only with 'Islam', submission to God's will; and God's plan of salvation determines human history with its prophets and saviours. To this psychological analysis, however, Spengler adds the biological theory that all civilizations follow the same typical course, leading from the first beginnings through the stages of growth to maturity, and finally passing through disintegration to an ultimate decay which bears within it the seeds of a new civilization. Spengler also attempts to explain the facts of interaction between two civilizations (facts which do not fit into the pattern of growth, blossoming and death) by a scientific metaphor; he speaks of 'pseudomorphosis' and assumes that the *Lebensgefühl* of a newly arising civilization pours into the hollow moulds of its dead predecessor as a mineral substance fills a crystal mould which is foreign to it.

In complete contrast to Spengler, but under the influence of his theory of the decay of civilizations, A. J. Toynbee shortly afterwards made a new attempt to explain the nature of world history. Whereas Spengler's morphology of civilization is determined by the fate of the German people, Toynbee's view of history depends upon the destiny of the British Empire. He rejects the view current in the nineteenth century which made the nation-state into the historical norm, and he makes the worship of nationality and the militarism of the nation-states responsible for the crises of Western civilization. The decisive historical norm he considers to be the civilization-communities, one of which is the Occidental civilization of Christian Western Europe and its colonies. But while Spengler regards a civilization as a biological structure, which can be characterized by a *Lebensgefühl* peculiar to it, growing, maturing, and decaying according to immutable natural laws, Toynbee regards every civilization as based on the achievements of a community united for common action. The birth, growth, and disappearance of a civilization are determined not by biological laws, race or environment, but ultimately by the free act of will of individuals in whom the *élan vital* is strongest and who, by their great talents, are able to save the community in time of crisis. A civilization-community of this nature does not grow through mere geographical expansion or through technical advances; in times of crisis only intensification provides the strength for composure and for the surmounting of external difficulties. Without this the crisis leads to collapse and decay, to conflict between the ruling minority and its subjects, the so-called internal proletariat in the mother country and the so-called 'external' proletariat —the primitive peoples within the sway of civilization. Disorders follow, interrupted by violent breakaways and calm spells. Often the ruling minority contrives to create a universal state with a definite political philosophy and the necessary officialdom, or the soldiery of the external proletariat may construct a universal state, or the internal proletariat may take over the religion of a foreign civilization and transform it into a universal religion; Toynbee, in contrast to Spengler, emphasizes the fact that civilization-communities are woven together by super-religions and universal churches, by philosophies and universal states. In analysing the decay of a civilization he devotes particular attention to the conflicts within the soul of a community in time of crisis, and concludes that deliverance is always sought through a saviour; in the present crisis of Western civilization he pins his hope to the Catholic church which, unlike the Protestant church, has no national ties.

Toynbee does not regard Islam as an independent civilization; for him Arabia in the sixth and seventh centuries was still a province of the Roman Empire, both politically and culturally, and hence he treats the pre-Islamic Arabs as belonging to the external proletariat which, according to his theory of the decay of civilizations, inevitably came into conflict with the Roman Empire. The form which this reaction was to take was decided by Muḥammad, in whose life—progressing from contemplative introspection to vigorous action—Toynbee sees a classic example of his theory that the creative individual gathers his powers in seclusion before entering public life. The substance of Muḥammad's message he considers to be monotheism and the Islamic theory of the state, both of which he traces back to the examples which the Roman Empire offered to an Arab observer in its religion and its political institutions. Toynbee regards the spread of Islam from the Atlantic Ocean to Central Asia as an attack upon Christianity which succeeded only as far as Byzantium was concerned; on the Iberian peninsula it gave rise to a counter-attack which not only hurled back the Muslims into North Africa but also led the Spaniards and Portuguese on voyages of discovery to all parts of the world. Like other

Christian critics, Toynbee has difficulty in finding his bearings in Islamic theocracy. From the experiences of the Christian church he postulates the principle that a religion which seeks the protection of the state or subjects itself to the state will, on balance, lose much more than it can gain; he is forced to admit, however, that the history of Islam contradicts this principle. As a corollary of this basic theory he describes the 'Abbasid caliphate as a rebirth of the universal state of the Near East which had been destroyed by Alexander the Great, and (unlike Spengler) regards the victory of Islam as having finally destroyed Hellenism; a further corollary is that he speaks of the universal church of Islam, from which, in his opinion, the new Arabic and Iranic civilizations were derived. It would be unjust, however, to reproach Toynbee for this theory, for the relation between politics and religion in Islam is in fact a problem about which Islamic students themselves have not yet reached agreement. Our survey must therefore end with the depressing conclusion that the lack of adequate preliminary work by Orientalists is mainly responsible for the fact that in Western historiography the portrayal and assessment of Islam as a historical phenomenon are still far removed from the perfection which Orientalists more than any others so ardently desire.

27. SOME REMARKS ON WEIL'S HISTORY OF THE CALIPHS

D. M. DUNLOP

Lecturer in Islamic History in the University of Cambridge

It was at Heidelberg in mid-February 1846 that Weil wrote the preface to the first volume of his History of the Caliphs. Who was this Dr. Weil, who thus attempted, practically for the first time, to undertake the enormous task of displaying the history of the successors of Muḥammad, the history, that is, of the Caliphate, an institution which bulks in general history as large as almost any other and with which, up to the time in which it flourished, only the Roman Empire and perhaps the Papacy are to be compared? Dr. Weil, before he came to write his History of the Caliphs, had had a remarkable and in some ways unique career, which undoubtedly put him in the position of being able to write it. Details of that career are to be found in the *Jewish encyclopaedia*, for Weil was descended from a Jewish family, and it may safely be said that the story of his early difficulties and ultimate success is not the least interesting of the biographies which feature in the pages of that remarkable work. Weil was also known to our contemporary Najīb al-ʿAqīqī, when he compiled his interesting book on European Orientalists, *al-Mustashriqūn* (Cairo, 1947); but for anything like a complete account of the author of the History of the Caliphs one will turn more naturally to the other work. It is from the *Jewish encyclopaedia*, then, that I extract the following on Gustav Weil.

He was born in Sulzburg, Baden, 25 April 1808; died at Freiburg-im-Breisgau, 29 August 1889, at the advanced age of eighty-one. Being destined for the rabbinate, he was taught Hebrew as well as German and French, and he received instruction in Latin from the minister of his native town. At the age of twelve he went to Metz, where his grandfather was rabbi, to study the Talmud. For this, however, he developed very little taste, and he abandoned his original intention of entering upon a theological career. In 1828 he entered the University of Heidelberg, devoting himself to the study of philology and history; at the same time he studied Arabic under Umbreit. Though without means, he nevertheless went to study under De Sacy in Paris in 1830, and thence followed the French military expedition to Algiers, acting as correspondent at Algiers for the *Augsburger Allgemeine Zeitung*. This position he resigned in January 1831, and journeyed to Cairo, where he was appointed instructor of French at the Egyptian Medical School of Abū Zaʿbal. (To this it may be added from Najīb al-ʿAqīqī, who evidently had his own sources of information on Weil, that while in Paris he studied Syriac under Quatremère, and exchanged German lessons for lessons in Arabic from the learned medical, Dr. Perron.) In Cairo he utilized the opportunity to study with the Arabic philologists Muḥammad ʻAyyād al-Ṭanṭāwī and Aḥmad al-Tūnusī. Here also he acquired modern Persian and Turkish, and save for a short interruption, occasioned by a visit to Europe, he remained in Egypt till March 1835. Weil returned to Europe via Constantinople, where he remained for some time, pursuing Turkish studies. In Germany he sought permission to establish himself as *privat-dozent* in the University of Heidelberg, receiving it, however, only after great difficulties. Weil had attacked Joseph von Hammer-Purgstall in a translation of al-Zamakhsharī's *Aṭwaq al-dhahab*, published at Stuttgart in 1836, and the faculty of Heidelberg, being unable to judge the matter, hesitated to appoint him *dozent* because of Hammer-Purgstall's high reputation. De Sacy's recommendation opened the way to him, which, however, was destined to remain rough and rugged. He gained his livelihood as assistant librarian, and was appointed librarian in 1838, which position he retained till 1861; in that year he became professor.

The most comprehensive work of Weil is his *Geschichte der Chalifen* (History of the Caliphs) in five volumes, 1846–62, which is virtually an elaboration of the original works of Muslim historians, whom in large part he studied from manuscripts; it treats also of the Egyptian and Spanish caliphates. This was followed by the *Geschichte der islamischen Völker von Muhammed bis zur Zeit des Sultan Selim*, published at Stuttgart in 1866, an introduction to the medieval history of the Orient. A number of his works had appeared earlier, notably a life of Muḥammad (*Mohammed der Prophet*) in 1843. After 1866 Weil confined his literary activity to the publication of reviews in the *Heidelberger Jahrbücher* and the *Jenäische Litteratur-Zeitung*. Honours from various states, including Baden and Prussia, were conferred on him. His collection of Arabic manuscripts after his death came to the University of Heidelberg, by gift of his children. In his own time Heidelberg University had been practically without Oriental manuscripts, as had already been remarked by a French reviewer of the History of the Caliphs.

It is to some of the contemporary reviews of Weil's book that I should like now to draw your attention. Here at least we get some kind of impression of how the History of the Caliphs struck informed persons on its first appearance. It was especially in France, it seems, that the book attracted attention. The reason appears to be that learned opinion in France, under the influence still of de Sacy, the first and in some ways the greatest of modern European Arabists, was already alerted for the appearance of a work of this kind. First, let me quote the eloquent words of Jules Mohl, like Weil of German origin and attracted to France by the reputation of the Paris Orientalists of that time. Mohl settled in France and became secretary of the *Société Asiatique*. In July 1846, shortly after the appearance of the first volume of Weil's history, he made an 'allocution' to the *Société* which included the following:

> M. Weil, professor at Heidelberg, has just published the first volume of a History of the Caliphs, which forms the continuation of his Life of Muḥammad. This subject is one of the most important that a historian can select; the extent of the Arab empire, the destruction of the ancient civilizations and the change of social conditions of the most cultivated part of the world make, of the formation of the caliphate, one of the greatest events of history. The caliphate itself has ceased to exist for six centuries, but the civilizing force contained in it was such, that the consequences of the movement which it impressed on the East still survive. Thus the task which the historian of the caliphate takes upon himself is difficult actually in proportion to the greatness of his theme, for it is a question for him not only to give the description of the Arab conquests and relate the history of their princes during six centuries; he has also to deal with the origin and development of a whole civilization; with the changes which this civilization has produced among numerous nations, different in race and character, who have in their turn reacted in different ways upon their conquerors; he has to deal with the influence which the principles and forms of the new administration have exercised on the condition of the provinces, the constitution of property, municipal government, legislation, indeed on all the interests of mankind. The caliphate is a unique fact in the history of the world which can only be compared from the point of view of spiritual power with the papacy.
>
> There is certainly no lack of materials for writing its history; general chronicles, chronicles of provinces and towns, biographies of illustrious men, works of poets and their commentators, collections of laws and legal decisions, works of theology and science, in short, all the parts of Arabic and Persian literature abound in facts of which each contributes directly or indirectly its tribute to this history. Already a certain number of the most important points have been treated in detail and not a month passes perhaps without the appearance in Europe of a work which adds something to the materials which may be disposed of. But in spite of all these efforts, only a small part of the sources of the history of the caliphate has been brought to light; the remainder is scattered in the libraries of Europe and the East. It is in this state that M. Weil has found his subject and has had the courage to confront it . . .
>
> The first volume of his work contains the history of the caliphate from the death of Muḥammad to the end of the Umayyad dynasty. This

volume includes only the political history, in the strict sense, of the period and the author reserves for later explanations of every kind regarding the social state of the country. His narrative is simple, he carefully preserves the actual words of the persons whose actions he relates, and he relegates to notes at the foot of the pages the critical discussions arising from doubtful points. The continuation will show whether in its present stage science is sufficiently advanced already to permit the composition of a history of the caliphate such as one would desire; in any case, one can see by what has already appeared that the work of M. Weil is a book of undoubted merit.

When in 1848 the second volume of the History of the Caliphs was published it was greeted by Mohl as follows (August of the same year), speaking of new works on the history of the Arabs under Islam:

First mention is due to the continuation of the History of the Caliphs by M. Weil of Heidelberg, whose second volume has just appeared. M. Weil has drawn the materials for his work to a great extent from the MSS. of the public libraries of Paris, Leiden and Gotha, which have been entrusted to him in the most liberal manner; the communication of them, which would have been impossible twenty years ago, witnesses strongly to the progress which the republic of letters has made in our time. One knows the strange jealousy with which the manuscripts in public libraries were guarded formerly; they were fastened with chains, as at Florence; the catalogue was hidden or its very existence denied, as at Rome and the Escurial; almost everywhere lending abroad was refused; it was almost as if they were regarded rather as relics than instruments of work. Today most of these barriers have fallen, and even in libraries where loans are not yet made abroad, as in nearly all the libraries of England, it is no longer this grim superstition which prevents it but ancient laws, which will disappear before the spirit of the age . . .

The subject of M. Weil's work is the political history of the caliphate of the East, and the second volume extends from the fall of the Umayyads to the death of the twenty-second caliph of the 'Abbasid dynasty. It was the epoch of the Arab empire's greatest external splendour, when their power and at the same time their literary and intellectual culture had attained their culminating point, but when already secret causes of decline were rapidly revealing themselves and leading to the defection of the provinces remote from Baghdād. M. Weil follows in detail the history of each of these revolts; but thereafter, to secure the unity of his plan, he immediately leaves these new states to themselves, when they have gained their liberty, and only occupies himself with them again in their relations with the caliphate. His judgement in this is perfectly sound, for most of these states had in common with the empire of

Baghdād only their origin and a fundamental resemblance in their constitutions; but their destiny and continuance depended on circumstances entirely remote from the caliphate.

In the *Journal Asiatique* for 1848 there appeared also, as well as this appreciation by Jules Mohl, another notice of Weil's second volume, unsigned, which contains somewhat more incisive criticism. This anonymous reviewer notes, what had escaped the attention of Mohl, that Weil had made use of Arabic manuscripts of al-Ṭabarī preserved in the royal library at Berlin. The words of the reviewer, translated into English, are as follows:

> The Arabic text of al-Ṭabarī has served him as principal guide, as far as the reign of al-Mahdī; and it is to this author that he is indebted for revelations which one looks for in vain in the later chronicles, and which cast a new light on the corrupt means employed by the 'Abbasids to attain to power. The correspondence of the Caliph al-Manṣūr with Abū Muslim and with the 'Alid Muḥammad ibn al-Ḥasan proves that the 'Abbasids sacrificed to their desire for ruling not only Arab nationality but also the fundamental principles of Islam.

The correspondence thus signalized by Weil and taken up by him into his second volume can now conveniently be read in the original in the Leiden edition of al-Ṭabarī. The anonymous reviewer praises the critical use which Weil has made of his sources. He makes the same remark as Mohl about the absence of information concerning certain states after their foundation, until they again come within the orbit of the caliphate, but notes that one has here a complete history of the Tahirids, Saffarids, Tulunids, Ikhshidids, Sajids, and Hamdanids, with a part of that of the Samanids and Dailamites.

It seems likely that the author of these remarks was the French Arabist Joseph Reinaud. Reinaud was at all events evidently responsible for some remarks on Weil's third volume, which appeared in the *Journal Asiatique*, June 1851, under the signature R—d:

> Here is the end of the important work, the publication of which was begun by M. Weil some years ago . . . This volume extends as far as the capture of Baghdād by the Tatars in 1258 and the total collapse of the eastern caliphate . . . M. Weil, wishing to give unity to the subject of his work has been obliged to sketch in broad traits the picture of the events which took place in the Middle Ages in the western part of the Muslim empire, an empire which then embraced a great part of the known world. In this volume M. Weil speaks especially of events of importance at Baghdād and in the ancient Chaldaea, as well as what was signalled by the domination of Buyid, Seljuq and Khwarizmian princes. One part he has taken care not to forget, i.e. the battles in

> which at the time of the Crusades our ancestors took part in Palestine and Syria and Mesopotamia, and which re-echoed through the East as well as the West . . . As one has already had occasion to remark, M. Weil has drawn from the sources. By his travels he has acquired a personal knowledge of Egypt and Syria. For the composition of his book he has consulted the collections of oriental manuscripts of Paris, Leiden and Gotha. Some of these volumes have even been communicated to him in Heidelberg.

Mohl for his part greeted the third volume in his rounded style:

> M. Weil, professor at Heidelberg, has published the third and last volume of his *History of the Caliphate*, in which he has treated of the three last centuries of that great empire, its internal struggles and its destruction. It is the first complete history of the caliphate, written according to the demands of European criticism and composed from the original sources, for the great work of Price (i.e. Major David Price, *Chronological retrospect or memoirs of the principal events of Mahommedan history*, four volumes, London, 1811–21) is only a compilation . . . while the work of M. Weil is a political history of the caliphate, where the authors are controlled by each other, the facts discussed and the authorities cited.

Mohl then returns to his previous criticism.

> The necessity of concentrating so many facts in a restricted space has forced M. Weil to confine himself almost exclusively to the political side of the Caliphate. Might we not hope that he would present us with . . . the social side of this empire . . .?

Weil's appreciation of his learned compatriot's praise must have been tempered by the remark with which it was introduced. For Mohl had begun his notice by saying that though the progress made by Arabic history would have appeared fantastic twenty years earlier, it still was far from corresponding to the actual requirements of science. This coupled with the reiterated remark about Weil's History of the Caliphs being, so to say, exclusively a political history certainly implies some censure.

Before proceeding to later views of the work, which will engage us presently, it may be of interest to learn what Weil himself thought about his history and see, if possible, how his own views developed. It is quite clear that he regarded it as a pioneer work. 'I have here,' he says, 'as in every work which lacks critical predecessors and is derived from manuscript sources, given account of all new facts in the notes.' Weil takes no notice of Price's *Chronological retrospect* and indeed among previous works mentions only a restricted presentation of the history of the caliphate in a periodical of the time, by G. Flügel. Flügel's merits as the editor of the *Fihrist* and otherwise are well known, but no doubt Weil was right in speaking of his account of Arab history under the caliphate as if it were of no special importance, and even as containing many mistakes.

The difficulties of the task before him were vividly present to Weil's mind, as they might well be to any man proposing to write a history of the caliphs. 'Even in the period handled in this first volume,' he wrote, 'it was often very difficult critically to sift the material, disfigured as it was by oriental phantasy, Muslim orthodoxy and political partisanship, and find out the bare historical truth. If even al-Ṭabarī's translator (Bal'amī), who served as the model to almost all later Persian historians, ventured, as can be seen from a number of passages given in the notes to the present volume, not only to leave out much which seemed to him non-essential or did not fit into his system, but even formally to falsify his author, what might be expected of independent historians who stood under no control? The Sunnites threw a thick veil over all defects which adhered to the first four caliphs, the old Companions and relatives of the Prophet. The Shi'ites deck out 'Alī especially and his descendants with all imaginable virtues. The adherents of the house of 'Abbās exert themselves to present the Umayyads to us as the most depraved of men. The pious Muslims of every party estimate the caliphs only according to their degree of piety, so that it is possible only by comparison of the different sources and the utilisation of their weaknesses and ineptitudes, through which they frequently betray themselves, to gain a sure historical basis.'

In the foreword to his second volume Weil emphasizes the point about the separating off of outlying provinces of the caliphate to form independent states, and how far he is going to deal with the history of these new states, which, as we saw, attracted the attention of the reviewers in France. He goes on to say that the second volume differs from the first also in that literary history is specially taken into account. The first beginnings of a written literature under the Umayyads, he says, scarcely come into contact with the political history, which forms the principal subject of the first volume. Under the 'Abbasids, on the other hand, with the help of Greek and Persian learning, the studies of the Arabs assume a scientific character, and a literature in the full sense of the word, as wide as all the interests of men, began to develop. Further, it developed in close association with political happenings and reflected often the policy of the caliphs themselves. Weil, we see, was unwilling or unable to follow the suggestion of one of his critics, and deal at large with social conditions, but at least he modifies the nearly exclusively political character of the history in the first volume, to admit a substantial amount about literature. In his third volume, he offers an appendix of twenty pages, on 'The advances of Arabic literature from the middle of the third to the middle of the fourth century of the Hijra', i.e. from the death of al-Mutawakkil onwards, when, as he says, literary activity became more and more divorced from the central power. The significance of this evidently is that his History after the second volume resumes its original character as a record of, in principle, political events.

Weil, like the conscientious scholar that he was, is careful to name his manuscript sources. The examination of these is instructive.

(1) The list in his first volume of 1846 begins with the *Dhakhīrat al-'ulūm wa-natījat al-fuhūm* of the mystic al-Bakrī (Brockelmann, ii, 334), a late writer (he died in 952/1547) whom no one nowadays would be likely to cite as an authority for the earliest days of the caliphate. Weil used MS. Gotha 1578, which is apparently unique. One may compare with this work the *Muḥāḍarāt al-abrār* of another mystic, the celebrated Muḥyī'l Dīn ibn al-'Arabī (died 638/1240), which contains a substantial amount of history, including short accounts of the reigns of most of the caliphs, and other material dealing with the early history of Islam. But it is very questionable if the *Muḥāḍarāt al-abrār* is to be relied on. One might hazard a guess that the same applies to the *Dhakhīrat al-'ulūm*.

(2) The second authority in Weil's list of manuscripts is the *Ta'rīkh al-khamīs fī aḥwāl anfas al-nafīs* of Ḥusayn b. Muḥammad b. al-Ḥasan al-Diyārbakrī, which he used in MS. Gotha 326. There are several copies in the British Museum, one in Cambridge, and I have myself seen another in the Fātiḥ Mosque in Istanbul. Al-Diyārbakrī (Brockelmann, ii, 381) is still later than al-Bakrī, Weil's first-named authority, since he died in 990/1582. His *Ta'rīkh al-khamīs*, which gives a detailed life of Muḥammad after Ibn Hishām and an account of the caliphs down to the Ottoman Sultan Murād, is by no means the kind of authority we should want to cite today.

(3) Weil's third-mentioned manuscript is al-Suyūṭī's *Ta'rīkh al-khulafā'*, of which there are now various editions and an English translation by Major H. S. Jarrett (Calcutta, 1881). Al-Suyūṭī is also very late (849/1445–911/1505), and though knowledgeable can scarcely be considered as more than a subsidiary authority. Weil used Gotha MS. 321.

(4) His fourth was a Paris manuscript of al-Mas'ūdī, *Murūj al-dhahab* (then No. 1815).

(5) His fifth manuscript was al-Dhahabī, *Ta'rīkh al-Islām*, i.e. a single volume from the Bibliothèque Royale of Paris, perhaps that numbered now 1880, but then No. 626. The importance of the great biographical compilation of al-Dhahabī is now well known. Weil must have been the first or one of the first to use it. It was arranged by its author in decades, within which were given the biographies of eminent persons who had died during the period, and it extended down to the year A.H. 700, in seventy classes. It has survived unfortunately only in a scattered state and perhaps incompletely. Details can be seen in Brockelmann, *GAL*, ii, 46–7. More

recently the manuscripts of the work were discussed by Joseph de Somogyi in *JRAS*, 1932.

(6) Sixthly, Weil cites the Paris manuscript of Abu'l-Maḥāsin b. Taghrī Birdī (Brockelmann, ii, 42), a respectable if late authority (he died in 815/1412), now Paris, No. 1551. This contains that part of Ibn Taghrī Birdī's *al-Baḥr al-zākhir fī 'ilm al-awwal wa'l-ākhir* (i.e. the swelling sea in the knowledge of first and last—surely a splendid title) which deals with the history from A.H. 32 to A.H. 71.

(7) Seventhly, Muḥammad b. Shākir al-Dimashqī al-Kutubī, *'Uyūn al-tawārīkh* (Brockelmann, ii, 48), i.e. a work, by the continuator of Ibn Khallikān, which is described as 'a history of caliphs and learned men, with special reference to Damascus'. Weil seems to have borrowed one of three volumes of this work preserved at Paris.

(8) He also had volumes 10 to 12 of the original text of al-Ṭabarī from Berlin. This was specially important. Kosegarten had already begun his work on al-Ṭabarī, but Kosegarten's third and last volume, when it appeared in 1853, giving al-Ṭabarī's Arabic text with a Latin translation, only came down as far as A.H. 23. The use which Weil made of al-Ṭabarī was no doubt one of the reasons which led to the appearance of the Leiden edition, published under De Goeje's general editorship from 1879 onwards.

(9) Ninth on the list is the *Futūḥ Miṣr* of Ibn 'Abd al-Ḥakam, which Weil borrowed from Ewald.

(10) Tenth was the *Kitāb al-ma'ārif* of Ibn Qutayba. Weil here characterizes the *Kitāb al-ma'ārif*, a manuscript of which he had received from J. H. Möller and which was shortly to be edited by Wüstenfeld, at Göttingen in 1850, as a work in which he 'found nothing considerable about the period dealt with in the present (first) volume, which was not already known to me from other sources'. This somewhat qualified appreciation he was afterwards to modify considerably. Even in 1846 he wrote,

> My supposition, which I have several times expressed, that many historians tend to ascribe later deeds to earlier caliphs, I found confirmed in regard to the conquest of Persia, which even by al-Ṭabarī is to a great extent placed in 'Umar's caliphate, while according to Ibn Qutayba (i.e. in the *Kitāb al-ma'ārif*) Rayy, a part of Fārs, Kirmān, Khurāsān, Sijistān and Ṭabaristān were conquered only under 'Uthmān. So it is also expressly said by this author that al-Ḥajjāj went direct from Medina to Iraq. Also he agrees with my opinion when he says briefly that al-Ḥajjāj ruled Iraq for twenty years, pacified it, and humiliated his opponents.

In 1846 Weil knew the Arabic historian al-Balādhurī as yet only in excerpts which he had received from Reinaud in Paris. By 1848, indeed already in October 1847, when the preface to his second volume was written, he had received at Heidelberg from Leiden their MS., No. 1903, which was a copy of al-Balādhurī's *Futūḥ al-buldān*. Later, Weil spoke of al-Balādhurī and this work of his, in a very interesting way, in the appendix on literature already mentioned as forming part of Volume III of the History of the Caliphs (1851). 'How much independent value this work has,' wrote Weil in that year, 'we cannot directly estimate, as we cannot yet compare it with those of his predecessors, whom he frequently cites, such as al-Wāqidī, al-Madā'inī, Ibn Kalbī, and others.' Then he goes on,

> More important, although to a great extent consisting only of short notices, and written in a dry chronicle style (*Chronikstyl*) is Ibn Qutayba's historical work, known as *Kitāb al-ma'ārif*, because it at the same time contains valuable explanations on the genealogy of the Arab tribes, as well as many valuable pieces of information concerning the culture and science of the two first centuries of the Hijra.

Weil adds,

> Ibn Qutayba spent the greatest part of his life in Baghdād and taught Tradition there, yet about the history of Baghdād which took place under his eyes he is extremely reticent, and from the accession of al-Wāthiq to the death of al-Muhtadī (A.H. 256) with which he ends, one finds practically nothing more than the dates of accession, birth and death of the caliphs.

The preference here given to the *Kitāb al-ma'ārif* over al-Balādhurī's *Futūḥ al-buldān* is interesting, and perhaps justified. Not that Weil underestimated al-Balādhurī, to whom he devotes another appendix in volume III, in which for the first time the contents of the *Futūḥ al-buldān*, afterwards to be edited by de Goeje (1870), became generally available to European readers. Only much later was the complete work translated under the title of *The Origin of the Islamic state*, by Philip K. Hitti and F. C. Murgotten (New York, 1916–24).

It is not possible to give all the new authorities in manuscript cited by Weil in the foreword to his second volume, except most cursorily. He has now got, in addition to al-Balādhurī already mentioned, the third volume of Ibn Khaldūn's history, the anonymous *Kitāb al-'uyūn wa'l-ḥadā'iq* (afterwards edited by de Goeje in *Fragmenta Historicorum Arabicorum*, vol. I), Ibn al-Athīr from A.H. 155–271, another volume of the '*Uyūn al-tawārīkh* of Muḥammad b. Shākir, Sibṭ Ibn al-Jawzī's *Mir'āt al-zamān* from 190–281, the *Mir'āt al-janān* of al-Yāfi'ī (another late author, who died 768/1367), the second volume of Ibn Taghrī Birdī's *al-Nujūm al-zāhira*, and finally, two works of which the identification was not altogether clear to Weil, the

Kitāb al-duwal al-munqaṭi'a of al-Azdī (Brockelmann, i, 321) and a Gotha codex (No. 261), later identified by Dozy as 'Arīb's continuation of al-Ṭabarī. Part of this manuscript dealing with the history of the Fatimids of Africa from A.H. 290 to 320, was translated into English as long ago as 1840 by John Nicholson.

This is undoubtedly a better, more workmanlike list than the first, and by this time Weil was acquainted with most of the books which would be considered necessary for anyone attempting to write the history of the caliphate today, though in some cases he had only odd volumes of Arabic works which he might now examine completely, if he wished, and of course nowadays he might expect to use most of them in a printed edition, more or less critical.

Weil continued to study these historical works, and in the appendix on literature in volume III, already several times referred to, he sets down some of his conclusions and impressions. Contrasting al-Ṭabarī with both al-Balādhurī and Ibn Qutayba, who, he says (referring to Ḥājjī Khalīfa, and not perhaps quite accurately) were content with giving short extracts of earlier works—al-Balādhurī at least frequently quoted local authorities on the Arab conquests, rather than books, though doubtless he often got from them book-answers instead of real tradition—in any case Weil speaks of the three volumes of the Arabic al-Ṭabarī, i.e. of course the original, which he got from Berlin and studied at Heidelberg. The three contained the years 70–159 of the Hijra, i.e. down to the death of al-Manṣūr. Weil found interestingly enough that al-Ṭabarī, in dealing with the life of Muḥammad (in the earlier part of his work, that is) goes somewhat more over to the miraculous and legendary, as he says, than Ibn Hishām, in the older *Sīrat al-Rasūl*. Here again we see that Weil knows a good source when he comes across it. It is likely that if he had been alive, he would have been very interested in the early recension of Ibn Isḥāq by Yūnus b. Bukayr (died 199/814, while Ibn Hishām, who made the recension usually studied, died 218/834), which has now come to light.

Still speaking of al-Ṭabarī, Weil goes on:

> Of the value of the Persian translation, which at the instance of the Samanid Manṣūr b. Nūḥ was made of this work in 352 and the Turkish translation which depends on it, mention has repeatedly been made in this book. If the translator (Bal'amī, that is) gave al-Ṭabarī's name to his work, although the Annals contained much which either seemed to him too detailed or did not fit into his system, this shows the reputation which al-Ṭabarī already enjoyed soon after his death. Apart from the many omissions and alterations, the translations are considerably different from the original text, in that they are no longer a collection of interrupted traditions, but form a connected account derived from

> these, with omission of the authorities and usually also without regard for the difference of the traditions. The same thing was done not only by the translators (of al-Ṭabarī), but also by later Arabic historians, e.g. Ibn al-Athīr who left aside the authorities cited by al-Ṭabarī and by so doing shortened the work by almost the half, although they were truer and exacter in presenting the facts. These works also were too voluminous for the mass of scholars, and there followed compendia, as Abu'l-Fidā', al-Makīn, and others. Not less than the various translators the continuations which later historians wrote of them speak for the great value of the Annals of al-Ṭabarī, especially those by the Sabian, Thābit b. Sinān, and 'Abdallāh b. Muḥammad [Brockelmann, Aḥmad] al-Farghāni.

Weil then mentions 'as a completion of al-Ṭabarī . . . the hitherto unknown works of Abū Faḍl Aḥmad b. Abī Ṭāhir Tayfūr and his son Abu'l-Ḥusayn 'Ubaydallāh'. The first, says Weil, reaches to towards the end of al-Muhtadī's caliphate and the latter till the death of al-Muqtadir. A Bodleian manuscript in fact contains Ibn Abī Ṭāhir's *Ta'rīkh Baghdād*, volume 6, from 204/218–883 (death of al-Ma'mūn). This was edited and translated into German by H. Keller (Leipzig, 1908). It has been described as a 'main source of al-Ṭabarī'. Once again Weil pointed forward to something which was to engage people's interest later. Another work the importance of which he recognized was the *Kāmil* of al-Mubarrad, destined to be edited in masterly fashion by William Wright, at Leipzig in 1864.

The two remaining volumes (IV and V) of Weil's History, which came out at Stuttgart in 1860 and 1862, with a new title, are no doubt of less interest, corresponding to their subject, which is no longer the once glorious caliphs of Baghdad, but their sad successors, the 'Abbasid caliphs in Egypt, who enjoyed less than the shadow of rule. I do not know whether it is by chance, or because the subscribers lost interest, that there are two sets of Weil's History in the Cambridge University Library which go only as far as the fourth volume. In 1866 Weil again submitted to the public a production of his with the title, already mentioned, of *Geschichte der islamischen Völker*. Thereafter he wrote no more big works.

One's impression is that the series of volumes on Islamic history had been less successful than the author had hoped. There was, so far as I know, no second edition, nor does the series, nor even the more generally interesting first three volumes, seem to have been translated into any foreign language. The work of course is very extensive and so not well adapted to translation, and most people who wished to use it were probably scholars and able to read German. There may have been other reasons which prevented its becoming popular, at least with the Arabists, which it seems never to have been. F. F. Arbuthnot, M.R.A.S., author of rather a poor book called *Arabian authors*, which yet reflects the range of interest common among British Orientalists at the time it was written (1890) speaks of Weil as 'the translator', with reference to his work on Ibn Hishām and the Arabian Nights, but does not mention the History of the Caliphs by so much as a word. Weil's work *Biblische Legenden der Muselmänner*, published in 1845, was translated into English in the following year, 1846, but there was no English translation of the *Geschichte der Chalifen*.

It may be allowed that he sometimes made mistakes, and I have noticed that in volume II under Hārūn al-Rashīd he appears to give a wrong motivation (Khazar Khāqān killed by an Arab) for the Khazar invasion (through the Caucasus into the lands of Islam) of the year 183/799. Similarly in volume I under 'Uthmān he denies that al-Ṭabarī has any notice of the defeat of 'Abd al-Raḥmān al-Bāhilī at Balanjar, whereas in point of fact he has several pages. Such mistakes, however, are practically unavoidable in dealing with the mass of material which makes up the history of the caliphs, and no one has suggested that we should stop reading Gibbon because of the mistakes set out from his works by J. B. Bury. The fact seems to be that Weil was sometimes what Gibbon rarely is—a little dull, and did not succeed in stimulating any of his foreign readers to translate him into their own languages. It is certainly somewhat remarkable that he is not mentioned in Reynold Nicholson's *Literary history of the Arabs*, or if the subject of Professor Nicholson's book renders that less surprising, that he is completely disregarded in the more recent works of Professor Hitti. There is one conspicuous exception to the general disregard of Weil among the English-speaking peoples, viz. Sir William Muir, and with Muir's position *vis-à-vis* Weil I propose now to deal.

Muir, as is well known, like Weil, published first a *Life of Mahomet*, then a history of the subsequent history of Islam ultimately entitled *The Caliphate: its rise, decline and fall* (editions from 1883). It is not simply that Muir and his Heidelberg predecessor produced works of similar title. Professor Carl Brockelmann within recent years wrote a *Geschichte der islamischen Völker*, and it would not, I think, be affirmed, in spite of the similarity of title, that he had submitted to Weil's influence. The case was different with Muir, who in the preface to the second edition of his *Caliphate* (September 1891) wrote:

> Towards the close, and especially for the brief chapter on the Caliphate under the Mameluke dynasty, I have drawn largely on Weil's admirable *Geschichte der Chalifen*, which indeed has been my constant companion throughout. I gratefully acknowledge my obligations to the late Dr. Weil. The more his great history is studied in connection with the original authorities, the more one is impressed with the vast research, the unfailing accuracy, and the dispassionate judgment of the author.

That indeed was a handsome tribute on the part of Muir, and it was deserved. It is difficult to estimate exactly how far Muir's work was based on the *Geschichte der Chalifen*. Muir quotes Weil not much more than half-a-dozen times, sometimes in the text, but usually in the notes, and always in the second half of *The Caliphate*. It would seem that Muir used his predecessor's work quite freely, but by no means slavishly. For example, on the question of the introduction of a specifically Muslim coinage, he differs from Weil quite sharply, and in another case criticizes his judgement (of barbarous conduct on the part of al-Mahdī). In one instance at least he specifically says that he has followed Weil. Weil's German volumes were available, and evidently not well known in this country. There was no reason why they should not be used, and it would seem that, as he said, Muir did in fact use them extensively.

Take the following account of the man who is often said to have been the real founder of the 'Abbasid dynasty, Abū Muslim al-Khurāsānī.

> He had drums of dog skin: when he wished to break up camp, he caused these drums to be beaten, and their uncanny sounds filled the troops with fear and alarm. Numberless men of Quraysh, Muḍar, Rabī'a and al-Yaman, as also the leading Persian families, among them many *faqīhs* and poets, owed their deaths to him. It is said that 600,000 persons were numbered (sc. as thus slain), apart from those who found their death in war or other public calamity. According to some he was of Arab, according to others of Kurdish origin, and it is reported that he had been a slave. He visited his harem only once or twice a year, for he considered the converse of the sexes as a form of madness. He was the most jealous man in the world. No one except himself entered his castle. All the requirements of the women were sent in through a hole in the wall. He is said to have slaughtered the mule on which his bride was brought to him, and to have burned the saddle on which she sat, lest any other man might touch them. None ate less than he, nor entertained more guests. In his bakery three thousand loaves of bread were baked daily, he had killed daily 100 sheep and a corresponding number of cattle and poultry. He had a thousand cooks, and for transporting his kitchen twelve thousand baggage animals were necessary. When he made the pilgrimage, he declared any man an outlaw who lit a fire, for he alone took upon himself the feeding of all who made pilgrimage with him. The bedouin fled before him, because they feared him as a shedder of blood. He died at the age of thirty-five years, and left only one daughter.

This somewhat disquieting picture of Abū Muslim is cited by Weil in a note from the *Kitāb al-duwal al-munqaṭi'a* of al-Azdī, a four-volume history which has never been published, used by Weil in a Gotha manuscript. It is most unlikely to have been seen by Sir William Muir, who yet has a note at the same place in his *Caliphate*, viz. the death of Abū Muslim, as follows: '600,000, we are told, met their death at his hands in cold blood, besides those slain in battle; a wild estimate, no doubt, but significant of his contempt of life. Apart from this, his character was popular and gave him the supreme command of men. Hospitable and generous, he held in Khorasan a court of great magnificence. Simple in respect of his harem, he was yet strangely jealous. The mule that brought his bride was slain and the saddle burnt, that none might ride again on it.' No source is given for this, but the indication certainly is that Muir has simply adopted it from Weil, as he was of course perfectly entitled to do.

There meantime at least we must take leave of Weil's History of the Caliphs. It is perhaps permissible to conjecture that the initial impulse to its composition is to be connected with the welcome accorded to von Ranke's celebrated *History of the popes*, first published 1834–37. Weil's great work has never enjoyed an equal reputation with von Ranke's. Yet it may be thought that on the whole the principal reason for this is the comparative obscurity, not to say exotic character, from the point of view of Europe, of the subject of which it treated. In one quarter at least, viz. in the works of Sir William Muir, the principal British historian of the caliphate, Weil's work has been very influential. It seems certain that this influence is not yet exhausted.

28. ISLAM AND SYRIA IN THE WRITINGS OF HENRI LAMMENS

K. S. SALIBI

Associate Professor of History in the American University of Beirut

To students of the *Sīra*, of early Islam, and of the regional history of Syria, the works of Henri Lammens are indispensable, in spite of their recognized faults. Most scholars would agree with Becker[1] that Lammens provided the study of the *Sīra* with a new basis; and none would underestimate his contributions on the history of the Umayyads. His *La Syrie, précis historique* (Beirut, 1921) continues to be the standard survey of the history of Syria since the Arab conquest, although it needs considerable revising. Lammens was, indeed, a scholar of undoubted originality, intelligence, and skill, and his work represents an important stage in the development of the Orientalist tradition.

While the appreciation of the Lammens contribution to Islamic studies has been almost unanimous, the recognition of his uninhibited prejudice, obvious even to the non-specialist, has been no less so. Lammens took little trouble to conceal the controversial motives which prompted his interest in Islamic history; and his basic ideas, derived from his contempt for Islam, dictated rather than resulted from his studies.[2] Fortunately, the pronounced nature of the prejudice of Lammens renders it easily discountable by the reader, and makes the editing of his works a comparatively easy task.

Henri Lammens was born in Ghent (Belgium), of Catholic Flemish stock, on 1 July 1862. At the age of fifteen he left for Beirut to join the Jesuit order there,[3] and made Lebanon his home for the rest of his life.

[1] C. Becker, 'Prinzipielles zu Lammens' Sirastudien', in *Der Islam* (1913), iv, 263 ff.

[2] For a recent criticism of Henri Lammens, see W. Montgomery Watt, *Muhammad at Mecca* (Oxford, 1953). 'There is much that is sound in what Lammens says,' he admits, '. . . [But] his high-handed treatment of the sources is unscientific. He rejects this and accepts that statement according to his own ideas and preconceptions and not according to any objective principle . . . The reason appears to be that Lammens [assumes] the truth of the theory he is trying to prove.' Ibid., p. 154. In spite of his frequent criticism of Henri Lammens, which at times approaches denunciation, Montgomery Watt makes frequent reference to his conclusions, often citing him as the authority. Later scholars were, perhaps, as guilty of inconsistency in their rejection and acceptance of the conclusions of Lammens as Lammens was in his treatment of his sources. On the other hand, even the most ardent supporters of Lammens have admitted his partiality. Thus J. M. Peñuela, a brother Jesuit who defends him most eloquently (*Mahoma, su carácter y personalidad*, offprint from *Arbor* (July–August, 1945), pp. 17–18), admits that the verdict of Lammens on Muḥammad was somewhat defective because of its one-sidedness: 'Lo que ha dicho es verdadero en su conjunto, pero no lo ha dicho todo.' Ibid., p. 75.

[3] A brother of Henri Lammens also became a Jesuit, but remained in Europe.

After one year of preliminary study at the Jesuit College in Beirut, he was transferred to the monastery of Ghazīr (Mount Lebanon), where he was enrolled as a Jesuit novice on 23 July 1878.

During his first eight years in Lebanon as student and novice, Lammens acquired an exceptional mastery of Arabic, as well as of Latin and Greek, and he appears also to have learnt Syriac. In 1886 he was assigned to teach Arabic at the Beirut Jesuit College, and he was soon publishing his own textbooks for the purpose. His first work of Orientalist scholarship appeared in 1889: a dictionary of Arabic usage (*Kitāb al-farā'id fi'l-furūq*), containing 1639 items and based on the classical Arabic lexicographers.

Lammens left teaching in 1891, and devoted the following six years to study and travel, with some interruption. He visited England, Belgium, Austria, and Egypt, and added a knowledge of English and German to his language equipment (which included French, his mother tongue, and Italian). In the meantime, he edited *al-Bashīr*, the Jesuit newspaper of Beirut, for one year in 1894. On his final return from his travels in 1897, he took charge of the administration and curriculum of the Jesuit College for three years, until he was assigned again to edit *al-Bashīr* in 1900. He resumed academic work at the College in 1903, teaching geography and history; and some of his lecture notes on Islamic history which date from this period were later published in his studies on pre-Islamic Arabia and on the Umayyads.[4]

With the establishment of the School of Oriental Studies at the Jesuit College in 1907, Lammens began his career as an Orientalist in earnest; and his appointment as professor at the newly-founded school enabled him to devote his whole effort to study and research. His well-known works on the *Sīra*[5] appeared during the first seven years following his appointment.

With the establishment of the French Mandate over Lebanon and Syria following the First World War, Lammens became the advocate of

[4] See the prefaces to *Études sur le règne du calife Omaiyade Mo'awia Ier* (Leipzig, 1908) and *Le berceau de l'Islam; l'Arabie occidentale à la veille de l'Hégire* (Rome, 1914).

[5] By *Sīra* is meant the literal Arabic biographies of the Prophet. Lammens seems to have used the term rather loosely to include *ḥadīth* of biographical and historical context or interest. He never attempted a systematic textual study of the *Sīra* proper, but rather used *Sīra* material in his critical monograph on the Prophet's life and career and on the early history of the Muhammadan movement. His first published study on the subject was an introductory essay entitled 'Qoran et tradition; comment fut composée la vie de Mahomet', in *Recherches de science religieuse* (1910), no. 1, followed by a number of monographs including 'Mahomet fut-il sincère?' in *Recherches de science religieuse* (1911), Nos. 1 and 2; 'L'âge de Mahomet et la chronologie de la Sîra', in *Journal Asiatique* (1911), xvii, 209–50; *Fāṭima et les filles de Mahomet; notes critiques pour l'étude de la Sīra* (Rome, 1912). He also published during this period his first series of studies on the Umayyads (see previous footnote), and a number of studies on pre-Islamic Arabia, including 'La république marchande de la Mecque vers l'an 600 de notre ère' in *Bulletin de l'Institut égyptien*, series V, vol. iv, 23–54, on which I shall comment later in the paper. Earlier work on the *Sīra* includes 'Le "triumvirat" Abou Bakr, 'Omar et Aboû 'Obaida', a paper read at the International Congress of Historical Sciences at Berlin in August 1908, which deals with the *Sīra* indirectly.

French policy in the Levant. One of his best-known works, *La Syrie* . . ., was written at the request of the High Commissioner, General Gouraud.[6] The esteem with which he was regarded by the French authorities enabled him to exercise an appreciable influence over Lebanese politics—an influence which he also wielded through those of his old students who were numbered among Lebanon's first political leaders.

Following the death of Louis Cheikho in 1927, Lammens became editor of the Jesuit learned periodical *al-Mashriq*, in which translations and adaptations of his work into Arabic had appeared, and continued to appear for the remaining years of his life. He died on 23 April 1937, following a stroke of paralysis; and he was mourned, among others, by a leading Muslim journalist of Beirut.[7]

Henri Lammens was both a militant Catholic and a genuine lover of *La Syrie*. He studied the geography and the history of his country of adoption with a tenderness that almost equalled his contempt for Islam. His love for Syria, in fact, may have been a projection of his hostility towards Islam and the Arabs.[8] Most of his holidays were spent in study tours of Lebanon, Syria, and Palestine; and he left many notes on the geography, archaeology, and sociology of the area.[9] In *La Syrie* . . ., which, aside from being an expression of his belief in the mission of France in the Levant, also reflects his devotion to Syria, Lammens traced the history of the country from the Arab conquests to the establishment of the French mandate, with a cursory glance over its ancient history as an introduction. Lammens also worked on a biography of Muḥammad, which has remained unpublished, possibly by express orders from Rome.[10] Judging by the hostile and derisive tone of his numerous monographs on the subject, the publication of this biography would have caused considerable embarrassment to the Holy See.

Lammens regarded Islam as an unfortunate historical accident in which the Syrian nation[11] became involved. Faced by the irresistible impact of this foreign cult, Syria had to absorb it, and to modify it into a less objectionable form, while maintaining its older Christian personality in the refuge of Mount Lebanon: *l'Asile du Liban*. In this difficult task which history set for Syria, Latin Europe was its traditional ally against the Saracens, both Arabs and Turks. Lammens depicted the Crusades as a welcome interruption to oppressive rule in Syria; and he heralded the

[6] See *La Syrie* . . ., i, p. i, and the comments on the book below.

[7] Anīs Nuṣūlī, in *Bayrut* (1 May 1937), no. 181; quoted by Tawtal in his biography of Lammens (*al-Mashriq* (1937), xxxv, 172).

[8] See below, in the remarks on his Umayyad studies.

[9] Most of those notes appear in the various numbers of *al-Mashriq*.

[10] This is the supposition of Zakī Muḥammad Ḥasan in his article on Lammens in *al-Muqtaṭaf* (December 1937), pp. 555–61.

[11] The concept of the Syrian nation was developed by Lammens in *La Syrie* . . . (see below), although the idea of a Syrian nationality had existed before.

French Mandate as the essential means for realizing the potential unity and integrity of the Syrian nation. 'Nation Melkite, nation Maronite . . . Cette terminologie captieuse ne devrait pas survivre au souvenir de la domination turque.'[12]

As a historian, Lammens was primarily concerned with the riddle of Muḥammad's personality and Prophetic career, the central problem of Islamic history. How did Islam come to being? Under what circumstances did its Prophet realize his spiritual calling, and wherefrom did he derive his religious ideas? Such questions had faced (and still face) the disinterested historian of Islam, as well as the Christian missionary struck by the almost complete immunity of Islam to his activity; and Lammens was both, historian and missionary. Muḥammad, to him, was a historical problem as well as a symbol of Islam's obstinacy and insensitiveness to the missionary influence. While, in general, he tackled the historical problem with the skill of the scholar, he frequently made savage attacks on the symbol as well, and sacrificed scholarship in the process.

Lammens developed his own technique of *Sīra* study by applying Goldziher's method of *ḥadīth* study to the critical analysis of the *Sīra*. Despairing of the *Sīra* as a historical source, Noeldeke had abandoned the attempt to understand the historical person of Muḥammad.[13] Lammens carried on with the abandoned work; and, by using the Qur'ān as a control, he demonstrated the possibility of the critical analysis of the *Sīra*, with interesting results.

Goldziher, whose *Muhammedanische Studien* had appeared in 1889–90, was extremely sceptical about the possibility of using the *ḥadīth* as a source for the history of early Islam. He considered it rather as a valid source for the period of later developments in Islam: the period during which the *ḥadīth* was actually being created. The compilation of the *ḥadīth*, he held, as well as its forgery, were begun during the Umayyad period by pious scholars who were neglected by the ruling dynasty, which set little count on religion. *Ḥadīth* scholarship became fully developed under the 'Abbasids, who patronized the pious traditionists, exploiting their work for political propaganda. Thus, according to Goldziher, the *ḥadīth* was basically anti-Umayyad; and few traditions supporting Umayyad political claims have survived the 'Abbasid purge.

The 'Abbasids, who considered their caliphate as an essentially religious institution (in contrast to the Umayyad *mulk*, or lay dominion), held the *ḥadīth* in high regard, for both political and legal purposes. Since the dominant school of Muslim jurisprudence held the Qur'ān and the *ḥadīth*

[12] *La Syrie* . . ., i, 5. Dots in the original.

[13] 'Weil ich mich reiferen Alter nicht mehr an die Charakteristik Muhammeds wagte', in *WZKM*, xxi, 298, No. 3. Quoted by Lammens in *Qoran et tradition* . . ., p. 5.

to be the exclusive bases of *fiqh* (law), and since Qur'anic and genuine *ḥadīth* materials were limited and, as such, inadequate for catering to the growing body of Muslim law, a considerable amount of *ḥadīth* had to be manufactured for the purpose. The forgery of favourable traditions was even necessary for those jurists who held that *ijmā'* (consensus of expert opinion) was valid as an additional basis for *fiqh*, thus diminishing the importance of the *ḥadīth* as a source of legislation.

The type of *ḥadīth* developed during the early 'Abbasid period reflected the political differences within the Islamic community. Each political faction compiled, and more often modified or fabricated, a body of traditions favourable to its position. Goldziher analysed the pro-'Alid and pro-'Abbasid *ḥadīth*, noting the manner in which each type reflected its peculiar political motives;[14] and his method was adopted by Lammens and applied to the biographical and historical *ḥadīth*, which he held to be a main basis of the *Sīra*.

While the Lammens technique of *ḥadīth* analysis was adapted from Goldziher, his use of the Qur'ān as the control in *Sīra* study was likewise adaptation rather than invention. Already in 1894 C. Snouck-Hurgronje, to whose works Lammens made frequent and respectful reference, had noted that orientalists were in agreement on the fact that the Qur'ān, along with the older *ḥadīth* (the latter subject to severe criticism), were the principal sources for the Prophet's life.[15] Snouck Hurgronje deplored the lack of a critical edition of the Qur'ān to help in the study of the *ḥadīth*[16] —a remark echoed by Lammens:

> Dans l'état actuel de nos connaissances, les innombrables allusions historiques du Qoran nous échappent en grande partie. Nous attendons toujours une édition critique, et la chronologie du texte demeure une question ouverte. En dépit de ses preventions—leur manifestation elle-même devient instructive—la Tradition ancienne, plus rapprochée des évènements, pouvait être en mesure de connaître les intentions du Maître, les personnes et les faits, visés par lui. Après avoir longuement pratiqué cette littérature, on peut, en procédant avec adresse, arriver à retrouver le noyau primitif et à dégager les récits traditionnels de leur gangue étrangère.[17]

In *Qoran et tradition . . .*, Lammens asserted that the traditional Arabic *Sīra*, like the modern Orientalist biographies of the Prophet, depended

[14] I. Goldziher, *Études sur la tradition islamique* (extr. and trans. from v. II of *Muhammedanische Studien* by Léon Bercher (Paris, 1952)). The arguments of the various chapters are given in summary.

[15] C. Snouck Hurgronje, 'Une nouvelle biographie de Mohammed', in *Selected Works* (Leiden, 1957), pp. 117–18; *Verspreide Geschriften* (Bonn and Leipzig, 1928), i, 329–30.

[16] *Selected works*, p. 127; *Verspreide Geschriften*, p. 341.

[17] *Qoran et tradition . . .*, p. 7.

mainly on *ḥadīth*, whereas the Qur'ān alone can serve as a valid historical basis for a knowledge of the Prophet's life and career. The historical and biographical *ḥadīth*, far from being the control of the *Sīra* or the source of supplementary information, is merely an apocryphal exegesis of the historical and biographical allusions of the Qur'ān. The value of a *ḥadīth* regarding the Prophet's life or career, he argued, would lie in its independence from the Qur'ān, where such independence can be clearly demonstrated. As a rule, he adds, a *ḥadīth* which is clearly exegetical of the Qur'ān should be disregarded.

Lammens admitted a vague oral tradition for the Medinese period of the Prophet's career, falsified through later attempts to adapt it to the Qur'ān. Its original form, he held, has to be re-established through criticism. Lammens also agreed that the earlier *ḥadīth* has a value *sui generis*, since it preceded the *tafsīr* (traditional exegesis of the Qur'ān). This early *ḥadīth*, he noted, must be studied in perspective with the Qur'ān; and any such *ḥadīth* pretending independence from the Qur'ān must be viewed with the utmost scepticism.

Although the *Sīra* thesis of Lammens did not remain unquestioned, it continues to serve as a working principle. The modern reaction in favour of the authenticity of the *Sīra*, represented by A. Guillaume and W. Montgomery Watt, has modified this working principle in some details without seriously affecting its essence. Lammens certainly provided *Sīra* scholarship with an important clue to the riddle of Muḥammad; and many of his own conclusions, as well as his technique, have been adopted and developed by later scholars.

Lammens has been criticized for some of his conclusions rather than his technique. Obsessed by his partiality against Islam, he applied his critical method masterfully when the source material reflected favourably on the Prophet, 'Alī, al-'Abbās, or the more revered of the Companions, or unfavourably on the Umayyads. On the other hand, he accepted uncritically any material that disparaged the Prophet (at least by modern standards of morality) or favoured the Umayyads. He is said to have held the view that pious Traditionists and *Sīra* writers could not have invented information that reflected poorly on Muḥammad; and, therefore, any such information which may have slipped in must be true. Lammens, however, did not always act on this principle, since he also held (whenever it was more convenient to do so) that standards of virtue and morality in pre-Islamic and early Islamic Arabia differed from the modern European standards, so that attributes distasteful to the modern European may have been highly thought of by the early Muslims. Thus he accepted the traditional accounts of the Prophet's prodigious virility (which, considering the standards of the day, may have been complimentary exaggerations) as certain proofs of the Prophet's sensuality; but, when faced with the necessity of explaining away the nickname *al-Amīn* (the loyal), by which Muḥammad was known to his contemporaries, he comments:

> A nous, hommes du vingtième siècle, un *amîn* qoraiśite paraitrait peut-être un coquin. Dans notre civilisation, deux mille ans de christianisme et de philosophie ont precisé, affiné jusqu' à l'extrème, le concept de la loyauté humaine. . . . La loyauté existe ou n'existe pas, mais elle ne peut se combiner avec une dose, même infinitésimale, de duplicité, de vues interessées. Jamais les Arabes ne haussèrent jusque-là.[18]

Partiality and inconsistency in dealing with the source material were not Lammens' only faults. His tendency to state as positive fact what he should have contented himself with suggesting was another. In his eagerness to discredit Muḥammad and his family and companions, he was not satisfied with doubting the validity of the *Sīra*, but went to the extent of contradicting it on very little, if any, grounds. Thus, in *Mahomet fut-il sincère*, he positively rejected Muḥammad's retreat to Mount Ḥirā' on the eve of his prophetic mission, basing his rejection on the following inconclusive grounds:

> Rien ne garantit l'authenticité de cette retraite. Elle cadre mal avec l'horreur de Mahomet pour la solitude,[19] avec sa repugnance notoire pour l'ascetisme. Nous la croyons plutôt calquée sur celles de Moïse au Sinai, du Christ au desert avant sa vie publique. Les montagnes sacrées abondaient aux alentours de la Mecque. En y plaçant la retraite du Maître, la tradition a essayé de leur conférer un caractère de sainteté islami que. . . . *Nous nous croyons donc autorisés à rayer le Mont Hira de l'histoire de la première vocation.*[20]

Another example of the high-handed manner in which Lammens forced his conclusions is provided by his *Fatima et les filles de Mahomet*. . . . In this monograph, which contains some of his most interesting *ḥadīth* and *Sīra* analysis, Lammens set out to prove that Fāṭima was not the favourite daughter of Muḥammad, and that the Prophet had never planned his succession through her progeny. All *ḥadīth* and *Sīra* material favourable to Fāṭima, 'Alī, and their sons, al-Ḥasan and al-Ḥusayn, is subjected to a searching criticism, with interesting and often valid results. Lammens, however, went further on to show that Fāṭima, in fact, was the, least favoured member of the Prophet's entourage, and that Muḥammad who cared little for his daughter's material and spiritual well-being, had the lowest possible opinion of her husband's intellect and general potentialities.

[18] *Mahomet fut-il sincère*, p. 4.

[19] Here Lammens depends on the *Musnad* of al-Dārimī (lithographed edition, p. 359), although it is not clear on what grounds he accepts the testimony of the *ḥadīth* of al-Dārimī and rejects all others on the subject.

[20] *Mahomet fut-il sincère*, p. 1. The italics are mine.

Fāṭima is depicted as a plain, sickly, and nagging woman, and no disparagement is spared her husband and sons. These positive conclusions are based partly on an almost entirely uncritical acceptance of the anti-'Alid material (which Lammens, on other occasions, viewed with the greatest doubt), and partly on stating the negative of the pro-'Alid material as positive fact. On the other hand, in his *Etudes sur le règne du calife omaiyade Mo'awia Ier*, he used the same technique to endow his favourite Umayyad with every virtue and every grace, to the extent of describing him as a tenderly loving son, a model father, and a devoted cousin.[21]

It is not the purpose of this paper to go into a detailed analysis of the individual works of Henri Lammens on the *Sīra* or on the Umayyads. It would be interesting, however, to summarize his thesis on the history of the Muḥammadan movement—a thesis which he was the first to develop in detail, and which has exercised a dominant influence over the subsequent scholarship on the subject.

Islam, as Lammens saw it, was the product of the urban and mercantile society of seventh-century Mecca. It was born in an atmosphere of high finance, and not in a nomadic environment. In *La république marchande de La Mecque . . .*, Lammens painted a vivid, though somewhat exaggerated, picture of Meccan politics and economy, tracing the rise of the city to economic importance on the eve of Islam.[22] In *Le berceau de l'Islam . . .*, he developed this idea further by demonstrating that Islam was actually the means whereby Qurayshite hegemony was finally secured over nomadic and agricultural Arabia. During the Arab conquests, the Quraysh of Mecca provided Islam with political and military leadership, while the nomadic tribes provided the military manpower.

In dealing with the Prophet's career, Lammens almost completely rejected the traditional accounts of the Meccan period; and later scholars have felt that he went too far.[23] Otherwise, while his biassed doubts of Muḥammad's sincerity have usually been discounted, his attempt to understand the Prophet's career in perspective with pre-Islamic Mecca has been accepted in the main by modern scholars. Lammens summarized his view of Muḥammad's original mission in his *Mahomet fut-il sincère*:

[21] . . . *Mo'awiya Ier*, p. 23: 'Le plus tendre des fils, il se montrera également père modèle et parent dévoué.'

[22] This part of the Lammens thesis has been accepted by later scholars, with some reservations regarding details. Cf. W. Montgomery Watt, op. cit., pp. 1–29. 'Scholars as a whole may not be quite so certain about details as Lammens appears to be, but it is clear that financial operations of considerable complexity were carried on at Mecca. The leading men of Mecca in Muḥammad's time were above all financiers, skilful in the manipulation of credit, shrewd in their speculations, and interested in any potentialities of lucrative investment from Aden to Gaza or Damascus. In the financial net that they had woven not merely were all the inhabitants of Mecca caught, but many notables of the surrounding tribes also. The Qur'ān appeared not in the atmosphere of the desert, but in that of high finance.' Ibid., p. 3.

[23] Ibid., p. xiii.

La mission, d'abord entrevue par Mahomet, se borne à une reforme mi-sociale, mi-religieuse des institutions mecquoises; ou, pour parler plus exactement, Mahomet ne separa jamais le sacré du profane: dogme, stipulations relatives aux héritages, aux testaments, tout sera par lui placé sur le même pied.[24]

Already in his *République marchande . . .*, Lammens had noted the necessity which Mecca felt for such a reform and the leadership of someone like Muḥammad, who could integrate tribal and sedentary Ḥijāz: 'Un chef pour les lancer, un programme pour les unir!'[25] But he criticized earlier biographies of Muḥammad which exaggerated the social reform aspect of his mission at the expense of the spiritual aspect, such as Hubert Grimme's *Mohammed* (Münster, 1892),[26] without agreeing with Becker that Islam began as a purely religious movement.[27] He stressed the fact that Muḥammad could not have won over to Islam groups like the *Anṣār* of Medina, who could not have been deeply concerned with Meccan social reform, without a spiritual dogma.[28] It is with hesitation, however, that Lammens admits Muḥammad's religious sincerity during the Meccan period: 'Pouvons nous refuser à Mahomet le bénéfice d'une conviction au moins initiale?'[29]

The once fashionable theory that Muḥammad was an epileptic, which was accepted by no less an Orientalist than Noeldeke,[30] was also criticized and rejected by Lammens:

Dans la description des phénomènes accompagnant l'inspiration chez le Prophète, certain détails trahiraient un désordre du système nerveux. Mais quelle créances méritent ces descriptions, ou l'exagération trahit chez le rédacteur l'effort maladroit et l'inéxperience de la mystique? Ne seraient-elles pas des tentatives enfantines pour interpreter les modalités d'une intervention surnaturelle?[31]

[24] *Mahomet fut-il sincère?*, p. 44.

[25] *République marchande . . .*, p. 54. Again later scholarship reflects Lammens' conclusions: 'In the rise of Mecca to wealth and power we have a movement from a nomadic economy to a mercantile and capitalist economy. By the time of Muhammad, however, there had been no readjustment of the social, moral, intellectual and religious attitudes of the community. These were still the attitudes appropriate to a nomadic community, for the most part. The tension felt by Muhammad and some of his contemporaries was doubtless due ultimately to this contrast between men's conscious attitudes and the economic basis of their life.' W. Montgomery Watt, op. cit., pp. 19–20.

[26] This is the work criticized by Snouck Hurgronje in *Une nouvelle biographie de Mohammed.* See fn. 14. Lammens, *Mahomet . . .*, p. 22.

[27] Ibid., p. 35, fn. 1, commenting on C. Becker, *Der Islam als Problem* (*Der Islam*, i, 5): 'Je n'oserais pourtant conclure avec l'auteur: "Les débuts de l'Islam sont exclusivement religieux." '

[28] *Mahomet . . .*, p. 22.

[29] Ibid., p. 1.

[30] T. Noeldeke, *Sketches from Eastern history,* trans. by J. S. Black (London, 1892), p. 25.

[31] *Mahomet . . .*, p. 11.

The view held by Lammens was that Muḥammad, 'le grand dormeur', as he called him, dreamed his revelations and his call to prophecy as a result of prolonged auto-suggestion.

Lammens, who considered the Prophet to have been, first and foremost, an adept Meccan politician, rejected the sincerity of Muḥammad during the Medinese period. With the growing political success of Islam at the time, the spiritual sincerity of Muḥammad diminished as his worldly ambitions grew. 'A mesure qu'il avancera, le Qoraišite calculateur apparaîtra davantage et finira par absorber le prophète.'[32]

The interest of Lammens in the history of the Umayyad dynasty ran parallel to his interest in the *Sīra*; and he followed the same approach in both cases.[33] He rightly held that most of the available sources for the history of the Umayyads were works of the 'Abbasid period and, as such, were partial towards the ruling dynasty and hostile to the fallen Umayyads. He rejected, therefore, most of the material unfavourable to the Umayyads, which he considered to be falsified through bias, and accepted all favourable material uncritically, on the principle that it had slipped in unintentionally. He also combed the poetical anthologies for incidental references, and was one of the first Orientalists to use this type of source material as extensively and as effectively; and his exceptional command of Arabic contributed greatly to his success there.

Lammens seems to have admired the Umayyads mainly because they were recognized, traditionally, as the black sheep of Islam. The fact that their piety and devotion to Muḥammad's faith was suspect, and that their ancestor, Abū Sufyān, was the leader of Quraysh in its struggle with the Prophet, raised them in his esteem, and enabled him to identify them as 'Syrians'.

[32] Ibid., p. 24. G. Levi Della Vida commented at some length on the *Sīra* studies of Lammens in his *Storia e religione nell' Oriente semitico* (Rome, 1924), p. 127 ff. He warns the readers of Lammens against his seductive arguments while stressing the importance of his contribution: 'Occore dunque al lettore delle numerose e svariate pubblicazioni che il Lammens ha dedicate a Maometto e alle origini dell'Islam stare sempre in guardia contro le seduzioni di un'argomentazione così sottilmente abile da sembrare talvolta persino capziosa e di uno stile così brioso ed efficace da fare spesso scambiare per una narrazione desunta da fonti esplicite e continuative ciò che non è se non un'ingegnosa ma ipotetica combinazione costruita sull'interpretazione soggetiva di centinaia di passi framentari, dispersi e oscuri. Tuttavia la cautela con la quale la grandiosa attività del Lammens va adoperata non deve far dimenticare nè attenuare i meriti eminenti che egli si è acquisati in un ramo di studi in quale appare tanto più irto di difficoltà quanto più profondamente e minutamente lo si esamina: col Lammens polemista si può non andar d'accordo, ma non si puo non inchinarsi, con rispetto e con riconoscenza, dinnanzi al Lammens erudito e critico.' Ibid., pp. 128–9.

[33] Lammens's work on Mu'āwiya has already been mentioned. Other works on the subject include *Etudes sur le siècle des Omayyades* (Beirut, 1930); *Ziād ibn Abīhi, vice-roi de l'Iraq, lieutenant de Mo'āwia I* (Rome, 1912); 'Un poète royal à la cour des Omiades de Damas', in *Orient Chretien* (1903), pp. 325–55; (1904), pp. 32–64; and 'Un gouverneur Omaiyade d'Egypte; Qorra ibn Šarīk, d'après les papyrus arabes', in *Bulletin de l'Institut egyptien*, Serie V, t. ii, pp. 99–115.

In the career of Mu'āwiya I, Lammens saw the moral triumph of the Syrian nation over conquering Islam:

> Le meilleur service rendu par 'Omar à la Syrie, fut d'y confier a Mo'âwiya le poste laissé vacant par la mort de son frère Yazîd. . . . Mo'âwiya visera à faire de son gouvernement une province modèle, a se concilier les indigènes. Dans le gouverneur s'annonce déjà le futur souverain, qui fixera en Syrie le centre du califat. Il commença par s'appuyer sur les tribus syriennes, sur les anciens sujets et alliés des Ghassanides. Il y choisit une femme, Maisoûn, la mère de son héritier Yazîd, auquel il tiendra également à donner une éducation syrienne. . . . Il compta sur (le) concours (des Syriens) pour l'aider à achever le dressage politique des nomades, amenés en Syrie par la conquête, pour initier ceux-ci à la discipline que les Syro-Arabes devaient à leur formation chrétienne, a leur passage par les camps de l'Empire [byzantin]. Ils fourniront les cadres de l'armée de Syrie, lui inculqueront la 'discipline syrienne' . . ., célebrée par tous les annalistes, et inconnue aux vieux Sarrasins. . . . Calife, il travailla à resserrer encore les liens qui le rattachaient aux Syriens. S'ingéniant à faire oublier sa qualité de souverain, il ne voudra paraître que leur élu, presque un égal, un 'primus inter pares'.[34]

In *La Syrie* . . .,[35] Lammens explained his concept of the Syrian nationality which, to him, was based on unity of land and of race.[36] He saw Syria as a clearly defined territory, bounded by excellent natural frontiers: the sea, the Taurus Mountains, and the Arabian desert. On the other hand, he recognized the rugged topography of the country as a barrier to political unity and to the development of national consciousness. 'La Providence, en dessinant les contours de ce pays, le prédestinait à devenir le berceau d'un peuple. Par contre, les accidents géographiques . . . retardaient indéfiniment l'éveil de l'idée nationale.'[37]

The Syrians, he held, were a race of remarkable uniformity, and of equally remarkable vitality. He noted their capacity for absorbing the constant infiltration of foreigners, particularly desert Arabs. Viewing the Arab conquests in this perspective, he comments:

> Cette puissance d'absorption chez la vieille race araméenne se manifesta encore mieux après la mort du Prophète (632) . . . En moins d'un quart de siècle, la Syrie vit affluer des tribus entières de Bédouins. Il pouvaient bien être cent mille. Ils auraient été le double, en quoi ce total—dont

[34] *La Syrie* . . ., pp. 63–9.

[35] Lammens noted in the preface that the book was written at the request of General Gouraud, the French High Commissioner, following the defeat of Fayṣal's supporters at Maysalūn in 1920. It was intended for use at a projected school for training administrative officials for the mandated territory: a school that was never actually set up.

[36] Ibid., pp. 1–8.

[37] Ibid., p. 2.

la moitié disparaîtra dans les guerres de conquête—pouvait-il modifier la composition ethnique de la race, diminuer sa faculté de réaction? . . . Après la mort de Mahomet, l'expansion, la conquête arabes aboutissent à la fondation du califat, d'un empire mondial. On l'a appelé arabe. En étudiant la période des Omayyades, nous verrons que ce fut en réalité un empire syrien.[38]

La Syrie . . . is no mere survey of events that took place in geographic Syria. It is an attempt to fit the history of the region in with the concept of Syrian nationality. It is an interpretative survey; and like other works of the same order, it tends to sacrifice absolute accuracy for ideas. Although Lammens admitted that consciousness of Syrian nationality had never been effective, he conceived the whole history of the country in terms of that concept. The book, as such, appears to reflect the effort of Lammens to create a Syrian nation that would conform to his ideas.

Within his concept of the Syrian nation, Lammens reserved a place for a Greater Lebanon, the origins of which he traced in the second volume of *La Syrie* . . .[39] From being a seventh-century headquarters of the Mardaites and the home of the Maronites, and later the settlement ground for some Syrian tribes,[40] Lammens saw Lebanon develop into a refuge for those Syrians who valued their freedom, becoming definitely so after the Ottoman conquest:

D'ailleurs, à tous ceux que révolte la tyrannie des pachas, la montagne s'ouvrait. Elle deveindra le dernier asile de l'indépendence syrienne. Des émirs y maintiennent, parmi des succès et des revers, une sorte d'autonomie vis-à-vis de l'autorité centrale. Leurs méthodes gouvernementales et politiques rappellent parfois celles du régime turc, faites de ruse et de violence. Mais ils s'occuperont efficacement de protéger leurs administrés. . . . Grâce a leur souplesse, la Syrie conserve encore jusqu'au 19e siècle un semblant d'histoire, de vie nationale, dont l'âge suivant recueillera le bénéfice.[41]

This theory of the *Asile du Liban*, of which traces can be found before Lammens, has had a dominant influence on subsequent scholars who wrote on the history of Lebanon.

Despite the fact that *La Syrie* . . . contains a number of mistakes and several undue assertions, and that it is in some ways out of date, it remains

[38] Ibid., pp. 7–8.

[39] Ibid., ii, 66 et seq. See also H. Levantin [pseud.], *Quarante ans d'autonomie au Liban* (Paris) [n.d.]

[40] *La Syrie* . . ., i, 81–3, 131–2; ii, 8–11. For the Mardaites see also . . . *Mo'âwia Ier*, pp. 14–22. In his presumptions on those two subjects, and particularly in the case of the Mardaites, Lammens trod dangerous ground, since the available material is far from being conclusive. Nevertheless, Lammens put forth his conclusions with his usual self-confidence.

[41] *La Syrie* . . ., ii, 63.

the best available survey of the history of Syria and certainly deserves a new edition. It represents an intelligent and forceful approach to the subject and places the various events and developments in an interesting perspective. Lammens made a good case for his *nation syrienne*; and, in some ways, he may have been right.

In general, the works of Lammens have received much criticism, mainly on the grounds of partiality; but it is important to note that later scholars have been as partial in their acceptance or rejection of his ideas and conclusions as he was in his treatment of sources. No scholar disputes the fact that Lammens was prejudiced; but a prejudice is not necessarily wrong.

29. TWO BRITISH HISTORIANS OF PERSIA

M. E. YAPP

Lecturer in the History of the Near and Middle East, School of Oriental and African Studies, London

In assessing an historian there are four general questions that need to be answered. These questions fall into two groups. First of all we want to know what information was available to the historian and the use he made of it, i.e. his sources and his technical equipment. Secondly we want to know with what preconceived ideas and with what object he approached his task. i.e. his prejudice. Within the general framework of these questions this paper will treat of two British historians of Persia—Sir John Malcolm and Sir Percy Sykes.

Malcolm and Sykes were chosen for two reasons. From the viewpoint of history they represent the first and the most recent attempts by British historians to write comprehensive histories of Persia and a comparison of their work spans a hundred years of the study of Persia from the Napoleonic to the First World War when British ideas of Persia were dominated by its position in relation to the North West Frontier of India.

Sir John Malcolm's *History of Persia* was published in 1815 in two portly volumes.[1] Malcolm's first motive in writing it was an official one: to produce information on an area which was becoming important in British diplomacy.[2] During the first years of the nineteenth century the danger of a French invasion of India caused the Indian Government to send a number of agents to negotiate treaties with and to collect information about the states lying beyond the North West Frontier of India. It was clear that the information collected needed to be more widely known. Accordingly the agents divided up the area between them, and each produced a book. Mountstuart Elphinstone wrote on Afghanistan;[3] Henry Pottinger on Sind and Baluchistan,[4] and Malcolm on Persia. In the first decade of the nineteenth century Malcolm had led three missions to Persia and he wrote, 'the prosecution of my public duties first led me to feel the want of a history of Persia'.[5] Malcolm's second motive was a more mundane one. The writing of the history was a sort of paid holiday for Malcolm. Malcolm had in fact begun it, at least in 1808, and in January 1809 he

[1] I have used the 1815 edition. Another was published in 1829.

[2] Cp. Edmonstone to Malcolm. Quoted Sir J. W. Kaye, *Life of Malcolm*, 2 vols. (London, 1856), ii, 60–1.

[3] Mountstuart Elphinstone, *An account of the Kingdom of Caubul*, 2 vols. (London, 1815).

[4] H. Pottinger, *Travels in Beloochistan and Sinde* (London, 1816).

[5] Malcolm, *History*, i, p. ix.

declared it to be 'in some forwardness'.[6] In the summer of 1809 however he was forced to put it aside for other diplomatic and literary work, and he did not take it up again until 1811 after his return from his third mission to Persia. For virtually the whole of 1811 he was writing his history in Bombay, drawing his pay and allowances as envoy and supplied with secretaries and writers and a house at Government expense.[7] The Governor General, Lord Minto, regarded it partly as a useful service but also as a reward for Malcolm.[8] At the end of 1811 Malcolm took leave for England to see the book through the Press. The third motive was fame. A few years earlier books on Asia had not been popular but in the early nineteenth century a combination of political interest aroused by events in India and the Egyptian expedition of Napoleon, of trading interest and of a general intellectual and romantic interest stimulated by the production of better books, had resulted in a much greater demand for books on Eastern subjects.[9] Accordingly Malcolm's book appealed not only to the politician and merchant requiring practical information but also to the Romantic interest in the fabulous associations of the names of Persia, Bukhārā, and Samarqand. In this moreover Malcolm's *History* joins with the works of James Mill, Sir Walter Scott, and James Morier. Malcolm himself received a European-wide fame and was honoured by the degree of LL.D. at Oxford.[10]

Much of the credit for this movement to make the East intellectually respectable must go to a rather pretentious intellectual named James Mackintosh.[11] Mackintosh had played a very prominent rôle in Whig thought in the 1790s and had become the friend of Malthus, Bentham, Sydney Smith, and Lord Jeffrey. In need of money, he had accepted the post of Recorder of Bombay. In Bombay, however, he felt himself entirely out of place in what to him was an intellectual backwater; as soon as he had amassed enough money, he returned to England. While in Bombay, however, he acted as a link between the intellectual world of London and the aspiring writers of Bombay and through the Literary Society which he founded had a large and beneficial influence on them. He wrote,

> I have laboured to excite and direct a general spirit of inquiry among those, whose only contribution to the increase of knowledge must be derived from Eastern stores. I have endeavoured to spread the general maxims of historical criticism which seem to have been hitherto . . . forgotten in Indian inquiries.[12]

[6] Kaye, n. i, 450. [7] Kaye, ii, 59–60. [8] Kaye, ii, 60.

[9] Cp. Elphinstone to W. Erskine, 28 March 1913, in Sir T. E. Colebrooke, *Life of Elphinstone* (London, 1884), i, 261–3.

[10] Kaye, ii, 141.

[11] For Sir James Mackintosh see R. J. Mackintosh (ed.), *Memoirs of Sir James Mackintosh*, second edition, 2 vols (London, 1836). [12] Mackintosh, i, 444.

His son wrote that 'no valuable work was undertaken during his residence in Bombay in which he had not some share by his advice or other assistance'.[13]

The evidence appears to bear out this claim. William Erskine and C. J. Rich were his sons-in-law. He instigated Wilks to write his *History of Mysore*. and Briggs to translate the *Fihrist*.[14] Malcolm first met him in 1808 and they became very close friends.[15] It was largely at Mackintosh's insistence that Malcolm began to write and Mackintosh read and corrected his manuscripts.[16] It seems reasonable to suppose then that Malcolm's book was considerably influenced by the discussions of the Literary Society and through Mackintosh by the intellectual world of the *Edinburgh Review*, and that this must have broadened Malcolm's intellectual horizon.

Malcolm's *History* falls into four main sections. The first 274 pages deal with the history of Persia down to the Arab conquest. This section is conceived in considerable detail but with distinct limitations. The first six chapters are devoted to an account of Persian history based on Firdawsī and certain Arabic and Persian writers. Such an account inevitably includes a great deal of a fabulous nature and omits a great deal of importance. Malcolm fully recognized this but defended his decision to limit the scope of his history on three main grounds. In the first place the Greek and Latin writers were already available in Europe and he wished to provide new information.[17] Secondly he observed acutely that a national myth both shaped and reflected the ideology of a nation.[18] Thirdly Malcolm argued that there were many facts buried in the legends and that these could only be uncovered by patiently and diligently comparing accounts of an event and not being deterred by the presence of obviously fabulous matter.[19] Against the views of Richardson[20] he argued that there was a notable correspondence between the Persian and Greek accounts and in his seventh chapter he attempted a number of rather unhappy identifications. The second part of Malcolm's *History* covers the period from the Arab conquest to the rise of Nādir S͟hāh. This occupies 369 pages and completes volume I. This section is not treated in the same detail as the preceding one; the reason Malcolm gives is that there is adequate information already available and all that is needed is to give a general and concise account of the successive dynasties which ruled Persia in this period.[21] The third section occupies the first 318 pages of volume 3 and is devoted to the history of Persia from Nādir S͟hāh to the establishment of the Ḳājārs where the *History* closes, before Malcolm's own arrival in Persia. This section is in much greater detail than the preceding one and

[13] Mackintosh, i, 242. [14] Mackintosh, i, 242. [15] Kaye, i, 408.
[16] Mackintosh, i, 118. [17] Malcolm, i, p. x. [18] Malcolm, i, 7. [19] Malcolm, ii, 74.
[20] J. Richardson, *A dissertation on the languages, literatures and manners of eastern nations* (London, 1778).
[21] Malcolm, i, 275.

the reason given by Malcolm is that from the rise of Nādir Shāh, 'every event will then derive an importance from its connexion with the present state of the Kingdom'.[22] The fourth section is not really history at all but is a general account of Persian life and occupies the remaining half of volume 2.

Although Malcolm's book sets out to be a comprehensive account of the history of Persia yet it suffers from certain limitations. It is designed essentially to provide practical information on Persia at the time that Malcolm was writing. For this reason we have the large section on Persian life, the extra detail on eighteenth-century Persia, and the stress on the legendary history because of its alleged revelation of the Persian character. Secondly it is written by a diplomat. Accordingly it is cut off at the point when to continue the history might lead to embarrassing diplomatic revelations.

Malcolm drew on three main sources. First of all there were the general works of European scholarship ('I have carefully consulted every European authority of eminence who has investigated the history and literature of the Oriental nations,'[23] he wrote modestly). Secondly he possessed a collection of Persian manuscripts that he had acquired on his travels in Persia and thirdly his assistants on his second and third missions had travelled widely and collected a great deal of first-hand information. To illustrate both some of the sources Malcolm used and the use he made of them, I want to discuss briefly his account of the ancient history of Persia.

There are roughly seven groups of sources for the ancient history of Persia. For the pre-Achaemenian period there is archaeological evidence derived from the Euphrates valley: this was discovered after Malcolm's time. For the Achaemenian period there are a number of coins and inscriptions in the cuneiform characters; at the time Malcolm was writing these had not been deciphered. Thirdly there is the fragment of Zoroastrian writing known as the Avesta. Malcolm did have some secondhand acquaintance with this. At Bombay he saw a copy of a document purporting to be an accurate account of the doctrines of Zoroaster known as the *Desātīr*.[24] This document was in fact a forgery but Malcolm took it to be genuine, although he thought it of little historical value. He also saw a book based on this document called the *Dabistān-i madhāhib*.[25] This book had attracted considerable praise from the foremost Orientalist of the preceding generation, Sir William Jones,[26] but Malcolm showed a justifiable scepticism of it and rejected its historical section on internal evidence.[27] Finally, and again in contradiction to Jones, he used the work of Anquetil

[22] Malcolm, i, 275.

[23] Malcolm, i, p. xi.

[24] Subsequently published Bombay, 1818.

[25] Written in the seventeenth century. English translation (Paris, 1843). See *EI*[2] *s.v. Dābistan al-madhāhib*.

[26] See Browne, *Literary history of Persia*, i, 54–5.

[27] Malcolm, i, 183–4.

du Perron[28] which he rightly thought to be the most authentic source then existing for Zoroastrianism.[29] The fourth group of sources is the inscriptions, seals, and coins and the small amount of historical writing in Pahlawī. Pahlawī still was not read generally by Europeans despite Perron's efforts, although Silvestre de Sacy had recently translated some of the inscriptions and Malcolm made use of this.[30] The fifth group of sources were the Arabic writers on Persia. Malcolm himself could not read Arabic, but he did obtain Persian translations of some of these and supplemented them with Persian histories written in Persian or in Indian languages. It is not always clear which of these he had seen himself and which he was quoting at second hand, e.g. the *Tārīkh-i guzīdae* of Ḥamdallāh Mustawfī. It is clear however that he did use the *Rawżat al-ṣafā* of Mīrkhwand and al-Ṭabarī. Al-Ṭabarī is disguised in the footnotes as 'Tarīkh Tubree' but information is attributed to this work in the text that could only have come from al-Ṭabarī. Malcolm was undoubtedly using Bal'amī's translation. The odd thing is that Malcolm did not realize that here was the most reliable source open to him. Odd because, apart from internal evidence, there is the authority of James Fraser who said, 'It is reckoned the most authentick History they have, and is much esteemed in the East.'[31] Malcolm however preferred to rely on a rare manuscript entitled *Zīnat al-tawārīkh* of 'Azīzallāh. Elliott and Dowson describe this work as 'a compilation of no value'.[32] I can find no more information about 'Azīzallāh, but it seems improbable that he was an Arab as Malcolm says, and presumably the copy Malcolm had was in Persian. In this case it casts some doubt, not only on Malcolm's judgement with regard to his sources, but also on his ability to read Persian, because he states that he had help in reading this from his Persian secretary.[33] Sixthly there is the Persian National Epic which finds its expression in Firdawsī. Malcolm states that he had several copies of the *Shāhnāma* available to him but the one he uses principally is the Calcutta edition of 1811.

The seventh and last group of sources for the ancient history of Persia is the various foreign writings. These include Greek, Byzantine, Syriac, Armenian, and Jewish. Malcolm had no access to any of these except the Greek and he deliberately excluded these from his narrative, although he brought the Greek historians into the seventh chapter for the purposes of comparison.

In effect, of these seven groups of sources Malcolm had no access or virtually none to three; three he used very partially and his principal reliance was on Firdawsī. This choice was partly the result of the state of

[28] Anquetil du Perron, *Zend-Avesta*, 3 vols. (Paris, 1771). [29] Malcolm, i, 193.

[30] Anquetil du Perron had used Pahlawī; and Silvestre de Sacy in his *Mémoires sur diverses. antiquités de la Perse*, (Paris, 1793), drew on Perron's vocabulary.

[31] James Fraser, *Nadir Shah* (London, 1742), second edition, Catalogue, p. 4.

[32] Elliott and Dowson, *Historia of India*, vii, 166–7. [33] Malcolm, i, 39.

knowledge at the time but partly also deliberate choice by Malcolm. In addition his use of this limited selection of sources does not always inspire confidence.

Malcolm's view of Persian history was not narrowly doctrinaire. He wrote,

> We must recollect that men are formed by habit and that all our sufferings and joys are comparative. . . . The feelings we receive from living in one state of society, disqualify us from judging of those of another. . . . It is proper and just that we should be grateful for the blessing of civilization; but we should not assume too great a superiority over those who continue in a more barbarous state.[34]

Nevertheless Malcolm finds Persian history depressing. Fundamentally Persia remains barbarian; there is no progress. The prevailing gloom is occasionally lifted by monarchs like Anūshirwān the Just or the first Seljuqs, but the prosperity is ephemeral, a weak ruler appears and the state of the country returns to its normal state of chaos and misery. Malcolm himself was a passionate believer in liberty but arguing that Asians do not know its value he was prepared to accept that they would prefer security and that this was more likely to be obtained under a strong despot than a weak one. This led Malcolm on to make some moral judgements from a standard which he would not have applied to a European nation. For example, he wrote a defence of Āghā Muḥammad's actions in establishing himself on the throne on the ground that a policy of terrorism was 'perhaps the only mode by which uncivilized nations can be preserved in peace'.[35] 'Abbās the Great's treatment of his sons is excused on the grounds that it was presumably necessary to save the state from anarchy.[36] This is a standard of judgement however that Malcolm does not push too far. He needs to see some positive advantage for acts of cruelty. Tīmūr falls somewhat below this standard and Sultan Muḥammad is entirely condemned.[37] In general, however, he does not condemn despotism as such: it is a symptom rather than a cause and its moral effects are worse than its material. To Malcolm the worst symptom of Persian decay is the debased morality of the people; the Persians are ignorant, deceitful, and capricious, and above all they are vain.

'One predominant feature, an overwhelming vanity distinguishes the whole nation.'[38]

Malcolm asks himself what is the reason for this lack of progress, this debased morality, and this constant succession of bloody and pointless wars. To the last he gives an ingenious answer. In civilized nations an army is drawn from the mass of the population and can be supported

[34] Malcolm, ii, 619–20. [35] Malcolm, ii, 272–5. [36] Malcolm, i, 565–6.
[37] Malcolm, ii, 20. [38] Malcolm, i, 622–3.

better in peace time, when resources are greater, than in war time. In barbaric nations, however, the army is recruited from a class apart from that to which the majority of the population belongs and they are unpaid. Consequently war is essential to keep the army disciplined, to keep it fed and paid and to avoid the danger to internal peace of disbanding it.[39] To the basic question of the lack of progress he produces the answer that it is due to Islam and especially to the position of women. Malcolm has no liking for Islam; its good features are taken from Christianity; for the rest it is

> a religion adverse to all improvement [which left its followers] debilitated and shackled by the chains of Bigotry, Superstition and Prejudice. What but Barbarism could be the result of such a doctrine.[40] There is no example of a Mahommedan nation having attained a high rank in the scale of civilization.

Why is this? There are two reasons. First of all there is the example of the Prophet and the character of some Muhammadan tenets which encourage warfare and violence.[41] Secondly there is the institution of polygamy and the seclusion of females which

> have, no doubt, had an influence, scarcely secondary to any other cause, in retarding the progress of civilization among those nations who have adopted this faith.[42]

Elsewhere Malcolm writes

> There is no condition of more consequence as connected with the conditions and character of a people, than the laws and customs which govern the relative situation and intercourse of the sexes. On it, perhaps beyond all other causes, depends the moral state of a country and its progress and general improvement. Many nations who have allowed their women to be publicly seen, have still remained in a barbarous state; but there is no instance of the inhabitants of a country in which it was the custom to immure them, and to deny them the benefit of education, ever having attained a forward rank in civilized life.[43]

Malcolm goes on to elaborate this and to describe the evils of the harem.

> The nations of Persia, like all Mahommedans, consider themselves entitled to an unlimited indulgence in the pleasures of the harem.

This leads to enervation and Malcolm produces the remarkable theory that the castration of Āghā Muḥammad by directing his energies from this outlet, was the direct cause of his winning the throne.

[39] Malcolm, ii, 139. [40] Kaye: n. i, p. 110. [41] Malcolm, i, 169–70.
[42] Malcolm, ii, 622. [43] Malcolm, ii, 587.

In the first place then the attitude to women leads to sexual excess and consequent enervation. In the second place the position of women encourages despotism; the Muslim is a despot in the house; therefore he is a despot in Government.

> It [Islam] has, by reducing one half of the human species to the condition of slaves, renders the other half tyrants, and thereby places an almost insuperable obstacle to the progress of improvement and civilisation.[44]

In the third place the attitude to women removes one of the main motives to good and great actions.

> The influence of women, when they hold their just station in society, is not more calculated to soften the rough manners and to subdue the angry passions of man than to stimulate him to generous, brave and bold actions. The admiration of highly cultivated females is more rarely given to personal beauty, than to valour, virtue and talent, and the hope of obtaining it constitutes one of the purest and highest motives to good and great actions. It has been before stated that the religion of Mahomet sanctions, if it does not inculcate, usages which keep the female sex in a subservient state. The followers of this faith, therefore, may be pronounced to be strangers to this refined but powerful motive of human action.[45]

It is apparent then that Malcolm considers sexual relations to be fundamental to understanding Persian history. Indeed, they seem to be an obsession with him. He is quite prepared to justify Āg͟hā Muḥammad's policy of terrorism but there is one aspect he will not accept. This is the (rare) practice of giving away the wives and daughters of rebellious nobles to the lower classes.

> No reasoning can reconcile our minds to a practice, which is at once infamous, inhuman and unjust; and which marks, perhaps beyond all others that have been stated, the wanton atrocity of a despotic and barbarous power.[46]

The success of the ancient legendary Persians is attributed principally to 'the great respect in which the female sex was held'.[47]

What was the origin of these ideas? The problem really resolves itself into two questions. Did Malcolm observe the symptoms correctly? And did he correctly identify the cause? With regard to the first question we should note first Malcolm's own account of his outlook.

[44] Malcolm, i, 169–70.
[45] Malcolm, ii, 587–8.
[46] Malcolm, ii, 455.
[47] Malcolm, i, 270.

I have studied perspicuity and I have sought truth; and my opinions, which are invariably expressed with freedom, may perhaps have some value from being those of a man whose only lessons have been learned in the school of experience.[48]

In other words Malcolm belonged to the depressing collection of simple, practical men who have been there. Now Malcolm's contacts with Persia were all those of an official diplomat; his job was to secure Persia's alliance and it involved him in some hard bargaining and liberal spending. It is said that he distributed money on such a scale that the Persians could only think he got a percentage of all he spent. Furthermore, on the whole, Malcolm had very little success. It is not surprising, therefore, that he found the Persian character so debased. Secondly Malcolm's view of the causes of this lack of progress was coloured by his whole outlook. He had sailed for India at the age of thirteen and since then he had lived in the romantic world of the Indian soldier and the rarefied and chivalrous world of Anglo-Indian society, where a European woman was a rarity to be cherished and guarded. He himself had just got married before his departure on his second mission to Persia. He wrote to his wife:

I feel a conscious pride that in possessing you, I possess the most powerful motive that man can have to honourable action.[49]

It is apparent that this notion was the product of a rather limited experience that had turned a naturally adventurous man into a proponent of Romantic chivalry. Yet it is precisely this notion which is at the root of Malcolm's explanation of the motivation of Persian history. He set up his own ideal of married relations as a decisive factor and finding it absent in Persia made its absence the mainspring of Persian history.

Like Malcolm, Sir Percy Sykes was an official. He transferred from the Indian Army to the Consular Service in Kirmān and Sīstān in East Persia, a very delicate frontier area in this period and the greater part of his many years of experience in Persia was confined to the Southern and Eastern parts. Sykes had several motives in writing his book. The first was intellectual. No comprehensive history of Persia had been written since that of Malcolm, which embodied the results of modern research. Sykes, however, did not feel that this justified his writing a history of Persia for its own sake; it was because Persia had exercised considerable influence on many other countries of Asia and through the Greeks on Europe itself.[50] This feeling is illustrated in the book by the many occasions on which Sykes pursues subjects not really relevant to his subject but which might attract the English reader. For example, he gives extended accounts of the life of Alexander the Great and of the Crusades and has a quite

[48] Malcolm, i, p. ix. [49] Kaye, i, 414.

[50] Sir P. Sykes, *A history of Persia*, 3rd edn., 2 vols. (London, 1930), i, p. xi.

unnecessary paragraph on the first British pilgrim to reach Persia.[51] Perhaps more importantly the book was intended as an up-to-date manual for people connected with Government. Sykes's apparent order of importance is brought out by his list of objects to be met by his *History*. First of all he hopes it may be useful to the British Government and to the makers of public opinion in Britain. Secondly he hopes it may be useful to students of Greek and Roman history who may want to know the Persian point of view (which Sykes claims to have aquired to some extent). Only thirdly does he hope that 'it helps Persians to realize more fully the splendours of their own history'.[52] Fourthly, Sykes appears to have intended the book to stimulate reform in Persia and the acceptance of the Agreement. He concludes his book, 'I refuse to abandon hope, however uncertain the situation may now appear, and I appeal to Persia to realize the truth as here set down by an old and true friend, and, in the new era that is dawning to play a part worthy of her splendid past.'[53] Finally Sykes was inspired by the fascination of 'romantic Iran' which drew him, while serving in India, to travel in Persia.[54]

Sykes's book is in two volumes. The first volume covers the period down to the early 'Abbasids; the second runs from about A.D. 800 to the period when Sykes was writing. In this second volume a disproportionately large amount is given to the nineteenth and twentieth centuries, and quite a large part, in strong contradistinction to Malcolm, to Sykes's own activities in South Persia during the First World War. The balance then is rather different to that of Malcolm. There is the same rather perfunctory treatment of the period from the Arab Conquest down to Nādir Shāh. The eighteenth century, however, is drastically compressed compared with Malcolm, but the more recent period comparatively enlarged, presumably with the same object as Malcolm of elucidating the present state of Persia. Unlike Malcolm, however, Sykes treats the more recent period comprehensively. This no doubt reflects the very changed diplomatic position of Persia after the First World War compared with that towards the end of the Napoleonic War. There is no longer any need to worry about offending Russia. The greatest change, however, is in the ancient history of Persia. Malcolm merely wrote up the legendary accounts of Persia by the Arab and Persian historians and compared them briefly with the Greeks. Sykes goes right back to the beginnings of civilization in the Euphrates delta and shows the gradual rise of Persia, giving great

[51] Sykes, ii, 42.

[52] Sykes, i, p. xii. There is a similar statement in Sykes's preface to his *History of Afghanistan* (London, 1940), 2 vols.; ii, p. viii. The order here is from the first edition. In the preface to the third edition he reverses this order and puts his hope that it may be of some service to the people of Persia first; i p. viii. His *History* was not however translated into Persian until 1944. Cf. also Sykes, *Ten thousand miles in Persia* (London, 1902), p. x.

[53] Sykes, ii, 540.

[54] Sykes, *Ten thousand miles*, p. 1.

attention to the reigns of Cyrus and Darius, a period entirely ignored by Malcolm, but which Sykes considers to be the greatest period of Persian history.

The most immediately striking thing about Sykes's Bibliography is that it does not include a single book in a non-European language. Sykes himself knew Persian, and in his history of Kirmān in his book *Ten thousand miles in Persia*, he used Persian manuscript histories. But in his comprehensive history in most striking contradistinction to Browne's *Literary history*, he relied entirely on translations and secondary sources. In the first half of the nineteenth century, for example, he draws virtually entirely on Watson's *History*. The second notable thing about Sykes's sources is that they seem to tell the story of Persia from the outside. Malcolm deliberately set out to write Persian history from the inside—as a Persian saw it; with Sykes, however, the picture is entirely reversed. For ancient Persia the sources are with some notable exceptions Assyrian, Babylonian, and Greek; for medieval Persia, Arab and for Modern Persia, European. This distinction can be overdone, especially with regard to the Middle Ages when Persian historians write in Arabic, but it still seems to preserve a broad truth.

To compare Sykes's book with that of Malcolm we might look at his sources for the ancient history of Persia. Whereas Malcolm relied largely on Persian-Arabic writings, Sykes extends his range to cover virtually all the seven groups of sources listed. The reason for this is partly the fact that research had progressed in all departments during the nineteenth century and partly Malcolm's deliberate exclusion of the classical sources for the Achaemenians, Parthians, and Sasanids. In the pre-Achaemenian period and Achaemenian period, Sykes could use the archaeological evidence derived from the excavations of the French at Susa and Woolley at Ur and the evidence of the cuneiform inscriptions deciphered by Rawlinson, Grotefend, and Larsen. For the Sasanids he could draw on the Pahlawī sources and even on Chinese missions. The effect of this is to produce a much enlarged and more comprehensive picture of activities affecting life on the Iranian plateau even if this could only be called Persian history by a stretch of the imagination. It is this section which illustrates most strongly the effect of the advances in knowledge and technique since the time of Malcolm and the choice of it as an example does distort the difference between the histories. A comparison of the later period would not reveal at all the same differences. In fact, Sykes's section on the ancient history of Persia is by far the most readable part of his book. The period from A.D. 600–1500 is a long series of battles described in great detail, and of inextricably confused events with no attempt to give life or meaning to them. It is really military history with political sidelights. Sykes is very much the victim of his material and his own interest as a soldier. When the material is not primarily political he presents a much more balanced picture of life in Persia, but when the material allows it he contents himself with a string of battles.[55] Economic and social history is disposed of in some such way as this:

> Little can be gleaned of the history of the masses of this period ['Abbasids to Mongols], but it is reasonable to suppose that it depended almost entirely on the strength or weakness, the justice or the injustice of the monarch and his governors. There is no doubt that, as a rule there was terrible oppression for this is the normal state of the East under an Asiatic Government.[56]

The simplest way in which to illustrate the nature of Sykes's prejudice is to turn straightway to the manner in which Sykes explains the motivations of Persian history. His explanations fall into two groups. In the first place Sykes is considerably interested, presumably as a result of his own interest in geography and travel, and from the writings of Ellsworth Huntington, in the influence of geography on history and on the effect of the drying up of Central Asia and the consequent emigrations, wars, and conquests. Secondly he is dominated by the idea of virility. Looking through his volumes one can multiply examples of this. It is luxury that causes the downfall of the Greeks, loss of virility the collapse of the Umayyads, 'cowardice, effeminacy and corruption' the defeat of the Safavids by the Afghans.[57] On the other side of the medal the most notable quality of the Achaemenians and the Parthians is their lack of effeminacy. Virility becomes the criterion by which history judges nations and individuals.

> The Persian nation (in 1722) had ceased to be virile and the verdict of history is that when it fell it fell deservedly through its own cowardice.[58]

> There is laid to his charge no great crime, but since lack of virility or valour is in autocratic monarchs a worse defect than many crimes, Yezdegird III . . . stands condemned, and rightly condemned, at the bar of history.[59]

Sykes derives from Persian history general lessons on the importance of virility applicable to Europe,

> To be the father of many sons, was, and still is described as proof of good fortune, and in this their attitude is surely more sane than that of the modern European who shirks the duty of a family.[60]

> Virility, expressed in valour and energy, is the best stock on which to graft other virtues.[61]

[55] Some of the deficiencies of this section of Sykes's book must be attributed to his failure to make use of the numerous editions of Arabic and Persian histories that appeared at this time, particularly in the Gibb Memorial Series.

[56] Sykes, ii, 56.

[57] Sykes, ii, 236–7.

[58] Sykes,ii, 226.

[59] Sykes, i, 502.

[60] Sykes, i, 172.

[61] Sykes, i, 171.

It is never quite clear precisely what virility is. Luxury and virility are usually defined as the negation of each other. It is not always easy to associate symptoms precisely with one or the other. Thus a fondness for women in Muḥammad Shāh is a sign of luxury; in Nādir Shāh a sign of virility. Nonetheless there are certain categories which can be established. The nomad is virile; the city dweller effeminate and the principal symptom of luxury is the harem. It often seems that the absence of civilization is virile and good and that the blessings of civilization are in fact the corruptions of luxury.

Having established this criterion, Sykes proceeds to make his moral judgements on the basis of them. The formulae run rather like this:

(1) Successful = virile = just = good.
(2) Unsuccessful = not virile = unjust = bad.

Timur was 'a great maker of history';[62] accordingly all his actions become good or justified by policy. Hārūn al-Rashīd's treatment of the Barmakids[63] and 'Abbās the Great's treatment of his sons[64] are justified on the same grounds. On the other hand a good man who failed is condemned.

> Ali stands out as the Caliph who was too noble and high minded for his surroundings.[65]

At the bottom of Sykes's judgements there is success worship and a Spartan ideology. The problem arises: where did these ideas come from? They were not religious. Sykes's religion was only a moral code, 'Good thoughts, good words, good deeds.' Their origin is surely in the Victorian public school and the ideals of a soldier. Sykes, himself, went to Rugby and Sandhurst. Perhaps the two greatest crimes in Dr. Arnold's canon were cowardice and lying. It is on these two points that Sykes condemns Persian ethics. He takes from Sa'dī, via Browne, two propositions. Firstly that desertion from a battlefield can be justifiable under some circumstances and secondly that an expedient lie is better than a mischievous truth. These he says show how distant Eastern ethics are from our own. Perhaps the direction of Sykes's thinking comes out most clearly in a passage in which he compares the Hellenistic Empire with the British. He says that the administrators of the British Empire are drawn from the public schools where they are trained to produce an average type 'which in many respects much resemble the best Greek ideals more closely than any other since the downfall of Hellas'.[65]

Finally, to attempt some comparison of these two writers. With regard to the sources the first thing that is apparent is the great advance in knowledge in a hundred years, although this is exaggerated in the examples used. Secondly it may be noted that both writers limit themselves in the

[62] Sykes, ii, 134–5. [63] Sykes, ii, 2. [64] Sykes, i, 575. [65] Sykes, i, 281.

use they make of the available sources. This, in its turn, leads to a comparison of their attitudes. There are certain similarities. They were not professional historians, their claim to authority was in both cases their experience of the country; they were officers, writing primarily for officers. From this point on, however, there are substantial differences. Malcolm was a self-educated, chivalrous Romantic; Sykes a product of the Victorian public school. In Sykes liberty is replaced by order and virility. Both men fall into the common error of writing about orientals and oriental nations, when they mean Persians and Persia, but one difference in their attitude is very noticeable. Malcolm, whose contact with Persia was on the whole rather humiliating, disliked the Persians and found their history depressing; Sykes, whose happiest years were spent in Persia, had a tremendous liking for the people of that country, and found their past 'splendid'.[66]

In conclusion it might be well to say something of the ideas behind this paper. I have over-simplified a complex subject and this is inevitable in a paper of this size. Its main motive, however, was to try and unearth some of the ideas which controlled these writers because their views have passed into historical currency. They represent first of all the spiritual attitude which dominated British writing on Persia down to Sykes and finds an even more notable expression in the work of Watson and Curzon. This is a phenomenon which is quite characteristic of British writing on India in the same period, but not in general of writing on the Middle East. This is because Persia, like Afghanistan, was of principal interest to Britain as a problem of Indian defence. Secondly I have stressed the personal factors which influence interpretation. In the case of Sykes this is not purely individual. The cult of the primitive found in his work is expressed by several writers on the Middle East and is responsible for the legend of the noble Arab of the Desert and has had its influence on British foreign policy. I have suggested here that it finds its origin in the Victorian public school, but it is a suggestion that is only tentative.

[66] Sykes, ii, 540.

30. HISTORICAL WRITING ON THE SUDAN SINCE 1820

R. L. HILL

Lecturer in Modern Near Eastern History in the University of Durham

Introduction

For the purposes of this paper 'the Sudan' means the Sudan within the limits of Egyptian, and subsequent Anglo-Egyptian, occupation.

Since 1820, the first year of the Turco-Egyptian penetration, the Sudan has not attracted the attention of any outstanding historian. Conversely, no single historian, outstanding or mediocre, has dominated any part of this period. There has been no counterpart to the elder Mill whose *History of India* (1819) provided an apologetic for two generations of British administrators and an Aunt Sally for the third. Nor was the Sudan a battleground of rivalries among historians, though the provenance of the Funj rulers of Sennar, the immediate predecessors of the Egyptians, has been for long in mild dispute. The great majority of articulate Europeans who thought of the Sudan at all, had their minds made up on all the significant issues in Sudanese history during the last 130 years—on General Gordon, on slavery, on the Anglo-Egyptian Condominium—with almost no opposition, at least in print, to the dominant view.

There are three discernible phases of historical writing on the Sudan from 1820 corresponding in time with the three régimes which existed during those years.

(1) The Egyptian period, 1820–81, sixty-two years poor in historiography whether in European languages or in Arabic.

(2) The Mahdist period, 1881–98, which gave rise to much frothy, popular writing, particularly on the theme of the African career and death of Gordon, but which has not until recently been studied by historians equipped for critical investigation.

(3) The Condominium period, 1899–1956, an alluring field of future historiography at present almost wholly unexplored.

Few historians have confined themselves rigidly to régimes; those writing on the *Mahdiyya*, for example, could not ignore the preceding Egyptian rule.

The Egyptian Period, 1820–81

Several circumstances have discouraged historical inquiry into this period.

The first has been the difficulty facing western students in examining the evidence. The principal primary documents, in Turkish and Arabic, are deposited in Cairo, in the Egyptian public record office (*Dār al-Maḥfūẓāt*) and in the archives of the Abdin Palace (*Qaṣr ʻĀbidīn* now *al-Qaṣr al-jumhūrī*). The Abdin archives have been closed to research since June 1955, though they may have been reopened lately without my knowledge.

The language barrier has not in the past deterred historians from writing of peoples whose languages they did not understand and of governors whose dispatches and orders they could not read. The need for literacy in Arabic and Turkish never occurred to the generality of writers on the Egyptian Sudan any more than his ignorance of Indian languages worried James Mill. Today, with the growth of a more scientific attitude towards the methods of historical investigation, the language barrier looks more forbidding.

The final deterrent to historians is the sheer dreariness and lack of relative importance of the subject as it appears to them. The Sudan was only a dependency of the Ottoman province of Egypt, and though the vice-consuls of the Powers in Khartoum sometimes wrote intelligent accounts of the state of the country, the consuls-general, in their remote offices in Alexandria, hardly knew of the Sudan's existence.

As might be expected there is a great poverty of Sudanese documents, but the possibility of future finds must not be excluded. The native chroniclers wrote annals, biography, and genealogy, important for the Funj period but much less important for the Egyptian. The main document, a composite chronicle by Ibrāhīm ʻAbd al-Dāfiʻ and three others (ed. Makkī Shibayka (Mekki Shibeika), *Ta'rīkh mulūk al-Sūdān*, Khartoum, 1947) carries the story to the time of the general governor (*mudīr ʻāmm*), Aḥmad Mumtāz Pasha (1871–2). The authors are cautious of criticizing the government, and their topographical purview is limited to the Nile valley. No state archive dating from the Egyptian occupation has survived in the Sudan; all that was not removed to Cairo in 1883–4 was destroyed by the Mahdists or left to decay.

The British traveller, Mansfield Parkyns, came near to writing a history of the Sudan. While he was in the country in 1845–8 he assembled manuscripts in Italian and French which seem to have been written for him by European residents. It is from these anonymous chroniclers that we get some of our least tainted impressions of the first twenty-five years of Egyptian rule. The first manuscript, the longest and the most informative, is written in the Italian of Central Italy. The second, a fragment in French, carries the tale to the late eighteen-forties. Both are among the Parkyns papers in the library of the Royal Geographical Society of London. English translations of portions of these manuscripts appeared in *Sudan Notes and Records*, xxxvi, 1935, and xxxvii–xxxviii, 1956–7. The third document, entitled *Journal fait durant un voyage au Sennar et à l'Hédjaz en . . . 1837 . . . 1840*, is in the Bayerische Staatsbibliothek, Munich. Adolphe Linant's manuscript, *Journal d'un voyage en Ethiopie . . . 1821 et 1822* (in the Griffith Institute, Ashmolean Museum, Oxford) is an essential witness of the Sudanese reaction to the imposition of Egyptian rule.

It is an almost humiliating experience to step down from these homely, informative, journals and chronicles to the level of the usual traveller's account during the second half of the Egyptian period. The best of the travellers during the earlier years of the occupation, G. B. English, F. Cailliaud, A. Linant, and G. B. Brocchi, are models of their kind, modest, observant, tolerant. But somewhere about 1870 (a more precise date eludes me) the tone of writing among almost all the foreign travellers changes. The newer men from the West have given up wearing Turkish *niẓām* dress and come clothed in outlandish modifications of European garb. They no longer feed off the country but bring tinned stores with them. They also bring a new mental attitude; it is as though they have been subjected to the influence of a new ideology at home.

Up to this time slavery and other indigenous institutions were accepted by the foreign visitors, with protests here and there where manifest injustice was present. The iniquities of the type of slavery practised by Christians in the Americas appear to have exhausted the fund of righteous indignation of anti-slavery opinion in Britain, at any rate until 1865, and nation-wide attention to slavery and the slave trade in Africa does not seem to have been drawn until after the abolition of slavery in the United States. From about that date British public opinion was increasingly sensitive to the problem of the slave traffic in the Nile Valley, the Foreign Office was converted and John Petherick was appointed British vice-consul in Khartoum in 1858. The appointment turned out to be unfortunate, nevertheless Petherick's book, *Egypt, the Soudan and Central Africa* (1861), probably had some effect upon public opinion in Britain, as did the writings of V. Schoelcher and E. F. Berlioux on the Continent. The climax came with the publication of Sir Samuel Baker Pasha's *Ismailïa* (1874), of which the sub-title was *Expedition to Central Africa for the suppression of the slave trade.*

This sub-title, as well as the text of the book, somewhat distorted Baker's terms of reference from the Khedive Ismā'īl who issued to Baker various administrative instructions one of which was an order to suppress the slave trade in the Equatorial regions. It may have been that Baker was intimidated by the anti-slavery pressure-group in Britain into allowing this distortion to appear in his book. The British and Foreign Anti-Slavery Society was the stronger from having an active, almost militant, Quaker element on the committee in the persons of Edmund Sturge and Joseph Cooper. These two controversial bruisers harried Baker and would have harried Gordon, Baker's successor in Equatoria, had not Cooper discovered in Gordon a fellow-warrior against the trade.

In spite of the justice of its aims the anti-slavery interest did harm to

British history-writing on the Sudan in that it intoxicated the weaker brethren among historians who accepted Baker's assertion as to the object of his mission, and who similarly misrepresented the later missions of Gordon. Gordon's single-minded obsession with the slave trade, his violence in attempting its abolition, combined with his ignorance of the place of the institution of slavery in the Sudanese economy, precipitated, if it did not cause, the Mahdist revolt.

Until our own day Orientalists saw nothing to attract them to the Egyptian Sudan, and histories of the Egyptian rule were written entirely from western source material. Such were H. Dehérain's *Le Soudan égyptien sous Mehemet Ali* (Paris, 1898) and O. Abbate Pasha's *Le Soudan sous le règne du Khédive Ismail* (Paris, 1905). These authors—and there were others—did not have access to the materials at the disposal of the Sudan Government official, Na'ūm Bay Shuqayr (Naum Shoucair), whose *Ta'rīkh al-Sūdān* (Cairo, 1903) was the first comprehensive history of the country to be published, and the first to make extensive use of Sudanese original documents and oral tradition for the Egyptian period. The lack of a translation of this work in a European language delayed for many years the advent of a balanced western appraisal of Sudanese history, for this was a time when European historians were themselves in process of fundamental intellectual transition.

Nearer our own day G. Douin, traffic manager of the Suez Canal Company, followed Na'ūm Shuqayr's path. He began by a study of the Sudan under the Khedive Ismā'īl and then, retracing his steps, wrote what he intended to be the first volume of a detailed history of the earlier period of the Egyptian occupation. This vast project was cut short by his death in 1944. Douin had his Turkish and Arabic sources translated for him by officials of the Abdin archives. The fact that a western historian of the Sudan was using original materials, even if in translation, represents a distinct advance in historiography. Using Arabic documents in the Egyptian State papers, and Arabic translations of the Turkish documents in the same archives, Professor Mekki Shibeika, the first professional historian to set his hand to the work, produced *al-Sūdān fī qarn 1819–1919* (Cairo, 1947), a short history of the century which contained the Egyptian and Mahdist periods together with the first twenty years of the Condominium.

The legacy of Egyptian scholars to historical studies of their own administration in the Sudan has been over-concerned with proving the strength of Egyptian claims to the sovereignty of the former appanage of the Ottoman *wilāya* of Egypt, and insufficiently concerned with the internal development of the area. It is therefore a literature of advocacy, of *parti pris*. It deserves close attention because it made the Arabic-speaking world aware of the ambiguous legality of the British protectorate over Uganda, and it gave publicity to Egyptian political interest in the Sudan. It originated in the Egypt of Muṣṭafā Kāmil and reached its maximum output in 1947–8 when the affairs of the Sudan were being brought before the Security Council of the United Nations. Dr. Muḥammad Ṣabrī's (M. Sabry), *Le Soudan égyptien (1821–1896)* (Cairo, 1947), and its Arabic version, *al-Imbarāṭūriyya al-sūdāniyya* (Cairo, 1948), are an example of what may with propriety be called the Wafdist school of historical writing on the Sudan. The logic is impeccable; it is the Blue Book logic of the political advocate, but the contents of the work bear no relation to the real Sudan of men and goats and camels; the text abounds in naiveties and solecisms concerning Sudanese internal history. In 'Abd al-Raḥmān al-Rāfi'ī's *Miṣr wa'l-Sūdān fī awā'il 'ahd al-iḥtilāl* (Cairo, 1948) we have a political tract so emotionally charged that it would be difficult, if not unjust to the author, to classify it as historical writing. Even Professor Muḥammad Fu'ād Shukrī, whose deep knowledge of the Khedive Ismā'īl's Sudan is based on European as well as Egyptian documentation, never lets us forget, in his *al-Ḥukm al-miṣrī fi'l-Sūdān* (Cairo, 1945), that he is an Egyptian, with a cause in his heart. In concentrating on the external aspects of Egyptian rule and ignoring events and institutions inside the Sudan, Egyptian historians in general have contributed less than their due share to an understanding of their régime.

The Egyptian revolution is still too young for us to detect in its historians the emergence of a clearly marked new trend in history-writing on the Sudan. It is not improbable that there will be a diminished concentration on the legalistic aspects of Egyptian sovereignty and a greater emphasis on the development of the Sudanese people under the stimulus of Egyptian culture and Egyptian institutions. We shall almost certainly see the beginnings of a reassessment of the achievements of Muḥammad 'Alī Pasha in the Sudan. In the biographical and administrative aspects of the Egyptian occupation Egyptian historians are obstructed by the absence of a dictionary of Egyptian biography comparable in scope and objectivity with the best national biographical collections of Europe and America. Many a distinguished Egyptian soldier, official and '*ālim* who served the Sudan, is now utterly forgotten. Anything which we can do to encourage our Egyptian colleagues to treasure their national biography will be to their, and our, advantage.

For the Egyptians have a great historical void ahead of them for their exploring; with the Sudan archives at their door they possess advantages for research denied to the greater number of foreign workers in Sudanese history. Not all Egyptian historians confine their researches to the arid field of international recrimination. Dr. 'Abd al-Raḥmān Zakī has written short regimental histories of units of the Egyptian army with long service in the Sudan, followed by *A'lām al-jaysh wa'l-baḥriyya fī Miṣr athnā' al-qarn al-tāsi' 'ashar* (Cairo, 1947), a collection of naval and military biographies, while Dr. 'Abd al-'Azīz 'Abd al-Majīd, in *al-Tarbiyya fi'l-Sūdān* (Cairo, 1949), has edited documents bearing upon the development of education in its widest sense under Egyptian auspices in the Sudan. My own *Egypt in the Sudan, 1820–1881* (Oxford, 1959), is an attempt towards a more general study of the régime.

The Mahdist Period, 1881–98

Genuine historical work on the Mahdist period—using the word 'genuine' in a technical and not a moral sense—is small in volume and extremely late in appearing. Colonel F. R. Wingate (the future sirdar and governor-general) wrote *Mahdiism and the Egyptian Sudan* (1891), a soldier's account, grounded on military intelligence reports and on such scraps of information as he could piece together. The book was perforce an outsider's view; to the writer Mahdism was the enemy. Works of detached scholarship could not have been written at the time, even less could the writings of escaped prisoners from the camps of El Obeid and Omdurman be judged apart from the dramatic context of the times. P. M. Holt, in his paper, 'The source materials of the Sudanese Mahdia' (*St. Antony's Papers*, No. 4, 1958), goes so far as to describe the work of Wingate, as author and editor, as war propaganda designed to prepare public opinion in Britain for the eventual reconquest of the Sudan; a conclusion which seems unassailable but which may require re-examination when the voluminous Wingate papers, presented in 1958 to Durham University by his son and biographer, Sir Ronald Wingate, are made available for research.

E. L. Dietrich was the first Arabist in the west to look to the Arabic sources of the Mahdist movement, and yet his 'Der Mahdi Moḥammed Aḥmed vom Sudan nach arabischen Quellen', published in *Der Islam*, xiv, 1925, was a compilation derived chiefly from Na'ūm Shuqayr. But this was an isolated essay, little more perhaps than an academic exercise; there were so many exciting themes to explore in the heart of Islam that western (and for that matter Arab) students may be forgiven for their reluctance to lose themselves in the African periphery. For many years a rich deposit of Mahdist state documents lay ignored in the archives of the Condominium secretariat in Khartoum, and we have had to wait for P. M. Holt to make use of them in his *Mahdist state in the Sudan, 1881–1898* (Oxford, 1958). A. B. Theobald's *The Mahdīya, a history of the Anglo-Egyptian Sudan*, 1881–1899 (London, 1951), which was not intended by the author to be more than a popular work, is the precursor of a more sympathetic approach to Mahdism.

It is pointless to pass moral judgements on the western contemporaries of the Mahdī; they arrived at conclusions on the evidence before them and, like ourselves, they were the children of their environment. If historical writing on the Sudan during the period of Egyptian rule gives some indication of what the middle classes in Europe were then thinking, historical work on the Mahdist rule, published during or soon after the Mahdist régime, introduces us to the new reading public born of compulsory, popular education. In Britain the crowds who read of Lord Kitchener's victory at Omdurman in 1898 were very different from the crowds who flocked to the Great Exhibition of 1851. At least half of the former would have received the bare bones of an elementary education and would be capable of reading the new kind of popular newspaper which the Harmsworths were producing for them. They now got their news superheated, news with a human story. The Mahdī (the stock epithet for the Imām was 'The False Prophet' which conveniently savoured of the Bible) and the Khalīfa 'Abdallāhi, were reported as monsters of cruelty. The reasons for the existence of Mahdism were never explained to them; it was not necessary that they should know, and they would not have understood the explanation anyway.

The British public in 1881–98 did not take their contemporary history of the Sudan from formal historians because there were none. They went rather to the war correspondents and the writers of fiction who, having left the Egyptian period well alone, now enter the bibliography of the Sudan in some force.

The novelist is the people's historian for, although the general public may have no head for cool, critical historiography, they can absorb simple, colourful detail founded on what is more or less the truth as far as it can be ascertained. And what G. A. Henty, Conan Doyle, Nat Gould, and A. E. W. Mason were doing for the English-speaking public, Jurjī Zaydān, with his *Asīr al-mutamahdī* (Cairo, 1892) did for the much smaller reading public in the Arabic-speaking lands.

The novelist in this popular rôle achieves an end unattainable by the formal historian: sales without scruples. The novelist has no need to be meticulous over the niceties of truth; the historian by the terms of his calling has a responsibility not only to his present readers but to posterity. He is bound, on the evidence available to him, to write what he believes to be the truth; he may not write trusting that posterity will not discover that he is a liar. The historical novelist writes under no such limitation. A. E. W. Mason, who created a fanatical ogre and called him the Khalīfa, did not have to bother about the feelings of the Khalīfa's sons and daughters, respected members of modern Sudanese society. And Mason was only embroidering Slatin Pasha's *Fire and sword* (1896) and the war correspondents' dispatches.

At the same time we would come away with a wrong impression of the reading public in Britain if we ignored the strong moral ingredient in popular historical reading. The twin influence of the anti-slavery movement and what we may rather loosely call Evangelical Imperialism continued to guide British thinking on the Sudan. The force of this joint interest is shown at its most powerful in 1884–5 in the torrent of writing on General Gordon.

The Condominium Period, 1899–1956

The foundation of the Anglo-Egyptian Condominium in 1899 marks the end of fifteen years of sensational and sometimes tendentious writing and the beginning of another, wholly different, literature, written mostly by British people employed in the Sudan whose experience gives to their contributions the character of eyewitness accounts. It is a dry, factual record, in parts unconsciously self-congratulatory, never consciously boastful. From the Orientalist's point of view it is somewhat parochial, as though the writers conceived of the Sudan as isolated from its neighbours. What is more important, it is a literature still in progress.

The journal *Sudan Notes and Records*, founded by a group of Sudan Government officials in Khartoum in 1918, enabled political officers, technicians, archaeologists, teachers, and Christian missionaries to publish information on a variety of subjects connected with their work and their hobbies. This journal provides the historian with a wealth of material. Yet, even here the reader confirms his impression of a sense of isolation from the rest of the Near East. This is due to the fact that most of the contributors had no knowledge of the Islamic past and no interest in the Arab present apart from the district in which the writers served. But it would be unscientific to judge their writings by irrelevant criteria; they were first and last practical, working men and women busy with the immediate problems, not of Araby but of the Sudan.

Historical work on the Condominium was late in coming for the reason that, whatever interest there may have been for specialists in comparative administration in its various branches, the reading public would have been small. There were no scandals, no great crises, to complicate the orderly march of government and add spice to historical inquiry. Serving officers and officials do not usually unburden themselves in public, and Sudan Government personnel were a model of this particular propriety. In course of time Sir Harold MacMichael published *The Anglo-Egyptian Sudan* (1934) at the end of his term of office as Civil Secretary. It is a plain account of the achievements of the Condominium from the beginning. The same writer's *The Sudan*, a vindication of British rule, followed in 1954.

The approaching end of the British connection coincided with the publication of several books by retiring political officers and doctors. K. D. D. Henderson edited the papers of the late Sir Douglas Newbold, Civil Secretary during the later stages of political transition, in *The making of the modern Sudan* (1953). Typical of the prevailing British view are J. S. R. Duncan's *The Sudan, a record of achievement* (1953) and *The Sudan's path to independence* (1957). The tone is friendly to the Sudanese, distant to the Egyptians, and in no doubt of the benefits of Condominium rule to the Sudanese. Further to the right stands H. C. Jackson who is pessimistic as to the future of Sudanese independence, not because of the weaknesses of the Sudanese but because of the malignity of the Egyptians. His two, partly autobiographical books, *Sudan days and ways* (1954), and *Behind the modern Sudan* (1956), re-echo the sentiments which we find in the Gordon literature: the same devotion to the Sudanese, the same dislike of the Egyptians. No reader of Jackson's entertaining books—he has also written a little history of the Sudan Defence Force in heroic vein—can fail to observe that the Old Alliance of Exeter Hall and Evangelical churchmanship lives on in British historical writing on the Sudan.

Meanwhile the gulf between British and Egyptian historians of the modern Sudan remains unbridged; each side refuses to recognize the existence of the other. The Egyptian thesis may be thus stated:

(1) The Mahdist rising was due almost wholly to foreign interference in the internal administration of the Sudan.

(2) The Mahdist movement was, and is, anachronistic.

(3) Egypt was tricked out of the Sudan in 1884–5.

(4) The Condominium in the Sudan was imposed on Egypt by *force majeure*.

(5) The unity of the Nile Valley is essential for Egypt and the Sudan. An independent Sudan is not a viable state.

The British attitude, broadly expressed in the literature of the Sudan, has been this:

(1) Egyptian rule in the Sudan was inefficient, corrupt, and cruel.

(2) The Mahdist revolt was a rising of an oppressed people, a shift in attitude since the reconquest of 1896–8. Contact with the Sudanese coupled with distrust of Egyptian aims in the Sudan contributed to the change.

(3) General Gordon was the exemplar of the British conception of justice and humanity.

(4) British rule was imperative to protect the Sudanese from further exploitation.

Only genuine historians (this time using 'genuine' in a moral sense) will be able to produce an intelligible interpretation out of this dark tangle of irreconcilables.

The Condominium period has not received enough attention by historians free from the embarrassing shackles of national and personal loyalties. Assuredly, historical criticism will not be withheld for much longer, though it is still idle to speculate over-seriously on the directions it will take. The historian may wish to examine the reasons which prompted the Sudan Government to segregate the southern Sudan from the Muslim North by an educational system apparently designed for the purpose. The confining of the languages taught in Government schools to Arabic and English (to the exclusion, for instance, of Oriental languages other than Arabic) may possibly be the subject of criticism. Students of the history of local government may inquire why the structure of local government over much of the Sudan is based on an adaptation of English practice when the legislators in Khartoum had the long experience of the Near East, the Ottoman system, and Arab prototypes, to draw upon. Social historians may direct their curiosity to the diverse influences which moulded the attitude of British administrators (political, medical, educational, technical in general) towards their work. On all these matters except the last the Sudan Government not only had a policy but explained it; the quality of future research in these fields must therefore represent investigation at its most judicial, or it will fail.

Conclusion

Among the pressing needs in Sudanese, as in Egyptian modern historical studies is the expansion of the kind of research which will lead to the making of a dictionary of national biography, a labour which will act as a training school for a team of Sudanese biographers captained by a trained scholar of the calibre of Professor Shibeika and inspired by the spirit of that father of Sudanese biography, S͟hayk͟h Muḥammad al-Nūr wad (i.e. ibn) Ḍayfallāh. The new Sudanese nationhood does not seem to have had the immediately depressing effect on historical research which was evident in Turkey at the outset of the Republic when men felt for the moment a weariness of the past. From Khartoum comes news of an apparently spontaneous enthusiasm for the study of Sudanese history, with no sign, up to the present, of the growth of a national myth. The Sudanese poets, the S͟hukrī chieftain al-Ḥardallū for one, are being printed or reprinted. Plans are at last being made, so it is said, for a comprehensive survey of the hundreds of domed tombs which cover the northern and central regions, in an endeavour to supplement the little now known of the country in the era of Funj dominion. In Britain two editors are believed to be working on a critical edition of Wad Ḍayfallāh's *Ṭabaqāt*. In the more recent field Saad Ed Din Fawzi's *Labour movement in the Sudan, 1946–1955* (Oxford, 1957), deserves to be matched by further studies in the by-ways of the Sudanese national movement. Some of these labours precede the period of this paper but are recorded without apology to emphasize that the historians are not idle.

31. SOVIET HISTORIOGRAPHY ON THE ISLAMIC ORIENT

R. N. FRYE

Aga Khan Professor of Iranian, Harvard University

It is not my intention in this paper to repeat material which has appeared in the surveys of Soviet Oriental studies in Russian in recent years.[1] Some of these Soviet publications have been summarized in English, French or German and are readily accessible.[2] Nor is the purpose here a discussion of Marxist theory as it has been applied to Soviet historical writings. This is more the task of the student of Soviet culture who is thoroughly conversant with the changes in Soviet policy and the nuances in the application and interpretation of Marxism or Leninism in various fields of learning. Rather it is my hope to investigate one field of Islamic history in which Soviet scholars have made some significant contributions to knowledge, and to come to some general conclusions from a limited study. I wish to discuss briefly the history of Central Asia in the ninth and tenth centuries A.D., as seen by Soviet Orientalists. They call this period 'the beginning of developed feudalism' in Central Asia. Some brief general remarks on the historical and methodological presuppositions of the Soviet scholars are necessary before proceeding.

At the outset one must recognize that Soviet Orientalists until recently have been little interested in the *history* of lands and peoples outside the Soviet Union. Histories of any Islamic peoples which have appeared have concentrated on Transcaucasia and Central Asia. I know of no history of the Umayyad or 'Abbasid caliphates, much less of the Fatimids, Islam in Spain, or the like. The best source of Soviet views on such subjects seems to be general world histories or articles in encyclopaedias published in the USSR. Unfortunately these are of little importance for the scholarly historian of the Islamic world. On the other hand, from them one may learn of the matters of interest and dispute among Soviet historians of the Orient, for example about one of the most important matters of dispute in recent years among Soviet scholars concerned with the Islamic world.

[1] Besides many articles there have been three volumes summarizing work in the Oriental area: I. Yu. Kratchkovskii, *Ocherki po istorii russkoi arabistiki* (Moscow, 1950); the two-volume work *Ocherki po istorii russkogo Vostokovedeniya* (Moscow, 1953–6), and N. A. Smirnov, *Ocherki istorii izucheniya Islama v SSSR* (Moscow, 1954).

[2] The work of Smirnov has been summarized and studied in *The Central Asian Review* (1956) and by N. Elisséeff in *Mélanges Massignon* (Beirut, 1956). A general account of Soviet orientalists is found in H. Jablonowski, 'Die Geschichte Asiens in der Sovethistoriographie nach dem zweiten Weltkrieg', in *Saeculum* (1957), viii, 298–311.

This is the question whether the prophet Muḥammad grew up in a slave-holding or in a feudal society. Marxism teaches that the history of any people or society must be analysed into five general and consecutive periods: primitive society, slave-holding, feudal, and capitalist periods, with the fifth, of course, Marxist-socialist society. The tide has swung recently in the USSR to the position that Muḥammad rose to power in the feudal period of Arab history, but just at the time of change from the slave-holding period.

When we turn to internal Soviet history we have a great amount of writing, even concerning the history of the Samanids and Karakhanids in Central Asia. We may divide these writings into four groups: (1) the large, general histories of the USSR or of large areas of the world; (2) local histories of Uzbekistān, Tājīkistān, and school textbooks of the same; (3) historical monographs on limited periods of the history of a republic, a district, or even a village; (4) detailed articles or books on art, archaeology, numismatics, and epigraphy. Books in the first category such as the *Survey of the history of the USSR*, published in 1956, give the overall orientation for history writing, and reveal changes in the 'line'. Publications of the second group are quite important because in them can be found both the latest results of work in categories three and four, plus the application of general ideas from category one to the local areas. In this group, characterized by books such as *The history of the Uzbek SSR* (second edition, Tashkent, 1955), and B. G. Gafurov, *History of the Tājīk nation* (Moscow, 1952), some documentation and bibliography lacking in the general histories may be found. These publications are usually the result of teamwork and serve as the authoritative 'college textbooks' on their subjects. The third group, above, is of most interest to historians of the Islamic world, for here we have research on manuscripts and archives producing special studies. Representative of such work are the books by N. V. Petrushevskii, *Survey of the history of feudal relations in Āẕarbāyjān and Armenia from the 16th to the Beginning of the 19th Centuries* (L. 1949), and A. K. Alizade, *Social-economic and political history of Āẕarbāyjān 13–14 cents.* (Baku, 1956). In the same category but of limited interest, though nonetheless important, are books such as S. A. Azimdzhanova, *On the history of Farg͟hāna, 15th cent.* (Tashkent, 1957), and M. S. Andreev, *The Tājīks of the K͟huf valley* (Stalinabad, 1953). In the fourth category we find the material for much of this paper. Here is a minimum of integration into large patterns of Marxist historical ideology, and here also is the research which is of greatest significance for the Orientalist and for the historian of Islam. The concern for somehow pragmatically justifying one's work within the Marxist interpretation of history is felt much less strongly in category four than even in three. Such publications as the journals *Oriental Epigraphy* and *Soviet Oriental Studies* contain many articles of prime interest for historians.

To illustrate this group, in art one may refer to the book by A. Yu. Yakubovskii, *The paintings of ancient Pandjikent* (Moscow, 1950), which is an art history of Sogdiana at the time of the Arab conquest with no apparent reference to Marxist doctrines. In archaeology, for example, the book on *The astronomical school of Ulug Beg* by T. N. Kary-Niyazov (Moscow, 1950) is an important contribution to the history of science as well as the cultural history of Samarqand under the Timurids. Numismatics, another sphere where Soviet scholars have made significant studies, will be elaborated below.

The history of the Samanids and Karakhanids has been elucidated by the numismatic work of A. A. Bykov, F. Davidovich, and the late F. Vasmer.[3] This is especially true of the Karakhanid rulers, for determination of their chronology and areas of rule depends to a great extent on their coinage since written sources are few and often contradictory. The Soviet Union with its large coin collections in the Hermitage Museum, in the Historical Museum in Moscow, and in Tashkent, is the only country where the coinage of the Karakhanids can be adequately studied. A revision of the list of rulers and the chronology of the Karakhanids in itself is not of great interest to a general assembly of historians. What is of importance, however, is first, new methods in numismatic history and, second, economic and social implications.

The Russians are the first to study in detail Islamic copper coinage. The reasons are understandable; in Western museums only silver and gold coins have been worthy of collection artistically and field archaeologists have been little interested in the usually poorly preserved copper coins. Western numismatists are few and usually have an enormous task of simply cataloguing coins with little time for economic or historical interpretations. One of the few articles in Western periodicals somewhat similar to Soviet work in this field is the article by R. P. Blake, 'The circulation of silver in the Moslem East down to the Mongol epoch', *HJAS*, 2 (1937), although Blake made little reference to actual coins. In the Soviet Union copper coins, 'the coinage of the masses' has stimulated field archaeologists in preserving and specialists later to study the great number of copper coins found on digs. Furthermore, one must remember that Marxist oriented scholars are interested in such basic source material for economic history.

What do the Soviet numismatic studies tell us about Samanid history?[4]

[3] For example, R. Vasmer, 'Die Münzkunde der Qarāhāniden', in *MSOS* (1930) xxxiii, 83–104. A. A. Bykov, 'A new hoard of copper Kufic coins from Tadzhikistan', in *Trudy Otdela numismatiki Gos. Ermitazha* (Leningrad, 1945), p. 1. E. A. Davidovich, 'Numismatic material for the history of the development of feudal conditions in Central Asia under the Samanids', in *Trudy Instituta Istorii, Akad. Nauk Tadzhikskoi SSR* (Stalinabad, 1954), xxvii, 69–117.

[4] M. E. Masson, 'On the Question of the Museiyabi "Black Dirhems" ', in *Trudy Instituta Istorii, Akad. Nauk Uzbekskoi SSR* (Tashkent, 1955), vii, 174–96.

It is now quite clear from the coins that Transoxania was really 'the other side of the river' from *dār al-Khilāfa* throughout much of the 'Abbasid as well as all of the Umayyad period. It was never considered an integral part of the central domains. In the tenth century we find that the monetary policy of the Samanids was directed towards the establishment of an independent area of trade and commerce in Central Asia apart from the Caliphate even though the rulers professed loyalty to the Caliph. From the hoards of coins found in the Soviet Union numismatists have been able to trace the areas of coinage and currency of various monies such as the Ghiṭrifī, Muḥammadī, and Musayyabī *dirhams*, and the progressive debasement of these coins. Soviet numismatists have shown in their studies the longer persistence of local copper or billon coins, in pre-Islamic form, in Central Asia, while silver, which was used in international trade, was minted on the caliphal model. The latter coinage, of course, attracted the attention of Muslim authors more than the former.[5] It is significant that the Soviet studies are based primarily on statistical surveys of distribution by find spots and by mint years. Only in Soviet Central Asia have conditions permitted extensive studies of find spots and full information on hoards of coins. Consequently the results are based on new analyses of new material, surely of interest to numismatists everywhere.

This specialized material is always interpreted in a general framework and I wish to disgress here on the background to and interpretation of Samanid history. The *Survey of the history of the USSR* (p. 13) says, 'the authors have tried as much as possible to portray the history of the peoples of the USSR (giving to each its special features and contributions to general history). Dividing this material into independent sections, at the same time they have endeavoured to show the common conformity to laws of history by the Russian people and other peoples of our country. Also they have tried to show the historical (economic, political, and cultural) relations between the peoples to the extent which relations existed in the period of the early Middle Ages . . . The history of the peoples of Central Asia and the Caucasus, from the ninth to the beginning of the thirteenth century, is a period of the development of feudal conditions, the aggravation of class differences, and the formation of a series of feudal states, as well as protracted struggles for independence.' Further we read (p. 497), 'in the sources on the history of Central Asia in this period, there is almost no information preserved about peasant uprisings against the secular and religious feudal lords'. And (p. 498), 'the historians, writing at the order of the rulers, and even themselves belonging to the highest stratum of feudal

[5] As Narshakhī says, 'Many copper coins were struck in Bukhārā by everyone of the Samanid dynasty, and of other rulers after the Samanids, but this has not been mentioned since there is nothing of interest in that.' Cf. *The history of Bukhara*, trans. R. N. Frye (Cambridge, Mass., 1954), p. 37.

society, were little interested in the movements of peasants and did not record the facts about this phase of history, although there were undoubtedly many of them [peasant uprisings]'. The authors of the first edition of *The history of the Uzbek SSR* (published as *History of the peoples of Uzbekistan* in 1950), had followed the written sources too closely, for in the introduction to the second edition we read that the authors in the first edition had 'insufficiently elaborated the periodicization of Central Asian history, had idealized certain episodes, and had given unnecessarily detailed accounts of the struggles of certain feudal groups at the expense of the real history of the masses'. After discussing the Arab conquests and their colonial policy, the struggle for independence led by al-Ḥārith b. Surayj in 734 and the politics of Naṣr b. Sayyār, last Umayyad governor of Khurāsān, are given considerable space. Naṣr, seeing the weakness of the Umayyad cause, tried to win over the local aristocracy, but it was too late. A mass movement had begun against the Umayyads and it was used by the 'Abbasids to consolidate their own power. The position of Abū Muslim is enigmatic for the Soviet scholars since he was a common man, but not concerned with the interests of the masses. He also did not hold to the aristocratic policy of al-Saffāḥ or to the people's party—the neo-Mazdakites or Khurramīs (Arabic *Muḥammira*). In any case the advent of the 'Abbasids weakened Arab rule in Central Asia. The anti-popular nature of 'Abbasid rule is revealed in the suppression of the popular Shi'ite revolt in Bukhārā against Abū Muslim, which was led by Sharīk b. Shaykh al-Mahrī. The further popular revolt of Muqanna' is connected with the pre-Islamic Mazdakite movement with a guarded idealization of both. The suppression of the anti-Arab or anti-caliphal revolts brings an end to the early feudal period of Central Asian history, and with the formation of the independent feudal kingdoms of the Tahirids and Samanids we are in the historical phase characterized by Soviet authors as the victory of the local aristocracy over the Arabs and the Caliphate.

To return to the coins, we find that the Samanids struck copper coins (*fals*), when they were nominally vassals of the Tahirids. Only the latter had the right to coin silver *dirhams*. The earliest Samanid *dirham* on record dates from 887, struck by Naṣr b. Aḥmad in Samarqand and preserved in the historical museum in Tashkent. From study of the copper coins Soviet scholars conclude that the Samanid kingdom was by no means a strong, centralized state. For the coins reveal that even the powerful founder of the dynasty Ismā'īl b. Aḥmad was not recognized as suzerain by his brother Isḥāq in Farghāna, while elsewhere in Central Asia allegiance to Ismā'īl was only nominal. The feudal forerunners of Seljuq *atabegs* and *iqṭā'* are found in the Samanid state.[6] By comparing the legends on the copper coins

[6] Perhaps one might also find Sogdian forerunners of the typical Central Asian theory of rule by *mamlūks* or slaves?

minted in such towns as Akhsikat, Shāsh, Isfijāb and elsewhere in Samanid domains the fortunes of the various branches of the Samanid family can be followed. From the beginning of Samanid rule when written sources tell us of strife between Ismā'īl and his brother Naṣr, we find here the only indication of family divisions which the coins now help to clarify. Unfortunately the written sources tell us very little about the later consequences.

Essentially there were two factions in the Samanid family from the start, the group which supported Ismā'īl and those who followed Naṣr. This division was of great importance in the assignment of feudal appanages, and played its part when Isḥāq revolted against his grand-nephew Naṣr b. Aḥmad b. Ismā'īl after the latter became *amīr* in Bukhārā in A.D. 914. Many districts of the Samanid state merely paid a nominal tribute to the ruler in Bukhārā while still ruled by native princes, such as Khwārizm, Khuttalān, Isfijāb, and Naṣrābād, where a Turkish family held sway. In these cases the relations between the local princes and their overlord in Bukhārā were similar to those which bound the Samanid *amīrs* to Baghdād.

It is not the place to go into details about the genealogy of the Samanids who ruled in Farghāna, or the independent feudatories of Isfijāb; suffice it to say that the striking of silver *dirhams* on the caliphal model was the sign of revolt against the central authorities who alone had the right to coin in silver. Further researches by Soviet numismatists have further elaborated the thesis that Samanid silver *dirhams* were used as money, as well as goods for their silver content, in Eastern Europe (the Volga region). In China and East Turkestan, on the contrary, silver was not wanted and trade with merchants from the Samanid domains was on a barter basis.

There is, of course, much more to say about the Samanids, the rôle of Qarmaṭī propaganda in Central Asia, art and architecture, government, bureaucracy, and a host of other questions which have been studied by Soviet scholars. In regard to literature, I cannot refrain from quoting Gafurov (p. 162) regarding the formation of the New Persian language in Samanid territory, 'As a result [of the tendency of various peoples of Transoxiana to unite economically, politically, and culturally] the development of East Iranian dialects and languages, evidently on the basis of one of the dialects located in the territory where Sogdiana, Ṭukhāristān and Khurāsān adjoin, was to form the common language of the Tājīks, which at that time was called *Darī*.'[7]

The feudal state of the Tājīk Samanids ended and the Turkish state of the Karakhanids with an elaborate system of *iqṭā'* with *iqṭā'dārs* replaced

[7] My views on this subject have been expressed in a lecture in Persian given at the Pohani theatre, Kabul, under the auspices of the University of Kabul on 17 January 1958. It is published in the newspapers *Anīs* and *Islāḥ* with an English version in the journal *Afghanistan*. See also my article 'Die Wiedergeburt Persiens', in *Der Islam*, 35 (1960), 142.

it. The entrenched landed aristocracy, the *dihqāns*, gave way to feudatories of the Ilak Khans or Karakhanids. This did not mean, however, a replacing of the Iranian by a Turkish aristocracy, for the two were blended. As the authors of the *History of Uzbekistan* say (p. 238), 'It would be erroneous, as was done frequently in the historiography of Central Asia, to oppose Transoxania as the world of Sogdian settlers to Semirechie as the world of Turkish nomads.' Turkish elements in Soviet Central Asia can be traced back to pre-Islamic times and the growing preponderance of Turkish speech did not mean the suppression of the Tājīk language, but rather the mingling of the two to form the ancestors of the tongues of modern Uzbeks and Tājīks. This was already foreseen at the end of Samanid rule when the *dihqāns* and Turkish generals between themselves held the power in the state.

The Ghaznavid state finds little place in Soviet investigations. In the *Survey* (above, p. 506), we find the following, 'F. Engels in a letter to K. Marx, 6 June 1853, wrote the following, characterizing the features of Oriental states, "the state in the Orient always had only three divisions: (1) financial (for the plunder of their own population); (2) military (for plunder outside as well as inside the country); (3) office of public works (for building)". These words clearly characterize the Ghaznavid state.' The Karakhanids receive a much fuller treatment than the Ghaznavids. I say they receive a fuller treatment than one would expect from the information in the sources, but we still know little about the dynasty.

The Soviet scholars tell us about the family rule of the Karakhanids, with members of the family ruling various parts of the total domains. They also tell us (*History of Uzbekistan*, p. 256) that the Ilak Khans and the Turkish warrior aristocracy continued the tradition of the union which had been concluded between the Turkish guard under the Samanids and the most reactionary part of the Islamic clergy. Under the Karakhanids the authority of the *imāms*, *sayyids*, *shaykhs*, and *ṣadrs* stood at the highest point ever.' The economic crisis under Karakhanid rule (decline of silver, debasement of coinage, fall of prices with the break up of large estates) is an interesting subject discussed by Soviet scholars. Again the new material comes from the rich coin collections, but a new source has been added. This source is to become of supreme importance after the Timurids, but it also has a relevance to earlier times. This source is the archives of the towns, local *waqfs*, or the like. The best examples of such studies are the book by P. P. Ivanov, *The economy of the Juibar shaykhs* (of Bukhārā) (Moscow, 1954) and the articles by O. D. Chekovich in *Istoricheskie Zapiski*, 'A new collection of documents on the history of Uzbekistan' (1951), 'Regarding the archival material on the history of Bukhārā' (1945), and others. Although these documents are all from the post-Timurid period, they refer to events as far back as early Samanid rule. From these A. A.

Semenov, in his article, 'On the question of the origin of the Samanids', *Trudy Akad. Nauk Tadzhikskoi*, SSR, vol. 27 (Stalinabad, 1954), was able to show that the Samanids came from a village near Termez. His other work on local archives has been just as fruitful.

From this necessarily brief survey of certain Soviet publications on Central Asian history one may draw some general conclusions, especially after comparison with work on related subjects elsewhere in the world. I believe one may say in general that the technical competence of the Soviet scholars, especially when it is directed towards specific problems, is excellent. Articles on the meaning of terms such as *iqṭā'*, *s̲h̲ākir*, *dihqān*, and the like, have brought new source materials to their clarification, and have thus made distinct contributions to our knowledge. The problems posed by archaeology, in the excavation of a site, are usually dealt with in a competent manner by a host of specialists on pottery, numismatics, architecture, etc. The number of trained specialists in the Soviet Union working on such problems, not to mention other problems of linguistics and ethnography, is quite beyond the estimates of most non-Soviet scholars in the Oriental field. Linguistic studies on various dialects of the many languages of the Soviet Union are of a high calibre, and this is especially true of Turkish and Iranian languages.

The core of the Near East, however, the 'Fertile Crescent' and Egypt in ancient times and the Arab world with Islam in the Middle Ages, has been little touched by Soviet scholars. One reason for this, of course, is geography, but another, and most important, reason is the concern which the people of all the Near East have ever evinced for religion. The written sources, pre-Islamic as well as Islamic, are permeated with religious sentiment. Indeed, one can hardly study this part of the world without a sympathy for religion since it is ubiquitous. Consequently one wonders whether Soviet contributions to the history of this part of the world, including Central Asia and the Caucasus, other than the technically specialized work just mentioned, can be of value to scholarship. So far the general studies published in the Soviet Union, mentioned above, show a lack of understanding of not only the spiritual, but consequently the cultural and social, development of man in this part of the world. The rigid periodicity of history, as taught by the Marxists, must be viewed by historians with greater suspicion than the prophetic utterances of a Spengler or a Toynbee. In spite of this, the linguistic, archaeological, numismatic, and such, studies in the Soviet Union have made the Russian language a necessary scholarly tool for scholars working on Oriental history.[8]

[8] Another reason for reading Soviet works is given by Gafurov (p. 458): 'Bourgeois authors, restricted by their class tendencies and methodological helplessness, were not able to portray the course of the historical development of the peoples of Central Asia, and many of these authors were engaged in the direct falsification of history.' This not only refers to Western scholars but Russians such as W. Barthold and F. Rosenberg, according to Gafurov.

32. SOVIET WRITING ON PERSIA FROM 1906 TO 1946

G. E. WHEELER

Director of the Central Asian Research Centre

During the past forty years a very large amount of material on Persian history has been published in the Soviet Union. So far, however, most of this material has escaped serious attention in the West, partly because Western students of oriental history seldom include Russian in their linguistic equipment, but chiefly because of the political and ideological restrictions to which Soviet historiography is generally believed to be subject. Neither of these reasons justifies the neglect of Persian history written in a country so intimately connected with Persia as the USSR.

No comprehensive history of Persia has so far been published in the Soviet Union, and the available material consists principally of articles in academic and other journals, together with a number of short books. By far the most scholarly and best documented part of the material is that concerned with ancient history, and of this there is a considerable amount; but the main Soviet emphasis is on modern history. For instance, more than threequarters of Ivanov's important outline of Persian history are taken up with the history of the nineteenth and twentieth centuries. The present paper only deals with Soviet writing on Persian historical events during the period of forty years beginning with the Persian revolution of 1906.

The ideological and political restrictions just referred to vary according to the current Communist Party line and also the policy of the day. The most important change—and one of which it is well to be aware at the outset—is in the Soviet attitude towards Tsarist policy. This is particularly apparent in the varying treatment which has been accorded to the Persian revolution. Again, it has always been incumbent upon all Soviet historians to find the Western capitalist world entirely responsible for all Persia's ills. But even here there have been certain changes of emphasis. Early Soviet criticisms of British policy in Persia were moderate in comparison with the charges which have been levelled against it during the past ten or twelve years, and while earlier writers either ignored or were favourably disposed towards American interest in Persia, the more recent tendency is to trace American imperialist designs on Persia back to the Persian revolution. Apart from one or two very brief intervals, Soviet historians have been uncompromisingly critical of all Persian governments which held power during the period under review.

The object of the present brief paper is merely to indicate the general nature of Soviet historical writing about a limited period of Persian history. To achieve this object certain representative incidents and phases during the period have been selected, and certain works of the principal Soviet writers on them examined. The subjects thus selected are: the Persian revolution of 1906; the setting up of the Gīlān Republic, 1920–21; Persia, 1921–41; and the separatist movement in Āẕarbāyjān, 1945–46.

Full details of the sources used are given in the text. It is hoped that these sources are representative but they are very far from exhausting all the published material much of which has not been available.

The Persian Revolution of 1906

The treatment of the Persian revolution by Soviet historians is quite different from that used by other, including Persian, historians. There is also a marked difference between earlier and later Soviet treatments: the earlier material is uncompromisingly critical of Tsarist policy and action; the more recent tendency is to show these as venial by comparison with those of Britain and America, and occasionally as right and farseeing. The latter tendency began to appear in 1937, when the first Marxist historian Pokrovskiy was discredited. Not much historical material was published during the War, but the same tendency was again evident in 1945 and increased in force from 1951 onwards.

The main source material on the Persian revolution is to be found in the following works: M. S. Ivanov's *Ocherk istorii Irana* (An outline of the history of Persia), Moscow, 1952; *Noveyshaya istoriya stran zarubezhnogo Vostoka* (New history of the countries of the non-Soviet East), vol. ii, Moscow, 1952; and Bor-Ramenskiy's article on 'The rôle of the Bolsheviks of Transcaucasia in the Persian revolution of 1905–11', which appeared in *Istorik-Marksist*, No. 11 of 1940. In addition to these, a large number of articles on Persian history is to be found in the periodicals and academic bulletins, and also in the two editions of the *Great Soviet encyclopaedia.*

The principal of the early works dealing with the revolution are: *Sovremennaya Persiya* (Modern Persia) by A. Sulṭānzāda, Moscow, 1922; *Kratkaya istoriya Persii* (Short history of Persia) by V. Gurko-Kryazhin, Moscow, 1925); and *Persiya v bor'be za nezavisimost'* (Persia in her fight for independence) by M. Pavlovich and S. Iranskiy, Moscow, 1925.

The Persian revolution is represented in recent Soviet historiography as the first phase of a Persian movement for 'national liberation' which, in spite of numerous setbacks has continued until the present day. Great emphasis is laid on the generally accepted fact that the Russian revolution of 1905 to some extent precipitated what is usually thought of by Persian and Western historians as the Constitutional Movement. Elaborate descriptions are given of the part played by Transcaucasian revolutionaries whereas this is barely mentioned in Persian and Western accounts. Tsarist hostility to the movement is generally confirmed, but recent writings tend to distract attention from this by representing British sympathy for the movement as 'hypocrisy'.

In support of the theory of the fundamental hostility of the British to the Persian revolution, Ivanov asserts that

> The British imperialists resorted to armed intervention against the Persian revolution earlier than Tsarist Russia. But with the aim of concealing their imperialist . . . policy the British carried out demagogic hypocritical and false propaganda about how they were helping the people of Persia to struggle for a constitution against the Shah who, according to them, was protected by the Russians. . . . It is just from such a false and demagogic position that the book of the British Persian expert, E. Browne, *The Persian Revolution, 1905–1909*, was written. . . . This crude falsehood about the attitude of Britain to the Persian revolution has not yet been properly unmasked. The British imperialists . . . at the time tried to give wide publicity to their false, demagogic version which has penetrated even into Russian literature. The facts decisively refute this . . . version.[1]

It is noteworthy that both Pavlovich and Gurko-Kryazhin use Edward Browne's works apparently as reliable sources.

The fact that after the reactionary *coup d'état* of June 1908 many of the Persian constitutionalists took refuge in the British Embassy is explained by Ivanov as follows:

> Several members of the *Majlis*, among them Taqīzāda, took refuge in the British mission. The British protected them not at all out of sympathy with the supporters of the constitution as British propaganda has falsely and hypocritically affirmed. The British imperialists were simply trying to save their agents amongst whom were several members of the *Majlis*.[2]

It is noteworthy that this is the sole reference to Taqīzāda, the outstanding figure of the *Majlis* and of the Revolution, in the whole of Ivanov's book. Still more remarkable is the fact that in Ivanov's very detailed account of the early months of the first *Majlis* 'The summoning of the first Persian *Majlis* and the struggle for the establishment of the fundamental law (October–December 1906)', which appeared in *Uchenyye Zapiski Instituta Vostokovedeniya*, No. 8, 1953, Taqīzāda is not mentioned at all. Earlier writers differ from Ivanov in their interpretation of the British attitude towards the Persian revolution. Pavlovich writes:

[1] M. S. Ivanov, *Ocherk istorii Irana*, pp. 216–17.

[2] Ibid., p. 226.

> . . . while in the early period of the constitutional movement, mass opposition and mass *bast* (asylum) were powerful factors in the struggle against the Shah . . . no less important a factor in this popular victory was the serious support which Great Britain gave to the constitutional party of Persia at that time. . . . It was not fear of Allāh or respect for sacred customs but merely fear of Britain that rendered the Shah's Government impotent before the *bast* of 15,000 people in the British embassy.[3]

Unlike Ivanov, Gurko-Kryazhin and Pavlovich make favourable mention of Taqīzāda as a leader of the Revolution and as the outstanding figure of the First *Majlis*.

Both Ivanov and Reysner[4] appear to assume that all Caucasians and Transcaucasians who came to Persia during the time of the Persian revolution were revolutionaries and that all these revolutionaries were, if not members, at least supporters of the Social-Democratic (i.e. Communist) Party. Recent Soviet writers tend to give a much more sharply defined and crystallized interpretation of the Mujāhid and Fidā'ī movements than is usually accepted. The Mujāhids, indeed, are not generally regarded as an organized political party at all. On this point Malik al-Shu'arā Bahār in his book *Tārīkh-i mukhtaṣar-i aḥzāb-i siyāsī* (Brief history of political parties), Tehran, 1945, says: 'In 1908 there were two political parties in Persia, one revolutionary and one moderate. In the same year, after the opening of the second *Majlis*, these two parties were given official status with the names *Dimūkrāt-i 'āmmiyūn* and *Ijtimā'iyūn-i i'tidāliyūn* and were presented to the *Majlis*' (p. 8). Bahār adds later (p. 12) that 'the Democratic Party was on good terms with the British, and British officials in the provinces were well-disposed towards it. The Moderate Party had good relations with the Russians.' He does not mention the Mujāhids as a party. Ivanov,[5] however, treats the Mujāhids as an established party and even gives in full their programme as decided on at the Mujāhid conference of September 1907. Ivanov and other modern Soviet writers mention the two parties described by Bahār but ascribe less importance to them. Thus Ivanov in a recent article[6] says: 'There were two basic factions in the second *Majlis*: the "moderates" . . . and the "democrats". . . . In the field of foreign policy the "moderates" turned to Britain and Tsarist Russia while the "democrats" . . . tried by relying on imperialist Germany and the USA to limit the position of the above-mentioned powers

[3] Pavlovich and Iranskiy, *Persiya v bor'be za Nezavisimost'*, p. 40.

[4] I. M. Reysner, 'The Russian revolution of 1905–7 and the Awakening of Asia', in *Sovetskoye Vostokovedeniye*, No. 2 of 1955.

[5] Ivanov, op. cit., p. 210.

[6] M. S. Ivanov, 'An episode in the history of the expansion of American imperialism in Persia (The mission of Morgan Shuster in 1911)', in *Sovetskoye Vostokovedeniye*, No. 2 of 1955.

and in particular of Tsarist Russia.' This differs radically from Bahār's description of party affiliations.

Both Ivanov and Reysner base their information about the Mujāhids and Transcaucasian revolutionaries on an article entitled 'The rôle of the Bolsheviks of Transcaucasia in the Persian revolution of 1905–11' by Ye. Bor-Ramenskiy which appeared in *Istorik-Marksist*, No. 11 of 1940. The basic meaning of the word *Mujāhid* has perhaps been overlooked by Soviet writers.[7]

On the presence of Transcaucasians in the Persian revolution and especially in the siege of Tabrīz confirmation is to be found in several non-Soviet sources. Kasravī Tabrīzī, for instance, in his *Tārīkh-i hijdah sālu Āzarbāyjān* (Eighteen years of Āzarbāyjānī history), Tehran, 1938, vol. iii (p. 67) says:

> What was most painful of all for the people of Tabrīz was the condition of the Caucasian Mujāhids and of the Georgian and Armenian Fidā'īs. These gallant men had come most energetically to the aid of Tabrīz and numbers of them had lost their lives for Persian freedom. Those who remained alive went into hiding at this time (i.e. at the time of the arrival of Russian troops in 1909) because the Russians considered them as their subjects and treated them worse than anyone else. Any they found they hanged out of hand. The fact is that from the day the Russians arrived in Tabrīz they (the Caucasians) dispersed and hid themselves where they could. The Tabrīzīs took this very hardly.

The Transcaucasian Russian subjects who infiltrated illegally into Persia were also the subject of reports from the Russian ambassador in Tehran, Hartwig, to St. Petersburg.

The general impression to be gathered from recent Soviet writings on the Persian revolution is that the influence of Russian revolutionaries and in particular of the Social-Democrat Party in Persia has been somewhat overstated. On the other hand, it should be remembered that Soviet historians alone have access to many Tsarist sources, for instance the Georgian State Archives used by Bor-Ramenskiy.

A good example of the change in Soviet historiography in the last fifteen years can be seen by comparing the versions in the old and new editions of the *Soviet encyclopaedia* of events in Persia in the period 1910–12. 'In 1910–11,' says the old edition of the *Soviet encyclopaedia*,[8]

> Russia tried several times by provoking the actions of various counter-revolutionary groups to return Muḥammad 'Alī (i.e. the deposed Shah of Persia) to power, and in 1911 even organized his landing on the shore

[7] Originally meaning a participant in a *jihād* or holy war, *mujāhid* is used in this sense and also as a champion of liberty all over the Muslim world.

[8] 'Persiya', in *Great Soviet encyclopaedia*, first edition, vol. 45 (1940).

of the Caspian Sea. After the failure of these provocations, the Tsarist government in December 1911, using as an excuse the activity of the American financial expert, Shuster, who had been invited by the *Majlis*, presented Persia with a series of ultimatums and by armed force put down the remaining strongholds of the revolutionary movement in Tabrīz, Rasht, and Anzalī, and in 1912, in Mashhad.

In the new edition of the *Soviet encyclopaedia* the comparable article[9] in dealing with the 1910–12 period does not mention either Muḥammad 'Alī's landing, or the Russian ultimatum, and counterbalances armed action by the Tsarist government with similar action by the British—a charge of which no evidence is given. Morgan Shuster's mission and the subsequent events are thus described:

> With the aim of exploiting in their own interests the contradictions between the imperialist powers, but in fact meeting the ambitions of the imperialists of the USA to gain control of Persia, the *Majlis* gave wide powers and the right of control over revenue and expenditure to the American financier M. Shuster and his assistants, who had been sent to Persia in 1911 by the State Department of the USA.

This latter version is typical of recent Soviet writing. Ivanov in a recent article[10] repeats the charge that Shuster was sent rather than invited to Persia with the following explanation:

> On 25th December 1910 the Persian Minister of Foreign Affairs . . . suggested to the Persian mission in Washington that they should turn to the State Department of the USA about the question of inviting to Persia financial advisers. . . . In January 1911 the State Department of the USA recommended to Persia five financiers led by Morgan Shuster. Formally, the American government took no part in the later discussions about the conditions upon which the financial advisers would be invited to Persia, but in fact Shuster and his assistants were sent to Persia by capitalist companies and by the State Department of the USA on whose instructions Shuster in future acted.

A remarkable feature of Sulṭānzāda and Gurko-Kryazhin's books is that they both speak approvingly of Morgan Shuster's mission to Persia in 1911 and thus condemn the Russian ultimatum to Persia at the end of 1911. 'The Russian Government,' writes Sulṭānzāda, 'with the agreement of London presented an ultimatum and forced Persia to dismiss the American instructors who had been invited by her to direct her finances and who had carried out their duties very conscientiously.'[11] Gurko-Kryazhin is still more emphatically in favour of Shuster:

[9] 'Iran', ibid., second edition, vol. 18 (1953).

[10] Op. cit., in note 6 above.

[11] *Sovremennaya Persiya*, p. 7.

In these difficult times . . . a literal saviour appeared in the person of an American financial adviser, Morgan Shuster (May 1911). Unlike all the foreigners who before and after this were in Persian service, he alone actually thought of the needs of the country and not of the interests of the power that had sent him, or of any financial or industrial group.[12]

In describing the ultimatum, Gurko-Kryazhin is equally critical of the Tsarist and British Governments:

The activity of Shuster, which liquidated the counter-revolution and promised the real survival of Persia, naturally aroused the fury of Britain and especially of Russia.

The Soviet Republic of Gīlān, 1920–1921

There are few incidents of modern Persian history about which Soviet writers are more at variance than that of the establishment of the republic of Gīlān, which arose out of the so-called Jangalī rebellion started by Kūchik Khān in 1918. The most recent and by far the most detailed account of this incident is that by M. N. Ivanova which appeared in *Sovetskoye Vostokovedeniye*, No. 3 of 1955. Earlier accounts are those of Iḥsān Allāh, published in *Novyy Vostok*, No. 29 of 1930,[13] Īrāndūst in *Istorik-Marksist*, No. 5 of 1927, and *Sovremennaya Persiya* by A. Sulṭānzāda, Moscow, 1922. All these accounts differ in their assessments of the objects and aims of Kūchik Khān's rebellion, in their estimate of the results of the movement and perhaps most of all in respect of the part played by Soviet military forces. Disentanglement of the conflicting Soviet accounts is rendered particularly difficult by the absence of any detailed collateral source material. The incident is dealt with only briefly by George Lenczowski in his *Russia and the West in Iran*, New York, 1949: but somewhat more fully from the Persian point of view in Manshūr Gurgānī's *Siyāsat-i dawlat-i shawravīhā dar Irān* (Soviet policy in Persia), Tehran, 1326 (Persian solar year). Ivanov deals with the matter at some length in *Ocherk istorii Irana*. By using all these sources it is possible to arrive at a fairly objective account, but here it will only be possible to notice some of the differences in the Soviet accounts.

The outstanding feature of Mme Ivanova's account, which being the most recent must be regarded as the most authoritative from the Soviet point of view, is the complete omission of any mention of the landing of Soviet armed forces under Raskol'nikov at Anzali on 18 May 1920, or indeed of any contact between Kūchik Khān's forces and the Bolsheviks. Iḥsān Allāh, on the other hand, describes how he and Kūchik Khān came to the conclusion that the revival and further success of the Gīlān

[12] *Kratkaya istoriya Persii*, pp. 60–1.
[13] As quoted by Lenczowski in *Russia and the West in Iran*, p. 56.

Revolution would depend on Soviet Russia. Following this line Kūchik went to Lenkorān, a province of Russian Āzarbāyjān.

> There he learnt that Kolomiytsev, the unofficial Soviet representative in Tehran who had been obliged to flee from Iran, was trying on his own initiative to get in touch with the Jangalīs. . . . In the early spring of 1920 the Jangalīs received a letter from a Bolshevik commander in the Caucasus informing them that the Bolsheviks would soon capture Baku. Evidently the Soviet forces were seeking closer liaison with the Iranian rebels in anticipation of their invasion of Iran. . . .[14]

Such recent Soviet authorities as Ivanov[15] and the *Noveyshaya istoriya stran zarubezhnogo Vostoka*[16] describe the landing of Soviet troops in Anzalī (although without mentioning Raskol'nikov by name), and the effect of this landing on the Gīlān revolution. Thus the *Noveyshaya istoriya* says:[17]

> In order to return the ships that had been taken away by the interventionists and to liquidate the threat from the British and White Guard forces stationed in Anzalī and Rasht, on 18th May 1920 a Soviet military and naval fleet arrived at Anzalī and landed a force which took the port and the town. The British occupying forces and the remnants of the White Guards . . . fled from Anzalī and Rasht in panic. . . . The Sepoy detachments of the British Indian Army which were stationed in northern Persia refused to fight against the Red Army. As a result of this successful operation the Soviet sailors with one blow liberated the ships of the Caspian fleet and liquidated the base from which the British imperialists and the White Guard bands were preparing to invade the Soviet republic. . . . The brilliant success of the Soviet fleet and landing party at Anzalī and the panic-stricken flight of the British occupying forces gave a powerful new impetus to the mass struggle of the peoples of Persia against the British imperialists. The national liberation movement developed with new strength in Gīlān.

The same line, although in somewhat milder terms, is taken by Īrāndūst. No Soviet writer mentions the date when Soviet forces were withdrawn, but Iranskiy says that the withdrawal of 'Soviet Āzarbāyjān troops' from Gīlān began on 26 May 1921.[18] The actual date is given by Lenczowski as 21 September 1921.

Mme Ivanova sums up her article as follows:

> In drawing up the balance sheet of the national liberation movement in Gīlān in 1920–21, it can be stated that this movement was directed against British imperialism and the feudal clique. At the same time it

[14] Ibid.

[15] Ivanov, op. cit., p. 279.

[16] Op. cit, i, 251.

[17] Ibid.

[18] Iranskiy, 'Five years of Russo-Persian relations', in *Novyy Vostok* (1923), Nos. 3–4.

made possible the liquidation of the Anglo-Persian Treaty of 1919 and eventually the overthrow of the Qājār monarchy. The national liberation movement in Gīlān showed that unlike the counter-revolutionary class of powerful feudalists and entrepreneurs who were supported by foreign imperialists, the broad masses of the people demanded an alliance with Soviet Russia since they saw in such an alliance a guarantee for their freedom and independence.[19]

Īrāndūst's 'balance sheet' is somewhat different.[20] First, he gives the Gīlān revolution a wider significance than does Madame Ivanova: while she sees the movement solely as 'directed against British imperialism and the feudal clique' Īrandūst distinguishes three strands in it: one, a national liberation movement directed against imperialism; two, a bourgeois-democratic movement directed against feudalism; and three, a proletarian-communist movement directed against the bourgeoisie. It is significant moreover that Īrāndūst throughout writes of the 'Gīlān revolution' whereas Madam Ivanova calls it 'the national-liberation movement in Gīlān'.

Sulṭānzāda's account of the end of the Gīlān republic differs from that in any of the other Soviet sources seen. After describing the 'serious conflicts' between Kūchik, the Central Committee of the Communist Party, and some of the Jangalīs he writes:[21]

These internal disturbances, skilfully inflamed by the Shah's agents, had a fateful influence on future events. When Kūchik returned to power for the second time (i.e. in May 1921) it was already too late. The intrigue of the Shah's agents and of the local landowners created an atmosphere of continuous treachery . . . which resulted in Hālī Qurbān, one of Kūchik's closest companions in arms, going over . . . to the side of the Shah's army. This unheard-of treachery sealed the fate of the Gīlān revolution: Hālī Qurbān, a Jangalī, knew perfectly all the ins and outs of the virgin forests, and soon after this Kūchik's forces were defeated and the whole of Gīlān was once more captured by the Shah's armies.

Hālī Qurbān is not mentioned at all by Mme Ivanova, who indeed lays all the blame for the final defeat on Kūchik himself. It is interesting that Sulṭānzāda does not mention Ḥaydar Khān, the Communist leader who is the hero of Mme Ivanova's account.

Sulṭānzada's contribution is of particular interest since he is violently attacked by Mme Ivanova as 'a traitor' and as the organizer of 'a counter-

[19] M. N. Ivanova, 'The National-Liberation movement in the Gilān province of Persia in 1920–21', in *Sovetskoye Vostokovedeniye,* No. 3 of 1955.

[20] Īrāndūst, 'Aspects of the Gilān revolution', in *Istorik-Marksist,* No. 5 of 1927, p. 135.

[21] Sulṭānzāda, op. cit., p. 50.

revolutionary group into which entered agents of the British and the Shah'. According to Lenczowski,[22] Sulṭānzāda, who was Minister of the Interior in the Gīlān Republic, was one and the same person as Ja'far Pīshavarī, who later led the separatist movement in Āẕarbāyjān in 1945–46, but Persian sources deny the truth of this.

Persia, 1921–1941

Soviet historians pay comparatively little attention to Soviet-Persian affairs in this period. Ivanov devotes two brief chapters to them, one called 'The overthrow of the Qājār dynasty' and the other, 'Persia under Riżā Shāh'.[23] The *Noveyshaya istoriya* devotes twenty-seven pages to the period 1918–21[24] but only eleven pages to the period 1922–28[25] and twenty-five to the period 1929–30.[26]

Only brief references are made in Soviet publications to the *coup d'état* of 1921, which is broadly attributed to British machinations. This charge is found not only in recent works but also in such contemporary studies as Iranskiy's article which appeared in 1923.[27] Sayyid Żiyā' al-Dīn, the principal figure of the *coup d'état*, is consistently described by Ivanov as a British agent. Both he and his lifelong political opponent Qavām became the special objects of Soviet historiographical criticism and obloquy.

There are accounts of the mutinies in Āẕarbāyjān and Khurāsān during 1926 which do not at all accord with Persian and Western versions. The account of Sālār-i Jang's mutiny in Bujnurd in particular seems to be based on the first exaggerated rumours which reached Mashhad in June 1926. Later it transpired that only one officer and forty men had actually mutinied and crossed the Soviet frontier. In describing the strike at the Anglo-Iranian Oil Company's installations in 1929, Ivanov[28] speaks of British troops being used against the strikers. There were in fact no British troops in Persia between 1921 and 1941.

Soviet writers are unable to see any redeeming feature in Riżā Shāh's reign. His sumptuary reforms are all represented as having some ulterior motive other than enlightenment and progress. Both Ivanov and the *Noveyshaya istoriya* attribute the compulsory emancipation of women to a plan to obtain cheap female labour for the factories. Even Riżā Shāh's curtailing of the authority of the clerical element is spoken of disapprovingly.[29] The construction of roads and the reorganization and regular payment of the army are seen merely as steps taken by the Shah to concentrate power in his own hands.

[22] Lenczowski, op. cit., p. 224.
[23] Ivanov, op. cit., pp. 301–11, 312–35.
[24] *Noveyshaya istoriya*, vol. i (see Note 15 above), pp. 235–62.
[25] Ibid., pp. 262–73.
[26] Ibid., ii, 190–215.
[27] Īrāndūst, op. cit., in note 19.
[28] Ivanov, op. cit., p. 327.
[29] Ibid., pp. 322–3.

The *Noveyshaya istoriya*[30] writes disparagingly of Riżā S͟hāh's linguistic reforms, and particularly of the attempt to remove non-Persian words from the vocabulary. Ivanov[31] complains that many of the 'Arabic, Turkish, and European words (thus replaced) had long been sanctioned by usage and formed part of the structure of the language'. The *Noveyshaya istoriya*[32] records that in 1935 'the new, officially accepted name "Iran" was introduced in place of the old word "Persia" '. It omits, however, to point out that this only referred to foreign languages; in Persian the name Iran had been used from time immemorial.

Ivanov only makes the barest mention of the Persian Communist Party's existence during Riżā S͟hāh's reign. The *Noveyshaya istoriya*, on the other hand, describes Persian Communist underground activities in some detail.[33]

The Separatist Movement in Āẕarbāyjān, 1945–1946

Persian and Western historians regard the movement which resulted in the Persian province of Āẕarbāyjān being removed from the jurisdiction of the Tehran Government from December 1945 to December 1946 as having been instigated by the Soviet Government and actively supported by the Soviet Army. Soviet writers on the other hand treat it as a spontaneous movement on the part of the people in which the Soviet Government played no part whatever. In no Soviet publication can any mention be found of the active rôle of the Soviet forces in support of the movement, of their failure to withdraw these forces by 2 March 1946 as stipulated in the Tripartite Agreement of 1942, or of their heavy reinforcement after that date. Not even the presence of Soviet troops in Āẕarbāyjān during the movement is ever referred to.

Apart from Ivanov's *Ocherk istorii Irana* the principal Soviet accounts of the movement are to be found in an article by Sergeyev entitled 'The struggle of democracy against reaction in Persia' which appeared in *Bolshevik*, Nos. 11–12 of 1946; Shteynberg's *Sovetsko-Iranskiye otnosheniya i proiski Anglo-Amerikanskogo imperializma v Irane* (Soviet-Persian relations and the intrigues of Anglo-American imperialism in Persia), a pamphlet published in 1947; Bashkirov's *Rabocheye i profsoyuznoye dvizheniye v Irane* (Workers' and trade-union movement in Persia), published in 1948; and Milov's *Iran vo vremya i posle vtoroy mirovoy voyny* (Iran during and after the Second World War), Moscow, 1949. The best Persian account of the events is to be found in *Marg būd bar gas͟ht ham būd* by Najaf Qulī Pasyān, Tehran, 1948. The fullest descriptions from the Western point of view are those given by Lenczowski in his *Russia and the West in Iran*, and in an

[30] *Noveyshaya istoriya*, ii, 202.
[31] Ivanov, op. cit., p. 324.
[32] *Noveyshaya istoriya*, ii, 202.
[33] Ibid., pp. 204 ff.

article entitled 'The battle of Azerbaijan, 1946' in *The Middle East Journal* (Winter, 1956) by Robert Rossow, who was an eyewitness of the affair.

Soviet accounts of the causes which led up to the establishment of the so-called National Government of Persian Āẕarbāyjān and of the measures, many of them progressive, adopted by that Government deserve careful attention, as the treatment of these aspects of the movement by Persian and American writers is sketchy and to some extent one-sided. Some of the incidents recounted by Bashkirov and Sergeyev may well be true. On the other hand, Bashkirov maintains that the Persian garrisons were surrounded by the Fidā'īs and compelled to lay down their arms; but Ivanov[34] states that all Persian troops except for the Rezāyeh brigade surrendered willingly and placed themselves at the disposal of the Āẕarbāyjān government. Neither makes any reference to the incident described by Pasyān when a Persian column proceeding to reinforce the Āẕarbāyjān garrison was halted at Sharīfābād by Soviet troops, whose commander threatened to open fire if the Persian force advanced.

The main difference between the Western and Soviet versions is that whereas the former, while accusing the Soviet government of starting the movement, admits the moral support given by the Western Powers to the Persian Government, the latter makes no mention of any direct Soviet interest in the matter at all. On the other hand, the intervention of 'British and American imperialists' on the side of the reactionaries is given great prominence. The dispatch of an Indian brigade to Baṣra and of two sloops to the Shaṭṭ al-'Arab at the time of the Anglo-Iranian strike is magnified into the dispatch of 'several divisions' to the Persian frontier and of naval forces to Ābādān 'in order to frighten democratic elements and encourage Persian reaction in Khūzistān'.[35]

Soviet writers tend to treat the Āẕarbāyjān independence movement as part of a general 'democratic' movement which developed in Persia after the end of the last war. Thus Ivanov deals with Āẕarbāyjān in his chapter called 'Persia after the Second World War' and interconnects it with the tribal revolt in Fārs and the strike in the Anglo-Iranian Oil Company's installations in Khūzistān. All three incidents he sees as part of the intensification of 'the struggle between democratic and reactionary forces' caused by the defeat of the Fascist army of Germany by the Soviet Union'.[36]

It may be seen from the foregoing how fundamental is the difference between the Soviet and Western treatments of historical events in Persia during the period under review, and particularly in respect of the part played in them by Russia and by the Western powers.

[34] Ivanov, op. cit., p. 370.
[35] Ibid., pp. 383–4. See also p. 387.
[36] Ibid., p. 365.

Among Western writers, many of whom were eyewitnesses of the events they describe, there is broad agreement about what actually happened; but there is a considerable difference of opinion, even among individuals writing at approximately the same time, about the causes leading up to events and about the policies of the various powers involved. In Soviet writing, on the other hand, differences in the treatment of events and in the diagnosis of their causes result not from differences in individual opinion but from changes in historiographical policy; for it should always be remembered that no literature can be published in the Soviet Union without the official imprimatur.

It is because rather than in spite of these considerations that Soviet writing on Persian history deserves from Western students of Persian affairs in general far more attention than it has received so far.

PART III

MODERN MIDDLE EASTERN HISTORICAL WRITING

33. THE HISTORIAN AL-JABARTĪ[1]

DAVID AYALON

Professor of the History of the Muslim Peoples in the Hebrew University of Jerusalem

The Enigma of al-Jabartī

In glaring contrast to the period of the Mamluk sultanate (1250–1517), which abounds in rich, most detailed and accurate source material, hardly surpassed either in quality or quantity by the source material pertaining to any other region of Islam, the period of Ottoman rule in Egypt (1517–1811, approximately) is conspicuous for the dearth of its historical sources written by contemporary inhabitants of the country.[2] This state of affairs, gloomy enough in itself, becomes even more gloomy in the light of the fact that the first seventy years or so of Ottoman rule are almost totally obscure. The very concise chronicles of Ibn Abi'l-Surūr al-Bakrī and al-Isḥāqī, which contain no more than the barest outline of the events, give only a faint glimpse of what happened in Egypt in the above-mentioned period. Thus the process of Egypt's transition from its Mamluk into its Ottoman shape is practically unknown except for the first few years (922/8/1517–22) of Ottoman rule described by Ibn Iyās. It is only after that transition had reached a very advanced stage that a somewhat clear picture of Egyptian history and society can be drawn from historical works compiled by contemporary Egyptian authors;[3] and it should be stressed in this connection that however important other kinds of sources may be—such as the Ottoman archives, and to a much lesser extent, the itineraries of European travellers—they are certainly no substitute for the works of the local historians.

Of the local historians of Ottoman Egypt, 'Abd al-Raḥmān al-Jabartī stands out as a giant among dwarfs. Moreover, but for his chronicle, the chronicles of the other historians of that period would have been of very limited value, because it is mainly as supplementary sources to his chronicle

[1] This article is an abridgement of a considerably revised version of the paper on al-Jabartī which was originally submitted to the Conference on the Historical Writing of the Near and Middle East. The full revised version was published in *BSOAS*, xxiii/2, 217–49.

[2] Such an abrupt decline and such an appalling contrast in the state of the historiography of two consecutive periods is, in my opinion, a unique phenomenon in Muslim history. I cannot find a full explanation for this phenomenon. For a partial explanation see p. 392, n. 4.

[3] This is due to a certain revival of Egyptian historiography at the end of the sixteenth and the beginning of the seventeenth centuries, the extent of which was, in my opinion, extremely limited. The local chronicles of Ottoman Egypt are, on the whole, quite reliable as sources of information, and some of them are quite detailed. The standard of almost all of them is, however, low. From what is said in this article it should by no means be concluded that the history of Ottoman Egypt cannot be reconstructed, if all kinds of source material pertaining to it are exploited.

that they acquire considerably added importance.[4] But to compare al-Jabartī only with the historians of Egypt under the Ottomans is to do him a great injustice, for he has an importance far transcending the period and the country with which his chronicle deals. In my opinion, al-Jabartī should be considered one of the greatest historians of the Muslim world of all times, and by far the greatest historian of the Arab world in modern times.

In his attempt to explain the appearance of a historian of al-Jabartī's calibre under such inauspicious conditions as those prevailing in Egypt under the Ottomans, the student of history is confronted with an enigma which does not really admit of a solution. It would have been far easier to show that a work like that of our historian could not have been written at all under those conditions. In studying the historiography of Ottoman Egypt, one cannot help feeling that al-Jabartī seems to come from nowhere and to go back to nowhere, as far as the study of history is concerned. He did not spring from any school of historians, nor did he create a school of his own. His monumental work is a purely isolated phenomenon. To this day nobody inside or outside Egypt has cared to continue it or tried to follow in al-Jabartī's footsteps.[5] Such a phenomenon of a solitary historian

[4] One of the main reasons for the decline of historiography in Egypt under the Ottomans lay in the fact that Egypt, which had been up to the time of the Ottoman conquest the centre of a big and powerful empire, became after that conquest only a province in an even bigger empire. Another important reason must have been the mass transfer of historical works from Cairo to Constantinople, a considerable number of which are still extant there. In view of the fact that such works are usually available only in very few copies, the devastating effects of their mass transfer are obvious. I have no information regarding any transfer of historians from Egypt to the Ottoman capital. Ottoman historiography from the sixteenth to the early nineteenth centuries had been far richer and on a far higher level than Egyptian historiography in the corresponding period (see B. Lewis, 'Some reflections on the decline of the Ottoman Empire', *Studia Islamica* (1958), ix, 126–7, and the same author's paper above, entitled: 'The use by Muslim historians of non-Muslim sources', pp. 184 ff., and F. Babinger, *Die Geschichtsschreiber der Osmanen*). Yet it did not seem to have affected or stimulated the latter to any appreciable extent. The works of Ottoman historians and travellers should also be considered as sources of no mean importance for the history of Egypt in the above-mentioned centuries. See also H. Jansky, 'Beiträge zur osmanischen Geschichtsschreibung über Ägypten', *Der Islam* (1933), xxi, 269–78.

[5] The great process of westernization which commenced in Egypt in the early nineteenth century, and the beginnings of which our author still witnessed, made it all the more difficult for the new generation of Egyptian historians to become the continuators of al-Jabartī, who wrote in the Muslim traditional historical style. In its attempt to write history, this new generation suffered from the weakening of its ties with the old Muslim civilization on the one hand, and from the difficulty in adopting the new European civilization on the other. Apart from al-Jabartī, 'Alī Mubārak was the only person in nineteenth-century Egypt who wrote a monumental historical (or, to be more exact, biographical-topographical) work (*al-Khiṭaṭ al-tawfīqiyya*). Though he cites al-Jabartī frequently, he cannot be considered his follower. *'Ajā'ib al-āthār* and *al-Khiṭaṭ al-tawfīqiyya* are very different in structure, contents, and aims. Besides, al-Jabartī's creative power was far superior to that of Mubārak, who was mainly a compiler. On 'Alī Mubārak see J. Heyworth-Dunne, *An introduction to the history of education in modern Egypt* (London, 1938), pp. 253–4, and Index; see also Gamal el-Din el-Shayyal's paper below, pp. 403 ff., 'A comparative study of Eygptian historiography in the nineteenth century.'

of genius rising to such heights out of his desolate surroundings,[6] is perhaps unique in the annals of Islam, and very rare in the annals of mankind.

The Decline of Historical Writing in al-Jabartī's Time

No one has given a better description of the decline of historiography in his time and of his contemporaries' aversion to it than al-Jabartī himself. After mentioning al-Sh̲āf'ī's saying that whoever knows history becomes wiser (*man 'alima al-ta'rīk̲h̲ zāda 'aqluhu*),[7] he says: 'The people of the past, since God had created mankind, took care to write history age after age and generation after generation, until the people of our time have left history and neglected it and discarded it and cast it off and considered it the business of persons without employment, saying: "History is nothing but legends of the ancients (*wa-'addūhu min s̲h̲ug̲h̲l al-baṭṭālīn wa-qālū asāṭīr al-awwalīn*)." By my life! The people of our time are excused (in their attitude towards history). They are preoccupied with more important things and, therefore, they do not want to tire their pens with such a kind of scrutiny. Time's conditions have been turned upside down. Its shades have shrunk. Its foundations have been shattered. Its events are, therefore, not recorded in a register or a book. Occupying one's time without benefit is sheer loss. Whatever happened and passed will never come back. It is only a person like myself—secluded as I am in the corner of obscurity and neglect and retired from employment unlike other people—who would keep himself busy in his solitude and would alleviate his loneliness by enumerating the Good and Evil of Time.'[8]

The depths to which historical learning had sunk in Egypt under the Ottomans may also be measured by the fact that in the very numerous biographies of learned men which al-Jabartī's chronicle contains, hardly any interest in history or in historical works is discernible. To my knowledge, only very few persons are referred to in his whole book as displaying an interest in history. There may be other references that have escaped me; but if so, this would not modify the general picture. Of all the above-mentioned biographies, none is dedicated to a historian. It is very doubtful whether al-Jabartī even knew about al-Dimurdās̲h̲ī and Muṣṭafā b. Ibrāhīm, the historians who died in the period covered by his chronicle.

From the passage quoted above, it is clear that had al-Jabartī not been debarred from an active life, the chances of his compiling this chronicle would have been greatly diminished. It was another fortunate accident for Muslim historiography that he happened to be the only survivor of all his father's children, whose number exceeded forty, and all of whom died

---

[6] The phrase 'desolate surroundings' refers only to the degree of interest in history manifested in Egypt under the Ottomans. In other Islamic cultural fields there was much ferment and lively activity. Without that rich cultural background in which al-Jabartī grew up, even a historical work far inferior to his chronicle could not have been written.

[7] i, 5, ll. 1–2.   [8] i, 5, ll. 6–13.

before reaching puberty (*wa-māta lahu min al-awlād nayyif wa-arbaʿīna waladan dhukūran wa-ināthan kulluhum dūna al-bulūgh wa-lam yaʿish lahu min al-awlād siwā al-ḥaqīr*).[9] Thus, al-Jabartī's opus has come down to posterity almost by a miracle. Had he not written his work, there is little likelihood that anybody else would have written anything similar.

Al-Jabartī's great historical achievement becomes all the more puzzling when one takes into account that his knowledge of either Muslim or Egyptian history in the Middle Ages seems to have been quite limited. In the opening of his book he enumerates in a rather disorderly fashion the works of Muslim and Egyptian (mainly Mamluk) historians,[10] and adds forthwith: 'I said: All these have become names without objects (*asmā' min ghayr musammayāt*), for we have seen from all this nothing but a few scattered and disorderly parts (*ajzā' mudashshata*) in some of the *waqf* bookshelves of the *madrasas*. Booksellers tampered with them. Inspectors and supervisors sold them, and they were transferred to the Maghrib and the Sudan. The very little that remained had gone (*dhahabat baqāyā al-baqāyā*) during the period of disorders and war. Then came the French and took whatever they found to their country. When I decided to compile (in its final form) what I had already drafted, I wanted to connect it with something which had happened before, but I did not find, after inquiry and search, anything except a few pamphlets, etc.'[11]

This unequivocal statement of our historian is of great weight. It is borne out in several ways. Al-Jabartī's historical introduction[12] is sketchy and disproportionate. The title of the famous chronicle of Ibn Iyās is cited wrongly (*marj al-zuhūr* instead of *badā'iʿ al-zuhūr*).[13] Throughout the book there are very few allusions—and these of an entirely casual character—to Mamluk history or historians. The only works which he can definitely be proved to have looked into—and even in these we do not know with what degree of thoroughness—are those of al-Maqrīzī. When he says about al-ʿAynī's chronicle of forty volumes, 'I have seen some volumes of it and they are very large, of the same format as (Ibn al-Athīr's) *al-Kāmil*' (*ra'aytu minhu baʿḍ mujalladāt wa-hiya ḍakhma fī qālab al-Kāmil*),[14] his wording seems to imply that he did not read them. Other Mamluk historians are indeed mentioned quite frequently in al-Jabartī's book, but almost exclusively in connection with their religious and theological treatises, and not with their historical ones. Neither was al-Jabartī well acquainted with the history of Ottoman Egypt before A.H. 1100, the year with which he opens his chronicle. His few allusions to events preceding that year are very deficient.

[9] i, 396, ll. 6–7.

[10] i, 5, ll. 25–6, l. 15.

[11] i, 6, ll. 16–20. The number of extant historical works in Egypt in al-Jabartī's time had, undoubtedly, been bigger than his estimate. But as many as these works had not been available either to him or to others, their existence did not change the situation.

[12] i, 13, ll. 17–21, l. 26.

[13] i, 20, l. 27.

[14] i, 6, ll. 10–11.

Al-Jabartī's Greatness

What makes al-Jabartī an historian of the first rank, in spite of the fact that his knowledge of both Islamic and Egyptian history was very limited, and that he wrote only a local history, is not only his outstanding natural gift, but also his profound emotional involvement in his subject. He is a great lover of his country, who shares its joys and sorrows to the full. It is as if he writes about his own flesh and blood. This is the spirit with which the book is imbued from beginning to end. The chronicle is a splendid combination of passionate warmth and scholarly detachment, which is only rarely overcome by any personal or other kind of bias.[15] The reader never loses the feeling of having his finger on the pulse of life and of sharing in the true atmosphere of the country and of the period. To this should be added our historian's concise, concentrated, and factual way of writing, together with his insight and his ability to go straight to the heart of things and draw a complete picture with a few broad strokes of his brush.[16]

How he Selected his Data

Al-Jabartī affords us a glimpse of the methods he employed in collecting and sifting his data. At the end of his narrative of the year 1225/1810–11, our author says: 'This year ended together with its events only part of which were included in our narrative. We could not include all of these events because of our being remote from the direction of affairs and because of our being unable to determine their genuineness and because of

[15] The objectivity with which he narrates the history of the French occupation can serve as a model to any modern European historian. On the other hand, it should not be forgotten that he was a product of his time and environment. Therefore, there is little point in criticizing, for example, his unsympathetic stand towards the non-Muslim minorities, or his favourable view of the English invasion of Egypt in 1807, or his failure to see anything positive in Muḥammad 'Alī's reforms. As for his collaboration with the French, it is hard to establish its scope. Besides, the fact of collaboration with the French was something he had in common with a very large section of the Egyptian *'ulamā'*. On his attempt, immediately after the French evacuation, to curry favour with the Ottomans by presenting them with a revised history of the French period of occupation (*Muẓhir al-taqdīs*), see *BSOAS*, xxiii, 1960, pp. 244–6. Still, his claim that in the compilation of his chronicle he did not intend to serve any powerful person or flatter any government (i, 6, ll. 31–3) is, on the whole, right. His uncompromising denunciation of such a strong man as Muḥammad 'Alī, who crushed his opponents without mercy, serves as a striking proof of his personal courage.

[16] As for al-Jabartī's language, there is no doubt that in numerous cases he ignores the grammatical rules of Arabic and uses not only colloquial, but also slang words (see his own apology in i, 7, ll. 4–7, and the remarks of Shaybūb, p. 101, and Maḥmūd al-Sharqāwī, i, 27–8, 83–4). But it should be noted that in this respect al-Jabartī followed numerous earlier Egyptian historians, who, mainly from the Mamluk period onwards, showed a growing inclination to use a living literary language which was more tolerant of colloquialisms in grammar and vocabulary than the literary Arabic of other branches of learning. Our author's language has still to be compared with that of the other chroniclers of Ottoman Egypt. For lexicographers, al-Jabartī's chronicle is a mine of information. It is to be regretted that, with the exception of G. Wiet's glossary to Nicolas Turc, pp. 289–314, there has been no serious attempt to collect and study al-Jabartī's vocabulary since the beginnings made by A. von Kremer in his *Beiträge zur arabischen Lexikographie* (Wien, 1883–4).

the distortions of the narrators, who add to their story or omit from it. I do not record any event before ascertaining its truth by means of independent and consecutive sources and by means of that event becoming widely known (*bil-tawātur wa'l-ishtihār*). Most of the happenings which I write down are of a general character (*al-umūr al-kullīya*) and, therefore, cannot be greatly distorted. Many a time I delayed registering an event until its genuineness had been established. Meanwhile, however, something new might have happened, which could have made me forget what preceded. I therefore used to record the event, the truth of which had not yet been determined, on a slip of paper (?) (*ṭayyāra*), pending its insertion, by the will of God, in its proper place during the revision (*tahdhīb*) of this writing (*hādhihi al-kitāba*).'[17] Earlier in his chronicle our author states that he included in it only such information which he could verify, that he invented nothing out of his own mind, and that God is (a) witness to the truthfulness of his words, for he can conceal nothing from His observant eye (. . . *mā waṣala 'ilmuhu ilayya wa-thabata khabaruhu ladayya . . . wa-lam akhtari' shay'an min tilqā' nafsī wa-Allāhu muṭṭali' 'alā amrī wa-ḥadsī*).[18]

The study of al-Jabartī's chronicle entirely confirms his above statements. In order to prove this, we shall choose two separate parts of the book: the one dealing with the first five decades or so of the period covered by the chronicle, and the other describing the French occupation.

The Chronicle as a Source for the Early Twelfth Hijra Century

In his reconstruction of the first half of the twelfth century A.H.—a period which he could not personally witness—he had a few second-rate sources from which to copy, including Aḥmad Chelebī b. 'Abd al-Ghanī, which he had used only partly. Now the reliability of al-Jabartī's narrative of this period can be proved in two ways. First, the same event is repeated several times in the chronicle and in the biographies, and there is usually no contradiction of note between the various versions. Second, we possess the chronicle of an eyewitness, al-Dimurdāshī, which deals with the years 1100–69/1688–1756, and which is called *Kitāb al-durra al-muṣāna fī akhbār al-Kināna*.[19] This chronicle, in spite of its poor style and bad structure, is a mine of accurate information. Al-Jabartī's narrative is entirely upheld in its essence by that of al-Dimurdāshī. The last-named only adds numerous

[17] iv, 124, ll. 20–5. On finishing his narrative of the events of A.H. 1217, our historian stresses again that he writes only about things of a general character, and explains why he does so (iii, 236, ll. 30–3). The fact that we find here and there in the book some details which may seem rather trivial to us should not serve as a proof to the contrary. Our historian's conscientiousness and accuracy are demonstrated, *inter alia*, by his reproduction of the numerous documents in his book without any editing of his own. In spite of his being shocked time and again by the horrible Arabic of many of the decrees and announcements of the French authorities of occupation, he reproduces them in his chronicle verbatim.

[18] i, 90, ll. 5–10.

[19] I used the British Museum manuscript (Or. 1073, 1074).

details and facts, some of which are extremely important, to the concise story of al-Jabartī.[20]

Al-Jabartī and the Mamluk Historians

At this juncture it is worthwhile to compare al-Jabartī with his predecessors, the historians of the Mamluk sultanate. These writers—some of whom rank with the foremost Muslim historians—also described in their chronicle the periods preceding their own. In doing so they had at their disposal the works of earlier great historians, from which they could simply copy. Yet in numerous cases they copied badly. By summarizing and paraphrasing the works of the earlier chronicles, they obliterated or dimmed—intentionally or unintentionally—many important issues. A study of the sources of the Baḥrī period, most of which are still in manuscript, clearly shows how dangerous it is to write the history of this period from the chronicles of the historians of the Circassian period.

There is another aspect in which al-Jabartī compares favourably with the Mamluk historians. It is true that few periods in Muslim history can be reconstructed as well as the Mamluk period, but this can be done because of the existence of so rich and, on the whole, excellent historical literature, which is as rich as it is varied, viz. chronicles, geographical and topographical works, encyclopaedias, biographical dictionaries, inscriptions, etc.—a formidable array, which can hardly be surpassed. Yet I do not think that any single Mamluk source is so rich, so concise, and so self-contained as al-Jabartī's chronicle in its four volumes of 1,372 pages.

The Chronicle as a Source for the French Occupation

As for the French occupation of Egypt, this short period of only three years is, in contrast with the centuries preceding it, extremely well documented. The contemporary and near-contemporary literature dealing with it is abundant, and it includes a great number of masterpieces in historiography written by European scholars, most of them French. Al-Jabartī's description of the occupation does not fall short of any of these masterpieces, and it remains one of the main and most reliable sources on this great event, both in Muslim and European history.

Those French contemporary historians who studied the French occupation and the period immediately following it placed extraordinary confidence in al-Jabartī. This confidence is reflected in the extent to which they relied on his chronicle. The famous *Histoire scientifique et militaire de l'expedition française en Égypte, d'après les mémoires, matériaux, documents inédits*, in ten volumes (Paris, 1830–4), dedicated to Louis-Philippe I, written by

[20] I have not yet compared systematically al-Jabartī's chronicle with that of Muṣṭafā b. Ibrāhīm al-Maddāḥ al-Qīnalī, also an eyewitness, who wrote the history of Egypt in the years 1100–52/1688–1739, or with that of Ibn 'Abd al-Ghanī.

top-ranking historians, some of whom were members of Bonaparte's expedition, and based on first-class documents, is undoubtedly one of the most important works on Egypt in the above-mentioned period. On p. 10 of vol. ix, the following statement occurs: 'L'historien arabe Abd-êr-Rahman, que déjà nous avons si souvent cité, trace de la position du peuple égyptien, immédiatement après le départ des Français, un tableau qui rend inutiles tous les détails que nous pourrions emprunter à d'autres sources.' Now, even a brief examination of the *Histoire scientifique* shows that its authors borrowed from al-Jabartī's manuscript much more than they had admitted by their quotations. They seem to have found very often that al-Jabartī's narrative was far superior to that of any other source at their disposal. Only a thorough comparison of the two texts will establish the full extent of their debt to our author.[21]

The Chronicle as a Source for Muḥammad 'Alī's Reign

The high standard of our author's historical writing is demonstrated not only by his narrative of the first half of the twelfth Hijra century and of the French occupation, but by practically any other part of his book as well. The last part of this book, dealing with Muḥammad 'Alī's rule and reforms, is of additional value and significance.

Few persons in the Muslim world in modern times have attracted so much attention and have been so acclaimed as Muḥammad 'Alī has been. The bulk of the vast literature written about this great man and about his period is, on the whole, very favourable to him. To a great extent this literature is biassed, consciously or unconsciously, in his favour for three main reasons. First, the ruling house of Muḥammad 'Alī made him and some of his successors the subject of systematic glorification. Second, many Europeans who visited Egypt in his time had been astounded by the process of swift changes on Western lines, which this country had been the only one in the Muslim and Eastern world to carry out with a zeal, energy, and determination hitherto unknown outside Western civilization. Third, Muḥammad 'Alī had achieved spectacular military successes. Few asked at the time whether the type and pace of the reforms, the military expansion, etc., were what Egypt really needed in the first half of the nine-

[21] For some of the passages, out of many, in which the authors of the *Histoire scientifique* do mention al-Jabartī, see iv, 90; vii, 412, 442; viii, 242–3. I am indebted to my students H. Harari, S. Magen, and D. Farhi for helping me in tracing al-Jabartī's immense influence on the *Histoire scientifique*. I am also indebted to my student, S. Moreh, for calling my attention to several passages regarding al-Jabartī's writing. The only other important Arabic source on the French occupation, written by Nicolas Turc and published by G. Wiet (*Chronique d'Égypte*, 1798–1804 (Cairo, 1950)), corroborates, on the whole, al-Jabartī's chronicle and supplements it. A systematic comparison of the two chronicles will undoubtedly shed additional light on our author's historical writing. A noteworthy step in this direction has already been made by G. Wiet in his notes to his French translation of Nicolas Turc's chronicle. Costa's unpublished history (in Arabic) of the French expedition (Wiet, op. cit., p. ix) is not known to me.

teenth century. Few witnessed the extremely cruel and barbarous methods which Muḥammad ʿAlī employed in accomplishing his grandiose plans. It may fairly be asked whether Egypt would not have been happier and more prosperous at the present time had the reforms and changes of the nineteenth century been carried out more slowly and with greater caution.

The student of history should, therefore, consider himself fortunate in having the other side of the picture, as depicted by an eyewitness like al-Jabartī, who described Muḥammad ʿAlī's rule in the blackest colours. His opinion and judgement cannot be brushed aside, for he was in a far better position than any other person writing on Muḥammad ʿAlī to compare that ruler's new order with the old order which he had destroyed and which our author had known so intimately. This is not to say that al-Jabartī's view of Muḥammad ʿAlī and of his régime should be taken at its face value. Far from it. He should definitely not be considered an entirely objective judge. His intense hatred of the new ruler prevented him from showing much understanding of his difficulties and from seeing the positive aspects of his rule and of his reforms. His ignorance of international affairs did not allow him to perceive the problems confronting Muḥammad ʿAlī in his relations with the outside world. Yet his chronicle serves as an excellent counterbalance to numerous other sources, which are extremely biassed in the opposite direction.[22]

The importance of al-Jabartī's chronicle for the study of Muḥammad ʿAlī's period is by no means limited to the fact that it gives us the other side of the picture. No less important is the extremely rich, varied, and accurate information which it contains on so many aspects of the early part of that ruler's reign. In spite of the numerous studies written on Muḥammad ʿAlī, it would be true to say that this information has not yet been exploited as fully as it deserves.

The Chronicle not a well-proportioned Work

From what we have said above it should not be concluded that al-Jabartī's chronicle, with all its great merits, can be considered a well-proportioned and harmonious work. The various subjects with which it deals receive very unequal attention and cannot, therefore, be reconstructed

[22] It should be noted in this connection that some very important European contemporaries held quite negative opinions about Muḥammad ʿAlī's reforms and rule. See, for example, Lane, *Manners and customs* (Everyman's Library), pp. 25, 113, 132–5, 228, n. 1, 562–4. Lane's view of Muḥammad ʿAlī became more favourable after the Egyptian evacuation of Syria, for Lane believed that he would then use his talents in the development of Egypt instead of wasting them on expansion. See also the opinion of Campbell, the British Consul-General in Egypt from 1833 (Sabry, *L'empire égyptien sous Mohamed-Ali* (Paris, 1930), pp. 115–16), and especially the opinion of the authors of *Histoire scientifique et militaire de l'expédition française en Égypte* in their description of Egypt's situation in 1834 (x, 477–90). A considerable number of the European consular representatives in Egypt and in Syria were also critical of Muḥammad ʿAlī's reign.

with the same degree of success. Mamluk society dominates the whole scene, and a most detailed and vivid picture of it can be drawn from our book. Mamluk leaders who became known in the West, like 'Alī Bak al-Kabīr, Muḥammad Abu'l Dhahab, Murād, Ibrāhīm, Muḥammad Bak al-Alfī, and others, rise in al-Jabartī's chronicle out of their real background and look far more human and natural than in the descriptions of European contemporaries (including Volney), to whom Mamluk internal relations and the principles of Mamlukdom were a completely or almost completely sealed book.

Very good and rich are the data furnished on the Ottoman element in Egypt and on that country's relations with the central Ottoman government. The Ottoman archives, however, may render al-Jabartī's chronicle a source of secondary importance on this particular subject, and perhaps on other important subjects as well. Extremely valuable is the information scattered all through the book on the nomads and semi-nomads, who were then very powerful and who had special connexions with the Mamluks. The biographies of the Ḥabā'iba, who headed the Niṣf Sa'd confederacy in Lower Egypt, and of Shaykh Humām, the head of the Hawwāra in Upper Egypt, are of the highest quality. The attention which al-Jabartī pays to the '*ulamā*' is as great as that which he pays to the Mamluks. As a matter of fact, the number of their biographies in his chronicle considerably exceeds that of the Mamluks. Yet the information on the '*ulamā*' is of a much more stereotyped character,[23] and therefore the picture of this class that is conveyed to us is much dimmer than that of Mamluk society.[24] The urban population (other than the ruling class and the '*ulamā*') is not well represented in the book. The information on the Christians and Jews is comparatively scarce, though by no means unimportant. The data on the economics and commerce of the country up to the rise of Muḥammad 'Alī leave too many gaps in the general picture, but even so, they can serve as a very important supplement to what we know from the *Description de l'Egypte* and from the itineraries of European travellers.[25] This statement

[23] A very considerable part of almost any biography of an '*ālim* is dedicated to the enumeration of the names of his teachers, the theological books and subjects which he studied, the treatises which he compiled, etc. Very little can be done with these stereotyped lists. This defect is not characteristic of al-Jabartī alone, but is common to numerous Muslim historians, a fact which renders the study of this most important class in Muslim society extremely difficult.

[24] Some aspects, however, of this class, such as the Azhar institution, the relations of the '*ulamā*' with the secular authorities, Sufism and the Dervish orders, are extremely well described by al-Jabartī. Heyworth-Dunne rightly says that 'The learned devoted much time and energy to the reading of Ṣūfī literature and by far the greatest proportion of the literary output was of this kind of writing and of Ṣūfī poetry' (*Introduction*, p. 10). This fact is strongly reflected in our chronicle. See also Heyworth-Dunne, *Introduction*, pp. 1–101, and Gibb and Bowen, *Islamic society and the West*, vol. i, part II, ch. VIII–XIII.

[25] Here, again, the Ottoman archives can greatly change the picture. Most of those parts of the *Description de l'Egypte* which deal with Egypt as the French army of occupation had found it, are of a very high quality. On the other hand, the sections dealing with the history of Egypt under the Ottomans are very poor.

does not include, however, the mint, the currency, and the prices, about which our author supplies unusually rich and valuable data. Of special importance is the fact that, in contrast to most Muslim historians, he repeatedly mentions the normal prices, and not only the prices in times of extreme shortage or extreme prosperity.

As for the peasants, al-Jabartī makes only casual mention of them. They remain obscure, as in most other Muslim chronicles. Some more light, however, is shed on this class in that part of the chronicle which deals with Muḥammad ʿAlī's land reforms.

Concerning the neighbouring countries, there is a wealth of information on the Ḥijāz and on its relations with Egypt. The information on the Wahhābīs, though not particularly rich, is highly important. Syria remains largely in the shade throughout the chronicle, except for its relations with Egypt and especially its invasion by ʿAlī Bak al-Kabīr and Muḥammad Abu'l-Dhahab. There is some valuable information on the Maghribīs, especially on the Maghribī pilgrimage caravan.

The Fortunate Combination

The great opus of al-Jabartī had thus been compiled by a man whose knowledge of and training in Muslim, and even Egyptian, history had certainly been quite limited. It came into being as a result of a fortunate combination of a great genius, profound involvement in the subject, and an extremely convenient position for acquiring first-hand and first-class information on contemporary Egyptian history.

An Approach to the Systematic Study of the Chronicle

It remains now to discuss briefly the question of how to approach the systematic study of al-Jabartī's chronicle. This leads us to point first at one of the most conspicuous characteristics of our author's work, namely, the comparative shortness of the chronicle on the one hand, and the great length of the biographies on the other, especially in the early parts (see also above). The narrative is thus frequently made too short, and is even mutilated. I believe that the first and by far the most urgent task in the study of al-Jabartī is to develop his narrative by merging the extremely rich historical data of the biographies with the chronological part into one whole. By so doing, the picture of the period will come out most clearly, vividly, and forcefully, and will serve as a sound basis for the study of the various aspects of Egyptian life. Moreover, the student of any of these aspects will be spared the trouble of proving many of his arguments, because the proofs will already be found in the correct and balanced narrative.

That the rewriting of the narrative should take precedence over all other studies concerning our chronicle may be shown in the following way. It may be proved beyond doubt that the key to Mamluk society, the main theme of al-Jabartī, is found in pp. 21–143 of the first volume which include the years 1100–42/1688–1729, i.e. up to the annihilation of the Qāsimīya by the Faqārīya. It is only after writing the narrative in full that Mamluk society in this period can be reconstructed, but once this is done, it becomes quite easy to follow the vicissitudes and internal relations of that society up to its extermination by Muḥammad ʿAlī.[26]

[26] The full version of the present article, as published in *BSOAS*, includes also the following sections:

How the chronicle was compiled, pp. 222–8
The chronicle's circulation before its publication, pp. 228–9
The chronicle's publication and translation,pp. 229–30
Al-Jabartī's immediate environment, pp. 237–44
Al-Jabartī's second chronicle (*Muẓhir al-taqdīs*), pp. 244–6
Non-historical works of our author, pp. 246–7
Appendix A: Note on the date of al-Jabartī's death, pp. 247–8
Appendix B: Al-Jabartī and ʿAbd Allāh al-Sharqāwī, pp. 248–9.

34. HISTORIOGRAPHY IN EGYPT IN THE NINETEENTH CENTURY

GAMAL EL-DIN EL-SHAYYAL

Professor of History in the University of Alexandria

The object of this study is to deal with three sides of the movement of historical writing in Egypt in the nineteenth century. First, I will trace the successive stages of its development and point out its various trends and currents. I will then try to give a clear idea of the various subjects which the Egyptian historians treated during that century, and of the cultural background which influenced their method and style. Finally I will discuss the aims of the movement and its effects on Egyptian society.

(1) *The Beginning of the Internal Cultural Revival towards the End of the Eighteenth Century*

Towards the close of the eighteenth century we detect the first signs of a spontaneous cultural revival. It was an internal movement which emerged from within Egypt away from any outside influence whether from the east or from the west. It was started by a group of Egyptian writers who appeared on the cultural scene and who were unequalled during the three preceding centuries either in their number or in the amount of material they produced. Ḥasan al-Jabartī excelled in mathematical and astronomical studies. In the field of literature there were such men as Muḥammad al-Shabrāwī, Ḥasan al-ʿAṭṭār (who occupied, at one time or the other, the post of Shaykh of al-Azhar), and Ismāʿīl al-Khashshāb. In the field of linguistic and theological studies there were Muḥammad Murtaḍā al-Zabīdī, and in history there was ʿAbd al-Raḥmān al-Jabartī.

It is most likely that this awakening would have taken the form of a national revival, bringing back to life the old glories and the legacy of the past. But this spontaneous awakening was interrupted by the advent of the French expedition. This was accompanied by a number of scientists and men of learning who brought in their train many aspects of a culture completely different from anything which the Egyptians had known. A number of Egyptian ʿ*ulama*ʾ made contact with those scientists, and visited the institute which they founded in Cairo and frequented the library and the press which they brought with them. They were overwhelmed with what they saw and started to compare their own culture with that which the French brought with them.

After that, many developments took place on the Egyptian scene. The French evacuated the country, some internal disturbances occurred,

Muḥammad 'Alī became governor of Egypt and a new régime was introduced. The new governor realized from the start that he had to copy from the West if his aim was a true revival and if Egypt was not to be left behind on the road to progress. New schools were opened, students were sent on educational missions to Europe, and in these circumstances the movement of writing came to a standstill while a movement of translation took its place and kept it all through Muḥammad 'Alī's reign.

(2) *Development of Historical Studies in Egypt in the Nineteenth Century*

What concerns us in this development is, first, to assess the position which history, as a subject, occupied and, second, to trace the movement of historiography. In my opinion it would have been possible for the revival started by al-Jabartī to carry on and for other historians to follow in his steps. Ismā'īl al-Khashshāb and Ḥasan al-'Aṭṭar, his two friends, showed an interest in history and an inclination towards historical writing. The first made an attempt when he wrote a work on history which he did not complete and which was in any case lost. The other was fond of reading books on history and geography and expressed his liking for the subject in the guidance which he used to give his students.

It would have also been possible for some of al-'Aṭṭār's students, such as Rifā'a Rāfi' al-Ṭahṭāwī, Muḥammad 'Ayyād al-Ṭanṭāwī, and Muḥammad 'Umar al-Tūnusī,[1] to become historians. Each of these showed his inclination towards historical studies in one way or the other. Rifā'a made his journey to Paris the subject of his book *Takhlīṣ al-ibrīz fī talkhīṣ Bārīz* and translated, with the collaboration of his students at the school of languages, many books on history. Al-Ṭanṭāwī was influenced by this tendency in his choice of the books which he read with his students in the literature seminars at al-Azhar. It was also apparent in the history books which he wrote during his stay in Russia. Al-Tūnusī showed the same tendency when he wrote about his two journeys to the Sudan, the first to Darfur and the second to Wadday, in which he dealt for the first time with the history of the Sudan.

But both the advent of the French expedition and the translation movement at the time of Muḥammad 'Alī put a stop to the movement of historical writing started by al-Jabartī, and directed all the efforts towards translation. At first this was restricted to books on scientific and military subjects, but when the school of languages was opened Rifā'a started to plan the translation of a number of books to cover the history of the world.

During the reign of Muḥammad 'Alī, Rifā'a and his students were completely absorbed in the movement of translation. It was hoped that they would soon take the natural second step and, instead of restricting them-

[1] Shayyal, 'Dr. Perron and the two sheikhs: Muhammad 'Ayyad al-Tantawi and Muhammad 'Umar al-Tunusi', *Bulletin of the Faculty of Arts*, Alexandria University, vol. ii (1944).

selves to translation, start composing their own books on history, after they had read and digested a great number of European historical books. The blow, however, which the cultural movement in general received at the hands of ʿAbbās I retarded this natural step for a while. When Ismāʿīl succeeded to the khedivial throne, Rifāʿa and his pupils resumed their efforts, this time writing and not translating. But they were no longer alone. A new group was headed by ʿAlī Mubārak and made up of members of educational missions who had completed their studies in Europe and whose field of specialization was engineering or archaeology.

Rifāʿa's group had an Islamic cultural background at al-Azhar. It was later blended with the French education which some of them received at Paris and others received at the school of languages. But Mubārak's group had a different cultural background. Their education was scientific. They had studied engineering, astronomy or archaeology. Later their education also had a French element. For this reason we notice that the members of these two schools of thought were influenced in their historical writings by the literary and scientific sides of French culture. This blending of the two cultures appeared clearly in their writings. They referred to al-Ṭabarī, Ibn ʿAbd al-Ḥakam, al-Masʿūdī, Ibn Khaldūn, al-Maqrīzī, al-Suyūṭī as well as to Voltaire, Rousseau, Montesquieu, and the orientalist Quatremère. In fact, this became characteristic of Egyptian historians in the nineteenth century. But while they benefited from the mixed culture, they did not forget their country or its history. On the contrary, their education in Europe drove them to pay more attention to the history of their own country and made them realize the necessity of rewriting it in the light of the latest findings of historical and archaeological research. Thus when they started to write they did not start with the history of Europe or the world but with the history of Egypt. In this respect Rifāʿa intended his first book to cover the history of Egypt from the earliest times to his own days, although he was only able to complete the first two volumes. As for Mubārak, the head of the second school, we find his most valuable book written on the topographical history of Egypt.

(3) *Currents and Influences which affected Historical Writing in that Century*

A. The National Movements

The next major influence was the reform movement towards the end of Ismāʿīl's reign. This was followed by the ʿUrābī revolution in the time of Tawfīq which ended with the intervention of the British and their occupation of Egypt. The bitterness and indignation which the Egyptians felt towards the British occupation gave birth to another national movement which was led, at first, by Muṣṭafā Kāmil. This national movement, with its two branches, had a clear effect on the writing of history towards the end of the nineteenth century. The writers directed their efforts towards dealing with the Egyptian affairs of the day and with the national movement itself. They also wrote about themselves and about the ruling dynasty of Muḥammad ʻAlī. However, they were not only occupied with themselves and their country but they kept at the same time an eye on the outside world which was ahead of them on the road to progress, especially Europe which had succeeded in dominating their country as well as other countries of the East. This appeared in their writings. Towards the end of the nineteenth century we find books written on the history of Egypt and others written on the history of the world, such as *al-Baḥr al-zākhir* by Maḥmūd Fahmī and *al-Kāfī* by Sharūbīm.

B. Archaeological Research

At the same time the efforts which the Europeans directed towards archaeological research since the dawn of the century did not fail to have their effect on the Egyptian historians who wrote during its second half.

These were the general currents and influences which affected the movement of historical writing in Egypt in the nineteenth century. But apart from these there were particular influences which also left their mark on the development of historical writing in Egypt during that century.

C. The Recognition of History as a Science to be taught in the Schools

One of these influences was the recognition of history as an independent science. For the first time history lessons formed part of the curriculum in the schools, special teachers were appointed to teach it, and history textbooks were written or translated for school use. All this was due to the efforts of Rifāʻa al-Ṭahṭāwī. He started teaching history in the school of languages. After this history was taught in the preparatory (intermediate) schools, then in the school of the Ancient Egyptian Language, in Dār al-ʻUlūm and finally in the Higher Training college. Some of the graduates of this last college were chosen to be sent to Europe to specialize in history. Later on some of the graduates of the Egyptian university were sent to Europe for the same purpose. Most of those members occupied chairs of history in the Egyptian universities after their return to Egypt. It was thanks to them and their students that historical studies in Egypt took a new turning both in the method and style of writing and in the actual subject matter.

D. Printing

Another factor which had a favourable influence on historical writing is the appearance and spread of printing in Egypt in that century. The first Arabic press to be introduced into Egypt was that brought by the French expedition in 1798. On their evacuation they took it with them and Egypt was left without one till Muḥammad ʿAlī established the Būlāq Press about 1822. This was followed by the foundation of many other presses which were attached to the ministries and the higher schools. In these presses history books, whether written or translated, were printed and could therefore have a circulation on a scale hitherto unknown in Egypt. As a rule, a thousand copies of each book were printed, especially in the case of textbooks. If we take into consideration that before that time the circulation of books was effected only through written copies we will have a clear idea of the difference in the effect of a book which was read by a thousand or more and another which could only be read by ten or twenty at the most.

E. The Press

Another very important factor, which had a marked influence, was the press. Egypt knew journalism for the first time in that century and more attention was paid in the newspapers of the nineteenth century to essays than to news. Thus many articles, sometimes even whole books, written or translated, were published in the Egyptian newspapers and magazines. Rifāʿa's book *Muntahā al-ījāz fī sīrat sākin al-Ḥijāz* (a biography of the Prophet) was serialized in this way in the magazine of *Rawḍat al-madāris*. Other books published in the same way were a treatise on the police organization of the Arabs, Turks, and Persians which was translated from the French,[2] and Mubārak's *Ḥaqā'iq al-akhbār li-waṣf al-biḥār* which appeared in the form of a series of articles in the same magazine and was latter collected and printed in book form. Many other books and articles were published in the same way in the newspapers *Wādī al-Nil*, *al-Liwā'*, *al-Mu'ayyad*, and in the magazines of *Rawḍat al-madāris*, *al-Muqtaṭaf*, *al-Hilāl* etc.

F. The Editing of Old Historical Manuscripts

The great number of presses which were founded both by the government and by private individuals gave the Egyptians the chance of a better knowledge of their old historical legacy, and a start was made in the editing and publication of the old books which contained that heritage. It was once more due to Rifāʿa's unceasing efforts that this was achieved. He succeeded in persuading Saʿīd Pasha to agree to this step and, as ʿAlī Mubārak tells us, the orders were given 'to print a number of old Arabic books at the expense of the Government. They were of great use in al-Azhar and elsewhere. They included the *Tafsīr* of al-Fakhr al-Rāzī, *Maʿāhid al-tanṣīṣ*, *Khizānat al-adab*, al-Ḥarīrī's *Maqāmāt*, and other books which were not available at that time.'

A similar step was taken at a later date by Muḥammad ʿAbduh. How-

[2] This is an Arabic translation of Behrnauer, 'Mémoire sur les Institutions de Police chez les Arabes, les Persans et les Turcs', *J.A.* 5e série (1866), xv, 461–509; xvi, 114–90.

ever, he did not depend on the support of the government, but formed in 1900 a society which he called the Society for the revival of Arabic studies.[3] This society published a great number of old Arabic manuscripts in linguistics, jurisprudence, literature, and history.

This was followed by other steps in the same direction. A number of publishers, journalists and men of letters in general, started to publish other books. In this way many of the works of old authors were printed. Among them were the works of Ibn al-Athīr, Ibn Khaldūn, Abū Shāma, Ibn al-Jawzī, Ibn Ḥajar, Ibn Baṭṭūta, Ibn Iyās, Ibn Mammātī, al-Balādhurī, al-Maqrīzī, al-Sakhāwī, al-Suyūṭī, Ibn Duqmāq, and al-Jabartī.

The Egyptians soon started to read these books, to become acquainted with their forgotten history and to know that they had many ancient glories in the fields of war, culture, and civilization. As a result of all this a new historical consciousness developed among them which kindled their national spirit.

G. Scientific and Historical Societies

Another factor which helped to spread historical consciousness and to promote historical studies was the forming of scientific societies. This too was unknown in Egypt before the nineteenth century. The research which was carried out under the auspices of these societies, and the books and treaties which were printed by them, dealt mostly with Egyptian history in its various ages.

The first of these societies was the *Institut Égyptien* which was founded by Napoleon in 1798. Most of the members of this Institute were chosen among the French scientists and men of learning who accompanied the expedition. The results of their scientific research were included in the immense and invaluable *Description de l'Égypte*. When the French evacuated Egypt the institute was closed down. It was reopened in Alexandria in 1859, during the reign of Sa'īd, under the name of *Institut d'Egypte*, and was later transferred to Cairo. Its members this time were chosen among both Egyptian and European scientists. It had a scientific *Bulletin*, as well as an annual memoir. In both of them many papers and articles were published on history in general and on Egyptian history in particular. This institute is still open and its bulletin is published regularly.

At the time of Muḥammad 'Alī a number of orientalists and European scientists founded in Egypt another society, which was called *La Société Égyptienne*.[4] This society was often mentioned in Dr. Perron's letters to his

[3] Adams, *Islam and Modernism in Egypt* (the Arabic translation), pp. 80–1; Muḥammad Rashīd Riḍā, *Ta'rikh al-ustādh al-imām*, iii, 247; i, 753; 'Uthmān Amīn, *Rā'id al-fikr al-miṣrī*, p. 38.

[4] Ya'qūb Artīn, *Lettres du Dr. Perron, du Caire et Alexandrie, à M. Jules Mohl, à Paris. 1838–1854* (Le Caire, 1911). Shayyal, 'Dr. Perron and the Two Sheikhs . . .', pp. 179–221.

friend Jules Mohl. In these letters he mentioned that it had been founded in 1835 with the purpose of building up a library which contains as many books as possible, especially books on the East, its history, geography, literature, customs etc.

Six or seven years after it had been founded the aims of this society developed and were soon to include the printing and publishing of books connected with the East. Later, a number of Egyptians who had European education joined the society. However, it was dissolved in the last quarter of the nineteenth century and its library was given over to Dār al-Kutub in 1874 on the recommendation of its last members, Ḥakakyān Bey, Kānnī Bey, and M. Thuborn.

Another society was founded in 1868 during the reign of Ismā'īl. It was called *Jam'iyyat al-Ma'ārif*[5] and its founders, who were Egyptian men of culture, intended it to be a purely Egyptian society. It aimed at the dissemination of culture through writing, printing, and publishing. It undertook the publication of a great number of old Arabic manuscripts on history, jurisprudence, and literature. Among these were *Usd al-g͟hāba* by Ibn al-At͟hīr, *al-Fatḥ al-wahbī*, *al-Muk͟htaṣar* by Abu'l-Fidā', and the history of Ibn al-Wardī.

The Khedivial Geographical Society was yet another of these cultural and scientific societies which appeared at the time of Ismā'īl. It was founded in 1875 with the aim of encouraging geographical research and publishing scientific production in that field. It had an extremely valuable scientific journal which it issued and still issues regularly and in which were published many articles and papers on geographic explorations and historical and archaeological findings which took place in the nineteenth century.

In the periodicals, proceedings, and publications of all these societies Egyptian and European historians published many of their articles and papers. Thus, next to the articles written by Casanova, Hertz, Mariette, and Brugsch, others bore the names of Maḥmūd al-Falakī, Ya'qūb Artīn, Muḥammad Muk͟htār, Aḥmad Kamāl, and 'Alī Bahjat.

(4) *The Effect of these Influences on Historiography*

The new schools, the recognition of history as a subject worthy of being taught independently in these schools, the spread of printing, the cultural and historical societies, the editing of old historical manuscripts, the interest taken in archaeology and archaeological research, the national awakening: these were the factors which left a deep impression on the writing of history and created what we may call a historical consciousness in Egypt in the nineteenth century. A great number of books were written

[5] 'Abd al-Raḥmān al-Rāfi'ī, *'Aṣr Ismā'īl*, i, 242–4.

and historical research claimed a wide range of subjects. Historians no longer confined themselves to the history of Egypt and Islam, but dealt with other problems which were not known in the Islamic period.

I shall try to give here a general idea of the various historical subjects with which the Egyptian historians dealt at that time.

A. The History of the World

The history of the world was one of these subjects. It was the first time that Egyptian historians wrote in this field. This development was a natural outcome of the new circumstances in which Egypt found itself during that century. Egypt was no longer cut off from the rest of the world as it had been all through the Ottoman period. While we do not hear of a single Egyptian who had visited Europe in the sixteenth, seventeenth, and eighteenth centuries we have a different picture in the nineteenth. Many Egyptians were sent during the first part of that century to study in Italy, France, Germany, and England. Many others went to Europe during its second half, to complete their studies, to visit museums and libraries, to attend conferences, to present and defend the case of their country or simply as tourists. These Egyptians studied the history of the world in European schools and universities. They also saw at close quarters the active movement of historical writing in the nineteenth century and read the writings of the European historians of that century. It was therefore natural for them to develop an interest in that branch of history.

In this field Rifā'a, in collaboration with some of his pupils, translated a number of French books which covered the history of the world in its various ages. One of these translated books, *The History of Charles V*, was written by the Scottish historian William Robertson (1721–93). Towards the end of the century two more Egyptians wrote on the history of the world. One of them, Maḥmūd Fahmī, a leader of the 'Urābī revolution, wrote *al-Baḥr al-zā<u>kh</u>ir*, in four volumes, during his exile in Ceylon. The other was Mī<u>kh</u>ā'īl <u>Sh</u>arūbīm, a Copt who wrote a similar book which he called *al-Kāfī fi'l-ta'rī<u>kh</u>*. Both writers depended on European sources.

It is true that earlier Egyptian and Muslim historians had written about the history of the world. But the borders of their world were those of Islam. They did not try to write about the nations which lay outside that world except for a few allusions about those which immediately adjoined the Islamic world, such as the Indians, the Turks, and the Byzantines. As for the European countries and their inhabitants the Muslim historians had a bad and distorted idea of them and generally held them in contempt. They believed that they lived in a world beset by ignorance and backwardness, which lay at a safe distance from the Islamic world with its flourishing civilization, and which had nothing to offer the Muslims. This opinion is reflected in the writings of Arab historians and geographers of the Middle

Ages. In this respect al-Masʿūdī, a tenth-century geographer, says, 'The peoples of the north are those for whom the sun is distant from the zenith . . . cold and damp prevail in those regions, and snow and ice follow one another in endless succession. The warm humour is lacking among them; their bodies are large, their natures gross, their manners harsh, their understanding dull and their tongues heavy . . . their religious beliefs lack solidity . . . those of them who are farthest to the north are the most subject to stupidity, grossness and brutishness.'[6]

A century later, Ibn Ṣāʿid al-Andalusī, a judge from Toledo, describes in his book, *Ṭabaqāt al-umam*, 'The Indians, the Persians, the Chaldees, the Hebrews, the Greeks, the Romans, the Egyptians and the Arabs' as the nations which had an affinity for knowledge. 'The Chinese and the Turks', he adds, 'come nearest to them in that respect.' As for the other nations, he mentions them in a contemptuous way when he says that 'Their bellies are big, their colour pale, their hair long and lank. They lack keenness of understanding and clarity of intelligence, and are overcome by ignorance and foolishness, blindness and stupidity.'[7]

This description was true when Europe lived in the darkness of the Middle Ages. The situation, however, changed completely at the beginning of the sixteenth century. Egypt and the Muslim Near East became isolated from the rest of the world and lived in a similar darkness to that which Europe knew in the Middle Ages. On the other hand the countries of Western Europe advanced by leaps and bounds in the fields of science, war, and economics. It was therefore natural for the Egyptians, at the time of their revival in the nineteenth century, to look west. They copied the sciences of Europe and learnt its languages, while Egyptian historians translated and wrote books on the history of the world and, in particular, on the history of those parts in Europe of which they had known nothing before. These were the first books on European history to appear in Arabic.

B. History of Adjacent Countries

Besides these books on general world history, a number of Egyptian historians took active interest in writing separate books on the history of some neighbouring countries which had some relations with Egypt. Ismāʿīl Sarhank Pasha, for instance, wrote his book *Haqāʾiq al-akhbār ʿan duwal al-biḥār* on the history of sea powers, counting Egypt as one of them. Muḥammad Farīd also contributed in this field. His book on the history of the Ottoman Empire was the only book to be written in Arabic on that subject at that time. Again, Muṣṭafā Kāmil wrote two books, one on the history of the Eastern question and the other on the history of Japan, while Jurjī Zaydān compiled a book on the history of Britain.

[6] This quotation is translated by B. Lewis, *The Arabs in History* (London, 1950), p. 164.

[7] Ibid., p. 165; and cf. above, p. 120.

The history of the Sudan was also one of the subjects with which the Egyptian historians dealt at that time. Two books which appeared on the subject were written by al-Tūnusī and took the form of travel books describing a journey to Darfur and another to Waddāy. Two more books on the history of the Sudan were written by Na'ūm Shuqayr and Ibrāhīm Fawzī.

Egyptian historians also wrote about the history of the Arabs and Islamic history. In this field Rifā'a wrote the biography of the Prophet, while Jurjī Zaydān wrote about the Arabs before Islam, the history of Islamic civilization, and the history of Arabic literature.

Some of these subjects were dealt with for the first time in Arabic and it was thanks to the Egyptian historians that the Arab reader was provided with his first books on them. Such was the case in the books dealing with the histories of the Ottoman Empire, the Eastern question, Japan, England, and the Sudan.

C. Personal Memoirs

Another form of historical writing which appeared in Egypt for the first time was personal memoirs. This was due to the fact that the Egyptians for the first time experienced the modern form of political life. They took part in political events and shouldered the responsibility of ruling or leading public opinion. Under these circumstances, the writers of the memoirs were usually men of the government or leaders of public opinion, such as 'Urābī, Muḥammad 'Abduh, 'Abdallāh al-Nadīm, and Maḥmūd Fahmī.

D. General History of Egypt

Apart from these new subjects which were dealt with for the first time, Egyptian historians wrote on other themes which were known before the nineteenth century. Some of them wrote on the general history of Egypt from the earliest times, or from the Arab conquest up to their time. In this category we can put Rifā'a's book in which he intended to cover the history of Egypt through the ages, but could only complete two of its volumes before he died; the first beginning with the time of the Pharaohs and ending with the Arab conquest, and the second dealing with the biography of the Prophet Muḥammad. Al-Jabartī's history also falls in this class of books, for he gives a concise account of Egyptian history since the Arab conquest and then talks in detail about its history in the eighteenth century and the first quarter of the nineteenth. We can also add to this list Zaydān's book on the history of Egypt from the time of the Arab conquest up to his time. The book is in two volumes and is called *Ta'rīkh Miṣr al-ḥadīth*.

E. Topographical History and the History of Towns and Cities

Another branch which the Egyptian historians of that century dealt with was topographical history and the history of towns and cities. This is one of the old types of historical writing which earlier Egyptian historians had initiated and in which they wrote a long series of books. The first historian to write on topographical history or *khiṭaṭ* was Abū ʿUmar al-Kindī and the last was Taqī al-Dīn al-Maqrīzī. They followed one another through the centuries except for the three centuries of Ottoman rule. This type of historical writing was renewed in the nineteenth century by ʿAlī Mubārak. In his valuable book *al-Khiṭaṭ al-tawfīqiyya al-jadīda*, which consists of twenty volumes, he wrote the history of Cairo and all the other towns of Egypt. He took al-Maqrīzī's *Khiṭaṭ* as a basis and followed it up to his time, i.e. up to the last part of the nineteenth century, making good use of the archaeological research which took place during that century. Some of his contemporaries wrote the histories of individual towns, whether these were still in existence or had long disappeared. In this field Aḥmad Kamāl wrote the history of Memphis and ʿAyn Shams (Heliopolis), ʿAlī Bahjat wrote the history of al-Fusṭāṭ in his book on the excavations there, and Muḥammad Masʿūd wrote a short history of Alexandria which he called *al-Minḥa al-dahriyya fī takhṭīṭ madīnat al-Iskandariyya*.

F. History of Egypt in the Nineteenth Century under the Rule of the Muḥammad ʿAlī Dynasty

Another topic which the Egyptian historians dealt with at that time was the history of Egypt in the nineteenth century and the history of the ruling dynasty in that period. Al-Jabartī started the long series of books written on that subject by his two books, *ʿAjāʾib al-āthār* and *Muẓhir al-taqdīs*. A number of historians followed in his steps. Khalīl al-Rajabī wrote a history of Muḥammad ʿAlī which is still in manuscript. Salīm Naqqāsh followed with his book *Miṣr liʾl-Miṣriyyīn*. This book consists of nine volumes of which the first three, which are lost, dealt with the history of the Muḥammad ʿAlī dynasty up to Ismāʿīl's time while the other six volumes dealt with the reign of Tawfīq and the ʿUrābī revolution. Other writers who wrote on the same subject are Muḥammad Farīd who compiled his book *al-Bahja al-tawfīqiyya* on the history of Muḥammad ʿAlī, and Jurjī Zaydān, whose book *Taʾrīkh Miṣr al-ḥadīth* deals in its second volume with modern Egyptian history.

G. Biographies

The writing of biographies was also one of the tasks with which the Egyptian historians occupied themselves in the nineteenth century. First there were the general biographical books, each of them containing the biographies of a number of famous men whether these were contemporaries or belonged to the past. Such were the books *Ashhar mashāhīr al-Islām fiʾl-ḥarb waʾl-siyāsa* on the famous leaders of Islam by Rafīq al-ʿAẓm, and the *Ḥumāt al-Islām* (protectors of Islam) by Muṣṭafā Najīb. Both of these books dealt with the heroes of Islam in early times. Other books which fall in the same category are *Mashāhīr al-sharq* by Jurjī Zaydān, *Nawābigh al-Aqbāṭ wa-mashāhīruhum fi'l-qarn al-tāsi' 'ashar* by Tawfīq Iskārūs, and *Tarājim a'yān al-qarn al-thālith-'ashar* (biographies of notables of the thirteenth century A.H.) by Aḥmad Taymūr.

Another category of these books dealt with individual biographies. The author would take the biography of only one person to be the study of his book. Among these books, which all dealt with the biographies of Egyptian notables in the nineteenth century, were Rifā'a's biography called *Ḥilyat al-zaman*[8] written by his pupil Ṣāliḥ Majdī, the biography of Maḥmud Pasha al-Falakī by Aḥmad Zakī, and Ismā'īl al-Falakī, the biography of Clot Bey, the founder of the medical school in Egypt, by Muḥammad Labīb, and the biography of Abu'l-Su'ūd by his son, Muḥammad Unsī.

The last category of these books was the autobiographies. One of the best examples in this respect is the autobiography of 'Alī Mubārak which he included in his *Khiṭaṭ*, in his description of Ibyār, his place of origin. Two more excellent examples are the autobiography of Muḥammad 'Umar al-Tūnusī which he wrote in his book *Tashḥīdh al-adhān* and the autobiography of 'Abdallāh al-Nadīm which he wrote in his book *Kāna wa-yakūn*.

H. The Historical Novel

Finally there was the historical novel, a genre which Egyptian writers knew for the first time towards the end of the nineteenth century. The first step in this field was taken by Jurjī Zaydān who wrote eighteen novels in which he tried to narrate the history of Islam and the Muslims from the time of the Prophet up to the nineteenth century. It is true that the novel as a branch of literature in general had been started earlier, by Muḥammad al-Muwayliḥī, in his novel *'Isā ibn Hishām*, but it was Zaydān who first used historical events as a theme for his novels. This art developed rapidly in the twentieth century and a number of writers distinguished themselves in it, such as Muḥammad Farīd Abū Ḥadīd, Najīb Maḥfūẓ, 'Alī Aḥmad Bākathīr, and Muḥammad Sa'īd al-'Iryān.

I. Historical Writing in Foreign Languages

A last feature which characterized the movement of historical writing in Egypt in the nineteenth century is that many Egyptians wrote their books and articles in European languages, particularly in French. This fact had no precedent among the Egyptian historians of the Islamic period. This becomes all the more conspicuous when we take into consideration that those Islamic historians and thinkers had known, and even excelled in, some foreign languages, especially Persian and Turkish. Among the

[8] Ed. (with Introduction and comments) by Gamal el-Din el-Shayyal (Cairo, 1959).

historians who knew Turkish were Ibn Duqmāq, al-'Aynī, Ibn Taghrī Birdī, and Ibn Iyās. Among the thinkers and men of letters, Ḥasan al-Jabartī knew Turkish and Persian well, while al-Murtaḍā al-Zabīdī excelled in Turkish, Persian, and Georgian. Yet we do not know of a single instance where one of those writers or, in fact, any other writer who used any language other than Arabic for his writings. This was due to the fact that Arabic was considered the language of science and letters in the Middle Ages.

The reason behind this new tendency among the Egyptian historians of the nineteenth century is that French had become the *lingua franca* of the day both in the field of letters and the field of politics. The Egyptians who used it for their writing were the members of educational missions who had completed their studies in France or those who had studied French in the school of languages.

The most prominent among this group of writers was Ya'qūb Artīn, who came from a family of Armenian origin. He received a European education and held many posts in the government. He became a tutor to some of the Khedive Ismā'īl's sons in 1873, a secretary for the European affairs of the Khedivial household in 1879 and a vice-minister of education in 1884.

He took a great interest in the cultural movement in general and in history in particular. Among his papers and treatises written in French are:

L'Instruction publique en Egypte (Paris, 1890). It was translated into Arabic by 'Alī Bahjat and printed in Būlāq in 1894.

La Propriété foncière en Egypte (Cairo, 1883). It was translated into Arabic by Sa'id 'Ammūn and printed in Būlāq in A.H. 1307.

Considérations sur l'instruction publique en Egypte (Cairo, 1894).

Apart from these books he wrote a great number of articles on historical subjects which were published in the *Bulletin de l'Institut Egyptien.*

Maḥmūd al-Falakī was another Egyptian who wrote in French. Among his books and articles are:

1. 'Mémoires sur le calendrier arabe avant l'Islamisme sur la naissance at l'age du Prophet Mohammed.' It was published in the *Journal Asiatique* in 1858. This paper was later translated into Arabic by Aḥmad Zakī, translator at the governorate of Ismailia, and printed at Būlāq.

2. *Mémoire sur l'ancienne Alexandrie* (Copenhagen, 1872).

He also published many papers in French in various scientific periodicals in Egypt and in Europe such as the *Bulletin de l'Institut Egyptien*, the *Bulletin de la Société Khediviale de Géographie*, the *Journal Asiatique*, and the publications of the Académie Royale Belge. One of the papers published by the Académie Belge was on the age of the Pyramids and the purpose of building them and was entitled 'L'Age et le but des pyramides lus dans Sirius.'

Among Egyptians writing in French was also Qadrī Pasha whose book *Notices géographiques* was published in Cairo in 1869. Another was 'Alī

Bahjat, whose book *Les Fouilles d'El Fustat* was translated into Arabic. He also contributed many articles on historical and archaeological subjects to the *Bulletin de l'Institut Egyptien.*

There was also Muḥammad Mukhtār who was the governor of Harar for some time when it was an Egyptian possession. His articles and papers are classed, up to the present day, among the most important works of reference on the history of that town. They were published in the *Bulletin de la Société Khediviale de Géographie du Cairo.* One of his chief articles on this subject was published in 1876 under the title *Notes sur les Pays de Harar.*

Others who wrote in French were Aḥmad Kamāl who published, apart from his Arabic books, many articles in the *Bulletin de l'Institut Egyptien,* and Aḥmad Shafīq whose book *L'Esclavage dans l'Islam* was translated by Aḥmad Zakī who added to it important historical comments. The translation was printed in Būlāq in A.H. 1309.

Thus historical research on a modern scientific basis was no longer confined to European writers or Orientalists. Egyptians now started to take an active part in this field. Valuable papers, written by them in French, appeared in historical journals both in Egypt and abroad, and next to the names of Casanova, Hertz, Mariette, and Brugsch, the names of Maḥmūd al-Falakī, Ismā'īl al-Falakī, Muḥammad Mukhtār, Ya'qūb Artīn, Aḥmad Kamāl, 'Alī Bahjat, and others were to be seen on the pages of these journals.

(5) *The Method and Style of Egyptian Historians in the Nineteenth Century*

The writings of the Egyptian historians in the nineteenth century differed greatly from those of their predecessors in the medieval Islamic period both in method and style. As a rule, the medieval historians used to depend on copying word for word from earlier writers when they dealt with periods before their own. The only original part of their writings was that in which they dealt with their own age. Only very few among them tried to criticize, analyse, or compare. Fewer still had the courage to give their own opinion in their writings.

Most of them also wrote their histories of Egypt or the Islamic world in the form of annals, giving the events year by year. Thus the facts which formed the material of their books were extremely disjointed and lacking in unity and continuity. Very few among them tried to write the history of separate countries, or to tackle separate subjects as Ibn Khaldūn did in his history.

But the Egyptian historians of the nineteenth century were different. They were influenced by the new scientific method that was followed in the European history books which they read, studied or translated. As a result of this they abandoned the annalistic method and dealt in their books with subjects, periods or countries, each in a separate chapter. This is evident in Rifā'a's book *Anwār tawfīq al-jalīl* and in the books written by Sharūbīm, Maḥmūd Fahmī, Sarhank, Jurjī Zaydān, and others.

The historians of the nineteenth century also tried to criticize, analyse, compare, and give their opinions and judgement on what they wrote, thus freeing themselves from the old method of copying.

One of the main features of their scientific method was using auxiliary sciences as a basis for the interpretation and understanding of history, such as documents, numismatics, archaeology, inscriptions, geographical explorations etc.

This method was rarely used by earlier historians. It is true that some Egyptian historians of the Islamic period had made use in their writings of inscriptions and documents, such as al-Maqrīzī in his *Khiṭaṭ* and al-Qalqashandī in his *Ṣubḥ al-a'shā*. But the historians of the nineteenth century made great progress in that direction. Al-Jabartī, for instance, includes in his *'Ajā'ib al-āthār* a multitude of documents and edicts issued by the rulers of Egypt, whether they were French, Turks or Mamluks. He points out this fact in the introduction of his book when he says that he consulted many inscriptions which he found on gravestones as well as the registers kept by clerks and officials. The same method was followed by 'Alī Mubārak in his *Khiṭaṭ*. Again Salīm Naqqāsh's book *Miṣr li'l-Miṣriyyīn* contained a great number of documents connected with the 'Urābī revolution, among them the complete proceedings of the trial of the 'Urabists. The same description applies to *al-Qāmūs al-'āmm li'l-idāra wa'l-qaḍā'* (Dictionary of Administration and Jurisprudence), in which the author, Philippe Gallad, collected a great number of laws, regulations, firmans, and treaties which the government issued in its official publications between 1840 and the closing years of the nineteenth century. The first writer to depend seriously on documents as one of the most important sources of history was Amīn Sāmī in his two books, *Ta'rīkh al-ta'līm fī Miṣr* (The History of Education in Egypt) and *Taqwīm al-Nīl*.

Of the other auxiliary sciences on which the writers of that century depended, numismatics forms the subject of a whole volume of 'Alī Mubārak's *Khiṭaṭ*, while archaeology and geographic explorations were of great use to such Egyptian historians of the second part of the nineteenth century as Rifā'a, 'Alī Mubārak, Aḥmad Kamāl, 'Alī Bahjat, and others.

But the change which the historical writing underwent in that century was not restricted to method. The style also differed greatly from that of earlier historians. At the beginning of the century, it is true, writers still followed the old style. This was evident in the rhyming titles which they used for their books. As regards the actual texts, they were written sometimes in rhymed prose (*saj'*) and at other times in simple and flowing style. The best example of this hesitation between the two styles is perhaps the writings of Rifā'a. In the first volume of his book called *Anwār tawfīq* he restricts himself to a great extent to *saj'*, while in the second volume he uses the simple and flowing style. Towards the end of the century historians and, in fact, writers in general left the old ornate style and used a simple style free from all the encumbrances which marred the writings of the later Ottoman period. In this respect, perhaps a useful comparison could be made between the styles of al-Jabartī or Rifā'a on the one hand and 'Abdallāh al-Nadīm or Muḥammad 'Abduh on the other.

Again we find great difference between the Egyptian historians of the nineteenth century and their predecessors in the Islamic period in the subjects with which they dealt. The majority of the earlier historians devoted their writings to political history and only rarely do we find any of them dealing with cultural, social or economical matters or with political institutions. But the nineteenth century historians wrote on all the branches of history. Besides the political history of Egypt and the world they wrote on the fiscal regulations of the land and on various systems of education. They also tackled such subjects as the political institutions at the time of the Prophet, slavery in Islam, the history of Islamic civilization, the problems of the Egyptian society in the nineteenth century, the 'Urābī revolution etc.

(6) *The Movement of Historical Writing in the Nineteenth Century and its Effects on the Egyptian Society*

The first sign of interest in history in the nineteenth century appeared at the time of Muḥammad 'Alī and took the form of translating a number of history books into the Turkish language on the orders of Muḥammad 'Alī and his son Ibrāhīm. However, the benefit of these translations was limited to the viceroy, his son, and some of the great officials of the state who knew the Turkish language.

After these a great number of books were translated into Arabic, mostly on science, medicine, and military subjects. The effect of these was also limited as it was confined to the students learning these subjects in the newly opened schools. But the books which left the deepest mark on the cultural movement at that time were those dealing with the humanities such as history, geography, philosophy, and logic, which were translated by Rifā'a and his students in the school of languages. Their benefit was equally felt by the graduates of the modern schools and the students and teachers of al-Azhar.

However, we find that Muḥammad 'Abduh tried to belittle the benefit drawn from the translations which took place at the time of Muḥammad 'Alī and on his orders by saying that their effect was confined to the schools in which those books were taught, and that most of them were stored after being printed till they were later sold to the paper dealers. This opinion is expressed in an article published in 1902 in the magazine *al-Manār*[9] on the occasion of the centenary celebrations of Muḥammad ʿAlī's accession to the rule of Egypt. Muḥammad ʿAbduh says: 'A great number of books were translated in various subjects such as history, philosophy, and literature, but were stored behind locked doors from the day they were printed till the last years of Ismāʿīl's reign. The government then wanted to empty those stores and put the books out for any one who wanted them. A number of them were read by some people. This shows that they were translated to satisfy the wishes of the European high officials who wanted to spread their culture in the country, but failed to achieve their purpose because the government of Muḥammad ʿAlī did not create a class of cultured readers to benefit from those books etc.'

It is evident, however, that Muḥammad ʿAbduh gives both an exaggerated idea of the situation and a harsh verdict on it. If his judgement was true in the case of books on scientific and military subjects, it certainly was not so in the case of the books translated in the school of languages, for educated Egyptians continued to read them all through the nineteenth century and during the first part of the twentieth, and there is a good deal of evidence to prove this fact. Among the books for which ʿAbdallāh al-Nadīm asked in order to read during his enforced solitude in his place of concealment was Rifāʿa's translation of Malte Brun's geography. Again, in an article written at the beginning of the twentieth century in which Muṣṭafā ʿAbd al-Rāziq criticizes the translation of Jules Simon's *Devoir* by Ṭāhā Ḥusayn and Muḥammad Ramaḍān, he mentions that he read the books translated by Rifāʿa and benefited from them. Referring to Rifāʿa's method of word-for-word translation he says: 'In Rifāʿa's translation which I have read, I found him extremely precise in applying this method, a fact which proves his great insight in modern sciences.'[10]

As for the books which were originally composed in Arabic, their effect was strong and widespread. This effect is particularly evident in two ways. The first is the creation of a historical consciousness which led the Egyptians to be interested in history generally and in the history of Egypt in the various ages in particular. The second is the kindling of patriotism and the strengthening of the national spirit.

As mentioned earlier, many factors combined to give these two effects. However, the most important among them, in my opinion, is the new understanding of ancient Egyptian history and of Egyptian civilization as one continuous entity. Connected with this was the pride which the new historians had in the glories of that history and civilization and the interest

[9] *Al-Manār*, v, pt. 5 (1902). This article was reprinted in the second volume of Muḥammad Rashīd Riḍā's *Ta'rīkh al-ustādh al-imām*.

[10] *Al-Jarīda*, Wednesday, 29 July 1914. The article was reprinted in *Min āthār Muṣṭafā ʿAbd al-Rāziq*, ed. ʿAlī ʿAbd al-Rāziq.

they took in archaeology and in preserving archaeological findings as patterns of that civilization in its various ages.

This new understanding and interpretation was started, as I mentioned earlier, by Rifāʻa al-Ṭahṭāwī, and was echoed and carried on by the historians who came after him.

In this respect, the biographies written in the nineteenth century also had a great influence on the Egyptian society. This is due to the fact that their authors no longer wrote about certain categories of people, such as physicians, grammarians or men of jurisprudence. Again, they did not write the biographies of all the notables in a whole century as was the case with the earlier historians in the Islamic period. The modern historians followed a different method. Each writer would select a specific group of heroes and great men and would then write their biographies pointing out the qualities of heroism and greatness in their lives and deeds. This was done by Rafīq al-ʻAẓm in his *As͟hhar mas͟hāhīr al-Islām*, by Muṣṭafā Najīb in his *Ḥumāt al-Islām*, and by Jurjī Zaydān in his *Mas͟hāhīr al-s͟harq*. Those biographies no doubt inspired the Egyptian youth with glimpses of heroism and put before their eyes a number of types of great men who believed in their ideals and who sacrificed greatly to attain them.

The same applies to the individual biographies written at that time. The biographies, for instance, of ʻAlī Mubārak, Abu'l-Suʻūd, Maḥmūd al-Falakī and others gave the history of self-made Egyptians who came from peasant origin and who were able, through sheer hard work, to attain the highest positions in the state and to render their country the greatest services.

Again, the books and treatises written on the national revival and on the resistance against foreign occupation, such as al-Jabartī's two books, those written on the ʻUrābī revolution, its causes and its aims, such as *Miṣr li'l-Miṣriyyīn*, and the personal memoirs written by the leaders of that revolution—all these left a deep impression on the Egyptians and were a strong factor behind the national movements which marked the twentieth century. In this field no one can deny the effect of these writings on the movements of Muṣṭafā Kāmil and Saʻd Zag͟hlūl and even on that of Jamāl ʻAbd al-Nāṣir.

Again, the interest taken in the legacy of the past, and the printing of a great number of old historical manuscripts acquainted the Egyptians with their glories in the Islamic period. This made them conscious of their past and led them to try to effect its revival.

One drawback of the movement of historical writing in the nineteenth century, however, was that it was not undertaken by professional historians who set themselves from the beginning solely to study, teach, and write on history. In this respect, with the exception of al-Jabartī, who devoted all his efforts to writing history, and Rifāʻa who qualified himself in one way or another for historical writing, the rest of the Egyptian historians in the nineteenth century were amateurs. They had their particular educational background which differed with their field of specialization, whether it was in law, engineering, literature, religion or war. Then they developed an interest in history and wrote in it.

This situation changed in the twentieth century. In its second decade some graduates of the higher training college were sent on educational missions to Europe to specialize in history. In 1925 the Egyptian University was opened and a special department was founded in it for the study of all branches of history. At the beginning, the task of teaching was put in the hands of some European professors and a number of those Egyptians who had completed their studies in Europe. Some graduates of this and of other universities (which were founded later) were sent, in their turn, on educational missions to specialize in history, while special sections for higher studies were opened in the history departments in them. It is the members of these educational missions and the graduates of these sections of higher historical studies, who occupy at present the chairs of history in the Egyptian universities. Their efforts and those of their pupils in writing, translating, and editing have a new and particular type which combines with the scientific basis of a balanced approach.

35. OTTOMAN HISTORIOGRAPHY OF THE TANZIMAT PERIOD

ERCÜMENT KURAN

Associate Professor of History, Robert College, Istanbul

The two-fold nature of the Tanzimat period, which extends, in its broad limits, from 1839 to 1908, has long been recognized as its most characteristic feature. Over these seventy years traditional institutions flourished side by side with new ones set up under European influence. Historiography in this period is no exception to the rule: we see works of history composed in the old-fashioned ways, while at the same time works inspired by European methods begin to appear and to develop into a completely modern style. In this study I shall try to show how these two distinct genres developed, endeavouring above all to define the influences operating in each, and even between them. I need not mention all the works published during that time, and shall restrict myself to those which I consider to be of some interest.[1]

Traditional historiography had behind it a noble past. It may have undergone Arab and Persian influence, but it had achieved an originality of its own, and the work of Turkish historians in the sixteenth and seventeenth centuries bears witness to the high level attained in this branch of study.[2] The decline of the Empire in the following century was not without effect upon Ottoman historiography; yet the traditional genre survived.

It cannot be gainsaid that the most important historical work of the Tanzimat period is the *Tārīkh-i devlet-i ʿaliyye* of Aḥmed Jevdet Pasha (1822–95) (12 vols., Istanbul, A.H. 1271–1309), a chronicle of events between 1774 and 1826. The author, appointed official historiographer after he had prepared the first volumes of his chronicle, devoted thirty years of his life to its composition. The amplitude of his sources, his critical sense, his faultless logic compel our admiration. Still, this work remains faithful to tradition, written as it is in annalistic form. Official promotions, elevations in rank and deaths which took place during each year are recorded in the classic manner. Nevertheless, when occasion warrants, Jevdet Pasha abandons his chronological system and accords his subject the ample treatment it demands. Thus his history took the form of a collection of chronicles and little monographs.

[1] Most of the works published during the Tanzimat have been noticed in the following study: Mükrimin Halil Yınanç, *Tanzimattan Meşrutiyete kadar bizde tarihçilik* (*Tanzimat* I (Istanbul, 1940), off-print).

[2] Cf. Bernard Lewis, 'History-writing and National Revival in Turkey', *Middle Eastern Affairs* (June–July 1953), iv, 219.

Jevdet Pasha's attitude towards Europe is very interesting. Although he received his education in the medrese, he is by no means a fanatic, like the historian and philologist 'Āṣim (d. 1819). For his chronicle he even used certain Western sources translated into Turkish and published in Egypt under Meḥemmed 'Alī Pasha.[3] Yet he remains a conservative, seeking a cure for the Empire's decadence in the improvement of ancient institutions, with no resort to European civilization. According to a contemporary writer, Jevdet Pasha might be regarded as 'the last disciple of Ibn Khaldūn'.[4] As shown by the introduction to his chronicle, which ultimately formed a whole volume of the last edition (1890), his notions of history and of human society rest essentially upon the ideas of that great Muslim historian-philosopher. It was he, indeed, who translated the sixth and last part of Ibn Khaldūn's Prolegomena.[5]

Jevdet Pasha's successor as official historiographer was Aḥmed Luṭfī (1815–1907), who left a chronicle covering the period from 1826 to 1861 (*Tārīkh-i Luṭfī*, 8 vols., issued, Istanbul, A.H. 1290–1328). This is a pallid work compared with his predecessor's, and is mainly a summary of newspaper articles.

Apart from Jevdet Pasha's chronicle, the best histories written in the traditional manner during the Tanzimat period were couched in the form of biographies. In justification may be mentioned the *Tārīkh-i 'Aṭā* of Ṭayyārzāde 'Aṭāullah (1810–77) and the *Sijill-i 'oṣmānī* of Meḥemmed Süreyya (d. 1909). The first (5 vols., Istanbul, A.H. 1291(?)–93) deals, after a long introduction on the Enderun (Imperial Palace School), with individuals educated there, whilst the second (4 vols., Istanbul, A.H. 1308–15) includes short lives of all men of note in Ottoman history. These are extensive works, but the information they contain, though useful, does not always correspond with the truth.

Even after the Tanzimat period there were those who continued to write history in the old way; the last of these was Ibnülemin Mahmud Kemal Inal (1870–1957), the author of an anecdotal work on the lives of the grand-viziers, starting with 'Ālī Pasha (1815–71).

The development of modern historiography in Turkey was slow, but sure. The proclamation of the Tanzimat by Muṣṭafa Reshīd Pasha (1800–58) had opened the Ottoman Empire, after 1839, to Western influences.

[3] For example, he used a summary of the Memoirs of Napoleon, printed in 1831 (*Tārikh-i Bonaparte* (Būlāq, A.H. 1247)). Jevdet Pasha was not the first to avail himself of Western sources. Before him, Shānīzāde 'Aṭāullah (d. 1826) who had learned French, drew on works in this language for his chronicle.

[4] Ahmed Hamdi Tanpınar, *On dokuzuncu asır Türk edebiyatı tarihi*, second edition (Istanbul, 1956), i, 141.

[5] Pīrīzāde Meḥemmed Ṣā'ib (d. 1749) had translated the first five parts. They were printed in Būlāq in 1857. Jevdet Pasha had them reprinted in the following year, in two volumes, and added as a third volume the portion he had translated (*Muqaddime-i Ibn Khaldūn*, 3 vols. (Istanbul, A.H. 1275–77)).

At first it was the actual content of European works which made them so welcome to Turkish historians.

The first part of the *Tārīkh-i devlet-i ʿaliyye-i ʿosmāniyye* by Khayrullah Efendi (1817–76) came out in 1854. He set himself the task of writing an Ottoman history, with a section devoted to each sultan. He got no further than Aḥmed I (1603–17) (18 parts published: the last in 1875). There was nothing original in this scheme, for Idrīs Bidlīsī (d. 1520) had tried it in the sixteenth century in his *Hasht bihisht*. Khayrullāh Efendi, apart from Eastern sources, had drawn largely from Hammer's celebrated history, and from the less important one of De la Croix. Though it was a somewhat composite work, and a feeble one at that, we can nevertheless look at it as a bridge between traditional and modern historiography.

The interest in Western civilization felt in intellectual Turkish circles deepened from year to year, and the number of Turks who learned Western languages grew in consequence. One of them, Aḥmed Ḥilmi (d. 1878), published a universal history in 1866 (*Tārīkh-i ʿumūmī*, 2 vols. Istanbul, A.H. 1285). This was a translation and adaptation from Chambers's Universal History.[6]

The way was now open: during the following years a number of European works were translated and published.[7] More numerous were those which formed the basis of adaptations. Aḥmed Midḥat (1841–1912) began, a series in imitation of the French *Univers*; this work deserves mention for its favourable reception (*Kāʾināt*, 15 vols., Istanbul, A.H. 1288–98). The author (or rather, the adapter) summarized the history of each country in a small volume, the last being devoted to the Ottoman Empire.

The second step in the development of historical writing in Turkey was the introduction of European methods. The need for text-books for the new schools obliged the Turkish intellectuals to prepare lucid and systematic history manuals. The first successful attempt was made in 1867 by Aḥmed Vefīq Pasha (1823–91) in his *Fezleke-i tārīkh-i ʿoṣmānī* (Istanbul, A.H. 1286). The writer, son of a Turkish diplomat, had studied for some years in a Paris lycée, a circumstance which enabled him to prepare a manual on French lines: Ottoman history is divided into six chapters, each chapter corresponding to a particular phase in the Empire's History, through the periods of expansion, greatness, and decline, from the origin of the Empire until the author's own time.

The writers who followed Aḥmed Vefīq Pasha in producing school books

[6] Some time later the same writer enlarged his work, developing the chapters dealing with Islam (*Tārīkh-i ʿumūmī*, 6 vols. (Istanbul, A.H. 1293–4)). These chapters are only a summary of the *Ṣāḥāʾ if al-Akhbār* by Münejjimbashi Aḥmed (d. 1702).

[7] The 'Enjümen-i dānish' academy, established at Istanbul in 1851, had ordered the translation of several historical works, including Voltaire's *Histoire de Charles XII*. With one exception, and that not worthy of note, none of these translations ever passed beyond the stage of manuscript. The academy, never very active, was dissolved in 1863. (See *EI*², Andjuman.)

adopted his classification. The last official historiographer 'Abdurraḥmān Sheref (1833–1925) wrote an Ottoman history for secondary schools (*Tārīkh-i devlet-i 'osmaniyye*, 2 vols., Istanbul, A.H. 1309–12), and this had its imitators even after the proclamation of the Turkish Republic.

The influence of Western historiography was felt equally in books meant for the general public. The *Netā'ij al-vuqū'āt* by Muṣṭafā Nūrī Pasha (1824–90) appeared in 1877; this is a work of synthesis on Ottoman history, which seeks to determine the causes and consequences of events (4 vols., Istanbul, A.H. 1294–1327). The author gave prominence to imperial institutions and economic problems. It is rather difficult to decide how the writer, who neither visited Europe nor knew any European language,[8] was led to adopt so scientific a method. Might it be that he had the happy notion of combining Aḥmed Vefīq Pasha's classification with Jevdet Pasha's analytical procedure? At all events, although it contains many mistakes, Muṣṭafā Nūrī Pasha's writing marks a distinct stage in modern Turkish historiography.

European methodology favoured the development of branches of history not hitherto in favour. Local history, previously restricted to the lives of a locality's famous men, was more and more devoted to a study of the past events of a region or town. The history of Trebizond by Shākir Shevket (*Trabzon tārīkhi*, 2 vols., Istanbul, A.H. 1294), of Mecca and Medina by Eyyūb Ṣabrī Pasha (d. 1890) (*Mir'āt al-ḥaremeyn*, 3 vols., Istanbul, A.H. 1306) and finally the *Mir'āt-i Istanbul* (Istanbul, A.H. 1314) by Meḥemmed Ra'īf (d. 1916) are some examples of a genre which was destined to lead to still better works after the Tanzimat period.

Memoirs were almost unknown in traditional historiography. Attempts at these in Turkey were certainly modelled on those written by prominent Europeans. Ẓarīf Pasha (1816–61) seems to have been the first Ottoman statesman to write his memoirs, though they were not intended for publication.[9] The historian and statesman Aḥmed Jevdet Pasha may have had the idea of incorporating his own memoirs in the *Teẕākīr* addressed to his successor as official historiographer, Luṭfī Efendi.[10] The Russo-Turkish War of 1877–78 was the occasion for the appearance of several memoirs. In fact, the Ottoman generals who had held commands in a war which turned out so disastrously for the Empire seized the opportunity to exculpate themselves by giving their own accounts of the events they took part in. Such are the memoirs of Aḥmed Mukhtār Pasha (1832–1919), later published under the title of *Serguzesht-i Ḥayātîmin jild-i s̱ānīsi* (Istanbul, A.H. 1328).

[8] Ali Fuat, 'Mansurî Zade Mustafa Paşa ve Netayicülvukua', *Türk Tarih Encümeni Mecmuasi* (January–August 1929), new series, i, 47.

[9] Enver Ziya Karal published them, with an introduction, in 1940: 'Zarif Paşa'nın hatıratı, *Belleten*, iv, 443–94.

[10] Cf. M. Cavid Baysun, *Cevdet Paşa, Tezakir* 1–12. (Ankara, 1953), Introduction, x.

Those distinctly European off-shoots of history, such as numismatics and sigillography, came to Turkey during the Tanzimat period. The pamphlet on Greek, Roman, and Islamic coins, *'Uyūn al-akhbār fi'l-nuqūd ve'l-āṣār* (Istanbul, A.H. 1279), from the pen of 'Abdullaṭīf Ṣubḥī Pasha (1818–86) had been the sole contribution of its kind.[11]

The final organization of the Imperial Museum of Antiquities at Istanbul in 1881 gave an impetus to the pursuit of these ancillary studies. Ismā'īl Ghālib (1847–95), Meḥemmed Mubārek, and Aḥmed Tevhīd Ulusoy (1868–1940) undertook the preparation of catalogues of Islamic and Turkish coins, published in six volumes (*Meskūkāt-i* [*qadīme-i*] *islāmiyye kataloğu*, Istanbul, A.H. 1309–22). Likewise, the catalogue of leaden seals preserved in the Imperial Museum was published by Halil Edhem Eldem (1861–1938) (*Kurshun Mühür kataloğu, 'Arab ve 'Ajem, Bizantin ve Osmānlı kurshun mühürlerine makhṣūṣ*, Istanbul, A.H. 1321).

European methodology extended to works of reference. Indeed, the historico-geographical encyclopaedia of Shemseddīn Sāmī (1850–1904) was written in imitation of the European ones (*Qāmūs al-a'lām*, 6 vols., Istanbul, A.H. 1306–16). With its subject matter drawn from Oriental and Western sources, this work is even now a practical tool of much use. Pride of place is given to articles relating to Islam and, in particular, to the Ottoman Empire.

The appearance of books owing their inspiration to European ideologies completed the development of modern historiography in the Tanzimat period. After 1860, a group of Turkish intellectuals had come to the conclusion that the creation of an Ottoman nationality was imperative, if the Empire was to be saved from complete dissolution. They aimed at uniting all Muslim communities under the aegis of an Ottoman nation, thereby reacting against the tendency of the Christian communities to separate from the Empire. These intellectuals, the 'Young Ottomans' took up the European idea of nationalism, and opposed Western imperialism in all its forms.

These ideological tendencies are reflected in the work of Namık Kemāl (1840–88). In the *Evrāq-i perīshān*, the first part of which appeared in 1871, he wrote a series of lives of Muslim heroes (Istanbul, A.H. 1288–1305). Here, Saladin, Sultan Meḥemmed II, Sultan Selīm I, and Emīr Nevrūz are vindicated as symbols of a Muslim idealism, of which the finest flower is Ottoman nationalism. His two great defenders of Islam were Saladin and Emīr Nevrūz, the one against Christianity, the other against the heathen Mongols.[12] In his view, Meḥemmed II was the founder of a

[11] Ṣubḥī Pasha had published a short historical work, based on Seleucid and Sasanid coins (*Tekmilet al-'iber* (Istanbul, A.H. 1278)). This book was intended to complete the first two volumes of Ibn Khaldūn's *Kitāb al-'ibar*, previously translated by the writer into Turkish (*Miftāḥ ul-'iber* (Istanbul, A.H. 1276)).

[12] N. Kemāl mentions in his introduction that he wrote the life of Saladin in order to demonstrate the untruth of the charges laid against the Muslim hero in Michaud's *Histoire des Croisades*,

Muslim state on a truly nationalistic basis, a state reinforced when Selīm I seized the Caliphate. Nāmík Kemāl's interpretation of history was thus in line with the feeling of his times. He endowed heroes with political and social intentions inconceivable before the time at which he was writing. All the same, he is perhaps the first historian to bring out the civilizing rôle of Meḥemmed II.[13]

Namík Kemāl's ideas were defined in the Ottoman history which he intended to complete in fourteen volumes. He got as far as 1479, but the printing of the work (begun in 1888) was stopped by the censorship of 'Abd al-Ḥamīd II (new impression: '*Os̱mānlí tārīḵẖi*, 4 vols. Istanbul, A.H. 1326–28). In this last work, the hero cult was pushed to such limits that exaggeration was inevitable.[14] Again, the writer labours to refute Hammer's opinions of persons and events in Ottoman history, which he does on logical rather than documentary grounds.[15] The work has thus acquired a polemical character, and this must cast some doubt on its objectivity.

This 'Ottomanist' ideology inspired but few historical works, nor could it prevent the dislocation of the Empire—both vanished together with the outbreak of World War I. A different ideology, that of 'Turkey for the Turks' was to have a greater influence on the modern Tanzimat historiography of the era.

After 1860, the invasion of Central Asia by Russia directed the attention of some of the Ottoman intellectuals towards those Turkish populations which were falling under the yoke of the common enemy. These peoples were Muslim, and moreover shared the same ethnic origin as the dominant element in the Empire. The study of the history of these Turks revealed to the Ottoman intellectuals a glorious past which had been buried by the traditions of Islam. Gradually there arose a national consciousness, steeped in Turkish history and culture, and distinct from the Ottoman ideology. The pan-Turkist ideas deriving from it met with catastrophe at the end of World War I; but it is no less certain that the new Turkish state which arose on the ruins of the Ottoman Empire drew all its strength from the moderate pan-Turkish ideology.

A strict correlation is to be found between the nationalistic aspirations of the Ottoman intellectuals and the works on Turkish history published during the Tanzimat period. Certainly it was to introduce the intellectuals

of which the translation had just been undertaken. This translation, undertaken by Aḥmed 'Ārifī, Edhem Pertev and 'Alī Fu'ād as a joint enterprise, was never finished, and only a portion of the first volume saw the light (*Emr al-'ajīb fī tārīḵẖ ehl al-ṣalīb* (Istanbul, n.d.)).

[13] Cf. Mehmed Kaplan, 'Namık Kemal ve Fatih', *Istanbul Üniversitesi Edebiyat Fakültesi Türk Dili ve Edebiyati Dergisi* (December, 1954), vi, 80–1.

[14] N. Kemāl assumes the truth of the legend, according to which Ertugrul Bey is supposed to have overcome a Mongol army with his four hundred men (Mehmed Kaplan, *Namık Kemal, hayatı ve eserleri*, thesis (Istanbul, 1948), p. 157).

[15] Kaplan, 'N. Kemal ve Fatih', pp. 81–2.

of the Ottoman Empire to the history of Turkistan, that in 1864 Aḥmed Vefīq Pasha had translated some of the writings of Abu'l-Ghāzī Bahādur Khān (1603–63) from the Chagatay into the Western Turkish dialect, under the style of *Shejere-i evshāl-i turkiyye* (Articles in the newspaper *Taṣvīr-i efkār*, Nos. 131 ff.; subsequently published separately, Istanbul, n.d.)[16]

The Ottoman intellectuals learned much from this work about the later history of the Eastern Turks. For ancient Turkish history they had only to consult those European works which dealt with it. In doing this, they became aware of a national heritage which they deemed worthy of respect. One of them, 'Alī Su'āvī (1839–78) (while in France as a Young-Ottoman refugee), wrote a newspaper article in which he sought to demonstrate the high value of the civilizations created by the Turks, from remotest times. (Article *Türk* in the first number of '*Ulūm*, published at Paris in 1869.) His sole source was the historical introduction to A. Lumley Davids' *Grammar of the Turkish Language*.[17] Of this he made free use, altering at pleasure those ideas which did not agree with his argument.[18]

None the less, Ottoman historians attached more importance to the military and political history of the ancient Turks than to their civilization. For them the essential was to give prominence to the power of Turkish states founded well before the Ottoman Empire. Süleymān Pasha (d. 1892) set his account of the pre-Islamic Turks in the framework of universal history. His work came out in 1876 (*Tārīkh-i 'ālem*, vol. 1: Antiquity, Istanbul, A.H. 1293) and includes a bibliography mentioning the well-known book by de Guignes, of which he makes full use for his chapter devoted to Turkish history.[19]

'Turkist' ideology is still more evident in the book which Nejib Asım Yazıksız (1861–1935) published in 1899, on Turkish general history (*Türk tārīkhi*, Istanbul, A.H. 1316). This was adapted, and largely remodelled from a French work vaunting the heroism of the nomad Turks of Central Asia.[20]

The war period which succeeded the Tanzimat was to prove a severe test for Turkist ideology. It emerged triumphant, if somewhat chastened.

[16] Bahadur Khan's work was not to be published in its entirety until after the Tanzimat period (*Türk shejeresi*, ed. Dr. Riza Nur, (Istanbul, 1925)).

[17] Ottoman intellectuals were not unacquainted with this work, since Fu'ād Pasha and Jevdet Pasha, in the *Qavā'id-i 'oṣmāniyye*, published in 1851, had utilized the French translation, which came out in 1836. However, its historical introduction had met with complete indifference until 1869.

[18] An example is given in Tanpınar, op. cit., p. 220.

[19] The work of de Guignes on the Turks and the Mongols, published in Paris between 1756 and 1758, was subsequently translated into Turkish by Hüseyin Cahid Yalçın, *Hunların, Türklerin, Mogolların ve daha sā'ir Tatarların tārīkh-i 'umūmīsi*, 8 vols. (Istanbul, 1923–5).

[20] This was the book by Léon Cahun, published at Paris in 1896 and entitled *Introduction à l'histoire de l'Asie*.

The historians of the young Republic followed the example of Fuad Köprülü (b. 1890) and concentrated upon the study of ancient Turkish civilization.

It transpires from the above account that the Tanzimat period was one of transition in Ottoman historical writing. The traditional genre did not cease to produce works of note, but Ottoman historians became more and more influenced by modern points of view. Their eyes were turned towards Europe. In fact, there could be no serious work published on Muslim history, when books of universal history were occupied with the past of Western states. This was a change advantageous for Ottoman writing. It was enriched by such new disciplines as memoirs and the ancillary branches of history; moreover, its horizon was extended by the Turkist ideology.

Yet, deficiency in historical criticism was always a blemish shared by all historians of the Tanzimat period. Jevdet Pasha himself is not free from this fault, for his masterly work is lacking in internal criticism. The editions of ancient texts prepared in those times were very defective, too. A superior contribution was not to be expected from writers with no special training; for the most part they were statesmen, generals, or journalists.

With the foundation of the 'Tārikh-i 'Osmānī Enjümeni' in 1911, a new age dawns in Ottoman historiography. The omissions of the previous era are filled in, and full advantage taken of the archives. Henceforth, historical research was to enlist the aid of professionals, some of whom received their training in the Faculty of Letters of the University of Istanbul, founded in 1900.

36. IRANIAN HISTORIOGRAPHY

FIRUZ KAZEMZADEH

Associate Professor of History, Yale University

It would not be an exaggeration to state that over the last generation the influence of the West has utterly changed the nature of Iranian historiography. So great has been the departure from traditional forms that works produced only some thirty or forty years ago seem to belong to another people and another age.

One must admit at the outset that modern Iranian historiography is undistinguished and contributes little that is of scholarly importance. However, the purpose of this brief study is not to pass critical judgement but rather to attempt to show how and to what extent the Iranians have absorbed both the technique and the ideas of their Western fellow-historians.

The abandonment of traditional form and content is revealed dramatically as soon as one begins to compare any nineteenth-century work with any recent publication. The historians of the Qājār period were essentially chroniclers. They described day by day, year by year, either briefly or in great detail, the activities of the Shah, gave dramatic, even if unreliable, accounts of battles and traced the intricacies of court intrigues. Their philosophy was fairly simple. Victories in war, prosperity, security, and order were attributed to the will of God and the wisdom of the sovereign, while defeat, famine, enemy invasion, and natural disasters were blamed on evil fortune or some occult force. The historians of the Qājār period commanded a readable and at times even a distinguished style. History writing was then a branch of literature. If the story read well, was instructive, and, most important of all, pleased the Shah, the author could be justly proud of his efforts.

Contemporary historians set themselves a different task. They still wish to be instructive, and admit this openly, justifying their enterprise in terms of its supposed didactic value. But the similarity ends there. The world of contemporary historians is much more complex, principally because it has been invaded by such Western importations as scientism, nationalism, scepticism, democracy, and, more recently, Marxism.

The influence of the West is clearly manifested in the critical spirit with which modern historians approach old Iranian historiography. In his work on Ancient Iran Ḥusayn Pīrnīyā criticized the *S͟hāhnāma* and other such 'sources' and rejects them, claiming that they are confused and full of errors. This reminds one of the attitudes of some of the nineteenth-century 'scientific' European historians. Pīrnīyā praises Western science for having provided history with such tools as philology and archaeology, tools that have made it possible for the first time to distinguish fable from reality and throw light on Iran's remote past.[1]

European nineteenth-century emphasis on environment is strongly reflected in the above-mentioned work. Pirniyā devotes much space to the discussion of the geographic factors which produced the world's earliest civilizations in the Nile valley and in Mesopotamia.[2] To him geography explains not only the national character of ancient Iranians but even their higher culture. They had to struggle with their rugged physical environment, Pīrnīyā writes, and '. . . struggle and endeavour became a life necessity for Iranian Aryans and so important that it entered their ancient religion'. Thus the differences in the religions of the Aryans of Iran and India are explained in terms of geography and environment.[3]

The influence of the West can also be seen in the sceptical attitude displayed by a number of Iranian historians towards Islam. The latter is not attacked directly but by implication. The Muslim conquest of Iran is usually deplored; the Arabs are often accused of having ruined the glorious civilization of the Sasanid period; the Zoroastrian past is invariably idealized. Usually no attacks are made on the substance of religion but the Muslim clergy is often presented in a most unfavourable light. Thus Ibrāhīm Taymūrī writes, referring to the 'fanatical and uninformed' mullās: 'This group opposed everything new, considering European discoveries harmful to Iran. For the sake of their own interests they kept the people of Iran in ignorance and superstition.'[4] Taymūrī, who is very critical of Nāṣir al-Dīn Shāh, nevertheless sympathizes with his efforts to decrease the power and influence of the mullās and deplores his failure to achieve this end.

Aḥmad Kasravī, a provocative though undisciplined and confused thinker, went much further in his attacks on religion. He even began to question some of the fundamentals of Islam, earning the hatred of the religious fanatics who finally brought about his assassination.

It is usually assumed that contemporary Iranian nationalism is of Western origin. There can be little doubt that Western influences were instrumental in fashioning the type of nationalism which exists in Iran today, but it would be naïve to close one's eyes to its native roots. The sense of nationality, pride in Iran's past, and hopes for her future, love of the Persian language, the consciousness of being a people apart from the Arabs or the Turks, and a conviction of cultural superiority—these are the feelings predating the birth of European nationalism. The importation of

[1] Ḥusayn Pīrnīyā, *Īrān-i bāstān*, second edition (Tehran, 1317), v. 1, p. 62.
[2] Ibid., pp. 24–5. [3] Ibid., p. 153.
[4] Ibrāhīm Taymūrī, '*Aṣr-i bikhabarī yā tārīkh-i imtiyāzāt dar Īrān* (Tehran, 1332), p. 22.

the latter into Iran served only to support and strengthen attitudes and patterns of thought which had already made part of Iranian culture for many centuries. Reading Herder or Fichte, acquiring some familiarity with Bismarck or Garibaldi, an Iranian intellectual had no difficulty reconciling their ideas with his own heritage. Even such nationalistic aberrations as the attempted 'purification' of the Persian language from Arabic loan words could be, and was, justified by invoking the name of Firdawsī and not of any European.[5] The blending of the native and foreign strains of nationalism created a virus of exceptional virulence from which no contemporary Iranian has entirely escaped.

Kasravī came close to being an extreme nationalist. He went so far as to attempt 'pure' Persian, achieving only an artificial and rather unpleasant style. 'Abdallāh Rāzī, the author of a well-known general history of Iran, though a moderate, assumed Iranian nationalism as a constant factor operative throughout Iran's history.[6] Taymūrī's criterion in judging historical personages is strictly nationalistic. Thus the barbarous eunuch, Āghā Muḥammad Khān Qājār, is praised for unifying Iran and restoring her strength. His savagery at Kirmān and Tiflis, the deep wounds he inflicted upon his own people, are apparently forgiven. Farīdūn Ādamiyyat goes even further in his biography of Mīrzā Taqī Khān, the Amīr Kabīr, creating a myth to satisfy nationalist desire for a hero more modern than Anūshirwān or Shah 'Abbās. On the strength of his Anglophobia Mīrzā Taqī Khān is proclaimed a great man, while his friendship with the Russians is passed over in silence.[7]

A good example of extreme nationalism can be seen in Nūrallāh Lārūdī's biography of Nādir Shāh, the nomad highwayman who freed his country from Afghan domination, raised her to power, and then proceeded to ruin her by bleeding her white in a series of useless wars. The book is of no scholarly value, but its violently nationalistic point of view won it the admiration of many Iranian intellectuals.[8] Nādir emerges from its pages as a great hero of whom Iran should be proud. Emotions are aroused, flags wave, swords flash, troops march. The will of God and the inborn heroism of the Iranians are said to have raised Nādir to purge the sacred land from the polluting presence of the barbarous Afghans.

> Iranians, do not forget! We are the sons of the soldiers who, obeying the orders of the King of Kings, and under such commanders as Xerxes, planted the banner of victory over the gates of Athens, the capital of

[5] It is very doubtful that Riżā Shāh or any of his advisers had ever heard of such things as the Pan-German League and its advocacy of the germanization of the German language as early as 1898.

[6] 'Abdallāh Rāzī Hamadānī, *Tārīkh-i Īrān* (Iqbāl, 1317, Tehran).

[7] Farīdūn Ādamiyyat, *Amīr Kabīr va Īrān yā waraqī az tārīkh-i siyāsī-yi Īrān* (Tehran).

[8] Nūrallāh Lārūdī, *Zindagānī-yi Nādir Shāh* (Tehran, 1319). It was highly praised by such writers as Yāsimi, Nafīsī and Shafaq.

Greece . . . We are the sons of soldiers who hunted down Kings and Emperors and threw them in the dust at the feet of their King of Kings![9]

It must be stated immediately that such chauvinistic outbursts are not characteristic of contemporary Iranian historical writing. Rather they represent the extreme to which some historians went, with official encouragement, under the intellectual and emotional impact of the then seemingly triumphant nationalism of Germany and Italy. Most Iranians were far too urbane, far too perceptive and sober to adopt such a tone. It should also be added that no serious Iranian historian has ever entertained racialist views which so often accompanied European nationalism. Perhaps one may hope that Iran's cultural traditions are too universal and generous to permit racism to find a home wherever Persian is spoken.

Whereas European nationalism easily fits into Iran's culture, democracy is totally alien to it. Few Iranian historians have concerned themselves with democracy, which perhaps is due to the nature of their discipline, history being an investigation of the past—not an attempt to peer into the future. The only period in Iran's long history when democracy, or at least some of the institutions associated with popular sovereignty, became a live political issue was the era of the constitutional movement beginning in 1906. The struggle against the Q̱ājārs who were strongly supported by Tsarist Russia, the turmoil, the momentous changes in the system of government, the hope of a brighter future, the sense of doom which overcame the nation when the agreement of 1907 was made public, the overthrow of Muḥammad 'Alī S̲h̲āh, the brutal Russian intervention in the north, all combined to endow the decade preceding the First World War with exceptional interest for the historian. Indeed, there have already appeared several large works covering the Revolution.[10]

Kasravī, himself a participant, devoted to it a large opus, his best.[11] Mahdī Malikzāda wrote a seven-volume History of the Iranian revolution and constitutionalism, a valuable, remarkably reasonable, and unusually well-documented effort.[12] However, Kasravī is not so much interested in democracy as he is in the independence of Iran. For him the Revolution is justified by its goal of making Iran free, strong, and prosperous once more. Individual rights, constitutions, parliaments, even a free press appear, at least by implication, to be sought only as instruments of nationalism. Malikzāda shows relatively more concern for democratic practices and institutions. However, it is quite evident that the impact of democratic

[9] Lārūdī, op. cit.

[10] E. G. Browne's book was written with such sympathy for Iran that one is tempted to include him among Iranian historians of the Revolution.

[11] Aḥmad Kasravī, *Tārīk̲h̲-i mas̲h̲ruṭa-yi Īrān*, second edition (Tehran, 1333).

[12] Mahdī Malikzāda, *Tārīk̲h̲-i inqilāb va mas̲h̲rūṭiyyat-i Īrān* (Tehran, n.d.), 7 vv.

ideas upon Iranian historians has been minor compared to the tremendous impact of nationalism.

Marxism, which has only recently begun to interest certain Iranian intellectuals, has not yet been reflected in any histories known to me. Perhaps the emphasis on British and Russian economic interests in Iran in Taymūrī's History of concessions in Iran[13] could be attributed to Marxian influence, but then one would have to admit that it was neither deep nor very obvious. The absence of outright Marxist histories is probably due more to political conditions in the country than to anything else.

Western influence can be traced not only in the realm of ideas with which Iranian historians interpret the past but also to their selection of subjects to be investigated. Few, if any, continue to chronicle the deeds of kings. Most look at a vaster scene. Kasravī, Malikzāda, and others who deal with the history of the Revolution, make at least some attempt to penetrate the surface of events and discover their underlying causes. Some investigate military history, while others do research in local history. Diplomatic history has attracted its share of attention. Maḥmūd Maḥmūd wrote a monumental History of Anglo-Iranian diplomatic relations in the nineteenth century.[14]

Modern techniques of historical research and writing are another importation from the West. Though some Iranian historians apparently have not yet become convinced of the desirability of documenting their statements, many are beginning to adopt the paraphernalia of Western scholarship. The works of Pīrnīyā, Taymūrī, Maḥmūd, and others, are carefully footnoted, provided with bibliographical information and acknowledgements of sources. Both Taymūrī and Maḥmūd go so far in their quest for authenticity as to reproduce photostatically a large number of documents on the pages of their books. All of this inevitably leads to greater accuracy and reliability and eventually may create a healthy respect for facts. Here Western influence has been entirely positive.

One hesitates to blame the West for the clearly evident deterioration of Persian style. Perhaps schools are not teaching the classics as well as they did a hundred years ago, or perhaps the dull jargon of modern Western social scientists has something to do with it, but not one of the books mentioned in this paper could compare in literary quality with that old, biased, inaccurate, unscientific, yet polished *Nāsikh al-tavārīkh*. Contemporary prose is drab, inelegant, and at times reminiscent of second-rate translations from a foreign language which some of it may very well be in fact.

[13] Cf. n. 4 *supra*.

[14] Maḥmūd Maḥmūd, *Tārīkh-i ravābiṭ-i siyāsī-yi Īrān va-Inglīs dar qarn-i nuzdahum-i mīlādī* (Tehran, from 1328 on), 10 vv.

37. DEVELOPMENT IN ARAB HISTORIOGRAPHY AS REFLECTED IN THE STRUGGLE BETWEEN 'ALĪ AND MU'ĀWIYA

N. A. FARIS

Professor of Arab History in the American University of Beirut

The fateful struggle between 'Alī and Mu'āwiya still agitates the minds of Muslims, scholars and non-scholars alike. Attention has been centred, for the most part, on that most controversial and, indeed, most confused incident of the arbitration. What happened then split the community once and for ever into the two major sects of Islam, the Sunnites and the Shi'ites. It also divided Arab chroniclers. For better or worse, no clear-cut record of the Umayyad position reached us; all the major early historians reflect Shi'ite leanings in varying degrees. Al-Dīnawarī (d. 282/985) is Persian-minded; al-Ya'qūbī (d. 284/897) is an out-and-out Shi'ite; al-Ṭabarī (310/923) is a little more moderate; and al-Mas'ūdī (345/956), perhaps because of his Mu'tazilite connections, is not free of Shi'ite bias.

All these writers flourished during the heyday of the 'Abbasids. Obviously they could not very well take the side of the Umayyads. At the same time it would have proved equally embarrassing to defend the 'Alid claims. A scapegoat had to be found, without, however, impugning the legitimacy of the Umayyad caliphate, as to question the Umayyad position would certainly lead to questioning the 'Abbasid as well. Better therefore to accept the legitimacy of the position of both 'Alī and Mu'āwiya and blame the whole tragedy on the cunning of 'Amr b. al-'Āṣ, and accuse Mu'āwiya only of 'changing the caliphate from a theocracy to a temporal state', just as Samuel did in the case of Saul.[1] The over-simplification is obvious.

A study of these sources[2] shows agreement on the cause of the conflict: Mu'āwiya's failure to swear allegiance to the new caliph, 'Alī, whom he accused of encouraging the rebels to kill 'Uthmān and of harbouring the criminals after they had performed their bloody deed, and 'Alī's insistence on extracting Mu'āwiya's allegiance at the point of the sword. They also agree that when the tide of battle finally turned against the Syrians, the situation was saved for Mu'āwiya by 'Amr's suggestion to raise copies of the Qur'ān on the spear shafts and call for arbitration by the Word of God. The raising of the Qur'āns should not necessarily be taken literally but

[1] I Sam. xii, 12.

[2] Dīnawarī, *al-Akhbār al-ṭiwāl*, ed. V. Guirgass (Leiden, 1888), pp. 149–232; Ya'qūbī, *Ta'rikh*, ed. M. Th. Houtsma (Leiden, 1883), ii, 218 ff.; Ṭabarī, *Ta'rikh al-rusul wa'l-mulūk*, ed. M. J. de Goeje and others (Leiden, 1898), vi, 3138–76; Mas'ūdī, *Murūj al-dhahab*, ed. C. Barbier de Meynard and Pavet de Courteille (Paris, 1914), iv, 304–41.

perhaps metaphorically, meaning a call for arbitration by appealing to the word of God. The point which was to be subject to arbitration was not which of the two men should be the rightful caliph but rather what was the verdict of the Qur'ān regarding the surrender of the murderers of 'Uthmān. Nevertheless, all the sources seem to bury this most important point amid a great deal of words and then proceed as though Abū Mūsā al-Ash'arī and 'Amr b. al-'Āṣ were named arbiters with terms of reference to select the next caliph. How this sudden shift took place is difficult to determine and more difficult to believe. Very likely nothing of the sort ever happened. What probably happened was that the truce arrived at to arbitrate the main cause of contention, namely the apprehension and the surrender of the murderers of 'Uthmān, split the followers of 'Alī with the result that he never again was able to resume the battle against Mu'āwiya. All subsequent accounts of the incident are nothing but an attempt to vindicate 'Alī and explain his unexpected and, to them, much regretted failure.

The sources state that 'Amr b. al-'Āṣ was fully aware of the trap he had fixed for 'Alī by suggesting that the controversy should be settled by arbitration according to the Qur'ān. He is reported to have said 'if 'Alī should accept the arbitration his followers would disperse, and if he should reject it, they would accuse him of unbelief'. In either case he was sure to lose. The other mistake 'Alī committed, which was perhaps the most damaging to his cause, was his failure to insist on keeping his rightful title in the document of arbitration, and allowing it to be dropped, against the explicit warnings of his advisers. As a face-saving device, which proved utterly useless, the example of the Prophet's usage in the Pact of al-Ḥudaybiyya was cited, if not by 'Alī himself, by his later partisans and apologists. By so doing he reduced his own position from that of a duly elected caliph to a mere claimant. And herein lies the secret in the sudden shift from an arbitration regarding the apprehension and surrender of the murderers of 'Uthmān to one the implied purpose of which was to determine who of the contenders should be caliph.[3]

All subsequent Arab historians reproduce in some form or another what the earlier historians had recorded, with the Sunnite group regretting the alleged trick of 'Amr b. al-'Āṣ but not casting any shadow of a doubt on the legitimacy of Mu'āwiya's caliphate, while the Shi'ite group follow in the main two schools of thought: a moderate one representing the bulk of the Shi'ites, and an extremist one representing the *ghulāt* or the *rāfiḍa*. The former also blames 'Amr b. al-'Āṣ for the fraud at the arbitration, but accepts the legitimacy of Mu'āwiya's caliphate, in whose favour al-Ḥasan is supposed to have abdicated.[4] The latter rejects not only the legitimacy

[3] Ṭabarī, vi, 3329–35.

[4] Ibn al-Ṭiqṭaqa, *al-Fakhrī fi'l-ādāb al-sulṭāniyya* (Cairo, 1339), p. 73.

of Mu'āwiya's caliphate but also the legitimacy of the caliphates of Abū Bakr, 'Umar and 'Uthmān.

Arab historical writings continued to echo these positions down to our own day. In the meantime Sunnī-Shi'ite schism continues to divide the Muslim community. From the tenth Christian century to the middle of the twentieth, political, social, and economic factors have contributed to the widening of the doctrinal and emotional gulf which separates the two groups and to the persistence of the argument. In 1957, Muḥammad al-Khāliṣī, a very well-known Shi'ite religious leader in Baghdād, lost the greater part of his following and influence simply because he advocated that Shi'ites revert in their call for prayer to the practice of the Prophet and therefore omit from the *ādhān* the words '*wa-anna 'Aliyyan waliyyu'llāh*' ('and that 'Alī is the friend of God'). A discussion of these factors, however, is outside the scope of this paper. Nevertheless these factors remain important in determining the attitude and the approach of modern Arab historians to this vexing issue between 'Alī and Mu'āwiya. One discreet Sunnite writer, residing at the time of writing in Baghdād, found it more convenient to dismiss the whole unsavoury episode with a few cursory paragraphs, both to insure the sale of the book in Iraq and to avoid contributing anything which might weaken the solidarity of the *Umma.*[5]

Leading modern Arab historians writing in Arabic, however, still follow the tradition of al-Ṭabarī and the other early historians. An examination of al-Khuḍarī's *Muḥāḍarāt ta'rīkh al-umam al-islāmiyya*[6] shows little departure from early Arab historians. Al-Khuḍarī accepts al-Mas'ūdī's account that Abū Mūsā al-Ash'arī and 'Amr b. al-'Āṣ had agreed to depose both 'Alī and Mu'āwiya and had embodied their decision in a signed document, but he rejects the alleged deception by 'Amr on the ground that the terms of reference stipulated that the community would be bound only by a verdict on which both arbiters agreed. For 'Amr to go back on the agreement and confirm Mu'āwiya would have been denounced as fraud and would not have been binding on the faithful anyway. At the same time al-Khuḍarī would have us accept a speech in which 'Alī is supposed to have stated that the two arbiters had disagreed and failed to reach any agreement.[7] Like all early Arab historians, he personalizes the whole conflict between 'Alī and Mu'āwiya, explaining it all on the basis of the personal antipathies and ambitions of the two major contenders.[8]

Another leading historian, Ḥasan Ibrāhīm Ḥasan,[9] adheres more or less to the traditional account of the early historians without attempting to explain some of the obvious difficulties. He, however, defends Abū Mūsā against his early and modern detractors who had levelled against him the

[5] Darwīsh al-Miqdādī, *Ta'rīkh al-umma al-'arabiyya* (Baghdād, 1931), pp. 257–60.
[6] iii (Cairo, 1354), 66–79. [7] Ibid., p. 74. [8] Ibid., p. 52.
[9] *Ta'rīkh al-Islām al-siyāsī*, second edition (Cairo, 1948), i, 286–9.

charge of gullibility and shortsightedness, and believes that Abū Mūsā acted with good faith and deliberation when he agreed to a decision unfavourable to ʿAlī and the Hashimites.[10] It may not be far amiss, however, to state that this readiness, on the part of Arab historians, to exonerate Abū Mūsā stems from the larger predilection, common to practically all later Arab historians, to revere and venerate the Fathers (*al-salaf al-ṣāliḥ*) in general and the Companions in particular, simply because they were Companions. Unlike the Disciples of Jesus, the Companions of the Prophet, if we are to believe Arab historians, produced no Iscariots.

For the last hundred and sixty years, however, the Arab East has felt the inroads of westernization in almost every walk of life. Modern writers are fond of dwelling on the material aspects of these inroads, often neglecting the more profound and more important intellectual aspect of the problem. This is in part the result of at least two factors: in the first place, it is easier to observe and to enumerate the material and physical inroads and to assess their far-reaching influence on Arab values and behaviour; in the second place the Arabs themselves often resisted and tried to reject the intellectual principles which lay at the base of the material. It is still held by many that the Arabs can accept the results of science without necessarily accepting all their intellectual implications. Nevertheless, western principles and methods of historical criticism have been able to find their way into the writings of some Arab historians and scholars. More and more these modern Arab scholars are paying added attention to the hitherto neglected social and economic factors surrounding early Muslim society. At least two main trends can be detected. The first emphasizes the Umayyad dynasty as the prototype of an Arab national state. This was particularly popular in the thirties of this century, and represents the conscious effort of Arab thinkers to lay the intellectual foundation of Arab nationalism.[11] The second is more recent and endeavours to idealize early Muslim leaders, particularly ʿUmar, ʿAlī, and other Companions known for their piety, and see in their lives the mainsprings and sum total of modern liberal ideals of social justice and democracy.[12] Among the best representative of this movement have been the famous Egyptian scholar and bellelettrist, Ṭāhā Ḥusayn, and an Iraqi Shiʿite sociologist, ʿAlī al-Wardī. Their approach to, and treatment of, the struggle between ʿAlī and Muʿāwiya offer a good example of the development of Arab historiography during the last few decades.

[10] Ibid., p. 289.

[11] See ʿAbd al-ʿAzīz al-Dūrī, *Muqaddima fī taʾrīkh ṣadr al-Islām* (Baghdād, 1949); Darwīsh al-Miqdādī, op. cit.

[12] See ʿAbbās Maḥmūd al-ʿAqqād, *ʿAbqariyyat al-Ṣiddīq* (Cairo, 1943); *ʿAbqariyyat ʿUmar* (Cairo, 1942); *ʿAbqariyyat al-Imām* (Cairo, 1943); Muṣṭafā Sādiq al-Rāfiʿī, *Waḥy al-qalam* (Cairo, 1936–41; Sayyid Quṭb, *al-ʿAdāla al-ijtimāʿiyya fīʾl-Islām* (Cairo, n.d.); George Jurdāq, *al-Imām ʿAlī: ṣawt al-ʿadāla al-ijtimāʿiyya* (Beirut, 1956).

Ṭāhā Ḥusayn is a very difficult man to evaluate. In some respects he has been overrated; in others his contribution has not yet been fully recognized. For the last three decades, his influence has been felt throughout the Arab world. He has been a pioneer in the field of historical criticism, a promoter of classical and European studies, a champion of compulsory education, and an ardent defender of academic freedom. 'Alī al-Wardī's career is still unfolding, but in spite of his being what might be called a 'beginner', he has already made a name for himself as an inconoclast and has aroused the hostility of conservatives, Shi'ite, and Sunnite alike. Each one of his five books[13] has elicited from his detractors an average of three works of rebuttal. Unfortunately, his keen observation and insight are somewhat marred by his undue use of sarcasm and by his insufficient care in the organization of his material. Nevertheless, his works make profitable and entertaining reading.

The struggle between 'Alī and Mu'āwiya is discussed by Ṭāhā Ḥusayn in the first two volumes of his *al-Fitna al-kubrā*,[14] particularly the second. But the material presented in the first is equally indispensable for a thorough understanding of the thesis. Wardī treats of the struggle first in his *Wu''āẓ al-salāṭīn*[15] and then in his *Mahzalat al-'aql al-bas̲h̲arī.*[16]

Of the two men, Ṭāhā Ḥusayn should be considered the precursor. But his verbose essayist style sometimes tends to conceal his thesis. Perhaps this is not fully unintentional. Wardī, on the other hand, is more direct, and being a trained sociologist, has brought to the discussion some very valuable considerations.

As they see it, the struggle between 'Alī and Mu'āwiya cannot be rightly understood without going back to the deeper causes of the conflict. The murder of 'Ut̲h̲mān in itself is an insufficient explanation, since it needs itself an explanation. One has to go back to the *Jāhiliyya* days and to the rôle the Umayyads played in Meccan society. Qurays̲h̲ enjoyed commercial hegemony over the tribes, but the Umayyads were supreme among Qurays̲h̲. The teaching of Islam ran counter to their economic interests and threatened their future with disaster. It was only natural for them to be the first to fight Muḥammad and the last to accept him, in spite of the close kinship which linked them to him. On the other hand, there seemed to have been no chance for Islam to endure without bringing Qurays̲h̲ to terms, some way or another. They had to be won over to the new order, either as followers or as partners. The Prophet solved the problem by reconciling the hearts of some of the most stubborn enemies of Islam,[17] the most prominent of whom was Abū Sufyān, the paramount Umayyad,

[13] *S̲h̲ak̲h̲ṣiyyat al-fard al-'irāqī* (Bag̲h̲dād, 1951); *K̲h̲awāriq al-lās̲h̲u'ūr* (Bag̲h̲dād, 1952); *Wu''āẓ al-salāṭīn* (Bag̲h̲dād, 1954); *Mahzalat al-'aql al-bas̲h̲arī* (Bag̲h̲dād, 1955); *Usṭūrat al-adab al-rafī'* (Bag̲h̲dād, 1957).

[14] i, '*Ut̲h̲mān* (Cairo, 1947); ii, '*Alī* (Cairo, 1953).

[15] Op cit., pp. 31–53, 112–241.

[16] Op. cit., pp. 368–32.

[17] *Sūra* 9, 60.

and by incorporating into Islam those pre-Islamic institutions most dear to the Meccan oligarchy, and bestowing on them Muslim significance. The first two caliphs made use of Umayyad talents in administration and military leadership since they were the only Meccans with such experience. So long as Abū Bakr and ʿUmar lived, however, the Umayyads were not able to recapture their former position. They were thwarted not only by the first two caliphs but also by the new aristocracy of Islam, whose nobility rested on ability, piety, loyal service to the new faith, and personal acquaintance with the Prophet and his usage. Converts to Islam in general, and from the various Arab tribes in particular, were reluctant to acknowledge any nobility except that of Islam, and Arabian Muslims were too conscious of their indispensable rôle in the conquests. In ʿUmar's own words, they were 'the main stay of Islam'. But with the death of ʿUmar and the election of ʿUthmān, the way was open for the revival of the old pagan aristocracy and the resurgence of its norms.

The reign of ʿUthmān was mainly occupied with the struggle of these 'aristocracies', the old aristocracy of pagan Mecca and the new aristocracy of Islam. The old aristocracy was predatory and viewed the new state and the conquered territories as their milch-cow; the new aristocracy thought in terms of a communal state, from the revenue of which every member was entitled to receive what was sufficient to meet his needs. The old aristocracy was intent on reviving the old order; the new aristocracy was deadly serious about the brotherhood of Islam and the equality of all Muslims; the only claim to distinction being in the field of piety. In fact it was a struggle between fundamentalism and virtual apostasy. The strong hand of ʿUmar was able to restrain the old aristocracy, and keep most of the Quraysh leadership virtually under forced residence in Medina, to forestall their possible abuse of their economic power over the conquered territories. ʿUthmān all but turned the temple over to the money changers. If Islam had been confined to Mecca and Medina, the Umayyad aristocracy, in all likelihood, would have prevailed. But with hordes of commoners embracing the new faith and expecting equal rights within the new dispensation, ʿUthmān and his Umayyad group had no chance. To make matters worse, the new aristocracy was led by ʿAlī and others like Abū Dharr, that articulate advocate of economic equality, and ʿAmmār b. Yāsir, an extreme proponent of equality within the faith and of the nobility of the pious. It must also be pointed out that leadership in Iraq was for the most part drawn from the religious classes (the Qur'ān readers), while in Syria Muʿāwiya had already, during twenty years of rule, built up a close-knit following which accepted Umayyad hegemony. The victory of ʿAlī and his religious supporters might mean a reversion to the strict and austere rule of ʿUmar.

ʿUthmān was getting on in years. His most likely successor was ʿAlī.

The Umayyads had to devise a way to forestall this dreaded event at any cost. Why not have 'U<u>th</u>mān assassinated and lay the crime on the person who would stand to benefit the most by his death, i.e. 'Alī?

According to Wardī, it was the Umayyads who engineered the murder of 'U<u>th</u>mān, with Mu'āwiya instigating the murder and Marwān working out the details.[18] As keeper of the caliph's seal, no one else could have written that letter which ordered the governor of Egypt to have the leaders of the rebellion killed, those same leaders to whom the caliph had already promised redress and pardon.

The struggle between the old aristocracy and the new was resumed after the death of 'U<u>th</u>mān. While the fundamentalists were busy arguing their religious points, the Umayyads were 'reconciling hearts' to their cause, including that of 'Alī's own brother. Even then, 'Alī was able to draw them to battle and almost defeated them. Once again the old aristocracy was able to save its skin by giving the fundamentalists still another issue to debate, another controversy over which to disagree. This was the appeal to arbitration. Their stratagem worked. With his own followers divided over religious and legal minutiae, 'Alī was never again able to resume his offensive against the Umayyads. His assassination made their military and political victory complete. To win the ideological victory as well, they proceeded to slander the memory of 'Alī and to emphasize alleged differences between him and 'Umar. In order to discredit him further, they made the Shi'ite movement a conspiracy against Islam, engineered by the Jewish convert 'Abdallāh b. Saba', who was alleged to have been an ardent follower of 'Alī. Both Ṭāhā Ḥusayn and Wardī, marshalling a great deal of impressive historical evidence, deny the existence of Ibn Saba' and make him the creation of Umayyad propaganda. The old aristocracy was back in the saddle. Their victory marks the final defeat of the new aristocracy of Islam. This is, after all, what the oft-repeated charge of the dispossessed that Mu'āwiya changed the caliphate of prophecy into a temporal state means. This is what it should mean.

Arnold Toynbee has stated that Islam came to an end with the Hijra. It is perhaps more accurate to state with Wardī that Islam came to an end with 'U<u>th</u>mān. 'Alī attempted a restoration but failed. Mu'āwiya built his Arab Empire on the ruins of Islam and the skulls of its new aristocracy.

[18] *Wu''āẓ al-salāṭīn*, p. 217.

38. REACTIONS TO WESTERN POLITICAL INFLUENCES IN 'ALĪ AḤMAD BĀKAT̲H̲ĪR'S DRAMA

UMBERTO RIZZITANO

Professor of Arabic Language and Literature in the University of Palermo

My aim in giving this paper on the reactions to western political influences in 'Alī Aḥmad Bākat̲h̲īr's drama, is to supply Near and Middle East non-orientalist historians with a documentation which they most probably do not know, this being additional data to the political and historical publications to which they generally refer. All these have, in fact, never permitted anyone to penetrate the soul of a people, to fathom what is at the bottom of a movement for independence or a nationalistic exasperation, or even to foresee the reactions of the masses to western policies regarding one or the other of the Near Eastern countries; although this is most important to western politicians.

No research work on the ancient and modern history of the Arab peoples, no study on western policy in the Near East can pretend to be exhaustive if its author neglects to know the soul of these peoples, as well as the limits and the aspects of what is called the 'conscience of the masses', which the writers try to present to us through their novels, poems, and dramas. This literary production is the true and precious auxiliary to history and, if it is unable to explain and show everything, it nevertheless illuminates, in many cases, facts which without it would seem obscure and it sometimes reveals to us the psychological reactions which the chronicles completely ignore. How many times the lecturer and no doubt some of the audience also, change an opinion on questions of Arab national or international policy after having attended a theatre show such as: 'The Struggle of the people' (*Kifāḥ al-s̲h̲aʿb*), 'The Prophet's Banner' (*al-Bayraq al-nabawī*), or of Bākat̲h̲īr's amusing comedy 'Juḥā's Nail' (*Mismār Juḥā*).[1]

The field chosen by Arab writers in Egypt, in the recent past as well as in modern times, to develop their ideas on national demands, is the narrative and the drama. The birth of Arab drama dates from the second half of the last century. At the same epoch, Arab actors from the Lebanon, where since 1847 Mārūn al-Naqqās̲h̲ had begun to acquaint the Lebanese public with this type of show, were encouraged to come to Cairo. At the

---

[1] The same opinions have already been expressed by colleagues such as Bernard Lewis in D. Sinor, ed., *Orientalism and History* (Cambridge, 1954, pp. 30-1, Cl. Cahen in 'Histoire economique et sociale de l'Orient musulman médiéval', *Studia Islamica* (1955), iii, 93-115, and F. Gabrieli in 'La storia moderna dei popoli arabi', *Relazioni del X Congresso Internazionale di Scienze storiche* (Roma, 4-11 Sett., 1955; Firenze, 1955), pp. 275-7.

beginning they had necessarily to limit their activities to the imitation of French productions, but, as soon as the Arab writers realized the importance of the theatre they leaned towards historical and political events such as the Crusades, Bonaparte's Expedition, 'Urābī's revolution in Egypt and so forth. Since then, the stage began to form a most adaptable link between the masses and their past and present. Today the best Egyptian theatre writers continue in this line, and if Maḥmūd Taymūr and 'Azīz Abāẓa dedicated themselves to the reconstruction of the past (the former through realistic drama; the latter through tragedy in verses), Tawfīq al-Ḥakīm thought of reducing to amusing sketches, certain phases of Egyptian contemporary and political life; others still, like Bākathīr, tried to interpret the reactions of the Arab people to foreign influences in the Near East.

The analysis of some of this young author's plays is my object here, but, my aim being limited to the historical contents of the play and to the didactic aim of the author, I shall avoid giving my personal opinion from a technical and ethical point of view as this would not be in the author's favour.

In these last few years, the efforts of the most sensitive of the Arab writers in Egypt have been concentrated on the Palestinian problem, which could have been resolved in the light of a more abundant moral and ethical documentation, if the representatives of international politics could have seen plays such as 'The Palestinian Veterans' (*al-'Ā'idūn min Filasṭīn*), 'The Zionist' (*al-Ṣahyūnī*), or 'al-Falūja'—the well-known centre of the useless Arab resistance—which, apart from their substantial value, are the sources of a documentation, unfortunately reserved to the *élite* of arabists, but which, on the contrary, should always form part of the reports which reach various Foreign Ministries.

In modern Egypt, the author, who through drama is able to express his ideas and those, I imagine, of his fellow citizens regarding western policy or, should I say, British policy towards the Near East in general, is Bākathīr, a Muslim (Ḥaḍramawṭī father and Indonesian mother) who emigrated, first to Indonesia then to the Ḥijāz, and finally to Egypt, where he is now a government official.

The dramaturge has come to the field of drama, which may be classified as memorialist and polemicist, after having spent an apprenticeship in other theatrical sections: the allegory in *Shehrazade*, the destiny of men in *King Œdipus*, the historical reconstruction in *Akhnaton and Nefertiti*, the comedy of manners, and so forth; and it is above all the atmosphere of exasperation created by Western influence in the Middle and Near East which activates his pen and increases his fruitfulness, showing his feelings which grow from his well accentuated, ardent and somewhat exalted Arabism.

Before, however, undertaking the analysis of the three dramas in question and in order to define my position towards these, I have to underline the fact that I shall limit any references to Bākathīr's dramas by sticking faithfully to his description of political events and politicians, never deviating from the well-known Latin saying, *relata refero*.

Bākathīr's work is very vast in the field of the plays already referred to before but quantity does not always equal quality, this is why I shall choose only three of his productions; honour of precedence being given to *Mismār Juḥā* (Juḥā's Nail), a character who was placed in the centre of Arab ludicrousness and of oriental humour, and to whom Bākathīr, in his scenic arrangements, leaves his well-known sagacious characteristic, giving him the additional merit of organizing a revolution which will culminate in the evacuation of foreign armies from Iraq. Behind 'Iraq' hides without much disguise, Egypt; behind 'foreign troops', British soldiers who occupied the Canal since 1882. But in order to understand his reference to the 'Nail' it is indispensable to say something.

Juḥā, who in the first place was the *imām* of a mosque at Kūfa and later became chief judge of Baghdād, is introduced to us concealing in his inner soul the desire to be useful to his country and to his fellow citizens, who for years have borne the sufferings caused by foreign occupation. It is not for him, of course, to take the lead of a people but rather, to think of a subtle way which would honour his fame. Nothing is easier for a character, introduced by oriental traditions as the symbol of craftiness and deceit, to find a way to rouse the people or rather to show the people undisguisedly the disasters due to foreign occupation. But, being unable, in view of his official position, to act in a direct way, he will make of his nephew Ḥammād his catspaw; this same Ḥammād, who after Juḥā's resignation as *imām*, had advised him to dedicate himself to agriculture by purchasing a piece of land with the proceeds of the sale of his house. They immediately agree. But Juḥā must, in the first place, give the house to Ḥammād in order to make him, rather than the judge, responsible for the trap which is hidden behind this sale. It is proposed to sell this house to a certain Ghānim, on the condition that a nail should be struck in the wall, giving the owner of the nail the right to enter at any time. This does not seem to have any great importance to the buyer, who never thought for one moment that such a small nail could put his newly purchased house to the entire disposal of Ḥammād. The latter became a very regular visitor, much to the dislike of the buyer, and they soon went to court, where they were compelled to submit to the wisdom of Juḥā, the chief judge of Baghdād. The hearing is presided over by the foreign military governor, who mentioned that the fault was Juḥā's for allowing this case to lie idle for seventy days, thus permitting such a trifle to develop into such large proportions, dividing the country into two parts. The moment came for Juḥā's first attack. Shouting to the governor that such cases lay idle without a solution for seventy years, and to the public, who were insisting that Ḥammād should extract the nail, the judge expresses surprise and disappointment to see his fellow citizens insisting on such a trifle as a small nail and completely ignoring the huge nail which has for so many years been stuck in their country. He then shouts to them, 'Order this foreign gentleman to extract this nail straightaway, or hasten to extract it yourselves.' At this, the governor realizes that he is in the midst of a revolution, roused by Juḥā who, arrested, leaves the Court singing:

> 'O, owner of the nail, draw this nail
> From the house of the free people
> As it is not your house.'

A few days later he received the visit of the governor in prison; he needed Juḥā's prestige to quell the rebellion, otherwise he would lose his job. Juḥā seizes this opportunity to dictate his conditions, which consist in the total and immediate evacuation of foreign troops from the country. Bākathīr ought to be doubly satisfied, to have given us a play, successful from a stage point of view and the characters (it was shown several times on the stage in Egypt and was chosen for a cinematographic adaptation), and at the same time to have foreseen a political situation some time prior to its realization.

A connoisseur of Shakespeare's plays (he translated *Romeo and Juliet* into Arabic) Bākathīr is inspired for his second play by *The Merchant of Venice*, and it is mainly the conditions imposed by Shylock the Jew to Antonio the merchant, guarantor of a loan with interest, which gives the dramatist the idea for the title and action of his new play *Shylock al-jadīd* ('The new Shylock')—let us remember these conditions:

> '. . . and in a merry sport,
> If you repay me not on such a day,
> In such a place, such sum or sums, as are
> Express'd in the conditions, let the forfeit
> Be nominated for an equal pound
> Of your fair flesh, to be cut off and taken
> In what part of your body pleaseth me . . .'

Antonio's body represents, in Bākathīr's artistic arrangement, the entire Arab States; the pound of flesh, Palestine, and the agreement between both characters, the 1917 Balfour Declaration, which is at the bottom of the creation of the Jewish Home. The Arab author's play takes place in Palestine and like Shakespeare's play is divided into two parts. In the first, entitled *al-Mushkila* ('The Problem'), Shylock is at the head of Palestinian Zionist activities which group around it a certain number of characters: Rachel, the deceitful and 'coquette' mistress of 'Abdallāh al-Fayyāḍ (nephew of Kāẓim Bey, an ardent Arab nationalist), Cohen, one of the most famous lawyers of his time, Jack, Chief of the Purchasing Committee, in charge of buying Arab land, and Benjamin who is at the head of Zionist propaganda. On the Arab side we have representatives of the most ardent anti-Zionist Arab Jews. The action, in his first part takes place among the frantic Zionist activities which aim at the expropriation of Arab lands. In their transactions they are helped by Rachel, their emissary, who makes use of her charms to get 'Abdallāh to sell his immense lands. We have, at this stage, to mention that 'Abdallāh is engaged to be married to Nādia, who lives in Cairo where she is studying and whom we shall meet again in the closing act, as a lawyer of the Arab cause. Nothing remarkable to add to these first scenes which are characterized by the various activities of both parties who are preparing to meet, or rather to clash, in the second part of the play, which is entitled, in too optimistic a manner, *al-Ḥall* ('The Solution').

Bākathīr now takes us to Palestine, in a Palestinian Court of Justice (note that the author does not fix the epoch of the case and limits himself to 'In the future'), where the twelve members of the International Commission of Arbitration are assembled, invited by the mandatory power to find a solution to the Palestinian problem. The other characters are those I have already mentioned. We are now watching one of the final acts in Court, in full Shakespearean atmosphere. In fact, the representative of the mandatory power concentrates the argument on one of the new Shylock phrases, 'You English, promised us a pound of flesh. Give it to us.' One can easily imagine the reactions of the Arab delegates and their furious attacks against the representatives of the International Commission, savagely conducted by Mīkhā'īl al-Jadd who, in a long speech—too long in my opinion for a theatrical show—gives a history of the birth and development of the question of the Jewish Home, underlining the political and military reasons which are at the bottom of the strange conduct of the mandatory power towards the Arabs.

We have now reached the last act of the second part of the play, which shows the participation of 'Urābī Pasha in the Arbitration Commission, convened this time by the desperate call of the Israelis who are at the end of their economic resistance. In fact, the pitiless boycott of the united Arab peoples compels them, according to the author's utopia, to seek the help of foreign powers, who will discuss the 'liquidation' of Israel. Regarding the punishment of the guilty, the Court returns once again to Shakespeare and to the sanctions he inflicted upon his hero, Shylock. It is above all 'Urābī Pasha who invites the Assembly to this analogical system. Bākathīr does not limit himself to these details, in the imitation of Shakespeare's drama, but he pushes his analogy between his play and the English one, up to the final act where he introduces Nādia, quite as Shakespeare's

Portia in *The Merchant of Venice.* The Court decides upon the sanctions against the Zionists, but Shylock, who follows the various Arab proposals, cannot survive, and commits suicide. The debates in Court are slightly tiresome but, one is however interested by the variety of proposals expressed by the different elements of Arab society today as represented by Bākathīr. His drama really aims at giving us to understand, that the solution of the grave Near and Middle Eastern problems necessitates the listening to many voices: the voice of the old Arab leading classes ('Urābī Pasha), of the new generation (Nādia, 'Abdallāh, and Fayṣal), of the nationalistic exasperation, and lastly of the Christian and Jewish minorities who live in the Near East. All these must not be forgotten by the West if they desire to collaborate with the Arab Orient; such are Bākathīr's wishes, who expresses them with all his enthusiastic Arabism which, this time does not permit him, as in *Mismār Juḥā*, to foresee the Palestinian situation which underwent a development, different to his expectations. The symbols are not excessively hermetically closed in Bākathīr's plays, this is why the titles of his dramas indicate, in general, the story. This being exactly the case with 'An Empire for Auction' (*Imbarāṭūriyya fi'l-mazād*) which was inspired in him by the 1948 Delhi Congress.

The first act shows only the struggle which takes place in England, between Labour and Tory. The characters of the play are logically those of the contemporary English politicians, hardly disguised by the slight corruption brought to their real names. The second act takes us to the cottage of a Tory leader where the triumph of the party in the elections is being celebrated. Mr. Sircle (Churchill), the most distinguished guest, is the character around which Bākathīr concentrates his attention and never misses an opportunity to describe the statesman with most realistic touches, thus revealing to us his exasperation against the British policy of the Near East. At a moment the wild and licentious joy of the guests is interrupted by the irruption in the cottage of the Commander-in-Chief of the British Army in the Near East, who is accompanied by the Minister of National Defence. The situation in Egypt is alarming, the Egyptian Commandos attack the British forces in the Suez Canal Area giving them no respite, the Afro-Asian nations are assembled at Delhi. In brief, the atmosphere created by Bākathīr is the downfall of the British Empire. Mr. Sircle, red with anger, reacts immediately and orders them to send the fleet and the Air Force to destroy Egyptian towns and villages in order to wipe out Egypt from the surface of the earth and thus give Israel a quieter existence. In this way, he will satisfy the wishes of Bernard Baruch and will insure at the same time, American aid to the United Kingdom, and after his great effort, he collapses shouting 'Baruch, Baruch, Baruch.' The third act takes place in the same cottage but, what a different atmosphere! The occupants follow with spasmodic anxiety the news given over the radio, to know the developments of the revolution which has broken out in London. The rebels pursue all party representatives and Mr. Sircle appears at the cottage disguised as a woman and hides in the attic. But, the rebels enter the cottage and everybody is arrested and thrown into prison. The ludicrous is easily attained in Bākathīr's scenes, but one is impatient to know the fate which the author reserves to the Empire. This is offered on auction, and the most tenacious buyers are the United States of America and Russia, but fortunately a third power is born at Delhi, the Afro-Asiatic Power which aims to avoid the auction sale because this Power fights for the freedom of *all* peoples which form part of the British Empire. As to the English themselves, they too shall be free, but reduced to the boundaries of their island. Now it is a question of destroying Mr. Sircle's freedom of activity; someone proposes to sell him on the Stock Exchange as he has now become an archaeological piece of work, but in the end, everybody agrees to hand him over to the Nuremberg Court.

Bākathīr's plays are an accusation to posterity, against western policy in general and British policy in particular in the Near and Middle Eastern states. But the dramatist, although sometimes exalted by his enthusiastic arabism, always knows how to differentiate between 'peoples' or 'masses of people' and the men at the head of these. The fault is always to be found at the top, the author gives us to understand, and the discontent of the Arab peoples towards the West has never been due to a conflict of ethnic or religious character but always the consequence of a policy which has never taken into consideration the 'Arab point of view'. But is there a unique Arab point of view which may be considered the economic, political, and social expression of arabism, of which so much is said these last few years and which is exalted by so many Arab writers?

PART IV

GENERAL THEMES

39. INTRODUCTORY REMARKS

A. H. HOURANI

Lecturer in the Modern History of the Near East in the University of Oxford

These two papers are alike in that they deal with very general ideas about how history—and in particular Islamic history—should be written, and also in that they are expressions of a rich and complex thought which only yields up its secrets, if at all, after a number of careful readings and fierce battles. In subject and treatment, however, they are very different, and it might seem better to treat them separately than together; but it is possible to see Professor Cantwell Smith's paper in a certain perspective opened up by some thoughts of Professor von Grunebaum. I shall therefore begin with von Grunebaum's paper, and deal with it rather more at length than the other.

For Professor von Grunebaum, the writing of history begins with a certain image in the historian's mind: it is an image of himself and the world, and it may be a reflection of what he is and what his world is, or it may be a reflection of what he would like himself and it to be, for the 'self-image' of a historian is closely related to his aspirations for his own society. It is this 'self-image' and these aspirations which turn his eyes to the past, where he may read a justification of the present or the future. The image is the motive force pushing him to the labour of recreating what is dead, but also it helps to decide what he will find when he looks at the past. It determines his choice of the 'shades' which he will summon back from the past, and the light in which he sees them. But to select is in some measure to distort, and sooner or later all those ghosts of the past which he has rejected will force themselves upon his attention, and compel him to change his image unless he wishes it to grow stale and sterile. Some images, however, distort the past less than others, and Professor von Grunebaum maintains that the 'self-image' of modern Western man enables more of the total reality of the past to reveal itself than any other: 'Western research of the last generations has been fortunate in the coincidence of its driving motivations . . . with the demands of factuality itself.'

What does he mean by the 'self-image' of the modern Western historian? It is, he maintains, the image of man and his consciousness as standing at the centre of his own universe; of man defined in terms of autonomous reason, obedience to whose precepts 'alone permits Western man to live in conformity and at peace with himself'; of this autonomous reason as aiming not only at control of the inner and the outer world, but also at a general understanding of it; and of the idea of philosophy, of a universal knowledge concerning the totality of being, as the norm of this understanding. The necessary condition of this general understanding, and therefore of Western man's knowing himself, is historical insight: the ability to see himself in the historical process and recognize his insights as provisional, and also to see the whole of his civilization as provisional, and view it against 'the totality of the cultural achievements of mankind'. Modern Western civilization is the only one which has fully recognized the cultural pluralism of mankind, the existence of a number of disparate civilizations.

Professor von Grunebaum contrasts the fruitfulness of such an image, as a motive for historical studies, with the comparative barrenness of the 'self-image' of certain modern Muslim historians, who have not yet, he maintains, been touched by the 'neo-humanism' of the West. He gives four or five examples of the 'self-image' of Muslim historians, and here my first doubt arises. Why has he chosen these examples and not others? Some of them seem to be extreme cases, not all of them are worth much analysis, and between them they do not include all the main attitudes current among Islamic historians today. If he is to prove his point, what is needed is a typology, a systematic survey of all types of Islamic attitude to the past at the present day.

A typology and critique of the various Western attitudes is also needed. I doubt whether the 'self-image' of the 'neo-humanist', as Professor von Grunebaum defines it, is in fact the only or the main motive force of Western historical study today. The idea of cultural pluralism for example seems to me a relatively new one, and one not yet fully received into the historical consciousness of the West. In Germany perhaps it was received earlier, but in the English-speaking world Hegel's philosophy of history has never been much studied, the influence of Dilthey has scarcely been felt, and the ideas of Max Weber are not yet fully digested. The idea of cultural pluralism, in so far as it exists among English-speaking historians, is largely derived from the first volumes of Toynbee's work; and while Toynbee has had a profound effect on the historical consciousness of the ordinary educated man, his impact on working historians has been limited, although not so limited perhaps as some of them would like to think. In general, it seems to me that Western historiography is more 'West-centred' than Professor von Grunebaum implies; as he himself admits, it has had, and to some extent still has, the idea of ancient Greece as its norm of human society, the *madīna fāḏila*. Side by side with the 'pluralistic historicism' of which he speaks there are other 'self-images' and normative ideas at work among Western historians. We must take account of Marxism, which has had a profound effect on our writing of history on this side of the Iron Curtain as well as the other; and of course we must take account of Christianity too, for the Christian image of man include the humanist image of which Professor von Grunebaum speaks, but includes it in a more complex whole.

It is Professor von Grunebaum's thesis that each 'self-image' is in some way at variance with the whole of historical reality, and there is no one of them which enables us to grasp the whole of the past as a whole. If this is so, there is room for a critique, which I hope Professor von Grunebaum will give us, of each type of image. This critique would define the limits within which a particular 'image' or approach to history enables us to understand a particular civilization or phase of history, or history as a whole—which, in other words, will define the conditions of objectivity for historians of each type. For there is some valid sense in which we can say that so-and-so is a good Marxist historian or a good Christian historian, while someone else is a bad one; and this does not simply mean that the good one has ceased to be a Marxist or a Christian and become something else, it means rather that he has been able to find in his being Marxist or Christian something of positive value for his understanding of history. A good Marxist historian would be one who knew how to use such Marxist concepts as that of class warfare in order to illuminate and not to distort the history of other civilizations than our own, and a good Christian historian would be one whose own faith and beliefs made it possible for him to discern, in other religions and the cultures which derive from them, not simply a rejection of the truth, but an inner consistency and value of their own.

There are dangers and limitations inherent in every approach to history, and such a critique might make us aware of them and help us to avoid them. Even the 'humanistic historicism' which, for Professor von Grunebaum, is typical of modern Western man has its dangers. He himself hints at them when he says that the world of modern Western man is 'a world in which operationally psychological truth takes the place of absolute truth'; there are many difficult problems implicit in such a statement. Similarly, in our discussion of modern Russian historians we have been told that they use a special language, which must be interpreted carefully if we are to understand what they are really trying to say. In inventing this language, they are not simply evading the censorship or the police, they also are dealing with this problem of how to be objective, how one can have a defined standpoint or system of beliefs and still be true to reality, and respect the 'given' as it reveals itself to our observation. Again, we have had an interesting paper and discussion about the Jesuit Lammens; I emerged from this with certain doubts about whether we had any right to do what we all did, that is, to accuse Lammens of being prejudiced. I am not sure that we are justified in saying that he prejudged matters, that he reached conclusions before really studying the material.

Perhaps that very quality in Lammens which has given rise to this accusation, his frankness in stating his own point of view and rejecting others, is a reflection of his struggle with the historian's problem, how to be loyal at the same time to one's own convictions or 'self-image' and to the 'given' in its totality.

This same problem, of how the Christian scholar should approach Islam, underlies the work of Louis Massignon. Not all of us perhaps would accept in its entirety his view of the relation of Christianity and Islam, but we have all felt the disturbing influence of a man of genius when reading what he has written. His work and that of other French Catholic scholars have given a new stimulus to our thought about the intellectual attitude of a Western Christian towards civilizations other than his own. In our times indeed we have seen a new development of the doctrine of the Church, its place in the world, the spiritual status of those who are not Christians, the idea of the 'baptism of desire', the inner structure and value of non-Christian civilizations, and the final question of *why* these civilizations still exist. (Connected with this last question is another, which Professor Lambton raised in regard to Shiʿism, but which exists for a believer in any kind of final revelation in history: what is the significance of the stretch of history which lies between the final revelation and the Day of Judgement?) Such ideas are reflected in the writings of men like Monsignor Journet and Father Danielou; and how effective they can be for the writing of history we can see in the works of Louis Gardet, the product of a man deeply rooted in his Thomist system of thought but who nevertheless can be objective about civilizations and religions other than his own.

It is in this perspective, it seems to me, that we can examine Professor Cantwell Smith's paper. It is an attempt to understand what Islam really is, and indeed what religion really is, by elucidating what Muslims mean or have meant when they use the word 'Islam'. He claims to have discovered a tendency for the word to change its meaning. There are, he maintains, four different ways in which the word has been used, and there has been a perceptible change from one of these meanings to another in the course of Islamic history. First of all, 'Islam' has been used in the sense of personal piety, submission, *taslīm*, a direct relationship of man and God. This was the normal way in which the word was used by the earliest writers, but later it was used to refer to an ideal religious system, a system of doctrines or what Professor Cantwell Smith calls the 'Platonic idea' of Islam. Later still it came to refer to the religious system as it has developed in history, the actual practice of Islam as it has grown up in time. In the modern age, finally, it is used most commonly to denote the civilization that was the historical expression of Islam. To illustrate this modern usage, Professor Cantwell Smith quotes the title of a work by 'Abd al-Raḥmān al-Badawī, *Atheism in Islam*; we regard this title as being significant, although it would have been meaninglesss or self-contradictory to Muslims in the past. Professor Cantwell Smith hints also at a fifth meaning, which is to be found in Lebanese colloquial usage; the word 'Islam' is used to refer to any group of Muslims, so that a Christian family in Beirut might say, 'Our neighbours are Islam.'

There are two questions which arise from Professor Cantwell Smith's thesis: first, did this development occur in the way in which he describes it, and secondly, if it did occur, what are the conclusions we can draw from it? I shall not deal with the second question, for he has put his paper forward as an interim report only, and has not attempted to draw many conclusions from it, although in his last paragraph he does hint at a conclusion, and ask whether the tendency of the word to change its meaning is not also a tendency 'to lose its relationship with God'. In regard to the first question, I wish to raise one point only. Does this division into four phases emerge from an empirical study of the material, or is it determined by Professor Cantwell Smith's own 'self-image'? I must apologize for putting my question in these terms, and injecting into this symposium of scholars a note of controversy, which may even be theological rather than historical, but when Professor Cantwell Smith has done us the honour of communicating to us his own thoughts about a very important matter, the least we can do is to take him seriously, and that means asking whether or not we agree with him. I read his paper more or less at the same time as I read his recent book, *Islam in modern history*; and out of my reading of both of them there arose certain doubts about whether his conclusions can be justified by an empirical study of the history of Islam, or whether what Professor von Grunebaum would call his 'self-image' has not led him to select and emphasize what agrees with his idea of true religion. The principle from which both his paper and his book start is that the reality of religion can be summed up in a direct call of God to the individual heart and a direct human response to it. Everything else, not only liturgies and customs and institutions but also systems of doctrine, is of human construction, a public interpretation of this private experience; it changes because human beings change, and if it does not change it may be dangerous, because it may obscure or even break the direct relationship. This may or may not be the true view of religion, but is it a possible interpretation of what Muslims, or indeed Christians, have thought about their religion in the past? I speak without any knowledge of Islamic theology, but it seems to me that if one tries to reduce the Islam in which Muslims have believed throughout history to its very minimum, one does not come down, except among a few mystics, to the direct call of God to the human heart in isolation. According to Muslim belief, God has revealed Himself not only by this call but by His Word, and not only in the secret of the heart but publicly through a line of prophets. The minimal conception of Islam includes not God and Man alone, but God, Man, the Qur'ān and the Prophet. If therefore we try to project upon a religion like Islam an idea of religion like Professor Cantwell Smith's, are we not in danger of distorting what has happened and also what is likely to happen? To adapt a phrase of von Grunebaum's, the past and future are closely and essentially connected with each other. To believe in a religion and to belong to a religious community imply some kind of responsibility towards the past; can a religion, simply by gradual development, change into something essentially other than itself, as Professor Cantwell Smith seems to imply in his book, or will not the future development of Islam be necessarily controlled by what it has been in the past?

40. SELF-IMAGE AND APPROACH TO HISTORY

G. E. VON GRUNEBAUM

Professor of Eastern History and Director of the Near Eastern Center in the University of California, Los Angeles

'The dream is but one; but diverse are the interpretations'
(Ṣā'ib, d. 1670)[1]

In the *Nekyia* it is the blood of the sacrificial victim partaking of which readmits the shades to a brief span of relevance to the living. Similarly, it is the aspiration of the living through the intermediacy of the searching historian that reinstills life or meaning—its intellectual substitute—to the facts and fictions of the past. And even as Odysseus fought off the shades so that Tiresias could drink, so the historian and the living generation through him must make their choice whom and what to revive or allow to continue forgotten. One may argue perhaps how much freedom of decision the historian possesses. His weapon to fight off those he wishes to stay outside of his consciousness is the context(s) into which he may fit the facts of the past, those contexts which in a sense are like lariats of different length and range, or else like magnets with which to single out or to capture responsive data lying buried in the sources that can be made to betray the past. But the contexts with which the historian is armed, as it were, reflect the aspirations of his time, or possibly merely his own, and the limitations implicit in those aspirations limit the freedom and the success of the historian before he has even begun his work. Completeness of evidence may be the aspiration of a time—as it is of ours—and yet completeness of comprehension of bygone events remains elusive. For the shades are too many and our methodological demand for the completeness of fact-finding does not do away with that hierarchy of relevance among the shades which ultimately must and will determine a selection.

Yet it is clear that ours is a historiogenic period, a period that craves contexts of maximum heuristic effectiveness, a period that is trying to adjust its contexts to the shades it expects to encounter. Or does it? It would seem that it does so only in certain areas and intellectual circles of the globe, those that are most simply and most nearly identified by speaking of the West and the Westernized. Outside of this geographic and intellectual sphere, the dominant aspiration and the self-image that parallels it dictate otherwise. The need to substantiate one's self-view

[1] The verse is quoted by V. Monteil, 'De la Perse à l'Iran (Itinéraire spirituel)', *Mélanges Louis Massignon* (Damascus, 1957), iii, 161–84, at p. 175.

through history, to find the justification of one's future in the past, is almost universal. But the needs of various self-views and aspirations for the future differ in the stylization they impose on known facts and the stimulus they give to the unearthing of hitherto unknown ones. Western research of the last generations has been fortunate in the coincidence of its driving motivations, first and foremost the will to self-understanding by means of understanding 'all' cultural solutions of the problem of living, with the demands of factuality itself. For the unrevived shades are only pushed away from the blood, they are not eliminated as shades.

We may, in a cave, turn our flashlight on this corner or that and take account of its structure overlooking deliberately the structure of the sections which we choose to leave without illumination. But those sections are still there and, if we do not pay heed, we will sooner or later be made to suffer from our neglect or be compelled to reorient our lighting. The wilful twisting and omitting of historical evidence will fairly soon make the context and its motivating aspiration seem stale and sterile—disillusionment is the emotional counterpart of this kind of intellectual failure. The aspiration compels the point at which the intellectual mastery of the past succeeds or fails. It is in this sense that the self-image of the historian or his society predetermines so to speak not only the results of his endeavours, but the specific cause and mode of their validity and their invalidation.

II

Any historiography is determined by content (data), function (of data within the context studied) and structure (of the data making them amenable to treatment within that context) on the one hand, and motivation or objective ('use'), method, and style of presentation on the other. The temptation to contrast the two sets of concepts as objective and subjective must be resisted because the contexts within which the data can be said to fulfil a function[2] do not possess a *Realexistenz* independent of the human observer; the same will have to be said of structure (i.e., the 'definable articulation', the 'ordered arrangement of parts')[3] which the data exhibit within the context. The researcher's objective which, at least from a psychological viewpoint, is hardly separable from his motivation, determines the context of the investigation, in other words, the principles of data selection and hence the perception or consideration of the data themselves.[4] The (research) objective and the data will, at best, converge like

[2] i.e., in the terms of S. F. Nadel, *The Theory of social structure* (Glencoe, Ill., 1957), 7, to show their 'adequacy in regard to some stipulated effectiveness'. [3] Ibid.

[4] An especially blunt statement of the aspiration is J. J. Winckelmann's (d. 1768) appeal to the student of classical art. '(The students) sollen . . . vorher eingenommen sich den Werken der griechischen Kunst nähern: denn in der Versicherung, viel schönes (*sic*) zu finden, werden sie dasselbe suchen, und einiges wird sich ihnen entdecken. Man kehre so oft zurück, bis man es

asymptotic curves; only in some cases such as the description of coins and the like, full coincidence may, to all practical intents and purposes, be claimed as capable of achievement.

The subjective acceptability of research results, is, however, not directly proportional to the closeness reached by those 'asymptotic curves'—rather it is partly by the period's methodological ideas and partly by the strength of the motivation, that the immediate conclusiveness of the objective is determined. Method must not be understood simply as the techniques of fact-finding of which the investigator disposes; but these techniques themselves need to be defined as accommodating or rather as deriving from the criteria of acceptability which the investigator and his society recognize as binding.[5] Credulity (or scepticism for that matter) in many cases is nothing but an expression of a society's disinterest in, or fundamental unconcern with the area in which it is allowed to prevail unless it betrays itself as part of the psychological machinery that is required to sustain and further a valued aspiration.

The style of historiographical presentation must be recognized as another instrument for the realization of the research objective. Stylistic patterns such as the annalistic or the declaratory (of certain royal inscriptions for instance) are in themselves limitative; their replacement bespeaks as much a shifting objective as does inquiry into (or: by means of) new contexts.

Considerations of this order make it obvious that between a society's motivation to support historiography, usually of a clearly defined type, and its self-image there exists a definite link. Descriptive (*konstatierend*) or normative ('pedagogical'), the self-image is reflected in motivation and objective of research and presentation. The connection tends to become painfully evident when the 'use' to which history is to be put is the adjustment of the collective self-image to that held by the observer and the minority within his society for which he is the spokesman. The varying judgements on the Greek *polis*, or the relative merits of Sparta and Athens, or on unitary and federative forms of organization in the Hellenistic world are apt to reflect the author's outlook on his society; his aspirations for its future and, in any event, the concerns that reflect his society's objectives (generally apprehended as its 'problems').

Objectivity, in this context, will mean first and foremost selfconsciousness

gefunden hat; denn es ist vorhanden.' *Geschichte der Kunst des Alterthums* (first published in 1764), Buch 5, Kap. 6, 13 (end) in *Winckelmann's Werke*, edd. H. Meyer and J. Schulze (Dresden, 1808–20), iv, 232; cf. W. Deonna, *L'expression des sentiments dans l'art grec* (Paris, 1914), pp. 80–3, where at p. 80 Winckelmann's advice is quoted from the French edition of 1802 (i, 484), in which the beginning of the passage is formulated more strongly than in the German original. 'Approchez-vous d'un esprit prévenu en faveur de l'antiquité.'

[5] Already J. J. Bachofen (1815–87), *Das Mutterrecht* (first published Stuttgart, 1861), in *Gesammelte Werke* (Basel, 1943 ff.), ii, 23, observes: 'Mit den Zeiten wechseln die Probabilitäten.' The dictum is quoted by E. Howald, *Humanismus und Europäertum* (Zürich and Stuttgart, 1957), p. 69.

about the nature of historical research and an ever-increasing but obviously never a complete willingness to strike historical situations, which examination of the sources (in the widest sense of the word) have proven unsuited for the purpose, from the dossier of arguments marshalled in support of one's aspirations; one may perhaps say, objectivity is an increased independence from history as an instrument of change which seems to be brought about most readily by having the possession of historical insight incorporated as an important trait in a society's self-image. Besides it is not merely a statement of fact that some proposed uses of history (or a segment of it) and some questions asked of it are more germane to the given material than others; it is in the nature of 'objectivity' as it has just been characterized that it will suggest more questions and 'uses' than can be pursued and consummated without an obviously arbitrary handling of the data consulted. In other words, a self-view that accepts one's historicity will protect the historicity of the dead and widen the areas of psychological response that make ever wider segments of the experience of the human past meaningful, i.e. utilizable in the service of currently effective aspirations. In this sense it may be noted that historical objectivity, viz. object orientedness, by placing it in the widest possible judgemental perspective, tends to liberate, or if you prefer, to purge the self-image from aspirations that are not *richtigkeitsrational*;[6] it assists in a rational adjustment of purposes where otherwise only a purposive rational adjustment of means to (non-rationally apprehended) ends would have been possible.[7] If such be the case, one may well postulate that distortions of a period's historiographic seizure of reality (not of course simple error, neglectfulness and defective information) are functions of peculiarities of the self-image of the society, as these are most easily understood by an analysis of its aspirations. The aspiration will determine what part of the total heritage potentially at a society's disposal activates the emotions.

Ṭāhā Ḥusayn (b. 1889) has noted this connection by denying the value of the *qudamā'* when they cease to inspire the living generation. So he sets

[6] For the concept cf. M. Weber, 'Ueber einige Kategorien der verstehenden Soziologie', *Logos* (1913), iv, 253–94, at pp. 254 and 257–63; Weber contrasts *subjektive Zweckrationalität* and *objektive Richtigkeitsrationalität*; the idea is taken up by S. F. Nadel, *The Foundations of social anthropology* (London, 1953), esp. p. 271 (where in note 1 the reference to Weber's study is inexact).

[7] The creative primacy of the self-image has been stated by Goethe in the famous lines of the *West-Oestliche Divan*:

Volk und Knecht und Ueberwinder
Sie gestehn zu jeder Zeit:
Höchstes Gluck des Erdenkinder
Sei nur die Persönlichkeit.

Jedes Leben sei zu führen
Wenn man sich nicht selbst vermisst;
Alles könne man verlieren,
Wenn man bliebe, was man ist.

himself the goal of recreating ancient history as an inspiration for the contemporaries.[8] When the Moroccan M. A. Lahbabi speaks (in a very different context it is true) of *la vérité des XIXe et XXe siècles* and then states that 'en analysant la vie, en expliquant et en décrivant ce qui *est* et ce qu'on doit *faire*, le philosophe accélère le mouvement d'émancipation de l'homme en lutte contre le matière et contre sa nature' he takes account of the incessant shifts in what the human mind will accept as conclusive and stresses, as we have done, but from a different vantage point, the liberating force of an 'open' and *richtigkeitsrational* oriented self-image. For, as Lahbabi states in another passage, in contrast to the animals, man has a transcendant image of himself to realize.[9] This philosophical assertion of the primacy of the self-view is at the same time (and in a sense not intended by the philosopher) a clue to the understanding of the concern for history in the contemporary Arab world.[10]

If the question is asked why the frequently observable discrepancy, not to say contradictoriness, of the ends and of the facts of a society's self-view does not result in either their adjustment or their mutual destruction, it must be said that, in the long run, such an adjustive or destructive process does in fact take place resulting in a replacement of current by new aspirations; but more importantly, it needs to be noted that contradictions and maladjustments of this order are as a rule only faintly perceived; or, to put it more accurately: they will be the less perceived, the stronger the emotional hold of the aspiration(s) which create the difficulties.

Periods of self-criticism are periods of aspirational shifts. As a matter of fact, the very aspiration that may, on the level of rational analysis, cause the maladjustments, will give for the time of its affective dominance, the necessary psychological cohesion to the *disjecta membra* of the self-image, and render bearable the chasm between the realities of the historical situation and the assumptions of its 'creative misinterpretation' in the service of the objectives for which the society believes it lives. It is more than fifty years since Th. Ribot said that the principle which confers unity within the sphere of 'la logique affective' and which 'régit la logique des sentiments toute entière' is the principle of finality. Psychologically, the

[8] *'Alā hāmish al-sīra* (Cairo, 1933), i, pp. 8^{16}–9^{2}; p. 9^{3-9}.

[9] M. A. Lahbabi, *Liberté ou libération?* (*A partir des libertés bergsoniennes*) (Paris, 1956), pp. 20, 21, 81–2. The nature, role, and in some cases, the primacy of the image are examined forcefully if impressionistically by K. E. Boulding, *The Image* (Ann Arbor, Mich., 1956); cf. e.g., the passage on p. 122: 'The history of the technological revolution must be written largely in terms of the dynamism of the image—the image of change as a good and desirable thing introduced by the various religious reformations, and the image of an orderly universe whose secret relations might be explored by experiment and observation.'

[10] Not with regard to historiography but to social and political attitudes the extremely interesting book by A. Memmi, *Portrait du colonisé précédé du portrait du colonisateur* (Paris, 1957), which deals with the French and the Muslims of Algeria, provides an illustration of the same truth; the analysis of the roles of religion, language, etc., that go into the several self-views, adds to the merits of the study.

coexistence of rationally incompatible affirmations is explainable on the ground that each one of them is experienced as necessary by individual or society. (Logically, of course, the contradiction cannot be concealed.)[11]

III

The nature and development of the Western attitude to and expectation from research in general and Oriental studies in particular as it appears to those Near Eastern scholars and leaders who identify with it has been formulated by Adnan Adıvar (d. 1955) in his introduction to the Turkish edition of the *Encyclopaedia of Islam*[12] He notes a difference of motivation between early and contemporary Oriental scholarship in Europe. 'In taking over early Eastern science and philosophy into their own language, the Orientalists were primarily concerned with improving their own knowledge and refinement rather than in making a scientific study of the East, and they were not seeking to discover anything original in Eastern languages and history. In this respect, these early Orientalists were engaged in an endeavour which somewhat resembles our [i.e. modern Turkey's] own activity in translation and adaptation from the West.' The Western scholar may hesitate to consider the translators of the thirteenth (and later) centuries as his predecessors in any but a formal sense; yet the parallel drawn with the assimilative tendencies of the contemporary East deserves attention. By the middle of the eighteenth century the framework of modern Orientalism is established. Adıvar finds it in the subtitle of d'Herbelot's (1625–95) *Bibliothèque orientale*[13] which, after the fashion of the age, describes its contents as 'everything necessary for an understanding of the Eastern peoples, i.e., their history, their real and legendary traditions, their religions, sects, governments, politics, more recent customs, and the organization and administration of their states'. In this 'more or less complete definition' of our studies we should miss primarily a statement of objective; as it is however quoted here not for its adequacy, but for its mirroring an Eastern view of our pursuits, a placing of d'Herbelot in the Western development may be dispensed with.[14]

Without trying his hand at an analysis of the Western motivation, Halil Inalcık declares the way in which Occidental scholarship deals today with Islamic history to be 'essentially scientific and objective'. What is decisive is that 'there is no other way for any serious student of the Islamic past. There is no need to say more about this. The scientific method is concerned only with discovering historical truth and explaining the causes

[11] *La logique des sentiments* (Paris, 1905), pp. 49 and 58.

[12] *Islam ansiklopedisi* (Ankara, 1943 ff.).

[13] Paris, 1697.

[14] Adnan Adıvar, 'A Turkish Account of Orientalism' (a translation of the introduction to the Turkish Edition of the *Encyclopaedia of Islam*), *The Muslim World* (1953), xliii. 266–82, at pp. 264 and 266.

which brought them forward.' This statement is to be read in the light of Inalcik's awareness of 'the dangers of requiring history to conform to current political views'. Such modern writers, Eastern and Western, 'who have a fanatical devotion to traditions are unaware that historical truth is beyond their reach . . . because they are bound to past errors and prejudices'. After rejecting the influence which some scholars in Islamic countries have allowed their nationalism to exert on their research, Inalcık asserts that, in his opinion, 'historical studies will form a strong foundation for the real cultural movements in Islamic countries today. The objective study of Islamic history with Western methodology will bring about general progress in all Islamic learning.'[15]

The epistemological presupposition of this statement of which Inalcık may not have been fully conscious, as well as the objective of the attitude for which he speaks had been expressed with his usual merciless precision by Atatürk: 'We shall take science and knowledge from wherever they may be, and put them in the mind of every member of the nation. For science and for knowledge, there are no restrictions and no conditions.[16] For a nation which insists on preserving a host of traditions and beliefs that rest on no logical proof, progress is very difficult, perhaps even impossible.'[17]

The self-image of Western man as it has been recognized in his intellectual history and at work in his present intellectual endeavours has been described by Edmund Husserl (1859–1938) in terms of 'the very idea that defines and constitutes him as Western man. That idea is no other than the idea of philosophy itself; the idea of a universal knowledge concerning the totality of being, a knowledge which contains within itself whatever special sciences may grow out of it as its ramifications, which rests upon ultimate foundations and proceeds throughout in a completely evident and self-justifying fashion and in full awareness of itself. Closely connected with this idea, whose first inception in Ancient Greece in the seventh and sixth centuries B.C. marks the historical beginning of Western man, is the idea of a truly human, i.e., philosophical existence, an existence oriented towards the ideas, ideals and norms of autonomous reason, which alone permits Western man to live in conformity and at peace with himself.'[18] Husserl proceeds to develop from this interpretation of 'Western man' a diagnosis of his present crisis which he finds in his having forsaken 'those

[15] 'The Study of History in Islamic Countries', *Middle East Journal* (1953), vii, 451–5, at pp. 454–5.

[16] Such transferability is considered in the writer's unpublished study, 'Specialization'.

[17] In a speech made to a meeting of teachers on 27 October 1922, *Atatürk'ün Söylev ve Demeçleri* (Ankara, 1952), ii, 44. The passage is quoted in a German version by J. Ritter, *Europäisch-asiatischer Dialog* (Dusseldorf, 1956), pp. 20–1.

[18] In the exposition of the relevant ideas of E. Husserl's posthumously published work *Die Krisis der europäischen Wissenschaften und die transzendentale Phänomenologie*, ed. W. Biemel (The Hague, 1954), the excellent analysis by A. Gurwitsch, 'The Last Work of Edmund Husserl', *Philosophy and phenomenological Research* (1956), xvi, 380–99; (1957), xvii, 370–98, has been utilized —largely because of the admirable manner in which Gurwitsch has coped with the problem of

very philosophical aspirations out of which Western science was born' and he proposes to remedy his malaise by leading him back to them through philosophy reunderstood. In our context it is not however the crisis of Western intellectuality that is of concern, but Husserl's and by his postulate, Western man's orientation towards 'the teleological idea of philosophy, that very idea which gives unity and meaning to the historical process as a whole. A teleological idea which, because it displays itself in the medium of history, by necessity undergoes transformations and yet preserves its identity, defines an *infinite task*. . . . The historical significance of a philosophical theory consists but in its contribution towards the infinite task.'[19]

The infinite task which Husserl assigns to philosophical theory, Western man has actually assigned to himself in every sphere of life; hence, his willingness to recognize his insights as provisional, his anticipation of his life work being superseded by subsequent correction and refutation, but also his conviction of the manipulability of the social and economic universe with the implied duty to strive after this-worldly perfection which he yet knows to be unattainable.

The insight into history that Husserl demands is not to culminate in knowledge of the past for its own sake; it is required to enable us 'to see and understand ourselves', and by such *Selbstverständnis*[20] 'to find our specific task within the infinite task'. It is true that Husserl confines his demands to the philosopher whom in our day comprehension of his position in history will guide towards assuming a specific task of renewing and transforming the very idea of philosophy through transcendental phenomenology.[21] But this restriction is justifiable solely by the purpose of Husserl's reflections. Essentially, self-understanding, unqualified by orientation to a specific object, is the purpose of Western man's immersion into history and, to spell out a significant implication, the cultural solutions to the problems of societal living which punctuate its flow. We can then accept Husserl's characterization of 'Western Man' as a human type who 'in der Endlichkeit lebend, auf Pole der Unendlichkeit hinlebt',[22] and whose historicity and 'wissenschaftliche Kultur' have the sense of 'Entwerden des endlichen Menschentums im Werden zum Menschentum unendlicher Aufgaben'.[23] The world which Western man uses as his material and as his stage is, to transfer an idea of Husserl's from epistemology to the philosophy of history, a world 'deren Sein aus subjektiver

finding English formulations for Husserl's statements. The passage quoted is from Gurwitsch, op. cit., xvi, 381–2.

[19] Ibid., xvi, 384–5. [20] For his concept of *Selbstverständnis* cf. *Krisis*, pp. 275–6.

[21] Gurwitsch, op. cit., xvi, 385. [22] Husserl, *Krisis*, p. 322; Gurwitsch, op. cit., xvi, 388.

[23] Ibid.; Husserl, *Krisis*, p. 325. The joyful realization of the infinity of the task of the searcher and the implied readiness to see one's lifework rendered obsolete by the efforts of one's successors shines through the analysis of his science which the great classicist, August Boeckh, was in the habit of presenting to his students in the University of Berlin. In his *Encyclopädie und Metholodogie der philologischen Wissenschaften*, which he offered no less than twenty-six times between 1809 and

Leistung ist'.[24] This world stands revealed 'as a correlate and product of subjective functions, activities, and operations'.[25] It is therefore, we may add, a world in which operationally psychological truth takes the place of absolute truth—an outlook that would seem to be made to order for the historian, but at the same time an outlook that it would be extremely difficult for a Muslim historian not so much to accept but to utilize towards the critical reshaping of an effective self-image. For it does imply the determination to place man and the structure of his consciousness in the centre and to acknowledge the autonomy of reason as an essential property of the idea of man.[26]

The teleological nexus in which man is placed, and which in retrospect appears as a nexus of causation, is in the case of contemporary Western society describable in terms of its central aspirations—the ever widening control and understanding of the inner and outer world. The coexistence of those aspirations is as characteristic of our civilization as are their accompanying methodological requirements of completeness and universality of information (and application). Specialization for control, generalization for understanding are, in a slightly oversimplified formulation, the objectives towards which we are pushed by somewhat conflicting internal drives. But generalization in the service of a 'self-understanding' that will be existentially satisfactory, factually correct and allowing for the development of control over the expanding human (political, social, etc.) and intellectual universe[27] presupposes specialized knowledge—a fact which assures the perpetuation of conflicting intellectual valuations and educational systems. The intellectual position of our civilization is however but

1866, he observes in discussing philological interpretation: 'Wenn also die fremde Individualität nie vollständig verstanden werden kann, so kann die Aufgabe der Hermeneutik nur durch unendliche Approximation, das heisst durch allmähliche, Punkt für Punkt fortschreitende, aber nie vollendete Annäherung gelöst werden.' (Quoted by K. Reinhardt, *Von Werken und Formen* (Godesberg, 1948), pp. 429–30.) An extreme formulation of the Occidental attitude was proposed by Nietzsche when he said: 'Die Grösse des "Fortschritts" bemisst sich sogar nach dem Masse dessen, was ihm alles geopfert werden musste.' (*Genealogie der Moral*, 2nd Treatise, Section 12.) In the Islamic orbit, this sense of the infinity of the human task, of the eternally provisional of the human achievement, that is yet striven for in gladness and without hesitation or discouragement, is met with only in the quest of the mystic; cf., e.g., the characteristic passage from the writings of Najm al-Dīn Kubrā (d. 1221) which F. Meier translated on pp. 92–3 of his book *Die Fawā'iḥ al-Ǧamāl wa-Fawātiḥ al-Ǧalāl des Naǧm ad-Dīn al-Kubrā* (Wiesbaden, 1957). The attitude to scholarship which Muḥammad al-Rāzī (d. 925) professes, *Opera philosophica*, ed. P. Kraus (Cairo, 1939), i, 300–3, seems to have died with him.

[24] Gurwitsch, op. cit., xvi, 398. Cf. Husserl, *Krisis*, p. 346: 'eine absolut eigenständige Geisteswissenschaft . . ., in Form einer konsequenten Selbstverständigung und Verständigung der Welt als geistiger Leistung.'

[25] Gurwitsch, ibid. For Husserl it falls to phenomenology 'to account for the world at large as well as mundane existents in particular, and for that matter, for all objective entities whatsoever, in terms of experiences, acts, operations, and productions ("Leistungen") of consciousness'; Gurwitsch, op. cit., xvii, 379.

[26] Cf. also Husserl's formulation, *Krisis*, p. 310: 'Unwelt ist relativ auf eine für sie fungierende Subjektivität—die Typik fungierender Subjektivität ist selbst historisch.'

[27] 'Specialization'.

incompletely assessed unless we realize one consequence of the peculiar combination of aspirations and epistemological assumptions to which we are dedicated (or, by which we are possessed) viz., that our self-understanding must needs be based on an understanding of other cultures. We are forced 'to review and reconstruct ourselves against the background of the totality of the cultural achievement of mankind' and this concern, connected as it is with our paramount objective and the collective self-extension or self-transcendence it demands, compels us to move towards a convergence of historical and anthropological research that is to culminate in a *Kulturlehre.*[28] At this point again, we are intellectually and emotionally well located for object-oriented historical research since the instructiveness in terms of our existential objective, of our conclusions with regard to our own past and the past and present of 'other' societies and civilizations is independent of their material content.

In this sense one may speak of the superior aptitude of the modern West for the analysis of civilizations. One may go further and describe it as the only civilization that has, in its concept of man, utilized fully his *Kulturenfähigkeit,*[29] i.e., his potential (and largely actualized) cultural pluralism.

[28] For more detail cf. the writer's study 'The Analysis of Islamic Civilization and Cultural Anthropology' to be published shortly, especially sections i and ii. Husserl, *Krisis*, p. 352, indicates how the pre-Socratic thinker comes to develop the concept of truth from the contemplation of the 'Mannigfaltigkeit der Nationen'. Note in this context the *Bildungsbegriff* developed by W. Schadewaldt, *Die Anforderungen der Technik an die Geisteswissenschaft* (Göttingen, 1957), p. 41. 'Auf dem Sich-Auskennen in den einfachsten Dingen, dem Sich-Auskennen in den Sachen und den Sachbereichen, baut sich danach organisch die Bildung auf als ein letztes und höchstes Sich-Auskennen im Ganzen der Welt, eine Orientierung meines gegenwärtigen Orts im Jetzt und Hier, in den grossen Zusammenhängen von Zeit und Raum, Natur und Geschichte.' The philosophical (or anthropological) assumption underlying our methodological requirement of 'completeness and universality of information' is very clearly brought out in this passage from Claude Lévi-Strauss, *Tristes tropiques* (Paris, 1955), p. 183: 'L'ensemble des coutumes d'un peuple est toujours marqué par un style; elles forment des systèmes. Je suis persuadé que ces systèmes n'existent pas en nombre illimité, et que les sociétés humaines, comme les individus—dans leurs jeux, leurs rêves ou leurs délires—ne créent jamais de façon absolue, mais se bornent à choisir certaines combinaisons dans un répertoire idéal qu'il serait possible de reconstituer. En faisant l'inventaire de toutes les coutumes observées, de toutes celles imaginées dans les mythes, celles aussi évoquées dans les jeux des enfants et des adultes, les rêves des individus sains ou malades et les conduites psycho-pathologiques, on parviendrait à dresser une sorte de tableau périodique comme celui des éléments chimiques, où toutes les coutumes réelles ou simplement possibles apparaîtraient groupées en familles, et où nous n'aurions plus qu'à reconnaître celles que les sociétés ont effectivement adoptées.'

[29] The expression is W. E. Mühlmann's; cf. his study 'Umrisse und Probleme einer Kulturanthropologie', *Homo* (1956), vii, 153–71, at p. 155. An anticipation of the modern Western approach occurs in the collection of essays by the Turkish author Kātib Chelebī (better known as Ḥājjī Khalīfa, 1609–57), published under the title of *Mīzān al-ḥaqq* and recently translated by G. L. Lewis as *The balance of truth* (London and New York, 1957), where we read on pages 29–30: 'It must . . . be known that mankind, ever since the time of Adam, has been divided. Every division has its own tenets and its own mode of behaviour, which seem at variance with those of other divisions. . . . Now the purpose of civilization and society, which is essential for mortals, demands that men of vision should acquire knowledge and become acquainted with the division of mankind into various sorts, and with the state and condition of every part. After gaining acquaintance with the classes of city-folk and the manners and customs of every class, they should

By basing its interpretation of man's psychological structure and, more particularly, its self-image on the fact of this human *Kulturenfähigkeit*, the West has developed a secular means to account for, functionalize, and perhaps allow to coexist a number of disparate civilizations without having to deprive them (intellectually) of their specific properties. From the religious viewpoint this attitude could have been reached through the acknowledgement that such pluralism was suggested if not demanded by the very fact of God's having created different peoples realizing themselves in different civilizations. But while the great religions accept the fact, the nature of religious truth precludes (or renders superfluous) the utilization of the experience of cultural pluralism as an essential means of collective self-understanding. Religious truth, and especially revealed religious truth, can and should be communicated to all; but the diversity of the societies that may be (made) receptive to it, while illustrating the ways of the Lord, has little to teach the faithful about himself.

The contrast of approaches that is inherent in the contrast of aspirations comes strikingly to the fore in certain contemporary studies of comparative religion in which the researcher places himself outside of his civilization and his own historical moment in order to judge both from the perspective of other civilizations (and other religions). The motivation for choosing a vantage point of such location is to be found in the problems dealt with and their choice depends, in turn, on the cultural or existential aspiration scholarship is called upon to serve. In his essay on *Symbolisme religieux et valorisation de l'angoisse*, M. Eliade places himself in the position of 'un observateur qui participe à une autre civilisation et nous juge à l'échelle de ses propres valeurs'.[30] Whether or not such abstraction from one's historical location is possible, the need is felt; and it is this need which constitutes the uniqueness of the Western position.

History has often been cultivated for the instruction to be gained from contemplation of the past (and especially its errors and catastrophes). The lesson derived however will always depend on the question asked. Thus, in the world of Islam for instance, it is generally found in an asseveration of the transitoriness of everything human and in the advice to adopt a pragmatic pattern of personal and especially political behaviour. To illustrate the familiar by somewhat unfamiliar examples. After Bayhaqī (d. 1077) has told the tragic end of Er-Yaruq and Il-Ghazi, he observes: 'And lo, what was the outcome of what the two generals did? All came to an end, one might say, as if it had never been. Time and the turning of the sky by the command of God have often acted thus and will often act thus

strive to acquire an outline knowledge of the bastions of the inhabitants of the habitable quarter of the earth, and of their condition. Thereafter the secret of the purpose of civilization is gradually revealed; . . .'

[30] *Mythes, rêves et mystères*, second edition (Paris, 1957), p. 61.

in the future.' The wise man is he who will not allow himself to be deceived by the favours of Time, *zamāna*, remains on guard and sees to it that he leaves behind him a good name.[31] Khwāja Ḥasan, the *kadkhudā* of Sultan Muḥammad joins Sultan Mas'ūd after the latter has brought about his master's fall—'not giving himself in the hand of Satan and taking the path of right and truth; for he was a man of perfect insight' who had experienced good and bad turns of fortune, 'had read the old books, *wa-kutub-i bāstān khwānda*, and knew the consequences of things (or: the end things will come to, *'awāqib-rā bi-dānista*)'; and so he preserves his position.[32] 'Insight into the history of man is a mirror in which the onlooker finds the verification of good and bad actions and which instructs the men of perfection and natural gifts. Through it God reminds those of His servants whom He finds worthy of such reminder and deserving of His recompense and His reward.'[33] Almost six centuries later, Kātib Chelebī asks of the ruler that 'like his mighty ancestors, he should read history, and draw the moral from the story of their illustrious deeds.'[34]

In reflecting on the fact, already noted elsewhere by the writer and again to be substantiated by the discussion of various recent works in the later part of this paper, that modern Arabic historiographical self-analysis has been satisfied with a somewhat crude psychological approach to its themes and has besides confined its attention almost totally to the Islamic, or better the Arab-Muslim sphere, one wonders whether the absence of the neo-humanistic strain (to use E. Spranger's expression) from the Arab nationalist ideology may not have something to do with its intellectual limitations.

The degeneration and obsolescence of European, and especially German, nationalism in some of its historical manifestations, must not induce one to overlook its connection with the humanistic movement which, in Europe, has been, since the Augustan period, if not before, the unfailing companion of national patriotism. The achievements of a Vergil, a Horace,

[31] *Tārīkh*, ed. Sa'īd Nafīsī (Tehran, 1319–32/1940–53), i, 279[13] ff.

[32] Ibid., i, 96, esp. ll. 8–9.

[33] Muḥammad b. 'Abd al-Malik al-Hamdānī (d. 1127), *Takmilat ta'rīkh al-Ṭabarī*, pt. I, ed. A. Y. Kan'ān, in *al-Mashriq* (1955), 49, 21–42; 149–72, at p. 25[8-10]. A remarkably wide concept of the scope of history we find in the Moroccan al-Yūsī (d. 1691); but its function remains confined to the intra-cultural one of legal and ethical illustration; cf. J. Berque, *Al-Yousi. Problèmes de la culture marocaine au XVII*e *siecle* (Paris and The Hague, 1958), p. 26. The relationship between history and religion is defined somewhat differently by another Moroccan, Abū 'Abdallāh Muḥammad b. al-Ṭayyib al-Qādirī, who died in Fez in 1773, *Nashr al-mathānī* (Fez, 1310), ii, 143, who allocates all that concerns religion in history, including for instance the history of coinage, weights and measures, the description of old mosques, etc., to religion. History itself may deal with any state or states, the foundation of towns or the life of important people. Although not part of religion it is good as long as it stimulates ethical behaviour. The passage is paraphrased in A. S. Tritton, *Materials on Muslim education in the Middle Ages* (London, 1957), p. 170, without indication of the author for whom cf. C. Brockelmann, *Geschichte der arabischen Litteratur, Supplement* (Leiden, 1937–42), ii, 687.

[34] Op. cit., p. 147.

an Ovid are motivated by the aspiration to equal the perfection of the Greek models. To introduce a Greek literary genre into Rome is an act of patriotic duty. The ennoblement of his nation is the first obligation of the poet; the pride felt in the great past and the potentialities of their people needs justification by a supreme creative achievement. The yardstick of such achievement has, in the Western orbit, always been sought in the Greek past. This is as true for the Scipios and their circle and the Augustans, as it is for the Elizabethans and the age of Louis XIV and again for the Italian Humanists and the Germans from Winckelmann to Spranger and Jaeger. To them the individuality of the nation and the individuality of the person are inseparable—the formation of the one not only entails but presupposes the formation of the other. The education of the individual can be accomplished only by his participation in the life of the nation; and conversely, the upward development of the nation is unthinkable without the spiritual and ethical growth of its citizens. Political power does not carry its legitimation in itself; it becomes legitimate when the ruler equals or outreaches the ruled *in spiritualibus*. The nation is the ever imperfect embodiment of *Deutschtum* or *Franzosentum*; *Deutschtum* itself is an idea, an unending process, in short, an aspiration.[35] Every European nation has risen to become a *Kulturnation* by following the example of Rome in attempting to find a spiritual expression of its national aspirations. To follow the example of Rome implies acceptance of the Greeks as the norm and hence that 'totale Lebensbeziehung zum Altertum' to which no part and no period of the Muslim development ever could be dedicated.[36] It has been the misfortune of the Arabs that the European sources of their nationalistic ideology (or in some cases the Arab transmitters themselves) represented a different strain of Western nationalism.[37]

[35] For the characterization of 'neo-humanistic nationalism', cf. e.g., E. Spranger, *Der Anteil des Neuhumanismus an der Entstehung des deutschen Nationalbewusstseins* (Berlin, 1923), esp. pp. 4–5, 5–6 and 11; E. Howald, op. cit., esp. pp. 3–7 and 23–41. A striking illustration for the contrasting approach of much of Arab nationalism is provided by Michel Aflaq, the leading theorist of the Syrian *Ba'th* party. Aflaq sees Arab nationalism as an existential rather than a rational fact; it exists independent of any Arab's positive acceptance of it. It is a destiny which binds him who is born into the Arab fold but which can also be adopted by him who has been associated with the Arabs in history and become one of them in thinking and feeling. Cf. L. Binder's analysis of Aflaq's ideas in his study 'Radical-Reform Nationalism in Syria and Egypt', *The Muslim World* (1959), vol. 59, pp. 101, 103, 104.

[36] Cf. Howald, op. cit., p. 7; the phrase is Spranger's as quoted by J. Kraemer, 'Die Bildungsideale des Islams und ihre gegenwärtige Problematik' in *Erziehung zur Menschlichkeit. Festschrift für Ed. Spranger* (Tübingen, 1957), pp. 273–89, at p. 278. It is no accident that the European Humanists were the first to be troubled by the relationship between past and present, who experienced the relevance of the past to the present and hence the phenomena of change and cultural survivals as problems.

[37] It will be useful to remember that Western consciousness of cultural structure is of relatively recent growth and that it was preceded by a rather naive awareness of what to us are minor contrasts in behaviour patterns; the quotation offered by A. Malvezzi, *L'Islamismo e la cultura europea* (Florence, 1956), p. 125, from F. Suriano's *Trattato di Terra Santa* (written in 1450) is a suggestive sample. The interest in things Christian observed by Ricoldo da Montecroce (d. 1320)

IV

How far removed the objective of contemporary 'Islamic research' specifically so-called is from that of Western(-inspired) historical self-interpretation and *Kulturforschung* may be documented from the statement defining such research which a prominent Pakistani, Muhammad Rafi-ud-Din (the Director of the Iqbal Academy at Karachi) recently published. Defining 'Islamic Research' as research that 'is centred around the contents of' Qur'ān and *Ḥadīth*, Dr. Rafi-ud-Din includes in it 'all that the Muslim scholars have written in the past or may write in the future (*a*) on the sacred books and (*b*) on books written about the sacred books. It excludes (*c*) all that Muslim scholars have written in the past or may write in the future on a subject other than Islam, e.g., on Medicine, Physics, Astronomy, Chemistry, Lexicography, History, Art or Literature. It excludes also (*d*) all research work that we may undertake on books written under (*c*) above. Moreover, since the contents of the sacred books are not intelligible to non-Muslims, as such, and non-Muslims cannot be expected to make them intelligible to others as sacred contents of the sacred books or even to have the intention to do so, Islamic research will also exclude (*e*) all research work done by non-Muslim scholars on the sacred books or on books written about the sacred books.'[38]

The author divides Islamic (as all) research in (1) mechanical and (2) original. The function of Original Islamic Research is double. '(1) It refutes directly or indirectly the wrong philosophical ideas that have become prevalent at the time and have begun to have an adverse effect on the faith of the Muslims. (2) It affirms the truth of Islam and defends Islamic beliefs and ideas by making use of all the right philosophical ideas that are available at the time.'[39] All research into matters connected with

during his visit to the Holy Land and especially in Baghdād (*c.* 1300) indicates a remarkable 'transcultural openness' among the educated Muslims with whom the Frater had to deal; cf. Malvezzi, op. cit., pp. 116–17, and the literature quoted on p. 147. Attention should be drawn to Sāṭiʿ al-Ḥuṣrī's *Muḥāḍarāt fī nushūʾ al-fikra al-qawmiyya* (Beirut, 1951; third edition, 1956), as an interesting survey of the rise of nationalistic thought in Western and Central Europe, the Balkans and the Turkish and Arab Near East.

[38] *The Meaning and purpose of Islamic research* (Karachi, n.d. [1957]); the book actually is a lecture held in December 1956), pp. 1–2. The uneasiness felt by some Muslim circles 'when observing non-Muslims who occupy themselves with Islam for purposes of study and observation' has been examined by C. A. O. van Nieuwenhuijze, 'Frictions Between Presuppositions', *Bulletin d'Informations* (of the Centre pour l'étude des problèmes du monde musulman contemporain at Brussels), March–April, 1958, v, 38–67, at pp. 39–47. To reserve Islam as a field of study to Muslims and thus to separate a group of peoples, a set of beliefs, a civilization from the common concern of scholarship is, of course, a fundamentally anti-humanist position. It is not necessarily but in actual fact accompanied by a lack of interest in the 'other' faiths, civilizations, etc., unless their analysis seems indicated for apologetic purposes. If carried to its logical conclusion, that is, if it were adopted by (all) other societies as well, this position would spell the end of any kind of universal history, history of religion, cultural anthropology, and the like; needless to say, it carries political implications as well.

[39] Op. cit., pp. 2–3.

what we should call Islamic civilization that are not covered by the definition of Islamic Research are merely 'Oriental Research' of which the Westerners have been the pioneers; it 'is entirely mechanical and concerns itself with translating, editing, annotating, summarizing, remodelling or indexing, ancient works of History, Philosophy, Religion, Lexicography, Science and Literature, written in the Oriental languages like Arabic, Persian, Sanskrit, Chinese, Indonesian and Turkish, etc.'[40] Apart from missionary, administrative, and political motivations the Western scholars were, in the pursuit of Oriental research, doubtless actuated also by their desire 'to satisfy their curiosity and to provide themselves with amusement by uncovering the hidden relics of an ancient civilization which according to them exists no longer and which has been superseded by a far superior civilization of which they are themselves the torchbearers. Their attitude is similar to ours in carrying out excavations at Taxila by means of which we lay bare to the world for their amusement or for the satisfaction of their curiosity the buried signs of a civilization which has ceased to exist for ever.'[41]

Could the misapprehension of our cultural aspiration and the unproductivity in terms of historical research of another be stated more clearly?[42] The goal of the Muslim Orientalist emerges as revealing 'the intellectual achievements of the ancient scholar of the East, which was the most cultured and civilized part of the globe till recently and showing their relation to the intellectual achievements of the present age'.[43] Still, research in this direction would not be Islamic research. On the other hand, a 'scientific interpretation of Islam . . . is a biological necessity for the Muslim community today and we can ignore it only at the penalty of death'.[44] To survive Islam must open an ideological offensive.[45]

The preoccupations directing 'Islamic' (but also 'Oriental') research as described and planned by Rafi-ud-Din limit it to apologetics. They reflect the absence in contemporary Islam of a positive secularist ideology, developed from the Muslim tradition itself which would parallel Western secularism as 'a positive system of values, based ultimately on Greek ideas of justice, order, reason and humanity'.[46] With the absence of self-

[40] Op. cit., p. 3. [41] Op. cit., p. 40.

[42] Cf. also, op. cit., p. 5: 'Since Oriental research is a mechanical process and has nothing original to give, it is characterized by its emphasis on petty things.'

[43] Op. cit., pp. 5–6. [44] Op. cit., p. 16.

[45] The philosophical basis of such an offensive as of any valid scientific introduction to Islam can only be Muḥammad Iqbāl's (d. 1938) Philosophy of the Self; cf. op. cit., pp. 22–3. The qualifications listed as essential for the Islamic research scholar, op. cit., pp. 24–5, remind one of those postulated by al-Māwardī for a candidate to the caliphate or by Abul Ala Maudoodi (b. 1903) for the *mujtahid*; cf. Maudoodi's communication to the International Islamic Colloquium at Lahore (29 December 1957 to 8 January 1958), *The Role of Ijtehad and the Scope of Legislation in Islam*, pp. 5–6.

[46] W. C. Smith, *Islam in modern history* (Princeton, 1957), p. 109. Smith goes on to observe that 'the Turks, alone among the Muslim peoples, have acquired such a positive secularism'.

understanding there comes almost of necessity a complementary absence of any understanding of the cultural differences between the Muslim and the Western worlds, a deficiency which is not even mitigated by an understanding of their religious components.

The intellectual situation from which Rafi-ud-Din speaks brings to mind the judgement pronounced by a young Arab intellectual on his own people who, in his view, have forgotten 'that all the self-knowledge, the history, the culture, even the ambitions of the Arabs, have been defined and articulated in and by the West in the last two hundred years. Even now there is no denying the fact that the Arab intellectual understands himself and his situation best, not in Cairo, Damascus or Beirut, writing or speaking in Arabic, but rather in Paris or London or New York, writing or speaking in French or English. His real task in the present crisis, for the next 50 years, is to find a way out of the Arab's paralysing solipsism, to come finally to understand the "other" instead of resting inertly in the "other's" understanding.'[47] The functional necessity for the great collectives to achieve self-interpretation through the understanding of the 'other' could not have been brought out more forcefully. And one seems to feel that Sharabi realizes that a shift in aspiration will have to precede the shaping of a creatively effective self-image. Changes in aspiration are *Umbrüche*—in the last analysis to be accepted as discontinuous leaps from one kind of human self-realization on to another; their nature is perhaps most readily discernible in certain reversals of artistic taste such as the sudden breakthrough of classicism in the 1750's and 1760's.[48]

V

The interdependence of self-image and subsequent historical action (and historiographical explanation) is of course confined to no particular period and to no particular civilization. It is the very universality of this connection that makes it important to retrace it. The ideological preparation for what was to become the Graeco-Macedonian conquest of the East by Isocrates (but also by Aristotle) as upholders of the essential superiority of the Hellenes over the Barbarians consists characteristically in the sharpening and inculcating of a self-view that would explain and justify the anticipated assumption of rulership. If the distance between Greek and Barbarian was as great as that between Man and Beast, Greek domination of the Barbarian was obviously called for. The elements that went to shape the self-image—in the Greek case, climate, the city as contrasted with the shapeless monarchies of the East, but also *paideia* and *dianoia*—will vary;[49]

[47] H. Sharabi, 'The Crisis of the intelligentsia in the Middle East', *The Muslim World* (1957), xlvii, 187–193, at p. 193.

[48] Cf. also Howald, op. cit., p. 28.

[49] For convenient reference, cf. e.g., G. Glotz, *La cité grecque*, second edition (Paris, 1953), p. 414. Note the insistence of Isocrates on the superiority vouchsafed the Greeks by the central

the functional relationship between image and action, aspiration and image, however, is constant.

Political pamphleteers (amongst whom Isocrates must be counted at certain stages of his development) will frequently argue their point on the basis of (what they would wish to be accepted as) the self-image of their own or another group. The interdependence of aspiration and image is almost amusingly illustrated by the great Jāḥiẓ (d. 869). Where he desires to make a recognized and respected place for the Turks in the Caliphate he blurs the ethnic distinctions between them and the Iranians and, above all, he emphasizes the assimilative effect of *walā'*, or clientship, which attaches the islamicized foreigner to the Arab tribe to which he wins affiliation. History records events that are suggestive of what may become possible in the future. Did not Ismā'īl, born of two non-Arab parents, become an Arab by divine command? Clientship emerges as the social instrument of that levelling of separatisms which religion requires when it pronounces the equality of the believers before the throne of God. Jāḥiẓ' objective, the attainment of unity in the obedience of the Caliph, colours, if it does not determine, the self-image he persuades the community to accept.[50] On another occasion however when Jāḥiẓ wishes to safeguard the prerogatives of the Arabs against the clients who claim equality on the basis of their *walā'* with the Arabs (and superiority as heirs of the cultural traditions of their Iranian ancestors which constitutes them as it were *dhawū'l-ḥaḍāratayn*) he exclaims: 'What is more irritating than to find your slave claiming to be more noble than yourself while he admits that he owes his nobility to the freedom you gave to him!'[51]

or intermediate position of their clime between the monarchies of the torrid zone etc., and the tribal peoples of the polar regions; the central position of their land was to be a point of pride with the Sasanian Persian as well as the Muslim Iraqi.

[50] Cf. *Risāla fī manāqib al-Turk* in *Tria Opuscula*, ed. G. Van Vloten (Leiden, 1903), pp. 1–56, and the recent analysis of the *risāla* by F. Gabrieli, *RSO* (1957), xxxii, 477–83: 'La Risāla di al-Gāḥiẓ sui Turchi', esp. at p. 480.

[51] *Risāla fī Banī Umayya* in *Rasā'il al-Jāḥiz*, ed. Ḥasan al-Sandūbī (Cairo, 1352/1933), pp. 292–300, at p. 300[4-5]; the *risāla* is better known as *Risāla fī'l-Nābita*, under which title it has been discussed and translated by C. Pellat in *Université d'Alger. Annales de l'Institut d'Études Orientales* (1952), x, 302–25. In our context the construction of Muslim history, and esp. of the *Rāshidūn* period, which Jāḥiẓ develops at the very beginning of his Epistle could also be cited in evidence of the interaction between aspiration and image. To add an example from a different historical context, J. G. A. Pocock, *The ancient constitution and the feudal law. A study of English historical thought in the seventeenth century* (Cambridge, 1957), pp. 16–17, states: 'By 1600 or thereabouts there was hardly any constitutional movement [in all of Europe] without its accompanying historical myth. No man granted us this liberty, it was said; it has been ours from beyond the memory of man; and consequently none can take it from us. In reply, the kings and their partisans tried to show that, in the words of James VI and I, "kings were the authors and makers of the laws and not the laws of the kings".' The purposeful romanticism with which the English of that period tended to envelop the common law as the result of immemorial custom and which dictated the reading of historical sources presents an interesting analog to some treatments of the Prophetic *sunna*. If Europe since the Renaissance has been trying to understand itself (in part) through an understanding of its past such an undertaking was possible only because it was

The criticism directed by Sāṭi' al-Ḥuṣrī against Ḥusayn Mu'nis would on the surface seem to be provoked by Mu'nis's view of the discontinuousness of Arab history.[52] In contrast to European history which, since the early Middle Ages, has known no breaks, and where each phase has grown organically from the preceding with the result that the modern Englishman, for example, experiences clearly the connections of the institutions under which he lives with *Magna Carta*; the major phases of Arab Muslim history are discrete. The age of the Umayyads is totally different from that of the *Rāshidūn*, and again from that of the 'Abbasids; the 'Abbasid caliph from the Umayyad, the society of Baghdād from that of Damascus. The changes are not developmental but *sprunghaft* and resemble new starts. 'So when today we aim to revive the past generations of Muslims, we actually aim to manufacture an unnatural phenomenon; we aim to shape our history on the European model. But while the contemporary Englishman feels that there exists a genuine connection between himself and *Magna Carta* and the *Habeas Corpus*, we feel truly that there is no real tie that would link us with the Banū Umayya or the Banū 'Abbās.' 'For this reason it is only natural that of all peoples the Arabs are least influenced by their past and least tied to it.'[53] Sāṭi' al-Ḥuṣrī does not find it too difficult to make his case for historical continuity in the Arab-Muslim world. In fact, he finds support in another statement of his opponents in which Mu'nis had stressed the survival of what one may call the 'Abbasid style of administration in modern Egypt.

The significant aspect of this debate is however neither Mu'nis's overstatement nor al-Ḥuṣrī's *mise-à-point*. It is the irreconcilable conflict of the aspirations underlying the irreconcilable conflict of the self-views that Mu'nis and al-Ḥuṣrī reflect in their presentation of Arab-Muslim history. Mu'nis does not find a commitment in the Arab-Muslim past—Arab history has always moved in unrelated phases; so one may conclude the future of the Arabs may be a new start, inspired perhaps by Western ideas and social models, in any event it can be conceived of as detachable from a past which is clearly experienced as an inadequate inspiration in the present situation. Quite different al-Ḥuṣrī! To him Arab-Muslim history is as naturally structured as any history could be and the Arab is as committed to it as any European to his. The shapers of the future, we may

generally agreed that this past somehow still survived and, in any event, was still meaningful. That the Muslim world, by and large, has not developed a comparable outlook on history is, in large measure and for its classical period, due to the fact that Muslim history was perceived as a self-sufficient whole, to whose interpretation neither the religious and moral morass of the *Jāhiliyya* nor the incidents that filled the annals of the peoples had anything significant to contribute.

[52] 'Ḥawla māḍī'l-'Arab' in his collection of essays *Difā' 'an al-'urūba* (Beirut, 1956), pp. 93–105.

[53] Ibid., p. 96.

infer, need to take the past into account—the 'Abbasids are as real to al-Ḥuṣrī as *Magna Carta* is to Mu'nis's Englishman.[54]

But the past has more than one lesson to teach. The early disintegration of the Muslim empire and, in addition, the fact that for the last millennium or longer there never had been a time in which Muslims had enjoyed political unity are proof that the road towards such unity must first lead towards the unity of the Arab-speaking peoples. Whether or not the political unity of the Muslims is an objective capable of realization, the political unification of the Arabs must be achieved before *al-waḥda al-islāmiyya* can seriously be attempted *bi-ma'nāhā al-siyāsī*. Those who put the unity of the Muslims ahead of that of the Arabs and those who go so far as to consider Arab unity as a danger to Muslim unity fail to distinguish between 'brotherhood in the faith', *al-ukhuwwa al-dīniyya*, and a 'political tie', *al-rābiṭa al-siyāsiyya*. Yet, while al-Ḥuṣrī is confirmed in his conviction by arguments drawn from history, geography and logic, he realizes that he will not be able to shake the beliefs of the religionists who, in our terminology, do not feel bound by history and whose aspirations deprive the logic of facts of its conclusiveness.[55]

VI

History is the battleground of aspirations; the self-image suggests the image of the past. Hence, the historical touch of Muslim apologetics, and hence also the need to demonstrate the glories of a past of which only selected episodes are accepted as significant and symptomatic in terms of prognostication. As early as 1923 Ṭāhā Ḥusayn (b. 1889) spoke of 'those who see in the study of history only an opportunity to glorify ancestors'; although he made it clear that he did not accept their approach 'he conceded that they represented an inevitable phase in the development of a country renascent but not yet great, attributing to its past the splendour that it lacked in the present'.[56] In 1947 Ṭāhā Ḥusayn completed his observation by noting 'Once the Modernists had gained a decisive victory over the Conservatives, they took to re-thinking Islamic history, and from 1933 onwards they produced a literature of religious inspiration which was avidly welcomed by the reading public.'[57] It is in this movement that

[54] The debate in 1952 between 'Abd al-'Azīz Sāmī and Sāṭi' al-Ḥuṣrī on the one hand and Muḥammad 'Abdallāh 'Inān on the other, whether the 'Saracens' who entered Switzerland in the tenth century were 'Arabs' or (non-Arab) 'Muslims' again reflects a difference in self-view which, in turn, is mirrored in the interpretation of historical data; ibid., pp. 106–13.

[55] Cf. Sāṭi' al-Ḥuṣrī, 'Bayn al-waḥdat al-islāmiyya wa'l-waḥdat al-'arabiyya' in *Ārā' wa-aḥādīth fī'l-waṭaniyya wa'l-qawmiyya*, third edition (Beirut, 1957), pp. 94–105, especially at pp. 95–8 and 101; the book was first published in 1947.

[56] P. Cachia, *Ṭāhā Ḥusayn. His place in the Egyptian literary renaissance* (London, 1956), p. 181, with reference to *Ḥadīth al-arba'ā'*, ii, 79–86.

[57] Ibid., p. 197, with reference to Ṭāhā Ḥusayn's study 'Tendances religieuses de la littérature égyptienne d'aujourd'hui', *L'Islam et l'Occident* (1947), 239–41.

Tawfīq al-Ḥakīm's *Ahl al-kahf* (1933) and the 'hagiographic'[58] biographies of the Prophet by Muḥammad Ḥusayn Haykal (1888–1956)[59] and 'Abbās Maḥmūd al-'Aqqād (b. 1889)[60] and of course Ṭāhā Ḥusayn's own series, the novelistic *'Alā hāmish al-sīra* (1933; 1937; 1946)[61] and the more historiographical *al-Fitna al-kubrā* (1947; 1953) are to be placed.

In the introductory section of his *'Uthmān*[62] Ṭāhā Ḥusayn allows us to recognize his double objective: the removal of the history of the *fitna* and its antecedents from the area of religious partisanship and the identification of impersonal circumstances rather than the weaknesses or evil intentions of certain personalities as the causes of the disturbances that led to the assassination of the Caliph 'Uthmān. It is a mistake to measure 'Uthmān by the aspirations of his two predecessors to establish political and social justice, aspirations that could not but fail, seeing that Abū Bakr and 'Umar were far in advance of their times. Ṭāhā Ḥusayn acknowledges his awareness of the religious implications which the events of the period carry for most Muslims even to this day. But he professes himself free from any bias of this kind. He insists on the uniqueness of the Islamic political order[63] yet feels that 'Umar perhaps did not go far enough in developing 'consultation'.[64]

One wonders whether Ṭāhā Ḥusayn is conscious of the typically Sunnite character of his attitude when, with a notable advance in the sophistication of historical analysis, he exculpates persons and blames conditions.[65] He draws a favourable portrait of 'Alī[66] in which he does not however depart from tradition. Where Ṭāhā Ḥusayn penetrates more deeply than his Muslim contemporaries into the course of events and the circumstances that brought it about he does so because of the greater scope of his psychological comprehension and because his objective of impersonalizing the tragic sequence of happenings provides him with cues which the conventional black-and-white narrative necessarily lacked; but the deepened understanding of the period which he achieves is not due to improved technical handling of the sources, to stricter canons of criticism, to greater sensitivity to anachronisms and the like. He does not hesitate to reject the testimony of all the historians concerning the reasons which led to Sa'd b. Abī Waqqāṣ's recall from the governorship of Kūfa on the simple ground

[58] The expression is M. Rodinson's, *Diogène* (1957), No. 20, p. 46, n. 17.

[59] *Ḥayāt Muḥammad* (Cairo, 1935; improved and enlarged second edition, same year). On the book and its critics cf. C. Brockelmann, *GAL*, S III 208–20.

[60] *'Abqariyyat Muḥammad* (Cairo, n.d.); cf. also his parallel works *'Abqariyyat al-Ṣiddīq* (Cairo, 1951), *'Abqariyyat 'Umar*, fifth edition (Cairo, 1948), and *'Abqariyyat al-Imām* (i.e. 'Alī), second edition (Cairo, 1947).

[61] Not 1946–7 as stated by Cachia, op. cit., p. 254; Brockelmann, op. cit., III 299–301, offers an analysis of the first two volumes.

[62] The book forms the first part of *al-Fitna al-kubrā*.

[63] E.g., pp. 31–2.

[64] Cf., pp. 48, 60–3.

[65] Cf. p. 49.

[66] pp. 152–3.

that those reasons reflect unfavourably on the third oldest of the *ṣaḥāba* and therefore cannot have been true.[67] Nor does he hesitate to utilize anachronistic traditions where they suit his purpose.[68] Yet he criticizes the thoughtless idealization of the early decades of the Caliphate by those who do so on purely religious grounds and he analyses shrewdly the motivations to the different interpretations which different Muslims place on the historical reports regarding the involvement of the *ṣaḥāba* in the opposition and in the revolt against 'Uthmān.[69] To remove the *fitna* from the causes of inter-Muslim cleavage and to demonstrate the uniqueness of the ideal Islamic order—these are the leading aspirations of Ṭāhā Ḥusayn's work. The desire to bring to life for his generation the tales of the past and to suggest a more subtle and, we may add, a more modern analytical approach even to semi-sacred history represent the other elements that have shaped and limited Ṭāhā Ḥusayn's presentation of historical events.[70] Fact-finding as such is not among them. To reintegrate the *fitna* in the consciousness of the educated as an ever meaningful chain of happenings is to Ṭāhā Ḥusayn clearly more important than the elucidation of moot points in the *fitna* itself.

It is not quite easy to extract the guiding vision from Subḥī Waḥīda's *Fī uṣūl al-mas'ala al-Miṣriyya*.[71] For one thing, it is in some respects a learned book or at least meant to be such. It offers the complete skeleton of a history of Egypt, oriented to its economic and social aspects; the presentation is, for the most part, based on somewhat haphazardly garnered secondary evidence; yet it is careful and avoids the shrillness of tone which is so rarely absent even from semi-political writing in the contemporary East. It is an apologetic book, but it lacks the aggressiveness that usually accompanies apologetics; it is also a constructive book even though it is difficult to see how the 'practising' statesman could utilize its insights. For the image which this Christian paints of his country's position in the world is too complex and too close to historical realities to allow for simple conclusions to be gained from it.

The Muslim conquest of Egypt was, in its effect, first and foremost an Arab conquest. It is remarkable how soon the arabization of the country

[67] pp. 90–5. The observation of R. Brunel, *Le monachisme errant dans l'Islam. Sidi Heddi et les Heddawa* (Paris, 1955), p. 24, comes to mind. '. . . Les biographes musulmans se soucient fort peu de la précision historique, leur objet principal étant trop apparemment de mettre leur sujet en concordance étroite avec l'orthodoxie, sans s'attacher à suivre la réalité et à la rendre fidèlement. Ils s'estiment en règle avec celle-ci lorsque l'épure répond à l'opinion personnelle qu'ils se font du sujet.'

[68] pp. 157–8.

[69] E.g., pp. 170–1.

[70] The subtlety of Ṭāhā Ḥusayn's approach to history is best appreciated when it is held against the conventional dullness of Aḥmad Amīn's accounting for the Muslim decline by reference to adverse external events that have befallen the Muslim world; cf. his *Ẓu'amā' al-islām fī'l-'aṣr al-ḥadīth* (Cairo, 1948), pp. 5–6, where the author does not betray any realization of the internal development that takes place within a political and cultural unit.

[71] Cairo, 1950.

was accomplished. The distinction between Christians and Muslims continues to this day; but Egyptian society of both religious camps has become irrecoverably arabicized.[72] The differences in Egyptian and Syrian, Syrian and Iraqi ways of thinking are not due to any differences in national consciousness. The Muslim empire was not structured by national entities. The very names of the ruling dynasties, the ease with which the Umayyads removed from their native Mecca to Damascus, the 'Abbasids enlisted Persian support, the Arab Fatimids founded their state in North Africa, transplanted it to Egypt and would, under favourable circumstances, have transferred its capital to Iraq, is evidence that the basis of the political society was not the nation, but that, on the other hand, its Arab foundation was everywhere strong enough to carry a political superstructure of varying geographical strength.[73]

It is understandable, and very largely justified, that Waḥīda emphasizes the continuity of Egyptian administration rather than the innovations introduced by succeeding régimes. But it would be unfair to charge him with blindness to the changing characteristics of the major periods through which Egypt lived—yet the sameness of an Egypt that experienced only one incisive transformation, viz. its arabization, remains the dominant motif. The homogeneity of what we should wish to call the orbit of Muslim civilization—in preference to Waḥīda's concept of an area deriving what uniformity it possesses from its arabization—militates in Waḥīda's vision against a strong sense of the 'individuality' of Egypt. The underplaying of the Muslim factor affecting Egypt as the result of the Arab conquest may be connected with Waḥīda's tendency to resolve the Christian-Muslim conflict as merely a social differentiation within the Arabic civilization of his country; at the same time he tries to isolate Egypt by a lengthy discussion of its own particular history before and under Islam; simultaneously, a third outlook asserts itself, that induces Waḥīda to oppose the views of those who explain the ills of present-day Egypt in terms of the natural disposition of its population, by deriving them from the general situation of the world after the discovery of the Cape of Good Hope—an analysis which incidentally leads him to reject the identification of individual powers as the culprits in the unsatisfactory state of Egyptian affairs.[74]

Waḥīda sees clearly the contradictory conclusions reached by his contemporaries in diagnosing Egypt's cultural position—one group led by Ṭāhā Ḥusayn holding that her intellectual kinship with the West compels her, in the conflict between Eastern and Western civilization, to range herself with the West; the other, best represented by Tawfīq al-Ḥakīm, that Egypt needs to adhere to the Eastern tradition as the one more closely in tune with what is best in mankind;[75] but the diversity of the aspirations that motivate him and, one may add, large sections of the society for which

[72] pp. 39–40. [73] Cf. e.g., pp. 42–3. [74] Cf. e.g., pp. 2–3. [75] p. 280.

he speaks, prevent him from subscribing to the objectives of either party. The outlook that appears to Waḥīda to be most readily compatible with those aspirations—even though in the view of this writer at least the tenet of arabization as the only major break in Egypt's history has not been completely harmonized with it—is an emphasis on the unity of the Mediterranean. Waḥīda insists on his awareness of the differences separating from one another each and every of the peoples that inhabit the shores of the Mediterranean, and again of the differences separating all of them from the Egyptians; yet he feels that those differences do not touch 'the major lines', *al-khuṭūṭ al-kubrā*, on which the lives of those societies are ordered; those who desire to take Egypt out of this Mediterranean context[76] are victims of a misunderstanding as serious as the misunderstanding of those who impute the unsatisfactory state of Egypt to innate defects in her population and so are led to despair of her future altogether.[77]

So the analysis ends in placing Egypt in a net of relations that justify the cultural tendencies of the Western-oriented, and separate her from the Asiatic Muslim areas, while leaving her within a region of arabization (rather than islamicization) that permits the merely arabicized Copt to identify in essentials with the arabicized Copt who has also been won over to Islam.

The future which Muḥammad 'Abd al-Qādir al-'Amāwī[78] envisages for Islam—seen variously and indistinctly as a religion, a social order, a political system and a civilization—is of very uncertain contours. The unlimited adaptability of the Qur'anic message makes it appear hazy. Its specific commitment to a programme in history would deprive it of its inspirational quality and it is almost exclusively by al-'Amāwī's statements on what the Islamic message is not that we can reconstruct what he believes it is. As he expects and aggressively provokes the opposition of the 'religious reactionaries', the atheists and those favouring an autocratic régime, we may assume that he stands for 'true' democracy, that is to say a democracy not on the Western model[79] but of a kind which is based on what he apprehends as the progressive character of genuine Islam. The tendency

[76] This context, we assume, accounts for the relatively minor effect of Greek rule which, to Waḥīda, actually was that of 'foreign kinsmen' (to use an expression which goes beyond Waḥīda's position).

[77] pp. 283–4.

[78] *Mustaqbal al-islām*, 2nd edition (Cairo, 1956).

[79] Western democracy is described with incredible superficiality on pp. 193–9; for the kinship of Islamic principles and democracy cf. pp. 204–5; see also p. 206, the statement that in Islam *ḥukm* is based solely on *shūrā*. The Qur'anic injunction *washāwir-hum fī'l-amri* (3: 153), 'And take counsel with them in the affair', has long been used in discussions of rulership. The Prophet's reliance on advice appears as an argument against unrestrained despotism in Niẓām al-Mulk's (d. 1092) *Siyāsat-Nāma*, ed. Ch. Schefer (Paris, 1891–7), p. 85 (English translation of the passage by A. J. Arberry, *Classical Persian Literature* (London, 1958), pp. 75–6), and again in Sa'd al-Dīn Varāvīnī's *Marzbān-Nāma* (written between 1210 and 1225), ed. M. M. Qazwīnī (Leiden and London, 1909), p. 176 (Italian translation by F. Gabrieli in *RSO* (1941), xix, 130).

that pervades all al-'Amāwī's thinking is to keep from Islam any particularization and limitation which the actual history of the Muslims (rather than Islam itself) may have imposed on it. History has no force to bind the later generations. True Islam was realized solely during the Prophet's lifetime, the reigns of the first two caliphs and the episodic rule of the Umayyad 'Umar II (717–20).[80] With the slate of memory wiped clean of the historical (administrative, political) experiences of the past, it is the turn of the articulations of the faith. Admittedly, religious beliefs need to be formulated; an *'aqīda* cannot be dispensed with;[81] but the *'aqā'id* will come to be or at least to contain retarding elements that are as responsible for the decay of Islam as, on the one hand, colonization, *isti'mār*, and on the other, the human inadequacy of the *rijāl al-dīn* (and of those rulers who claimed to be God's representatives on earth).[82] The constrictive character of any definition of the nature of Islam implies a condemnation of sectarian movements. Al-'Amāwī turns against attempts such as those made by

[80] E.g., p. 205. Al-'Amāwī's classical (non-Shī'ī) predecessors such as, for instance, the Ibāḍī Abu Ḥamza 'Abdallāh in his famous address of A.D. 747 (trans. by G. Van Vloten, *Recherches sur la domination arabe* (Amsterdam, 1894), pp. 76–8, from Abu'l-Faraj al-Iṣfahānī, *Kitāb al-aghānī* (Būlāq, 1285), xx, 106–7) and Jāḥiẓ himself, loc. cit., pp. 292^{5-6} (trans. Pellat, loc. cit., p. 310), extend the golden age through the first six years of 'Uthmān's rule. Jāḥiẓ does not mention 'Umar II, while Abū Ḥamza gives him credit for his intenions but judges him to have failed in carrying them out. Thābit b. Qurra (d. 901) held that the Arabs were to be envied for three personalities: 'Umar b. al-Khaṭṭāb, Ḥasan al-Baṣrī and al-Jāḥiẓ; his statement is quoted by Tawḥīdī, *Baṣā'ir*, pp. 194^{11}–198^{6}. In Thābit's characterization of 'Umar (pp. 195^{3}–196^{7}) there occurs (p. 195^{9}) the significant phrase: *wa-mazaja al-dunyā bi'l-dīn wa-a'āna al-dīn bi'l-dunyā.* This phrase is missing in the much shorter version of Thābit's discourse on 'Umar in Yāqūt, *Dictionary of learned men*, ed. D. S. Margoliouth, second edition (London, 1923–6), vi, 69^{10-19} (quoted from Tawḥīdī's *Taqrīẓ al-Jāḥiẓ*).

[81] *Mustaqbal al-islām*, p. 17.

[82] Ibid., pp. 14–16. The dislike for definition and explicitation of dogma is as old in Islam as doctrinal searching and dispute. The well-known *qāḍī* Abū Ḥāmid al-Marwarūdhī (d. 362/972–3), e.g., compares in a poem the situation of the *mutakallimīn* in their disputes with that of travellers through the desert who, under the direction of an incompetent guide, find themselves in the evening precisely where they set out in the morning. Cf. Tawḥīdī (d. 1023), *al-Baṣā'ir wa'l-dhakhā'ir*, ed. Aḥmad Amīn and Aḥmad Ṣaqr (Cairo, 1373/1953), pp. 60–1. This attitude coupled with scepticism regarding the ability of human reason to cope with theological problems is frequently expressed during the first great theological debate of Islam. Ibn 'Abbās is made to reply when asked his views on *qadar* that this concept is like the sun: the longer you stare at it the more your eye will be blinded; ibid., p. 40^{11-11}; cf. also p. 126. The anti-theoretical attitude and the horror of definition carries over into nationalistic writings of our times; cf. e.g., Michel Aflaq's view that nationalism should not be enclosed 'in a framework of narrow definition', that theory deadens and leads to inaccuracy, a position, incidentally, which makes his own efforts at circumscribing the nature of Arab nationalism look somewhat paradoxical (cf. Binder, op. cit., pp. 101, 107). The Egyptian, Anwar al-Sādāt, *Revolt on the Nile* (London, 1957), p. 53, declares in a similar vein that he has always distrusted theories and purely rational systems. The intellectual vagueness of the conceptual framework of the aspirations voiced impressively in Anwar al-Sādāt's *Qiṣṣat al-waḥda al-'arabiyya* (Cairo, 1957; briefly discussed together with a translation of the first chapter by A. Miquel, 'Patriotisme égyptien et nationalisme arabe', *Orient*, ii/1 (No. 5, 1958), 91–112) and the definition of Arab nationalism, *qawmiyya*, offered by the Third Congress of Arab Writers (Cairo, 9–15 December 1957; French translation ibid., pp. 44–5) also reflect a state of mind for which *Gefühl ist alles* . . .

Goldziher or M.ʿA. al-ʿAqqād to explain the rise of the sects and the *fitan* in Islam as the results of large historical issues; he interprets those movements as merely the consequence of over-subtlety and insincerity on the part of the newly converted, or of personal ambition of certain leaders and the like.[83] Nor is there any conflict between reason and religion as such; where a conflict does obtain, it is between reason and the *ʿaqīdat rijāl al-dīn* and their personal *sulūk*.[84]

Al-ʿAmāwī insists that there is nothing in the nature of Islam that would necessarily have led to the Sunnī-Shīʿī as to any other sectarian division; the split between Sunna and Shīʿa is due exclusively to political circumstances.[85] As a matter of fact the Shīʿī ideology is a 'foreign body' introduced into Islam by people such as 'Abdallāh b. Saba' who had undergone but an outward conversion.[86] The contemporary Shīʿī cannot be accused of insincerity, remoteness from religion (*al-buʿd ʿan al-dīn*) or the desire to destroy Islam; the instigators of Shiʿism however must be charged with those defects and intentions.[87] The murder of Ḥusayn is the blackest deed recorded by history[88]—only the enemies of Islam stood to gain by it; so it is they who must be identified as its engineers.[89] All Muslim sects, the author insists time and again owe their existence to extra-religious motivations, primarily to a desire to damage Islam.[90] The Islam al-ʿAmāwī has in mind is never clearly defined, but from his criticism of the sects and of the Muʿtazila, who are accused of removing the faith from the essentials by introducing the excessive refinements of philosophic reasoning,[91] there emerges an image of Islam as the smallest common denominator of what any Muslim community ever conceived Islam to be,[92] a set of attitudes justifiable from the Qur'ān and elements of the Sunna, elements that are selected so directly and naïvely in response to current objectives that the arbitrariness of the selection in terms of both the Muslim *ʿilm al-ḥadīth* and Western critical scholarship goes unnoticed. In the last analysis Islam is, to al-ʿAmāwī, what the 'right-minded' people in any community want or experience it to be. More than anything else, it is an identification, a banner, a cause; it can be defined by negation rather

[83] Ibid., pp. 131–5. Al-ʿAmāwī's attitude continues the irritation felt by classical orthodoxy with the attempts to conceptualize the idea of *qadar* and the like. Ibn Khaldūn, too, was sensitive to the socially disruptive effect of theological argumentation but found comfort in the conviction that the science of speculative theology was no longer needed since heretics and innovators had been eliminated and the orthodox leaders had built a fence around religion; cf. *Prolegomena*, ed. E. Quatremère (Paris, 1858), iii, 36–43; trans. F. Rosenthal (New York, 1958), iii, 44–54.

[84] Ibid., p. 188. [85] Ibid., pp. 149–50. [86] Ibid., p. 154. [87] Ibid., pp. 156–7.

[88] Ibid., p. 159 pult. [89] Ibid., pp. 158–61. [90] E.g., ibid., p. 185. [91] Ibid., pp. 180–1.

[92] The question whether ignorance of doctrine and aberrant practice exclude from the community, i.e., confer the status of *kāfir* on an individual or a sub-community, has been argued throughout the history of Islam. The latitudinarian view, which is also the only practicable one in backward and tribal areas with a strongly persisting *ʿurf*, holds that the profession of faith suffices to preserve the status of 'believer'. On the problem cf. e.g., L. Gardet and M.-M. Anawati, *Introduction à la théologie musulmane* (Paris, 1948), pp. 333, 340 and 433–5.

than assertion; for al-'Amāwī has a horror of fixation, be it by theological definition, juridical stipulation or the bare factuality of history. What all heretics have in common, in fact the quality that constitutes them deviants and outsiders is precisely the urge to define Islam, circumscribe doctrinal implications and acknowledge historical precedent outside of the timeless romanticism of that *Rāshidūn* period that never was.[93]

There is a hint that the very universalism of the Islamic Revelation carried with it the dangers of sectarian division, considering the appeal of its message to peoples of different backgrounds.[94] There is besides a realization that Islam is 'of one piece', that its bases support one another, that its religious and political aspects are inseparable.[95] But these insights are, as it were, not really understood. For the author brushes them aside to insist again and again that differences in religious views within Islam sprang from the hidden hostility to it on the part of Arabs and non-Arabs[96] and the detrimental influences of the *mawālī* on the Islamic life are dwelt upon at length.[97] Islam is a political system—but only three of those who ever held sway over the community were Islamic rulers; the others merely ruled in the name of Islam, but Islam cannot be held responsible for their administration.[98] Little wonder that al-'Amāwī's horror of history does not lead him to any comprehension of the past or of the historical process as such.

The summary of pre-Islamic history[99] which is offered to illustrate the degradation of the world before the coming of the Prophet makes no effort whatever to provide accurate information.[100] What we may call deliberate ignorance continues into the presentation of the Muslim period; it is hardly conceivable that an educated Muslim could be as defectively informed on the history of his faith and the faithful as al-'Amāwī shows himself to be. Argument from psychological *a priori* is readily admitted: 'Alī being what he was (the characterization is based on unsifted tradition) could not have been opposed to Abū Bakr's accession.[101] The report of 'Uthmān's death is taken indiscriminately from Ibn Sa'd and Ibn Khaldūn.[102] The events of the ninth century are stylized to bear out the prejudgement that the period was moving away from Islam.[103]

[93] For this romanticism cf. e.g., op. cit., p. 122. Ibn al-Muqaffa' (d. 757), 'Risāla fi'l-ṣaḥāba' in M. K. 'Alī, *Rasā'il al-bulaghā'*, fourth edition (Cairo, 1954), p. 126^{14-15}, designates the first four caliphs as *a'immat al-hudā*, a term that brings out their normative position very forcefully; cf. also the expression *sunan hādiya* used by Aḥmad b. Abī Ṭāhir in his famous letter to his son (written in the reign of Ma'mūn) and quoted by E. I. J. Rosenthal, *Political Thought in Medieval Islam* (Cambridge, 1958), p. 75.

[94] Op. cit., pp. 127–8. [95] Op. cit., pp. 52–5. [96] Cf. e.g., op. cit., pp. 118–19.

[97] Op. cit., pp. 97–101; the *mawālī* as forgers of *ḥadīth*, p. 95.

[98] Op. cit., pp. 113–14. [99] Ibid., pp. 52–114.

[100] The materials used and the 'facts' narrated are very similar to those presented by Abu'l-Ḥasan 'Alī al-Ḥasanī al-Nadwī, *Mādhā khasara al-'ālam bi'nḥiṭāṭ al-Muslimīn?*, second edition (Cairo, 1370/1951), pp. 21–64.

[101] *Mustaqbal al-islām*, pp. 119–22. [102] Ibid., p. 106. [103] Ibid., pp. 110–13.

The reduction of Islam to an idea evasively located in the Holy Book and manifested but for a brief span in a human society eliminates any relation of this idea to history. Islam is described as capable of informing each and every historical situation,[104] but strictly speaking it has been realized only in two brief episodes. Al-'Amāwī's Islam could, but hardly ever did, validate history, nor did history ever validate Islam,[105] if al-'Amāwī's position is taken seriously. Al-'Amāwī's Islam—an extreme and, within the Muslim world, somewhat atypical instance of an aspiration to which history and hence historiography are valueless—empties history of any meaning to a believer and deprives him of any motivation to investigate its course. Divested of any function in the realization of al-'Amāwī's objective—the rebuilding of his society by means of an identification projecting past history onto a pre-existing revelation—history bows out. The vanishing of the lifegiving context makes the data of the past sink below the threshold of distinctness. The Muslim reformer remains alone with a Book and the fiction of the short-lived blissful origins; he is free to remould his society in the name of an ideological entity that will shift its shape to accommodate his aspirations. But this freedom is gained by the sacrifice of history, that very history whose next phase al-'Amāwī intends to re-form.

[104] Ibid., p. 92.

[105] To vary the expression used by W. C. Smith, *Islam in modern history* (Princeton, 1957), p. 32.

41. THE HISTORICAL DEVELOPMENT IN ISLAM OF THE CONCEPT OF ISLAM AS AN HISTORICAL DEVELOPMENT

WILFRED CANTWELL SMITH

W. M. Birks Professor of Comparative Religion and Director of the Institute of Islamic Studies, McGill University

Introduction to the Problem

When human beings think or talk about religion in general or any one particular religion, they do so under three main heads. The first is personal, the second and third are systematic and institutional. The first, the personal, considers the life of the spirit, the quality of faith, for a specific individual: it is immediate, concrete, and existential. My faith is my own, in a highly personal and private sense, and is different from my brother's, and indeed even different from what it was ten years ago. Any man's religious life is a dynamic human reality. To conceptualize it is precarious and doubtless always inadequate, though sometimes important.

The second and third considerations are more impersonal, are community possessions: the religious systems to which whole bodies of people 'belong'. The system may be conceptualized in two ways: as ideal, or as historical reality. Between ideal and actuality, essence and existence, there is always a well-known gap; probably in the case of religion that gap yawns at its widest, since here by the very nature of religion the ideal tends to be at its loftiest and purest, whereas the actuality (apparently by the very nature of man and his society) has sometimes proven highly corruptible and almost always immensely involved, subject to the influence and even domination and distortion of a great variety of other factors.

In addition, then, to my Christian faith which is utterly my own and no one else's, a quality of my personal life and of my eternal destiny, not directly observable by others, there is 'Christianity' in general, an abstract system which in some sense I share with millions of others. Or rather, there are two Christianities: 'true Christianity' or the ideal which the theologian tries to formulate but which he knows transcends him, on the one hand, and on the other the Christianity of history, which the sociologist or other observer notes as a human, sometimes all too human, complex.

The relation of John Doe's Christianness (the fact or quality of his being or becoming a Christian) to Christianity in general, or to true Christianity, is a serious and difficult question—for him, for a philosopher or an historian observing him, and for a student of *Religionswissenschaft*.

The same sort of consideration applies in the case of Islam. To put the matter in other terms, the word 'Islām' is used in at least three distinct ways, to refer to three related but different things. First, there is the Islam, the self-commitment, the *taslīm kardan*, of an individual Muslim: his own personal submission to God, the act of dedication wherein he as a specific and live person in his concrete situation is deliberately and numinously related to a transcendent divine reality which he recognizes and to a cosmic imperative which he accepts. Secondly and thirdly there are the Platonic ideal and the empirical actuality of the total system of Islam as an institutionalized entity. This is a generalized pattern, of the religion in the one case as it ideally is, at its conceivable best, in the other case as tangible reality, a mundane phenomenon historical and sociological.

We may designate these three as Islam the active personal faith, Islam the religious system as transcendent ideal, and Islam the religious system as historical phenomenon. In the first case, the term 'Islam' is a *maṣdar*, a verbal noun, the name of an action rather than of an institution; it is the response of a particular person to a challenge. That person's whole being is involved, in a transaction, as it were, between his soul and the universe; and, according to his conviction, his eternal destiny is at stake. It involves a decision, private and inalienable. His personal submittingness—if we may use such a term—is, of course, quite distinct from any other person's. Between this action (*islām*) and the fact of his personal faith (*īmān*) the relation is not altogether straightforward and has been much discussed; yet in general the two are of the same order of ideas. 'Islam' here may not mean exactly what 'faith' means (and no one, Muslim, Christian, or philosopher, has ever been able satisfactorily to translate religious faith into words); but it means something comparable.

In the second and third cases, 'Islam' is the name of a religion. On the whole, there is a tendency here for believing Muslims to use the term in the second sense, as an ideal, and for outside observers to use it in the third, as an historical-sociological actuality. This is because men generally tend to talk about other people's religions as they are and about their own as it ought to be. If they have no faith of their own they usually think of all religion as observably practised. As a result, insiders and outsiders may use the same words but be talking of different things.

However, this distribution of meanings is not absolute. Believers also recognize that their religion has in fact had a history, a mundane application, an objectively institutionalized development; and although they may regard this as perhaps but a sorry reflection of the transcendent ideal, yet they may still call it Islam, in its earthly version as it were. Similarly non-believers, although they cannot share with the faithful the notion that ideal Islam is eternal and universal, a pre-existent idea in the mind of God, a final truth, yet may and often do postulate an ideal entity, Islam, which transcends the practice of the community and transcends perhaps even the concepts of individual Muslims.

Accordingly, we may stress the point that the word 'Islam' has three kinds of meaning, without postulating what that meaning in any case is. There is room for wide divergence as to what constitutes the personal piety of the individual Muslim; as to what the ideal of 'true' Islam essentially is; as to what has been the actual quality of the Islam that has observably existed over now many centuries in time and over increasingly many areas in geographic space and with many, not yet always clearly elucidated, ramifications in human society. We also leave open the difficult and subtle question of the relation between the three things, which are obviously connected at the same time as obviously different. We would certainly not aspire to closing the discussion as to what Islam is, in any of these realms. Rather our suggestion is that the threefold discrimination here put forward may help to let that discussion be carried forward more fruitfully.

In particular, our purpose in the present paper is to give an historical dimension to such discussion. Our concern is with the history of ideas. Understanding is furthered, we feel, not only if we clarify the concepts that we are using, as a first step towards refining them so that they may serve with more adequate justice to represent in our minds that to which they refer. Understanding is also furthered perhaps if we may appreciate more clearly the historical process by which the concepts now available to us have come to be used with the content with which today we are using them.

Our long-range ambition, we may confess, is to come closer to an understanding of what Islam (and, ultimately, religion) really is. In the meantime, however, we content ourselves with the veriest prolegomenon to this, namely a preliminary concern with certain instances of what people at various times and places have thought it to be.

In particular, it has seemed to us on investigation that although today the word 'Islam' is used in the three senses mentioned, this was not always so; or at least that the relative proportion of usage was in the past greatly different. Indeed we are somewhat impelled to the conclusion that the concept of Islam as a religious system, and especially as an historical system, is increasingly dominant but relatively modern.

We have found that a similar historical development is in evidence in other religions also.

Through the centuries of man's religiousness in general, and particularly within the development of each of the individual world religions, there seems discernible a long-term trend towards self-conscious systematization. What begins as active practice and faith gradually becomes, or is thought to become, definable pattern. The personal experience, behaviour, or belief of individual or group is abstracted and generalized, is conceptualized as an independent entity. Religion in general, and particularly the great religions, have been undergoing an historical process of reification.

In an as yet unpublished address[1] we have tentatively examined this process for the concept of religion in general and for the religions other than Islam. We have also touched on the Islamic instance, stressing the similarities and the differences in its conception. Our conclusion was that the Islamic religion, for various reasons which are susceptible of study, has been in some ways from the beginning the most reified of all the world's religions; and yet that like others it began (was proclaimed in the Qur'ān) as a ringing personal summons to individual men and women to have faith in God and to commit themselves wholeheartedly to His commands, with the institutions and conceptualized system of what we now call Islam the result of that faith and commitment. We suggest that that result has come into historical existence and (then?) into conceptual thought more gradually and indeed in its modern form much more recently than is usually recognized. Such a process of tardy reification is readily demonstrable for Christianity, 'Hinduism', and the rest. We have come to believe that Islamic history evinces something comparable, and the present study is an attempt to investigate this.

The fundamentally rewarding task would be to make a study of the history of the word 'Islam': to discover the evolution of its usage and meaning over the centuries and the variety of connotations that it has evinced in the course of its historical development. We have been recently reminded that 'the history of Islam has yet to be written'.[2] One preliminary approach to that historical study of the religion might be the historical study of the word. Clearly it would be a formidable task, perhaps the work of a lifetime. What we are attempting here is very considerably less ambitious, a first step towards that preliminary approach. Yet despite the quite limited scope, already the results seem suggestive. That they have significance is made the more probable in that this verbal study confirms the development suggested independently by other considerations.[3]

The term *islām* in the Qur'ān itself has been the object of considerable study, both by Muslims and recently by Western scholars.[4] The two groups differ in that the latter, regarding the text as expressive of the mind of

[1] 'Is Islam the name of a Religion?', delivered at Princeton University, January 1957. 'Should the Great Religions have Names?' delivered at the University of Tehran and the American University at Cairo, February 1958.

[2] R. Brunschvig, in G. E. von Grunebaum, ed., *Unity and Variety in Muslim Civilization* (Chicago, 1955), p. 47, citing A. J. Wensinck from article 'Ṣalāt' in *Handwörterbuch des Islam* (Leiden, 1941).

[3] In our studies noted in note 1 above.

[4] Most notably Ringgren, *Islam, 'aslama, and Muslim* (Uppsala, 1949). See also the abstract of an as yet unpublished paper, D. H. Baneth, 'The original meaning of *islām* as a religious term; a renewal of a medieval interpretation' in *Proceedings of the Twenty-Third International Congress of Orientalists, Cambridge* 1954 (London, n.d.) [*c.* 1955?]. Prof. Baneth was kind enough to let me see the manuscript of the whole. James Robson, ' 'Islām' as a Term', *The Muslim World* (Hartford, 1954), 44: 101–9, adds nothing to Ringgren for the classical period. Dawid Künstlinger, ' "Islām", "Muslim", "aslama" im Ḳurān', in *Rocznik Orjentalistyczny*, Lwów, 11; 128–37 (1935) should also be consulted.

Muḥammad, aim at reconstructing the historical meaning of the seventh century A.D., whereas Muslims, regarding it as expressive, if we may say so, of the mind of God, may legitimately interpret it in the light of a continuingly contemporary understanding of its timeless validity. For our purposes, of the study of the historical development of the concept 'Islām' in the minds of men, in all its senses, a rewarding and manageable study would be an investigation of the history of *tafsīr* relating to this word. Muslims and outsiders may disagree as to what Islām really is (and in the nature of the case a Muslim must equate what it really is and what the word means in the Qur'ān). Yet they may come together in discussing how specific persons at certain times and places have understood it. In the matter of the Qur'ān text, historical consideration may well be focused on what it probably meant to the seventh-century Arabs who first heard it. This can be supplemented, of course, with internal considerations of what in their own context the words must mean.

In the case of the term *islām* in the Qur'ān we have two observations to put forward. The first is that the word is relatively little used. It occurs eight times in all, *īmān* forty-five times. Similarly *mu'min* in its various forms is more than five times as frequent as *muslim.*[5]

Secondly, where it is used, it in some cases inevitably carries our first sense of the word, as an act of personal faith. That is, it is inevitably a *maṣdar.*[6] In other cases it may do so. We ourselves do not necessarily find a systematic, institutionalized sense even in the classic verses where it is customary nowadays to see the religion as being named. *Inna'l-dīna 'inda'llāhi'l-islām* (3: 19) may be read as stating the essential religious truth that 'the proper way to worship God is to obey Him'. We will not, however, repeat here our reasons supporting this and similar interpretations. We may assert, however, that there is no instance in the Qur'ān where (as often happens later) the dynamic sense of the term as personal faith is patently absurd or grammatically intolerable.

For subsequent centuries we cannot, as we have said, at this stage investigate the whole history of the word *islām*. What we have done is to take a highly restricted but not insignificant body of material, namely the titles of books in Arabic. Even this we have further restricted by considering (except for the modern period) only those titles entered by Brockelmann. His *Geschichte der arabischen Litteratur* lists in the index some twenty-five thousand titles, of works written over the entire course of Islamic history from the beginning until about 1938. We have gone through this list, culled out all instances where the word *islām* appears[7] and arranged these

[5] Our study is based on the admirable concordance of 'Abd al-Bāqī, *al-Mu'jam al-mufahras li-alfāẓ al-Qur'ān al-karīm* (Cairo, 1364[*c.* 1945]). For fuller discussion see our studies noted at note 1 above.

[6] E.g., *Wa-kafarū ba'da islāmihim*, 9:74.

[7] We have also entered on cards all titles from that index in which the following terms appear:

in chronological order. For the modern period (from A.H. 1300) we have supplemented Brockelmann from other sources, though not extensively. The conclusions that seemed to us to arise from an examination of these data will constitute the body of our study, Part II. Before concluding this introductory section we may make certain general observations on our method and on the actual construction of our lists.

Our list of titles is unquestionably imperfect. To begin with, I myself have doubtless missed the odd entry in the Brockelmann index that has escaped my hurrying eye. Moreover Brockelmann, I find, and it is hardly surprising, has made occasional slips, both in his index and elsewhere. Further, there are such possibilities as that what appear in such a listing to be distinct works may sometimes prove on examination to be rather divergent titles from various manuscripts of the same treatise. The next step in this investigation, and unfortunately I have not yet been able to take it except for modern works, would be to check these titles against the works to which they refer. The process of doing this, though lengthy, would be useful and would undoubtedly modify the material here presented in some of its details. I have, with apologies, taken the liberty of presenting my results at this interim stage because of the time limit imposed by the Conference and because I see no reason to suppose that the conclusions to be inferred from the results would be seriously modified in principle. It is the general trends that seem to emerge, rather than the details, that are of interest.

A large-scale question is that the massive work of the new Institute for Manuscripts of the Arab League in Cairo is in process of superseding Brockelmann, or anyway of revealing his catalogue as limited. However, his listing remains a very sizeable sampling, not inadequate for the discerning of trends.

Another objection that might be made is that classical and medieval Arabic book titles were often highly stylized and not always informative of the subject-matter of the work. For one thing, however, I have found on examination that this is not as extensively true as is sometimes thought, and in any case there is no forceful reason for questioning the validity on this basis of such generalizations as are induced from such occurrences of our terms as are found—this practice perhaps reduces the number of occurrences but not the relative distribution or the meanings when the terms are used. Besides, the use or the lack of use of a term in a title, whatever may be the cultural-conventional reasons for it, does I feel bear some relation to the fixing or lack of fixing of that idea in currency.

I have arranged the material in three lists. The first (List A) is of all Arabic titles that I have found up to the year 1300 *hijrī* containing the

islāmī, muslim, īmān, īmānī, mu'min, dīn, dīnī, adyān, diyāna, milla, and in certain senses (those relating to religion) *niẓām.* Except for *islām* we have not yet studied the collections systematically.

word *islām*. It is based squarely on Brockelmann, not only for entries but in general for dates and references. I have added one item not in his list, of an early work recently published in Cairo; this happened to come to my notice, and perhaps does not disrupt the objectivity of the study. The items are listed chronologically according to the date of death of author, so far as feasible.

The second list, B, is for titles more recent than 1300 *hijrī*. Its items are arranged so far as feasible according to the date of first publication. All Brockelmann entries are included, and in addition such works as happen to be in my personal collection or came to my attention in the two libraries in which I did most of the detailed work for this study. It lists works in Arabic in which the term *islām* figures, whether translations or originals; in general, pamphlets are excluded. A fair number of entries have been checked from Brockelmann against the original works. The desideratum that remains is to make this survey more nearly complete—a task of not too great proportions.

The third list, C, enumerates a handful of titles proffered to me by persons in Cairo as the result of my discussions. I have separated them from List B because they occur as illustrations of a point already made, materials serving a thesis rather than vice versa; I felt that it would distort the objective and inductive nature of the study to base it on a list constructed in part *ad hoc*. Some of these titles are such striking exemplifications of certain usages, however, that it seemed worthwhile to append them.

Let us turn, then, to consider the lists,[7a] to see what inferences arise.

II

A Study of the Preliminary Data

To begin with, the number of entries in our lists is significant. For list A it is rather small, but not negligible. In classical and medieval Muslim times religious books were numerous, but titles on 'Islam', although they do occur, are considerably less common than today. (In classical and medieval Christendom, so far as I have been able to discover, no one ever wrote a book on 'religion' or on 'Christianity'.) In all, I have found in Brockelmann to 1300 *hijrī* eighty-four titles. The proportion to the total number of titles listed is tiny.[8]

The proportion to titles in which the word *īmān* occurs, is also interesting. From a comparable study of Brockelmann's index, not here listed,[9] I have found *īmān* used in fifty-six titles until 1300 *hijrī*. In other words,

[7a] On the lists, see below, p. 502.

[8] I have no figure for how many of the approximately 25,000 titles in Brockelmann's index, from which this list is constructed, are of works before 1300 *hijrī*. A rough guess might put the number at 15,000 to 20,000.

[9] Cf. note 7, *supra*.

during these centuries, *islām* slightly outnumbers *īmān* in titles in a ratio of three to two.[10] We have already seen that in the Qur'ān the ratio was one to five, in favour of *īmān*. In modern times, this ratio climbs to over thirteen to one.[11] That is, *islām* gets much less attention than *īmān* in the Qur'ān, gradually comes to get slightly more attention as Islamic history proceeds, and today is vastly more considered.[12]

Let us turn, next, to the meanings that attach to the term 'Islām' in the various instances. The context often makes reasonably clear that the author is using the word in one sense or another.

To begin with, one finds several cases in which the work evidently is referring to 'Islām' in the personal sense—of commitment, *taslīm*, the act of faith. In these cases, a substitution of the word *taslīm* for *islām*, though it might change the significance slightly, is meaningful and not absurd. This is fairly clear in such a work as al-Sullamī's *al-Farq bayn al-īmān wa'l-islām*, which explores the difference between having faith and submitting to God. We would add al-Ghazzālī's *Fayṣal al-tafriqa bayn al-islām wa'l-zandaqa*, or the mystic Ibn al-'Arabī's *al-I'lām fī mā buniya 'alayhi'l-islām*, and Ibn Taymiyya's *Risāla fi'l-islām wa'l-īmān*.

In two striking instances the usage is not only specifically personal but indeed individual: al-Wā'iẓ al-Bakrī al-Baṣrī's *Islām al-Ṭufayl b. 'Āmir al-Dawsī* and al-Marṣafī's *Tanzīh al-kawn 'an i'tiqād islām Fir'awn*, where it is exclusively a question of the *islām*, the commitment, of one man.

Even if one thinks, as a non-Muslim or a non-religious Muslim is likely to do, of *islām* in these two cases as a technical term, with an institutional rather than a divine reference, it is still obvious that it would mean 'becoming a Muslim' (and one may draw attention to the verb, 'becoming'). And even so we would feel that in a case where the author or reader is pious, he would be thinking of the content of the becoming-a-Muslim concept, which is a religious content, that is an act of surrender to God.

Again, in the case of Ibn Rajab al-Hamdānī's *Ghurbat al-islām* (The Strangeness of Islām) (8th/14th century) recently published by a *shaykh* of the Azhar, the title of the work is perhaps not in itself at once lucid, and indeed the modern editor writes a 60-page introduction largely concerned with explicating terms to show why Islām in its true sense is indeed 'strange' or rare; in the course of this he remarks that the word *islām* has two meanings, self-surrender to God without an understanding faith, and

[10] That is, 84 to 56.

[11] In the Brockelmann index, for the present century *islām* occurs 52 times (our list B), *īmān* four times. The entries in B not from Brockelmann are not here considered since they were compiled *ad hoc*.

[12] It is interesting to reflect on how much more prominent a role in such a situation as modern Pakistan is played by the concept of *islām* than by the concept of *īmān*. Might one suggest that perhaps the fundamental fallacy of the 'Islamic state' advocated was the assumption that Islam can be considered without giving attention to the question of *īmān*?

with it.[13] (It may also be mentioned that the title-page carries the legend *wa-yusammā kashf al-kurba bi-waṣf ahl al-ghurba*—whether this means that the title, *Ghurbat al-islām*, is not actually original, or not as old as the text, is not clear to me.) In any case the allusion is to a *ḥadīth* affirming that *islām*, presumably in its 'true' sense of genuine surrender to God, is rare.

Somewhat similar considerations would doubtless apply to the mystic 'Alī al-Idrīsī's *Bayān ghurbat al-islām*, and to al-Ghazzālī's *Risāla fī manba' al-islām*.

Titles with the doublet phrase *al-īmān wa'l-islām* (8 times so, 6 times vice versa) begin about the 8th/14th century. Other works that we have considered so far in this group are also late, the only earlier ones being the Ibn al-'Arabī mentioned (7th/13th century) and the two of al-Ghazzālī (d. 505/1111). To this group should possibly be added, we would feel, two works from the end of our period, in the 13th/19th century: both by an Indian Shī'ī author, Dildār: *Huṣām al-islām fī naqḍ ma dhakarahu 'Abd al-'Azīz fī bāb al-nubuwwa*, and *'Imād al-islām fī 'ilm al-kalām*; the latter being alternatively entitled *Mir'āt al-'uqūl fī 'ilm al-uṣūl*.

There is a further group of titles, beginning as early as the 3rd/9th century and continuing without serious interruption to the 13th/19th, with our term in the form *sharā'i' al-islām* (5 times, and twice in the singular), *qawā'id al-islām* (3 times, and once in the singular), *arkān al-islām* (3 times), *qawāṭi' al-islām*, and so on. In this case it does not seem to me possible to say clearly at first glance in what sense the word *islām* is being used. It could mean the action of submitting to God, or it could be the name of a religion as a systematic ideal in the sense that we are exploring. There are some indications that suggest the former. For example, al-Maqdisī's *Lawāzim al-islam wa'l-īmān* (MS., uncertain date) is again of that class that correlates *islām* with faith, making it in my judgement unambiguously personal, as in the other instances that we have been considering. (It may be mentioned in passing that I have found no title of any work of the present century mentioning *islām* and *īmān* in the same breath.) Again, as late as the 12th/18th century, in the case of an Indian author writing in Arabic, two manuscripts of his work have survived, one bearing the title *Farā'iḍ al-islām* and the other *Farā'iḍ al-īmān*. Again, a slightly more recent author has left a work entitled *Farā'iḍ al-dīn wa-wājibāt al-islām*, where the *farā'iḍ* could logically be either *farḍ kifāya* or *farḍ 'āmm*. To me it somewhat seems that the use of *wājib* here, with its implication of moral responsibility, rather strengthens the suggestion that the author had in mind the individual person, who, after all, is alone able to take on that responsibility. The question here, and with *farā'iḍ* and *lawāzim*, turns on one's attitude to duty.

In all the cases being considered in this group, properly to determine

[13] Op. cit., pp. 27–8.

the meaning that the word had for the author in each instance, one would of course have to read the book with imaginative care; and I have not been able to do this as yet. Sometimes it is not even an available resource: for example, al-Ṭabarī refers in his Chronicle to a work that he has written entitled *Basīṭ al-qawl fī aḥkām sharā'i' al-islām*, and in his Commentary to *al-Laṭīf min al-bayān 'an aḥkām sharā'i' al-islām*, which are quite possibly alternative titles to the same treatise, but in any case no manuscript has survived, or at least up to 1938 or so none had been discovered.

In any case, a question as to what was in the author's mind is not the whole story. For, whatever a writer may intend, his words (as all of us who write learn sometimes to our sorrow) have to stand in their own right, and people who hear or read them may read into them meanings of their own. Once a book exists, if its words can mean or appear to mean a certain thing, then whether or not the author intended them to mean that they may nonetheless contribute to the currency of that idea. In the matter that we are discussing, it is not impossible that phrases like *sharā'i' al-islām* may have been launched with Islām meaning religion in our first sense, as personal reverence and morality, but may have contributed to the ambiguity by which it eventually came to mean the religion in our second sense, the institutional system. The puritanical founder of the Wahhābī movement has a book listed as *Faḍl al-islām*. This is reminiscent of late nineteenth- and early twentieth-century writings in the field of apologetics bearing such titles as *Faḍā'il al-islām*. However, though I do not have access to Ibn 'Abd al-Wahhāb's work, which so far as I know has not been published, yet knowing what one does of his general point of view and his *da 'wa*, I should be surprised if he meant by 'Islām' here what the apologists now mean by it. To him it was a moral imperative to be obeyed rather than an idealization to be admired or defended. This is one of the many points where I must do more research.

In somewhat similar case are the six titles (beginning 7th/13th century) bearing the words *ahl al-islām* and one with *millat al-islām*. Perhaps *jamharat al-islām* should also be added here?[14] Here again in two instances the full phrase is *ahl al-islām wa-l-īmān*—which again suggests the personal response to a challenge. Nonetheless it would seem to me that there is a certain ambiguity here, and phrases such as this and those of the preceding group doubtless helped to ease a transition from *islām* as personal commitment to Islām as a systematized ideal.

This transition is illustrated further in the phrase *shaykh al-islām* applied 3 times to Ibn Taymiyya, twice to Ibn Ḥajar, once to al-Bulqīnī, 3 times to persons not designated in the sources. One should add also *Ḥujjat al-islām* for al-Ghazzālī (MS. of uncertain date) and presumably the Shī'ī *Rūḥ al-islām* (13th/19th century) for Salmān. The usage *shaykh al-islām*

[14] Cf. *infra*, 19.

begins from the first half of the 6th/12th century, very considerably earlier than Süleymān the Magnificent's or the Safavids' first establishing of a formal, official post with that name.

Another difficulty which arises here, and indeed besets us throughout this work, is the problem of not being sure whether the titles as given in Brockelmann are in fact as ancient as the works that they describe, or whether they may not have been added under the pressure of later style. An example of this process is the work of al-Wāqidī, entitled when it was written in the second century presumably *Futūḥ bilād al-'Ajam wa-Khurāsān* or the like, but published in a modern edition with the new title *Futūḥ al-islām bi-bilād al-'Ajam wa Khurāsān.*[15] For example, the work *Tarjamat shaykh al-islām al-Bulqīnī* is listed as found in two manuscripts, one in Istanbul and one in the Escorial—but the latter omits the words *shaykh al-islām* from the title, which leaves one wondering whether this usage is indeed as old as the fall of central Spain after all. Again, Ibn Qudāma's tribute to his mentor is variously listed as *Tarjamat Taqī al-Dīn b. Taymiyya* or as *Manāqib shaykh al-islām Ibn Taymiyya.*[16]

However, until more meticulous and thorough research is feasible in this rather virgin field, we must presumably accept the titles given and the dates of the authors to whom the works are prescribed; the latter as in any case indicating a minimum date for the introduction of a new connotation or usage, even if there be a possibility of its being misleadingly early.

Finally within this category we turn to consider a work of Ibn Taymiyya himself called *al-Ḥisba fi'l-islām.* We must note that this is the first time, and apparently the only time until the present century, that the phrase *fi'l-islām* is used. This is a most interesting wording, and it has developed far in our own day, as we shall presently be noting. The use of *fī* makes quite clear that Islām is an entity, something with parts, something that things can be inside of or outside of—not in the Ṣūfī sense of *bāṭin* and *ẓāhir* but in the concrete sense of an organized observable pattern. This is the modern sense to a lot of people. Yet it is obvious when one reflects on it that the terminology *kadha wa-kadha fi'l-islām* could not be used by men for whom the term *islām* signified in its Qur'ān sense a personal relationship between the soul and God.

We have now surveyed all but 17 of the titles in which the word *islām* occurs during the first thirteen centuries of Islamic history. We have discovered that so far the term is either correlative with *īmān*, actually or potentially, the designation of a man's personal acceptance of responsibility before God, or else is used in such a context as to be ambiguously either this or the idealized ideal; except for the Ibn Taymiyya work just

[15] The work may be spurious (so Horovitz in *EI*, first edition, s.v. Wāḳidī); that at least the title is not original is evident from his other titles as given in *Fihrist* s.v. or in Brockelmann.

[16] Cf. S II 128/4b_2 with S II 119, last line.

noted, where the ideal is perhaps clearly indicated. Chronologically, except for al-Ṭabarī's use of *Sharā'i' al-islām* these titles begin with al-Ghazzālī.

We turn finally to examine these remaining 17. Two of them are by non-Muslims. One is the recent (12th/18th century) work, rather curious, of a Christian entitled *Taḥiyyat al-islām fī mā warada bi'l-salām wa'l-muṣāfaḥa wa'l-qiyām*. The other is early, and in fact is the first recorded work altogether by anyone in whose title the word *islām* appears. It has not survived, but the name is reported as given in a passing reference in al-Jāḥiẓ as the work of a certain Yūnus b. Farwa who was a member of the sceptical and rather ribald circle of Bashshār b. Burd at the court of al-Mahdī. I venture to call him a non-Muslim because of his associations and because he reputedly dedicated to the Byzantine emperor this treatise with the title *Mathālib al-'Arab wa-'uyūb al-islām*.

This relates to the point on which we have remarked above, which we have elaborated in our previously mentioned papers,[17] and to which we shall return for the modern period: namely, the significance of the use by outsiders of a name to designate a religious system in which they do not themselves believe.

There remain then 15 titles. I have set them aside for separate consideration, because in them we seem to see a transition towards the development of a new and more mundane meaning of Islām, where this term designates not the religion of the Muslims but the Muslims themselves, the community or its historical culture.[18] In some cases the transition is only partial, in some cases perhaps complete.[19]

If these cases are carefully considered, reflection seems to lead one to conclude that the word *islām* has become the name not even of a religion but of a culture or a community. It apparently signifies not the relationship of obedience and submission of the individual before his Creator, nor even the ideal pattern of such relationships systematically organized into a group order to which the life of the community ought to conform. It signifies rather the life of the community as it actually is and has been, without consideration as to what it ought to be.

The use of the phrase *mulūk al-islām* is worth attention. Parenthetically

[17] Note 1 *supra*.

[18] In modern Bayrūtī dialect this has reached a point where *jīrunā islām* is colloquial for 'the people next door are Muslims'.

[19] Three titles require special mention. Muḥammad Kurd 'Alī, in his prefatory remarks (p. 10) in his Damascus edition (1365/1946) of Ẓahīr al-Dīn al-Bayhaqī's *Ta'rīkh ḥukamā' al-islām*, states that this title is recent, the original being *Tatimmat ṣiwān al-ḥikma*. With regard to al-Balawī's *Ādāb al-islām*, the Balawī (6th/12th cent.) citation implies that the title as well as the work itself is from the pen of the 3rd/9th century writer Abū 'Ubayd. The word *islām* here as a literary term is contrasted with *jāhiliyya*; Christian writers in the period after the Prophet would presumably be hospitably included. One may compare the fact that, apparently, the term *islāmī* is first used (Lane s.v.) in literary rather than religious or even historical discussions in the same sense. Al-Shayzarī's *Jamharat al-islām* is included here, although it is debatable whether this entry should rather (or also?) go with the group *ahl al-islām*, *millat al-islām*, above. See 14 *supra*.

we may note that it follows by three centuries and more the introduction, not in literature but in politics, of a title such as *sulṭān-i Islām* for an actual ruling prince: the Seljuq Sultan Sanjar in the early part of the 6th/12th century is referred to by this title in a Persian *sawgand-nāma* and is called *malik-i islām* by al-Ghazzālī himself in a Persian letter; and the Īl-Khānī, and Safavid rulers later are repeatedly called *pādishāh-i islām*.[20] We may discern in such cases that *islām* has not altogether lost its transcendent reference: the idea is not only that the ruler is a ruler of Muslims, but that he has the moral responsibilities and spiritual prerogatives and authoritative legitimacy of ruling them *ad dei gloriam* as it were. The point of giving him such a title was to affirm that his being ruler, despite his not being *khalīfa*, was part of the proper, the Islamic, order of things.

Similarly in some of the book titles that we are considering. The full titles of two of the more recent (9th and 10th/15th and 16th centuries) suggest this: *Nuṣḥ mulūk al-islām bi'l-ta'rīf bi-mā yajibu 'alayhim min ḥuqūq ila'l-bayt al-kirām* and *Taḥdīr a'immat al-islām 'an taghyīr binā' al-bayt al-ḥarām.* In earlier cases, however, there seems little to suggest this. Al-Maqrīzī's *mulūk al-islām* in Ethiopia means perhaps little or nothing more than Muslim kings, or perhaps more accurately Muslim kings of a Muslim community. And in *ḥukamā' al-islām* (and perhaps *jamharat al-islam*?) does *islām* mean anything more than the Muslim community? Similarly al-Bayyāsī's modern-sounding reference to *ṣadr al-islām* presumably has in mind the appearance of Islām on earth as an historical phenomenon. If one thinks of Islām in its strictly theological sense, according to Muslim conviction, it appeared with Adam and has reappeared at least with each of the prophets.

This secularizing tendency, if we may call it that, culminates in the small group of history works that form virtually a series stemming from the seminal work of Shams al-Dīn al-Dhahabī (8th/14th century). This monumental and influential political and intellectual history from the time of the Prophet Muḥammad to his own day was widely copied, imitated, abridged, revised. Let us consider its title, *Ta'rīkh al-islām.* This phrase can have two possible meanings, so far as I can see. It cannot mean the history of a personal commitment, of an individual attitude to God's command: that would conceivably be *ta'rīkh islāmī* or *ta'rīkh islāmikum* or *ta'rīkh islām fulān*, but this would be rare—a sort of spiritual biography. What *ta'rīkh al-islām* could mean would be, first, the history of the religion, as an organized system; and secondly, the history of the Muslim community.

The former has never been written. It is a fascinating subject, and is one that I myself have occasionally dreamed of some day attempting: a history of the religion of Islām, its development as a religious *Weltanschauung* across

[20] See A. K. S. Lambton, 'Quis Custodiet Custodes: Some reflections on the Persian theory of government, I' in *Studia Islamica* (Paris, 1956), 5:129.

the centuries, the changes that it has undergone as it has been adopted by different peoples, in different conditions, and at different times. Muslims, on the whole, not only have not written such an account but to some extent theoretically preclude themselves from writing it—for to a believing Muslim in the modern mood Islām if conceived as a religious system tends to be conceived as fixed, as given by God: it does not change from one place or one generation to another, it has no history. The inappropriateness or at least the radical nature of this suggestion becomes perhaps clear if one translates 'history of Islām' by the revealing phrase *taṭawwur al-islām* or *taṭawwur dīn al-islām*. It is perhaps not rash to predict that such a book will first be written by a non-Muslim (though one would like to hope that this prediction will be proved wrong).[21]

The other meaning that the words *ta'rīkh al-islām* could have, and actually the one that they have had, is the history of the Muslim community. The concept that the community has a history is straightforward enough and is theologically quite acceptable. What is curious in this case is the meaning that the word *islām* then takes on. Does it not, as we have remarked, designate then not an ideal but an actuality; not what God asks of men but what men choose to give Him?

This concludes our survey of the classical and medieval periods; but before turning to the present century we should note that this last way of looking at Islām is the normal one for outsiders. This is the accepted meaning of the term 'Islām' for non-believers. For example, the standard Western Orientalist has tended to look at Islām as a mundane phenomenon, an historical reality that he objectively studies. For him it is not an idea in the mind of God, but a purely human construction on the stage of history. I personally do not share this; and indeed part of my present study in trying to wrestle with the problem of an outsider attempting to understand a religion not his own is pushing me to the conclusion that such understanding requires a fairly serious revision of many of our terms and concepts. At the very least one must learn to view Islām not only as an objective historical phenomenon but also as the ideal that lies behind it, not the overt behaviour of the Muslim but the inner aspiration of his heart. Even this, I feel, will eventually have to be refined, if not superseded. It would seem to me highly possible that we shall come to recognize that a religion, and therefore religious history, and therefore human history, cannot be properly understood without an effective awareness of its transcendent dimension.[22]

In the meantime, however, it is not surprising, and perhaps was

[21] Since writing the above sentence, I am happy to find that apparently my prediction is to be proven wrong, for my colleague, Dr. Fazlur-Rahman, is undertaking to write such a history.

[22] Cf. the present writer's *Islam in modern history* (Princeton, 1957/London, 1958), pp. 8–9, n. 5; and in general chapter 1 there.

inevitable, that outsiders in the first instance have approached Islām in this unidealist fashion, have seen it as something totally within the empirical world. The result is that this is the meaning that the term 'Islām' has come to have in European languages.

The importance of this point for our present study is that we seem to find in this matter as in others a powerful impact of the modern West on the Muslim community itself, or at least on those sections of it that read, and often think, in one of the European languages.

Turning then, to our list B, and studying the usages that it displays, we find ourselves asking whether there has not been during fairly recent times in the Muslim world an increasing and now widespread tendency to use the word 'Islām' in the sense of the tangible historical reality that has actually existed.

In list B we find a small number of works that continue the older tradition from the medieval period. Such usages are very soon greatly outnumbered and for modern-type books replaced by the newer and more mundane meaning. The tendency is again illustrated by the many modern books being published and widely read in our century entitled *Ta'rīkh al-islām*. There are many examples of this, and one may add the extremely popular series of Aḥmad Amīn, *Fajr al-islām*, *Ḍuḥā' al-islām*, *Ẓuhr al-islām*, *Yawm al-islām*.

One gets also titles such as *Ta'rīkh ṣadr al-islām*, and if one considers the title *Mabādi' al-islām* one realizes that this phrase might mean 'the principles of Islām' as a systematic ideal, but instead the author means 'the beginnings of Islām' as a systematic actuality.

Similarly when a man writes a book called *Ashhar mashāhir al-islām fi'l-ḥarb wa'l-siyāsa* or *al-Mustashriqūn wa'l-islām* one may, of course, be quite sure that by 'Islām' he is not thinking of *taslīm kardan*. May one not also surmise as in the former case certain and in the later case probable that he is not even thinking of the ideal religious system but more likely of the historical civilization? Similarly a title such as *al-Islām fi'l-Ḥabasha*. In this case, the word *islām* must designate the historical religious situation as it exists. The ideal pattern of Islām, in its systematic sense, is presumably the same in Ethiopia as anywhere else. If one writes, or for that matter reads, a book *al-Islām fi'l-Ḥabasha* obviously one has in mind not the transcendent pattern of Islām but one of its actual historical expressions.

This point is further clarified if we go back to the phrase of Ibn Taymiyya *al-Ḥisba fi'l-islām*. Presumably Ibn Taymiyya's work is at a theoretical level, a treatise on *ḥisba* as it ought to be, according to ideal Islamic prescription. One can imagine a quite different work by, let us say, a Western economic historian; his study might well have the same title, but it would discuss *ḥisba* and the *muḥtasib* not as they ought to be but as they actually were in the history of a given time and place. For instance, such a study would include any corruption that may have taken place. By comparing these two concepts one can forcefully see the difference in the two meanings of *islām*.

This is illustrated precisely when de Boer's work entitled *The History of philosophy in Islam* is considered. This was translated also into Arabic as *Ta'rīkh al-falsafa fi'l-islām*. It is clear that the phrase *fi'l-islām* here means something different from what it means in Ibn Taymiyya's *al-Ḥisba fi'l-islām*.

The same difference occurs in the phrase *fi'l-islām* between *al-Mujaddidūn fi'l-islām, 100 H.–1370 H.* and *Ḥuqūq al-nisā fi'l-islām*. With this last compare *al-Rizq fi'l-islām*, *al-zawāj fi'l-islām*, etc., and with the former *Ta'rīkh al-qaḍā fi'l-islām* and a few other *fi'l-islāms* that we shall consider presently. Attention may be drawn to the point that the first title here incorporates boundary dates, illustrating almost explicitly that an historical rather than a timeless Islam is in mind. Our hypothetical Western economist's work fancied above might well be entitled (and strictly would have to be entitled, at least implicitly) 'The *ḥisba* in Islam from year A to year B'; whereas Ibn Taymiyya's work on the *ḥisba* in Islam could not accept dates.

The de Boer translation brings us to what I am beginning to believe was perhaps crucial in this matter: the question of an impact from the West, from non-Muslims. That this has been operative is suggested, apart from its inherent plausibility, by a careful scrutiny of some of the works published. For example, the only two books of Shaykh Muḥammad 'Abduh in whose title the word *Islām* appears were both written in explicit reply to outside attacks on Islām—that is, attacks on what non-believers thought Islām to be. The earlier work was in answer to a European article; the later, *al-Islām wa'l-radd 'alā muntaqidīhi*, 1902, is an answer to the non-Muslim Arab Farāḥ Anṭūn. It is perhaps of interest to note that the word *Islām* in the earlier article reproduces the same word used in the Arabic translation of Hanotaux's originally French article, a translation that was published in the Cairo journal *al-Mu'ayyad* and provoked his response.[23]

Again, the first work, very influential and often revised and republished, of perhaps the most energetic, most prolific, and most characteristic of the writers introducing the new attitude, Farīd Wajdī, was, from its second edition, entitled *al-Madaniyya wa'l-islām*. It was not only an apologetic for

[23] Brockelmann, S III 320, speaks of Hanotaux's article as in *Ta'rīḫ* II 382/95, and Muḥammad 'Abduh's reply as 395/411. In the second edition (Cairo, 1344) of vol. 2 of Rashīd Riḍā, *Ta'rīkh al-ustādh al-imām* it is pp. 401–14, and the six answers of 'Abduh are given pp. 415–68. The Hanotaux article is cited there as translated by Muḥammad Mas'ūd (Bey), then one of the editors of *al-Mu'ayyad*, and published therein 1317 (=1899–1900) as *Qad aṣbaḥnā'l-yawm izā' al-islām wa'l-mas'ala al-islāmiyya*. The French original was phrased: 'Face à face de l'Islam et la question musulmane.'

Islam in dispute with two Frenchmen, B. Constans, and J. Simon, but was actually first written in French and then translated also into Arabic.[24] Another of the modern works in which *islām* appears in the title in the historical sense was *al-Islām, khawāṭir wa-sawāniḥ*, which is a translation of H. de Castries. The very fact that the word *islām* can be translated from a non-believer's language into Arabic by a Muslim without discomfort is significant.[25]

Besides the translations, there is the writing of books in Arabic by non-Muslims. One of the first, and most influential, was *Ḥaḍārat al-islām fī dār al-salām*, by a Christian Arab (Cairo, 1888 and in later editions); a work that is said[26] to have been a forerunner of the still more popular and effective Christian writer, Jurjī Zaydān.[27]

To come to a later period, one may note such a work as *Ta'rīkh al-ḥarakāt al-fikriyya fi'l-islām—al-ḥarakat al-ijtimā'iyya* (Jerusalem, 1928), which is a Marxist history, in which *islām* means an historical phenomenon, as the phrase *fi'l-islām* once more suggests.

In fact, during the formative period of the first three decades of the present century *hijrī* (roughly, from the 1880's to the First World War), I have found that works that are either translations from the French or are by non-Muslim Arabs form a quite substantial proportion of the titles in which the term *islām* appears; and that they use this term chiefly in its systematic-historical sense. If one adds also those instances where Muslim writers are explicitly answering outsiders' attacks on *islām*, then during this period approximately one half of the usages are in this sense non-indigenous.[28] Since that period, however, Muslims themselves have adopted this usage, and nowadays it considerably exceeds any other meaning for the term in Arabic titles.

Indeed, I have come to believe that these years should be examined to see whether they do not constitute a critical point in the development of the thinking of Arab intellectuals about Islām; and whether during this time the transition did not take place, and take place quite largely under Western impact, to this non-transcendental reference.[29]

[24] The title of the first Arabic edition (Cairo, 1316/*c.* 1898) was (Brockelmann, loc. cit.), *Taṭbīq al-diyāna al-islāmiyya 'alā nawāmīs al-madaniyya.*

[25] Worth investigating, perhaps, is the question as to why Wajdī translated the French 'Islam' by the Arabic *al-diyāna al-īslāmīyya* in 1898 and by *islām* in 1904 (cf. preceding note).

[26] Brockelmann, S III 184.

[27] Cf. *infra*, 29.

[28] Of twenty-five titles in our list B, covering the modern period up to the First World War, four are by Christians, three are translations, and from five to seven at least are explicitly answers to non-Muslims. A more thorough study may show that still more should be included in this last group. For instance Brockelmann characterizes Abu'l-Maḥāsin Yūsuf al-Nabhānī, the author of two of these works, as a great defender of Islam against Christian culture (S II 763). Is the editor of *Futūḥ al-islām bi-bilād al-'Ajam wa-Khurāsān* perhaps a non-Muslim?—and so on.

[29] The resultant outlook on Islam I have analysed in chapter 3 ('The Arabs') of my recent *Islam in modern history*. The present study has led me to question whether the process that

Similarly later, in 1927 in Cairo there appeared *Ta'rīkh falsafat al-islām* by Muḥammad Luṭfī Jum'a. This does not mean a history of the philosophy of the religion of Islām, nor even a history of Muslim philosophy of religion; but simply a history of such general philosophy as has occurred within Muslim civilization. It is instructive, therefore, to learn that this book was criticized in an article by Maḥmūd al-Khuḍarī in Cairo as being but a plagiarism from the work of the German orientalist Munk.[30]

In these various ways, then, through books in European languages read by Muslims, through books in Arabic and other Muslim languages written by non-Muslims, through the translations, as well as perhaps through the waning of a lively personal faith among some members of the Muslim community themselves, the word *islām* in a non-believers' meaning would seem to have established itself in the languages and perhaps even the thinking of the modernized Muslim world.

In the 1930's, a writer in a sense protests against this development, and in a sense acquiesces in it, by publishing a book entitled *al-Islām al-ṣaḥīḥ*. By this time one hardly noticed it; whereas a thousand or perhaps fifty years earlier it would not have occurred to him or to his readers that there was any other kind of Islām to write about.

The secularizing tendency culminates perhaps in a work published in Cairo a few years ago which included in its title the astonishing phrase *al-Ilḥād fi'l-islām*. To reflect on these words is to realize how profoundly the meaning has changed!

My attention has been called, in line with this last phrase, to certain other titles in which the usage of *fi'l-islām* betrays a similarly novel conception.

To sum up, then. We may say that to an outsider it would seem that there has been a tendency over the centuries and especially in modern times for the connotation of the word 'Islām' gradually to lose its relationship with God, first by shifting from a personal piety to an ideal religious

resulted in that orientation is not to be looked for in the writings of the period here under consideration, as perhaps an important turning point. I would also wonder whether I should not refine some of the interpretations. To take one example: the wide effectiveness of Jurjī Zaydān's *Ta'rīkh al-tammaddun al-islāmī*, 5 vols. (Cairo, 1902–7) is recognized, in popularizing among Arab Muslims their sense of past cultural glory. One may ask whether the title of his book did not introduce into modern Arabic thought the concept 'Islamic civilization' as such. (I have not searched out whether al-Afghānī had used precisely this concept.) In my recent study I referred, of course, to this work (p. 54; cf. p. 94 n. 2), but treated Zaydān as almost peripheral to the modern Arab Muslim's developing religious consciousness, because of his not being a Muslim. As a result of my present investigation, however, I am forced to ask whether conceivably his not being a Muslim is in itself of significance; whether rather than being peripheral, his contribution specifically as a non-Muslim might not be of prime consequence. For my argument went on to show that the modern Muslim's concept of Islām, exemplified in the case of Wajdī, comes close to the concept of a non-believer. Perhaps the non-Muslim has (unwittingly) played a more central role in the modern disintegration of Muslim religious thinking than we have recognized.

[30] Brockelmann, S III 276.

system, a transcendent pattern, then to an external, mundane religious system, and finally by shifting still further from that religious system to the civilization that was its historical expression.

Note

This paper, as submitted to the Conference, comprised basically two parts: one was a presentation of data, the other an interpretation of those data. The interpretation is given here. For reasons of space and cost, the other part is omitted. It consisted of a list in chronological order of all books in Arabic that the author could find in which the word *islām* appears. The construction of the list is explained above (pp. 488–90). Professor Cantwell Smith writes: 'In some ways the list that I compiled was more important than the interpretation that I was induced to give to it. For others might wish to query my interpretation, but it is important that we be talking of the same facts.' If anyone should wish to pursue the questions raised here the author is ready to forward a duplicated copy of the list (of some 150 titles) to any interested enquirer addressing him at McGill University, Montreal.

INDEX[1]

of authors and titles

[1] The editors wish to thank Mr. T. J. Heywood for his work in preparing the index.